INCREASE MATHER

LONDON: HUMPHREY MILFORD

OXFORD UNIVERSITY PRESS

INCREASE MATHER

THE FOREMOST AMERICAN PURITAN

BY

KENNETH BALLARD MURDOCK, Ph.D.

Instructor in English at Harvard University

"It is a *trite* (yet a *true*) assertion, that historical studies are both profitable and pleasant. And of all historical narratives, those which give a faithful account of the *lives* of eminent saints, must needs be the most edifying."—INCREASE MATHER.

CAMBRIDGE

HARVARD UNIVERSITY PRESS

1925

PRINTED AT THE HARVARD UNIVERSITY PRESS
CAMBRIDGE, MASS., U.S.A.

TO

MY FATHER AND MOTHER

PREFACE

THE fact that Increase Mather has a generally recognized claim to be considered the greatest American of his generation and the further fact that he was both a leader and a representative figure in a most important and too imperfectly studied period of the history of this nation, have led to the writing of this book. Therefore I have tried not only to give a "life" of Mather, based upon all the material now available, much of it unused before, but also to retell in some measure the story of his time in New England as it is revealed in the tale of the character and activity of its foremost citizen. If this double purpose mars my work, considered purely as biography, I hope that it may be justified to some extent as history, in so far as it serves to shed more light on Puritan days in this country.

I have no illusions as to the completeness of the picture. Mather bibliography I have left to more expert hands than mine; I have made no attempt to go deeply into all the problems of Congregational history raised by Mather's writings, nor have I tried to record every known fact about his life. Errors and gaps there must be, but I hope that in spite of them there is no essential point in Mather's life left quite untouched.

The footnotes are designed to give brief references to the sources and authorities whence I have drawn my conclusions. I hope that their presence may not prove discouraging to those to whom notes always suggest "pedantry" or an intention to address scholars alone. It seemed unwise to omit them, lest inconvenience be caused to anyone specially interested in the subject of the book; and I think that it is still entirely possible to read the text without being hindered in any way by the fact that the notes have been printed for those who may care to refer to them. For those who find the annotation inadequate or desire further discussion of some controversies or problems, I offer a general reference to a thesis, "The Life and Works of Increase Mather," presented by me in 1923 to the Faculty of Harvard University, and now deposited in the Harvard University Library.

In quoting unpublished documents I have tried to reproduce the originals so far as this is possible in type. In the case of Mather's own writing, however, ordinary symbols do not always suffice to reproduce what he wrote, for his abbreviations are curious, and, at times, he indulges in what is virtually shorthand. At times, too, the illegibility of his manuscripts makes it necessary to interpret a vague scrawl by a word which is not easy to trace in the lines of the original. I have dared to do this in no case where the sense is affected by my conjectural reading, without putting my guess in brackets. In using Mather's "Autobiography" I have ordinarily copied not from the original but from a careful transcript owned by the American Antiquarian Society, but I have compared this with the original whenever there is involved a proper name or any other word the reading of which might seriously affect my conclusions. In using printed records I have referred to and followed the printed text. The letter "s," however written or printed, I have always given in its modern form.

It is, perhaps, only fair to say that my purpose has not been to eulogize Increase Mather, nor merely to defend him against certain unfounded accusations. My creed is not one of which he would have approved; my personal predilections are not towards Puritan theology or modes of life. But, in writing a biography, based upon the facts which can be discovered, I have found it impossible to avoid the conclusion that he has often been misjudged. I hope that I have said no word in his favor except when the evidence has supported my statement. Where what we can be sure of makes possible no decision, I have felt that it was quite as fair to admit that he may have been right as to follow the traditional line of least resistance to the conclusion that a Mather was always wrong. I should not choose Puritan Boston as an abiding place, but I have yet to discover any facts which deprive me of my respect for many of those who did.

To thank all those whose help has made my work more easy and delightful than it could otherwise have been, is impossible in the limits of this preface. Among the books I have used, I owe a special debt to Barrett Wendell's "Cotton Mather," which sets a standard for sympathetic and scholarly understanding of the Puritans, and to Mr. J. T. Adams's "Founding of New England." With the latter I have ventured often to disagree but, written as it is with a point of view of to-day, its restatement of the history of the early period of New England is both stimulating and useful. Apart from books I owe much to librarians, ministers, and scholars, both in England and this country, whose courtesy and interest have been unfailing, and through whom I have had access to much material not otherwise to be secured. I cannot omit specific notes as to the very great kindness of the American Antiquarian Society and its librarian, Mr. Clarence S. Brigham, and the similar generosity of the Massachusetts Historical Society. Mr. Julius H. Tuttle, librarian of the latter society, has been constantly helpful. Mr. William G. Mather of Cleveland, and his librarian, Mr. Thomas J. Holmes, have been most liberal in allowing me to utilize their collections, and Mr. Mather's generosity has furnished the illustrations for this book. Mr. Albert Matthews has been an unfailing resource in time of perplexity. Professor George L. Kittredge has aided me in many ways, and was good enough to read a part of my manuscript. Miss Fanny B. Chandler, who acted as my secretary during much of my work, and my long-suffering wife, who has patiently given hours to the reading of proof, stand high among my benefactors. In England, Sir Charles Firth, the authorities of Dr. Williams's Library and of the Royal Society, the Reverend Andrew Leggatt of Dorchester, and Miss Edith F. Carey of Guernsey, gave invaluable assistance.

To Professor Chester N. Greenough I ventured to dedicate the thesis in which this book originated, and I cannot now present this work without further recognition of my obligation to him. He first called my attention to the need for such a biography, and his help made possible the completion of my task. My highest hope for these pages is that they may bring to some few readers a share, at least, of the enthusiasm which his wisdom and skill impart to those who, like myself, have been fortunate enough to study the literature and history of America as his pupils.

K. B. M.

CAMBRIDGE, MASSACHUSETTS
April 1925

CONTENTS

xi

LIST OF ILLUSTRATIONS

xiii

Except as otherwise noted, the originals from which the illustrations are reproduced are in the possession of the author.

INCREASE MATHER

CHAPTER I

INTRODUCTION

TWO centuries ago there died in Boston a man who had been for fifty years a true leader of his time. "The most powerful man in all that part of the world," [1] Increase Mather's achievement was the highest development reached by a family whose name is writ large in the annals of four generations of New England. Richard, renowned among the founders of the early Massachusetts church; Cotton, the apotheosis of intense Puritan character; and Samuel, a steadfast patriot of Revolutionary Boston, strong figures as they were, all lacked the rugged symmetry of growth and concord with their times, which make the abiding interest in Increase Mather's career.

To the student of New England history — religious, political, or literary — the great Mathers reveal themselves in lights varying in vividness according to the interests of the observer. The wanderer in the field of early American literature comes on Cotton Mather at every turn. Salem witchcraft is a favorite historical hunting-ground, and here again Cotton is to the fore. And, of course, he who would learn of educational or religious aspects of colonial days, can hardly spare the name of one of the Mathers. The general reader, however, preferring beaten paths to narrow byways of research, is apt to confront no one but Cotton face to face, and, for such a one, he alone of all his family survives as a personality apart from the historical impress of his deeds. It was his fortune to have in his nature an epitome of the most fervid traits of New England Puritanism; and the fact that his light shone most clearly in the days when the ideals he championed were beginning to wane, lends the force of contrast to the impression he makes. And, finally, he has found a sympathetic and discerning biographer whose art filled his subject with the breath of life. [2]

Yet, great as Cotton was, his father was greater. Increase Mather's life has a breadth of activity that makes it widely

1. Moses Coit Tyler, *A History*, ii, 68.
2. See Barrett Wendell, *Cotton Mather* — an admirable biography.

appealing. The long continuous developing of his character and accomplishment offers to the biographer a satisfying theme. Imbued from birth with Puritan ideals, he fought to maintain them while they were alive, with power and support in his world. It has been said that he "went in and out among men and dealt with open-air questions," and in so doing he "became the most prominent New Englander of his time" and "held the chief influence in the colony." [3] He "may be pronounced one of the strongest and most interesting men produced in the American colonies." [4] "To the last, he was a sovereign man throughout New England, illustrious for great talents and great services, both at home and abroad." [5] "There is no man who compares with him in the New England of his day in ability, leadership, or influence, or who more sincerely labored for what he deemed the abiding interests of the Kingdom of God." [6] In secular affairs "he moved, the commanding figure, through the political agitations of the time"; [7] and, from the point of view of literary history "his writings certainly have considerable merit. His style is far better than that of his son — simpler, more terse, more sinewy and direct, less bedraggled in the dust of pedantry; it has remarkable energy." [8]

It is in such phrases that Increase Mather is described for us. Brief summaries of his prowess in this line or that, comment on his connection with one political event or another, and an occasional short biographical sketch — these are his memory's only shrine. They leave many sides of his life unrecorded. His character, the influences that went into its making, his learning, his use of it in writing, his interest in science, and the process by which his personality was shaped and impressed itself on his world, are fit material for biography. From these elements the present work attempts to give to the reader of to-day a picture not wholly incomplete of one who was "for many years the most influential as well as the most learned man in New England," [9] and is still by nature and achievement worthy of close acquaintance and a share of living fame. If the task be half-way well done, Increase

3. Katharine Lee Bates, *American Literature*, pp. 41, 44.
4. W. P. Trent, *History*, p. 72.
5. Tyler, *A History*, ii, 69.
6. W. Walker, *Services of the Mathers*, p. 70.
7. Bates, *American Literature*, p. 41.
8. Tyler, *A History*, ii, 70.
9. J. F. Jameson, *History of Historical Writing*, p. 47.

Mather, renowned in his own day for his accomplishment, reveals himself to us as by intrinsic qualities of personality a man for all time.

First of all, of course, such a work aims toward collecting and arranging the many bits of concrete fact on Increase Mather's life. State papers, college records, contemporary accounts, his diaries, his autobiography, and his son's biography of him, form a treasure trove. Some of these documents were avowedly written for posterity, and elimination of the harsher traits of their subject is to be expected in them; but, used with due caution, they have unquestioned historical value; and, of course, some of the contemporary authorities on Mather, as well as his private papers, contain evidence which is proof against the most rigid criticism. Later biographical sketches too often display opinion or conjecture warped by a point of view out of harmony with Mather's time and its standards.[10] It is far safer to rely on trustworthy documents dating from his own period, written by his friends or foes, or penned by himself with no thought of their surviving for the use of readers in the twentieth century. True insight into his character can come only from such sources, and the narrative of his life can be more safely drawn from them than from any account colored by later theory or prejudice.

But, however sure we may be of our facts, in the use of them there must be constant selection and frequently we shall find interpretation necessary. The dates and texts of thousands of Increase Mather's sermons are preserved, but to cite them adds nothing to a useful analysis of him. Such selection of material is obviously dictated, but far more difficult is the problem of understanding such matter as one decides to use. Starting with the same historical landmarks, in the fields of witchcraft or the Andros revolt, various authors have followed diverging paths. Perhaps there is no infallible protection against this; but if the standpoint of reader and writer be firmly established and maintained, the insidious distortion that grows from standards differing with the opinion of one man or one age may be avoided. The point of view safest for us is, if we may attain it, that of the seventeenth century. We shall need an attitude of sympathy

10. Most of these deserve no special mention, since the material they contain is accessible in the other authorities cited. Most useful are J. L. Sibley, "Increase Mather," in *Biographical Sketches*, i, 410–470; W. Walker, "Increase Mather," in *Ten New England Leaders;* and B. Wendell, *Cotton Mather*, which has much to say of Increase Mather.

toward the Puritan spirit, and a resolve to judge Increase Mather, not by preconceptions foreign to him in nature and time, but by the ideals he understood and lived for.

Manifestly, to clamber up to such an observation ground is hard. For a writer not a Calvinist to lead equally unsympathetic readers back through three centuries to a time when God was vengeful and discipline was a cardinal point in life, to guide them from a diffusely free-thinking world to one where religion was as vigorous as it was narrow, is no small task. If the way is stony, the surest aid is a memory of the historical conditions in England and America, of contemporary literature in the Old and New World, and of the state of learning at the time. To encourage such mindfulness the story is told throughout with frequent allusions, if nothing more, to the intellectual and political progress of the period. If the goal be reached and we can read of the verifiable facts of Increase Mather's life with a background drawn not from our era but from his, we shall come near meeting him face to face. We are to gauge his stature by what others did who lived with him and before him; we are to measure his writings by what others produced from the resources that were his; and we are to appraise his character in relation to current influences of training and environment. If he excelled his fellows, it matters little whether he met modern tests. If he wrote better prose than his contemporaries and won their praise, it is a fact of meaning for literary history, even though to our eyes, myopic through difference in standards, his books seem dull. Such contact with the seventeenth century need not and will not blind us to the changes of later years; and though we see as nearly as may be eye to eye with him, we may still applaud when his ideas seem by the experience of later years to have been proved of enduring value.

The final problem is again one of selection. Somehow we must apportion our attention to the diverse branches of his many activities, with reference at once to the charm they held for him and to the indication of character they offer us. Remembering that "the spiritual force animating a new religious movement attracts the intellectual energies of the period, and furnishes them a new reality of purpose," [11] and that the spirit of his day decreed that his life-work should be primarily for the church, no preoccupation with ecclesiastical concerns should blind us to elements in

11. H. O. Taylor, *The Mediæval Mind*, ii, 427.

him which persist when Puritanism dies. For literary history, his style, his use of sources, and the structure of his books, are matters of weight. Though he seems to have written with an eye fixed on the statement of things dear to his time rather than on the manner of expression, the means by which he gained his end are of importance in relation to what came later. Thus some study of his books becomes for us a main thread in the web. Similarly, his service to Harvard, his relation to the state, and his interest in science, culminating in his plea for the radical and much-feared experiment of inoculation, to him all minor parts of a universally consuming devotion to God, are all lines of his thought worth following because they are often connected with the broader history of his period and ours.

Drawing from facts so far as we can make sure of them, selecting and interpreting by the standards of his era, we may outline, perhaps, the fundamentals of his life. Here and there a gap may be bridged by conjecture, admitted frankly as such, provided this guessing be based on probabilities inherent in his nature and his time, and with the reservation that no such additions may alter the firmer lines fixed by safer means. The background comes from history, from details of the material side of his world, and from some reconstruction in our minds of the influences he knew. Against these ground colors, the portrait finally takes shape when light and shade are introduced in the softening or intensifying of some one deed or thought in accord with its power to reveal to us qualities essential to his nature, and as fundamental now as then. A living picture can be made on such a plan. The brush is faultily guided if the result lack life. Yet to think of a biography as a portrait gives too static an impression. Say rather that, rightly seen, Increase Mather's life is as a tree growing great against a background familiar but changing year by year. At times there is blending with the woods behind, at times a rugged contrast in a light from a new angle, but always there is the sweep and greatness of a living thing transforming manifold forces into indomitable growth.

Mists of controversy occasionally make the vision waver. Such veiling we find when we try to see Mather clearly against the background of the "witchcraft delusion." Denunciation of all concerned, eager efforts to disentangle the relation of Cotton Mather and his father to the blaze of excitement over the devil and his works in Salem, and the ease with which certain writers have found it possible to believe that the two men played identical parts,[12] have complicated written history. But in such cases our point of view may save us. Forget the nineteenth century's decrying of the folly of a darker past, and remember the seventeenth-century scholar's view of Satan and his power among men. Remember that much we believe sincerely to-day, two centuries from now will be an antiquarian's delight. It is not given us to know how time will judge, any more than it was Increase Mather's fortune to guess that more than one fundamental commonplace of life would seem to his descendants mere delusion. To judge by criteria he could not know is to condemn unheard; to assess the meaning of his acts by the tests available to him is to go far toward understanding what he did, and why.

More baffling is the question that confronts us on every page — what was Puritanism? Increase Mather was a Puritan; yet which of us can define the name? The facts are too far out of our reach. We are dealing not with events, dates, or simple motives, but with a state of mind, complex, radically opposed to most of our ideas, and yet, for those who owned it, a primary force. There have been as many attempts to state the true inwardness of Puritanism as there have been sincere and earnest students of early American history; and only in those rare cases where the written word is the product of close study of Puritan writings, Puritan deeds, and the thought of the years that came before them, do we find a foundation of rock. Original sources — the documents of the Puritans themselves — are too numerous, too broad in scope, and, some modern writers would have us believe, too insincere, to serve our ends.

There are, fortunately, a few axioms by which we may chart a course through shoals of controversy. They are agreed to by most students and are founded on search among Puritan words, books, and acts. Briefly, then, we may say that Puritanism was the school of thought dominating the lives of certain dissenters from the rites of the Church of England, some of whom, early in the seventeenth century, founded the colony of Massachusetts Bay. Puritans, as we use the name, refers to these men. The vigor of their belief is shown in two aspects — their religious faith and organization and their conduct of civil affairs. In creed they were Calvinists, believing essentially in a doctrine which assured eternal life to certain fortunate ones predestined to sal-

12. Cf., for example, J. T. Adams, *The Founding*, pp. 451–456, especially p. 455.

vation. The rest of mankind were immutably condemned to ever-lasting torment. The elect remained the elect, and the damned remained the damned. This rigid classification could not be changed. The animating principle in the scheme was each man's desire to know whether he was to be saved. He who could consistently lead his life always in harmony with God's will could consider himself elect. Thus the Puritan strove valiantly to exercise his will in accord with God's, and while striving, analyzed and reviewed his every thought and deed, weighing and trying them in the never-ending effort to be sure that his spirit was so attuned to the Divine wish that he might hope to escape the fires of eternal punishment.[13] The God presiding over this system was rigorous and stern, exerting his power directly upon every affair of human life and avenging human misdeeds by prompt interventions of His might. The Devil, too, was a personality with a direct influence in earthly matters, and a vigorous and ever-present enemy of God-fearing men. Good Puritans were sure that Satan had power to do them harm and was to be met with in the daily walks of life. His messengers were active. Only prayer and devotion to God could protect against his wiles.

With such beliefs, the formal side of religion was expressed in a church the services of which were patterned on what were believed to be Biblical models. The result was the early Congregationalism of New England. To follow God's will was the aim of every Puritan, and God's will was written down once for all in the Bible. Hence, not only in the church but also in secular matters, religion was the centre of life, and the Bible was an infallible guide for government and a complete body of law for every human activity. The clergy were the interpreters of the divine writings, and inevitably, therefore, interpreters of the fundamental law of the Puritans' world. In the Scriptures they found rules for every man and every sphere. No act of life, however trivial, was beyond the reach of such laws.

Yet, with this belief and this discipline, men were no less human. To them their faith, grim and repellent as we find it, was warm and glowing to such a degree as to give their lives all the intellectual stimulus, all the inspiration, and all the absorbing interest they could crave. Their intense concentration on individual spiritual progress, and the advance of the state toward

13. Cf. B. Wendell, "Some Neglected Characteristics of the New England Puritans," in his *Stelligeri*.

what they believed to be godliness, eclipsed all else. Naturally, in such a world there was no place for ideas of religious liberty or freedom of conscience, and few Puritans thought of them. God's law was revealed in the Bible, interpreted by His agents, the clergy, and departure from it meant departure from the Divine Word. Where anyone who wavered by ever so little from harmonious following of God's will could feel sure of everlasting death, differences of religious opinion showed not merely "freedom of conscience" but hopeless unregeneracy. To punish a man who failed to accept Puritan rule in all its aspects, to banish him, or to take his life, was but to protect the church and state decreed of God by just human chastisement of one already sentenced by divine preordination. Inevitably Puritanism was intolerant; inevitably it was often cruel. Tolerance and gentleness would have meant faintness in the pursuit of its central ideals.

Our bundling together of loose strands plucked from the skein of Puritanism leaves much unsaid.[14] The love for learning, the zeal for education, the neglect of art in favor of more practical pursuits, are all traits untouched. Such omissions are repaired in the pages which follow, for in every year of Increase Mather's life there is material of use to him who would know the Puritan. And, after all, though our view of the mental attitude of early New England be incomplete, it matters little for our ends. Our goal is a visioning of Increase Mather's life and nature. The medium in which he worked was Puritanism. Whatever we think of it, the life of the man absorbed by it has meaning and validity. One thing alone we must grant, the sincerity underlying his point of view. Whatever Puritanism was, it was real to him. However we may decry it as unenlightened or cruel, or praise it as fundamentally concerned with the noblest of aims, we cannot forget that in it, with its faults and virtues, there was power to occupy the energies of an intellectually active and vigorously human man. The qualities that made him "the greatest of the native Puritans"[15] are eternal. Their outward expression was dictated by his times. Their appeal for us lies in their essential strength, and their harmonious fusion into a character of potentiality for any age and, in his own period, developed in leadership and power.

14. See, for further statements, J. F. Jameson, *History of Historical Writing*, p. 34; G. E. Ellis, *Memorial History of Boston*, i, 161; J. C. Bowman, "The Hated Puritan," in *Weekly Review* (N. Y.), v, 10; and, especially, S. P. Sherman, "What is a Puritan?" in *The Genius of America*, pp. 35ff.

15. Wendell, *Cotton Mather*, p. 287.

RICHARD MATHER'S BIRTHPLACE AT WINWICK

CHAPTER II

THE MATHERS IN ENGLAND

SOME time in 1614 there sat beneath a hedge in Lancashire a boy of eighteen, weeping bitterly "to lament his misery before God."[1] Such was Richard Mather's religious coming of age. Boy as he was, the effect of Puritan teachings was for him an intense conviction of the power of the Lord, and of his own unworthiness. His emotion drove him from the hospitable table of Edward Aspinwall, of Toxteth, near Liverpool, to seek solitude for repentance and prayer. From this dawning of religious feeling sprang his consecration to the Puritan church. With his boyish fears at his first spiritual awakening, began an unswerving devotion to his faith, passed on as a heritage to his descendants, and transformed by him and them into service which brought renown to their family name.

For generations before Richard's day Mathers seem to have been known in England, especially in Lancashire,[2] and there are still members of the family proud of their heritage. But it was only with the beginning of the seventeenth century that there rose from the old stock a man with a sound claim to distinction. Just what it was in the character of the times at the accession of James the First that fanned into a blaze the love for learning and the ability for leadership that smouldered in the Lancashire Mathers, we can only guess. Perhaps the breath of inspiration was in the increasing opportunities for education, in the beginnings of greater power for the yeomanry, or in the widespread effect of Puritanism on traditional ideas. Certain it is that in 1596 an old timbered house in Mather Lane, in the tiny village of Lowton, a part of the parish of Winwick in Lancashire, became the birthplace of a man who was to gain more than local prominence and, in Puritan circles, enduring fame.[3]

1. Increase Mather, *The Life and Death of... Mr. Richard Mather* (reprinted, Boston, 1850), p. 48.

2. For the name Mather, see H. Harrison, *Surnames of the United Kingdom*, vol. 2, and C. W. Bardsley, *A Dictionary of... Surnames*.

3. *Dictionary of National Biography*, and W. Beamont, *Winwick: Its History and Antiquities* (2d ed.).

Richard Mather's parents "*Thomas* and *Margarite Mather* were of Ancient Families in *Lowton* aforesaid, but by reason of some unhappy Mortgages they were reduced unto a low condition as to the World." [4] We know little more, except that the father of Thomas, and the grandfather of Richard, is said to have been one John Mather.[5] The family seems, so far as one can tell, to have been of the yeoman class.

To his parents Richard Mather owed the privilege of an education as good as the time and place allowed. A harsh schoolmaster, William Horrocke, then in charge of Winwick school, "very severe and partial in his discipline," caused his pupil to "desire that his Father would take him from School, and dispose of him to some other Calling." [6] But Richard could write later: "God intended better for me, then I would have chosen for my self; and therefore my Father, though in other things indulgent enough, yet in this would never condescend to my request, but by putting me in hope that by his speaking to the Master, things would be amended, would still overrule me to go on in my Studies." The father's determination to educate his son, proof against the boy's own pleas, was not immune to the arguments offered by his slender purse. "Popish merchants" came from Wales to Warrington, and there, two miles from Winwick, heard of young Richard as "a pregnant youth." Needing an apprentice, they applied to his father for him. It was the stern schoolmaster who restrained Thomas Mather, sorely tempted "to accept of this Motion, because now his Estate was so decayed, that he almost despaired of bringing up this his Son as he had intended." Horrocke was "importunate with" Richard's "Father still to keep him at School, professing that it was great pity that a Wit so prone to Learning should be taken from it . . . or that he should be undone by Popish Education." "The Perswasions of the Master . . . prevailed," and Richard continued to study, boarding at the school in winter, and in summer travelling each day the four miles through the quiet countryside between the old house in Lowton and the town of Winwick.[7]

Horrocke was not the only influence to defend Richard Mather against Popery. One "Mr. *Palin*, then Preacher at *Leagh*,"

4. I. Mather, *The Life and Death*, p. 43.
5. H. E. Mather, *Lineage of Rev. Richard Mather*, p. 25.
6. I. Mather, *The Life and Death*, p. 44. For Horrocke, see *DNB*, article "Richard Mather," and Beamont, *Winwick*, pp. 91, 92.
7. I. Mather, *The Life and Death*, pp. 44, 45.

impressed the boy with "such a plain, powerfull and piercing efficacy . . . as was not to be seen in the common sort of Preachers in those dayes, by means whereof some Illumination . . . was wrought in him." [8]

Mather's first step into the world came in 1611, when he was but fifteen years old. Projects for American colonization and troubles in Ireland probably had affected him hitherto quite as little as James I's difficulties with Parliament. To him the translation of the Bible in the great King James version may well have seemed of less immediate interest than the fact that in the same year he was to leave Lowton for what must have appeared a considerable adventure — the twenty-mile journey to Toxteth Park, and the beginning of his duties as schoolmaster there.

In 1611, the tenants of Sir Richard Molyneux, owner of a piece of property known as Toxteth Park, formerly a holding of the crown, and to-day swallowed up in Liverpool, resolved to set up for their children a grammar school.[9] It was to Horrocke that they applied for a teacher,[10] and so Richard Mather, who would have preferred to go on as a student in one of the universities, but was, because of the necessities of his family, left no choice, became at fifteen a full-fledged schoolmaster. "The Lord helped him in those his young years to carry it with such Wisdome and Love and Gravity amongst his Scholars as was to admiration, so as that he was by them both loved and feared, beyond what is usual, even where there are aged Masters." [11]

His success gave him local reputation, at least, and he had a chance to continue his own studies in the course of his work. Religiously, too, the experience was of influence, for at Toxteth he lived with the family of Mr. Edward Aspinwall, "a Learned and Religious Gentleman" and undoubtedly a Puritan in sympathies. Add to this that Richard Mather heard sermons from Mr. Harrison, "then a famous Minister at *Hyton*," and one sees why this boy, faced with problems beyond his years, was bowled over by a conviction of his own sinfulness and of the saving powers of the Puritan's faith.[12]

8. I. Mather, *The Life and Death*, p. 46. Leagh was the village now called Leigh.
9. V. D. Davis, *The Ancient Chapel of Toxteth Park*, p. 1.
10. *Ibid.*, p. 9.
11. I. Mather, *The Life and Death*, p. 47.
12. *Ibid.*, pp. 47, 48.

After the first stormy access of religious feeling, "Being thus become a *New Creature*, he was the more eminently a Blessing in the Family, and in the Calling which the Lord has disposed of him in: And such notice was taken of him, as that even from places remote Children were sent unto him for Instruction and Education; and many were, by the Lords blessing upon his Endeavours, fitted for, and sent unto the *University*. Some years having been past over . . . he resolved . . . to spend some time in one of the Universities. . . . Accordingly he went to *Oxford*, and continued for some time there in *Brazen-Nose Colledge*." He delighted in the books and learned men he found there, "But his heart being afore this touched with the fear of God, the great Superstition and Prophaness which he was forced there to behold, was no small grief unto him." [13]

Once again his education was interrupted, for before he took his degree, the people at Toxteth called him back, "desiring that he would . . . instruct not so much their Children as themselves, and that not in meer Humane Literature, but in the things of God." [14] In name they were members of the Church of England; they were Puritans at heart. Naturally enough they did not care to go three miles to St. Nicholas' Church in Liverpool [15] to be ministered to with rites they did not approve. Mather's preaching was more to their mind. "After due Consideration, for weighty Reasons he accepted" their call, and on November 30, 1618, he preached his first sermon. [16]

James I's policy toward Puritans was strict enough to make episcopal ordination necessary for this minister of twenty-two. He accepted it at the hands of Thomas Morton, Bishop of Chester. The story is told how, after the ceremony, the Bishop startled him by singling him out with the words: "I have something to say to you betwixt you and me alone." He then asked Mather to pray for him. "For I know," said Morton, "the Prayers of men that fear God will avail much, and you, I believe are such an one." [17] If the story be true, and it comes to us from Richard himself, through his son Increase, such notice from the Bishop, who was known as "a great patron of good and learned

13. I. Mather, *The Life and Death*, pp. 48, 49.

14. *Ibid.*, p. 49. It appears that Mather was not the first minister at the Toxteth Chapel. Cf. *Transactions of the Historic Society of Lancashire and Cheshire*, lxxi, 90.

15. V. D. Davis, *The Ancient Chapel of Toxteth Park*, p. 2.

16. I. Mather, *The Life and Death*, pp. 49, 50.

17. *Ibid.*, p. 50.

men," [18] must have been flattering to this newest preacher in his diocese, and, if it became known abroad, must have augmented Mather's reputation. The incident seems typical of Morton, who belonged, according to Baxter, "to that class of episcopal divines who differ in nothing considerable from the rest of the reformed churches except in church government," and was placed by Clarendon with "the less formal and more popular prelates." [19]

Richard Mather, thus settled in his daily work at Toxteth Park, found time enough free from his parish cares to sue for the hand of Katharine Hoult, or Holt, daughter to Edmund Holt of Bury. She "had (and that deservedly) the repute of a very godly and prudent Maid." [20] Her father had no love for Puritans, but his wife and many of her family were years later called by Increase Mather "singularly pious and prudent." [21] Such comment from an ardent Puritan suggests, at least, that to Mrs. Holt Richard Mather's religious opinions were not so repugnant as they were to her husband. Whatever his scruples against a nonconformist son-in-law may have been, they were overcome by September 29, 1624, for on that day his daughter's marriage to Richard Mather took place. [22]

The couple moved three miles, to "Much-Woolton," where Mather bought a house of his own. He preached each Sunday at Toxteth, but his influence was extended, for in alternate weeks he lectured at Prescot, and was often called to preach in other parishes. [23] In 1629, too, at the request of the Lord Mayor, he gave two monthly sermons at Liverpool, winning thus a wider influence than had yet been his. [24]

In 1625 James I died, and Charles succeeded him. The new King brought an ecclesiastical policy far less tolerant of the sort of nonconformity Mather was coming more and more to uphold. Six years before, Bishop Morton had been replaced by John Bridgeman. The latter was no more unsympathetic toward the Puritans than his predecessor, but he had to contend with official interest in the affairs of his diocese. In 1633, Laud became Arch-

18. *DNB*, article "Thomas Morton, 1564–1659."
19. *Ibid.*
20. I. Mather, *The Life and Death*, p. 51.
21. *Autobiography.*
22. I. Mather, *The Life and Death*, p. 51.
23. *Ibid.*, p. 52.
24. J. A. Picton, *Selections from... Archives*, p. 200.

bishop of Canterbury, and in August of that year, Bridgeman, probably under pressure from his superiors, suspended Richard Mather for failure to use the ceremonies of the established church. "Some Gentlemen in *Lancashire*" interceded, among them one Simon Byby, "a near Alliance" of Bridgeman's, proved on another occasion a good friend to John Cotton.[25] By their efforts Mather was in November restored to the ministry. Undaunted, "he more fully searched into . . . and handled the Points of *Church-Discipline*" in his preaching.[26]

By this time he seems to have been committed fully to the "Congregational Way," a form of worship the importance and nature of which will become clearer in connection with the establishment of the Mathers in the colonies. His activities promptly got him into further trouble, for visitors from Richard Neal (or Neile), Archbishop of York, the man who had first brought Laud to the notice of the King, and one who declared himself "a great adversary of the Puritan faction," came into Lancashire.[27] In 1634 Mather was summoned before them at Wigan. In his own words, he stood "before them without being daunted in the least measure, but answered . . . such words . . . as the Lord put into" his "mouth, not being afraid of their faces at all." He was sentenced to suspension for nonconformity, and in this latest crisis his friends seemed powerless. Later in his life he told how he had torn up the certificate of ordination he had received from Morton, thus protesting against the ceremonial it represented. We may well believe that this took place before 1634, when his views seem to have been definitely fixed in regard to all the rites of the established church. Before the court at Wigan, we read, he declared that he had never in his ministry worn a surplice; and his son reports with evident satisfaction that one of the court remarked, "It had been better for him that he had gotten Seven Bastards." [28]

From this time his thoughts seem to have turned to New England. Characteristically, he drew up detailed arguments as to why he should hazard the long voyage to the New World. He seems to have convinced himself. To remove from a corrupt

25. I. Mather, *The Life and Death*, p. 54. For Byby and Cotton, see T. Hutchinson, *A Collection of Original Papers*, i, 275.
26. I. Mather, *The Life and Death*, p. 54.
27. *DNB*, article "Richard Neile."
28. I. Mather, *The Life and Death*, p. 56.

church to a purer; to remove from a place where the truth and the professors of it were persecuted, to a place of more quietness and safety; to remove from a church where the discipline of Christ was wanting, to a church where it might be enjoyed; to remove from a place where the ministers of God were unjustly inhibited from the execution of their functions, to a place where they might more freely execute them; to remove from a place where there were fearful signs of desolation to a place where one might have well-grounded hope of preservation, and of God's protection [29] — these were some of the objects to be achieved by his pilgrimage. In this list we find no word of universal religious toleration to be set up in New England. To Mather and similarly minded men, as to his sons who followed after, New England was to be the home of one religion which, however radical and subversive of tradition it may have seemed in Wigan, in Boston was to be as firmly established and as explicit in its demands as the religious order against which it was a great revolt.

Talk with Lancashire friends, and letters from Hooker and Cotton,[30] whose desertion of England had won them prominence in Massachusetts, strengthened Mather in his plan. In April, 1635, in his thirty-ninth year, with his wife and his four sons, Samuel, Timothy, Nathaniel, and Joseph, the eldest a boy of nine, he set out from Warrington for Bristol. Picturesqueness is added to the scene, if we believe that to avoid detention he was forced to travel in disguise.[31] Seven days were used in the journey of one hundred and twenty miles to Bristol. How they were inspected and licensed to leave the country, how they sailed on June 4, in the *James*, of their delays in getting to sea, their sickness, the wonders they saw, and of their escape from shipwreck and coming to anchor at last at "Nantascot" on August 16, we may read in Richard Mather's graphically detailed "Journal."[32] On August 17, 1635, the family went ashore at Boston, and from that day dates the fame of the line of Mather in New England.

It took independence of character to be a Puritan in the early seventeenth century, and Mather's life in England shows that he by no means lacked the courage of his convictions. It took

---

29. I. Mather, *The Life and Death*, pp. 57ff.

30. Thomas Hooker and John Cotton, two divines prominent in early New England. *Ibid.*, p. 68.

31. *Ibid.*, p. 69.

32. Reprinted in *Dorchester Antiquarian and Historical Society Collections*, Number 3, Boston, 1850, pp. 2ff.

intellectual vigor and sound learning to achieve as much as he had achieved in the first forty years of his life. Willingness to undergo hardships for what seemed a good and true cause was needed for him to undertake the long voyage to Boston. His qualities may well have been shared by his wife, and a large part of the burden must have been hers to bear. Doubtless she did it well. The character of his parents accounts for much in their most famous son Increase, and those to whom in later years he was to give his name.

CHAPTER III

PURITAN EMIGRANTS

IN Richard Mather's "Journal" for August 16, 1635, we read
"came y^t night to ancre ... before Boston, and so rested y^t
night with glad & thankefull hearts y^t God had put an end to o^r
long journey." From the deck of the little ship they looked out
on "a most pleasant harbor," such as they had never seen before,
"amongst a great many of Ilands on every side." Timber-covered
hills, salt marshes, and natural meadow lands, with here and there
a pale column of smoke marking some one of the villages about
the bay, made a pleasant picture to travellers weary of the sea.
But in the hearts of Richard and Katharine Mather there must
have been emotions other than mere thankfulness for their
journey's end.

At our safe distance it is hard to remember what real terrors
were known in the early seventeenth century to lurk behind the
smiling landscape of Massachusetts. It is only too easy to forget
the chill of strangeness that struck to the heart of a Lancashire
man viewing for the first time the awakening of English life on
the shores of New England. Instead of villages of seasoned timber
and stone, comfortably gray with age, here were scattered log
huts or barn-like houses, with newly made clapboards covering
beams recently cut from the surrounding forests. Instead of
fields matured by centuries of tillage, and enclosed by hedges or
trim walls, Mather saw in what was to be the home of his last
years woods broken only by rough clearings or by the broad
natural meadows stretching down to the sea. Above them rose
the bare hills of Boston, one crowned by the newly built beacon.[1]

The very lack of underbrush held meaning, perhaps, for the
Mathers may well have known that the Indians had burned over
the ground to give clear passage for their hunting parties.[2] With
such thoughts came the memory that the red-skinned "Children
of the Devil"[3] held great terror for those who sought to do God's

1. W. Wood, *New Englands Prospect*, p. 40; J. G. Palfrey, *History*, i, 395.
2. W. Wood, *New Englands Prospect*, p. 16.
3. Cf. Cotton Mather, *Magnalia*, book I, chap. 1, section 2.

work in a wilderness community. Perhaps they might be converted to a Christian mode of life, but the bears and wolves were sure to prove even less tractable neighbors. Somewhere, too, there may have lurked a momentary dread of "the kingly Lyon" as an enemy still more to be feared.[4]

Richard Mather had gone too far to turn back. The courage that led him to cross "one of ye greatest seas in ye world," [5] and the spirit that supported him before the court at Wigan, were ready to brave dangers on these unfriendly shores. Just in so far as we can realize what this courage and this spirit were, and translate ourselves into the position of those of our ancestors who were imbued by them, can we hope to understand the world in which the two Mathers laid the foundations for the enormously significant career of their son Increase. If we fail to catch their fervor, then Richard, Increase, Cotton — all the Mathers, and their fellow founders of New England — become mere historical abstractions of a grim and repellent type. If we cannot share their warm devotion to their ideal, the picture of Puritan New England becomes cold and lifeless, and the great figures fade into the dimmest of gray. We are handicapped by three centuries of change, and by the numbing influence of historical distance. Facts that were to Richard Mather the very elements of daily life are for us but sentences in a textbook, remote and colorless on the printed page. To him the affairs of the Boston in which he landed were as vividly clear as the political situation in England which led to his intrepid setting out across the sea. To him the meaning of the government of Church and State in New England was as apparent as is to us the latest venture in "self-determination." The causes and theories from which the new structure arose were quite as well established in his mind as are in ours the essential changes wrought by the European war. In facing his new world he had chiefly to overcome the perplexities caused by new surroundings, new climate, and the material beginnings of a new colony. When we try to stand beside him, however, our difficulty is less in appreciating the externals of frontier life than in picturing plainly enough the form of state and the type of church which made early Massachusetts what it was. Above all, it is hard for us to do what is most of all necessary — to share

4. W. Wood, *New Englands Prospect*, pp. 20, 21; T. Lechford, *Plain Dealing*, pp. 111, 112.

5. R. Mather, *Journal*, p. 31.

in some degree the enthusiasm that made this government, this church, and this great colonial venture, not a dream of some philosopher in his closet, or the material for history of distant antiquity, but an intensely living fact.

We can hope to feel the power of this enthusiasm only through recalling the circumstances from which it had its birth. On the one hand, the teachings of Calvin, the growth of popular education in England, and the restless search of many men for the purest and most primitive way of service to God, come at once to mind. On the other side, we cannot forget the tendency of the English Church after the Reformation to grow quite as rigid as the establishment against which it had rebelled, nor the inevitable realization by English kings that a strong ecclesiastical force, obedient to the royal will, was essential to the effective exercise of royal power. Against this background stand those brave men and women who despaired of the Church of England, and, for preferring to its rites a different form of worship, which they believed to have been ordained by Holy Writ, incurred the penalties of the English law, fled to Holland, and suffered there the homesickness of loyal Englishmen on foreign soil. They dreamed of a colony of their own, under the English flag, but with their own forms of worship, so much purer, they warmly believed, than any England knew; and in their amazingly courageous migration to Plymouth they made their dream a fact. Their complete separation from the established church shows how far Puritanism had developed in 1620. Their facing down of perils which, they knew too well, beset them reveals, as we read of it in Bradford, a first great blazing up of that placing of service to God before service to man, that eager search for the true way of life, and that hot vigor in turning the religious ideal into the practical basis of daily life, that made New England possible.

Beside these pioneers there stand those other Puritans whose protest against the English Church was less fundamental but quite as sincere. Their difference was not in creed or doctrine but purely in matters of government and ceremonial. Increase Mather says, "we agree with other reformed churches," and adds that it was "what concerns worship and discipline, that caused our fathers to come into this wilderness." [6] They insisted that the local congregation must be an integral unit, independent of others, and that its basis must be a covenant of its members

6. *Religious History of New England*, p. 7.

agreeing together to form a church. Over such bodies of believers there were to minister men deriving their powers from the congregation, with jurisdiction only in spiritual matters.[7] And, of course, the guide in every concern of life was the word of God which must be admitted to be directly revealed in the pages of the Bible.[8] We must not think, because no one of these tenets had to do with the creed or the fundamental doctrine of the church, that the points at issue were any the less grave. God was to be strictly obeyed, and His written commands followed in detail. The ceremonies of the Church of England were not directly ordered by Holy Writ. Hence they were not to be tolerated by him who feared God.[9] To protest against them was but to observe the divine will. Nothing could be more important to the true Puritan. We need not try to see just what he thought, so long as we realize that he did think, and thought so deeply that his conclusions were to him something to be upheld not only with words but with deeds. For them he would face the utmost in hardship, and defy perseveringly the perils of sea and land.

Men who felt thus were the settlers in and about Boston. In their ranks were a number of university men, many of them educated at Puritanically inclined Cambridge. Richard Mather's reasons for leaving England to follow them five years after their great migration were the same that theirs had been. It was to the State they had built that he came, and under their government he established himself. As we have seen, neither he nor they wished universal tolerance. Their aim was to build their own church in their own way. It was still considered part of the English establishment.[10] Its members were English subjects, their numbers were few, their difficulties great, and the country strange to them. All this Richard Mather understood, just as he was prepared to find in the Massachusetts of 1635 a community where the government and the religious system were both based on such directions as could be found in the Bible, where the ministers were often learned and always regarded as the final authorities on Scriptural interpretation, and where, accordingly, they held great power in the state. Originally it was held that

---

7. Cf., in general, *Religious History of New England*, pp. 1–73; H. M. Dexter, *Congregationalism;* and W. Walker, *A History of the Congregational Churches.*

8. Cf. Chapter 4, note 6, *post.*

9. Cf. Palfrey, i, 113, 114.

10. Idem, i, 312; C. Mather, *Magnalia*, book I, chap. 4, section 1; and T. G. Wright, *Literary Culture*, pp. 15, 16.

the religious and the civil governments were quite distinct; but inevitably, with Holy Writ as the guide for both, and the ministers as the sole interpreters of its pages, the line of division was often blurred. Mather knew, and we must not forget, that it was with a definite idea of founding not only a church but a harmonious Bible government that the Puritans came.[11] Their success or failure can be read in his life, and his son's. Both influenced profoundly the course of Puritanism in the New World.

Religion and government were the greatest concerns of the Puritan, and foremost in Richard Mather's mind. They were topics that left little room for minor things. In England such men as Jonson, Massinger, Ford, and John Milton dominated the literary scene. But in Plymouth and Boston, literature was a minor matter, and such books as were written live for the most part not as art but as earnest records of human experience, or concise statements of definite religious views. To the New Englanders of the time, art was less important than the record of solid realities, and books were valued only for the sound doctrine they might contain. Poetry and drama were luxuries out of place in a frontier community where practical learning and instruction in religious and civil business were staple needs. Moreover the Puritans were for the most part men tasting for the first time the fruits of education. Most of them came from families without learned background, and to them the opportunity to study had come as a rare privilege offered by the changing times. Naturally, then, they turned to the classics, to the solid cornerstones of scholarship, and to those books most packed with learning. (They found no time for mere works of art. They wrote to teach, and read to learn. Scholarship, not literature, was their goal.)

All this, and much more, Mather accepted without thought, as part of the very texture of his everyday world. Many another aspect of his times, forgotten by us, deserves to be recalled, but even with what has been said we may perhaps understand him and his illustrious son so far as we deal with the mere events and facts of their lives. But we cannot hope to appreciate how the Mathers felt on that memorable evening when they first walked through the newly laid out streets of Boston, unless we try constantly to revive in ourselves the spirit that gave them courage and life.

11. *Religious History of New England*, pp. 12, 13.

It was a spirit of sincere loyalty to an ideal, and to a church and state founded upon it. Their minds knew no doubt where their great purpose was involved; and doubts of a later day should not affect us when we would follow them with sympathetic minds. Unquestionable sincerity was theirs, great hardihood, great perseverance, and, judged by their results in the wilderness, great skill. Calvinists we cannot be, perhaps, nor can we see in every incident the direct interposition of God. Few of us can create for ourselves an Almighty so stern and rigorous as Richard Mather's, or accept the doctrine that only a chosen few are God's elect, and by Him saved from hell. Each of us, aided by the accumulated experience of three hundred years, can pick flaws in the government and policy of the Puritans. But is there one of us who can quite resist men who served their faith with such deep earnestness? They were radicals when it was far easier to be reactionaries; they were pioneers when the wilderness held unusual dangers; they were state-builders in spite of every material difficulty; they were church-builders unaided by the force of tradition; and they were, above all, sincere and single-minded in word and act. Grant them admiration for what they achieved, share their spirit for one moment, and the task of forgetting the twentieth century for the seventeenth is done, and with clear consciences and stout hearts we may land in Boston with Richard Mather. With him, we shall be ready to meet and face unafraid what the morrow may bring forth.

CHAPTER IV

THE SETTLEMENT OF THE MATHERS IN NEW ENG-LAND. — THE BIRTH OF INCREASE MATHER

AS we leave the *James* with Richard Mather, and enter the Boston of 1635, there are still details that waken our interest, although they were to him the veriest commonplaces. We may puzzle over the validity of the charter [1] by which Massachusetts was owned, and under which John Haynes was then governor. We may question the justifiability of the colony's determination to protect their patent against revocation or alteration from England.[2] We may stop to consider the way in which New England's political problem, the government of a large settlement by those few men to whom the charter gave power, and the admission of enough new members to the corporation to ensure its permanency without endangering its orthodoxy, had been solved. We shall find no ideals of universal suffrage, abstract democracy, nor any motives other than the practical ambition to preserve Massachusetts as a Bible commonwealth, the stronghold of a particular faith.) We shall discover that the authority was in the hands of Winthrop and other good Puritans, elected by church members alone.[3]

How this "aristocratic republic" appealed to the large part [4] of the population whose interests in New England were not primarily religious, or who, for one reason or another,[5] had not joined one of the churches springing up in and about Boston, may seem to twentieth-century eyes a grave question. To some of us the Puritan political scheme may seem fundamentally wrong. The harshness of our judgment increases in proportion to our belief in democracy as we know it as the ideal rule for all states. But Mather saw Massachusetts as a refuge for one sect, where others than the orthodox had no right to disobey the laws piously made

1. *Lectures on Massachusetts History*, chap. 11.
2. Palfrey, vol. 1, chap. 10.
3. *Mass. Rec.*, May 18, 1631. For Winthrop, see R. C. Winthrop, *Life and Letters of John Winthrop*.
4. Channing, i, 347ff.
5. *Lectures on Massachusetts History*, p. 61 n.

for them.[6] He could regard calmly what was probably the most discussed affair of the day in Boston, the banishment of the too vociferously conscientious Roger Williams.[7] To the Puritans this seemed, not persecution, but a necessary weeding out of heresy striking at the very root of the structure of the New England they believed in; and the checking of an unorthodoxy made dangerous chiefly because of the vehemence of its expression.[8] Mather could see current affairs as the colonial leaders saw them. He could trace in their actions the unswerving pursuit of a clearly visioned goal. To it we are too often blind. Thus we make the whole record of the early years of Massachusetts seem an unintelligible chaos of oligarchic intolerance. Once more we must see with Puritan eyes. Only thus can we understand the times and the men who dominated them.

Seeing for the moment as Richard Mather saw, we shall find the people in the streets of Boston in no way strange. Their doublets and buckled belts, their hose, the ruffs of the gentry, and the broad-brimmed hats — and perhaps here and there a bit of forbidden lace — were simply English costume, worn by Englishmen in new surroundings. There were social distinctions here as at home. "Mr." and "Mrs." were titles to be claimed only by those of undoubted prominence, by ministers or magistrates, while the lesser members of the colony contented themselves with the humbler "Goodman" or "Goodwife."[9]

But, obvious and normal as all this seemed, the Mathers cannot have been indifferent to the physical setting of the Puritans' colonial experiment. They found themselves in a city of less than five thousand souls,[10] with "thirty houses"[11] and many less pretentious dwellings, pleasantly situated on a peninsula between the "Bay of Roxberry" and the "Charles-River." There was interest for newcomers in the fishing boats at the wharves, the fences against the wolves, the heaps of furs from Indian traders, the granaries of maize, the fabrics woven at Rowley, the freshly

6. *Lectures on Massachusetts History*, pp. 31ff. On the Bible as the basis of the Puritans' law, cf. R. C. Winthrop, *Life and Letters*, ii, 445; W. Walker, *Creeds and Platforms*, p. 203; and J. Winthrop, *History of New England*, i, 240.

7. W. Walker, *A History*, pp. 136, 137; O. S. Straus, *Roger Williams*; and Channing, i, 381.

8. J. Winthrop, *History of New England*, especially i, 209, 210. Cf. in general, Palfrey, i, 300, 388.

9. On the foregoing details, see *Memorial History of Boston*, i, 123, 486, 487.

10. F. B. Dexter, *Estimates of Population*.

11. J. Josselyn, *An Account of Two Voyages*, p. 20, and Palfrey, ii, 62 n.

felled timber from the woods, and the beginnings of roads throughout the countryside.[12] These were all sights satisfying to a family venturing its all in a spot of wilderness recently reclaimed by the chosen of God. To admit that Mather and his brethren were deeply concerned with such practical affairs as the prosperity of the fisheries or the Indian trading expeditions is not to be forced to follow some modern writers in the difficult leap to the belief that worldly considerations eclipsed religious ones in the minds of the founders of Massachusetts. (Practical necessities of life were inevitably to the fore in their thoughts.)They were faced with the problem of self-support in a strange country; they knew that only by active trade could colonists be induced to join them; and they knew that though they as leaders had come from motives largely concerned with their religious faith, their state could not survive long with leaders alone. Laborers, tradesmen, and craftsmen were all needed for the colony's life. No one knew better than Mather and his spiritually minded brethren that a starving town could never nourish a vigorous church.

To the visitor in Boston in 1635, the prospects for Massachusetts must have seemed bright, and to the Puritan there was good augury for the permanence of his ideal state. Comfortable houses were rapidly replacing the huts of the early settlers, the wharves bore witness to the beginnings of commerce, while indoors the abundant variety of food showed that, for the present, famine was not to be feared.[13] To us, perhaps, the absence of luxury, of amusements, of the visible tokens of an interest in art, strikes a chill. To the Mathers and their friends such deficiencies passed unnoticed, or, if seen, were welcomed, for was there not always the church? Was not the church to them, in the fervency of their faith, the centre of all life? The cold and cheerless meeting-house offered them the warmest and most glowing interest man could have. Worship was not worship merely, but the gratification of the longing that dictated their every step, the apotheosis of all hobbies, and the all-sufficing substitute for worldly recreations and unprofitable ways of passing time, given by God to be devoted by men to His work. With worship went the need and desire for learning, for in knowledge lay greater opportunity for service to the Church.[14] Thus, between the

12. For these details see W. Wood, *New Englands Prospect*, p. 39, and Palfrey, ii, 52–54, 58.

13. Palfrey, ii, 56, 57, 59, and E. Johnson, *A History of New England*, p. 210.

14. Cf., for example, I. Mather, *The Life and Death*, pp. 75, 88, 89.

rudely finished study of his home, still redolent of new wood, and the severely austere meeting-house, many a Bostonian found more than enough of intellectual excitement to fill the hours that his labors in conquering the material hardships of frontier life left him for such joys.

Others, no doubt, found their solace in other ways. They sought profit in sound coin of the realm rather than in accumulated credit for a future life. They may well have felt a bitter sense of injustice at paying taxes to support a church with which they were unsympathetic, and complained, justly enough, we may think, against subjection to a government in which they had a voice but no vote.[15] But their leaders loved the church and believed in it, and, to them, men who did not share their belief were outcasts in this world and the next, without right to dictate in a commonwealth governed by the Puritan interpretation of the Bible and consecrated to one form of service to God. Naturally then, Mather and his fellow thinkers went their way quite untroubled by ideals of a rule better than Winthrop's, and mercifully ignorant of the political theories that in centuries to come were to change the world for their descendants. Boston Puritans in 1635 believed that they were building on a sound basis. Problems might occur, but such men as Richard Mather, by nature and experience, were strong enough to face them down.

The newcomers on the *James* were warmly received. A Puritan preacher known in England, in New England was sure to be hailed with delight. A man with university training and a student and lover of books found many of similar experiences and tastes in Boston. An able writer on points of religious controversy, such as Richard Mather was soon to prove himself, was to the colonial leaders a most grateful prize.[16] It was among friends that he set to work to build up a new home, admired Governor Winthrop's house, talked to such reverend men as Wilson and Hooker,[17] and enrolled himself and his wife as members of the Boston church.[18] There were about him many university graduates, and there are

15. Channing, i, 343; J. T. Adams, *The Founding*, pp. 172, 213ff., 388; and *Lectures on Massachusetts History*, p. 63. That taxation for the support of the church did not seem to some Puritan leaders to be the best method is shown by Cotton's views, reflected in J. Winthrop, *History of New England*, i, 144, 145 and n.

16. E. Johnson, *A History of New England*, pp. 104, 105.

17. For John Wilson, see C. Mather, *Magnalia*, book III, chap. 3. For Hooker, see G. L. Walker, *Thomas Hooker*.

18. J. Winthrop, *History of New England*, i, 218 n.; I. Mather, *The Life and Death*, p. 74.

abundant records revealing the existence of good libraries, the importation of books, and their circulation among the townsfolk.[19] For a man who loved his own well-filled bookshelves [20] Boston was no intellectual desert. For a good Puritan it was a plain well watered by sound literature and the teachings of enlightened men.

The books soon to be produced in New England were, indeed, more to Mather's mind than what we now regard as the best work of the time in the mother country. A printing press of their own relieved Massachusetts writers from the necessity of trusting their manuscripts to a long sea voyage.[21] There were printers in the colony before they found a place in several quite as well-settled communities in England,[22] and the defects of the books they published are far more apparent to us than they were to those who read the sheets fresh from the press. To contemporary readers the first publications in Massachusetts appealed through their timeliness. No flavor of antiquity marked them then, but their value was obvious to every New Englander who would read the newest expressions on the most important matters of every-day life. The beginnings were slow and small, but the first literature of the colonies suffers little when compared with what practical, hard-working Puritans printed elsewhere.[23] There was no Milton in New England, and such poetry as saw the light, though no worse than much which found a hearing at the same time in England, lacks any merit to preserve it for our day. There was no Ford, no Ben Jonson, no Heywood, and no Shirley in Boston, for which every faithful devotee of the new state gave thanks; but there was Thomas Hooker to expound religion, William Wood to describe the material side of life, and Richard Mather himself — all three far better suited to Boston's early needs than dramatists whose art seemed to the colonists irretrievably profane and vile.

Books and reading were alluring, but Richard Mather's mission was practical. He had come to resume the preaching interrupted in England; and we read that, while he "abode with his Family for some Moneths in *Boston* . . . . Motions from sundry Towns were

19. Cf. T. G. Wright, *Literary Culture*, chaps. 2, 3, 4.
20. See references to books owned by Richard Mather, in J. H. Tuttle, *The Libraries of the Mathers*, and Mather's will, *Ibid.*, p. 277.
21. Cf. R. F. Roden, *The Cambridge Press*.
22. Cf. T. G. Wright, *Literary Culture*, pp. 80, 81.
23. Cf. *Ibid.*, p. 84.

soon presented to him," desiring him to undertake "the work of the Ministry amongst them." Plymouth called, as did Roxbury and Dorchester,[24] and, no doubt, he made the trip to the two last-named villages, as an aid to his decision. Roxbury, "a faire and handsome Countrey-towne; the inhabitants of it being all very rich," was "well woodded and watered; having a cleare and fresh Brooke running through the Towne," in which "there is great store of Smelts." [25]

All this was attractive, but it was on Dorchester, a mile away, that his choice fell. He "referred himself to the Advice of some judicious Friends; amongst whom, Mr. *Cotton* and Mr. *Hooker* were chief . . . and their Advice was, That he should accept of the Motion from *Dorchester*." [26] A wise decision, for his chosen field was "the greatest Towne in New England; well woodded and watered; very good arable grounds, and Hay-ground, faire Corne-fields, and pleasant Gardens, with Kitchin gardens." [27] There was opportunity here, since most of the first church in the town had moved to Connecticut, and Mather lost no time.[28] By April 1, 1636, a group was prepared to take the covenant required to form a new church. Prudent and far-sighted Puritan councils had seen that, with church membership as the test for the franchise, the forming of new churches must be supervised, and made subject to the consent of the magistrates and the existing congregations.[29] Winthrop tells how Mather and his followers were, on their first application, thought to be "not meet at present to be the foundation of a church" — but in explaining the defects in their belief, he excepts Mather himself as one whose orthodoxy was beyond cavil.[30] By August 23, however, the defects were remedied and "a Church was Constituted in *Dorchester* according to the Order of the Gospel, by Confession and Profession of Faith; and Mr. *Mather* was chosen *Teacher* of that Church." [31]

To remember just what was the scene enacted in Dorchester on that summer day of 1636 is to see more clearly essential elements of the time. Preaching, prayer, — both at length, — the

24. I. Mather, *The Life and Death*, p. 74.
25. W. Wood, *New Englands Prospect*, p. 39.
26. I. Mather, *The Life and Death*, p. 74.
27. W. Wood, *New Englands Prospect*, p. 39.
28. I. Mather, *The Life and Death*, p. 74; S. J. Barrows and W. B. Trask, *Records of the First Church at Dorchester*, Introduction.
29. I. Mather, *The Life and Death*, p. 75; *Mass. Rec.*, i, 168.
30. J. Winthrop, *History of New England*, i, 219.
31. I. Mather, *The Life and Death*, p. 75.

presence of representatives from the churches of neighboring towns and of a delegate of the civil government, a public confession of faith by the congregation, and their offering of evidence to support their sincerity, their cross-examination by the ministers, the bestowal upon them of the right hand of fellowship from other parishes, and, finally, the public acknowledgment of the covenant, binding the congregation together as a church "to walke togeather as a right ordered Congregacoñ of Cht."—these are the broad outlines.[32] In them we see the dawning realization of the need for close relations between individual churches and between the religious and civil establishments, the emphasis on definite evidence of conversion and public profession of fidelity, and, most of all, the democratic basis of the church in its creation from a voluntary consociation of would-be servants of the faith.[33]

At least thirty-five men were members of Mather's church when he took up his duties as "teacher," and laid on his capable shoulders the task of "attending to doctrine and therein administering a word of knowledge."[34] His parish was large, for Dorchester then comprised territory now divided among half a dozen towns.[35] There was plenty of work to be done, and the little meeting-house, standing near what was later the corner of Cottage and Pleasant streets,[36] absorbed much of Richard Mather's time. There was also his family to be cared for, and educated, and he had his own studies to pursue. Moreover, he soon found writing to be done to aid the Congregational cause. There were few idle hours in his day, even though his good wife "had taken . . . all Secular Cares, so that he wholly devoted himself to his Study."[37]

There were no established schools as yet, and the teaching of four sons was a task not to be evaded by a Puritan to whom books had proved the key of life.[38] The eldest boy was Samuel, nine years old. Two years younger was Timothy, and Nathaniel was but five when he first saw Boston. On May 13, 1637, Eleazar was

32. E. Johnson (*A History of New England*, pp. 214–216) describes the founding of a New England church. The text of the Dorchester church covenant is in Barrows and Trask, *Records*, pp. 1, 2.

33. The churches, once formed, do not seem to have been democratic in government. Cf. H. M. Dexter, *Congregationalism*, pp. 424–429.

34. Barrows and Trask, *Records*, p. xvii; W. Walker, *Creeds and Platforms*, p. 211.

35. *Memorial History of Boston*, i, 430.

36. *Ibid.*, pp. 435, 436.

37. I. Mather, *The Life and Death*, p. 77.

38. Palfrey, ii, 46; S. G. Drake, *The Pedigree of the Family of Mather*.

born.[39] Surely the Mathers found abundant interest and many problems within their own four walls. Some of their cares were shared by the new college across the river in Newtowne,[40] for Samuel Mather graduated with the second class it sent out, in 1643. Timothy never went to college, but Nathaniel followed Samuel, graduating in 1647, and returning at once to England.

There were preoccupations other than those concerned with growing youth. With that habit of introspection so typical of Puritanism, and rife among the Mathers, Richard grew uneasy as to his own religious state, and gladly availed himself of the help of the Reverend John Norton in putting his fears to rest.[41] There was literary work, too, for two sets of questions on church government came from English Puritans to their brethren in Boston. The larger of these Mather set himself to answer, and in so doing he covered clearly and ably the fundamentals of Congregationalism in New England.[42] A few years later he answered another English questioner, in his "Apologie of the Chvrches in New-England." [43] A third work of a different sort must have been even more exacting in its demands on his time. "The Whole Booke of Psalmes Faithfully Translated into English Metre," familiarly known as "The Bay Psalm Book," appeared as the work of John Eliot, famous for his work with the Indians, Thomas Welde,[44] his co-laborer in Roxbury, and Richard Mather. Chiefly remembered to-day as the third production of the new press at Cambridge, and by its rarity made dear to the bibliophile, it was to contemporary readers a scholarly work of sound religious value. Its popularity leaves no doubt as to its reception by those for whom it was designed.[45] And, though we may find its form barbarous, we cannot well forget what obstacles its authors overcame. To do so much, in their inexperience and their remoteness from centres of learning, was real achievement. Nor may we forget the authors' own defence of their method and statement of their aim. "If therefore the verses are not always so smooth and elegant as some may desire or expect; let them consider that

39. J. L. Sibley, *Biographical Sketches*, i, 78ff., 157ff., 405ff.; S. G. Drake, *The Pedigree of the Family of Mather*.

40. J. Winthrop, *History of New England*, i, 318 and n.

41. I. Mather, *The Life and Death*, p. 76.

42. W. Walker, *The Services of the Mathers*, pp. 63ff.; H. M. Dexter, *Congregationalism*, p. 426.

43. W. Walker, *The Services of the Mathers*, p. 65.

44. For Eliot and Welde, see *DNB*.

45. Cf. R. F. Roden, *The Cambridge Press*, chap. 2; M. C. Tyler, *History*, i, 274–277.

Gods Altar needs not our pollishings:... wee have respected rather a plaine translation, then to smooth our verses with the sweetnes of any paraphrase, and soe have attended Conscience rather then Elegance, fidelity rather then poetry, in translating the hebrew words into english language, and Davids poetry into English meetre; that soe we may sing in Sion the Lords songs of prayse according to his owne will." [46]

Beyond Mather's study door the world was moving fast. By 1639 the population of Massachusetts had grown to more than eight thousand,[47] Anne Hutchinson had provoked a storm of discussion, and her judges had sown the seeds of recriminations to be heaped on them by their descendants;[48] the churches had held their first Synod;[49] attempts against the Charter had been resisted,[50] and Harvard had been founded.[51] There was news from England, too. Prynne, Bastwick and Burton suffered at the hands of Laud, Ship-money became a topic for popular debate, and the fires soon to destroy Charles I's power burned more brightly. And through it all the Dorchester Church heard from their Teacher, now fast becoming a leader in Massachusetts, a "way of Preaching" which "was plain, aiming to shoot his Arrows not over his peoples heads, but into their Hearts and Consciences." "The Lord gave him an excellent faculty in making abstruse things plain." Constantly he gave himself to study and prayer, fought off temptation, and by patience, judgment, and the fear of God, won a measure of fame.[52]

He has served us well as a guide. His life has given us a clue to the experience of a typical Puritan emigrant, and an inkling of the problems such men faced. With his eyes we have seen Boston in its infancy. In his characteristics, we have found the germ of those qualities which were to develop fully in his son. For Richard Mather and his wife the birth of a boy, on June 21, 1639, was but another proof of God's love.[53] For us it is the dawning of the life we are to trace in its varied meaning for the men and the times

46. Preface.
47. F. B. Dexter, *Estimates of Population.*
48. Cf. J. T. Adams, *The Founding of New England,* pp. 171, 172; B. Adams, *The Emancipation of Massachusetts,* also denounces the Puritans' course toward Mrs. Hutchinson.
49. W. Walker, *History,* pp. 142ff.
50. Palfrey, i, 556, 557.
51. *Mass. Rec.,* i, 183.
52. I. Mather, *The Life and Death,* pp. 75, 81–83, 85.
53. *Parentator,* pp. 2, 3.

which saw its course. On June 23, Increase Mather was baptized at the Dorchester church.[54] His name, we read, was given "because of the never-to-be-forgotten *Increase*, of every sort, wherewith GOD favoured the Country, about the time of his Nativity." [55] If this be so, it is peculiarly fitting, for never throughout his life were the fortunes of Increase Mather unaffected by the progress of Massachusetts, and his influence was always felt in the state. In him flowered the vigor which brought his father from the mediocrity of his early environment to leadership in the colony. Richard's fervor lived again in Increase, and even such minor things as the Dorchester Teacher's habits of work, his diary writing, his summaries of his faults, his grateful epitomizing of his causes for thanksgiving, and his promises to the Lord, were to be aids in his son's climb to eminence. Thirst for study, talent for preaching, and the ability to write for his fellow men with what to them were inspiration and power, fell by inheritance to Increase Mather's lot. How he welded his birthright, his training, and his experience into a character singularly qualified to do an unprecedented work among his fellows, is the keynote of the interest held for us by the chronicle of his long and active life.

54. Barrows and Trask, *Records*, p. 151.
55. *Parentator*, p. 5.

CHAPTER V

BOYHOOD

CHILDHOOD was uninteresting to biographers of Puritan tastes. That they told of Increase Mather's career, with hardly a word on the days before he left college, is characteristic of his time. Deeds done for the church were of excelling interest to our earliest American biographers, and a child too young to be a preacher, and still innocent of any valid religious experience, offered little to the diligent chroniclers who gloated over the spiritual conquests of his later life. Of course, an exceptional child might be worthy of attention even from Jonathan Edwards,[1] but what we are wont to call the "normal boy" was, to those who saw him in the seventeenth century, most often merely a living proof of the power of the sin born in man. Until at some sober later day he acknowledged God, and joined a church duly professing the orthodox Congregational way, he was an unfit subject for such a "life" as those with which the "Magnalia" abounds. Education was necessary, and the finished product was to be admired. The raw material was not to be borne in mind. In the glory of the man, the Puritan too easily forgot what had been the promise of the child.

In a different age, and concerned with a being of flesh and blood rather than a pious lay figure, we cannot so easily pass by his youth. Elements of it we have already seen. His parents' concerns, their motives and traits, were more than once reflected in him, and a knowledge of them opens a loophole for a glimpse of the child who was the father of Increase Mather, the man. We have glanced, too, at events of his day in his world, and to look more closely is the best way to see in truer colors the determining conditions of his early growth. He lived in the house of a leader in local affairs, and to a sharp-eared boy such talk as he heard at home must have offered both interest and excitement. Frontier life, experience teaches, is not dull, and the Mather home was set in the midst of a frontier community. Remembering his heritage, and searching for the more striking incidents of the Boston and

1. Cf. his account of Phebe Bartlett in his *Faithful Narrative of the Surprising Work of God.*

the England of the sixteen-forties, we may sketch the scene that figured largely in shaping the early development of a Puritan man of affairs.

The first broad outlines are plain enough. Increase Mather was only two years old when Strafford was executed. Edgehill, Marston Moor, and Naseby were fought before he passed his sixth birthday. He may have been old enough to be stirred by the news which told New England that the Scots had surrendered the King and that the army was in possession of London. Less than two years later the windows of Whitehall looked out upon the execution of Charles I, and in the streets of Boston men heard the tidings, gravely conscious of their import. By 1650, two of Richard Mather's sons were in England, and their letters, written during the events leading up to the Protectorate, must have given their younger brother a vivid sense of the reality of affairs abroad.[2] Here was a safeguard against a provincial point of view for Increase Mather, and for us a valuable reminder of how closely Boston Puritans were in touch with their old home. The youngest of them knew how the Commonwealth arose, of the fighting at Dunbar and Worcester, of the fall of the Long Parliament before Cromwell, and how the Protectorate began and waxed in power.

So also Richard Mather's youngest son could not easily close his eyes to events at home. There were obvious effects from the cessation of emigration from England. As Winthrop writes: "The parliament of England setting upon a general reformation both of church and state, the Earl of Strafford being beheaded, and the archbishop (our great enemy) and many others . . . imprisoned and called to account, this caused all men to stay in England in expectation of a new world, so as few coming to us, all foreign commodities grew scarce, and our own of no price."[3] Increase Mather may, on the other hand, have been quite unconscious of annexations to Massachusetts, of the dangers seen by his elders in the sway of Presbyterianism in England, or the political implications of the forming, in 1643, of the "United Colonies of New England."[4] He was not yet four years old when this confederation of Plymouth, Connecticut, New Haven, and Massachusetts, was begun; but a few years later, even without

2. J. L. Sibley, *Biographical Sketches*, i, 78ff., 157ff.; *MHS Coll.*, Series 4, vol. viii.
3. J. Winthrop, *History*, ii, 37.
4. Palfrey, vol. i, chap. 15; vol. ii, chaps. 4, 10.

our perspective, he surely realized its meaning as "an act of absolute sovereignty on the part of the contracting states," [5] and in it he must have read, as clearly as we can, the colonists' desire to free congregational New England from the interference of a Presbyterian parliament. Surely he saw that they had seized a most opportune time to put through this measure so vital to their future.[6]

Easier for a boy to grasp were the difficulties with the Indians, or attempts at their conversion. When he was seven years old, Increase Mather may have heard John Eliot preach to his savage converts at Dorchester.[7] Surely he knew of the calling of the Synod in 1646, for was not his own father a leader in its debates?[8] Perhaps, with a boy's feelings, he noted the now famous date in 1647, when by law was established in Massachusetts a system of common schools.[9] Certainly the college across the river held from his earliest days a share of his interest and respect. His older brothers graduated from Harvard while he was still very young, and the eldest became the first fellow of the College.[10] Through their eyes he saw the beginnings of higher education in New England; by the family fireside he joined in the loyal mourning for the death of John Winthrop,[11] and, indoors or out, he found himself with every passing year more and more a part of the busy little world that to him was home.

If town government, a school system, territorial growth, alliance with other colonies, and opposition to English rule held no less meaning for him than for us, if all the events of the first decade of his life helped to mould his view of the world, we can trace in even blacker ink and with a firmer hand the shaping influences he found in his father's house. Here Richard Mather in the full tide of his power stands boldly out. His congregation, answering the drum or horn on Sunday morning, saw him in the pulpit of the meeting-house, a leader in more senses than one — not merely their minister but a strong figure throughout the commonwealth. After the prayer, and the exposition of a selection from the Bible, they sang a psalm as he had translated it, and

5. Palfrey, i, 630.
6. Idem, vol. i, chap. 15.
7. Idem, ii, 194, 195; *Lectures on Massachusetts History*, pp. 305ff.
8. H. M. Dexter, *Congregationalism*, pp. 436ff.
9. *Mass. Rec.*, ii, 203; Palfrey, ii, 262, 263.
10. J. L. Sibley, *Biographical Sketches*, i, 78.
11. March 26, 1649.

after the long sermon, they received his blessing. In the afternoon they came again to pray, and to be preached to once more.[12] Accounts of such services give us a sense of mental chill, but to his hearers Richard Mather's ministrations were the event of the week, and the warmth and vigor of his teaching gave them intellectual stimulus and inspiration for life. They were not alone in their benefits from him. In England were printed books from his pen; and when the Synod of 1646, or 1647, finally endorsed what we know as the "Cambridge Platform,"—"by far the best statement of Congregational principles which the seventeenth century produced,"[13]— most of the finished version was the product of Mather's thought.[14] This "terse, clear, and well-balanced summary,"[15] alone would have made its author a father for any Puritan boy to be proud of. Nor was he forgetful of wife and son, for there are recorded his resolutions for their welfare, his desire "to be more frequent in religious discourse and talk," and his determination "to be more careful in catechising children." He adds "and therefore to bestow some pains this way, *every week* once; and if by urgent occasions it be sometimes omitted, to do it twice as much another week."[16]

Against the background thus outlined there is room for a more intimate portrait of the young Increase Mather than can be made from such materials as the influence of family and environment. Like clear brush-strokes of vivid color, suddenly bringing out the dominant note of the picture, his own words shape our vision of his youth. His mother, "*Twice a Mother* to him," looms large in the tale of his early years, and her words live worthily to-day. "Child," she told him, when he was but a small boy, "if GOD make thee a Good Christian and a Good Scholar, thou hast all that ever thy Mother Asked for thee."[17] Her prayer for him was earnest, her confidence deep, and her love always great. There is no better corrective for the harsh black and white of the conventional likeness we cherish as that of the typical Puritan, than the reading of such diaries or autobiographies as Mather's. They reveal how hotly the love of parent and child burned in a

12. Cf. H. M. Dexter, *Congregationalism*, pp. 452ff.
13. W. Walker, *The Services of the Mathers*, p. 67.
14. I. Mather, *The Life and Death*, p. 87; W. Walker, *Creeds and Platforms*, pp. 157–237.
15. H. M. Dexter, *Congregationalism*, p. 438.
16. C. Mather, *Magnalia*, book III, part ii, chap. 20, section 13.
17. *Parentator*, p. 3; *Autobiography*.

world where home ties were strong, and discipline, if severe, was made light by loyal and devoted family life. Increase Mather displays his mother in the tenderest of lights. As he sat at her feet, learning to read, or as his father's hand guided his in his first essays toward the strangely crabbed handwriting that was to be so ready a tool in days to come, there was moulding for his later career.[18] But there is one sentence of his that gives the crowning touch. Later, his mother's urgings toward scholarship bore fruit, but very precious to-day are his words: "Until I was fourteen years old, I had no love to, nor delight in my books." [19] True, he led his class,[20] but a memory of him as a boy who preferred to school tasks more active pursuits, is an antidote to many a misconception about the man who found an active share in worldly affairs always quite as appealing as quieter hours at his desk. His life was to lead him far from his study; his able dealings were to be not only with books but with men.

Comfortably aware that we are concerned, not with a "young old man" like Samuel Mather,[21] or with a priggish and canting half-grown Puritan, we may come close to understanding how the events and surroundings we have glanced at helped to guide Mather's progress to manhood. Training began early in those days, and, willing pupil or not, he quickly learned to read and write. His father added instruction in the elements of grammar, both Latin and Greek.[22] Probably by the time he was nine or ten, he went regularly to the schoolhouse near the church for such teaching as one Henry Butler, then a student at Harvard, could give.[23] When he was twelve he could read Cicero "ex tempore," "and make and speak true Latine in Verse and Prose, *suo ut aiunt Marte*," and "decline perfectly the Paradigm's of Nouns and Verbes in the Greek tongue." [24] Much else he must have learned from what he saw and heard, from the life of Nature so close to his door, and from such boyish escapades as were possible in the Boston of his time.[25] Surely his father's library had its effect in

---

18. *Autobiography*. Of his handwriting, Jeremy Belknap said: "It was the most crabbed handwriting that ever I had to decipher" (*MHS Coll.*, Series 5, iii, 153).

19. *Autobiography*.   20. *Ibid.*

21. C. Mather, *Magnalia*, book IV, part ii, chap. 2, section 3.

22. *Autobiography*.

23. J. L. Sibley, *Biographical Sketches*, i, 297ff.

24. He went to Harvard "in the latter end of 1651" (*Autobiography*). See the early rules for admission to the college in *New England's First Fruits*, p. 26.

25. Cf. *Lectures on Massachusetts History*, pp. 465ff.; A. M. Earle, *Customs and Fashions in Old New England*, chap. 1.

determining his tastes, though most of it he was probably too frankly boyish to undertake. Among his own books, preserved to-day, one bears an inscription dating it during his early years. George Downame's "Abstract of the Duties Commanded in the Law of God," in which Increase Mather wrote his name in 1651, was a tabular analysis of the Ten Commandments, written by a bishop of the English church who, although at one time, at least, a strong advocate of episcopacy, was ever opposed to "popery," and always a thorough Calvinist. From a father's point of view here was a highly satisfactory gift for a youngest son preparing to take by his entrance to College his first step away from home.[26] Other books he must have had before 1651, but except for the classics there were probably few among them which we should classify otherwise than as church history or theology. When religion was the chief topic among leaders, one could not begin too early to read along such lines. And, even as a boy, Mather must have been unfeignedly interested in many a book which we should cast aside as fit only for students in a narrow field. He lived when intellectual life meant theological study, and current literature meant the newest works on religious topics.

In England, of course, there were published during these years books which have not lost their power and charm. Between 1639 and 1657 there appeared such things as the poems of Carew, Vaughan, Crashaw, and Waller, Herrick's "Hesperides," Izaac Walton's "Lives" and his undying "Angler," Browne's "Religio Medici," Baxter's "Saints Rest," Taylor's "Holy Living," Hobbes's "De Cive" and his "Leviathan," the "Oceana" of Harrington, and Milton's "Areopagitica" and "Eikonoklastes." Some of these Richard Mather may have bought and read. Others he would have rejected as idle and vain creations. Often the works from which we should turn most quickly are those he would read most eagerly and place in the hands of his son. Unfortunately, from his point of view, English literature was not entirely dominated by writers of one faith, or confined to the business-like statement of the ideas of practical church-builders.

America was better ordered, standards were clearly defined, and literature held narrowly to the interests of Mather and his fellow leaders in this newly created Puritan world. Publication from the Cambridge Press continued steadily, and the products filled shelves in Boston homes. There were catechisms, almanacs, and

26. J. H. Tuttle, *The Libraries of the Mathers*, p. 324. For Downame, see *DNB*.

here and there a more pretentious book whose title reveals its contents. John Eliot's "Indian Primer or Catechism" and his translation of the Book of Genesis into the Indian tongue, point to two phases of the settlers' contact with their predecessors on Massachusetts soil. In 1647 there was a new edition of the "Bay Psalm Book," followed by a revised version in 1651. The next year there appeared "The Summe of Certain Sermons upon Genes: 15.6," by Richard Mather himself, and the "Cambridge Platform" was printed at the same press three years before. Charles Chauncy's "Gods Mercy, shewed to his People in giving them a faithful Ministry and Schooles of Learning for the continual supplyes thereof," and John Cotton's "Spiritual Milk for Boston Babes in either England," [27] by their titles alone show what popular interest made it worth while to print. Among such new books of the day, then white and crisp with the ink just dry on their unthumbed pages, there were sound treatises by New England authors, printed in England and shipped to Boston for the delight of the faithful there. If there came with them Thomas Lechford's "Plain Dealing," with its frank statement of the woes of Boston's first lawyer, a man who found a theocratic régime far from agreeable, it was a book that Richard Mather very possibly kept from his son, but its influence was offset by such pamphlets as "New England's First Fruits; In Respect first of the Indians. 2. Of the Progresse of Learning in the Colledge at Cambridge," defending as eloquently as contemporary conventions in style allowed, the practices of the dwellers on Massachusetts Bay. The unorthodoxy of Roger Williams was answered by no less a person than John Cotton.[28] Edward Winslow, defending New England's policy against such malcontents as Samuel Gorton and Robert Child, wrote his "Hypocrisie Unmasked." And, as the first generation of the colony was thinned by death, the deeds and beliefs of its leaders were recorded in what seemed at the time such worthy memorials as John Norton's "The Life and Death of that Deservedly Famous Mr. John Cotton." [29]

There are, moreover, three books published in Increase Mather's youth which have some claim to permanence. Nathaniel Ward of Ipswich, under the pseudonym of "Theodore de la Guard," wrote "The Simple Cobler of Aggawam," and several editions appeared in England in 1647.[30] Even though we read

27. For these books, see R. F. Roden, *The Cambridge Press*, chaps. 3, 4, 5.
28. Cf. M. C. Tyler, *History*, i, 252–254.
29. *Ibid.*, p. 219.   30. *Ibid.*, pp. 229–241.

it with complete lack of sympathy for its doctrine, and contempt for its denunciation of what Ward saw as the vices of his day, we cannot escape the discovery that in the vigor of its prose, violent and unbridled as it too often is, there is power undulled by time. If to our ears its sentences ring clear, how great must have been their sound to readers in tune with the ideas expressed! More prosaic, and enduring for its historical value rather than any literary merit, is Captain Edward Johnson's "Wonder-Working Providence of Sion's Saviour in New England." Its frank, matter-of-fact manner, and its striving toward transmission of its author's spirit, even by such ill-judged methods as frequent and alarming attempts at verse, give it a flavor which has not lost its zest; and, as a picture of events and the age when it was written, the sturdy militia captain's pages offer much worth reading more than once.[31] But most interesting of all is "The Tenth Muse lately Sprung up in America" — that *rara avis* in colonial New England, a book of poems. Anne Bradstreet was too good a Puritan not to repel us by the strong tincture of theology in her verse, and her choice of Du Bartas as a model was, by modern standards, unhappy.[32] Yet he who reads her work patiently, comparing the finish of her lines, not to more polished metres but to those written with the resources and ideals that were hers, will find much to admire. The most captious must find imbedded here and there in the "Tenth Muse" bits of deep feeling, clear picturing, and vivid fragments of authentic poetry.[33]

Current books, the events of active days in the colony, and the inspiration of parents and home, all went into the making of the Increase Mather who, at twelve years old, entered Harvard. He still lacked, as we have seen, any preoccupation in favor of scholarship,[34] but the college offered him far more than a mere course of study designed for hopeful candidates for the pulpit. There were other students to live with and new teachers to guide him. There was a chance to add to a sound home training experience in a wider field. There was broader scope for his thoughts and ambitions, and, above all, a chance to begin for himself the shaping of a worthy inheritance into a character of individuality and strength.

31. M. C. Tyler, *History*, i, 137–146.

32. *Ibid.*, p. 282.

33. *Ibid.*, pp. 277–292.

34. He must, however, have met the rules for admission in respect to character and conduct. Cf. *Harv. Rec.*, i, 28, 29.

CHAPTER VI

HARVARD COLLEGE. THE CHOICE OF A LIFE WORK

ON October 28, 1636, three years before Increase Mather was born, the General Court of Massachusetts voted £400 "towards a schoale or colledge," and in the next year "the most eminent men of the colony" were appointed "to take order for a colledge at Newetowne."[1] The enterprise first took definite shape when there died in Charlestown an English nonconformist minister, one John Harvard.[2] He bequeathed one half of his estate, and all his books, to the college.[3] This was a gift "equal to, if not double, that which the colony had ventured even to promise."[4] His benevolence made possible the establishment of the institution that still bears his name.[5]

Harvard College was first under the unworthy guidance of a certain Nathaniel Eaton. He was soon succeeded by Samuel Shepard,[6] of Cambridge, whose pious care prepared the way for the period of wise and firm control which dated from the landing of Henry Dunster in the fall of 1640. The newcomer accepted the post of "President," and in his achievement, his ability finds proof.[7] By charters granted in 1642 and 1650 his task was lightened by the appointment, first of Overseers, and then of five Fellows and a Treasurer. The last-named officers were subject to the powers reserved to the Governor, Deputy-Governor, the magistrates of the colony, and the ministers of the six nearest towns, who acted as overseers or visitors of the college.[8] With them Dunster drew up rules for admission, laws, and forms for degrees. He secured funds for the building of a president's house, and gave from his own property one hundred acres of land. Pursuing a wise policy in attempting to concentrate the

1. *Mass. Rec.*, i, 183, 217.
2. Cf. H. C. Shelley, *John Harvard.*
3. Quincy, i, 460, 462; *New England's First Fruits*, pp. 23, 24.
4. Quincy, i, 9.
5. *Mass. Rec.*, i, 253.
6. Quincy, i, 13, 14; J. Winthrop, *History*, i, 370–376.
7. Quincy, i, 14–22; *DNB*; J. Chaplin, *Life of Henry Dunster.*
8. *Mass. Rec.*, ii, 30, iv, 12–14.

educational aspirations of all New England in Harvard, he led Shepard to ask the Commissioners of the federated colonies to aid in the support of such scholars as were in need. To this end it was suggested that "every family throughout the plantation . . . contribute a fourth part of a bushel of corn or something equivalent thereto," and the Commissioners recommended accordingly. Yet in 1647 there were still uses for more money. The library lacked books, especially on law, philosophy, physics, and mathematics, and the college building was in want of repair.[9] There were constant appeals from Dunster, necessary in spite of gifts from far-sighted supporters; and the lack of books remained even after Sir Kenelm Digby and others gave freely to the library.[10]

To Increase Mather such a sketch of Harvard's history would have been unnecessary. He had grown up with the college, and came from a household where its progress was eagerly watched. Leaving the Dorchester fireside, with his brother Eleazar,[11] to seek for such accommodations as students could hope for in Cambridge, it was the physical aspect of Harvard that was of most interest to him. The college building was an "edifice . . . very faire and comely within and without, having in it a Spacious Hall . . . and a large Library." "Chambers and Studies" were "fitted for and possessed by the Students, and all other roomes of the office necessary and convenient, with all needful offices thereto belonging."[12] But when Increase Mather came there, the structure was, according to Dunster, in a decaying condition.[13] That so new a building was so soon out of repair does not speak well for the solidity of its construction, and gives some idea of its character. The President's house stood near it, and on the next lot was the house of Edward Goffe, where some students were allowed to live. Before Increase Mather graduated, still another building was added to the group; for by a shrewd appeal to the Society for the Propagation of the Gospel, money was secured for "the Indian college," "built plain but strong and durable." Ostensibly it was to house such Indians as found their way to Harvard, but, apparently, this new brick house, large enough for twenty scholars, was by no means preempted by the natives, and

9. Quincy, i, 14–22 and Appendix to vol. i.
10. *Harv. Rec.*, pp. 199, 200.
11. J. L. Sibley, *Biographical Sketches*, i, 405ff.
12. *New England's First Fruits*, p. 24.
13. Quincy, i, 17.

during Increase Mather's acquaintance with it, it housed not only English scholars, but also the colony's printing press.[14]

From their windows the students looked out "on a large plain, more than eight miles square, with a fine stream in the middle of it, capable of bearing heavily laden vessels." [15] The village of Cambridge was "compact closely within it selfe," although "of late yeares some few stragling houses have been built." Its "well ordered streets" were "comly pompleated[16] with the faire building of Harver Colledge."

In such surroundings Increase Mather began his work for his degree. Harvard offered a training not widely different from that afforded by English universities, and in 1651 few doubted its excellence.[17] The college had been founded "to advance Learning, and perpetuate it to Posterity," by men "dreading to leave an illiterate Ministery to the Churches";[18] but the religious aim was not unduly harped upon. The charter of 1642 gave power to the President and governing boards "to make & establish all such ord^rs, statutes, & constitutions as they shall see necessary for the instituting, guiding, & furthering of the said colledge & the sev^rall memb^rs thereof . . . in piety, morality, & learning"; and in 1650 the object of Harvard was declared to be "the advancement of all good litterature, arts, and sciences" and the "education of the English and Indjan youth of this country in knowledge and godliness." [19] Taken at their face value, such statements are not unsuited to a liberally minded university of to-day; nor was the curriculum exclusively devoted to the technicalities of religious education.[20] In the first year were studied "Logic, Physics,[21] Greek Etymological Syntax," and, in the Greek language, practice in "the precepts of Grammar in such Authors as have variety of words." Additional studies were "Hebrew and Eastern Grammar," "practise in the Bible," "Reading of Rhetorick to all Scholars," "Divinity Catecheticall," "Common Places," [22] and "Declamations," with a provision that "Every Scholler may

14. See A. McF. Davis, The Early College Buildings; Harv. Rec., p. 208.
15. Long Island Historical Society Memoirs, i, 384, 385; E. Johnson, History, p. 201.
16. "Completed"? E. Johnson, History, p. 90.
17. T. G. Wright, Literary Culture, pp. 19–22, and references given there.
18. New England's First Fruits, p. 23.
19. Mass. Rec., ii, 30, iv, 12.
20. Cf. Quincy, i, 45–48.
21. "Natural Science in general." Cf. New English Dictionary, "Physics," definition 1.
22. Exercises or theses on set themes. Cf. Ibid., "Commonplace," definition 2.

declaime once a moneth." In the winter, time was given to history, and, in summer, "the Nature of Plants" was taught. The second year advanced in Greek to "Prosodie and Dialects," "Poesy, Nonnus,[23] Duport,[24] or the like," and Chaldee appears in the schedule. "Ethicks" and "Politicks" [25] replaced "Logick" and "Physics," but the other subjects of the first year were studied further. In his last term the scholar learned "Arithmetic, Geometry and Astronomy," and in Greek he was expected to "perfect . . . Theory before noone, and exercise *Style, Composition, Imitation, Epitome* both in Prose and Verse, afternoone." The year's work was completed with the addition of "Syriack." Predominantly linguistic and classical, with only a hint of science, the course led to a degree conferred when the candidate "on proofe" was found "able to read in the Originalls of the *Old* and *New Testament* into the Latine tongue, and to resolve them *Logically;* withall being of godly life and conversation," provided he could obtain "at any publick Act . . . the Approbation of the Overseers and Master of the Colledge." [26] Such a training, though admirably adapted to equip a man for the Puritan pulpit, was not planned for embryo divines alone. One remembers that Dunster sought books to aid his pupils "whose various inclinations to all professions might thereby be incouraged." [27] In seventeenth-century eyes, Harvard's course was by no means without breadth.

A glimpse at the Library confirms this. John Harvard's bequest was representative of the whole collection, and a study of its contents gives a clue to the educated taste of the day. Three quarters of the books were theological, and of these perhaps half were commentaries on the Bible, dealing almost equally with the Old and New Testaments. Many sermons found a place, but there was little space for religious controversy. Jesuit writers rubbed elbows with the works of sound Puritans. The classics filled a good-sized shelf, and one cannot pass unnoticed Chapman's Homer and North's Plutarch. Grammars and dictionaries, Greek, Hebrew, and English, flanked by "half a dozen books of

23. Nonnus, fifth-century Greek poet, author of a paraphrase of the Gospel of St. John in Greek hexameters.

24. James Duport, 1606–1679, Regius professor of Greek at Magdalene College, Cambridge. Cf. *DNB.*

25. Probably ethics, in the public or social sense. Cf. *NED.*

26. The foregoing account of the curriculum is from *New England's First Fruits,* pp. 28–30.

27. E. Hazard, *Historical Collections,* ii, 86.

extracts, or phrases, as Ocland's Anglorum Prælia, La Primaud-
aye's French Academy, and Peacham's Garden of Eloquence"
made up a section of reference works. English literature, as we
know it, was little represented save for Bacon's Essays, and the
poems of Quarles and Wither, and two tracts and Camden's
Remaines are the insecure foundation of the collection on English
history. A smattering of science, of scholastic philosophy, of
logic, of medicine, and two books on law complete the literary
mixture.[28] Such a collection was not inadequate material for a
"liberal" seventeenth-century education,[29] and Mather had
added resources in his father's library, and such books as he
owned himself.[30]

It is not in the curriculum or on the bookshelves that we find
most evidence of Harvard's Puritanical tone. The laws or rules
reveal more of what we like to consider as typical early Congregational rigor. Latin was to be used at all times, the Scriptures
were to be read so that twice a day each student could give "such
an account of his proficiency therein, both in *Theorettical* observations of the Language, and *Logick*, and in *Practicall* and spirit-
uall truths, as his Tutor" might require. He was not to forget
that the main end of life is to know God, that Christ is the foundation of all sound learning. He must eschew "all profanation of
God's Name, Attributes, Word, Ordinances, and times of Worship," and study "to retaine God" and the love of His truth.
Punctuality, diligence, and good behavior at lectures were
demanded. No student might "frequent the society of men
leading an unfit or dissolute life." No one, without the consent of
his tutor, or the call of his parent or guardian, might "goe abroad
to other Townes." Twice a day each pupil reported to his tutor,
and gave an account of his reading. In 1650, the use of tobacco
was forbidden except by the special consent of the President, with
the permission of parent or guardian and the recommendation of
a physician, and, even when allowed, smoking was to be carried
on "in a sober and private manner." Public meetings or gather-
ings during college hours were banned, and no scholar might drill
with a military company unless he was known to be of "Gravity,
& of approved sober & virtuous conversation." For three weeks

28. I have drawn my account of Harvard's library directly from A. C. Potter's
Catalogue of John Harvard's Library, p. 192.
29. Cf. E. A. Savage, *Old English Libraries*, chaps. 6 and 7.
30. See J. H. Tuttle, *Libraries of the Mathers*.

before Commencement, on two days each week, all students of two or more years standing were required to sit in the Hall, "to be examined by all comers in the Latin, Greek and Hebrew tongues, and in Rhetoric, Logic, and Physics"; while candidates for the degree were "to be examined of their sufficiency according to the Laws of the College." Breaches of discipline were punished by "Admonition," and a third offence made the culprit liable to correction by more vigorous means, unless he were an adult, in which case he was reported to the Overseers for public reprimand.[31] Such laws made a world that was no Paradise for idle youth or for rebels against Puritan theories; but their strictness is more apparent in the light of present conditions than in contrast with the rules of seventeenth-century universities elsewhere.[32]

Admitted to Harvard, Increase Mather and his brother transcribed these College regulations and signed them, agreeing to keep the copy as a reminder "of the duties whereto their priviledges oblidged them."[33] Their names, as befitted their rank in the colonial social system, were then listed at the head of their class.[34] What they studied and how they were disciplined we have seen; one would give much to know how Increase Mather responded to the major influences of instructors and fellow students. Dunster, inspecting the "manners" of his pupils, delivering his Biblical expositions at morning and evening prayers, and preaching at "publick assemblies on the Lord's day at Cambridge where the students" had "a particular gallery allotted unto them,"[35] may have been for some an inspiration and guide.

Mather's first impressions came most vividly, however, from Michael Wigglesworth and John Cotton. Of the former he writes: "I was his Scholar at my first Admission into the Colledge"; and "this worthy man" is called "a blessing as a Tutor."[36] We know Wigglesworth as a sincere and true-hearted Puritan. His "Day of Doom," even in pages which seem to us incredibly stern, displays an earnest believer, and, for his time, no mean poet. Surely there burned in his infirm body eternally valid

31. For the college rules, see *New England's First Fruits;* Quincy, i, 515ff.; and *Harv. Rec.,* p. 190.

32. Cf., for example, J. B. Mullinger, *Cambridge Characteristics in the Seventeenth Century,* chap. 2.

33. C. Mather, *Magnalia,* book IV, part i, section 4.

34. Cf. *Harvard University Quinquennial Catalogue,* 1920, p. 135 n.

35. C. Mather, *Magnalia,* book IV, part i, section 4.

36. I. Mather, Introduction, in C. Mather, *A Faithful Man Described.* Boston, 1705.

qualities of soul.[37] He was a man who could appeal to his pupils' hearts; the other whose impression on Increase Mather is recorded was of a sort to stimulate a student's mind. John Cotton wrote and preached vigorously reasoned doctrine, and made his abilities felt in church and state. Austere he seems to us, largely from the beliefs he taught. To his contemporaries he was an example in learning, and a leader in thought. To Richard Mather he had been adviser and comforter; to his son he was a figure whose memory endured. "Although I had little of personal acquaintance with Mr. Cotton, being a child not above thirteen years old when he died, I shall never forget the last sermon which he preached at Cambridge, and his particular application to the scholars there, amongst whom I was then a student newly admitted." [38]

No word of Mather's hints at the education he gained from his contact with other students. We know that in college with him were such men as Thomas Shepard, later a force in colonial affairs, Samuel Nowell, to become in after years Treasurer of Harvard, Gershom Bulkeley, the Connecticut physician and surgeon, John Cotton the younger, later united to Mather by a family bond, Robert Paine, believed to have been the foreman of the jury which years afterward tried the Salem witches, Thomas Graves, the Charlestown physician, who became Mather's opponent on points of doctrine and went so far as to uphold Andros during the revolt against his rule, and Elisha Cooke, who was to clash with Mather more than once during their joint embassy to England in 1690.[39] Such a list, chosen at random, contains a few whose potentialities may well have been great enough to mark them in youth. There were others, of course, for in the three years from 1657 to 1659 twenty-four men took their degrees. Of these, nearly two thirds became ministers, and others taught or preached for a time.[40] However little we have in exact records, we cannot escape the fact that there were abundant and varied human influences in Mather's Harvard, nor can we doubt what type of aspiration was most common in this little world.

In his own case, circumstances decreed that the formal routine

37. Cf. J. L. Sibley, *Biographical Sketches*, i, 259ff.; J. W. Dean, *Sketch of the Life of Rev. Michael Wigglesworth;* and M. C. Tyler, *History of American Literature*, ii, 27-35.

38. I. Mather, Preface to C. Mather, "Johannes in Eremo," in *Magnalia*, book III, part i.

39. Cf. J. L. Sibley, *Biographical Sketches*, vol. i. For Cooke, see pp. 229ff *post.*

40. Sibley, vols. i, ii.

of the college should not be his. The greatest turning-points of these years, supremely important for his later life, came elsewhere than within college walls. Some time at the end of 1652,[41] his parents, fearing for his health and distrusting particularly the diet furnished the students,[42] sent him to Ipswich to continue his work toward the degree under the minister of that town, John Norton. It was a momentous change. Norton is labelled to-day stern, fiercely bigoted, and absolutely convinced of his own infallibility, undeterred by doubt, and unrestrained by pity,[43] but he was known in his own time as "Thou Noble Norton," and praised in such lines as

> But Christ hath given his blessing from above
> Unto thy workes the World with light to fill.[44]

He is best seen as one of the most complete embodiments of the thoroughgoing Puritan character. Intolerant, cruel in his treatment of foes of the commonwealth, hot-tempered, and implacably strict in his tenets, he was a diligent student and a learned writer, and, to those of his faith, a strong leader and a cherished friend. For Increase Mather he was one "whose memory I have peculiar cause to love and honour." [45] Already distinguished as the author of the first Latin book written in Massachusetts, he was soon to be chosen as Cotton's successor in the first church at Boston, and won further honor, and a chance for even greater service, in his appointment as an agent from the colony to the king.[46] His fame in 1652, and his clear promise of further achievement, were sufficient to mark him in Richard Mather's mind as an ideal teacher for his son. There were closer ties, too, between Mather in Dorchester, and Norton in Ipswich; for the latter had helped his colleague through a period of mental unrest, and we know that "Mr. Mather ... consulted him as an oracle ... and found him so accomplished and experienced a person, that he maintained a most valuable friendship with him to the last." [47]

41. J. L. Sibley, i, 410. In his *Autobiography* Mather says that he went to Ipswich after he had lived in Cambridge "about a year." The last quarter bill against him in the Steward's Account Books of the College is, according to Sibley, i, 405, dated 10–10–52 (Dec. 10, 1652).

42. *Parentator*, p. 6. *Autobiography* refers to the college diet.

43. J. T. Adams, *The Founding*, p. 259.

44. E. Johnson, *History*, p. 104.

45. See note 38, *ante*.

46. Cf. *DNB;* T. Hutchinson, *Collection*, ii, 65–93; C. Mather, *Magnalia*, book III, part i, chap. 2.

47. *Ibid.*, book III, part i, chap. 2, section 13.

When Increase Mather began his life under Norton's roof in the "good Haven Towne" of Ipswich, with its "faire built" houses "with pleasant Gardens and Orchards," [48] he was, one remembers, although "free from any *Scandalous Outbreakings* of Immorality, . . . nothing more than outwardly *Moral*." [49] In other words, he was a boy without zeal for learning, though of good ability, and was possessed of no consuming passion for religion and its works. The college, with its aspirants for the ministry, its exhortations from prominent divines, and its theological training, may well have done much to make him tinder easy to kindle to a blaze of religious devotion. John Norton was admirably fitted to carry on the process, and instil the feelings and ambitions that made ministers of Boston boys. Yet the final spark came not from training or teachers, but from a sudden bitter taste of life.

The story is best told in Increase Mather's own words:

In the year 1654, the Lord in mercy visited me with a sore disease, which was apprehended to be the stone. . . . I was soon (by the Lord's blessing) recovered. This sickness set me upon prayer to God, and caused me to reform many vain, wild courses and extravagances of my life. Also, from this time I became very studious, which before I had not been. Nevertheless, after some months of health I began to forget God again, though not so as in the former years of my childhood & vanity. But in the latter end of that year, God took away my dear mother, who had so often prayed for me. About which time the Lord broke in upon my conscience with very terrible convictions and awakenings. In the months of March & April, and in the latter end of May, 1655, I was in extremity of anguish and horror in my soul. Once at Dorchester, when my father was gone abroad on a public occasion, and not to return for a day or two, I shut myself up in his study, and wrote down all the sins which I could remember I had been guilty of that lay as a heavy burden on my spirits. I brought them before God, and cried to him for pardoning mercy; and at night burnt the paper which in way of confession I had sorrowfully spread before the Lord. Everyone observed that I was strangely changed. Some of my companions derided me for my now strictness and tender conscience. I acquainted no man with my troubles, save only that I wrote some letters from Boston [50] to my father, telling him what

48. E. Johnson, *History*, p. 96.
49. *Parentator*, p. 6.
50. Norton was then living in Boston.

anguish my soul was in, and desiring his earnest prayers to God for me. I wished for another opportunity to spend a day in secret prayer and fasting before the Lord, to humble myself for all my past transgressions. I knew that on the election day, the other scholars who boarded with me at Mr. Norton's would be from home; & therefore I resolved to spend that time from morning to night, where none but God should see. Accordingly I went into a little garret of Mr. Norton's study, & shut the door. And all the family being abroad, I poured out my soul in complaints before God that day. I prayed to God that he would show me mercy. At the close of the day, as I was praying, I gave myself up to Jesus Christ, declaring that I was now resolved to be his servant, I his only, and his forever; and humbly professed to him that if I did perish, I would perish at his feet. Upon this I had ease and inward peace in my perplexed soul immediately; and from that day I walked comfortably for a considerable time, and was careful that all my words and ways should be such as would not offend God.[51]

Sickness, and the first sight of death, were then as now reagents powerful in awakening religious feeling in a youthful soul. The final touch came with his dying mother's last request. Reminding him of the text, "They that turn many to righteousness shall shine as the stars for ever and ever," she urged him to enter the ministry.[52] The sight of her dead face, and the memory of her voice fresh in his ears, completed the first great stage in his education. Never in future was he to be in doubt as to his goal.

The rest of his period of training served simply to confirm his clear vision of his aim. In Boston, after Norton came there in April, 1653,[53] he carried on his work with the new interest that came from the sudden crystallization of his purpose. There were changes in the college to watch, for Dunster had fallen into "the snares of Anabaptism," [54] and for daring to express his views was forced in October, 1654, to resign the presidency.[55] John Norton and Richard Mather were the two men chosen to ask Charles Chauncy to fill the vacant place.[56] That this mission of his father

51. *Autobiography.*   52. *Ibid.*
53. C. Mather, *Magnalia*, book III, part i, chap. 2, sections 19, 20. Norton probably lived at the present corner of Washington and Milk streets, in the house formerly occupied by John Winthrop. Cf. *Memorial History of Boston*, i, 481 n., and H. A. Hill, *History of the Old South Church*, i, 131.
54. C. Mather, *Magnalia*, book IV, part i, section 5.
55. See references in note 7, *ante.*
56. *Harv. Rec.*, pp. 206, 207.

and his instructor was successful cannot have failed to interest Increase Mather. The new President, his leanings toward England conquered, and his doubts as to salary set at rest,[57] bound himself to silence as to such of his beliefs as were unorthodox for the time and place. He was a man known in his day for unquestioned learning, and his inaugural address, and his diligent administration, won general praise.[58]

For Increase Mather a more immediate influence was Jonathan Mitchell. As a boy he had come from England on the *James* with Richard Mather, and, still a young man, was now minister in Cambridge and tutor in the college. To one pupil, at least, his teaching was a delight; and even late in life Mather remembered him and spoke of him in the warmest tones.[59] A hard student and a learned preacher, he was beloved for the human qualities of meekness and charity clearly discernible in all we read of him. For a young aspirant for the ministry, in the first blush of fervor, one could not choose a better guide. The charm of his personality was needed to aid in overcoming the annoyance caused to Increase Mather by the delaying of his graduation for a year. His father, too, insisted that he remain to take his degree, even though others of his classmates left in protest against the new rule which lengthened the college course;[60] and, finally, in 1656 [61] he returned to Cambridge, and, probably on August 12,[62] he took his first degree as Bachelor of Arts.[63]

Cotton Mather tells of the presentation of his father's thesis. The picture strikingly sums up a few of the chief elements of

57. Quincy, i, 466, 467.

58. Cf. *DNB*; *MHS Coll.*, Series 1, x, 171–180; and C. Mather, *Magnalia*, book III, part ii, chap. 23, and book IV, part i, section 5.

59. *Autobiography*; J. L. Sibley, *Biographical Sketches*, i, 141–157; and C. Mather, *Magnalia*, book IV, part ii, chap. 4, Epistle Dedicatory.

60. *Autobiography*; *Parentator*, p. 14, speaks of "some reasons of state" as causing the lengthening of the course. A. Matthews ("Harvard Commencement Days, 1642–1916," in *Colonial Society Publications*, xviii, 309ff.) says that, in 1653, the course of study was changed from three to four years. There was a double Commencement in 1653. The *Autobiography* gives, as reasons for the change: "the President, being desirous to keep the students as long in the College as might be, and some other reasons occurring." Sibley gives, in Appendix to vol. 1, a list of all men of whom record is preserved as members of the college from 1642 to 1658. Several of these, contemporaries of Mather, took no degree, and they may be those said to have left because of the lengthening of the course.

61. *Autobiography*; *Parentator*, p. 14.

62. That is, the second Tuesday in August. Cf. *Colonial Society Publications*, xviii, 309ff.

63. *Harvard University Quinquennial Catalogue*, p. 136.

Increase's early life.[64] We read that the President "upon a Dislike of the *Ramœan* Strains in which our Young Disputant was carrying on his Thesis, would have cut him Short, but Mr. *Mitchel* Publickly Interposed, *Pergat, Quæso, Nam-doctissime disputat.*" Peter Ramus, the greatest French philosopher of the sixteenth century, a brilliant and useful educational reformer, who prepared the way for many later developments in thought, principally by freeing men's minds from the "yoke of Aristotle," had early impressed Richard Mather.[65] Michael Wigglesworth, the beloved tutor, studied him, and fell under the spell of the "Ramœan" confidence in the power of reason and in the observation of human nature as the basis of philosophy.[66] His commencement, then, reveals in Increase Mather the force of home training, the effect of a favorite teacher, and the courage to defend a thesis unwelcome to a President firmly wedded to Aristotelian theories.[67] It is significant, too, that his most recent tutor saw promise in his pupil, and intervened to save him from interruption. Such a scene picks out some of the threads we have followed in the story of his youth, and closes fittingly enough the record of these early years.

Leaving college behind him, he faced experiences and tasks which were to lead to further development and expansion of his nature. With the rest of his generation, he had seen the establishment of institutions for which he was to fight as for the ideals of youth. Much that grew in his early days was to endure. Much else was to change, or, perhaps, to vanish before the shifting ideas of a newer day. For him, as for those who were boys with him, was the labor of warding off, on the one hand, a desire to cling rigidly to all that he grew up with, and, on the other, the temptation to follow too readily innovators whose necessary work threatened much that was better left unmarred. To such problems he brought a character hewn from good material, forged in the fire of Puritan home life and education, and tempered by the chill shock of sickness and bereavement. With his realization of a goal in life, came the power to turn the steel of his nature toward a definite end. Further polishing there was to be, further

64. The scene is not alluded to in *Autobiography*, but is described in *Parentator*, pp. 14, 15.

65. C. Waddington, *Ramus*, pp. 10, 399, 400; I. Mather, *The Life and Death*, p. 49.

66. J. L. Sibley, *Biographical Sketches*, i, 267.

67. *Parentator*, p. 14.

sharpening from learning, travel, and contact with men; but before he left college there was shaped a personality strong as a well-balanced blade. With it he was to cut through the thronging events of the next half-century and more, the broad pathway of a vigorous and useful life.

CHAPTER VII

EXPERIMENTAL YEARS
ENGLAND, IRELAND, AND GUERNSEY

"THE whole Auditory were greatly Affected with the *Light* and *Flame*, in which the Rare Youth Appear'd unto them." So writes his loyal son of Increase Mather's second sermon, preached on Sunday, June 28, 1657, in his father's church at Dorchester.[1] A week earlier, on June 21, his eighteenth birthday, he had made his first appearance in the pulpit, "at a Village belonging to *Dorchester*," and had chosen for his text, "And Enoch walked with God: and he was not; for God took him." His second sermon was preached on the sixth verse of the ninth chapter of St. John, "concerning the excellency of Christ." His account of its reception is brief: "The Lord was pleased to give great acceptance of my labors with serious Christians. Some did, with many tears, thank me & bless me."[2]

How his time had been spent since he graduated in August of the previous year, is not recorded. Probably he lived in Dorchester in his father's house. There was plenty to occupy him. Family changes had taken place, for on August 26, 1656, Richard Mather had married John Cotton's widow, and her daughter, Maria, came with her to her new home.[3] New faces by his fireside, his new zeal for learning, and the affairs of a busy period in the colony, were quite enough to absorb Increase Mather in the winter of 1656 and 1657.

Puritanism had now gripped firmly the reins of authority in Massachusetts, and with an assured control, came naturally increased strictness in the exercise of power. This is summed up in the persecution of the Quakers, which began in 1656 and ran its course for several years. Discussion has raged on all sides of the affair. Defenders of the Puritans have harped upon the civil disturbances caused by the strenuous seventeenth-century Quaker, so different from all that later centuries have taught

1. *Parentator*, p. 15.
2. *Autobiography.*
3. S. G. Drake, *The Pedigree of the Family of Mather.*

us to associate with his sect; and persecutions elsewhere have been pointed out, to show that New England was not alone in her methods, however ill-advised, and worse, they seem. Others have sought truth by neglecting the persecutors' explanation of their motives, in favor of the complaints of the victims.[4] One may most safely rest his case to-day with some such statement as that of Hutchinson: "The most that can be said for our ancestors is, that they tried gentler means at first, which they found utterly ineffectual, and that they followed the examples of the authorities in most other states and in most ages of the world, who, with the like absurdity, have supposed every person could and ought to think as they did, and when [with?] the like cruelty have punished such as appeared to differ from them. We may add, that it was with reluctance that these unnatural laws were carried into execution." [5] Beyond this, later history has not gone.

For us the point of view is to be that of 1657. We must remember that for a Boston citizen of the year to punish a Quaker was not mere idle cruelty, but necessary defence of the integrity of his state. Placed in the shoes of a leader of the time, believing as he did, and equipped with his understanding of his position in the community, and the purpose of that community, any one of us would have acted much as he did. And it is helpful, too, to bear in mind that, even while Puritanism reigned, men saw the errors of their past. Cotton Mather, so often a stalking horse for the darker side of his times, writes of the Quaker persecution: "If any man will appear in the vindication of it, let him do as he please; for my part I will not." [6] He surpasses some later writers in being able not only to see the wrong that was done, but to realize what seemed the need for it.

As for Increase Mather, a Puritan diligently preparing for the "priesthood," instinct with hot belief in his creed and with desire for its success, he might well have seen the first attacks upon the Quakers, not as the opening of a dark page of cruelty, but as the beginning of a crusade against evil. Yet the only record we have of his views shows him as more moderate than his times. His son

---

4. J. T. Adams, *The Founding*, seems to me to neglect unduly the civil disturbances of the Quakers, and to cite, except for the formal records of the laws passed, only works written from the Quaker point of view. If these are to be considered, surely the arguments urged by the Puritans in their own defence should be read also. Cf. also, Palfrey, ii, 461, 483, and *Lectures on Massachusetts History*, pp. 75ff.

5. T. Hutchinson, *History*, i, 198.

6. *Magnalia*, book VII, chap. 4, section 2; *Parentator*, pp. 57, 58.

tells us "Mr. *Mather* . . . little Approved some *Unadvised* and *Sanguinary* Things that were done by them who did all; particularly, the Rash Things done unto the *Quakers*." [7] If this be refuted as partisan testimony, one has only fancy left to guide, and a guess that he was temperate in his views is quite as valuable as one that he was not.

On other matters we have surer evidence. His thoughts were turning from New England to his brothers abroad. Nathaniel was at Barnstaple in Devonshire, and Samuel preached in Dublin.[8] The former had written: "Tis incredible what an advantage . . . it is to have been a New English man"; and the latter urged that Increase be sent to him in Ireland.[9] This influence was supported elsewhere. Of the Harvard graduates before 1656, more than one third went back to England at some time after leaving college.[10] Clearly the mother country was believed to hold opportunity for nonconformists from the colonies, and there is here more than a hint that Englishmen in New England were English still. Most naturally, a student, after draining Harvard's resources, looked enviously toward the older universities and crowded libraries across the sea.

For Increase Mather, his brother's call to Ireland must have had especial appeal. That country, since the Marquis of Ormond surrendered Dublin to the Parliament, had been a favorite field for the sowing of Puritan seed.[11] Cromwell's commissioners were sent there to propagate the Gospel, to encourage preachers, and to advance learning, and they had repeatedly sought to enlist in their cause ministers from England and the Puritan colonies abroad.[12] From its foundation Trinity College, Dublin, had Puritanical leanings, and it was now a centre of Parliamentarian interest.[13] Samuel Mather was a fellow, John Owen a trustee, and, in Puritan circles, its provost, Samuel Winter, was widely and favorably known.[14] A chance for further study, for

7. *Parentator*, p. 57.

8. See lives of Samuel and Nathaniel Mather in J. L. Sibley, *Biographical Sketches*, vol. i.

9. *MHS Coll.*, Series 4, viii, 5; *Autobiography; Parentator*, p. 15.

10. Sibley, *Biographical Sketches*, vol. i.

11. Cf., in general, St. J. D. Seymour, *The Puritans in Ireland*.

12. *Ibid.*, pp. 62, 63, 103, 113, and references there given.

13. W. M. Dixon, *Trinity College, Dublin;* W. Urwick, *The Early History of Trinity College;* and J. P. Mahaffy, *An Epoch in Irish History.*

14. J. W. Stubbs, *History of the University of Dublin*, pp. 89ff.; Mahaffy, pp. 293ff. For Owen, see *DNB*. For Winter, see references given in note 24, *post*, and *DNB*.

the beginning of his career in surroundings where the leaders, among them his own brother, thought as he did, cannot have failed to interest Increase Mather. Its attractiveness may well have outweighed for him such trifling drawbacks as the fact that, in Ireland as in New England, Quakers were proving themselves foes, to be banished or jailed.[15] Whether or not his longing for England in preference to the colonies, a desire dominant through much of his later life, played a part as early as this, there was sufficient reason for his feeling "a marvellous inclination & bent of spirit" toward Dublin.[16]

On July 3, 1657, he sailed from Boston. His father blessed him, and they both wept at parting, "not expecting to see one another again in this world."[17] Probably Increase Mather believed, as he began his five weeks' voyage, that he had looked for the last time on the clustering houses of Boston.

From Massachusetts to the England of Evelyn and Pepys was a change calculated to impress any voyager, however prepared by education or insight into current affairs. Mather arrived in London at a time when Cromwell's power seemed safe, when the English church had succumbed before the Puritans, yielding some of its choicest monuments to be defaced by their too zealous hands, and when the intrigues of Charles II seemed least destined for success. Yet Royalist feeling was by no means dead, and in proportion to the greater stakes involved, the elements hostile to the beliefs of the Mathers were more varied and more in force than in rigidly controlled New England. All this was intellectually stimulating, and an age that boasted of a Hobbes, a Herbert, and a newly founded Royal Society, cannot have been sterile of inspiration to an active-minded youth. In literature, John Milton is a name to conjure with, and Thomas Fuller, Archbishop Usher, and Jeremy Taylor represent religious controversy with dignity and force. Herrick, Carew, Vaughan — valued still for elements of perennial charm — were then vilified or praised according to their readers' individual views. English prose was driving strong roots, newspapers were springing up here and there, and all the tangled social forces of a period of political upheaval were manifested in the external features of the day. From a historical standpoint, the ten years before the

15. Seymour, pp. 131, 133.
16. *Autobiography*.
17. *Ibid.; Parentator*, p. 16.

Restoration offer unlimited scope for study; to a colonial visitor they must have been at once confusing and absorbing. For Mather, of paramount importance was the dominance of the type of worship which he had been taught to uphold. Dissensions in politics and the undercurrent of enmity from religious foes, however vividly seen in the light of later days, were, at the time, hardly more than half-heard rumblings beneath the surface of a righteously ordered world.

He landed at Portsmouth, and rode thence to London. After a fortnight there, he continued his journey to Lancashire, where his father's friends warmly welcomed him. They entertained him until September, when he sailed from Liverpool to Dublin. Samuel Mather had not seen his brother for more than seven years, and so different was Increase at eighteen from the Dorchester schoolboy whom his brother remembered, that he had to introduce himself with the letters he had brought. Once recognized, he was greeted with affectionate hospitality by his brother and his sister-in-law. Under their guidance he lost no time in turning his visit to account by beginning study at Trinity College.[18]

Nothing of the seventeenth-century Trinity College remains to-day. A small quadrangle of red brick buildings then limited the activities of some two hundred students; but even the wide view from the windows is now greatly changed. Formally opened in 1593, the college, under various leaders, among them Bishop Laud himself, had grown in importance. In 1657 its directors were Puritans, and its rules, like those of Harvard, were strict. The curriculum, too, did not differ widely from Harvard's, and its emphasis was on the classics. Candidates for the Master's degree studied mathematics, and "performed . . . exercises in Disputations, Orations, &c., required by the statutes of the college."[19] In the library were more than four thousand books,[20] and in this, as in other respects, Trinity must have seemed to a New Englander the gate of opportunity.

With Increase Mather, studied or taught several who later climbed some few steps toward fame.[21] No one of them seems, however, to have been of more than passing interest to him. The provost, Samuel Winter, left a deeper mark, and his son,

18. *Autobiography.*
19. Dixon, pp. 12, 80, 78 n., 79 n., and chaps. 1, 3, 4; Stubbs, pp. 44, 45.
20. Dixon, p. 221.
21. Urwick, pp. 73–83.

Josiah, a classmate of Mather's, came completely under the spell of this stranger from overseas.[22] Samuel Winter has been called in our time "at once a shrewd man of business, an energetic worker in things spiritual and temporal, and a godly divine, broad-minded to a degree that can scarcely be realized, especially by those who lump the Puritans of the Commonwealth together, and imagine that their outstanding features were hypocrisy, love of names compounded of Biblical texts, and nasal psalmody." [23] A seventeenth-century biographer confirms this estimate, as does Winter's own notebook.[24] If narrowness and intolerance were fostered in Boston, there was an antidote here in Dublin. And, if Winter was of influence with Increase Mather, his brother Samuel also was a guide to him; and Samuel too is remembered for broadness of mind on at least one occasion, "when the power was put into his hands to attack the Episcopalian clergy both in Dublin and Cork," and he "refused to do so, on the ground that he had been called into Ireland to preach the Gospel, not to hinder others from doing it." [25]

There was to be discipline other than that of contact with human forces and college rules; for in October Increase Mather's work was delayed by the measles, and in the next month came the smallpox.[26] Moreover, it was the "severest winter that any man alive had known in England. The crowes feete were frozen to their prey. Islands of ice inclos'd both fish and fowl frozen, and some persons in their boates." [27] In spite of all, on June 24 Mather had completed his course, and "proceeded *Master of Arts.*" [28]

At the ceremony there cropped out dramatically one of the ledges that underlay his Puritanism, for he stoutly refused to wear cap or hood, and managed to convert another student to his principles. He was undeterred by the proctor, or by the scholars who jeered at him as a "Precisian." But, when it came to his formal part in the exercises, he tells us that many were so

22. *Autobiography.*

23. Seymour, p. 28.

24. J. W., *The Life ... of ... Dr. Winter.* Was the author Josiah Winter, or, as *DNB* suggests, Winter's brother-in-law, Weaver? Winter's notebook is in MS. at Trinity College library. It is described in Seymour, pp. xiii, 36ff.

25. *Ibid.,* pp. 39, 91; C. Mather, *Magnalia,* book IV, part ii, chap. 2, section 9. Cf. also, *MHS Coll.,* Series 4, viii, 549, 550.

26. *Autobiography; Parentator,* p. 17.

27. J. Evelyn, *Diary,* March 7, 1658.

28. *Autobiography; Parentator,* p. 17.

pleased with him that they "did publicly *Hum*" him, a vanity which he "never saw practised before nor since." [29]

It has been suggested that "humming" was a sign of derision rather than of favor,[30] and that the demonstration was misconstrued by its object. Certainly it would not be surprising if this New Englander, with all the confidence of nineteen years, and the obstinacy to stand out against cherished collegiate forms, by no means robust, and endowed with ideas far narrower than those of his fellows, failed to win their hearts. It is so much the greater tribute to him if the humming was kindly meant; and, whether it was or not, Winter's treatment of him shows that, however the students felt, the provost had no doubts.

From him came to Mather an appointment as "Fellow" [31] of the college. The office was refused, but the Lord Deputy and Commissioners were not behindhand, and they gave him a place as preacher at Magherafelt, an Ulster town. Though it was but a mere handful of houses with "a few straggling people," and its church was still in ruins from the Rebellion of 1641,[32] it was at least a parish of his own. Thither he set out, but at Dundalk he fell sick, and, discouraged, came back to Dublin.[33]

Three illnesses in a year led him to decide that the "moist Irish air" did not agree with him, and his thoughts turned to England. Henry Cromwell assured him that he should never want encouragement in Ireland; but more attractive was the news that his brother Nathaniel had secured for him an invitation to settle at Sedwells in Exeter.[33] There was temptation in the memory that, as Ireland was to New England, so England was to Ireland, in respect to opportunities for learning and power. To neglect an interest in such considerations as this is to make unintelligible much of Mather's life. To remember them is not to think of him as merely ambitious, but simply as faithful to his aim. If God's work was worth doing at all, the greater the posi-

29. *Autobiography.*

30. *DNB*, article "Increase Mather."

31. The *Autobiography* says: "The fellows in the college are chosen ... by the other fellows; only it is in the power of the Provost to choose one"; but it is not clear from the Statutes that the Provost ever had such power. It may well have been Winter's influence which procured the appointment, or the word "Fellow" here may be used to mean simply "tutor." Mr. Albert Matthews tells me that he has some evidence of the use of "Fellow" in this sense at Harvard, previous to this time, and Mather may have written with this meaning in mind.

32. Seymour, p. 113; *Autobiography*; *Parentator*, p. 18; and W. H. Maitland, *History of Magherafelt*, pp. 1–5, 6, 36.

33. *Autobiography*; *Parentator*, p. 18.

tion of him who carried it on, and the broader his field, the more acceptable his success.

In July, 1658, Mather arrived in London. There he met a man whose friendship was to last for many years and to play a part in his later career. At the present juncture, too, it proved of great service. John Howe [34] had been ordained some years before at Winwick, and it may have been through Richard Mather's friends there that he came to know Increase. He was a man holding a position of unique power among nonconformists, for he had been domestic chaplain to Oliver Cromwell, and the new Protector, Richard, continued him in office at Whitehall. Tall and graceful, this Puritan who "preached incomparably"[35] and salted his talk with occasional bits of humor, inveighed sturdily against the fanatical notions of the court, quite undeterred by the sentiment of his hearers. For this he seems to have won respect. Certainly he had power enough to be an able champion at Whitehall of such men as Bishop Ward of Salisbury, and Thomas Fuller.

He had been curate at Great Torrington in Devonshire when he first preached before Cromwell. Though the length of his sermon quite exhausted the patience of his intrepid listener, it was of a quality that won him his high post by the Protector's side. With characteristic independence, he longed for a humbler sphere. Courtiers, even of the Roundhead stamp, were not so amenable to his teaching as simple country folk in Devon, and he never ceased to long for Torrington. Indeed, he insisted that he be allowed to spend a quarter of each year there, and that he be authorized to appoint a substitute with full salary to conduct his favorite parish in his absence.[36]

When Increase Mather returned from Ireland, Howe was still in London, still uneasy there, but still persuaded to remain by such advisers as Richard Baxter. Like Winter, he saw promise in the young student from New England and he suggested that he go as his substitute in Torrington.[37] Nathaniel Mather was not so powerful a man as Howe, nor was Sedwells so good a post as the Devonshire parish. So Increase writes: "I . . . spent the

34. See *DNB*, and E. Calamy, *Life* of John Howe, prefixed to the London, 1724, edition of Howe's works.

35. R. Thoresby, *Diary*, i, 295, 296.

36. For these details as to Howe, see references in note 34, and J. P. Hewlett, Introduction, in his edition of Howe's writings.

37. *Autobiography*.

following winter in Torrington for the most part, only one month I continued with my brother Nathaniel, who was the preacher at Barnstaple," but nine miles away. Torrington was historic ground, as the scene of a Puritan victory, and from its hilltop commanded a broad view of the rolling country of a lovely district of Devon. But neither this village, nor the harbor town of Barnstaple with its fresh memories of seafaring hardihood, offered permanent settlement.[38]

Oliver Cromwell had died in the autumn of 1658, and his successor, Richard, was quickly in difficulties. On April 22, 1659, he was forced to dissolve Parliament, and a month later he abdicated. With his going, Howe became free to return to Torrington. Mather, and his faithful brother, Nathaniel, must have foreseen the turn of events. During the winter the latter seems to have approached his father-in-law, William Benn,[39] minister of All Saints Church, in Dorchester, Dorset, disciple of John White to whom New England owed so much,[40] and an influential Puritan, and interested him in Increase's welfare. Certainly Benn recommended [41] the young preacher to Colonel Bingham, Governor of Guernsey,[42] who sought a chaplain for the English garrison in the island. The place was offered to Increase Mather. He accepted it, and by April, 1659, when Evelyn wrote: "A wonderfull and suddaine change in yᵉ face of yᵉ publiq . . . several pretenders and parties strive for yᵉ government: all anarchy and confusion; Lord have mercy on us," [43] Mather was safely out of England.[44]

At Guernsey he was quartered in grim old Castle Cornet, long a stronghold of the Royalists against the island folk.[45] There he preached to the garrison each Sunday morning, and, in the afternoon, rowed ashore to hold service in the Town Church on the waterfront of "Petersport." The laxity of the time and place evoked earnest sermons on the fourth commandment, and he

38. For Torrington and Barnstaple, cf. J. B. Gribble, *Memorials of Barnstaple;* R. Polwhele, *History of Devonshire,* iii, 412, 413; T. Westcote, *A View of Devonshire in 1630,* pp. 327, 328; and R. N. Worth, *History of Devonshire,* chap. 18.

39. See *DNB; Nonconformist's Memorial,* ii, 126; *MHS Coll.,* Series 4, viii, 31 n.; and W. Densham and J. Ogle, *The Story of the Congregational Churches of Dorset,* pp. 115f.

40. *Ibid.; DNB.*

41. *Autobiography.*

42. See R. E. McCalmont, *Memoirs of the Binghams,* pp. 158, 159, 166, 167, and Appendix.

43. Evelyn, *Diary,* April 25, 1659.

44. *Autobiography.*

45. F. B. Tupper, *The Chronicles of Castle Cornet,* and *History of Guernsey.*

GREAT TORRINGTON CHURCH, DEVONSHIRE

records proudly that he "caused considerable external Reformation in this particular."[46]

Guernsey, with its French traditions, its peculiar customs, and its foreign flavor, offered much to an English traveller and student. Moreover, various godless rites, the people's tendency to celebrate festivals outlawed by the Puritan canon, and the island's distinction as a favorite playground of the Devil, of witches, and other infernal messengers, made it a peculiarly fruitful field for the labors of a divine more concerned with Biblical command than folklore, and much less interested in popular gaiety than in universal churchgoing.[47] But Mather's restlessness was still unsatisfied. His brother Nathaniel once again found a place for him, at Sandwich, but once again he rejected it. For a time he considered going back to Dublin, but from Samuel Mather there came a discouraging picture of the changes there. Finally, a congregational church in Gloucester, inspired by its minister, James Forbes, called him to the ancient church of St. Mary-de-Lode, in that town, and this offer won him over.[48] He was not easily contented — Ireland, Torrington, and Guernsey had each proved less attractive than the trial of new fields, and on December 18 he sailed once more for England.[49]

At Gloucester he lived with Forbes, who was a Scotsman, and, of course, a nonconformist, preaching during these years in Gloucester Cathedral, "with great success, but to the apparent danger of shortening his life."[50] Mather delivered his morning sermons in St. Mary's Church, just outside the Cathedral gate, in the square where Bishop Hooper was burned for his resistance to popery.[51] Inside the building was the tomb lovingly declared by an unsceptical age to be that of Lucius, the first Christian king of Britain.[52] It was hallowed ground for an antiquarian and an admirer of martyrs, and the Cathedral itself, where Mather held forth in the afternoons,[53] had even more of the spell of an

46. *Autobiography; Parentator*, p. 19. In Mather's time the Castle was not connected with the mainland.

47. See the histories of Guernsey, and especially E. MacCulloch, *Guernsey Folklore*. Cf., of course, Hugo's *Les Travailleurs de la Mer*.

48. *Autobiography; MHS Coll.*, Series 4, viii, 550, 551.

49. MS. *Diary* in American Antiquarian Society library, labelled "1660," contains some pages referring to this Journey; *Autobiography*.

50. *Nonconformist's Memorial*, ii, 249, 250.

51. *Autobiography; Parentator*, p. 20. For St. Mary's Church, see T. D. Fosbrooke, *An Original History*, pp. 341ff. For Hooper, see *Ibid.*, pp. 185, 186.

52. *Ibid.*, p. 341; *Autobiography*.

53. *Ibid.*

historic past. The beauty of the "noble fabric"[54] may have been decried as vanity of the flesh, even after its harsh correction at the hands of Cromwell's too zealous vandals; but its size and dignity must have appealed to a young divine educated among the bleak meeting-houses of New England.[55] All in all, Gloucester, that "handsome Citty, considerable for the Church & monuments,"[54] had much to recommend it. Forbes was an ideal comrade. Frequent imprisonment and the final penalty of excommunication failed to swerve him from his nonconforming path. Such stern devotion to his faith qualified him to inspire a young disciple, himself not without tough fibre, and ardent in his first labors for his church. Mather felt that he need seek no further.[56] Entering heartily into Forbes's task of building up what was to become a permanent Congregational establishment in Gloucester, he declared himself content to settle there. This time not his own restlessness but external events drove him to move.

He "saw a change of times at the door." "But the court which is without the temple leave out, and measure it not: for it is given unto the Gentiles; and the holy city shall they tread underfoot forty and two months," was the text of a sermon in which he prophesied "sufferings for the faithful." In the face of the storm he turned once more to Guernsey.[57]

He left Gloucester on February 2, 1660, and travelling by way of Bristol, Glastonbury, and Yeovil, reached Weymouth on the 8th. There he stayed till the 16th of March, when he sailed for Jersey. After a fortnight in that island, he came to Guernsey, on April 7.[58] On May 31, 1660, Charles II was proclaimed in "Petersport."[59]

The event was celebrated "with ringing of bells, and feux-de-joie and great rejoicing; half of all the companies of Militia of this island, of the most expert, being under arms." The proclamation was read by Abraham Carey, the provost, in six places, one of which was at the church door. Messengers were sent to congratulate Charles.[60] But with so much of what had made

54. Evelyn, *Diary*, July 31, 1654.
55. Cf. T. D. Fosbrooke, *An Original History*, pp. 233ff.
56. *Autobiography*.
57. *Ibid.*
58. MS. *Diary*, "1660."
59. P. LeRoy, *Note-Book*, p. 25.
60. *Ibid.*, pp. 25, 26.

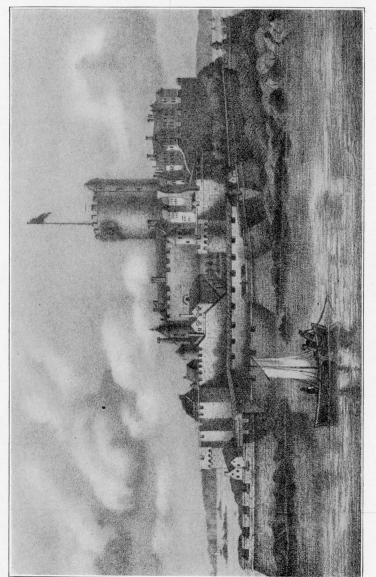

CASTLE CORNET, GUERNSEY

England and Guernsey a promised land for him, crumbling about his feet, Increase Mather, amid the rejoicing in the castle and the streets of "Petersport," refused to drink the king's health.[61]

If this were overlooked, he left no doubt as to his attitude by refusing to sign papers sent by General Monk, now Duke of Albermarle, to all government officers, "the purport of which was that now we believed the times were and would be happy." "A naughty & malicious person," said to have been a certain Ashton, and a chaplain at Jersey, took pains to tell Monk that his failure to get signatures from Guernsey was due to Mather's influence.[62] The duke ordered the governor, "Colonel Weaver," to have the rebellious Puritan brought before him; but the command was disobeyed, and Mather writes of Weaver, "God moved his heart to stand my friend, by which means I escaped the trouble, which, in that matter, I had been threatened with."[63] More dangerous was Captain Sharp, arriving as lieutenant-governor, on April 24, 1660; for he returned the muster-roll without Mather's name.[64] On another list his favorite Latinization of Crescentius for Increase had appeared, so that it was declared that Increase was not an officer in Guernsey. Therefore he was held to be entitled to no pay. In this crisis, M. Martin, a deacon of the French church in Petersport, made deposition to such good effect that the arrears of Mather's salary, of £120 a year, were paid in full.[65]

With these sharp contacts with the new régime, virtually ends Mather's first experience away from Boston. Sir Hugh Pollard, the new governor of Guernsey, insisted on conformity, and Mather was forced to leave on March 1, 1660–61. He remarks, with some satisfaction, it seems, "Thus was I persecuted out of two places, Gloucester and Guernsey, before I was twenty two years of age."[66]

Till June he lived, now in Weymouth and now in Dorchester, preaching continuously, but without salary.[67] At Weymouth there had been an Independent congregation during the Com-

61. *Autobiography.*
62. *Ibid.; Parentator*, pp. 20, 21.
63. *Autobiography.* I have not been able to find that any "Colonel Weaver" was ever governor of Guernsey, but LeRoy, *Note-Book*, p. 25, refers to "Generall Wayver" as governor.
64. *Autobiography;* LeRoy, *Note-Book*, p. 25.
65. *Autobiography.*
66. *Ibid.*
67. *Ibid.; Parentator*, p. 22.

monwealth, and such leaders for it as George Thorn, and John Wesley, grandfather of a famous namesake.[68] These men were still at work when Mather joined them, and no doubt planned measures to keep their flocks together even after their meetings were frowned on by law. Here was religious pioneering and the best of experience for a young divine.

In Dorchester, a town bound by close ties to New England, and famous for more than one good Puritan, Mather found similar work to be done. William Benn, the Congregational leader, had been ejected by the Restoration from the Church of All Saints, which his congregation had usurped under the Commonwealth. He was now meeting the loyal members of his flock and worshipping with them in private houses, laying the foundations for a Congregational Church that still endures.[69] Mather's aid must have been welcome, and he may have recognized a special claim upon him in the family connection between his brother Nathaniel and Benn.

Such work, however, was not the sort to hold a young man with his way in the world still to make. If England could give him nothing but a chance to work without pay toward the care of young and struggling churches, he might better return to Massachusetts where the first throes of religious establishment were safely past. The signs of the times were clear. Puritan supremacy had gone, great churches in large towns were no longer to be his, and a man of his cloth could hope for nothing but the humblest of posts. Four hundred pounds a year was offered him, he tells us, if he would conform, but this he "durst not do." [70] He considered going to Holland to join Nathaniel, but Samuel Bellingham, who had once invited him to make the journey, had been forced to hasten his departure, and the plan came to nothing.[71] It was as a last resort, it would seem, that he decided to revisit his birthplace. He longed to see his father, and hoped that he might find a place in New England "for some time." This does not sound as if he contemplated more than a brief stay there, and when, on June 29, 1661, he sailed for home, it was not eagerly, but simply "with submission to the will of God." [72]

68. Cf. J. Hutchins, *The History and Antiquities of Dorset*, ii, 418ff.; W. Densham and J. Ogle, *The Story*, pp. 367ff.; and *Nonconformist's Memorial*, ii, 161ff., 164ff.

69. Densham and Ogle, *The Story*, pp. 113ff.

70. *Autobiography*; *Parentator*, p. 22.

71. *Autobiography*; *MHS Coll.*, Series 4, viii, 6.

72. *Autobiography*; *Parentator*, p. 23. He sailed from Weymouth.

CHURCH OF ST. MARY DE LODE, GLOUCESTER

His ship was bound for Newfoundland, and he landed there after a voyage of somewhat more than a month.[73] With him he had brought many books; for the size of his library three years later [74] points clearly to the fact that his first experience in the bookshops of London had led him to buy much. Indeed, in the case of a few volumes, his own inscriptions show that they were selected during his travels. The works of William Fenner, in the second collected edition, for example, he bought for twenty shillings [75] — the current price of the then current doctrine of "this pious divine," with his "plain, zealous, and alarming" style.[76] Of "association" interest are two other books. One, Samuel Winter's "Summe of diverse Sermons Preached in Dublin," marked as the gift of the author's son at Dublin in 1658,[77] evidences once again the partiality of Josiah Winter for his classmate. The other, the "De Bono Unitatis," a warning to the English church by that doughty theologian, John Amos Comenius, a man of some interest to New Englanders of the day, is inscribed as Increase Mather's gift to his father in 1660.[78] And, finally, one cannot overlook a copy of Plautus among these sober neighbors.[79] One Puritan, at least, did not exclude profane works, if they were classic. The hint given by the buying of this book is abundantly borne out elsewhere in his library.[80]

Books were tangible products of his voyagings, but the experience and impressions he had gained were of far greater significance, and quite as obvious in the record of his later life. The maelstrom of English social life before and during the Restoration floated to the surface many great figures, and Mather, tossed in the same whirlpool, had moored himself by several of them. Winter and Samuel Mather were men of ability and liberal minds. Howe, rigid in belief, but by the power of personality enabled to hold an uncoveted place near the governing force of England; Cromwell seen through Howe's eyes;[81] Forbes, with his stern consistency of belief; and Colonel Bingham, a soldier, and practically minded politician who relished the preaching of a

---

73. *Parentator*, p. 23.
74. J. H. Tuttle, *The Libraries of the Mathers*, pp. 280–290.
75. See Mather's copy, now owned by the Boston Public Library.
76. B. Brook, *Lives of the Puritans*, ii, 451, 452.
77. The book is now owned by the American Antiquarian Society.
78. Cf. *Colonial Society Publications*, xxi, 181; H. Criegern, *Johann Amos Comenius als Theolog*, p. 66; F. A. Hanus, *Educational Aims and Educational Values*, pp. 193ff.
79. The book is now owned by the American Antiquarian Society.
80. Cf. pp. 76, 126, 127 *post*.   81. *Parentator*, p. 18.

good Puritan in his garrison church — these are all names which stand out in the record. Strong men, active times, Ireland, England, the thronging seventeenth-century London, Guernsey, quiet Devonshire hillsides, books, contact with thought, narrow and broad, Congregational and Presbyterian, all gave abundant material for reflection on the long voyage home. And with the sudden change of scene on the king's return, he had tasted what he fondly believed to be unrighteous persecution, and had learned by experience what it is to work for one's faith in a land where official sanction is withheld. Through it all he had kept unscathed what, though we may see them as narrow and dusty tenets, were to him and his class in his age clearly flaming ideals. If his father had protested against the rites of the established church and had rejected not only the surplice, but his native land, in order to build anew elsewhere, so Increase, less reasonable in the fervency of his faith, had spurned collegiate gowns, declined the royal health, and left unsigned the Oath of Allegiance. His creed had stood the test before which many another's had yielded, the inducement to purchase by conformity a far better living than any loyal Puritan could command in the new world. Four hundred pounds a year may have been an exceptional bait, to be distrusted as such; but, young as he was, he had received in Guernsey more than his father, with all his eminence in the colonies, could be given by his faithful church.[82] There were comfortable rewards for those in England who chose to read the Common Prayer, and, moreover, the temptation was not one to be measured in shillings and pence. Mather's heart was in England, he had left home planning a life-work abroad, and he returned only as a last resort, submitting to the Lord's will. Carp as we may in the twentieth century, there was, in Increase Mather's adherence to a point of faith, nobility to pass current for all time.

The seeds of experience had been thickly sown, and they sprang later to abundant growth. His desire for England waxed with his years. If he had left Boston a boy, he came back a man. Like a man, leaving the ship which brought him from Newfoundland, at the first sight of his father, he "wept abundantly for joy." This, he writes, was "the first, & I think the only time that I ever wept for joy." [83]

82. The *History of Dorchester*, p. 181, notes that the £100 granted Richard Mather was, for the period, liberal compensation.

83. *Autobiography.*

JOHN HOWE

From a painting in the National Portrait Gallery

CHAPTER VIII

BEGINNINGS IN BOSTON

INCREASE MATHER arrived at home on a Saturday evening. Eleazar, his brother, had just returned from Northampton, and the next day the two young men led the services in their father's church. "The Comforted Old Patriarch, sat Shining like the Sun in *Gemini*, . . . hearing his two Sons, in his own Pulpit entertain the People of GOD, with Performances, that made all People Proclaim him, *An Happy Father*." [1]

This was in September, 1661, and it was not until 1664 that Increase Mather was formally installed at the Second Church in Boston.[2] The interval forms a natural stage in the tale of his life. It was a period of settlement, and of aspiration rather than achievement. There were desires forsaken in the face of necessity, and ideals pruned back by contact with actual church problems. Yet it was, withal, a time of great significance for his life.

Boston had changed since he left it. The leading town of a district of perhaps thirty thousand people, its houses were "for the most part raised on the Sea-banks and wharfed out with great industry and cost, many of them standing upon piles, close together on each side the streets as in *London*, and furnished with many fair shops," and "their materials" were "Brick, Stone, Lime, handsomely contrived." It had also its "Town-house built upon pillars where the Merchants may confer" while "in the Chambers above they keep their monethly Courts." A public library, too, was planned for. "Their streets are many and large, paved with pebble stone, and the South-side adorned with Gardens and Orchards. . . . On the North-west and North-east two constant Fairs are kept for daily Traffick thereunto. On the South there is a small, but pleasant Common where the Gallants a little before Sun-set walk . . . till the nine a clock Bell rings them home." [3] We can reconstruct the picture more accurately than

---

1. *Parentator*, p. 23.
2. *Ibid.*, p. 25; *Autobiography*.
3. F. B. Dexter, *Estimates;* J. H. Benton, *The Story of the Old Boston Town House;* J. Josselyn, *An Account of Two Voyages*, p. 125; *Colonial Society Publications*, xii, 116f.

that of earlier Boston, for here and there to-day throughout New England we find some broad-beamed old house that has faced down the changes of years since 1661.

But, although the town was "rich and very populous, much frequented by strangers," [4] to a man who had known London it may well have seemed stale and unprofitable. Similarly, perhaps, there was little enticement in invitations to minister to congregations in "Barnstaple," so much less developed than the English town which bore its name, in Windsor, in the "Sea-Town" of Guilford, or in Plymouth, "the elder sister of all the united Colonies." [5] Half a dozen other towns sought Mather's services, but he turned his back quickly enough on all but the two largest settlements, Boston and Dorchester. Though the former ultimately won him, it was in the latter, in its church and his father's old house, that he first found immediate interest in the colonies.[6]

There lived his step-sister, Maria.[7] She was the daughter of John Cotton, by his second wife, and her mother had married Richard Mather some years before. Increase Mather was thus brought "into acquaintance with her," and perhaps his thoughts had sometimes turned back to her from England. Certainly when he was once at home he lost no time, for in March of the next year their marriage was celebrated.[8] One would go far for a glimpse of their wooing; but Puritan training did not encourage romantic expression, and the family archives hold no written record of young love. That it did not exist is not to be assumed. Such matters, perhaps unworthy in the sight of God, were not readily committed to paper; and remembering this, the great tenderness with which Increase wrote of his wife is all the more striking. Her son called her a "Gentlewoman of much Goodness in her Temper; a Godly, an Humble, and a Praying Woman."[9] Increase Mather wrote that in her the Lord gave him "a great Blessing" for she was "Singularly Conscientious, Humble, Pious, Prayerful" and the "Dear Companion of" his "Pilgrimage on Earth." To her children she was to be "a Tender Mother (if

4. Josselyn, *An Account*, p. 125.
5. *Autobiography*; Josselyn, *An Account*, p. 120; E. Johnson, *History*, p. 98.
6. *Autobiography*; S. J. Barrows and W. B. Trask, *Records*, p. 22.
7. *Ibid.*, p. 21.
8. March 6, 1661–62. *Autobiography*, and entry in Increase Mather's Bible, owned by the Massachusetts Historical Society.
9. *Parentator*, p. 24.

there was such an one in the world)," and at her death, more than fifty years later, her husband wrote with more than a hint of deep feeling of his "Dear, Dead Consort." [10] She had been "of a very loving, tender disposition." "I kept close to my study," he writes, "& committed the management of the affairs of the family to her. When I have been absent from my family, I was easy in my spirit because my heart did safely trust in her, who did me good, & not evil, all the days of my life. She was always very careful not to do anything which she thought would trouble me. Her honor to me was too great, for she has said to many that she thought I was the best husband, & the best man in the whole world."[11] Her heart, hemmed in by Puritan restraint, disciplined by the responsibilities of managing a household in colonial Boston, clearly was warm with love for her husband. His simple phrasing shows, as plainly as any emotional outburst of a romantic era, the tenderness of age born of the love of his youth.

On the morning of the twelfth of the following February there was born to Maria and Increase Mather a son, and three days later he was baptized by Mr. Wilson "at ye old church in Boston."[12] The name of Cotton was given him in honor of his mother's father, and the pitch of fame to which he carried it needs no comment here.[13] Increase Mather loved all his children dearly. To them he wrote: "[you] are all of you so many parts of myself and dearer to me than all things which I enjoy in this world";[14] and his firstborn became singularly precious to him. Cotton's relation to his father was to be at once that of disciple, companion, and champion, and from the days when he lay in his cradle in his first winter, many hopes clustered about his head.

He was born in Boston, in the house which had been the home of his grandfather Cotton and the birthplace of his mother. Its broad rooftree sheltered Increase Mather and his wife for the first eight years of their married life.[15] It stood very near the present Pemberton Square, and seems to have been a double house. One half was once occupied by Sir Henry Vane, and the northern half by John Cotton.[16] Possibly the Mathers had all of

10. I. Mather, *A Sermon Concerning Obedience & Resignation to the Will of God*, pp. i, 38–40.
11. *Autobiography*.
12. Entry in Increase Mather's Bible (see note 8).
13. *Autobiography*; B. Wendell, *Cotton Mather*.
14. Letter prefacing *Autobiography*.
15. Entry in Increase Mather's Bible (see note 8); *MHS Proc.*, xviii, 14.
16. Cf. *MHS Coll.*, Series 5, v, note on pp. 59–62.

it. In any case, the northern part was theirs. Nothing remains of the old house, but it seems to have been "an old square house of the usual pattern," [17] and from an occasional one of its contemporaries still preserved we may guess at its character. Dignity, sturdiness, and simplicity of design, and the sound effect of fine proportions, mark the seventeenth-century builder's work in America.

We generalize blindly to-day as to the Puritans' contempt for art, and, in the same breath, acknowledge the broadly satisfactory nature of their handiwork. We find beauty in their furniture, plain and rugged always, but never without the quality that comes from strength and balance in design,[18] and at the same time deny to its makers any interest in beauty. True, they planned for use, not ornament, but they had an eye for dignity and proportion, and builded better than they knew. So when they wrote, save for an occasional lapse into forced decoration of style, just as some bits of their furniture show here and there too much elaboration,[19] they wrote to instruct, to guide, or to warn, but gave worth to their pages by a sincere purpose dignified by a plain and vigorous form. Conscious artists in architecture or literature they may not have been, but unconsciously they observed traditional standards of beauty of line and power of phrase.

Accordingly, when we follow Increase Mather inside his new home, we shall find antidotes for many a misconception of to-day. The Puritan's fireside is austere to us, because he wrote and talked about austere things; but it was not alone in the Mather house that love of wife and children brought warmth. In the back of our minds we think of early New Englanders as ascetics, as men blind to beauty, and concerned only with repression and discipline. Yet within their doors there were chests of drawers, chairs, or tables, beautiful in themselves. On their tables were bits of pottery admired to-day. In their kitchens was pewter, for use and not for show, that we are glad to display upon our shelves.[20] They did not shun good things of the table, nor were

17. *MHS Coll.*, Series 5, v, pp. 59, 60, 62, 63.

18. Cf., for example, W. Nutting, *Furniture of the Pilgrim Century.*

19. *Ibid., passim.*

20. Cf. *Ibid.; MHS Coll.*, Series 5, vols. v, vi (Sewall's *Diary*), Series 6, vol. i, especially p. 4 n.; I. W. Lyon, *The Colonial Furniture of New England*, pp. 219ff. and its references to Puritan inventories.

they deprived of them. They drank good beer and wine;[21] and, if Puritanism be blamed for its attempt to control the smallest daily acts of its followers,[22] their tankards and wineglasses brimming on their tables point a moral to him who believes that the twentieth century has left Puritan narrowness dead and far behind.

Yet from Increase Mather's point of view the crowning glory of the house was not in the furniture, not in the "pendulum clock" that ticked on the wall beside the great fireplace, nor in the silver tankard that shone on the pine table, but in the books that lined his study's shelves.[23] "I have ever since any of you can remember," he told his children, "loved to be in no place on the Earth, so much as in my Study." [24] Any student of his day would have found resource there, and any book-collector cause for pride. On October 18, 1664, he entered in his diary, "Wrote catalogue of my books," and the list is fortunately extant.[25] It contains nearly seven hundred titles, and represents nearly a thousand volumes. There were sturdy quartos with bindings then undulled by time, neat octavos, and a mass of smaller books and pamphlets to fill the narrower spaces. To-day items for the antiquarian and bibliophile, the bulk of his library was then the current output of the press. There was room, of course, for the sixteenth century, with its Renaissance educators and its church reformers, and they held proud posts.

A man's books give the key to his character and tastes.[26] To follow around Mather's shelves is to see him more clearly. He was a professional divine, and by far the greater part of his collection was made up of Biblical commentaries, treatises, and sermons. The Latin church fathers rubbed elbows with seventeenth-century English Puritans. Historians occupied a good-sized row, and treatises on geography and books of travel point to interests broader than those concerned with his daily task. Of peculiar fascination is a group of books on science, or what passed for science in his time. Here is Lazare Rivière's [27] "Practise of

21. E. Johnson, *History*, pp. 246, 247; W. Wood, *New Englands Prospect*, p. 15.
22. Cf. J. T. Adams, *The Founding*, p. 79.
23. The clock and tankard are referred to in his will. See C. Robbins, *History*, pp. 212ff.
24. I. Mather, *Sermon Concerning Obedience & Resignation*, p. ii.
25. MS. *Diary*, "1660"; J. H. Tuttle, *The Libraries of the Mathers*, pp. 280–290.
26. For Mather's books, discussed below, cf. *Ibid*.
27. A French physician, 1589–1655.

Physick," a book with the illuminating title of "The Causes of Pestilence," an up-to-date medical treatise by Dr. Thomas Willis,[28] then alive and practising in England, a "Body of Chymistry," the "Physica" of another contemporary, Jean Magirius,[29] Scribonius[30] in a sixteenth-century edition, Thomas Cogan's "Haven of Health," and, more familiar to our ears, the "De Augmentis Scientiarum" of Bacon, and his "Natural History." Euclid appears, with a commentary, and Ramus, as we should expect, is represented by more than one volume. Finally, the classics make a brave showing. Tacitus, Juvenal, Persius, Cicero, Demosthenes, Horace, Plautus, Seneca, Æsop, Lucian, Sophocles, Lucan, and Ovid's "Art of Love," shelved with the works of Charles Chauncy, John Davenport, John Cotton, and other New England authors, reveal two sides of Massachusetts Puritanism, and correct the fatally easy generalization which asserts that men of Mather's type, because they wrote and read along the line of their beliefs, were blind to all else and ignorant of the great profane literature of the world.

Abandoning classification, and tumbling out on the table a heap of books, chosen at random for their connection with elements in Mather's life, or for their appeal to our modern eyes, one may have a composite impression which will serve in lieu of a detailed bibliographical study of Mather's library list. In such a heap would be "The Theatre of God's Judgements," a collection of tales "from Sacred, Ecclesiastical, and Prophane Authors" showing God's punishment of transgressors of His laws, written by the schoolmaster of Oliver Cromwell.[31] Beside it is "The World of Wonders" by H. Stevens, hiding under its English title a translation of Henri Estienne's famous "Apologie pour Herodote."[32] Here are literary kinsmen of what was to be the most famous of Increase Mather's own works.[33] Robert Fabyan's[34] chronicle of England from the arrival of Brutus to the sixteenth century, known in his day as "The Concordance of Histories," lies open before us. The "Adagia" of Erasmus is better known to-day,[35] as is, perhaps, Buchanan's great Scottish

28. Cf. DNB.   29. 1615–1697.
30. Roman physican of the first century.
31. See DNB, article "Thomas Beard."
32. Cf., for example, C. H. C. Wright, History of French Literature, p. 205.
33. See pages 170–171 post.
34. Cf. DNB.
35. Cf. H. O. Taylor, Thought and Expression in the Sixteenth Century, i, 166.

history.[36] Of the Puritans, Owen, Mede, and Baxter [37] are seen at once, and William Prynne's great tirade against the theatre, the "Histrio-Mastix," [38] called by Voltaire "a very bad book," [39] but which is, none the less, a "*magnum opus* of Puritan enthusiasm and learning."[40] Here and there a book has an inscription marking it as the gift of Richard Mather, and five of his works were in his son's hands. Milton's "Apology for Smectymnuus" and his "Defensio pro Populo Anglicano" catch one's eye, and a collector of Americana would delight in "The Planter's Plea," the "Anti-Synodalia," and kindred works. Calvin's immortal "Institute"[41] is here, of course, and, lest we form too narrow an idea of the tastes of the collector, the works of Robert Bellarmine, a cardinal so derided by the Dutch Puritans as to have a wine jug modelled in his likeness and crowned by them with his name.[42] Fuller's "Church History" is familiar,[43] "Hall against Long Hair" has an alluring title,[44] and "Willet and Holland de vocal Judgment of witches"[45] is an entry which arouses our curiosity when we keep later events in mind.

In a far different field is Grotius on the power of the temporal government in church councils;[46] and Sir Walter Raleigh's politically advanced "Prerogative of Parliaments,"[47] and a mass of pamphlets on current political topics, reveal the interest of at least one ecclesiastic in the policies and problems of the state. One cannot turn away without a glance at the numerous compilations or collections, books of ready reference, flanked by grammars and dictionaries of various languages. There is the "Herwologia Anglica" of Henry Holland,[48] the "Anglorum

36. Cf. *Cambridge History of English Literature*, iii, 164.
37. Cf. *DNB*.
38. *DNB; Cambridge History of English Literature*, vi, 403, 406; A. W. Ward, *History of English Dramatic Literature*, ii, 412f.
39. In his *Sur la Consideration qu'on doit aux Gens de Lettres*.
40. A. W. Ward, *History of English Dramatic Literature*, ii, 412f. An entry in the "1660" MS. *Diary* shows that Mather was reading the *Histrio-Mastix* on Dec. 13, 1664.
41. H. O. Taylor, *Thought and Expression*, i, 402-423.
42. Cf. R. Chambers, *The Book of Days*, i, 371, 372.
43. For Thomas Fuller, see *DNB*.
44. Thomas Hall, 1610-1665. See *DNB*.
45. I have not identified this book positively, but see *Cambridge History of English Literature*, iv, 325.
46. *De Imperio Summarum Potestatum Circa Sacra*. Cf. J. L. de Burigny, *The Life of ... Grotius*, pp. 85, 365.
47. *Cambridge History of English Literature*, iv, 64.
48. I thus identify Mather's entry "Herologia Anglorium." Holland's book, containing brief lives of famous men, appeared in 1620.

Prælia" so much in favor with Elizabeth's Privy Council,[49] and Matthias Prideaux's "Introduction to the Reading of History."[50] Its pages shed light on the critical views of the time. It sums up, with the assurance of a Wells, the earth's history to the accession of Charles I, classifies history, asks engaging questions to stimulate the student, and delivers itself of harsh opinions on the profane romances or "bastard histories" of an earlier day.[51] What wonder that the tales of Arthur do not find their way to this Boston house, or that there are lacking the lighter works of the Elizabethan "merrie England"? Yet, save for this absence of fiction, of poetry, of current English literature, redeemed only by such items as Fuller's "Worthies" or "Herbert's poems," it is hard from a seventeenth-century vantage-point to pick flaws in the Mather library as a collection for a man broad in culture and active in mind.

One would turn gladly enough from the books, to catch a glimpse of their owner in the flesh. "It was Commonly said, *It was a very Edifying Thing, only to see him in our Public Assemblies; His very Countenance carried the Force of a Sermon with it.*"[52] No portrait of him at this time is preserved, but we may believe that his stature, his strongly modelled face with its high cheekbones and long, straight nose, and, most characteristic of all, his long narrow hands with their slender fingers, were distinctive features then as well as twenty years later.[53] Fortunately, if we lack evidence as to externals, we do find hints here and there of more fundamental elements in his make-up. It was during these years that he wrote the first of the diaries preserved for us. In them there are, here and there, vivid sidelights on the writer. We see in his "heart serious" or "heart various"[54] at the close of each day's entry his effort to appraise his progress in his task of walking with his will in strict accordance with God's. In his constant debates as to whether he should accept the call of the Second Church in Boston, his worries about salary,[55] his longing to move elsewhere,[56] and, by preference, to England,[57] there is

49. Cf. A. C. Potter, *Catalogue*, p. 193.
50. See *DNB*, article "John Prideaux, 1578–1650."
51. M. Prideaux, *An Easy and Compendious Introduction for Reading all sorts of Histories*, pp. 348, 349.   52. *Parentator*, p. 40.
53. See the 1688 portrait of Mather, reproduced as frontispiece to this book.
54. MS. *Diary*, "1660"; *Parentator*, p. 40.
55. *Autobiography*; MS. *Diary*, "1660," entries Feb. 15, March 15, 1664. Cf. also, C. Robbins, *History*, pp. 11, 12.
56. MS. *Diary*, "1660," entry Feb. 17, 1664.   57. *Autobiography*.

seen the working of his remembered successes abroad, and the desire for the home country that ran in his blood. And a still more human side appears in his visits to his neighbors, his dinings out, his many callers, and the repeated occurrence in his diary of the great names of his Boston — Wilson, Allen, Richards, Way, Collicott, Mayo, Clark, Higginson, and Hutchinson.[58] He is thus revealed, not as the dour minister locked in his study, or the ascetic shunning the world, but as the man of "very *Gentlemanly Behaviour;* full of *Gravity,* with all the Handsom *Carriage,* as well as *Neatness,* of a *Gentleman.*" [59] He was welcomed by clergy and laymen, sought for as a preacher, and known as a travelled and learned man and a cultured friend. He did not waste his words, but he loved "good talk." [60] If its charms lured him from work, what he lost in erudition he gained in a knowledge of men that stood him ever in good stead. Young as he was, his potentialities marked him early as a prominent figure in Boston streets.[61]

Such a man surely discussed with his friends the complaints against Massachusetts, brought before Charles II, the sending of John Norton and Simon Bradstreet as agents of the colony in England, the aftermath of the Quaker disturbances, and the King's demand that the restriction of the franchise on religious grounds be abolished. Probably he sympathized with the temporizing policy which delayed action on this royal order so fatally aimed at the roots of Congregational control in New England.[62] We may be sure that he read and rejoiced in Michael Wigglesworth's "Day of Doom," so popular in its day, and so thoroughgoing in its Calvinism.[63] Dryden and Cowley were certainly of less moment to Mather than this poet of New England soil. But nothing in current literature or current politics concerned him quite so closely as the great controversy which, culminating in these years, divided the church and enlisted the best writers on each side. It was a dispute which touched every resident of the colony.

58. MS. *Diary,* "1660," *passim.*   59. *Parentator,* p. 186.
60. *Ibid.,* pp. 39, 40, 186.
61. *Parentator,* p. 24, tells us that he preached alternately in Boston and Dorchester during the first winter after his return. Then he seems (*Autobiography*) to have stayed at the Second Church, Boston. He left the Dorchester church formally in 1663 (Barrows and Trask, *Records,* pp. 22, 41). He was admitted to the Boston church March 10, 1664. C. Robbins, *History,* p. 263.
62. Cf. Palfrey, ii, chaps. 12, 13.
63. See R. F. Roden, *The Cambridge Press,* pp. 95-100; M. C. Tyler, *History of American Literature,* ii, 27-35.

Simply stated, the problem was one of admission to the church. The original Congregational rule was that, to be admitted into full rights as a church member, an applicant must show evidence of a demonstrable religious experience and a valid regeneration of spirit. The first settlers were, like Richard Mather, men to whom Congregationalism was the core of life. They found no difficulty in experiencing intense spiritual conviction, and in kindling in their hearts a faith proof against the terrors of the sea. But their sons, in a time and place where their religion was established and could be seen more as a matter of course, had no such opportunities for inward victories of soul. Were they, therefore, although baptized in infancy, to be denied admission to the church? According to strict Congregational law they must be excluded; but, if they were, who was to carry on the living religious organization? [64]

The question was discussed at a meeting of ministers in 1657, and simmered until 1662, when the General Court, perceiving the danger which lay in indecision on a point so fundamental to the whole colonial structure, summoned a Synod to solve the problem. Increase Mather was interested in the ministers' first debate, and in England he helped his brother publish their results.[65] It was natural, therefore, that when the church council of 1662 was formed from delegates and ministers of the various churches, he was chosen to accompany his father in representing Dorchester.[66]

The heated arguments, the volleying of texts in support of one position or another, and the various doctrines upheld, concern us less than the result of the Synod, printed in 1662.[67] This declared, in brief, that a man of sober and virtuous life, even though not fired by any verifiable religious experience, might claim membership in the church, provided he had been baptized in youth, but could not be admitted to communion. His children were entitled to baptism, but not to partake of the Lord's Supper. This made at once two classes of church membership, communicants and non-communicants. This dualism, the presence of rights conferred by inheritance beside those due to men of

64. On the controversy which followed, see W. Walker, *Creeds and Platforms*, pp. 238, 339, and H. M. Dexter, *Congregationalism*, pp. 467ff.
65. Walker, *Creeds and Platforms*, p. 261, n. 5.
66. Barrows and Trask, *Records*, p. 39.
67. Walker, *Creeds and Platforms*, pp. 301ff., 238.

authentic religious experience, held possibilities of complications of many sorts.

By far the majority of the Synod [68] voted for the plan outlined above, but there was an active minority. With it sided Increase Mather and his brother,[69] inspired from afar by John Davenport of New Haven,[70] and led in the council itself by President Chauncy. They opposed not only most of the influential divines of the day, but especially Jonathan Mitchell,[71] the beloved tutor of college days, and their own father.

Chauncy printed a protest against the decision of the Synod.[72] John Davenport followed suit. With his own essay he included a preface, the first published work of Increase Mather.[73] The book was promptly answered by Richard Mather and Mitchell, the former turning his arguments against Davenport, and the latter combatting the views of his erstwhile pupil.[74] One may read in the "Magnalia" the main contentions that Increase urged,[75] and his Preface repays study from more than one aspect.

He begins with an apology for his work, and a frank avowal of his respect for his opponents. The cause of truth demands, however, that Davenport's voice be heard. He defends the minority opinion briefly but adequately against such charges as that its upholders were few; that they denied the need for the church's care of children; and that they argued from mere weakness and wilfulness. There are then propounded the seven arguments summarized in the "Magnalia." The seventh seems the key to

68. H. M. Dexter, *Congregationalism*, p. 471.

69. Hutchinson, *History*, i, 224 n.

70. *MHS Coll.*, Series 4, viii, 188, 189; F. B. Dexter, *Sketch of the Life and Writings of John Davenport.*

71. Cf. H. M. Dexter, *Congregationalism*, p. 472.

72. His *Anti-Synodalia Scripta Americana*, 1662.

73. The full title is: "*Another Essay for Investigation of the Truth, In Answer to two Questions*, Concerning

      I.   The Subject of Baptism.
     II.   The Consosiation of Churches.

By John Davenport, etc. . . . Cambridge, Printed by Samuel Green and Marmaduke Johnson, 1663." The copy in the New York Public Library bears on the title-page the inscription "John Cotton his booke given him by his Brother, Mr Increase Mather"; and at the beginning of the "Apologetical Preface to the Reader" there is written, apparently in the same hand, "Written by the Reverend Increase Mather." The authorship is ascribed to Increase Mather in *Parentator*, p. 52.

74. *A Defense of the Answer and Arguments of the Synod met at Boston in the year 1662.* Cambridge, 1664. A summary of the answer is in C. Mather, *Magnalia*, book v, part iii.

75. *Ibid.*

the position taken by the rebels against the Synod. "There is danger of great Corruption and Pollution creeping into the Churches, by the Enlargement of Baptism." There spoke the desire to defend the integrity of the church.

Most interesting to us is the Preface's moderate tone, and the judicial statement of its doctrine. There is no trace of the scurrilous pamphleteer or hot-headed fanatic. We see, rather, an argument for the cherished belief of a scholar who could use a line from Seneca, or lean on support afforded by an array of citations from church writers from Augustine to Cotton. Their number and variety prove the work to be that of a man who could use the books he owned. His reading had kept pace easily with any demands likely to be put upon it by Synodical debates. From the point of view of style there is, perhaps, nothing to detain us. There is, however, clear phrasing, logical arrangement, and skilful use of persuasive methods in controversy. And on every page there is the seal set upon the written word by the style of the English Bible. Its translators found their native tongue a medium capable of stateliness without loss of picturesqueness and charm. Many a good Puritan, consciously or not, let their habits of phrasing guide his pen. So also Mather, at work on his Preface, saw the power of their means. Thence came the resonant effectiveness of his Preface's last words: "*Now the Lord grant, that his People may have* one heart and one way (*and that it may be the* right way, *even the* way which is called Holy) to serve him, for the good of them, and of their Children after them. *And the God of* Truth *and* Peace, *lead us by his Spirit into* all Truth, *through him who is made unto us of God*, the Way, and the Truth, and the Life." [76]

Courage was needed to push Davenport's book and Mather's Preface toward publication. It could only be done against what were, for a young and untried minister, great odds. Increase did not flinch. To Davenport he wrote: "I have your writings still in my hands. I offered the Synod to read them, but ∩ʳU.Ƨ7.U [Mr. Norton] advised them not to suffer me." How Norton's temper must have blazed at these signs of unruliness in his pupil! Mather continues: "I let them have a coppy of them, which was genˡˡʸ transcribed." Some of the court would gladly have ruled out the arguments, "but the major pte were not soe violent." It was moved that the essay be printed. "All the answer that could

76. *Preface*, p. 14.

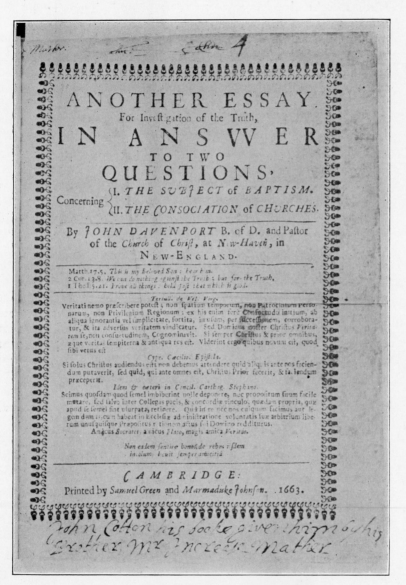

TITLE-PAGE OF DAVENPORT'S "ANOTHER ESSAY"

be obtained was that wee might doe as we would, but they would not vote for such a thing, & wee must count it a favour that wee were not Cõmanded to be silent. ... yoᵂ may see which way things are like to be Carried."[77]

In Mather's view in the Synod one sees the strict Congregationalism in which he had been trained asserting itself, backed by the same rigidity of character that marked his nonconformity in the face of opposition abroad. To him the "Half-Way Covenant," as the Synod's decision came to be called, meant a lowering of the standard of church membership. Nineteenth-century theologians could see how, in the movement he opposed, the decline of Congregationalism was begun, and the seeds of New England Unitarianism were sown.[78] If they were right, then Increase Mather at twenty-three fought for the purity of the church to which he had dedicated his life.

His position was sound in theory, but in practice there were difficulties, inevitable and grave. Mitchell showed that, if the old rule of admission to the church was maintained, there must be a relaxation in the test of religious experience. Otherwise there could be found no new members through whom the church might live. And, standards once lowered, religiously untested persons might come, in time, not merely into rights of baptism, but to the communion table itself. Practically he had weight on his side. In opposing him, Mather had none the less founded his belief on the rock that underlay his church.

Increase Mather's boldness won both friends and enemies. A year later someone at table declared that he "had acted disorderly in opposing yᵉ Synod, and that being disorderly was as bad as drunkenesse or scandale."[79] His father's lack of sympathy with his opinion was no light thing, though their relations stood the test unscathed.[80] In Boston, however, he won praise as well as blame. His views were those of Mr. Mayo, minister of the Second Church, who urged him to share his pulpit.[81]

The appeal came to a man much perplexed as to his future course. Mather had debated with himself, sought advice from

---

77. *MHS Coll.*, Series 4, viii, 205, 206.

78. H. M. Dexter, "Two Hundred Years Ago in New England," in *Congregational Quarterly*, iv, 29.

79. MS. *Diary*, "1660," entry for June 21, 1664.

80. *Parentator*, p. 52.

81. W. Walker, *Creeds and Platforms*, p. 266. Cf. also, *MHS Coll.*, Series 4, viii, 78.

friends, and still had not decided where to take up his work.[82] His desire for England was stifled finally, no doubt, by the firmness with which the Restoration government set its face against nonconformity; but there were still vexations of spirit as to the salary he might hope for from the Boston church. It was not until May 24, 1664, after prayers and a public day of fasting, that his scruples were put to rest. On that day he was formally installed as Teacher of the Second Church in Boston, and received his charge from the hands of his aged father.[83]

A look ahead reveals much. By 1668 Increase Mather had abandoned his strict doctrine on baptism,[84] and in 1675 he published two books in support of the "Half-Way Covenant." So, too, his intolerance, great enough to be noted by his son, who is himself mocked to-day as the very symbol of inflexibly rigid views, yielded before the tolerant adaptation of his ideas to practical necessity that marks his later years.[85] In his autobiography he is silent as to his first writing and his arguments in the Synod, but we need not be ashamed for them. His youthful theories were sound in principle. In changing them he revealed the practical strain that guided him everywhere in his career and made possible for him achievement, not in the sphere of the abstract but in the world of men. If, before 1664, he was a theorist, with a narrowness that came from lack of experience in the daily conduct of a parish in a rapidly growing community, his more hard-headed traits triumphed in the end. If only by the "Half-Way" method could the church reach men, what mattered points of theory? His was an ideal of service, and service, he came quickly to know, could be achieved by no rule so strict as to exclude those whom, by milder measures, it might hope to win. So also one need not blink the fact that he regarded a sufficient salary, a house, and proper respect, as imperative needs. So they were, unless he were to be an impractical idealist, crying in a wilderness. To work among men he must be able to hold the place that a minister's authority logically demanded, and on which it depended, in part, for its strength. He must be learned, if he were to teach, and books were not to be bought for love. Practical policy replaced theoretical strictness; ideas gave way in

82. *Autobiography;* MS. *Diary,* "1660."
83. *Autobiography; Parentator,* p. 25.
84. *Ibid.,* p. 53.
85. *Ibid.,* Article 13.

favor of working methods of service. He turned from an ideal of ascetic holiness, such as a mendicant friar may have had sometimes, to a clearly visioned and deftly executed purpose to conquer, not in philosophical discussion in some unearthly realm, but in the heart of the man in the seventeenth-century Boston street. That he changed his doctrine on baptism, or that he grew more tolerant, shows not weakness but strength — the courage to leave a chill pinnacle of thought to play his part among men of flesh and blood, in quest of the preëminent ideal of practical human service to God.

CHAPTER IX

THE TEACHER OF THE SECOND CHURCH

MATHER became Teacher of the Second Church harassed by doubts and hedged in by terms. "Under my hand I expressed, that, if hereafter the Lord should call me to greater service elsewhere, or, in case of personal persecutions wherein not they but I shall be aimed at, or want of health, or if I should find that a competent maintenance for me and mine should not be afforded, then (my relation to them notwithstanding) I would be at liberty to return to England, or to remove elsewhere." [1] Yet for fifty-nine years he served the Second Church and gave it the central place in his thoughts.

Until 1674 his course was outwardly uneventful, but this period is, for the biographer, doubly precious. Then began the self-expression that gives us the truest measure of his life. Diaries, sermons, and printed books give us now a chance to see the man apart from the turmoil of the busier days to come. And, from the point of view of character, his inner life from 1664 to 1674 has a dramatic quality of its own.

He cannot be seen, of course, apart from the affairs of the day. No one lived then in Boston without knowing of events abroad. In England there was war with the Dutch, and their guns echoed in the Thames. There was the smoke and glare of the Great Fire of London, the political stir of the fall of Clarendon, the forming of the Triple Alliance, the Declaration of Indulgence and its withdrawal, and the relief which came with peace with the persistent Dutch. Ever present was the aspiration of the new government toward a firmer imperial control, and its inevitable consequences for the colonies.[2] Meanwhile there were Dryden's plays, Robert Boyle's scientific questings, John Bunyan's soul searchings, and, above them all, "Paradise Lost," "Paradise Regained," and "Samson Agonistes."

Against this English scene, New England shone in duller lights. There was no dramatist in the colonies, for which good Puritans thanked their God; but there was no Milton. There was no

1. C. Robbins, *History*, p. 21. 2. Cf. J. T. Adams, *The Founding*, chap. 13.

Clarendon, but there was an Endicott, however bigoted, and a Bellingham, to resist the efforts of the Royal Commissioners to bring the American colonies of Charles II's empire more closely under control. In the controversy between the king's representatives and the colonial leaders, appears the basic problem of the day. If Colonel Richard Nicolls, Sir Robert Carr, Colonel George Cartwright, and Samuel Maverick[3] accomplished nothing in Massachusetts, it was not through weakness or lack of royal authority, but because they faced New Englanders imbued with the idea that their American home was theirs by charter, to be ruled in virtual independence and with constant jealousy of all trespass on the domain of their fathers' faith. The leaders may not have spoken for the majority, and their position may have been legally unsound; but to a son of Richard Mather there seemed to be no room for dispute. And, in his shoes, in a land believed to be the stronghold of God's elect, any of us might share his views unashamed. Such men as he were right in that they were following logically what they knew as the sole way of truth — the maintenance of a faith decreed by the word of God. So when the Puritans of Boston observed the letter of the King's order, and ignored its spirit, by replacing the former restriction of the franchise to church members by a limitation identical in result,[4] they saw it not as evasion but as righteous use of the readiest weapons in defence of their Bible state. To uphold their government was a greater duty than to submit to any ideal of tolerance. God's behest could not be ignored to meet the plans of an earthly king. What wonder that, when the Royal Commissioners sat in his congregation, Mather, from the pulpit, "lifted his heart to God!"[5]

United the Puritans may have been against royal encroachments, but harmony was sometimes lacking within the doors of their own churches. The Synod's decision was not universally approved, and the First Church of Boston, on the death of their first leader, Mr. Wilson, took the occasion to oppose the "Half-Way Covenant" by calling to their pulpit John Davenport, the staunchest foe of the new order.[6] There was a split in the ranks of the congregation, and Mather, by his opposition to the rebel-

3. Cf. Palfrey, ii, 580, 581; J. T. Adams, *The Founding*, p. 330.
4. *Ibid.*, p. 331; Channing, ii, 69.
5. MS. *Diary*, "1660," July 24, 1664: "Being commissioners at meeting lifted my hrt to God."
6. Cf. H. A. Hill, *History*, chap. 1.

lious faction, gave prompt notice of his change from his views of 1662. There was room for deep concern when a third church was formed by those of Wilson's old congregation who disagreed with Davenport. Such a rift in church unity threatened the whole frame of things.

There were other gloomy portents. More than one citizen must have been worried by the troubles that were to lead to a disastrous Indian war, and everyone knew that the college was in a state of discontent. Chauncy, until his death in 1672, carried Harvard safely through stormy financial seas, relieved by such timely aid as Portsmouth's contribution; but his successor, Leonard Hoar, coming with abundant recommendations from England, faced graver dangers. Dissensions sprang up within the college walls, and an investigation by the General Court prefaced its demand that Hoar improve the state of things. In 1675 he resigned. Whatever the root of the trouble, whatever led members of the Corporation to give up their offices in the midst of Hoar's régime, it is obvious that disputes within the college, the hope of New England Puritanism, struck chill to devout advocates of the New England way.[7]

Increase Mather notes again and again the deaths, during these years, of the first generation of settlers, and the change in the people's attitude. An interest in New England solely as a church state was giving place to a more worldly view. In such signs he saw impending woes for the colony. With troubles at home, with the royal and colonial governments at odds,[8] it was plain that the times were critical. For men of his ideals there were sure to be shocks in store. Characteristically he expressed this in his sermons, and stoutly preached the faith of Boston's earliest years.

His interest in the times was, moreover, by no means academic. The man who had refused the king's health at Guernsey, and had seen in the Restoration promise of evil days, continued to carry his opinions into practice. When Whalley and Goffe, condemned by Charles II for their share in his father's trial, fled to New England and took shelter with John Davenport in New Haven, more than one Puritan saw in the chance to aid in their escape a way to oppose royal tyranny.[9] Although there was a half-

7. Quincy, i, 27–30, 31–34; C. Mather, *Magnalia*, book IV, part i, section 5.
8. Channing, ii, 65; J. T. Adams, *The Founding*, pp. 336, 337.
9. *Lectures on Massachusetts History*, pp. 321ff.; F. B. Dexter, *Memoranda; MHS Coll.*, Series 4, viii, notes to pp. 122, 123; Channing, ii, 66, 67; Palfrey, ii, 494ff.

hearted search for the regicides, in obedience to the king's commands, they never lacked for friends. Increase Mather stood in close relation to them, and for years their letters found their way out of the colonies in his care.[10] Naturally he did not welcome the Royal Commissioners' visit to Boston.

A greater interest than this, however, he found in observing the progress of his own spirit. The pages of his diaries are filled with introspection. There are noted not only the books he read, the texts he preached from, and the incidents of his busy days, but also his temptations and his state of mind. To-day much of this seems to cry "cant." Yet, read further, the diaries reveal no hypocrite absorbed in morbid self-analysis, but a man writing of what seemed most real in life, his relation to God and to God's will. His notes were penned without reference to some twentieth-century reader, estranged from Puritanism, and prone to scent hypocrisy in any outspoken expression of religious feeling. He was writing for himself and the God he worshipped. Nothing in life was so important as the search for assurance of salvation and for signs that one was numbered among the elect.[11] A diary was but the daily balancing of the account of the writer's success or failure in doing God's will. To falsify his figures would be to deceive himself. Where eternal life was at stake self-deception would have been worse than idle. A Puritan diary read in any other light is unintelligible.

Mather's diary from 1663 to 1667 is preserved.[12] In it, and his letters, we find many details as to his daily course, and hints as to more general and immensely significant features of his life. His many callers, and his frequent dinings out, continue. He reads widely, and writes his sermons and learns them carefully by heart. A certain T., or Tim, perhaps the only one of his brothers not avowedly a servant of the Lord, gives him pain by wickedness. He travels to the college across the river, and as far as Exeter, New Hampshire, or to Northampton by way of Lancaster and Hadley,[13] the latter the hiding-place of Whalley and Goffe.[14] He sees a rattlesnake, but "Ye Lord prevented evil by his good

10. *Lectures on Massachusetts History*, p. 342.

11. Cf. B. Wendell, *Stelligeri*, pp. 47ff.

12. Owned by the American Antiquarian Society. It is marked "1660," and referred to here as MS. *Diary*, "1660."

13. MS. *Diary*, "1660," June 26, July 13, 1665; Aug. 9, Sept. 10 to Sept. 20, 1664; June 6 to 23, 1665.

14. *Lectures on Massachusetts History*, pp. 342ff.

providence." [15] He gets up at three o'clock in the morning "to see ye blazing star the people spake of," and at five, after the clouds have thinned, "there appears a Comett with a long tayle towards the Northwest." [16] He spends the rest of the morning in reading about comets, and, a few days later, rises early once more to get a better view of the "blazing star." [17] And, again and again, he adds to the record of his days reflections on the "little care" shown him by the church. "God help me & remove me to some other place that may be more for my comfort," he writes, and adds later: "My special silent request unto God was that he would remove me from Boston to some other place yet more for my comfort if it would be more for his glory."[18] He finds Mr. Way agrees with him in saying, "yt if the way of maintenance be not altered," he has just cause of complaint.[19] His candid interest in worldly details is flanked by his recognition of his "temptations to vainglory,"[20] and his struggles therewith. Worst of all, he is "grievously molested with temptations to atheism," but his experience with prayers that have been answered saves him. He prays constantly, and sets down his "Causes of Humiliation before the Lord" beside his "Requests to God in Jesus Christ." He finds reason for humility in "the sins of his unregenerate state," his "failings in every place where" he has lived, "& in every relation" he has sustained, as well as in "the sad divisions in Boston." He bewails his "pride, passion, sloth, selfishness, sensuality, earthly mindedness, unbelief," and "hypocrisy." And his aspiration is summed up as "*The threefold wish of the chief of sinners. I wish! I wish! I wish! That I might do some special service for my dear God in Jesus Christ.*" [21] Some prayers are heard,[22] and the generosity of Sir Thomas Temple,[23] who came to Boston after giving up the governorship of Nova Scotia, and of Captain Thomas Lake,[24] a merchant and "an eminently faithful servant of God," who joined the Second Church in Boston in

15. MS. *Diary*, "1660," June 21, 1665.
16. *Ibid.*, Dec. 5, 1664.
17. *Ibid.*, Dec. 8, 1664.
18. *Ibid.*, Feb. 24, March 22, 1664-65.
19. *Ibid.*, April 22, 1665.
20. *Ibid.*, Oct. 12, 1665.
21. *Autobiography.*
22. *Ibid.; Parentator*, p. 34.
23. For Temple, see *DNB*, and C. Robbins, *History*, p. 281.
24. For Lake, cf. I. Mather, *The Life and Death*, pp. 102-106. His daughter later became Mather's second wife.

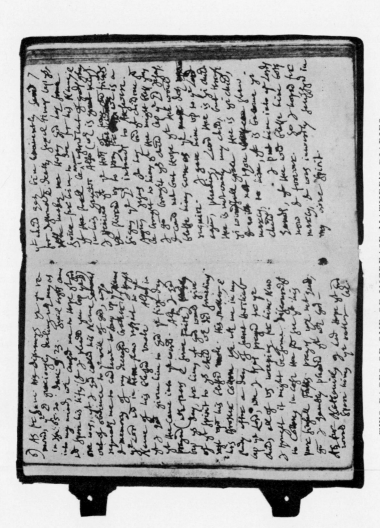

TWO PAGES OF ONE OF INCREASE MATHER'S DIARIES

1670, relieved him from his financial straits. In gratitude he lists "those special mercies which I have cause forever to bless God for." Characteristically he includes among them his early conversion, his education, his employment in the ministry, his travels, called "a great mercy ... in many ways," his books and manuscripts, and the casting of his lot in "the most public place in New England."[25]

Such gleanings define our image of this Puritan, bound heart and soul in his faith, but never forgetful of the world. Piety and zeal do not cut him off from men; the tale of his visitors and visits plants him firmly in the tableau of the daily human life of Boston. Religious feeling never blinds him to earthly needs. This blending of practical temper, "Yankee shrewdness" if one will, and devotion to things of the spirit, grows year by year, and the union lies behind his whole career. His faith had no being except in practical expression. His piety found its true value in its effect on other men.

His contemporaries may have known the side he reveals in his private papers less well than we do, but their contact with his spoken word, and his printed works, was more direct than ours can ever be. To the humblest citizens of seventeenth-century Boston, his books dealt with affairs of the moment, and, once within the doors of the Second Church, the actual tones of his voice sounded in their ears. We are blinded in our reading by a spirit hostile to his, and we know of his preaching only at second-hand.

"His Delivery had something Singular in it. He spoke with a Grave and Wise *Deliberation:* But on some Subjects, his Voice would rise for the more *Emphatical Clauses,* as the Discourse went on: and anon come on with such a *Tonitruous Cogency,* that the Hearers would be struck with an *Awe,* like what would be Produced on the Fall of *Thunderbolts.*"[26] He never read sermons, though he made notes which he did not use. "He wished, there were more *Speaking,* and less *Reading,* in our *Sermons:* and would have had the *Preacher* to be more of a *Speaker;* even so much, that the Necessary *Vigour* and *Address,* of proper *Preaching,* might not be lost."[27] In style "He much despised what they call *Quaintness....* though he were such a *Scholar,* yet his *Learning* hindred not his Condescension to the Lowest and Meanest Capacity: aiming to shoot not over the *Heads,* but into the

25. *Autobiography.*   26. *Parentator,* p. 216.   27. *Ibid.,* pp. 216, 217.

Hearts, of the Hearers. He was very careful to be *understood*, and *concealed* every other *Art*, that he might Pursue and Practise that one *Art* of *Being Intelligible*. . . . A *Simple Diet*, he counted the most *Wholsom Diet*." [28] He learned early the lessons later so vigorously taught by Joseph Glanvill, for whom "the first Rule and Character of Preaching" was that "it should be PLAIN." [29] One shares Cotton Mather's wonder at the statement that his father used a style "Affected and Quaint," [30] and on the evidence we have, apparently unknown to the accuser,[31] we can easily dismiss the charge. Finally one finds a statement of what we have already discovered. "It was his perpetual endeavour therewithal to Preach very *Scripturally*." [32] He believed no language could equal the Bible's, and at his son's ordination preached on the use of its words as the best means of securing in sermons the Divine spirit.[33] By such means he held his congregation, swelled its numbers,[34] and led "Thousands and Thousands" to say "they never knew a more *Compleat Preacher*." "Competent Judges" declared "*He never Preached a Sermon but what was worthy of the Press*." [35]

He found outlet for his abilities not only in the pulpit, but also through the colonial press. Changes in his family and in his church and personal trials dictated many pages. Insight into the books written in these years is most easily found through knowledge of the conditions that surrounded their birth.

From 1664 to 1670 his days were divided between the church in Clark's Square, or his father's pulpit in Dorchester,[36] and his

28. *Parentator*, p. 215.

29. J. E. Spingarn, *Critical Essays of the Seventeenth Century*, ii, 273ff., especially 277. Cf. also, *Ibid.*, i, pp. xxxvi–xlv.

30. J. Oldmixon, *The British Empire*, i, 112; *Parentator*, p. ix.

31. Oldmixon says that Increase Mather's sermons would bear him out, if any had been printed (p. 112). When Oldmixon wrote, many of Increase Mather's sermons had been printed, some of them in England. Oldmixon evidently criticized what he had not troubled to read.

32. *Parentator*, p. 215.   33. *Ibid.*, pp. 215, 216.

34. The admissions to membership in the Second Church from 1660 through 1673, according to a copy of the original records now owned by the church, were:

1660	11	1664	7	1668	1	1672	17
1661	3	1665	10	1669	3	1673	17
1662	3	1666	7	1670	13		
1663	5	1667	5	1671	No record		

Obviously in the matter of new members, the church continued to prosper with Mather's coming.

35. *Parentator*, p. 214.

36. Barrows and Trask, *Records*, p. 59.

own study. In the latter year, perhaps to save the time wasted on his walk from his door down Hanover Street, across the Mill Creek, and through Middle Street, past the "Red Lion Inn"[37] to the church, he moved to "y^t house wch was bought of Mr. Anth. Chickley."[38] It stood on what is now the westerly side of North Square,[39] and was bought by the trustees of the church as one step in their renewed attention to his welfare.[40] From here it was but a few yards across the Square to his pulpit. His neighbors made the district the "court end" of the town.[41] At his moving he took with him not only his wife, and Cotton, then seven years old, but also a son, Nathaniel, born the year before, and two little daughters, Maria and Elizabeth, aged five and four.[42] The Lord continued his mercies in the new house,[43] and a third daughter, Sarah, was born on November 8, 1671, and a son, Samuel, saw the light on August 28, 1674. Though they often robbed him of sleep,[44] Mather thanked God for his children, and their preservation to him.[45]

Meanwhile Cotton was showing a precocity that gave promise of what he was to become. By 1674 he was enrolled at Harvard, at the age of twelve.[46] His childhood was not without its anxieties for a devoted father, for the boy suffered from an impediment in his speech, and Increase Mather more than once "fasted & prayed before the Lord" because of it. One day, he writes, "I called" Cotton "& his mother into my study. We prayed together, and with many tears bewailed our sinfulness, and begged of God mercy in this particular, and solemnly gave the child to God upon our knees, begging the Lord to accept of him. I cannot but hope that the Lord has heard me, and will, in some comfortable measure remove this evil in his own time. However, whether God will hear me or no, I am resolved to trust in him, & so let him do with me & mine as seemeth [Him?] Good."[47]

37. See Memorial History of Boston, i, 548–551.
38. Entry in I. Mather's Bible, at the Massachusetts Historical Society.
39. E. G. Porter, Rambles in Old Boston, pp. 319ff. The site is marked to-day by the Paul Revere House, one of the seventeenth-century landmarks of Boston.
40. Ibid., p. 319.
41. See Memorial History of Boston, i, 550, and S. A. Drake, Old Landmarks and Historic Personages of Boston, p. 160.
42. Entry in Increase Mather's Bible.
43. "God has blessed & increased my family" (Autobiography).
44. Cf. MS. Diary, "1660," Aug. 28, 1666; Jan. 1, 1666–67.
45. Autobiography.
46. B. Wendell, Cotton Mather, pp. 35–37.   47. Autobiography.

The time that was left from such cares was abundantly filled by work at his desk. He set out to write a life of his father-in-law, John Cotton, but the book, if ever completed, never found its way into print.[48] It was in 1667 that John Davenport wrote for him the preface to what was the second of his printed writings, and the first worthy to be called a book. Two years later the volume was printed, with the title "The Mystery of Israel's Salvation."[49]

The subject of the treatise was the doctrine that the Jews would be converted and Christ would come again. Mather held that the thousand Apocalyptical years were still to come; that Christ's return would occur before another thousand years had passed; that His second advent was to be preceded by the conversion of the Jews; and that, finally, there would be a long and glorious day on earth for the elect.[50] Such a book, lighting up vague passages of Scripture by learned interpretation, had for Puritans the same spell held for us by a sound explanation of a fundamental scientific fact directly affecting our lives.

It is interesting to find Davenport in his preface harping upon the timeliness of the book. Mather's material was so up to date, indeed, as to call for some apology. "Neither let anyone be offended with the seeming *Novelism* which is in these notions," he writes, " . . . new discoveries of old truth ought not to be branded with the odious name of *Novel opinions*." The topics he treated are still discussed in some quarters, but for most of us they have lost interest. It is none the less worth while to remember that they were not only interesting to his contemporaries but had for them the charm of novelty.

If we cannot read the book in the spirit of those who bought it fresh from the press, we may still find in it paragraphs worth noting. We find effective use of references to current affairs, to the Great Fire of London, to the latest comet, and to church

48. MS. *Diary*, "1660," July 28, 31, Aug. 4, Nov. 25, 1665.

49. The title-page reads: "The Mystery of Israel's Salvation, Explained and Applyed: or, A Discourse Concerning the General Conversion of the *Israelitish Nation*. Wherein is Shewed, 1. *That the Twelve Tribes shall be saved*. 2. *When this is to be expected*. 3. *Why this must be*. 4. *What kind of Salvation the Tribes of* Israel *shall partake of* (viz.) A Glorious, Wonderful, Spiritual, Temporal *Salvation*. Being the Substance of several Sermons Preached *by* Increase Mather, *M. A.* Teacher of a Church in *Boston* in *New England*. [Several lines of Scripture] Printed in the Year 1669." There is a later title-page, in which, instead of the last line of the first one we have "*London*, Printed for *John Allen* in *Wentworth-street*, near *Bell-Lane*, 1669."

50. See Mather's own summary in his Preface to the Reader.

dissensions in Boston.[51] We find that not only Davenport but also William Greenhill and William Hook, both prominent Puritans, considered the book worthy of endorsement, and wrote prefaces for it.[52] The latter points out that it is "written in a plain and clear stile, only richly trimmed in the border," calling attention to Mather's wisdom in freeing the text from crowded references to his authorities. Marginal notes gave the scholarly reader the clues he wished. As to the style, Mather's own words suffice. "Only remember," he wrote, "that this *Discourse* is the substance of several *Lecture-Sermons* preached in the ordinary course of my Ministry to a plain Auditory, and therefore not Elegancy of phrases or *wisdom of words* (I thank Christ I have learned to slight such vanities in the sacred and awful things of God.) But (as far as the nature of the subject will permit) Truths plainly delivered, are to be expected."[53] Here and there is a poorly turned sentence, or a stilted phrase; but everywhere there is steadily advancing, clearly wrought exposition not unworthy of many a more famous scribe.

Printed in England, and perhaps also in the Colonies,[54] the book must have enhanced Mather's reputation greatly. But "vainglory" was sharply checked. In July, 1668, Jonathan Mitchell died. This brought grief to his pupil, to whom he was ever beloved.[55] The hand of the Lord did not pause, and in April of the next year, Richard Mather, visiting his son in Boston, fell ill. In the Dorchester church records for the 23d of this month, one reads: "Mr. Mather ye teacher of this Church departed this lif about 10 of ye Clock on ye evening before being ye first teaching officer y^t have taken away by death since ye first gathering of ye Church wch is now 32 yeers & 8 months Compleate." No words from two centuries' distance can do justice to the "inexpressible loss and sorrow" of the loyal son who saw his father die.[56] We know how much of Puritanism was bound up in Richard Mather, and how faithfully he had served according to his lights. One can guess the double grief of the son, who lost

51. Pages 39, 160 n., 161.

52. These two prefaces are signed W. G. and W. H., respectively. For their authorship, see *Parentator*, p. 62. For both men see *DNB*.

53. Mather's Preface to the Reader. The range of his reading is shown by his long list of references, printed at the end of his book.

54. J. L. Sibley, *Biographical Sketches*, i, 438.

55. I. Mather, *Epistle Dedicatory*, in C. Mather, *Magnalia*, book IV, part ii, chap. 4.

56. I. Mather, *The Life and Death*, pp. 78–80; *Autobiography*; Barrows and Trask, *Records*, pp. 9, 10.

not merely a dear human father but a father of much that to him and his friends was best in New England. Richard Mather remained teacher to the last. On his deathbed he found time to urge Increase to see that "the Rising Generation . . . be brought under the Government of Christ in his Church," pointing his words with an explicit plea for the Half-Way Covenant. "Thus did that Light that had been shining in the Church above Fifty years, Expire." [57]

Increase, preaching in Dorchester and Boston, writing and publishing, entertaining English visitors,[58] and winning his people's love, bore bravely his load of sorrow. He saw his father laid in the Dorchester churchyard where one may still trace the worn letters on the gravestone.[59] He had, with his brother Timothy, to carry out the terms of his father's will, and there was his aged mother-in-law to shelter. Nor was there long respite from grief, for barely three months later his brother Eleazar died in Northampton.[60] His widow and his church turned to Increase, who came from Boston late in August. There the burden of the last years claimed its toll, and he fell sick of "a fiolent fever" which brought him "near to the gates of death." In the little town, "godly Christians met together to fast and pray for his life." By winter he was able to go home. But nerves made taut by hard study and deep feeling were not easily calmed, and, until March, "the hypochondrical affection" made him "unable to go abroad." On March 13 he began his service again, and once more preached each week.[61]

With the shock to tired mind and body, came, once more, heightened religious zeal, and he cast about eagerly for new roads to God's service. He found them in planning books that should do good. "I considered with myself that if I should write & publish my Father's life it would be a service not only honorable to my Father, but acceptable & honorable to the name of God." [62] He planned other books, too, and much of his literary activity in the next few years dates back to the troubled days of his illness. More than once he wrote pages harking back to this time of strain, and to the latest of New England's calamities, the

57. I. Mather, *The Life and Death*, pp. 79, 80.
58. J. L. Sibley, *Biographical Sketches*, ii, 398.
59. Cf. N. B. Shurtleff, *Topographical and Historical Description of Boston*, p. 285.
60. C. Mather, *Magnalia*, book III, part ii, chap. 20, section 19.
61. *Autobiography*.   62. *Ibid.*

RICHARD MATHER

death of John Davenport.[63] In 1670, Increase Mather felt as strongly as ever in his life the impermanence of this world. His mood was one of passionate desire to do some last service before he, too, should be called to face trial by God.

Out of this sprang his life of his father.[64] The preface was dated in September, 1670, and the book was printed at Cambridge in the same year. Enough has been quoted to give some idea of it. All that has been said of the straightforward manner of the earlier books holds true here. Moreover, the subject is nearer our interests, and we read the little biography to-day without boredom and, often, with admiration for a simple dignity that comes close to art. It was published anonymously, only the preface being signed, but there can have been little mystery in its readers' minds. Whoever was believed to be its author, its clear narrative, picked out with anecdote,[65] surely won it a hearing. Not only the Dorchester congregation, to whom it was dedicated, but good New Englanders everywhere, must have read it; a biographer overseas put it almost bodily into a work of his own,[66] and we to-day, if not quite deaf to seventeenth-century thought, may easily linger on many a page.

It was but the first fruit of the time of stress. Even though Mayo, old and infirm, had to give up his active preaching,[67] and threw more and more of the church burdens on his colleague's shoulders, Mather still found time to write. In 1670, probably, he signed himself "M. I." to the preface to a pair of his brother Samuel's sermons.[68] Even a foreword gave Increase Mather space to denounce religious ceremonial, to warn his readers against the

63. March 15, 1670. C. Mather, *Magnalia*, book III, part i, chap. 4, section 2.

64. The full title is "The Life and Death of That Reverend Man of God, Mr. *Richard Mather*, Teacher of the Church *in* Dorchester in *New-England. . . . Cambridge:* Printed by *S. G.* and *M. J.* 1670." The book is reprinted in the Collections of the Dorchester Antiquarian and Historical Society, Number 3, Boston, 1850. All references in this book are to that edition.

65. Cf. pp. 50, 73, 84–86.

66. *Parentator*, p. 73; S. Clark, *The Lives of Sundry Eminent Persons*, pp. 126ff.

67. H. Ware, *Two Discourses*, p. 6.

68. The full title is: "A Testimony from the Scripture against Idolatry & Superstition, In Two Sermons; Upon the Example of that Great Reformer *Hezekiah*, 2 *Kings* 18: 4. The first, Witnessing in generall against all the Idols and Inventions of men in the Worship of God. The second, more particularly against the Ceremonies, and some other Corruptions of the Church of *England*. Preached, the one *September* 27. the other *Septemb.* 30, 1660 By Mr. *Samuel Mather*, Teacher to a Church of Christ in *Dublin* in *Ireland.*" No imprint. There is no date given, but Roden lists the book under 1670 and on p. 135 gives the reason for this dating.

opinions, while praising the learning, of Grotius, and to reveal, once more, how deeply he himself had read.

One of his resolves after his father's death had been to publish "some discourses wherein the rising generation should be especially concerned . . . for God's glory, and the good of souls." [69] These he found in some of Eleazar's sermons, and he printed them with a preface, dated March, 1671, and dedicated to the Northampton church.[70] He explains his motive, saying: "*But especially I was inclined to Publish what is here presented to you, because the dying Counsel which my Reverend Father . . . left with me, was, that I should seriously endeavour the good of the Rising Generation in this Country.*"

Two months later, he dated the preface of still another book, this time one from his own pen. "The First Principles of New England" was written in 1671, although not printed for nearly three years.[71] He made here his first published statement of his change from his views of 1662, by collecting testimony from the writings of the most respected New England divines as to the subject of baptism and in support of the Half-Way view. He had access to much material, printed and unprinted, and marshals a brave array of authority to support his new opinions. To his extracts from other writers, he appends a persuasive preface of his own. Addressing himself to those who still opposed the decision of the Synod and were active in the controversy over the founding of the Third Church, he writes: "Brethren I was once of your perswasion, and thence can with the more *Love and Compassion* speak unto you." He avoids the dogmatic, and leaves argument to his quoted authorities, which ranged from Cotton and Hooker to "*sundry eminent Divines of the Congre-*

---

69. *Autobiography.*

70. The full title is: "A Serious Exhortation to the Present and Succeeding Generation *in New-England;* Earnestly calling upon all to Endeavour that the Lords *Gracious Presence* may be continued with *Posterity. Being the Substance of the* Last Sermons Preached By *Eleazar Mather,* late Pastor of the Church in *Northampton* in *New England.* . . . *Cambridge:* Printed by *S. G.* and *M. J.* 1671."

71. The full title is: "The First Principles of *New-England,* Concerning *The Subject of Baptisme & Communion of Churches.* Collected partly out of the Printed Books, but chiefly out of the *Original Manuscripts* of the *First* and chiefe *Fathers* in the *New-English Churches;* with the Judgment of Sundry Learned Divines of the *Congregational Way* in *England,* Concerning the said Questions. *Published for the Benefit of those who are of the Rising Generation in* New-England. By *Increase Mather,* Teacher of a Church in Boston in *New-England.* . . . *Cambridge* Printed by *Samuel Green,* 1675." The preface is dated "From my Study in *Boston* N. E. 1. of *3d Moneth,* 1671 *Who is* less then the least of all Gods mercies and Saints. *Increase Mather.*"

gational way in *England.*" That one still may feel the skill and persuasiveness of the book's method, is a tribute to its writer, and there is no support here for the belief that Puritanism expressed itself only in dogmatic style.

In the early summer, his nerves were still in revolt, and he "went to the springs at Lynn, & tarried there some weeks to see what might be done for . . . relief." Terrified by dreams which "sorely molested" him, he drank the waters and prayed for healing from the Lord. He became "much melted and moved" and felt some confirmation of his "hope that God was indeed to accept of some service" from him. On July 24, on his way home, he met "a poor godly woman — her name was Mansfield" who "desired those that rode with" him "to go forward, for she must needs speak with" him. He stopped, and "O, Sir, (said she, with much affection and tears,) I am troubled at my condition. I an afraid that I grieve the good Spirit of God by not being cheerful as I ought to be. I am dejected, & my soul disquieted; and when I meet with afflictions, I lay them too much to heart, and I doubt hereby offend so gracious a Father as God has been to me." To a thoroughgoing Puritan, such an encounter revealed the hand of God, and Mather writes: "I was astonished to hear her speak, and to come to me for relief in her temptations. And concluded that this poor woman, (who little thought so herself) was a messenger sent of God to me, for she spake to my then condition, as if he that knows all things had put words into her mouth." [72]

But, even though he was buoyed up by so direct an admonition to conquer his "special infirmities," there were months more of melancholy, of harassing dreams, and of prayers and fasting for divine aid. The news of his brother Samuel's death came at the close of this period. He prayed, and in answer there came a mood in which his heart was "exceedingly melted." "Methought," he writes, "I saw God before my eyes, in an inexpressible way, so as that I was afraid I should have fallen into a trance in my study." [73]

For Mather's practical temper, the best reply to such profound stirrings of soul was in activity, and in the spring he finished another "savoury book." [74] By now Mayo was unable to continue even a nominal relation to his church and its sole conduct devolved on his comrade in the pulpit. [75] With increased respon-

72. *Autobiography.*
73. *Autobiography.*
74. *Parentator,* p. 74.
75. *Autobiography.*

sibility Mather worried more as to the scanty rewards the people gave him, and grew to hate fiercely the debts he was forced to incur.[76] Written in such times, his book might well have been slighted; but "Some Important Truths about Conversion"[77] shows no signs of scanted labor. It was made up of sermons preached to the Second Church, and was printed in London in 1674, though it was finished in June, 1672. John Owen[78] wrote a preface. After speaking of "that respect" which he bore to "the worthy Author," who is "known unto all, unto whom he is known," to be a "person of singular good Learning and Reading" (a valuable tribute coming from so great an English Puritan), he comments on the style, saying, "Whatever else the Author aimed at, it is evident that *plainness, perspicuity, gravity* in delivering the Truth were continually in his eye, nor hath he come short of attaining his Design. . . . He hath in this Discourse abandoned all Additional Ornaments whatever," and revealed himself as "a Workman that needeth not to be ashamed." This criticism is just in its summing up of the quality that makes this book, like the others, still worthy of attention from the point of view of style. As to contents, it is a plea for valid conversion, a true awakening of God's grace, in all who read it. Such conversion is the sole means of salvation, and comes only through the saving mercy of Christ. Everywhere the redeeming power of the Saviour is the dominant note. God's predestination as to who shall be subject to this saving grace is not discussed. The point is simply that anyone may have been included among the elect by divine decree, and, therefore, everyone must pray for Christ's mercy and prepare his heart for it, so that, in its coming, he may find assurance of salvation. The old problem of reconciling predestination and free will is involved, of course, if one reminds himself of it; but in reading the book one finds the accent, not on such riddles, but on the humane nature of the Son of God. Like Manfred's abbot, Mather

> Did not speak of punishment
> But penitence and pardon.

76. *Autobiography.*

77. The full title is: "Some Important Truths about Conversion, Delivered in sundry Sermons, By Increase Mather, Teacher of a Church at *Boston* in *New-England.* . . . *London,* Printed for *Richard Chiswell, at the* Rose and Crown in *Pauls* Church-yard, *Anno* 1674."

78. For John Owen, one of the great English Puritans, see *DNB.*

JOHN OWEN

From a painting in the National Portrait Gallery

Such correction of our favorite belief in Puritan grimness deserves to be read. But it is no milk-and-water doctrine after all. The great sign of regeneracy is the spiritual combat Mather knew so well.[79] "There never was any man that did believe, but he found hard work of it. Those things then shew, that it is an hard matter to obtain Salvation. Carnal hearts would be pleased well with it, if Ministers would sow pillows under mens elbows, and tell them that they might easily get to Heaven. But Truth saith otherwise, God saith otherwise" (p. 241). The Puritan saw life as a continual struggle toward the right, and an eternal conflict with the flesh, but it was no uninspiring fight. Mercy and love played a part that made the warfare of life seem to the true believer full of warmth and zest.

Though for Mather the skies are lightening, and he is now "through the Mercy of God in present health," he fears lest death be near. He alludes to church divisions, pleads for "humane learning" as indispensable to true religion, and attacks the Church of Rome. There is one relapse into preaching of "hell fire" that is almost drastic enough for the nineteenth century, and foreshadows almost word for word a fulmination of Jonathan Edwards.[80] Finally, in this random turning of the leaves, one hits upon Mather's expression of his feeling towards his church. It is a fitting summing up for the book and a crisp expression of his devotion to the chief duty of his life. To his congregation he writes: "*All things are yours;* my Gifts (such weak ones as they are) my Time, my Studies, all them are yours."[81]

Ill health and financial troubles passed, and Mather wrote three more books before 1674. One need not stop long for the first, the printing of a sermon preached in 1673 with the title "The Day of Trouble is Near."[82] It points out the manifest evils of the day as auguries of wrath to come. Urian Oakes, Mitchell's successor in Cambridge, soon to become president of

79. Cf. pp. 46, 47.

80. Page 224; and compare selection from Edwards in E. C. Stedman and E. M. Hutchinson, *Library of American Literature*, ii, 389.

81. Preface.

82. The full title is: "*The Day of Trouble is near.* Two Sermons *Wherein is shewed,* What are the Signs of a Day of Trouble being near. *And particularly,* What reason there is for *New-England* to expect *A Day of Trouble.* Also what is to be done, that we may escape these things which shall come to pass. Preached (the 11th day of the 12th Moneth, 1673. being a day of Humiliation in one of the Churches in *Boston.* By *Increase Mather,* Teacher of that Church. . . . *Cambridge:* Printed by *Marmaduke Johnson.* 1674."

the college,[83] introduced the book to the "Christian Reader," and pointed to Mather as "this vigilant Watchman and wise Discerner of the Signs of the Times."[84] His vigilance and discernment light upon such particulars as pride. "And what *Pride* is there? Spiritual Pride, in Parts and common Gifts of the Spirit, and in Spiritual Priviledges; yea carnal, shameful, foolish Pride, in Apparel, Fashions, and the like. Whence is all that rising up, and disobedience in Inferiours towards Superiours, in Families, in Churches, and in the Commonwealth, but from the unmortified Pride which is in the hearts of the sons and daughters of men? . . . Are there no biting Usurers in *New-England?* Are there not those that grinde the faces of the poor? A poor man cometh amongst you, and he must have a Commodity whatsoever it cost him, and you will make him give whatever you please, and put what price you please upon what he hath to give too, without respecting the just value of the thing" (p. 22). There is a modern note in this statement of seventeenth-century vices, and a skill in pulpit address, well worthy of a later day. The conclusion is: "Alas! we have changed our Interest. The Interest of *New-England* was Religion, which did distinguish us from other *English Plantations*. . . . When-as now we begin to espouse a Worldly Interest, and so to chuse a new God, therefore no wonder that War is like to be in the gates" (p. 23). But there is a note of comfort. "Though troubles come, why should we be dismayed thereat? for a glorious issue and happy deliverance out of all these troubles, shall certainly arise" (p. 18). And the lesson is plainly stated as, "Why then, up and be doing. If thou hast but one Tear in thy eyes, if thou hast but one Prayer in thy heart, spend it now" (p. 31).

The call was not unheeded, for, if something better than tradition be believed, one of those who heard the sermon was moved to change the manner of his life. Thence dates an alliance at the root of Mather's later political power, and the convert to "The Day of Trouble" found himself, before twenty years had passed, in its author's debt not only for spiritual gain but also for worldly rank. The full story belongs to later times. For 1674 the episode stands out as bearing witness stronger than pages of criticism to the fact that this sermon was effective as uttered from the pulpit, and its power was not lost upon men.

83. J. L. Sibley, *Biographical Sketches*, i, 173–183.
84. See Oakes's Preface.

As for the preface to Samuel Torrey's "Exhortation unto Reformation," [85] it holds no point of interest not revealed in Mather's other works, except that it is one more proof that the name of this "least of all saints" [86] was one which carried weight with buyers of books.

The last work of this period, the "Wo to Drunkards," [87] has a peculiar claim on us. Unlike most of the treatises of its writer, its subject is still a current topic. We are used to read, on this subject, matter far more intolerant than this Puritan booklet. Perhaps we are right and they were wrong, but Increase Mather's contemporaries did not shun wine, but its abuse; not drinking, but excess. Instead of hearing cries for the abolishment of the saloon, one reads of alehouses and taverns. "I know that in such a great Town as this, there is need of such Houses, and no sober Minister will speak against the Licensing of them; but I wish there not more of them then there is any need of " (p. 29). Again: "Drink is in itself a good creature of God, and to be received with thankfulness, but the abuse of drink is from Satan; the wine is from God, but the Drunkard is from the Devil" (p. 4). For once it is not the Puritan who excels us in preaching repression and absolute denial. Possibly he realized that the exercise of temperance and moderation was a character-forming process. Certainly he believed that these qualities should have scope to work.

No less striking is the fact that this unenlightened Puritan age did not fight a perennial evil with archaic weapons. "Excess damages the body," says Mather, and anticipates in elementary fashion the physiological argument of to-day (pp. 9 ff.). He is as apt as we are, in his choice of Scripture; and though he shares our own tract writers' delight in references to "hellfire," it is

85. The full title is: "An Exhortation unto Reformation, Amplified, By a Discourse concerning the Parts and Progress of that Work, according to the Word of God. Delivered in a Sermon Preached in the Audience of the General Assembly of the *Massachusetts* Colony, at *Boston* in *New-England*, May 27. 1674. Being the Day of Election There. By *Samuel Torrey*, Pastor of the Church of Christ in *Waymouth*. . . . *Cambridge*: Printed by *Marmaduke Johnson*. 1674."

86. The preface is signed: "Less then the least of all Saints, Increase Mather. Boston, N. E. 26. 5. 1674."

87. The full title is: "*Wo to Drunkards*. Two Sermons Testifying against the Sin of Drunkenness: Wherein the *Wofulness* of that Evil, and the Misery of all that are addicted to it, is discovered from the Word of God. Preached by *Increase Mather*, Teacher of a Church in *Boston* in *New-England* . . . . *Cambridge*: Printed by *Marmaduke Johnson*. 1673. And Sold by *Edmund Ranger* Bookbinder in *Boston*."

not he who makes such allusions a weapon too eagerly used. "Do not think," he declares, "that I love to scare you, with the dark visions of that Eternal Night which is hastening upon your Souls. Do not think, my Brethren, that I delight in terrifying you with the sad tidings of Hell and Death. Indeed, sometimes I am forced to it. *Knowing the terrour of the Lord, I* seek to *perswade you* by those Arguments; nevertheless I take no pleasure to tell you thereof. But now that I am speaking to you of the pardoning grace of God, me-thinks I am in my Element: I could be glad to stay and dwell here, and to enlarge myself much to you, would time and strength permit me" (p. 33). Are these the words of a Puritan, the foe to tolerance, to liberty, the champion of a merciless faith always relentless and grim?

Aside from its contents, the sermon is admirably shaped to its purpose. There are plenty of homely illustrations, more than one passage of vigorous phrasing, and a construction planned for effect. One reads, to choose at random, "The Drunkards Credit is crackt, and lost amongst all sober men; and therefore wise men carry towards such, as they would do to a person of no Credit, whom they dare not trust. Trust a Drunkard with an Estate, and when he is in his Cups hee'll send it going: Trust him with a Secret, and when he is drunken hee'll discover it; Trust him, and when he is drunken he will undo himself and his friend too" (p. 9). Like preachers of all times, he plays on the readiest means, the influential men in the pews. "There are sundry of you that stand in some Publick Capacity, *Townsmen, Constables, Grand Jurymen,* &c. Behold, the word of the Lord is unto you in particular this day; I lay the solemn charge of God upon you, that you do your utmost towards the suppression of this abounding iniquity. Kill this Serpent, before it be grown too big for you" (p. 29).

In 1674, Increase Mather undertook two new public offices, and stood upon the threshold of a larger career. He was proved an author more prolific than any other in New England. His books were greeted by the faithful at home and abroad. In the church, his task had been well done. In the town, he was welcomed and sought. Most important of all, his heart was tested by sickness, bereavement, and the temptations that assaulted him had broken harmless against the strong wall of his devotion to God. He worked himself into emotional transports of worship, and, with all the abandonment of a mediæval fanatic, revelled in his struggle toward Heaven. He examined himself constantly, and, if one will, morbidly. He saw in the commonest happenings of the day, direct signs of God's hand. But above all was his dominant practical strain. Idle dreams were not the only fruits of these years. Hence he craved a chance for self-forgetful service, and, in the same breath, complained of his scanty wage. Hence he was tempted to vainglory and tinged with earthly mindedness, though many of his days were spent in fasting and prayer. There was no basic incongruity, for his belief was not one to flourish merely in solitary ecstasies, nor could his nature stop short of tangible achievement. Puritanism demanded both emotion and action. Mather was by temperament a Puritan, and one who expressed himself best in the everyday affairs of the world. His imaginative and emotional side was the driving force. His practical temper, degenerating at its worst to material yearnings and personal ambition, served him well in carrying him beyond good words to good works, from speculation to accomplishment, and from love of God to trenchant service of His will. Thus the troubles of his spirit brought forth not merely fasting but more and more sermons, and books "which being wholly *practical* . . . speak to the life of Religion."[88] His grief for father, brothers, and teachers led him not merely to fears and repinings, but to staunch resolution to bear, himself, the standard of those who had gone before. Life was a stern fight, but he battled joyously in the intensity of his faith. The Bible was the guide, and for him its truest teaching lay, not in Old Testament laws, but in its revelation of the mercy of Christ.[89] His creed was one for strong men. His cry was not for peace or holy calm, but for a chance to strive and serve. He loved deeds above words, and aspired toward definite tasks. In doing them he thrust himself head and shoulders above his fellows, but he could not rest. Trained in the fight, he still sought service, and opportunity lay waiting.

88. I. Mather, *Some Important Truths*, Preface.

89. J. T. Adams (*The Founding*, p. 80), says that the Puritans drew their texts almost exclusively from the Old Testament. I have found no evidence for this. For some examination of just how much the Puritans used the Old Testament as compared with the New, see K. B. Murdock, "The Puritans and the New Testament," in *Colonial Society Publications*, xxv, 239ff.; and printed separately, Cambridge, 1924.

CHAPTER X

PUBLIC LIFE

ON May 27, 1674, the General Court "granted that there may be a printing press elswhere then at Cambridge," and, "for the better regulation of the press," voted that there be added to the former licensers, Thomas Thatcher and Increase Mather.[1] A rigid governmental censorship of all that was printed in New England sounds to-day like bigotry run mad. Yet the colonies were not more stern than the mother country; the Puritan was no more intolerant than Charles II. Censorship of the press was sanctioned by English custom, and although the licensing acts expired by limitation in 1679, a common-law doctrine was promptly found to cover the case, and its application was, in effect, almost as thorough as the licensing system had been. Leaders in both Englands knew the power of the press, and the need for its control. The Puritans of Massachusetts, with an eye for logical organization, saw its relation to education, and for nearly forty years had kept printing under the wing of the College. The starting of a press in Boston was proof of colonial growth, and Increase Mather's appointment to share in its regulation, testifies to the standing he had won.[2]

His duties do not seem to have been arduous. The seven years after Mather's appointment were "so free . . . from all disturbances on account of disorderly printing, that the occasional filling of vacancies in the board of licensers gives the only notice of its existence." As late as 1685 the censorship was still in force, and "before the abrogation of the charter . . . and the institution of a government not of their own choosing, the people of Massachusetts as a whole could not feel any serious deprivation in restrictions upon the freedom of the press." [3]

More important at the time, and in relation to what followed, was Mather's entry, in the same year, upon another public

1. *Mass. Rec.*, v, 4.
2. Cf. C. A. Duniway, *The Development of Freedom of the Press in Massachusetts*, especially pp. 23ff., 55, 56, 58, 59.
3. *Ibid.*, pp. 54, 57, 58, 61, 62.

office. On December 11, 1674, a vote of the Harvard College Corporation reads "ffor the filling up the corporation in its number of seaven. The sd society doth also unanimously choose the Revd Mr Urian Oakes & Mr Thomas Sheppard & Mr Increase Mather as ffellowes of the sd Colledg." On March 15 following, this action was confirmed by the Overseers. The appointment was to a post reserved for recognized leaders. That Mather was faithful to his trust appears in the record that during the next nine years he attended all but four of the twenty-three Corporation meetings for which minutes are preserved.[4]

Hoar resigned the Presidency on the day that Mather was finally elected as Fellow. Urian Oakes was chosen to fill Hoar's place, but refused, contenting himself with assuming the active guidance of Harvard, becoming President in all but name.[5] This state of affairs continued for four years, during which Mather wrote in his diary: "The Colledge is still desolate." [6] Efforts were made to remedy this condition. The Reverend John Rogers was elected President, but declined, and Stoughton vainly sought for a candidate from abroad.[7] Mather himself, closely in touch with Oakes, was more than once suggested for the leadership. Oakes told him in May, 1675, that all the scholars knew he might have the place if he would. Far from accepting it, he was inclined to lay down his Fellowship to quiet rumors that he sought higher office. His friends expostulated and told him that if he would "accept of ye Presidentship, it" would be "selfe denial." [8] And, in 1681, after Oakes had relented, accepted the President's chair, and died in office, the records read "Reverend Mr Increase Mather was chosen President of Harvard Colledge." [9] In answer he "told ym, yt except ye church to wch" he was "related sld consent to my leaving ym" he "cld not," and he believed "yy wld not consent yrunto." He hated the thought of leaving Boston, and feared lest his congregation consent to part with him, so that he would be "voted out of ye Town." His qualms were unnecessary; his church refused to give him up, and he declined the call.[10]

4. Cf. *Harv. Rec.*, especially pp. 59, 231.

5. *Ibid.*, p. 231; J. Quincy, *History*, i, 35.

6. Entry in Mather's diary for 1675–76 (ed. by Green), for March 25, 1675. Cf. also, entry for Oct. 7, 1675.

7. J. Quincy, *History*, i, 35; *Harv. Rec.*, p. 238.

8. *Diary*, 1675–76, May 28, June 18, 1675.   9. *Harv. Rec.*, p. 68.

10. MS. *Diary*, 1680–84, Sept. 8, 1681. Cf. also, I. Mather, *Practical Truths*, Preface (1682), and *Autobiography*.

There is no better clue to much that is often misread in his later connection with Harvard, than the memory that he not only never sought office, but twice refused to become President.

Though his church transcended in Mather's mind any claim of the college in remote Cambridge, he found many ways to serve the latter. He aided the Treasurer in the management of legacies, urged Oakes to become President, and when the place was vacant again, voted for his good friend, Samuel Torrey, to fill it.[11] He conducted at least two Commencements, and, whatever his interest on other grounds, found in Cotton's admission as a freshman an added tie to Harvard.[12] Like more than one genius since his day, Cotton Mather did not easily adapt himself to college. His father prayed for his success, and worried over what seems to have been a seventeenth-century outbreak of hazing. Samuel Danforth and Urian Oakes were complained to, and the difficulty blew over.[13] There was balm for all wounds in Cotton's Commencement, for Oakes, in his oration, praised not only the pupil but the father, whom he named "the most watchful of guardians, the most distinguished Fellow of the College."[14]

There are few red letter days in Harvard's progress from 1675 to 1685. Its history is written in dissensions, difficulties in securing a leader, occasional bequests, and elections of new Overseers or Fellows. Yet, even in this stagnant time, it sent out year by year handfuls of graduates, and maintained the foundations on which Mather and later leaders were to build.[15] Two hostile accounts, written in these years, paint the picture in its darkest aspect, telling of the college hall so thick with smoke that a Dutch visitor declared, "This is certainly a tavern"; of the students ignorant of Latin; and of the Library "where there was nothing particular."[16] The old college building partly collapsed in 1677, but the new Harvard Hall, begun in 1672, was almost ready to replace it, though, "by reason of the . . . Indian warre," it was "not yet finished."[17]

11. *Harv. Rec.*, pp. 67, 69, 239, 243.
12. *Ibid.*, pp. 240, 241; *Autobiography;* MS. *Diary,* July 27, 1682; *Diary,* June 22, 1675.
13. *Ibid.*, July 16, 26; *Harv. Rec.*, p. 228.
14. J. L. Sibley, *Biographical Sketches,* iii, 6, 7.
15. *Ibid.*, vols. ii and iii; J. Quincy, *History,* vol. i, chap. 2.
16. *Long Island Historical Society Memoirs,* i, 384, 385.
17. T. Hutchinson, *Collection,* ii, 238; A. McF. Davis, *Early College Buildings,* pp. 15, 16.

There is more in these words than concerns Harvard, for "the
... Indian war" was New England's first great trial by the
sword.[18] With our tradition of years without warfare on American
soil, and ignorant as we are of the actual horrors of Indian raids,
we too easily forget how devastating was New England's introduction to battle. If the "armies" were too small to deserve the
name,[19] if the fighting was occasional, and the advances mere
guerilla raids, there were laid waste, none the less, sixteen towns
in thinly settled Massachusetts alone. One man in every sixteen
of military age was killed.[20] If the shock of the United States'
greatest and most recent war seems profound, how severely must
the colonies have been shaken by a conflict taking a toll far
greater in proportion than that of the European strife. And,
when one remembers that here was fighting, not three thousand
miles away but at the colonists' very doors, one sees why the
College building was delayed, and why the brand of Philip's
War burned deep in the minds of all who survived it.

Mather, least of all, was heedless of its bloody course. Before
his eyes, the prophecies of his "Day of Trouble" were coming
true, and, nurtured on Puritanism and Scriptural lore, he saw
the whole struggle as the vengeance of God upon his people.[21]
The stamp of this idea is on all he wrote in these turbulent years,
and from it came strength for his rooted belief that the Lord
reveals himself in human affairs and punishes sin by calamities
on earth, just as He repays good deeds by salvation from the
perils of this life. The warning seemed obvious, and, in his
pulpit, Mather used it to the full. In private prayer he strove
to atone for his share in the sins that had brought condign chas-
tening to the colony.[22] If from such preaching and such thought
came a too superstitious attitude toward the smallest daily event,
it was but one more expression of the emotional effect worked in
all countries and in all times after great wars, acting here upon
men prepared by traditional beliefs to see in earthly conflicts
evidence of the all-powerful anger of God.

The immediate influence upon Mather has special interest

18. Channing, ii, 76–79, 92; G. W. Ellis and J. E. Morris, *King Philip's War*; J. T.
Adams, *The Founding*, chap. 14.

19. I. Mather, *Brief History*, p. 211.

20. For various estimates, cf. Channing, ii, 79; Palfrey, iii, 215; J. T. Adams, *The
Founding*, p. 363.

21. I. Mather, *Brief History*, p. 42.

22. Cf. *Diary*, 1675–76.

for us. These were memorable days, and only history could preserve their lesson for generations to come. From a vantage-point in the social centre of the colonies, Mather had watched the shifting fortunes of the war, and had interpreted the news of each day in accordance with his faith. He knew his literary leadership in New England, and, always sensitive to all that affected his rank in the community, saw the prestige to be gained by the historian of the war. As an experienced preacher, too, he saw homiletic possibilities in a chronicle of the strife. Accordingly, he hurried to the press his "Brief History of the War with the Indians." [23]

The detailed narrative of King Philip's War need not concern us, but the book claims attention from other points of view. Primarily, it was Mather's first essay toward the writing of history, and his first book not essentially theological in theme. It is the effort not so much of a preacher driving home truths of doctrine, as of "an *Historian* . . . endeavouring to relate things truly and impartially," and doing his best not to "lead the *Reader* into a Mistake." He showed his literary judgment, and brought refutation for those who would see in all Puritans mere dogmatists and pedants, by telling the tale without crowding Biblical references, and comparatively unencumbered by citations of learned works. When one has said that his pages show obvious marks of haste, that his fear lest his "defective manner of management in this History renders it unprofitable" because of "the other employments" he had, is sometimes justified, and that the book is not soundly selected and critical history, with insight into the broader relations of events, but merely a day-by-day chronicle of happenings reported by letters and word-of-mouth accounts delivered when the news was fresh, one has told the worst. On the other side there remains the value that comes from the very

23. The full title is: "A Brief History of the Warr With the *Indians* in Nevv-England, (From *June* 24, 1675. when the first English-man was murdered by the Indians, to *August* 12. 1676. when *Philip*, aliàs *Metacomet*, the principal Author and Beginner of this Warr, was slain.) Wherein the Grounds, Beginning, and Progress of the Warr, is summarily expressed. Together with a Serious Exhortation to the Inhabitants of that Land.—By *Increase Mather*, . . . Boston . . . 1676." This was also printed in the same year in London, without the "Exhortation," although the title-page still referred to it. The omission was due to the fact that the English publisher printed from an imperfect copy (*MHS Coll.*, Series 4, viii, 576). There was a reprint in 1862, by S. G. Drake, to which all references in this book are made. That Mather felt a keen rivalry with other writers is suggested by his correspondence in regard to Hubbard, a fellow historian. For example, John Cotton writes him there are more mistakes than truths in Hubbard's book (*MHS Coll.*, Series 4, viii, 232); and again (*Ibid.*, 233, 234). Mather apparently quoted Cotton, to the latter's dismay. See his letter (*Ibid.*, 234, 235).

journalistic quality of his method. A collection of facts, undigested though they be, made at the time of their occurrence, has abiding historic worth. And Mather's telling of the story is marked always by directness and an eye for the stirring and significant in incident. He who would form a vivid picture of King Philip's War may go farther and fare no better.[24]

More than one page deserves reading. Among them, there is Mather's statement of his aim. He writes: "I earnestly wish that some effectual Course may be taken (before it be too late) that a just *History of New-England*, be written and published to the World. That is a thing that hath been often spoken of, but was never done to this day, and yet the longer it is deferred, the more difficulty will there be in effecting of it" (p. 37). To this idea he returned again, urged by his friends; and, a score of years later, his son came near accomplishing the task outlined.

There is illumination of a different sort in Mather's justification of the acts which brought on the war. It is relegated to a Postcript, saving the body of the book for the narrative itself. Its pages may not meet all criticisms of the Puritans' course with the Indians, but they leave no doubt, at least, as to what the English believed their rights to be. It is doubtful whether, in all the tragic history of the contact of white man and Indian on this continent, there is much to choose between Puritans and their successors. By its nature the problem was difficult, and for finite mortals, faced not with the problem of writing history on grounds of abstract theory, but with that of conducting a practical day-by-day relation with the savages, the riddle seems to have been proved by experience to be insoluble without injustice or worse.

The practical nature of the case is often to the fore in Mather's account. Relating how the war began upon "a day of solemn Humiliation" in Plymouth, he comments, "The Providence of God is deeply to be observed, that the Sword should be first drawn upon" such a day, "the Lord thereby declaring from Heaven that he expected something else from his People besides Fasting and Prayer." Akin to this spirit is the desire to see God as well as man expressing Himself in deeds, turning the weapons of the English upon their own soldiers, as a payment for sins, and manifesting His might in prodigies.[25] God's hand was in every affair of life; the Bible revealed His power on earth. These

24. Cf. pp. 36, 37.   25. Cf. pp. 55, 119, 120, 158.

beliefs, and the emotional receptivity encouraged by public calamity, made Mather's harping on the "remarkable providences" of God eminently fit for the edification of his readers, and the expression of his own faith.

Finally, one may not overlook several bits of good narrative. Mather often used to the full the dramatic possibilites of his subject. Telling of Captain Hutchinson's flight, he relates: "Hundreds of *Indians* beset the House, and took possession of a Barn belonging thereunto, from whence they often shot into the House, and also attempted to set fire to it six times, but could not prevail, at last they took a Cart full of Flax and other combustible matter, and brought it near the House, intending to set it on fire; and then there was no appearing possibility, but all the *English* there, Men and Women, and Children must have perished, either by unmerciful flames, or more unmerciful hands of wicked Men, whose tender Mercies are cruelties, so that all hope that they should be saved was then taken away, but behold in the Mount of Difficulty and Extremity, *the Lord is seen.*

"For in the very nick of opportunity God sent that worthy Major *Willard . . .*" And there follows the tale of the rescue.[26]

"Thus have we a brief, plain, and true Story of the *War* with the *Indians* in *New-England*, how it began, and how it hath made its progress. . . . Designing only a *Breviary of the History of this war*, I have not enlarged upon the circumstances of things, but shall leave that to others who have advantages and leasure to go on with such an undertaking" (p. 201).

One needs no better summary of the book, than this by its author. However modest its design, it must have created something of a sensation when it first appeared on the counters of Edmund Ranger, or John Foster, its publisher, "over against the Sign of the Dove."[27] In England an edition came out from the shop of Richard Chiswell[28] in the same year as the Boston issue, and we have some evidence that it was eagerly received.[29]

With what has been said of King Philip's War, one sees why it was the great historical feature of New England history in 1675 and 1676. Estimates of the affair vary, and it is the fashion to belittle the achievement of the colonists in bringing it to success.[30]

26. Pp. 67, 68. Cf. also, p. 85.
27. T. G. Wright, *Literary Culture*, p. 115.
28. Cf. *DNB; MHS Coll.*, Series 4, viii, 576.
29. *Ibid.*, vii, 239, 581; but see also, *Ibid.*, 576.
30. Cf. J. T. Adams, *The Founding*, pp. 349–351.

Mather would have agreed to this. He is careful to say "that as to *Victoryes* obtained, we have no cause to glory in anything that we have done, but rather to be ashamed and confounded for our own wayes. . . . God hath let us see that he could easily have destroyed us, by such a contemptible enemy as the Indians have been in our eyes, yea, he hath convinced us that we our selves could not subdue them" (p. 206). More serious, and with less relation to fact, is the charge that such barbarities as marked the English conduct of the war were due to the clergy, whereas "the people were more merciful than the ministers." [31] Yet it was the clergy who pleaded for the conversion of the Indians by the Gospel, and urged their protection from white traders.[32] It was the people who murdered Indian captives in cold blood,[33] and it was Increase Mather, a minister, who deplored their acts.[34] It was the divines who led in the effort to restore friendly inter-course between the two races in New England.[35] The only color for the theory of a merciful people opposed to cruel church lead-ers has been drawn from the affair of Philip's son, who was cap-tured, and, for a time, threatened with death.[36] Because his fate had to be decided by the civil authorities; because the civil authorities asked advice of the ministers; and because some of them queried whether the boy, child though he was, should not be put to death, the clergy have been charged with barbarity.[37] The fact remains that he was not executed, but sold into slavery, a punishment which seems inhuman to-day, but was by no means so brutal in seventeenth-century eyes. It was then quite as reasonable a proceeding in the case of a dangerous political foe, as was an exile to St. Helena in a later age. The sparing of the life of Philip's son cannot be shown by any evidence what-soever to have been the work of the people as distinct from the ministers, whereas we have exact records showing that more than one divine favored the merciful course.[38] Only by unsupported

31. J. T. Adams, *The Founding*, p. 362 (but cf. *Ibid.*, p. 357).

32. I. Mather, *Brief History*, Preface, p. 99. Cf. also, any life of John Eliot, the Indian missionary.

33. Ellis and Morris, *King Philip's War*, p. 132; *MHS Proc.*, xxxiii, 405; *American Antiquarian Society Transactions*, ii, 482.

34. T. Hutchinson, *History*, i, 307; *MHS Proc.*, xxxiii, 403.

35. Cf. I. Mather, *Serious Exhortation*, pp. 25, 26.

36. Palfrey, iii, 221 and n.; J. T. Adams, *The Founding*, pp. 362, 363.

37. *Ibid.*, p. 362.

38. *MHS Coll.*, Series 4, viii, 690. Cf. also, Eliot, as referred to in J. T. Adams, *The Founding*, p. 362.

conjecture can New England citizens of 1676 be translated into the rôle of humane advocates for the representative of a race which had pillaged their homes and slain their wives.

Mather has had to take his share of the groundless accusation brought against the clergy, because of one letter which he wrote to John Cotton, a professed advocate of the death penalty. He declared that he believed "some effectual course" should be taken with Philip's son, remarking that, if Hadad had not fled, "David would have taken a Course that" he "should never have proved a scourge to the next Generation." [39] This letter is mild, when read in the light of Cotton's explicit plea for the boy's execution,[40] and certainly all it contains applies quite as well to the condemnation of the captive to exile and slavery, as to sentencing him to die. If Mather believed the youngest of New England's foes should be killed, it is strange, in view of his habit of speaking plainly, that he did not say so. It is even more curious to read elsewhere that he had been rebuked for urging a friend not to wish the hanging of Indians, lest their innocent blood cry out.[41] Clearly the case against Mather, as an individual, is not proved. Moreover, the ministers as a class cannot be shown to have been cruel judges, restrained only by the will of a more humane people.

There was more to do than to chronicle the events of the war years. New England was more than once in dire need, and to the leaders of the Second Church, especially to Mather, came opportunity to win help for them from abroad.[42] Also, since the war was God's vengeance upon sinners, the ministers were called upon to decide what had been done amiss, and where lay means of amendment and reformation.[43] Mather turned eagerly to the task. Urged by him, the General Court met to consider the necessary reforms.[44] It has been said that they decided that the Lord "was then engaged in burning towns and murdering women and children along the frontier, because Massachusetts had become somewhat lax in persecuting the Quakers, and because her men had begun to wear periwigs and their women to indulge in

39. *MHS Coll.*, Series 4, viii, 690. Of this, J. T. Adams, *The Founding*, p. 362, says: "Increase Mather... called for the lad's blood!"

40. *MHS Coll.*, Series 4, viii, 689.

41. *MHS Proc.*, xxxiii, 402.

42. *Parentator*, p. 76; *Autobiography; MHS Coll.*, Series 4, viii, 9, 261ff., 690ff.

43. I. Mather, *Brief History*, pp. 98ff.; *Mass. Rec.*, v, 59ff.

44. *Parentator*, p. 76; *MHS Proc.*, xxxiii, 399ff., entry for Nov. 9, 1675.

'cutting, curling and immodest laying out theire haire.'" [45] Such statement, following that of an avowed enemy of the Puritan régime in New England,[46] can be made only on a basis of prejudice, or in ignorance of what the Court actually did. What they recommended in reality was the correction of immodest and extravagant dress (which included modes of dressing the hair), the bearing of "due testimony . . . against such as are false Worshippers, especially Idolatrous *Quakers*, who set up Altars against the Lords Altar, yea who set up a Christ whom the Scriptures know not" (this is by no means an explicit plea for "persecution," be it noted); the taking of measures to prevent drunkenness, the abolition of unnecessary Taverns, and the prohibition of profanity, and of sabbath-breaking. There is a plea that "there may be no more such oppression, either by Merchants or day-Labourers as heretofore hath been," an appeal for safeguarding the Indians against the evil influence of the English traders, and, finally, an appeal for Christian education for the children of the colony.[47] To summarize such a document by referring to the only two of its items which seem out of place to-day, when hairdressing and Quakers are not considered public dangers, is like judging the date of a poem by a single, carefully chosen archaic word. Read as a whole, this Puritan declaration shows in all but one of its main clauses the stuff that reformers' dreams are made on in the twentieth century as in the seventeenth. The same things that Mather and his contemporaries saw as crying evils are to-day favorite topics for discussion by school committees, legislatures, and the press. Even in our enlightened age, labor problems, standards of dress, and Sunday laws are of interest. Such matters are the property of no one age or sect.

But, however sound its judgments, the General Court could not check misfortune. Boston, with its many homes mourning their losses in the war, and its pulpits thundering admonitions lest God find further cause to chasten, passed from the shock of battle to the terrors of an epidemic, with coffins meeting one another in the streets.[48] Fire was a third trial. On November 27, 1676, Mather wrote in his diary: "A dismal day. Near my dwelling a fire broke out about 5 h AM. & consumed Houses & many

45. J. T. Adams, *The Founding*, p. 349.
46. Mr. Adams chooses to follow a letter of Edward Randolph, printed in R. N. Toppan, *Edward Randolph*, ii, 225ff., especially 244.
47. I. Mather, *Brief History*, pp. 98ff. 48. *MHS Coll.*, Series 4, viii, 383, 384.

goods. Among others my house & the house appointed for solemnizing the publick worship of God were consumed. Yet there was ... great mixture of mercy with judg^t for tho' the wind was high yet it rained much wch prevented the house from taking fire so soon as else would have been. Also divers houses being blown up & the wind suddenly fallen though this end of the Town was in extreme danger the wind being southeast many habitations are yet spared." [49] Sewall adds: "Mr. Mather saved his Books and other Goods." [50] "There were burnt down Mr Increase Mather's house, Mr Jeremiah Cushings, Thomas Moores, tenements all of them, which brought him in 70 or 80£ p^r Ann Rents, Lieut Way's House, Dr Stone's houses, Mr John Winsle's, Mr Anthony Checkley's new house with sundry others that were considerable. About 5 houses were blown up which was a means to prevent the spreading of the fire. About 70 or 80 families dispossessed of their dwellings & lodgings some losing all they had." [51]

The town's one fire engine was overmatched by this first "Great Fire" of Boston. Ladders, long-handled hooks, swabs on poles, were called into play, and householders, aided by the rain, battled fiercely to save their goods. [52] Yet, when the roar of the flames had ceased, a large part of the North part of the town lay in ruins, the Mather family was homeless, and their church a heap of ashes. But the precious books, so dear to Increase's heart, were saved except for a few, and the generosity of one of his flock helped to make good the loss. [53] Less devastating than the second great fire of 1679, [54] the conflagration of 1676 was to the Second Church and its Teacher a cruel blow.

The Mathers, for the first day or so afterward, were "kindly entertayned at Mr. Richards." [55] On November 29, after spending the morning drying the books, they moved to Captain Bredon's old house, which, with the street before it, had made the stage for the colonists' final dramatic defiance of the Royal Commissioners. [56]

49. *Diary*, 1675–76 (p. 47 of the reprint).   50. *MHS Coll.*, Series 5, v, 29.

51. Capt. Lawrence Hammond's journal, in the reprint of I. Mather's Diary for 1675–76, p. 54.

52. N. B. Shurtleff, *A Topographical ... Description*, p. 641.

53. *Autobiography; Parentator*, p. 79; J. H. Tuttle, *The Libraries*, pp. 291ff.

54. Cf. *Diary*, Aug. 8, 1679.

55. *Ibid.*, Nov. 27, 1676; *Memorial History of Boston*, 1, 578.

56. *Diary*, Nov. 29, 1676; A. H. Thwing, *The Crooked and Narrow Streets*, pp. 61, 62ff.

The controversy then momentarily ended by the refusal of Massachusetts to comply with the royal command was still alive. Its development gave every loyal New Englander more worries than Indians, disease, or fire.[57] England's imperial policy found the Bay Colony a thorn in its path. The charter was to the colonist the keystone of an independent government. He was by no means scrupulous in observing England's laws for her outlying possessions, and he lent to her imperial aspirations a most unsympathetic ear.

With 1676 England began a new and more vigorous attempt to enforce her will, and one of her first acts was to send Edward Randolph to New England as the special messenger of the crown. Loathed by Mather and his followers, he was by no means without dexterity as a diplomat.[58] He suffered from an inability to lose, himself, what he most blamed in the Puritans — a belief that his own church and the government he represented were best for New England. Royal authority and the English church must replace local institutions as the established rule for the colonial church and state.[59] Randolph and his masters, it has been urged, stood for tolerance and religious liberty, as opposed to Puritan persecution and narrowness.[60] One needs no more than a glance at Randolph's letters to see the utter fallacy of such an idea. He sought tolerance just in so far as the Puritans sought it in their migration to America. In other words, he sought it not at all, save for one church. He did not insist that the English church merely stand beside the Congregational in New England, or that an Episcopal school be founded to take

57. Cf. Channing, ii, 157–164; Palfrey, iii, 7–9; J. T. Adams, *The Founding*, chap. 15.

58. Cf. Channing, ii, 160, 161.

59. See Randolph's letters in R. N. Toppan, *Edward Randolph*. It must be remembered that, when Randolph urged English laws for the colonies, he urged laws which regarded the Episcopal church as the official religious institution of the state. He lists, among laws repugnant to those of England: "No person whatsoever shall joine any persons in marriage but a magistrate" (Toppan, ii, 233). To alter this law, to establish ecclesiastical marriages, would be to strike at a fundamental tenet of Puritanism. Nor was Randolph content to make both civil and ecclesiastical marriages legal, which would have been the obvious course of tolerance, but wrote to the Bishop of London: "but one thing will mainely helpe, when no marriages heereafter shall be allowed lawfull but such as are made by the ministers of the church of England" (*Ibid.*, iii, 148). To pass such a rule would be to force all Puritans who married to do so by a ceremony of which they thoroughly disapproved, administered by a Church they disliked. Other points in which Randolph urges general regulations, which would mean the giving up of fundamental Congregational tenets, can easily be found in his correspondence in Toppan.

60. Cf. J. T. Adams, *The Founding*, pp. 395ff.

those for whom Harvard was too narrow.[61] Preferably, Congregational Harvard was to be stamped out, and the Puritan meeting-house was to be thrown open to all who would be admitted to the English church.[62] He was shrewd enough, probably, to see that this meant the destruction of Congregationalism, which differed from the parent establishment chiefly in the very restrictions of admission and discipline which he proposed to destroy. Right or wrong from a legal point of view, the colonists saw in the English policy the undermining of the foundation on which their fathers had built their state; and, probably, those among them who are called to-day "liberals" for their adherence to Randolph's views,[63] acted simply from indifference to the theocratic ideal and interest in the material advantages of harmony with the mother country. They could hardly have cherished any illusions that "religious liberty" or tolerance for all creeds would result from the proposed change in régime.

The colonial case was put first into the hands of Stoughton and Bulkeley, who went to England as agents, but with very limited powers.[64] Against them, Randolph was volubly reciting his list of Massachusetts' errors, with some neglect of the line between falsehood and truth.[65] Sometimes his statements were obviously untrue. Sometimes they were quite as obviously based on fact. A third group of charges arose from a fundamental disparity in the thinking of the colonists and that of Englishmen at home. For example, Randolph declared that English citizens

61. Cf. Toppan, *Edward Randolph*, iv, 90; vi, 245, 246; iv, 132.

62. Randolph declared, April 8, 1678, that the King had ordered that "all persons of good and honest lives should be admitted to yᵉ Sacrament of the Lord's Supper, and their Children to Baptisme," and complained that this ruling was ignored. To obey it would have been to destroy Congregationalism, not to be tolerant for all sects. It will be noted that Randolph here does not refer to the establishment of Anglican churches beside Congregational ones, which would have been the course of tolerance, but to admitting people of good behavior to communion, without any of the tests which seemed so important to Puritans, and played so large a part in the distinguishing of their polity from others. (*Ibid.*, ii, 293.) Cf. also, *Ibid.*, ii, 312ff.

63. Prominent among these were Governor Simon Bradstreet, William Stoughton, and Joseph Dudley. The Governor's attitude was a weak desire to please everyone. See Palfrey, iii, 362. Dudley was a politician first of all. On Stoughton see n. 64.

64. *Mass. Rec.*, v, 99ff., 113–117. William Stoughton was moderate, and favored submission to the English demands. He was a generous benefactor to the college, and often a good servant of New England, though he suffers from his vigorous prosecution of the Salem witches. For his life see Sibley, *Biographical Sketches*, i, 194ff. Peter Bulkeley, son of Peter Bulkeley, first minister of Concord, was Speaker of the House of Deputies, and believed to be opposed to the English view. Palfrey, iii, 293, 294.

65. Palfrey, iii, 296ff., especially 301, 301 n.

had been executed in Massachusetts on account of their religious views. This the colonists denied, for the civil disturbances of the Quakers, and their utter disregard for the sentences imposed upon them, were made grounds for their suffering the penalty of death.[66] From their point of view the Puritans' assertion was true, but to an Englishman, unimpressed with the theocratic ideal of the integral relation of civil and religious discipline, their defence seemed quibbling, or even falsehood.

The English authorities gave a decision which, even to the most prejudiced eyes, seems absolutely just.[67] They supported the original Massachusetts charter, but objected, quite reasonably, to making the word of God the basis of laws involving life and death so long as it could be interpreted only by fallible human means. They pointed to the legislation which punished stubborn and rebellious children by death, fined those who celebrated Christmas, and opposed heresy, as being, with other colonial decrees, repugnant to the terms of the charter. Similarly they opposed the rule that all marriages must be civil, and touched here a point close to the Puritan's heart, since the illegality of ecclesiastical marriage was a cardinal point in the Congregational system. Here alone, perhaps, the English opinion worked not for tolerance, but attacked a main tenet of the Massachusetts church.[68] The colonial agents were told that the royal decision as to boundaries must be final, that their state must sue for forgiveness of its offences, observe the laws of England, and repeal such of its own as conflicted with them. Finally, the religious test for the franchise was denounced. In answer, the agents resorted to quibbling by declaring that the right to vote was no longer related to church membership. It was a pitiful evasion. The statement, true in theory, was quite disproved in practice.[69]

In the face of the English ruling, the General Court in Boston proved defiant. The Lords of Trade, constantly besieged by Randolph, were outraged, and with reason, at the flouting of royal orders. The Attorney General ruled that the violations of the charter justified its revocation, and the Lords of Trade urged

66. R. N. Toppan, *Edward Randolph*, ii, 266, 276ff.

67. *Cal. State Papers, Am. and W. I.*, x, 118ff.; J. T. Adams, *The Founding*, pp. 382, 383.

68. *Religious History of New England*, p. 24.

69. J. T. Adams, *The Founding*, p. 384; Toppan, *Edward Randolph*, iii, 8, 44ff., 47ff.

bringing *Quo Warranto* proceedings against it. Randolph, in spite of the agents' warm opposition, was made Collector of Customs for New England. Reluctantly the colonists made concessions here and there, but they clung fast to their idea of virtual independence.[70]

The agents returned in 1679, bringing the King's letter in regard to the franchise and increased toleration. Randolph met hostility on every side when he undertook his new duties,[71] and the colony, once more resorting to delay, waited several years before sending new agents to England to answer the King's commands. This Fabian policy was opposed by Mather, who believed that delegates should be promptly chosen and sent to defend the colony in London.[72] None the less, even after John Richards and Samuel Nowell had been appointed [73] as messengers to the King, their sailing was postponed, and they had not left Boston by the end of the year, when Randolph appeared fresh from renewed efforts in England on behalf of the *Quo Warranto*. With him he brought a new royal order.[74] This provided for more assistance for the Collector of Customs, demanded that the Navigation Acts be obeyed, and insisted once more that agents be sent. Early in the next year the General Court read this letter, and Richards and Dudley were chosen to go to England [75]—the one a radical in his desire to uphold the power of the colony, and the other a politician eager to turn the event of the moment toward the building of personal power.[76] As diplomats they were acceptable, for the most part, but the authority given them was insufficient to make any action of theirs of use. Matters had gone too far for them to check.

Controversy has been busy with every detail of these relations between New England and the mother country up to 1683. The proper interpretation of more than one fact in the record still offers ground for dispute. It seems safe, none the less, to believe that the issue was clearly drawn between England's imperial

70. Toppan, *Edward Randolph*, i, 124. Cf. in general, Palfrey, vol. iii.

71. Toppan, *Edward Randolph*, iii, 61.

72. *Diary*, 1675–76 (page 51 of reprint, entry for October 17, 1680).

73. *Mass. Rec.*, v, 304, 307. For Randolph's views as to Richards, cf. T. Hutchinson, *Collection*, ii, 273. For Nowell, cf. Sibley, *Biographical Sketches*, i, 335ff.

74. Toppan, *Edward Randolph*, iii, 110ff.

75. *Mass. Rec.*, v, 333; T. Hutchinson, *History*, i, 334; *MHS Coll.*, Series 4, viii, 49ff.

76. For Dudley, see E. Kimball, *The Public Life of Joseph Dudley*.

policy and New England's zeal for autonomy. If only the leaders were busy on the colonial side, the fact remains that the mass of the people, if contrary-minded, did not express themselves, and one has only inference to guide as to their attitude. Many of them must have followed their magistrates and ministers in accepting the tradition that their commonwealth had been erected in the interests of one faith. Such men cannot have welcomed the English plan to remodel their community into a British colony dominated by the Church of England, and bereft of its original theological tone. To them the brand of tolerance urged by England was not tolerance, but the direst intolerance in all that concerned their chosen frame for church and state. Current events led them to hope for little for their creed at the hands of a Stuart king.[77] On the other hand, another class in the colony, more interested in trade than in worship, sought no more for Massachusetts than the government which, though soon to fail, then seemed to work well in England.[78] A third group, perhaps, comprised the politically minded, who sought office rather than any one ideal of government.

Broadly speaking, the larger towns were most inclined to temporize, for their interests were most cosmopolitan. The country districts and their representatives were less exposed to material influences, and clung more narrowly to their fathers' beliefs.[79] Though we may grant that the party which favored submission to England aimed in the direction of the progress of later years, it is still unfair to forget that, to the Puritans, preservation of the old order meant not only New England's independence and continued power for the Congregational clergy, but also the maintenance of what had come to seem to them the only way of life sanctioned by God. To desert it would have seemed falsehood to an ideal, and treachery to what they saw as the best interests of mankind.

Mather's stand on such questions is plain. The established order in New England was to him an article of faith, inculcated by inheritance and training. Though he would amend the system here and there, by such means as the Half-Way Covenant, and was never in his life a slave to authority but was often an advocate of what was newest and most progressive in thought,

77. Cf. letters to Mather in *MHS Coll.*, Series 4, viii, 510, 617, 618, 642.
78. For the parties in Massachusetts, cf. Palfrey, iii, 359.
79. Cf. J. T. Adams, *The Founding*, pp. 373, 374.

his belief in the validity of the essentials of the Congregational Way was incapable of change. His intellectual curiosity led him more than once in advance of his contemporaries, but it was his weakness, if it be a weakness, to hold rooted convictions as to right and wrong. The church in which he had been nurtured was right, and for it no change or progress was needed or to be conceived of. To ask him to alter his view on this point would have been much as if one of us were asked to alter our rooted idea that two and two make four, in preference for some other theory hailed as newest and best. If one admits that this certainty as to the truth of their creed had a stifling effect upon the Puritans, one must also admit its large share in their achievement as colonizers. Without it could hardly have come the steadfastness of purpose that led them to brave a stormy sea and a bleak land.

From 1675 to 1683, then, Mather was, at the very least, a deeply interested spectator of the political activities of the time. As we have seen, he longed for action, not delay. With John Richards, the representative of his views abroad, he had close relations. For him, he conducted at least one delicate negotiation with the Governor; and in Richards's absence, his wife and children were confided to the care of the Teacher of the Second Church.[80]

But, however great Mather's concern with public affairs, a variety of other interests helped to make up the rich activity of his life. At home his children were growing up. Cotton took his first degree at Harvard in 1678, and, three years later, received his A.M. from his father's hands.[81] His loyalty to Increase began early, and he writes in 1681, "About this time I bought a *Spanish Indian*, and bestowed him for a *Servant*, on my Father." Again, two years later, "I was owner of a Watch, whereof I was very fond, for the Varietie of Motions in it. My Father was desirous of this Watch, and I, in a manner, gave it him, with such Thoughts, *I owe him a great deal more than this*." In 1681 Cotton began to work as pastor of the Second Church, aiding his father there. "And I," he writes, "am herein a Colleague to a *Father*; yea, to a *Father*, given mee from the Dead, and one of my greatest Blessings." Among his "causes for thanksgiving" he lists "The Smiles of God, upon my *Father's Family* . . . But espe-

---

80. *MHS Coll.*, Series 4, viii, 499, 500, 494.
81. *Ibid.*, Series 7, vii, 26; J. L. Sibley, *Biographical Sketches*, iii, 7.

cially, the Life and Health of my dear *Father*, whom I may reckon among the richest of my Enjoyments." [82]

The devoted Cotton was the oldest of nine children. The youngest, Catherine, was born in 1682 in the new house built for Mather at the corner of what are now Hanover and North Bennett Streets, near the Second Church, which had been rebuilt in North Square.[83] Hannah was born in this house on May 30, 1680, and Abigail, the next youngest, was born in April, 1677, during her father's stay in Captain Bredon's former home.[84] "Little doe children think, wt affection is in ye Heart of a Father," Increase Mather wrote in his diary;[85] and his son Nathaniel, fourteen years old in 1683, repaid his father's love.[86] One after another the children fell sick and their father prayed beside their beds, deserting the study where he "could doe little . . . bec. of childrens sickness."[87] Only one of them died in childhood— little Catherine, who "dyed June 11: 1683."[88]

We know that Mather tried "to be exemplary unto others . . . in the habite of his wife and children,"[89] and his care for them is reflected in page after page of his diary. There are prayers, too, lists of blessings for which he thanks God, and notes as to causes for humiliation. Again and again he deplores his sins, the "publick state of things," the "Troubles like to come on N. E. from abroad," and the "vnsuccessfullness of" his "Labors." "I doe but cumber ye ground," he writes. He is grateful that "God hath given" him "esteem among his people" and has preserved his and his family's health. He asks for more grace and "wisdome to goe in & out bef his people, over whom Hee hath set me." He begs the Lord to "subdue ye Heathen," keep Boston "from ys Terrible disease of ye small pox . . . & suff[er] not ys disease to spread here."[90] He has premonitions, and records how in 1676 he "was strongly possessed with fears that Boston would be punished with the judgment of fire." Thus moved, he preached on the text "*I said, surely thou wilt fear me, thou wilt receive*

82. *MHS Coll.*, Series 7, vii, 20, 22, 36, 53, 63.
83. Entries in Increase Mather's Bible; E. G. Porter, *Rambles*, pp. 210ff.; *Memorial History of Boston*, i, 192 n.; *MHS Coll.*, Series 4, viii, 237.
84. Entries in Increase Mather's Bible.
85. April 7, 1675.
86. Cf. *MHS Coll.*, Series 4, viii, 19.
87. *Diary*, April 9, 1675; and *Ibid.*, for 1675 and 1676, *passim*.
88. Entry in Increase Mather's Bible.
89. *MHS Coll.*, Series 4, viii, 574.
90. *Diaries; Autobiography.*

instruction; so their *dwelling should not be cut off, howsoever I punished them.*" The fire followed hard upon this.[91] If such a chronicle seems to us to reveal idle crediting of vague forebodings remembered only after the fact, to him they were precious hints that God might have been willing in some measure to make known His purposes to His servant upon earth.[92]

Prayer and heartburnings could not suffice. There was work to do, and, lest he waste time, he drew up a plan for his days.

"The first day of the week, besides my public labors, to attend catechising, and personal instruction in my family as time shall permit.

"The second day of the week, A.M., to read a text with some commentator upon. To study part of a sermon. P.M. to read some author, & study.

"Third day, A.M. Read context, study sermon. P.M. Endeavor to instruct personally some or other at home in the summer time. Read authors.

"Fourth day, read commentators, Study. P.M., read authors; study.

"Fifth day, Read commentators. Sermon. At lecture, to endeavor amongst ministers to promote what shall be for public advantage.

"Sixth day, A.M. Read commentators; study. P.M. Read authors; study.

"Seventh day. Read commentators. Prepare for Sabbath.

"Only allowance must be given for visitations and diversions, and necessary avocations not foreseen." [93]

The last clause means most of all, for his activities were too many to be confined to any rigid scheme. His correspondence with friends at home and abroad, and his continued visits and visitors, make clear once more his eagerness for participation in the affairs of men.[94]

91. *Autobiography; Parentator,* p. 78.
92. On such premonitions, cf. B. Wendell, *Cotton Mather,* pp. 52, 53.
93. *Autobiography.* The same material is in *Parentator,* p. 38.
94. Cf. letters in *MHS Coll.,* Series 4, vol. viii.

CHAPTER XI

LITERARY LEADER AND SPOKESMAN OF THE PEOPLE

IF the years from 1675 to 1683 were filled with the excitement of political change, and for Mather marked by the eventful progress of his family and church, they still offered him time to exercise his scholarly bent. Learning was an integral part of his conception of his task, and reading and study filled many of his days. He bought books from England and from the counters of Boston booksellers on King's Street or Prison Lane. The titles he chose forbid one's picturing him as the narrow-minded preacher deaf to all but the echo of his own thoughts. If he received from his brother Nathaniel a treatise on the millennium, from John Davenport's son his father's vindication of Congregationalism, or from Richard Russell the very useful "Fulfilling of the Scripture," by Robert Fleming; if he bought Dike's "Worthy Communicant" and Perkins's "Reformed Catholike," there were also books broader in subject, such as Horn's "De Originibus Americanis," another volume of Ramus, and, most interesting of all, Paul Pellison's history of the French Academy.[1] So also, when "the Honourable Mrs. *Bridget Hoar* made him to take what he Pleased from the Library of her Deceased Husband," he chose books of no one type.[2] His selection included not only purely theological works, but general writings, such as Gesner's "Bibliotheca," "Pembrook's Arcadia," Cicero's "Orations," two volumes on tobacco, and such scientific books as Parkinson's "Garden Flowers" and "Theatre of Plants," Horstius's Medical works, and Helmont's "Ortus Medicinae." And when Richard Chiswell sends him upon order thirteen books, we find that seven are on theology, but the rest are the "Discovery of Pigmies," "Horologicall Dialogues," Barbette's "Chirurgery," Leybourne's

---

1. All these books from Mather's library, with inscriptions dating them, are in the library of the American Antiquarian Society, except Horn, which is owned by the Massachusetts Historical Society.

2. Cf. J. H. Tuttle, *The Libraries of the Mathers*, p. 291, and *Parentator*, p. 79.

"Dialling," Hooke's "Motion of the Earth," the work of a pioneer in his field,[3] and Stephenson's "Mathemat. Compendium." These books, one remembers, were Mather's own choice, and ordered by him from London.[4] Chiswell knew, too, that his correspondent was eager to keep in touch with the newest writing, and added a few books of his own selection. Two of these were medical, two political, and two "best sellers" by Sir Matthew Hale, of which the bookseller wrote: "I know not any two books have come forth these 20 yeares, that have sold so great a number in so short a time."[5]

Another shipment from London "for Mr. Mather" is, perhaps, the most interesting of all. It was sent on September 5, 1683.[6] The sermons of his old friend, William Benn, of Dorchester, and Richard Baxter's "How to Do Good to Many" may be classed as theology, but we find three copies of Chamberlayne's "Compendium Geographicum" revealing broader interests. Medicine is represented by Samuel Haworth's "The True Method of Curing Consumptions"; and a work called "Miracles no Violations of the Laws of Nature" points forward to Mather's "Illustrious Providences." For history, or politics, we find "The Compleat States-man," a life of Shaftesbury. There is also "The Woman's Advocate, or Fifteen real Comforts of Matrimony . . . With Satyrical Reflections on Whoring, and the Debauchery of this Age. By a Person of Quality of the Female Sex"; suggesting that human concerns were not foreign to one Boston reader! And as for two copies of "The London Jilt, or the Politick Whore; shewing all the artifices and stratagems which the Ladies of Pleasure make use of, for the intreaguing and decoying of men; interwoven with several pleasant stories of the Misses' ingenious performances," the least one can say is that these were not the adornment most to be expected on the shelves of a narrow-minded cleric. Undoubtedly the book was written by someone who, like Defoe, professed a zeal for moral edification; but quite as certainly his "pleasant stories" were sometimes read by those with other motives. That Mather owned them shows, probably, that he was cognizant of a fact some teachers and divines have forgotten, and realized that to guide men into righteousness

3. Cf. *DNB*.   4. *MHS Coll.*, Series 4, viii, 575-577.
5. *Ibid.*; for Hale, see *DNB*.
6. W. C. Ford, *The Boston Book Market*, pp. 114ff. The original list is owned by W. A. Jeffries, Esq., of Boston.

one must not be wholly ignorant of things of the world. To-day ministers read the reports of social workers as to the more sordid conditions of life; then a divine found similar material in "The London Jilt."

Mather bought books to read them, and in 1675–76 one finds him going through many varied pages. Cicero, Franzius's "History of Brutes," several histories, Moxon "Of Globes," Paget's "Chronography," and Purchas, are sandwiched in among treatises by learned divines. "The Life of Richard 3" appears, with no other identification; and even more alluring is the sound of the "Cabinet of Mirth." 7

In the face of this one cannot believe that there was in New England "for the average citizen" an "absence . . . of almost any books other than theological, and of any intellectual stimulus other than the sermon." 8 Admitting, of course, that Mather was not "the average citizen," and that the size of his library and breadth of his reading place him above his fellow towns-people, there is still abundant evidence that they, too, had access to literature of all sorts. Boston had a library, and so had Harvard. Boston booksellers' lists of importations testify to the wide range of books, popular and learned, within reach of every passer-by.9 Yet one reads: "Among the numerous contemporary writers whom our educated colonists might have been reading had they been in England, we may mention, at hazard, Locke, Hobbes, Butler, Marvell, Sir Thomas Browne, Milton, Taylor, Izaak Walton, Bunyan, Fuller, Clarendon, Herbert, Dryden, and Herrick. . . . Of all this varied intellectual life, it may be said that practically nothing reached the vast majority of New Englanders." 10 Such a statement weakens in the face of the fact that of this list all save Hobbes, Walton, and Herrick can be shown certainly to have been known in colonial New England.11 Marvell, Milton, Taylor, Fuller, and Herbert were in Mather's library; 12 before his death at least one public library owned Locke and Clarendon; 13 he quoted from Sir Thomas

7. T. G. Wright, *Literary Culture*, pp. 130ff. Paget's *Chronography* may have been Ephraim Pagit's *Christianographie*, 1635, and often reprinted. Cf. W. T. Lowndes, *Bibliographer's Manual*, i, 344, for the "Cabinet of Mirth."

8. J. T. Adams, *The Founding*, p. 370.   9. Wright, *Literary Culture*.

10. Adams, *The Founding*, p. 371.

11. I have searched no further than the lists given in Wright's *Literary Culture*.

12. J. H. Tuttle, *The Libraries*.

13. Wright, *Literary Culture*, p. 185.

Browne,[14] his son knew Butler,[15] Dryden was quoted by New Englanders,[16] and the booksellers in Boston sold Bunyan.[17] The "Pilgrim's Progress" was printed in Boston in 1681.[18] If the scanty records preserved show thus much, one may be sure that other libraries unlisted and sales unrecorded would, if known, do their part to dispel the popular delusion that the Puritan was blind to all beyond his own door. The book trade in New England flourished, and English books were its support.[19] Without readers this could not have been the case, and the Puritan need not fear comparison with his descendants. Like them, he had his own tastes. He preferred Herbert to Herrick, or Milton to Clarendon, just as some of us desert Ezra Pound for Masefield, or Wells for Bryce, without bringing discredit to our education.

Mather's reading, and the events among which he lived, find more than one reflection in what he wrote. In the front rank of the governors of the College, he sought supremacy elsewhere, and he knew how well leadership among New England writers would serve the personal prestige which was so important an asset in the prosecution of his work in church and town. Thus, from 1675 to 1683 the press turned out his books, year by year, histories, sermons, theology, and even a page or two of up-to-date science.

He never forgot that the writing of New England history was a necessary task awaiting a willing hand. In 1677, he finished his "Relation of the Troubles which have hapned in New-England, By reason of the Indians there: From the Year 1614 to the Year 1675."[20] His authorities are still recognized, except that modern historians envy him the sight of "a *Manuscript Narrative* of the *Pequot War*" from Davenport's library (p. 45). He states clearly the theory on which he wrote. "I am not altogether ignorant of what is commonly and truly observed, viz. That those *Histories* which are partly *Chronological* are the

---

14. Cf. I. Mather, *Essay . . . Illustrious Providences*, chap. 4.
15. He refers to *Hudibras* in the *Magnalia*.
16. Wright, *Literary Culture*, p. 150.   17. *Ibid.*, p. 123.
18. S. A. Green, *Ten Fac-simile Reproductions . . . Various Subjects*, pp. 13, 14.
19. Wright, *Literary Culture*, especially chap. 7.
20. The full title was: "*A Relation Of the* Troubles *which have hapned in* New-England, *By reason of the* Indians *there:* From the Year 1614. to the Year 1675. Wherein the frequent Conspiracyes of the Indians to cutt off the English, and the wonderfull providence of God, in disappointing their devices, is declared. . . . By Increase Mather. . . . Boston. . . . 1677." It was reprinted by S. G. Drake as the "Early History of New England," Boston, 1864. All references in this book are to this edition.

most profitable; and that they that undertake a Work of this Nature, should go by Prescript of that so much celebrated Verse, *Quis, Quid, Vbi, Quibus auxiliis, Cur, Quomodò Quandò.* which I have endeavoured to remember" (pp. 46, 47). He recurs to his favorite literary doctrine, saying: "Nor hath that Maxim been wholly forgotten, *Stylus Historicus quo simplicior eo melior.* And J may expect that *Ingenuous Readers* will act according to that which a learned man in his *Historica* layeth down as a Theorem, *Historici legantur cum moderatione et venia,* h. e. *cogitetur fieri non posse ut in omnibus circumstantiis sint Lyncei.* I have done what I could to come at the Truth, and plainly to declare it, knowing that that is (as useth to be said) *the Soul and Sun of History,* whose Property is, Μόνη τῇ ἀληθεί ἁ θυείν" (p. 47). There are worse guides for the writing of history.

For us the book has the value of a faithfully compiled story of events, with nothing in style or plan to mark it for special comment, after our glance at the chief features of his very similar history of King Philip's War. The "Relation" suffers less from hasty composition than its predecessor, and the bony chronological structure is better veiled by more skilful transitions and more closely knit narrative. Once more there is an eye for the dramatic and picturesque, and no pages are more readable than those given to anecdotes of various encounters between the English and the Indians. We read, "He . . . doth also *Relate* another Particular no less pleasant; namely, that whereas the *Pequots* observed, that the English, being willing to show as much Mercy as would stand with Justice, did only captivate and not kill the *Squaws,* some great Indian Boyes would cry, *I Squaw, I Squaw,* thereby to escape with their Lives" (pp. 183, 184). Writing in such a vein does violence to the conventional picture of the dour and nasal Puritan, but it is welcome, and one regrets that the next paragraph begins "But to be Serious —".

The book closes on a note that sounds again and again in Mather's work in these years — his faith that two sorts of men settled New England, "some that came hither on Account of Trade and worldly Interests, by whom the Indians have been scandalized," and "others that came hither on a religious and conscientious Account, having in their Eye the Conversion of the *Heathen* unto Christ." The former have met the Lord's displeasure, while the latter have prospered. "*This is the Lord's doing and it is marvellous in our Eyes*" (pp. 238, 239).

The book found readers, and favor enough to lead such friends as Samuel Whiting and Nathaniel Morton to write: "Let me beg one request of you, that you would set pen to paper in writing a History of New-England since the coming of our chief men thither... which I hope you may easily accomplish, having by your diligence and search found out so much history concerning the Pequot war," or "I would propose vnto you . . . that you would please . . . to be Instrumentall to sett on foot and put forward a Generall History of New England." [21] Time never offered for Mather himself to write such a book, but it is probable that he was "Instrumentall to sett" it "on foot," for the first who achieved the task "in a polite and scholar-like way" was his eldest son.

There was more work for Mather's pen in non-historical fields. From his sermons he prepared a series of little books, and between 1675 and 1683 the list of his writings includes "The Times of Men are in the Hand of God," "The Wicked Man's Portion," "Renewal of Covenant the Great Duty," "Pray for the Rising Generation," "A Discourse Concerning the Danger of Apostasy," "Returning unto God," "Heaven's Alarm to the World," "The Latter Sign," "A Sermon Wherein is shewed that the Church of God is sometimes a Subject of Great Persecution," and a series of "sundry sermons" under the title of "Practical Truths Tending to Promote the Power of Godliness." Five of these books were printed more than once, two of them appearing in three impressions.

Some elements are common to all of them. There is a style tuned to the needs of the pulpit, always Scriptural, almost always direct, and, at times, dramatic. There is constant care for emphasis, and time and time again one finds the main theme repeated like a refrain, or by position given unique force. In content there is everywhere harping upon the sins of the day, most of all upon New England's falling away from the religious ideal of its founders. "The interest of New-England is now changed from a religious to a worldly interest; and in this thing is *the great radical Apostacy of New-England*." [22] Reform is constantly urged. Mather's readers are to express their zeal in renewing the old church covenants and in supporting the minis-

21. *New England Historical and Genealogical Register*, ii, 198; *MHS Coll.*, Series 4, viii, 594ff.
22. I. Mather, *Call from Heaven*, 1685 ed., p. 89.

try, and, most of all, they are to seek God through prayer. But to save themselves would not be to save New England for all time. In her youth, her "rising generation," lay her hope. Mather saw the strategic place to battle for the life of the old faith, and in sermon after sermon he reverts to insistent pleas for sound education of children, and the gift to them of the blessing of a disciplined and Christian home.

These strains run through all the writing of these years, but there is no one of Mather's volumes without some paragraph or two of interest in and for itself. "The Times of Men," completed early in 1675, is built about the idea that "*it becometh us, not to censure those that are made* Examples *of* divine Severity; *and yet with Humility and an Holy Fear to take notice of the solemn works of God.*" [23] With all its stress upon the swift judgment of God, for reasons sometimes beyond human ken, the book is not cheerless, for if life and death and all human concerns are in God's hands, "they are in the best hands that possibly can be" (p. 12). There burns the faith that triumphs over the sternest articles of the Puritan creed.

Either the "Times of Men" or the "Wicked Man's Portion" seems to have been the first book printed in Boston.[24] The latter, a sermon preached on the occasion of the execution of two men "who had murthered their master," [25] is marked by directness of utterance, pointed by examples of the punishment of the wicked, and dignified by its resistance of the obvious temptation to sensationalism offered by its theme. Most striking of all, is its address to the murderers, with its picture of Christ's place as the great Redeemer. "And know, that Jesus Christ the Son of God, Came to *Save the chief of sinners.* There is Merit and Righteousness enough in Jesus Christ. Hee was bruised for our Iniquityes, and wounded for our Transgressions. The wounds of Christ can

23. The Preface is dated 9ᵗʰ of 4ᵗʰ Moneth, 1675. The quotation is from the Preface. The full title is: "*The Times of men are in the hand of God.* or A Sermon Occasioned by that awfull Providence which hapned in *Boston* in *New-England*, the 4ᵗʰ day of the 3ᵈ Moneth 1675. (when part of a Vessel was blown up in the Harbour, and nine men hurt, and three mortally wounded) wherein is shewed how we should sanctifie the dreadfull Name of God under such awfull Dispensations. By *Increase Mather*, Teacher of a Church of Christ. . . . *Boston*, Printed by *John Foster* 1675."

24. R. F. Roden, *The Cambridge Press*, p. 139.

25. The full title is: "*The Wicked Mans Portion* or A Sermon (Preached at the Lecture in Boston in *New-England* the 18th day of the 1 Moneth 1674. when two men were *executed*, who had *murthered* their Master.) Wherein is shewed *That excess in wickedness doth bring untimely Death.* By *Increase Mather*, Teacher of a Church of Christ. . . . *Boston*, Printed by *John Foster.* 1675."

make amends for those wounds which you gave your Master, when you slew him. The Blood of Christ can satisfie for the blood which you have shed. Jesus doth deliver from the wrath to come. And he doth not exclude you from salvation by him, if you doe not by Impenitency & Unbelief exclude your selves. Neither can the death you suffer hinder the Salvation of your souls, in case you truly repent and believe. Yea Hee (the blessed Son of God) was hanged upon a Tree, though Hee never knew any sin, only for the sins of his people, and therefore he hath sanctified all maner of deaths unto those that shall beleive on Him. Oh Consider of it and let it break your Hearts" (p. 23).

In the first of these two sermons Mather wrote: "Possibly some may wonder, that I should so frequently appear in this way, who am the least amongst my Brethren; and also one that hath his Head and Hands and Heart, otherwise full of thoughts and Labours. The Truth is (although I should not be weary in well doing, yet such is mine infirmity as that) I am weary. And if the Lord give me to finish two small Treatises, which I have upon the Anvill, (and which I doe confess my Heart is much upon) . . . I doe not Purpose (although I should live much longer then I think I shall) to be any more troublesome in this way." [26] Yet his pen did not flag, and in 1677, because of the "concurrent desires" [27] of the Dorchester church, he published the sermon he had preached to them on what he saw as the great need of the day, the "Renewal of Covenant." [28]

Mather felt that there was no better way to restore the zeal of the first enthusiastic years in Massachusetts, than to reaffirm publicly one's religious purpose and faith, and his Dorchester sermon, now printed, expresses this idea. The book contains an interesting passage on the use of the Bible. "Others have objected, that we find nothing in the New-Testament concerning a *Church Covenant*. And suppose it were so indeed, Is the old Testament Apocrypha in these dayes?" Such a statement is hardly intelligible if, as we are urged to believe, the Old Testament was the Puritans' avowed favorite. Much is explained in the comment, "Its a solid Notion, that things abundantly

---

26. I. Mather, *The Times of Men*, Preface.

27. I. Mather, *Renewal of Covenant*, Preface.

28. The full title is: "*Renewal of Covenant the great Duty incumbent on decaying or distressed Churches.* A Sermon Concerning Renewing of Covenant with God in Christ, Preached at *Dorchester* in *New-England*, the 21. Day of the 1. Moneth 1677. being a Day of Humiliation There, on that Occasion." Boston, 1677.

insisted on in the Old Testament, and matters about which there was no occasion for controversie in the Apostles time, are sparingly mentioned in the New Testament." [29]

"Pray for the Rising Generation" [30] carries in its title sufficient clue to its contents. The diction is heavy, and perhaps overloaded with Scripture, but the argument for the efficacy of prayer, its necessity for children, and the need of good examples for them, is none the less plain.

Mather's election sermon for 1677, preached before the "general Assembly," was printed in 1679.[31] One or two paragraphs make clear points of the gravest import to all who would read the Puritan aright. Mather turns to the deputies and magistrates, and exhorts them to enforce the laws, to check the disturbances common on Saturday nights (a modern note!), and to urge the renewal of covenants. The need of New England is for discipline in homes and churches, and for the calling of worthy men to office. "Let it be your Care, that none but faithful ones . . . be employed as Publick Preachers" (p. 103).[32] Toleration is a danger. "Truly sinful Toleration was Solomon's great Iniquity, whereby he did forsake the Lord" (p. 104). "Do we not find that all the godly reforming Magistrates, spoken of in Scripture, thought it their Concern to pull down false worship, as well as to set up the true Worship of God?" "Sinful Toleration is an evil of exceeding dangerous consequence" (p. 105). One reads, and at once the grim figure of the conventional Puritan, fabricated from conjectures of a later day, seems to gain reality. But before we add Mather to those who would put Quakers to death for their opinions, we may well pause to read "Yet it is far from

29. Preface.

30. The full title is: "*Pray for the Rising Generation*, or a Sermon *Wherein Godly Parents are Encouraged, to Pray and Believe for their Children*, Preached the third Day of the fifth Month, 1678. which Day was set apart by the second Church in *Boston* in *New-England*, humbly to seek unto God by Fasting and Prayer, for a Spirit of Converting Grace, to be poured out upon the Children, and *Rising Generation* in *New-England*" (Cambridge, 1678). A second impression was printed in Boston in 1679, and bound with "A Call from Heaven." A third impression appeared in the 1685 edition of the last-named book. All references here are to the 1685 edition.

31. The title is: "*A Discourse* Concerning the Danger of Apostasy, Especially as to those that are the Children and Posterity of such as have been eminent for God in their Generation. *Delivered in a Sermon, preached in the Audience of the general Assembly of the* Massachusets *Colony at* Boston *in* New-England, May 23. 1677. *being the day of* Election *there*." This was printed with the "Call from Heaven" in both editions of that book.

32. The references are to the edition of 1685.

my design in speaking this to stir up Magistrates to that which the Scripture calls *Persecution:* it were better to err by *too much indulgence* towards those that have *the root of the matter in them,* than by *too much Severity.* Nay, as to those that are indeed Heretical, I can for my own part say with Luther, *ad judicium sanguinis tardus sum,* I have no affection to *sanguinary* punishments in such Cases. And certainly there are other wayes to suppress Hereticks besides *Hereticide"* (pp. 107, 108).

Driven from one position, our Puritan-baiting tendencies find refuge in the thought that, at least, we have here the Puritan minister attempting to control not only the church but the state, in contradiction to the Congregational theory which kept the two apart, and in violation of all principles save those of dogmatic tyranny. But Mather once more cuts the ground from beneath our feet. His function is to preach, to state the case of religion, not to dictate or control. "For a Minister of Christ to be a Merchant and entangle himself with the Affairs of this life, against the express charge of yᵉ Holy Ghost; or for them to be Gospel Lawyers, to handle the *Code* instead of the Bible, and study the Statutes of the Land instead of the Statutes of Heaven; for them to appear as Advocates, and plead Causes in civil Courts of Judicature, it is very uncomely" (p. 120). Nor may the magistrates control the church. "There is indeed one particular insisted on, which is now become a matter of Scruple and distast to some amongst us, *viz.* that which concerns the *Magistrates power in matters of Religion.* But as it was by me either intended or expressed, I know not to this hour why any one should be offended at it. I may better speak in this cause than some others, as having my self had experience what it is to have Conscience imposed on, and therefore would be loth that any truly conscientious should be burdened; and it is sufficiently known that I have a greater latitude and *Indulgence* in the point of *Toleration,* than many better than myself have. Nevertheless, I judge it most unreasonable that *pretended Liberty of Conscience,* should be an *Asylum* for the profanest errors to take Sanctuary in: As though men must therefore have Liberty to Profane *Sabbaths* or *Sacraments.*"[33] Here speaks Mather's dominant belief that where right and wrong, as the Puritan saw them, were concerned, there could be no question of tolerance. His vigorous confidence as to this, and more than a hint of the force of his

33. Preface.

character, stand out in his "What I have to say, if it were in a Church full of Kings, I would speak it."

Both the sermons last considered were printed more than once. "Pray for the Rising Generation" appeared by itself, and then as a part of two editions of a small volume made up of a group of sermons, all directed to New England youth. Both impressions contained also "The Danger of Apostasy." The whole volume bore the name "A Call from Heaven to the Present and Succeeding Generations," [34] and it contains two sermons we have not yet seen.

The first, on 1 Chronicles, 28:9, is an appeal to parents to bring up their children in true religion. There is a strangely archaic note for us in its assertion that election to salvation tends to follow family lines. But, if it be undemocratic and out of date to believe that godly parents are most likely to have offspring whom God will number among His chosen, there are redeeming pages. One reads: "If Parents truly fear God, their children shall fare the better for it; Yea, let me tell you, that then if any of them dye in their Infancyes, you need not doubt of their Salvation" (p. 20). What has become of the unhappy children in "The Day of Doom," [35] tortured eternally by the chance of an early death? What becomes of modern critics of the seventeenth century, who love to quote Wigglesworth's grim verses, as typical of his creed? Perhaps Mather had progressed beyond his old college tutor. Certainly he makes clear what cannot be repeated too often — that, conservative though he may have been, it was not the past for the sake of the past, that he upheld. "The Wise Man," he remarks, "doth justly condemn the folly of those, that are alwayes saying and complaining, *what is the cause that the former dayes were better then* these? . . . there is in men an aptness to Morose Repinings, like the Poets old Man, *Laudator temporis acti, se puero;* which is not from wisdome; such complaints often proceeding from igno-

34. The full title is: "*A Call from Heaven* To the Present and Succeeding *Generations.* Or A Discourse Wherin is shewed, I. That the Children of Godly Parents are under special Advantages and Encouragements to seek the Lord. II. The exceeding danger of Apostasie, especially as to those that are the Children and Posterity of such as have been eminent for God in their Generation. III. That Young Men ought to Remember God their Creator." Boston, 1679. There was a second edition, Boston, 1685, to which all references here are made.

35. Cf. M. C. Tyler, *History*, ii, 31, 32.

rance in History, or non observation of the vices of those of former, and virtues in some of the present generation." [36]

The other sermon in the same volume, still unconsidered, was addressed especially to the young men of New England. It does not spare its allusions to hell-fire. Yet the climax returns to the heart of all Christianity, the love of Christ. "*Look unto Jesus Christ.* O betake your selves to him. . . . Goe to him by Prayer, and to God by him. Some of you, when you are asked that Question, *do you pray*, Answer, I cannot pray. You would do it, you say, but you know not how to pray. Why, get into a secret place, and there lift up thine Eyes and heart to the Lord Jesus, and if thou can'st say nothing else, yet say, *O thou Son of God have mercy on me! O convert me, and save my poor Soul!* who knoweth but the Lord from on high, may look upon thee, since the Lord Jesus himself hath said, *They that seek me early shall find me*" (p. 114).

On March 17, 1679–80, the Second Church renewed their covenant, and Mather preached to them on "Returning unto God." [37] There is nothing to detain us in this sermon, printed a few months later; and the next of his public discourses to find its way into print is concerned less with his activities as preacher and writer than with his interest in matters of science. We may leave it—with "The Latter Sign," still another sermon, published in 1682—for the present, and turn to "A Sermon *Wherein is shewed that the* Church of God *is sometimes a Subject* of Great Persecution." [38] From France came news of the Protestants' sufferings under Louis XIV, and Mather hastened to remind his people that they, too, had cause to fear. Sins they had, and Satan was strong. God might well send persecution to chasten them. They had quarrelled foolishly among themselves. "Have not we been like foolish little Birds, Pecking at one another, until the great Kite be ready to come, and devour one as well as another?" (pp. 19, 20.) Faith once more conquers fear. "If per-

36. I. Mather, *Call from Heaven*, Preface.

37. The full title is: "*Returning unto God the great concernment of a Covenant People.* Or A Sermon *Preached to the second Church in* Boston *in* New-England, *March* 17. 16$\frac{79}{80}$. *when that Church did solemnly and explicitly* Renew their Covenant *with God, and one with another.*" Boston, 1680.

38. The full title is: "A Sermon *Wherein is shewed that the* Church of God *is sometimes a Subject of* Great Persecution; Preached on a Publick Fast At *Boston* in *New-England:* Occasioned by the Tidings of a great *Persecution* Raised against the *Protestants* in *France.*" Boston, 1682.

secution do come, the event of it will, by the overruling Hand of divine providence, be good" (p. 22). Terror is not necessary, but rather "Labour for Syncerity" and thankfulness to God. Remembering what was to come, there is a hint of unconscious irony in the words "Never any people in the world, had greater cause of Thankfulness unto God, than we have had. In respect of our *Civil* Libertyes; wherein we have been admirably priviledged; and which God has to a wonderment, continued to us" (p. 23).

His last published sermons before 1684, included in a little book of "Practical Truths," are, perhaps, the most readable of all.[39] They are based primarily on the New Testament, and though such titles as "Sleeping at Sermons is a Great and a Dangerous Evil," and "It is the Property of a Sincere Godly Man Not to Sit with Vain Persons," are, if one will, characteristically Puritanical, the greater part of the book deals with the essentials of Christianity in all ages, prayer, personal consecration, and communion with the church. The charm — and charm is not an inept word, if one will but take pains to read the book — lies most of all in the writer's enthusiasm, in his faith and his devotion to his readers. He is eager that they share with him the spiritual absorption that gave meaning to his life. To them, his "Most Dearly Beloved," he writes: "And if I (who, you will all say, have not been wont to flatter you) take notice of some vertues, wherein the Lord hath caused you to excel, and shine as lights unto others, *I* trust *I* shall therein, follow the holy Example of the Lord Jesus Christ, who doth not only reprove the failings, but take notice of the Graces in His Churches, before all the world." [40] Where is the "grim" Puritan, and his ideal of a stern and tyrannical God?

Mather's book was printed at the expense of certain members of the Second Church.[41] It was well adapted for its readers. Their queries are answered, as, for example, when the common objections to prayer, still heard, — "I have n't time," "I am ashamed," — are put to rest. And even in the least "modern" of all the sermons, the argument against sleeping at sermons,

39. The full title is: "Practical Truths Tending to Promote the *Power of Godliness:* Wherein Several Important *Duties*, are Urged, and the Evil of divers common Sins, is Evinced; Delivered in Sundry Sermons." Boston, 1682.

40. Preface. One wonders why John Higginson thought the book would have been more useful without the preface. Cf. *MHS Coll.*, Series 4, viii, 282.

41. Preface.

theoretical objections are supported by eminently practical suggestions as to how to keep awake!

The book, of course, is written with an eye on the man in the street. So, perhaps, were the histories; but there is a third class of Mather's writings, more limited in range, more scholarly in tone, and designed for those to whom theological problems and doctrines were of deep concern. Such was the "Discourse on Baptism," [42] following hard upon "The First Principles of New England." Its defence of the Half-Way Covenant is not argument for argument's sake, or talking for victory, but a plea made persuasive by moderate utterance. Mather tried to avoid "such bitter invectives against Dissenters, as Polemical writings are many times full of." [43] He says, "These things should make us wise & moderate in our notions," for "they that have a righteous Cause are wont to be . . . zealous for the Truth" (p. 75). "I shall finish with the *Words* of that famous *African Synod* fourteen hundred years agoe, being come to the *Conclusion*, of the Controversie then under debate, concerning the Subject and time of Baptisme they yet say, *Neminem Iudicamus si diversum in hac re senserit*, we Censure no man, albeit as to this Question, he be not altogether of our Judgement" (p. 76).

Mather returned again to the controversy on baptism in his "Divine Right of Baptism" [44] — this time an argument against the Baptists on the ground that they would deprive children of their right to be placed in infancy under the protection of the Church. The "Anabaptists" had given trouble in New England. They had installed as minister a man excommunicated from the Congregational church, and, when their meeting-house was closed to them, they persisted in assembling publicly before its barred doors rather than worship unmolested in a private house.[45] To Mather these were attacks upon the true faith, and manifest disturbances of the civil peace. Naturally there is some acidity in his strictures on the "blasted Error" of "Antipedobaptism" (p. 20). Against it he urged even "the light of nature." He

42. The full title is: "A Discourse Concerning *the Subject of Baptisme* Wherein the present Controversies, that are agitated in the *New English Churches* are from *Scripture* and *Reason* modestly enquired into." Cambridge, 1675.

43. Preface.

44. The full title is: "The Divine Right of Infant-Baptisme *Asserted and Proved from* Scripture and Antiquity." Boston, 1680.

45. *MHS Proc.*, xxxiii, 399ff., entry for March 13, 1679–80, and *Memorial History of Boston*, i, 195, n. 3.

denounces Baptists roundly enough, points to their kindred with the turbulent Anabaptists in Europe, and writes: "Are they not generally of a bad Spirit? Bitter enemies to the Lords most eminent Servants? yea, to his faithful Ambassadors, spitting the cruel venome of Asps against them." There is cogency in his "To snarle at the Shepherds is no sign of a sheep" (p. 21). Yet there is relief from intolerant gloom in such lines as "I do not . . . Judge simple Antipedobaptists as Hereticks. I have known of that way not only in *New England*, but in *England* and in *Ireland*, that I believe were sincerely Conscientious" (p. 20); and "My design in writing these things, is not to stigmatize all that through weakness of Conscience scruple Infant Baptism; some of which, their error notwithstanding, [I] could imbrace with both arms, for I believe God hath received them" (pp. 24, 25). President Oakes, introducing the book, writes: "It is sufficiently known to those that know the Author, that he is none of the Ishmaels of the times, that have their hand against every man, and love to be taking a Dog by the Ears . . . or to be dabling in the waters of strife. . . . They that know his Doctrine and manner of life, cannot but know that the life of his Spirit is in the things of practical Divinity, and the great Design of his Ministry is to promote the power and practice of piety in the greatest instances . . . I dare undertake . . . his design . . . is not to traduce . . . those that are otherwise minded, or expose them to severities & sufferings on the bare account of their opinion."[46] Nor is the modern reader likely to disagree.

Out of the war grew Mather's "Earnest Exhortation,"[47] full of warnings to his people. Quarrels, profiteering, and excessive demands of labor are things to be banned. The Indians are to be converted, not harried and oppressed. Once more there is no sign of the conventional Puritan of outworn interests and zeal for deeds of blood.

As the "Earnest Exhortation" was coupled with one of his histories, so to the other he joined "An Historical Discourse Concerning the Prevalency of Prayer."[48] This was written to

46. Preface.

47. The full title is: "An Earnest Exhortation *To the Inhabitants of* New-England, *To hearken to the voice of God in his late and present Dispensations* As ever they desire to escape another Judgement, seven times greater then any thing which as yet hath been." Boston, 1676. The book was bound with the first Boston edition of Mather's "Brief History of the War," separately paged.

48. The full title is: "*An* Historical Discourse Concerning the Prevalency of Prayer.

prove "that *New-Englands* Late Deliverance from the Rage of the Heathen is an Eminent Answer to Prayer." This Mather did by collecting instances of signal mercies shown to men in answer to their pleas to God. Whatever our judgment may be as to the witnesses he relied on, they were of authority in his time, at least, nor may we forget that it is possible sometimes to be sceptical as to the evidence used in some modern treatises of the power of prayer.

But sinful Massachusetts did not limit Mather's pen. In 1682 a little volume of his saw the light in Amsterdam. Written in Latin, its title was "Diatriba de Signo Filii Hominis, et de Secundo Messiae Adventu; ubi de modo futurae Judaeorum Conversionis; Nec non de signis Novissimi diei, disseritur"—a sufficient index of its content.[49] Obviously it is a book for theological scholars, a New Englander's effort to take his place in the larger world of religious learning. For us, the fact that the book was published in Holland, and that he hoped for its success, praying characteristically that God might "owne" his "labors in writing that work,"[50] is, perhaps, its greatest claim to interest. There were here seeds for a reputation not confined to Boston, and in the tale of Mather's later years, their full flowering finds proof.

Historian, preacher, and scholarly writer, Mather was eminently equipped to lend useful support to any book to be sold in Boston. Accordingly we find him more than once signing the prefaces to works by other hands. A second edition of his brother Eleazar's "Serious Exhortation" contained a new preface by Increase Mather.[51] He performed the same office for James Fitch's "The First Principles of the Doctrine of Christ," arguing for the writing and use of catechisms.[52] Samuel Torrey also

Wherein is shown that *New-Englands* Late Deliverance from the Rage of the Heathen is an Eminent Answer to Prayer." Boston, 1677. A reprint is in S. G. Drake, *Early History of New England*, p. 241.

49. "Diatriba de Signo Filii Hominis, et de Secundo Messiæ Adventu; *Ubi* de modo *futurae Judæorum Conversionis; Nec non de* signis *Novissimi diei*, disseritur." Amstelodami, 1682.

50. MS. *Diary*, 1680–84, June 22, 1682.

51. The full title is: "A Serious Exhortation to the Present and Succeeding Generation *in New-England*, Earnestly calling upon all to endeavour that the Lord's *Gracious Presence* may be continued with *Posterity*. Being the substance of the Last Sermons preached By Mr. *Eleazer Mather ... The second Edition*." Boston, 1678.

52. The title is: "The first Pinciples [*sic*] of the Doctrine of *Christ*...." Boston, 1679. Mather's preface is dated 4.m. 23.d. 1679. Fitch was minister in Norwich, Connecticut.

turned to him, for an introduction to the "Plea for the Life of Dying Religion";[53] and after Oakes's death, "New Englands Samuel," a "Seasonable Discourse," found among his lecture notes, was given to the press by Mather, who added a preface of his own.[54] His "Nor is there anything more offensive to the Lord Iesus then luke-warmnesse in profession, or having a Name to live, and being dead," reveals much. There is more than a hint of his understanding of his times, in the question, "Are not some weary of that *Theocracy*, or *Government* which God hath established amongst us, as to sacred, and civill respects, willing for a change in both?"

For Samuel Willard he wrote two prefaces. The first, for "Covenant-Keeping, The Way to Blessedness,"[55] has nothing to mark it for special attention, but the second gives a valuable glimpse at Mather's views on current affairs. Willard, although Randolph believed him to be inclined to tolerance,[56] had no love for Anabaptists, and in his "Ne Sutor Ultra Crepidam"[57] answers what he dubbed their "Late Fallacious Narrative."[58] Mather's preface sums up his views on toleration, sketched elsewhere, and puts so plainly the Puritan side of the controversy in regard to persecution of other sects, that much of it deserves quoting. "Certain Complainants," he writes, "say they understand that the present Honourable Governour of this Colony, had threatned this poor people . . . with death: which report of theirs, is like too many particulars in their vindication, an *utter mistake*. . . . The Governour . . . hath sometimes moved, that an old severe Law made against those that should manifest any publick contempt of that ordinance of *Infant Baptisme*, might be lenifyed." As to persecution for opinions we read: "I have been a poor labourer in the Lords Vineyard in this place upwards of

53. The title is: "A Plea *For the Life of* Dying Religion *from the Word of the Lord.*" Boston, 1683.

54. The full title is: "*A Seasonable Discourse* Wherein *Sincerity & Delight in the Service of God* is earnestly pressed upon *Professors of Religion.*" Cambridge, 1682.

55. Boston, 1682. Mather's preface is dated November 15, 1682.

56. R. N. Toppan, *Edward Randolph*, iii, 148.

57. The full title is: "*Ne Sutor ultra Crepidam.* Or Brief Animadversions Upon the *New-England* Anabaptists Late Fallacious *Narrative; Wherein the Notorious Mistakes and Falshoods* by them *Published, are Detected.*" Boston, 1681.

The sub-title of this book has sometimes been listed as a work by Increase Mather. This is probably due to a confusion of the sub-title with the knowledge that Mather wrote the preface for it. No copy of a book by Mather with such a title has been found, so far as I know.

58. This was a book by John Russell, a Baptist.

twenty years: and it is more than I know, if in all that time, any of those that scruple Infant-Baptisme, have met with molestation from the Magistrate meerly on the account of their Opinion." On tolerance in general: "It is evident, that that Toleration is in one place, not only lawful, but a necessary duty, which in another place would be destructive; and the expectation of it irrational. That which is needful to ballast a great ship, will sink a small boat. If a considerable number of *Antipædobaptists* should (as our Fathers here did) obtain Liberty from the State, to transport themselves and families, into a wast *American wilderness,* that so they might be a peculiar People by themselves ... if now *Pædo-Baptists* should come after them, and intrude themselves upon them, and when they cast men out of their society for moral Scandals, entertain them: Surely they would desire such persons; either to walk orderly with them, or to return to the place from whence they came. And if they would do neither, they would think that such *Pædo-Baptists* were blame-worthy: let them do as they would be done by; and deal by us, as they would have us to deal by them; were they in our case, and we in theirs." As to the treatment of New England Baptists, "those of their perswasion in this place, have acted with so much irregularity and prophaneness, that should men of any other perswasion whatsoever, have done the like, the same severity would have been used towards them. . . . They say those of the Congregational way in *England, plead for Anabaptists liberty as for their own.* . . . When I was in *England,* I did so myself; and if I were their now, I would do so again: but that they should plead for liberty unto such practises, as our Anabaptists have been guilty of is not easie to believe." Here is argument from fact, not theory, and a view determined not by abstract ideas but by conditions of time and place. The last few pages sum up the Puritans' view so that he who runs may read. "Finally, let me intreat the Brethren to believe, that some of us would shew as much indulgence unto truly tender Consciences, as themselves. It is not so long since our own Necks bled under an intolerable yoke of Imposition upon Conscience; as that we should forget what it is to be so dealt with; or exercise that severity towards any, that we have ourselves complained of, in others." Tolerance is the ideal, but in practice there are problems. "But the Brethren will readily own, that some men have pretended Conscience, when pride & perverseness in the will, have been at the bottom: They will also confess, that a meer pretence of Conscience, is not enough to bear men out in an evil practice. All the difficulty is, in discerning the one of these from the other. ... If men will call unjustifiable *Practices* by the name of their *Opinion;* and when their evils are born witness against, make out cries, that they suffer for their Opinion, and for their Conscience: How is it possible, for those to help them, who desire to keep their own Consciences pure, and without offence towards God, by being faithful according to that capacity the Lord hath set them in?" When we can answer such a question adequately, we may fairly attack the Puritan view. Until we can, and it is not easy, we may grant that those whose case Mather stated, for their day and according to their lights, acted not quite without reason.[59]

A last group of books brings us to a new and less known side of Mather's thought. In England, science was developing fast.[60] In New England, though it be true that Puritanism offered poor soil, some seeds of the new investigating spirit took root. One remembers that the younger John Winthrop corresponded with, and became a member of, the Royal Society,[61] but it is less often recalled that he was not alone among New Englanders in his scientific bent. Least of all do we bear in mind that Increase Mather, ardent divine as he was, was a pioneer in stimulating scientific research. In 1681 he published a sermon "Heaven's Alarm to the World." [62] At first sight this is as radical an example as could be wished for, of the theological as opposed to the scientific view. He wrote frankly, "Concerning those admirable; and amazing works of God, which are by us called *Comets*, as under a *Physical* and *Mathematical* Consideration, there are many that have published their Sentiments, and some to good purpose and edification. The scope of the ensuing discourse is only (that being proper for one under my circumstances) to make a *Theo-*

59. Some interesting sidelights on the opinion of Mather's contemporaries as to his preface to Willard's book, and as to toleration in general, are found in the letters printed in the *MHS Coll.*, Series 4, viii. Simon Bradstreet, Harvard 1660, writes from London in 1681, saying that Mather might well have gone further in his attack on the Baptists (p. 477). He referred to "that cursed Bratt Toleration" (p. 478).

60. Cf., for example, H. D. Traill and J. S. Mann, *Social England*, iv, 553ff.

61. Cf. *DNB*, and T. G. Wright, *Literary Culture, passim.*

62. The full title is: "*Heavens Alarm to the World.* Or A Sermon Wherein is Shewed, *That fearful Sights and Signs in Heaven are the Presages of great Calamities at hand.*" Boston, 1681. There were two impressions of this work, the second being Boston, 1682. It was also printed in the *Kometographia.*

logical Improvement thereof." [63] He then urges that, in accordance with traditional belief as to comets, the "blazing star" of 1680 may well be regarded as a warning to New England. Two years later, in "The Latter Sign," [64] a sermon on the comet of 1682, he returns to the same view, but it is striking to note that the new astronomy has left its mark. He begins to realize the possibility that comets may not be prodigies revealing God's anger, but normal products of natural law. Even so the lesson is not lost, for "Divines lay it down as a Principle of Truth, That *Things, which proceed from Natural causes, if Unusual, are Signal*" (p. 29).

Before looking at his third book on this theme, a glance at the ancient doctrine of comets may not be out of place. [65] The theological party supported the belief that heavenly apparitions were God's signs of warning to men, and this idea held sway throughout the sixteenth century. If a Copernicus, a Paracelsus, or a Scaliger (whom Mather read), [66] denounced the old view, Polydore Vergil, Jean Bodin, or John Knox and John Howe, were spokesmen of the great mass of people who still held the old theory. Tycho Brahe and Kepler made discoveries that shook the traditional faith, and Thomas Browne early had his doubts. [67] But even in the late years of the seventeenth century, "we have English authors of much power battling for this supposed scriptural view"; and Ralph Thoresby, though well enough informed to be a member of the Royal Society, in 1682 firmly cherished the old doctrine. Even to the end of the seventeenth century, the oath usually required of professors of astronomy in Europe forbade their teaching that comets obeyed natural laws.

But the sceptics were busy. Bayle, writing after 1680, did much to replace dogma by science, and the new discoveries of Tycho Brahe and Kepler fermented in men's minds. These

63. Preface.

64. The full title is: "The Latter Sign Discoursed of, In A Sermon *Preached at the Lecture of* Boston *in* New-England *August*, 31. 1682. Wherein is shewed, that the Voice of God in Signal Providences, especially when repeated and Iterated, ought to be Hearkned unto." No imprint. Bound with the *Kometographia*.

65. For a convenient summary, see A. D. White, "A History of the Doctrine of Comets," in *Papers of the American Historical Association*, vol. ii, No. 2; or vol. i, chap. 4 of the same writer's *A History of The Warfare of Science with Theology*.

66. He refers to Scaliger's views, and had cited him earlier in his *Mystery of Israel's Salvation*.

67. A. D. White, *A History*, i, 178ff., chap. 4; T. Browne, *Pseudodoxia Epidemica*, book vi, chap. 14.

scientists placed comets among the heavenly bodies, denying them fellowship with meteors and other "appearances in the neighborhood of the earth." This, we are told, "dealt a blow at the very foundations of the theological argument, and gave a great impulse to the idea that comets are themselves heavenly bodies moving regularly and in obedience to law." Hevel worked to develop the new theory, and its victory came finally with Halley's and Newton's proof that comets are subject to law and that their coming can be foretold. Some still clung to the old idea, others compromised by saying that comets "might be heavenly bodies moving in regular orbits, and even obedient to law, and yet be sent as 'signs in the heavens.'" Such was Semler's view in 1770; and even in the nineteenth century there were outcroppings here and there of belief in the power of comets to influence dwellers on earth.[68]

Both Halley and Newton completed their scientific pioneering in regard to comets after 1680.[69] In writing his "Kometographia," published in 1683, Mather was a contemporary student of the same phenomena.[70] He does not here confine himself to theology, but says, "I have added some things of the *nature, place; motion of Comets*, which only such as have some skill in *Astronomy* can understand."[71] He accepts definitely the new theory that comets are heavenly bodies, although we are assured that this idea was so opposed to the theological view as to be fatal to it.[72] He maintains that they move regularly, like the planets, and that they may be of exactly the same nature as the true planets. He is doubtful as to their origin, but thinks they are probably groups of small stars collected into a body. We have not progressed far from this view.[73] He notes that comets move faster than planets. He doubts whether "the time of any Comets appearance" can "certainly be prædicted before hand," but admits that "some very learned men have supposed the knowl-

68. A. D. White, *A History*, i, 181, 183, 196ff., 201–203, 204, 205.

69. *Ibid.*, pp. 203, 204.

70. The title is: "КОМНТОГРАФІА. Or A Discourse Concerning Comets; *Wherein the Nature of Blazing Stars is Enquired into:* With an Historical Account of all the Comets which have appeared from the Beginning of the World unto this present Year, M.DC.LXXXIII. *Expressing* The Place in the Heavens, where they were seen, Their Motion, Forms, Duration; and the Remarkable Events which have followed in the World, so far as they have been by Learned Men Observed." Boston, 1683.

71. Preface.

72. *Kometographia*, pp. 1–3; White, A *History*, ii, 201, 202.

73. Cf. J. A. Thomson (ed.), *The Outline of Science*, p. 22.

edge is obtainable," and calls their belief "a *probable conjecture*" (p. 16). Though he thinks that there are direct physical effects upon the earth from cometary influence (pp. 132, 133), — an idea by no means dead, as one remembers, when our world last passed through a comet's tail, — [74] he says flatly: "The great Revolutions and Conjunctions of the *Planets* come to pass according to the ordinary course of nature" (pp. 19, 20). He condemns astrology and its practitioners, with a special attack on that "*blind but insolent Buzzard*, William Lilly." [75] In short, he is quite abreast of the scientific thought of the day in his remarks as to the phenomena he studied. When he applies his observations to theology, he takes his position, not upon the dogmatic assertion of the traditional theological theory, but, instead, upon the newer compromise maintained for a century after him. "There are who think," he writes, "that inasmuch as Comets may be supposed to proceed from natural causes, there is no *speaking voice of Heaven* in them, beyond what is to be said of all other works of God. But certain it is, that many things which may happen according to the course of nature, are portentous signs of divine anger" (p. 18). From history he draws instances of comets' preceding earthly calamities, and, for his own part, is content to hold that a comet, however subject to fixed law, is none the less a warning sign. God rules planets, comets, and the universe. If heavenly apparitions occur at fixed seasons, known to men, can men therefore ignore the fact that God may purpose, at the same fixed seasons, to chasten the world? Modern science, with its detailed explanation of phenomena, does not answer the prime question as to the moving cause, which Mather held to be the Lord. With a faith as great as his, the mere fact that a comet appeared periodically could not shake his conviction that God wished periodically to warn his children. Even so, the most he says is that "blazing stars" are "*most commonly*" signs of evil portent, and he admits that some may herald good things. All that he insists upon is that they precede earthly changes and, as there is room left to fear the worst, "It is certainly much better for men to prepare for the worst, then that Judgement should overwhelm them in their sin" (pp. 133–135).

Whatever one thinks of the theological compromise he proposes, his book quite defies classification as one which "supports

74. Cf. also, White, *A History*, i, 205.
75. Cf. *DNB*, and note Evelyn's *Diary*, Sept. 3, 1699.

the theological cometary theory fully."[76] Instead, his doctrine is most cautiously expressed. Nor is it fair to say that the scientific view was a source of alarm to him,[77] for, far from showing fear, he makes Kepler and Hevel two of his main authorities, cites Tycho Brahe, and Robert Hook, and makes repeated use of the publications of the Royal Society.[78] He accepts some of the newest scientific tenets, and his attempt to combine them with his religious views results in a position held by others for a century after him, and not wholly abandoned to-day.

One must admit, perhaps, that in the matter of comets, Mather was in the front rank of his time. How many other New Englanders can be shown to have reached the same advanced plane of scientific thought? How many men in England, not professional scientists, are abreast of him? Yet even if one clings to the convenient popular doctrine that he was a Puritan blinded to truth by the muffling of dogma, and ignores his books, there are obstacles even harder to down. To Mather Joseph Eliot writes in 1678: "when your engine comes from London to advance speech so incredibly . . . if it wil promote any thing toward our confabulation at this distance, or if it were much nearer than you mention in your letter, I should think the better of Squire Morland."[79] Now Sir Samuel Morland, tutor of Pepys, Fellow of the Royal Society, mathematician and inventor, was one of the chief mechanicians of the time.[80] An interest in his work marks a minister in remote New England as by no means a close-minded and provincial preacher. Whatever the "engine" was,[81] the man who heard of it three thousand miles away, and ordered it, is not one to call devoid of intellectual curiosity.[82] And, finally, there is positive evidence that on one point Mather, in his eager interest in scientific progress, anticipated his fellow townsmen by many years.

In 1683, says Mather, "I promoted a design for a private philo-

76. A. D. White, *A History*, i, 195.   77. *Ibid.*, i, 196.
78. On Brahe's opposition to the "theological" view, cf. *Ibid.*, vol. i, chap. 4.
79. *MHS Coll.*, Series 4, viii, 377, 378.
80. Cf. *DNB*.
81. One cannot be sure what the "engine" Mather was interested in was. Morland invented the speaking trumpet — perhaps the reference is to this. The editors of the *Mather Papers* point to a reference in *MHS Coll.*, Series 4, vi, 500ff., which seems to suggest " a foreshadowing of the magnetic telegraph." See *Ibid.*, Series 4, viii, 377 n.
82. This statement, obviously contradicted repeatedly by the facts of Mather's life and work, — see especially p. 395 of this volume,— is made by V. L. Parrington, in the *Cambridge History of American Literature*, i, 49.

sophical society in Boston, which I hope may have laid the foundation for that which will be for future edification." Cotton Mather called it "a *Philosophical Society* of Agreeable Gentlemen, who met once a Fornight for a Conference upon Improvements in *Philosophy* and Additions to the Stores of *Natural History*." [83] A Dutch scholar is said to have used material they collected,[84] and "One that had a share in that Combination . . . now a Fellow of the Royal Society in *London*, afterwards transmitted communications thither" from the observations of this first scientific "academy" in Boston.[85] Cotton Mather clearly refers to himself, and the dates of some of the phenomena described in his letters to the Royal Society make it plain that more than a little of his material may have come from the fortnightly meetings of his father's club of "agreeable Gentlemen." [86]

That the institution did not survive is not strange. The political upheaval of the next few years, "the Calamity of the Times,"[87] struck a death-blow to more than one Boston enterprise. The important fact is that Mather's society, while it lasted, discussed matters worthy of the attention of the Royal Society as late as 1712, and that it actually did what so sound a judge as Jonathan Mayhew declared was still too far advanced for the Boston of 1760.[88]

Books and men were absorbing, but the centre of Mather's life was still his church. When fire drove his congregation from their first building, he housed them wherever the hospitality of his fellow ministers offered. A striking sidelight on his character

83. *Autobiography; Parentator*, p. 86; MS. *Diary*, 1680–84, April 23 and Mar. 25 1683.

84. "From which [the proceedings of the Boston society] the learned *Wolferdus Senguerdius* a Professor at Leyden had some of the Materials, wherewith his *Philosophia Naturalis* was Enriched." *Parentator*, p. 86. A hasty examination of the *Philosophia Naturalis* reveals nothing directly credited to the Boston society, but, of course, their work may have been used none the less, without definite mention of its source.

85. *Parentator*, p. 86.

86. Cotton Mather became a member of the Royal Society. See G. L. Kittredge, "Cotton Mather's Election into the Royal Society," in *Col. Soc. Pub.*, xiv, and reprinted separately, Cambridge, 1912; and Idem, "Cotton Mather's Scientific Communications to the Royal Society," in *American Antiquarian Society Proceedings*, xxvi, 18ff. His letters to the Society are accessible in the Gay Transcripts at the Massachusetts Historical Society. Examples of his describing phenomena observed prior to the time of the establishment of the Boston "Society" are to be found in the volume of transcripts of his letters, pp. 133, 136, 148. On p. 108 he relates an episode of 1687 — perhaps this too came through his father and his friends.

87. *Parentator*, p. 86.

88. MS. vol. of "Hollis Papers," at the Massachusetts Historical Society, p. 5.

comes from the diary of that shrewd observer and sound business man, Samuel Sewall, who remarks: "One might gather by Mr Willards speech that there was some Animosity in him toward Mr Mather: for that he said he chose the Afternoon so that he might have a copious auditory: and that when the Town House was offered him to preach to his Church distinct, said he would not preach in a corner." [89] Jealous of his own prestige and of his church's standing, Mather was not inclined to take a second place even when he and his flock were without a roof to shelter them. Part of his attitude is explained by his character, in which a strongly practical bent ran often into something very like ambition. The deeds that were the expression of his faith, satisfied him best when their results were visible in the respect they won. At the same time, it was not mere self-seeking, or desire for eminence, that drove him sometimes to seem eager for public notice. Fundamental in his belief was the idea that the humblest divine was God's servant. [90] For such a one to be slighted was for the world to ignore the voice of Heaven. So also, for a minister to fail to preserve the dignity of his post, was to be false to a trust. Such is the argument Mather expounds to Michael Wigglesworth, now his colleague in the ministry. The older man wished to marry his "servant mayd." Not common snobbery or arrogance appears in Mather's entertaining remonstrances to his friend. Rather there is here pride in his profession, and a desire to uphold the sanctity of his cloth. [91]

By 1677 Increase and Cotton Mather ministered to the Second Church, unmolested by outside interference. Yet even in the church there were critics to be met. At dinner with the magistrates, Governor Leverett, Mather says, "reflected on me, on ye account of some passages in my serm^n. viz. yt strangers sd, yt yy had seen more drunkennes in N. E. in halfe a yeare yn in E. in all yir lives. Hee sd yt yy yt sd so lyed. And yt yr was more drunkennes in N. E. many years agoe yn yr is now, yea at ye first beginning of ys Colony." Mr. Stoughton suggested pleasantly that Mather preach a recantation sermon. But he was not easy to quell. "I told him, no, but if men wld not accept my Labors God will." And, privately, he reflects with a hint of acidity, and what one suspects was a pun: "As for ye Gover-

89. *MHS Coll.*, Series 5, v, 30.

90. His views on this are expressed in his sermon on "Sleeping at Sermons," in his *Practical Truths*.

91. *MHS Coll.*, Series 4, viii, 94, 95.

nor, He hath bin ye principal Author of ye multitude of ordinaries w^{c}h be in Boston, giving licenses wn ye townsmen wld not doe it. No wonder yt N. E. is visited wn ye Head is so spirited." [92] Again, on another day, "After ye church was gone," Captain Thomas Lake, soon to die in Philip's War, and Mather's good friend John Richards, told him "yt wn ministers did lay a solemn charge vpo^{n} people, it might take in ye ignorant, but no rational men wld regard wt was sd ye more for yt." His conception of the clergy's place is clear in his reply that "Truth had ye more Authority with it wn it came in such a way, as wn a Father injoyned ys or yt duty, yr was ye more weight spoke in wt was sd, bec. it came fro^{m} a Father." And he reminded them of the text, "Obey them that have the rule over you, and submit yourselves: for they watch for your souls, as they that must give account, that they may do it with joy and not with grief: for that is unprofitable for you." [93]

In the main, however, his sermons, his public services, and his visits to those who needed what he could give, sufficed to keep him firmly at the head of his people. His church gained nearly twice as many new members in the nine years from 1675 to 1683, as in the preceding nine years.[94] The most successful season in this respect, save one, was 1677, when twenty-eight members were added. One suspects that the lesson of the war, as Mather taught it, struck home. The greatest year of all was 1681, when thirty-five persons joined the Second Church.[95] Such facts carry refutation of the theory that religious interest was waning, and of the statements of travellers admittedly hostile to the Congregational way; nor can the citation of one individual, who wrote years later,[96] shake the force of the original record.

It is only on the personal side that we lack facts on Mather's life. Plain as is the tale of his activities, one would like a closer view of the human aspect of the character that carried him through them. Surely there was power of personality in the successful preacher, which lent force to his pleas. As for his appearance, we may get some idea of it, perhaps, from a mezzotint

92. *Diary*, Jan. 27, 1675–76.   93. *Ibid.*, Feb. 4, 1675–76.

94. For the preceding nine years there were 80 admissions; for the years in question, 143.

95. My figures are from a MS. copy of part of the original records. The copy is owned by the Second Church.

96. J. T. Adams, *The Founding*, p. 373, cites, as evidence of the state of feeling in the years before the loss of the charter, a letter written by John Bishop, in 1687.

owned by the Massachusetts Historical Society, which probably dates from 1683.[97]

The picture is sadly marred by time, but enough remains to show us a rather full oval face, a long broad nose, and a wide, half-smiling mouth. There are heavy lines under the eyes, suggesting the mark left by Mather's close study and his illnesses. It is not a beautiful portrait, but, allowing for the crudeness of drawing, one sees in it a face expressive of character, and one worth looking at more than once.

Whatever his appearance, Mather was certainly seen by his contemporaries as a leader, a fact proved once more in 1679 when it is he who prevails on his fellow workers to ask the General Court to call a Reforming Synod, to answer two questions: "What are the euills that have provoked the Lord to bring his judgements on New England?" and "What is to be done so that those evills may be reformed?" [98]

The delegates met in September, 1679, and Mather was prominent in their councils. At the close of the first session he was chosen, with Oakes and others, to draw up for the Court the Synod's result. In October this work was ready, and printed as "The Necessity of Reformation." At its presentation, Mather preached "a very Potent Sermon." [99]

The same committee had been charged with the preparation of a new Confession of Faith. "Mather and Oakes had been in England while the Savoy Synod was in Session," and their proposed "platform" for the local church was, with few changes, the Savoy Confession.[100] This was presented to the second session of the Synod, held in May, 1680. At that time, "though there were many Elder, and some Famous, Persons in that Venerable Assembly, yet Mr. *Mather* was chosen their *Moderator*." [101]

97. Cf. K. B. Murdock, *The Portraits of Increase Mather.*

98. W. Walker, *Creeds and Platforms*, pp. 412–414, 416.

99. *Ibid.*, pp. 416–419; *Parentator*, p. 85. The result of the Synod was printed with the title: "The Necessity of Reformation With the Expedients subservient thereunto, asserted; in Answer to two *Questions* I. *What are the Evils that have provoked the Lord to bring his Judgments on New-England?* II. *What is to be done that so those Evils may be Reformed? Agreed upon by the Elders and Messengers of the Churches assembled in the Synod At* Boston *in* New-England, Sept. 10. 1679." Boston, 1679.

In view of Cotton Mather's statement (*Parentator*, p. 85), the book is usually included among Increase Mather's works. For a reprint of it, see Walker, *Creeds and Platforms*, pp. 423ff.

100. *Ibid.*, pp. 420, 421, 340–408.

101. *Parentator*, p. 87.

He served, and carried the meeting to a successful end, though "he was then Ill, under the Approaches & Beginnings of a *Fever*." This was to be for him one more of the serious sicknesses that checkered his life, and, for the town, an occasion of fasting and prayer for his recovery.[102] Early in September he began to preach again,[103] and that he had regained by 1683 not only his health but his vigor of speech, is proved by the year's events.

We have seen that by this date English hostility to the Massachusetts Charter had gone dangerously far. The agents had been worsted in their unequal combat with the Stuarts' imperial policy, fostered day by day, as it was, by that indefatigable foe of Puritans, Edward Randolph. Delay and evasion could no longer serve the colony's turn. It was a time for leadership and action. Increase Mather, foremost in the college and in church councils, influential in a large Boston congregation, known abroad, and proved a skilful and popular writer, was ideally equipped to defend New England. Silence in such times would have been for him treachery to his faith.

Opportunity came quickly. In October, 1683, a *Quo Warranto* "against the Charter and Government" of Massachusetts was issued, and Dudley and Richards returned to Boston. Close upon their heels came Randolph, bearing the *Quo Warranto* itself. With it arrived a royal "Declaration" promising that, if the colony would make full submission to his will, the king would simply regulate and alter the Charter, as seemed best to him.[104] The Governor, Simon Bradstreet, and the Assistants, with a prudent eye on political considerations, voted to answer humbly in accordance with the king's pleasure. The deputies, representing the outlying towns, less interested in trade than in the keeping of the established order, opposed the vote.[105] In Boston a meeting of the freemen was called, to consider what answer they should make toward the breaking of the deadlock.

Though the freemen were all church members, and thus inclined, perhaps, to vote to keep the Charter, which seemed indispensable to the success of Congregationalism, there were among them, none the less, many men who knew the value of temporizing in a matter likely to affect the relations of the colony

102. *Autobiography; Long Island Historical Society Memoirs*, i, 380.
103. MS. *Diary*, Sept. 6, 1680.
104. T. Hutchinson, *History*, i, 338; *Memorial History of Boston*, i, 375.
105. Hutchinson, *History*, i, 338, 339.

and the mother country in regard to trade. They included some, as we have seen, not wholly under the clergy's spell. There were varied opinions and classes, merchants with English interests beside men for whom the world began and ended in Boston, in the crowd that filled the Town-house on January twenty-first, 1683–84.[106] They had read the king's "Declaration," and also Mather's "Elaborate Answer to it," [107] with his assurance that they would "act neither the part of *Good Christians*, nor of *True Englishmen*, if by any Act of theirs they should be Accessary to the *Plot* then manageing to produce a *General Shipwreck of Liberties*." They had heard his foes call him the "Mahomet of New England," and when, at the request of the Boston deputies, he appeared before them in the crowded Town-house that January day, they knew him as a man committed to a policy.[108] His fame made his words tell, and the most hostile in his audience must perforce have listened with some degree of respect.

In Cranfield's words, Mather indulged in "insolent speeches."[109] The scene is pictured best, possibly, in his own record: "I made a short speech to the freemen in these words: 'As the question is now stated, (viz., whether you will make a full submission & entire resignation of the Charter, & privileges of it to his Majesty's pleasure,) we shall sin against God if we vote an affirmative to it. The Scripture teaches us otherwise. . . . Nor would it be wisdom in us to comply. We know that David made a wise choice when he chose to fall into the hands of God rather than into the hands of man. If we make a submissive & entire resignation, we fall into the hands of men immediately. But if we do it not, we keep ourselves still in the hands of God, & trust ourselves with his providence. And who knows what God may do for us? Moreover, there are examples before our eyes, the consideration whereof should be of weight with us. Our brethren hard by; what have they gained by their readiness to submit & comply? Who, if they had abode by their liberties longer would not have been miserable so soon. And we hear from London, that when it came to, the loyal citizens would not make a full submission and entire resignation to pleasure, lest, haply, their posterity should

106. MS. *Diary*, Jan. 21, 1683–84; *Autobiography* and *Parentator* (p. 90) give Jan. 23 as the date.

107. *Parentator*, p. 90. Mather's answer may be the document printed in *MHS Coll.*, Series 3, i, 74.

108. *Parentator*, p. 90; *Autobiography*.

109. *Cal. State Papers, Am. and W. I.*, vol. xi ⚹ 1683.

curse them. And shall we do it then? I hope there is not one freeman in Boston that will dare to be guilty of so great a sin.'" [110]

Mather surely realized, as he spoke, how much depended on his words. If he did not foresee how much the result of this, his first important entry into politics, was to affect his career in future years, he cannot have ignored its meaning for New England at the moment. If his appeal were heeded, there would be not only a vindication of his personal power, but a heavy weight to turn the scale of general opinion in the colony. If, on the other hand, the townsmen tamely threw themselves upon the royal mercy, it must seem to him a personal defeat and a death-blow to what he passionately believed were the highest ideals of New England.

The issue was not long in doubt. From the crowd in the hall, one man, outraged by the speech, rose, and left "in great heat." [111] Then "Many of the Freemen fell into Tears; and there was a General Acclamation, *We Thank you, Syr! We Thank you, Syr!*" The question was put, and carried against submission, without a single dissenting vote. "This act of Boston had a great influence on the country." [112]

110. *Autobiography; Parentator*, p. 91.
111. R. N. Toppan, *Edward Randolph*, iv, 244.
112. *Parentator*, p. 92; *Autobiography*.

CHAPTER XII

"ILLUSTRIOUS PROVIDENCES," AND THE FLIGHT TO ENGLAND

FOR New England the meeting of the Boston freemen, however great its influence on opinion, worked little practical result. England's plans, and the current of political development, had gone too far to be checked. But to Mather not only did it prove that, at forty-four, he was a man of personal power in Boston, and one whose word was to be reckoned with in public concerns, but it opened for him a new field. The next five years of his life were marked by an increasing interest in civil affairs. Thence came troubles, abuse, and, finally, his bold entry into what is, in many ways, the most actively interesting of all his undertakings — his mission to England.

The years from 1683 to 1688 were, of course, a period of the most profound public unrest in New England. No one in Boston who thought at all could deafen himself to the news that matters of vital moment were on foot. No one lived those years without realizing that then if ever were needed leaders to speak for all the parties in the political turmoil. Mather "behaved with so much prudence, as to give no room to take hold of any part of his conduct." [1] Yet he was not idle, and his voice and pen were lent more than once on the side of what be believed to be the right.

In all these troubled years, he never failed to find time for his church. He remained first of all Boston's leading divine, and no mere civil disturbance shook his unswerving loyalty to his pastoral work. In the college he won new prominence, and to it he turned yearly more of his active interest. Finally, as an author, he did not allow his star to wane. Year by year Boston presses printed his sermons and treatises. Boston booksellers sold them over their counters as the unquestioned "leading books" and, almost certainly, the "best sellers" of the day. And from the remote twentieth century, we mark this period as the birth-time of Mather's most enduring literary work.

1. T. Hutchinson, *History*, i, 366.

His activities can be seen only against the turbulent historical background of these years. No period in New England's history, perhaps, has been more written about. None, perhaps, offers more scope for controversy and debate. For us the bare facts may suffice, with such hints as we can get as to how they appeared at the time. Evaluation of the events of 1683 to 1688, from the point of view of later history, subsequent political theory, or twentieth-century doctrines of democracy, remains as far outside our range as it was beyond Mather's ken.

Briefly, then, the old charter of Massachusetts was declared vacated on October 23, 1684. Colonel Kirke, whose name still connotes cruelty in the exercise of authority, and was justly anathema to the Puritans, was appointed as the first royal governor under the new régime.[2] He was never sent to take up his duties, and Randolph assumed the credit, laying the saving of New England from the Colonel's "lambs" to his own diplomatic zeal.[3] Mather, on the other hand, believed that here was an answer to his eager prayers, and confirmation of what he saw as a heaven-sent consolation vouchsafed directly from above![4] Whatever the reason, it was not Kirke, but that first of New England's long line of adroit politicians, Joseph Dudley, who received James II's commission as chief executive in New England. Suspected by the more ardent defenders of the charter as a half-hearted worker in their cause, hailed by Randolph at first as a pliant tool and then rejected as a dangerous recalcitrant, he had by no means an easy course to trace.[5] Yet, on the whole, with such power as was given him, he governed justly. He saw that it was a time for gradual change, and for education of the people in the ideals of the new form of government. He detected a few, at least, of the weaknesses in the new scheme of things, and hoped to correct them. He received the king's commission from Randolph on May 14, 1686, two days after he had been defeated for election to the Court of Assistants. Not the vote of the people, or any part of them, but the royal decree, was now New England's law.[6]

2. Cf. *DNB; MHS Coll.*, Series 5, v, 87 n.
3. Cf. J. T. Adams, *The Founding*, pp. 407, 408, and references given there. Kirke's troops in Tangier were called his "lambs." Cf. *DNB*.
4. *Autobiography*.
5. E. Kimball, *The Public Life of Joseph Dudley*, pp. 17, 33, 34; R. N. Toppan, *Edward Randolph*, iii, 145–149, iv, 103–110.
6. Kimball, pp. 23, 24, 25.

Dudley faced no active resistance. Various members of the General Court sought to persuade him not to accept the royal appointment.[7] Increase Mather was present at one such conference, and Dudley, before his inauguration, sought his advice and support.[8] Advice he secured, no doubt; support he did not. He went on without it. For the time, opposition to the new government contented itself with wordy protests.

By the new commission, Massachusetts was placed in the hands of a president and a council of seventeen, all appointed by the king.[9] Hitherto the basis of the government had been an elected assembly. If the old system had been intolerant and undemocratic in denying the franchise to all who were not church members, the new plan was certainly in greater contradiction to any theory of direct popular representation. The President of Massachusetts now governed also Maine, New Hampshire, and the "King's Province" of Rhode Island. Thus the government of New England lay in the hands of a few men appointed by a king across the sea, and no one, whatsoever his position in the community, might vote as to who should make his laws. The Council had complete military, judicial and executive power. It could not legislate, or impose new taxes, but it could spend what was received from the revenue system already in force.

The members of Dudley's Council were wisely chosen. They represented well enough the territorial interests involved, but not so adequately the various social classes of the population. Seven of the councillors from Massachusetts had formerly been Assistants, but they were nearly all of one political color, and of them but three had won election when the voters last expressed their choice. They were enough in touch with Massachusetts standards and moods to avoid too decidedly unpopular measures. Moreover, they spoke for the old "liberties" of New England in asking the king for a popular assembly. This was denied, but the Council's request helped to keep such discontent as there was, smouldering unseen. If an individual offered resistance, here and there, he met prompt and sharp reproof.[10]

Dudley's rule was short. His successor was not equipped with the same insight into the temper of the colony. Sir Edmund

7. Kimball, p. 25; *MHS Coll.*, Series 5, v, 139.
8. T. Hutchinson, *History*, i, 352 n.
9. Kimball, pp. 27ff.
10. *Ibid.*, pp. 29, 32, 35.

Andros, an Englishman, who had proved his ability as royal governor of New York, landed in Boston on December 20, 1686.[11] Some of the colonists may early have suspected him as a "tyrant," and since their day he has been painted more than once as a model despot.[12] Most of his shortcomings may be explained as due to lack of tact, rather than to any desire to set up an oppressive rule. Nor should we forget that he had royal orders to carry out. His Council, however, found little to do, and came more and more to leave all the power in the governor's hands.[13] To Mather, Andros may well have seemed a sinister figure, for his very name harked back to the days when his father was in power in Guernsey, and when the government he represented "persecuted" Increase out of that island.[14] The colonists as a whole, however little predisposed to dread the new governor, soon found cause for complaint.

Official fees were increased, legal business was centralized in Boston, and, worst of all, land titles were said to have been impaired by the fall of the charter. Thus every owner of real estate in New England must pay for the validation of his right to his holdings, and the fees for this, at times, ran high. Moreover, Andros and his Council had power to impose such taxes as they wished.[15] At once the cry of "taxation without representation" was raised, and for upholding it John Wise of Ipswich and others were imprisoned.[16] This doctrine had quite as much power to inflame the popular mind in the seventeenth century as in the eighteenth.

As for the church under Dudley and Andros, the new government was committed ostensibly to liberty of conscience. It insisted upon the right of the Church of England to hold service, and refused to impose any political disabilities upon any citizen for his failure to meet a religious test. Thus far the new régime, seen from our safe distance, worked clearly for toleration and liberal ideals. Curiously enough, a government in most respects arbitrary, depriving New England of such popular control as she

11. *MHS Coll.*, Series 5, v, 159ff.

12. For views of Andros, see *Andros Tracts;* Channing, ii, 173ff.; and J. T. Adams, *The Founding*, pp. 411ff.

13. E. Kimball, *The Public Life*, p. 44, and references given there.

14. Amias, father of Edmund Andros, was made bailiff of Guernsey in 1651, but did not take office actually until 1661.

15. J. T. Adams, *The Founding*, pp. 414-425; Channing, ii, 179-185.

16. For Wise, see J. L. Sibley, *Biographical Sketches*, ii, 428ff.

had had, was, at the same time, the champion of liberty for religions, and the opponent of the old exclusive supremacy of one sect.[17] At the same time, the theory did not always appear so well in practice, and more than one event under the new laws was by no means reassuring to liberal-minded advocates of tolerance. The Church of England was to be not merely tolerated but especially privileged.[18] An English governor in New Hampshire, Bostonians remembered, had jailed a Congregational minister for his refusal to read the Anglican service.[19] Behind the scenes there was a movement toward setting up in the colony the supremacy of the established church of the mother country. Much of this must have been public knowledge, and lovers of toleration cannot have been impressed by proposals to tax Congregational churches to support the form of worship Andros favored.[20] If it be true that the Puritans had done the same thing in the interests of their church, it does not alter the fact that the change from the dominance of one sect to the dominance of another was merely change, not progress. And to the Puritans, still believing that their charter had been rightfully granted and had authorized them to form a church-state on Congregational lines, Andros's commandeering of the Old South Church for the English service seemed aggression against traditional rights.[21] Certainly it was no example of tolerance, inasmuch as the English chaplain had been allowed to minister to his congregation in the Town-house.[22]

To-day we may be thankful that the new government came. None of us would wish to live in a Puritan town, perhaps, and there are unlimited possibilities for conjecture as to what might have happened if the Congregational way had been suffered to flourish in close alliance with the civil power of the colony. But, to the Bostonians of the sixteen-eighties, the ultimate gain for liberty was not the most apparent feature in connection with the post-charter administration. To the Puritans it meant the loss of their position as leaders of the religious establishment.

17. J. T. Adams, *The Founding*, p. 420.

18. *Colonial Society Publications*, ii, 54.

19. J. Belknap, *History*, i, 204–211.

20. Randolph wrote to the Archbishop of Canterbury, in 1686: "I humbly represent to your grace, that the three meeting houses in Boston might pay twentey shillings a weeke, a piece ... towards the defraieing our church charges." T. Hutchinson, *Collection*, ii, 292.

21. J. T. Adams, *The Founding*, pp. 420, 421; and *MHS Coll.*, Series 5, v, 171.

22. *MHS Coll.*, Series 5, v, 141.

It meant the coming to New England of the same power that persecuted their fellow nonconformists in England. Red coats and gold lace, sword-play, may-poles, celebrations of Christmas, and the gaiety of Andros's followers, were direct violations of the Puritan's code of public morals. Suggestions that no marriage should be legal unless made according to the Book of Common Prayer, or that Congregationalists should contribute to support English forms of worship, seemed death-blows to their religious system. To the clergy, the new order meant a loss of power, and the exaltation of rivals for church leadership. Yet they were temperate, for the most part, in word and act, under the royal rule, and if Mather be taken as an example, there is little to show that their prime concern was with their own loss of prestige. To them the most serious innovation was the violation of the standards they held to have been divinely laid down for worship and conduct. To have ignored the danger would have been to make their life-work a mockery and to yield tamely to what they must see as an invasion of a new Eden by the sin of the world.[23]

Here and there, historians, mindful of later progress toward religious liberty in New England, suggest that the days under Andros were times when a cruel and narrow-minded group of ministers and church members opposed an enlightened people who welcomed the change in affairs as the dawning of freedom.[24] Fascinating as such visions are, they fade when one deals with the facts. One cannot fix the image of the Puritan preacher as the bloody persecutor restrained only by a progressive people. Too often the divine wrote and preached moderately, urging persuasion rather than force. From 1683 to 1688 there is only conjecture to support the idea that the clergy under Andros mourned the loss of their unquestioned supremacy, while the people heaved grateful sighs. Indeed, some of the ministers welcomed James II's proclamation of religious liberty, even in the face of shrewd objections from those who dreaded opening the door to equal opportunity for all creeds. As for the people, every church member lost his vote. If he was a sincere Puritan, he found about him many breaches of the rules of life he held to be right. If he was no more than a professing churchman, he was still likely to be imbued with the traditional idea of the colony's charter privileges. As for the man not a church member, and never a

23. *MHS Proc.*, xxiii, 399ff., entries for March 16, April 17, 23, 27, and May 1, 1687.
24. J. T. Adams, *The Founding*, pp. 396, 422.

voter, he was often, obviously, a church-goer and more or less moved by what he heard in the meeting-house, and, consequently, opposed to much that Andros brought. Finally, leaving religion out of account altogether, no man of property, no man with any legal business on his hands, can have failed to chafe now and then under the new management of official transactions and the new taxes. The only New Englander likely to find Andros and his Council ideal rulers, or an improvement on the old leaders, was the man who owned no property, paid no taxes, and had no interest in Puritan manners and rules of life, or the citizen who was so ardent in his devotion to the Church of England that he regarded the chance to hear its services read as a privilege outweighing disenfranchisement and royal taxes. There is not material here for a very substantial picture of an irate clergy, bent on intolerance and persecution, confronted by Edmund Andros and a "people" delighted at losing such popular representation as they had had, revelling in the chance to pay their earnings to the governor's agents, and serenely aware that the new system was working toward a freer New England to come years later.

As for Mather, he continued busily following out his many-sided career. Whatever his growing concern with public interests, the staple elements of his life-work were not neglected.

At home the progress of his seven children gave him a chance to put his strict views on religious education into force. Nathaniel, a hard student, was finishing his course at Harvard. In 1685 and 1686 he published two almanacs, and his promise brought joy to his household.[25] There were shadows, too; for one more loss, this time of a brother, helped to teach Increase Mather that his family were by no means beyond the all-powerful hand of God. His brother Timothy, Richard Mather's second son, a leading citizen of Dorchester, died on January 14, 1685, after a fall from a scaffold in a barn.[26] He, alone among the brothers, had not entered the ministry, and there is in the writings of his brother and nephew a marked silence as to his life. Probably he did not seem to them pious enough to be worthy of his ancestry, and his brother Nathaniel wrote from Dublin, "I desyre to mourn over poor Tims case . . . that his heart should work in so quite con-

25. C. Mather, *Magnalia*, book IV, chap. 10; J. L. Sibley, *Biographical Sketches*, iii, 321ff.

26. *History of Dorchester*, p. 248.

trary a way argues a very evill and unhumbled frame." [27] Yet his death cannot have passed unmourned by his two surviving brothers.

There was consolation for more than one such loss in Cotton Mather's continued progress in godliness and leadership. He was beginning to follow in his father's footsteps as a writer, and by 1688 he had printed a poem, an almanac, an elegy on Mr. Nathaniel Collins, and two sermons.[28] We remember that by 1683 he was at work as his father's colleague in the Second Church. On May 13, 1685, he was formally ordained there. He writes, "With a Soul, inexpressibly irradiated from on High, I went into one of the vastest Congregations that has ever been seen in these parts of the World"; and "In the Afternoon, my Father having prayed and preached . . . intimating he knew not but that God might now call him out of the world . . . the *Ordination* was performed, with a more than ordinary Solemnitie, producing a greater Number of moved Hearts and weeping Eyes, than perhaps have been at any Time here seen together." [29]

The next year, on May fourth, he tells of another important family event. "I was *married*," he writes, "and the good Providence of God caused my Wedding to be attended with many Circumstances of Respect and Honour above most that have ever been in these parts of the World." [30] His bride was Abigail Phillips of Charlestown, daughter of a colonel, a leading citizen, and a good church member. "'Tis said was a great Wedding." [31]

After living in Charlestown for a few months, Cotton and his wife came back to Boston, and he writes: "I took an *House*, wherein my Father lived, in the years 1677, and 78"—a dwelling which was, as we have seen, close to the church, and conveniently near Increase Mather's door.[32]

With his son becoming more and more of an active ally and fellow scholar, Increase did not desert his books. His diaries testify to his reading, and a few volumes still preserved were acquired during these years. Most interesting to us are George Herbert's "Priest to the Temple; or, the Country Parson," and Jeremy Taylor's "Discourse of the Liberty of Prophesying. Showing the Unreasonableness of Prescribing to Other Mens

27. *MHS Coll.*, Series 4, viii, 18.
28. J. L. Sibley, *Biographical Sketches*, iii, 42ff.
29. *MHS Coll.*, Series 7, vii, 98, 99.   31. *Ibid.*, Series 5, v, 136.
30. *Ibid.*, 126, 127.   32. *Ibid.*, Series 7, vii, 129.

Faith, and the Iniquity of Persecuting Differing Opinions." [33] This was, if not "the first or the fullest statement of the principles of toleration," still "the most fruitful in its effects upon the English mind." [34] Its presence in Mather's hands in 1686 points to the fact that he by no means ignored the claims of liberty of conscience.

As for his own writings, he published from 1683 to 1688 eight new books. Three of them reached second editions. Boston presses also reprinted some of his earlier work.

Of the new publications the earliest was "An Arrow against Profane and Promiscuous Dancing." [35] Ostensibly written by the ministers of Boston, the book was ascribed by Thomas Prince to Mather, and his autobiography confirms his authorship.[36] We know that at a meeting of ministers where dancing was discussed, he "struck at the Root, speaking against mixt Dances." [37] The book is simply a denunciation of mixed dancing, basing its argument on the Scriptures and the authority of learned writers. Now, if ever, New England should shun such errors. "Is this a time for *Jigs* and *Galiards!*" [38]

Similar in tone, and equally conditioned by the changing scene in Boston, was a "Testimony against Several Prophane and Superstitious Customs." [39] No one of Mather's writings is less suited to twentieth-century readers, and none more clearly displays the Puritans' strictness as to what seem to us moral inessentials. Beginning with an attack on "Stage-Plays," and a declaration of the barbaric paganism involved in the setting up of a may-pole, Mather devotes his first discourse to "Health drinking." His definition of the term makes his charges seem

33. *New England Historical and Genealogical Register*, xxvii, 347. Mather's copy of Taylor is now owned by the American Antiquarian Society.

34. *DNB*, "Jeremy Taylor."

35. The full title is: "An Arrow Against *Profane and Promiscuous* Dancing. *Drawn out of the Quiver of the* Scriptures. *By the Ministers of Christ* at Boston *in* New-England." Boston, 1684. One of Mather's books published between 1683 and 1688 is not discussed until Chapter 16. See pages 272, 273 *post.*

36. J. L. Sibley, *Biographical Sketches*, i, 446. In the *Autobiography* Mather writes: "This caused me to write that little discourse about profane & promiscuous dancing then printed."

37. *MHS Coll.*, Series 5, v, 104.

38. Page 21.

39. The full title is: "A Testimony Against several Prophane and Superstitious Customs, Now Practised by some in New-England. The Evil whereof is evinced from the Holy Scriptures, and from the Writings both of Ancient and Modern Divines." *London*, 1687.

sounder than they otherwise might. "An Health is that which doth Oblige men to Drink such a quantity of Liquor, as an Indication of their Praying for the Health or Prosperity of such a Person, or of such a Design." The attack is essentially one upon drunkenness and customs which lead men to it. As for gambling, it is "Best and safest to abstain." Christmas celebrations are condemned as keeping alive a pagan festival, and savoring of Catholicism. It is a comfort to find one point on which we can still see Mather's seriousness as not wholly out of proportion to his subject. In good round terms he denounces cock-fighting, and pleads against cruelty to animals. The book closes with a lament that such evils as have been mentioned dare show their heads in New England.[40]

It is a relief to turn back to printed sermons on more fundamental themes. "The Greatest Sinners Exhorted and Encouraged"[41] is essentially a plea that men may repent and turn to Christ. If there is emphasis on the idea that the Day of Judgment is to be a day of wrath for the wicked, one is nowhere allowed to forget the saving power of Jesus. "If any man come to Jesus Christ, He will in no wise to cast him out."[42] A fruitful life is the best means of glorifying God. The love of God is the greatest of earthly happiness. God is the greatest good man can know. In communion with him is bliss, in Christ is salvation, and for men the call to repentance and conversion sounds clear. Such doctrine is not too harsh for any Christian, however relaxed the times in which he lives. The style is always straightforward and simple, sometimes pointed with a vivid expression or a well-turned climax, and continually persuasive in tone. Modern types and punctuation would lend to this little book the air of a tract by no means out of date.

The "Mystery of Christ"[43] is a more elaborate work of the same sort. Of it Mather said, "*I will confess to you, that no Subjects ever insisted on by me, have had so much of my heart, as these which I now present unto you*" (p. 5). He preaches of the nature

40. Preface and chap. I, pp. 12, 39.

41. The full title is: "The *Greatest* Sinners Exhorted and Encouraged *To Come to Christ,* and that Now Without *Delaying.* Also, The Exceeding *Danger* of men's *Deferring their Repentance.* Together with a *Discourse* about *the Day* of *Judgement.* And on *Several other* Subjects." Boston, 1686.

42. Title of the first section of the book.

43. The full title is: "The Mystery of Christ *Opened* and *Applyed.* In Several *Sermons,* Concerning the Person, Office, *and* Glory *of* Jesus Christ." Boston, 1686.

of Christ, His redeeming power, His divine Sonship, His combining in one person the God and the man, and, above all, the strength and beauty of His love. Here speaks what made Puritanism more than a dry husk of dogma, the passionate absorption of the true believer in an enthusiastic personal devotion to the divine ideal as revealed to men in Jesus Christ. Such flaming religious feeling does not lose its appeal, and few pages of this book need be corrected to fit it to be read by, and to lend inspiration to, an ardent Christian mystic of the present. Avowedly, the love of the Son of God and His power, constituted for Increase Mather the heart of religion. "*I have . . . in the Course of my Ministry among you (you know) preached concerning* Christ *more than on any other subject*" (p. 1). His notes in his autobiography show how preëminently the New Testament was the basis of his preaching. As for the style of the book, we are told, "*it would have bin easy to have discoursed on such mysterious subjects, after such a* Metaphysical strain *as none but Scholars should have understood anything*," and "to make an *ignorant* man understand these *Mysteries* in some good measure, will put us to the tryal of our skill, & trouble us a great deal more than if we were to discuss a *Controversy* or handle a subtile point of Learning in the Schools" (p. 4). With a desire for simple exposition, and a realization of the difficulty of attaining it, Mather wrote a book of which Urian Oakes, who read it before his death, could say "*they* [the sermons] *are* in my opinion *very much to the purpose*, recommended to intelligent Readers by their *Solidity* & *Succinctness*, comprizing in a *little room* the choicest Notions that refer to the Subjects discoursed on: They are also well *levelled to the meanest Capacityes*, and thereby singularly fitted to the ends designed." [44] There is no fault to be found with this criticism. Somewhat different in aim is the "Sermon Occasioned by the Execution of a Man," [45] a timely printing of an address delivered on an occasion of great popular interest. One James Morgan, a confessed murderer, was sentenced to death, and Increase Mather was called upon to preach the Lecture sermon before the execution. It was a day of excitement, and "a crazed woman" broke

44. See reverse of title-page.
45. The full title is: "A *Sermon* Occasioned by the Execution of *a man found* Guilty *of* Murder *Preached at* Boston *in* N. E. *March* 11th 168$\frac{5}{6}$ (Together with the *Confession*, Last *Expressions*, & solemn *Warning* of that Murderer to all persons; *especially to Young* men, to beware of *those* Sins which brought him to his *miserable End.*)" Boston 1687. This title is that of the second edition.

up the first attempt at a meeting, but finally the crowd moved to the South Church and there the sermon was preached.[46] The murderer opportunely declared that drunkenness and failure to go to church worked his undoing. Accordingly Increase Mather denounced these two sins. He mourns that "of later years, a kind of Strong Drink hath been *common* amongst us, which the poorer sort of people, both in Town & Country, can make themselves drunk with, at cheap and easy rates." He condemns cruelty of all kinds. He paints in a few paragraphs a sufficiently lurid picture of the torments of the damned. But the climax is once more not admonition, not repentance through fear, but the mercy of Christ. If the criminal be sincere in repentance his soul may be saved. "Go to *Christ* for life . . . look unto the Lord *Jesus* that you may live and not dye forever. . . . Don't think you shall be saved only because good *men* have *pray'd* for you, or for the *Confession* of your *sins* which you have now made, or for the sake of anything but Christ. And I pray the Son of God to have Compassion on you." [47]

Different again, is "The Doctrine of Divine Providence," published in 1684.[48] It forms, in some ways, an introduction to Mather's most widely read book. It expounds the doctrine that "the God of Heaven has an over-ruling hand of Providence in whatever cometh to pass in this world." [49] "There are some events of providence in which there is a special hand of Heaven ordering of them." Such are remarkable preservations and deliverances, remarkable judgments upon men, amazing changes in the world or in particular nations. The existence of Providence is proved from the very existence of the universe. "A Wheel must have an Hand to guide it or it will presently Turn out of the way and fall to the ground." Apparent contradictions to natural law are manifestations of God's will. "*Hence see the reason why little inconsiderable things do occasion great matters to be brought to pass amongst men in the world.* It is because he that sits upon the throne doth wonderfully over rule all. He maketh little matters like the small wheel of a clock which sets all the rest a-going or like the hinges of a great gate upon which all turns." The works of God are wonderful, even the action of natural laws.

46. See *MHS Coll.*, Series 5, v, 111, 123–126.
47. Pp. 25, 18, 19, 35 (second ed. 1687).
48. The full title is: "The Doctrine *of Divine* Providence Opened *and* Applyed: *Also* Sundry *Sermons* on Several other Subjects." Boston 1684.
49. Title of chap. 1.

"That Law and Course of Nature which He hath Established in the world, is a great and marvellous work. His ordering of Times and Seasons, Heat and Cold, Seed-Time and Harvest, Summer and winter, Day and Night in their several Vicissitudes, These are wonderful works." He adds a truly Gilbertian collection of cases in which "the punishment fits the crime." God punished New England for her abuse of the Indians, by a cruel war. Obviously man must avoid the judgments of Providence by adhering to the will of God. Sins of omission are as dangerous as those of commission. Hence the colony is in danger. "And is not *Mercy* neglected too? . . . mercy to the souls of men is neglected." Once more there is a plea for church discipline and family prayer, and an argument *ad hominem.* "And why do men amongst us neglect prayer and reading the Scriptures in their Families, and in their Closets . . . but because of their worldly Incumbrances? Again *Carnal Fears,* and a sinful Bashfulness have a great influence into mens neglects of duty. Why don't they make a profession of Religion? They are afraid they shall be accounted Hypocrites, or that some of their old vain companions will deride them." The final note is not one of fear, or authority, but of the delight of serving God. Men should desire to live long to serve Him.[50]

Such teaching had long been stock in trade for good Puritans. In a day of growing interest in scientific observation, however, mere statement of truths or abstract doctrines did not satisfy. Here lies the root of Mather's "Illustrious Providences," [51] of all his books the most readable to-day, and of unequalled importance, perhaps, for the student of his life and thought.

Few selections of early American prose, and few histories of American literature, pass it by. That it is marked by a style far better than that of the average colonial Puritan is often noted. Its importance as one of the few bits of evidence on the writing of narrative in the pioneer days of New England is mentioned also, though less frequently. But its significance as one of the first scientific writings in America, is, for the most part, neglected.

50. Pp. 2, 21, 22, 29, 30, 45, 78, 79, 98, 99, 107.
51. The full title is: "An Essay for the Recording of Illustrious Providences: Wherein An Account is given of many Remarkable and very Memorable Events, which have happened in this last Age; Especially in *New-England.*" Boston, 1684. This was reprinted as "Remarkable Providences Illustrative of the Earlier Days of American Colonisation," ed. by George Offor, London, 1856, and London, 1890. To this last edition all references here are made.

Here and there, of course, someone notes, as did Tyler and Poole,[52] that there was a scientific inclination revealed in the method and material of the book. Very recently, Professor Murray of Dublin has gone comparatively far in upholding its place as an evidence, not of blind credulity, but of scientific progress in its day.[53] Still, however, one finds selections from it usually concerned with the more incredible of the "providences" described, and comments on it emphasize most often its usefulness as a clue to the superstitious views of its writer.[54] To read such selections, or to try to gain to-day an idea of the book, without going to its pages, is to form an impression far wide of the truth.

In the first place, one needs only to read the book to discover that it is not a mere defence of, or treatise upon, witchcraft.[55] The historical echoing of the Salem delusion, which occurred a decade after the "Illustrious Providences" was written, has made most interesting to historians those pages which deal with witches. Discovering that in Mather's book he considered witchcraft and apparitions, together with all the other wonders of New England, some writers have been prone to forget all else in favor of those pages which treated this peculiarly malignant phase of colonial superstition. Yet, after all, witches and witchcraft fill but a small part of the volume, and all that Mather said of such phenomena is supported by authorities who then were still authorities. In no way does he go beyond the scientists of his time, who, generally speaking, believed in witches, and regarded demonology as a legitimate field for scientific research. This has been made so clear by Professor Kittredge and others, that one need not go into it here.[56] Suffice it to repeat, that witchcraft is but one of many topics treated in the "Illustrious Providences," and that it is treated, by seventeenth-century standards, sanely. What was the main theme of the book? We are more fortunate

52. Cf. M. C. Tyler, *History*, ii, 73; W. P. Trent, *History of American Literature*, p. 73 (which speaks of Mather's "by no means feeble style"); and W. F. Poole, in *Memorial History of Boston*, ii, 158, 159. Tyler says, "It cannot be denied that the conception of the book is thoroughly scientific; for it is to prove by induction the actual presence of supernatural forces in the world."

53. Cf. R. H. Murray, *Dublin University and the New World*. See especially, pp. 57, 58.

54. Cf., for example, Trent, *History*, p. 73.

55. Cf. W. Walker, *Ten New England Leaders*, p. 201; but see reference to Poole, cited in note 52, *ante*.

56. Cf. G. L. Kittredge, *Notes on Witchcraft*.

than literary investigators are wont to be, in that, in this case, we know just why, and with what aim, the book was written. In 1681, at a ministerial convention, Increase Mather suggested that a collection be made of instances in which God's hand had revealed itself in New England.[57] The value of such a compilation was obvious. It would support, more convincingly than anything else could, the truth of the Puritans' cherished doctrine that God punishes or rewards sinners and saints by direct acts of providence revealed upon earth. It would accord with the trend of the day in substituting for collections of Divine Judgments, culled from standard histories, narratives of similar manifestations actually observed on colonial soil. It is this feature of the plan that marks it first as scientific — its reliance upon observation. It was an effort to supply from experience facts from which might be derived, by induction, a theory already abundantly proved by written authority.

That such a view is not reading too much into Mather's design, is proved by a glance at the author, and what he said of his work. He was, throughout his life, keenly interested in current science. We have seen that he took an advanced position in regard to comets, admitting earlier than most of his brethren the possibility that they were governed by natural law, and accepting definitely a scientific fact which, we are told, was fatal to the theological view of such heavenly bodies, and, therefore, to be shunned by divines. We have read of his Philosophical Society in Boston. He bought and read the newest scientific books,[58] and imported to the colonies at least one new invention of ingenious Samuel Morland. Moreover, one may not forget that after he was eighty years old he joined his son in the highly unpopular cause of inoculation. Even so, he might, of course, have been content to be unscientific in the "Illustrious Providences," where there were theological axes to grind. He puts doubt to rest, however, for, after rehearsing the plan of his book and explaining how much, perforce, has been left unsaid, he adds: "I have often wished that the Natural History of New-England might be written and published to the world; the rules and method described by that learned and excellent person Robert Boyle, Esq., being duely observed therein." He would not

57. C. Mather, *Magnalia*, book VI, section 1; I. Mather, *Danger of Apostasy* (in 1685 ed. of *Call from Heaven*), pp. 98, 99.
58. Cf. his diaries, and J. H. Tuttle, *The Libraries*.

decline the task himself, did his other duties permit him to undertake it. Now Boyle's rules for the writing of "Natural History"[59] are as sane now as when they were written, and Mather's reference to them, coupled with his explanation that the "Illustrious Providences" was less complete than he would have liked, and but an essay toward a larger work,[60] makes it quite clear that his aim was not purely theological. He would write scientific natural history, and, no doubt, believed he had done so. And his contemporaries were not likely to question it, though we, with two centuries' more training, may find fault with every page.

In the first place, then, Mather's book was written as a scientific and historical recording of phenomena observed in New England. True, it aimed at religious instruction, but how much of an advance it represents over other books of the time written with the same purpose is seen first in that it deals chiefly with New England, or with events of which New Englanders had direct information; and, second, in that its basis is not written authority, but observation. On both these points it differs radically in method from similar works of edification.

This is best seen in a glance at one or two such books. Mather knew, for example, Samuel Clark's "Mirrour or Looking-Glass both for Saints and Sinners," which reached its fourth edition in 1671.[61] Its title explains its contents: "The wondrous workes of God in Nature, and the curious, costly, and stupendious workes made by Man, with the cheifest curiosities of antient and moderne times." A similar volume was the same author's "Looking-glass for Persecutors; containing Multitudes of Examples of God's Severe, but Righteous Judgments, upon bloody and merciless Haters of his Children in all Times, from the beginning of the World to this present Age. Collected out of the Sacred Scriptures, and other Ecclesiastical Writers, both Ancient and Modern." Its second edition came out in 1675. We have found also, in Mather's library, "The Theatre of God's Judgements," by Thomas Beard and Thomas Taylor. The sub-title describes it as "a Collection of Histories out of Sacred, Ecclesiasticall, and Prophane Authors, concerning the admirable Judgements of God upon the transgressours of his commandments." Again,

---

59. *Philosophical Transactions*, 1665, 1666, vol. i, no. 2, pp. 186–189; R. Boyle, *Works*, ii, 1ff.

60. Preface.

61. Cf. Mather's diaries; and, for Clark, *DNB*.

we know that he owned "A World of Wonders," by "Henrie Stephen." The tales in this book obviously adapted themselves to the ends of Puritan preachers. Later than the "Illustrious Providences" one remembers, too, Sinclair's "Satan's Invisible World Discovered," published in England in 1685. Its preface declares that all its stories "may be attested by Authentick Records, or by famous witnesses." Therefore, "what belief can be given to any human histories, and matters of Fact, related by famous Writters, as much may be given to these . . . Relations." In 1697 William Turner printed his "Compleat History of the Most Remarkable Providences, Both of Judgment and Mercy, which have Hapned in this Present Age. Extracted from the Best Writers, the Author's own Observations, and the Numerous Relations sent him from divers Parts of the Three Kingdoms."

It is plain that only the last-mentioned of these books comes near Mather's use of up-to-date local observations rather than old writers, and Turner makes it clear that he considered Mather his predecessor in the field.[62] The author of the "Illustrious Providences" went beyond the other contemporaries and successors we have looked at, and was more consistent even than Turner in his use of the stories of eye-witnesses rather than printed accounts in books. For example, Turner tells some stories because he finds them in Mather. Mather, on the other hand, nine times out of ten based his relations on what had been seen and directly reported to him, or upon what he himself had had opportunity to observe. Of course, his purpose was in part that of Clark, Beard, Taylor, and the rest. He wished to point a moral, but he chose a method most favored in his day by scientists, and not generally employed in the pulpit. He deserves a place, not with superstitious divines, but on the same plane with Glanvill and Dr. Henry More, who were serious students in "psychical research," and seekers for empirical proof of what had hitherto been forced upon men's minds by authority alone.[63]

Written with such a method, the book is, briefly summarized for convenience, a collection of narratives of New England happenings. They are classified by subject. There are accounts of "Sea Deliverances," "Remarkable Preservations" from dangers of various sorts, and stories of the vagaries of thunder and light-

62. See Turner's foreword, "To the Courteous Reader."
63. Cf. *DNB*, articles "Joseph Glanvill," "Henry More"; also, H. S. and I. M. L. Redgrove, *Joseph Glanvill and Psychical Research in the Seventeenth Century*.

ning. There are "Philosophical Meditations" on such scientific topics as the theory of lightning, of magnetism, and of "Antipathies and Sympathies" in nature. The supernatural is discussed, and witchcraft. An argument for the existence of "Dæmons and Possessed Persons" and "Apparitions" follows, and one notes that here, as elsewhere, the existence of marvels is not upheld simply because historians vouch for them, or because they have Scriptural authority, but because they are supported by the products of what was, however crude and prejudiced, still the "psychical research" of interested observers of the time. The next chapter, most often neglected, does not preach superstition, but attacks it, laying bare the hollowness of many popular beliefs. Then comes a series of stories of the wonders wrought by and for the deaf and dumb, tales of "remarkable tempests," of "Judgements," and, finally, a section on "some events at Norwich."

The materials for all this were gathered by the approved modern "questionnaire" method,[64] and in most cases Mather's sources are verbal relations of eye-witnesses, or letters from observers outside of Boston. And, though it is easy to be struck by the sprinkling of incredible fables, the reader cannot ignore the fact that much of what is told is by no means beyond belief. We still know of remarkable escapes from shipwreck, or perils on land, and we still write of them. We still know that the deaf and dumb can be taught to speak and hear.

We do not, however, use such facts to support religious doctrines, and Mather did. In this lies the first archaic element of the book. Yet it by no means clouds the accuracy of many of the observations recorded. A grave defect, however, is the uncritical use of evidence. A story told as true by a Puritan divine in New England was, for Mather, sufficiently vouched for. The testimony of witnesses passed current with too little investigation of their skill as observers, or their devotion to truth. Hence the book is not proof against scepticism of later days. Yet we may not forget that Mather showed rudimentary critical ability,[65] and that the seventeenth century's view of what was evidence was not ours. In addition, marvels are most often told of remote

---

64. Preface to *Illustrious Providences*.

65. He is careful to say that "circumstantial mistakes" may have crept in, though he has tried to print things of the truth of which he was "well assured" and about which he has received "credible" information. See *Illustrious Providences*, Preface.

lands, and remoteness can be measured only in the time taken for travel to the place in question. Thus, in the New England of 1684, where transportation was no more advanced than in pagan Rome, an event at Lynn was considerably removed in time from an investigator in Boston.[66] English scientists believed in miracles of nature related as happening in China, though they would have known they were false if they were reported to have occurred in London. So Mather, distant from the scenes of some of the events he wrote of, was handicapped in investigating their truth, and was the more ready to credit them because they took place in parts of the country he did not know. That this tendency in him was shared by good scientists, and that he was not unduly credulous by their standards, becomes clear when one glances at the transactions of the Royal Society for these years. One finds there a willingness to credit many strange tales told of distant lands; and even in regard to English observations, one must suspend one's critical faculties quite as much to read a volume of the "Philosophical Transactions," as to read the "Illustrious Providences."[67] Indeed, some of the contents of this book, and

66. "The occupation of three whole days in a visit from Boston to Salem, by fords and on foot, gives an impressive picture of the locomotion of that early period [1631] of the colony." *Memorial History of Boston*, i, 118.

67. In the *General Index or Alphabetical Table, to all the Philosophical Transactions, from the Beginning to July, 1677* (London, 1678), one finds, for example, these items:
(1) "Animals drink very little, some not at all, in the hotter countries."
(2) "Porcupins kill Lions by shooting quills."
(3) "The Blood of the Negro's is black, which seems to be the cause of their black skin."
(4) "A man relieved from inveterate and outrageous madness by the blood of a Calf."
(5) "Flames and flashes from the sea."
(6) "Lakes turning Copper into Iron, and causing storms when anything is cast into them."
(7) A paragraph of entries on monstrous births, including "A Calf deformed, and a great Stone found in a Cows womb."
(8) "A Nutmeg, called thieving, one alone put into a whole Room-full of Nutmegs corrupts them all."
(9) "A Stone of excellent vertues found in the head of a serpent in the Indies." ("This stone will extract poison from wounds, and, if put into milk, will give up the poison again.")
(10) "Rain, how caused or attracted by Woods and certain trees."
(11) "Rain in a vale of Jamaica turns suddenly into Maggots, as it falls upon Garments."
(12) "Scotland: Extracts from thence about extraordinary Winds there, Lakes, Frosts, a petrifying Water."
(13) "Serpents, having an head on each end of the Body."
One notes that in the case of (1), (2), (3), (9), (11), and, to a lesser degree, (13), credulity is aided by the remoteness of the events.

much similar material, was communicated to, and considered by the Royal Society nearly thirty years later.[68] And we must see the Royal Society, none the less, as abreast of the science of its day.

It is quite unjust, too, to think of Mather's book as one which absorbed indiscriminately every proffered tale. He states expressly that he has tried to print only matters of the truth of which he is "well assured," and about which he has received "credible" information.[69] Moreover, one of his wildest stories, sharply ridiculed in recent years as a proof of his "stupid credulity," is not included in the body of his book, but relegated to the preface,[70] with the simple comment that it is from a manuscript sent to him — and sent, be it noted, by a man of some scientific reputation in England.[71] Mr. Drake assures us that these things Mather "believed ... implicitly." The most he says, however, is that they are contained in the manuscript; and, as we have seen, he denies them a place in the body of his work. To twist this into a statement of implicit belief, is a considerable feat.

Furthermore, Mather was not without enemies, some of whom

In the *Philosophical Transactions*, vol. xiii (1683), pp. 93, 94, we read of a murrain in Switzerland, imputed by some to witchcraft, but "more probably from some *Noxious* Exhalations thrown out of the Earth, by three distinct *Earthquakes* perceived here ... in the Space of one year."

On p. 169 of the same volume we learn how a man "had some of the organic parts of his body transformed into, or affected after the nature of a Dog."

In vol. xiv (1684), we learn how the Trade Winds are caused by the "breath" of sea plants (p. 489), that "Thunder and Lightning owe their matter from the sole breath of the Pyrites" (pp. 518, 519), that in some places it has rained iron, copper, stones, but not silver or gold (p. 518). There is nothing harder to swallow in the *Illustrious Providences*. It is difficult to see why Mather is called superstitious, and the Royal Society scientific.

68. See Cotton Mather's letters to the Royal Society in 1712, copies of which are among the Gay Transcripts in the library of the Massachusetts Historical Society; and G. L. Kittredge, "Cotton Mather's Scientific Communications to the Royal Society," *American Antiquarian Society Proceedings*, xxvi, 18ff.

69. Preface.

70. S. G. Drake, in his *Early History of New England*, pp. xviii, xix, refers to this story. It is found in the preface to the *Illustrious Providences*.

71. All Mather says of the story is: "One strange passage more I shall here relate out of the MS. which we have thus far made mention of." But Drake says "this circumstance ... though it came second hand to our Author he believed ... implicitly" (*op. cit*). Mather had the manuscript from John Davenport, and says he believes that it came originally from "Mr. Hartlib." Samuel Hartlib, friend of Milton, Marvell, and Boyle, was "intimately acquainted with the small group out of which grew the Royal Society." He wrote much on agriculture. See *DNB*, article "Samuel Hartlib (d. 1670)."

criticized his book. Had it contained matters incredible to them, or errors of fact they could detect, they would surely have hastened to expose them. Instead, we find indignant critics questioning not the truth of certain stories, but their application to their sect,[72] and the indefatigable Robert Calef, though he is sceptical in 1700 as to the old doctrine of "remarkable providences," pokes no holes in Mather's facts.[73]

It is often forgotten, too, that Mather did not merely collect evidence, but wrote some of his own reflections on scientific matters.[74] He was not a Newton or a Boyle, but there was only one of each. He was not a great original thinker in science, but he was an intelligent reader of men who were. So, if he upholds the belief that the Devil causes thunderstorms (p. 88), no more unreasonable, perhaps, than the view that the source of such tempests lay in "pyrites," a theory seriously considered by the Royal Society,[75] he also decries as superstition the hanging of horseshoes over doors, or the use of herbs and charms to drive away spirits.[76] He frankly declares that many stories of witchcraft are false (p. 124). He discusses magnetism, and other scientific topics of the day, and wisely supports his ideas by references to current writers who were leaders in contemporary science. Among the names thus cited, one notes, of course, the contributors to the "Philosophical Transactions" of the Royal Society. He refers also to Kenelm Digby, Kepler the astronomer, Thomas Browne and his "Vulgar Errors," Boyle's experiments recorded in his "Usefulness of Natural Philosophy," the "Philosophical Conferences of the Virtuosi of France," [77] the "Ephemeridum Medico-Physicarum Germanicarum," [78] pioneer learned scientific journal in Germany, the books of Glanvill, and of Dr. Henry More, together with a host of others. Many of them had recognized scientific standing in 1684, and no one of them was outlawed by the learned world of that year.

72. Mather's tales of the Quakers were answered by George Keith in his *Presbyterian and Independent Visible Churches*, pp. 214–230, as well as by John Whiting in *Truth and Innocency Defended*, pp. 132–135; but they do not question the truth of the events recorded, confining themselves to a denial that the participants were Quakers.

73. See Robert Calef, *More Wonders of the Invisible World*, ii, 108ff.

74. *Illustrious Providences*, chap. 4.

75. Cf. note 67, *ante*.   76. Chap. 8.

77. Cf. *MHS Coll.*, Series 3, x, 71.

78. "Miscellanea Curiosa Medico–Physica Academiæ Naturæ Curiosorum, *sive* Ephemeridum Medico-Physicarum Germanicarum *Curiosarum*." The first volume is dated "Lipsiae, 1670," and the publication continued regularly thereafter.

Even from so brief a sketch as this, touching only one or two features of the book, and neglecting altogether the fruitful questions as to how Mather selected from the material offered him, or how,he treated narrative in writing up the stories told him, there is enough to lead one to reread the "Illustrious Providences." Where else can one turn in seventeenth-century America to find the same use of the most recent scientific publications? How many English Puritans wrote with the same grasp of such material? In all the books which collect remarkable occurrences, for purposes of religious teaching, where is one with so little dependence on mere traditional authority, or one so truly scientific in its preoccupation with events, not as retailed in books, but as seen by men in a given part of the world and in modern times? Admit, of course, that the theological point of view sometimes gives Mather theories far from ours; confess that he was too uncritical in his use of evidence, and one still faces the fact that he was abreast of his time, that he chose his method soundly, that much of his material still has value, that he was familiar with more than one point of up-to-date science, and that he succeeded in his attempt to write a real chapter of New England history. Best of all, we have the answer to the old riddle as to why a man so sagacious in statecraft was stupidly credulous in other matters.[79] We can reconcile the book with the man, as his deeds reveal him, only when we read what he wrote in reference to his contemporaries, and see that in method and material he is treating, for the most part, not superstition, but science. We may add, then, to the importance of the "Illustrious Providences" as a literary work, its importance as a leader among works of "popular science" in America. And, if its own significance does not justify our noticing the book thus, the reflection that it appears in its true colors only when read in connection with the world and life whence it sprang, is in itself of value. Only by such reading can any Puritan writer of America, be he witch-finder or Indian missionary, politician or religious theorist, win his due from critics of to-day.

Aside from the scientific interest of the book, few of its pages can be dull to the antiquarian, the seeker after the curious in narrative, or the student of folklore. There is, moreover, much good story-telling, and always a certain sharpness and directness in the recital of facts. There is, when we compare his narratives

79. Cf. S. G. Drake, *Early History*, p. xviii.

with the original versions as they came to him,[80] proof of editorial skill and the seal of a historian with a respect for sources. In style the book has the good qualities of Mather's early historical writing, and suffers less from marks of haste. Whatever its faults, Benjamin Franklin would not have been ashamed to own some pages of the "Illustrious Providences." Any New England writer of the day would have been proud to sign it; and in England there were few in the seventeenth century who wrote narrative with more simplicity and strength of phrase.

More and more Mather must have been called from his study by the claims of his church. With new religious rivals, no meeting-house of the old Congregational way could afford to be without the best efforts of its teacher. Measured in terms of the new members admitted, the years 1684 to 1688 show a decrease, but by no means a stagnation of interest.[81] Mather's preaching is revealed to some extent in his printed sermons, and faithful Samuel Sewall adds here and there an illuminating note. He tells us, for example, how Mather preached at the ordination of Charles Morton, although he disapproved of the form employed.[82] As he grew older, he grew further and further away from the boy who had refused to recognize such an innocent rite as the wearing of academic robes at Trinity College.

Obviously the church demanded his presence in Boston. Quite as obviously, the college across the river was too hopeful a plant to be left to wither. So, in 1685, after President Rogers left office, and after Joshua Moodey had been elected and had declined, one reads in the College records: "The Reverend Mr Increase Mather was requested to take special care for ye Government of ye Colledge, & for y^t end to act as President till a further settlem^t be orderly made." It was a compromise by which the strongest man Harvard could claim became virtually President, though his first interest, his church, kept him from taking up residence in Cambridge and becoming in fact the active controlling force of the day-to-day work of the College. The salary ordinarily paid to the President was now shared with John

80. For such narratives see, for example, John Russell's letter, Aug. 2, 1683, John Whiting's, Dec. 4, 1682, and John Higginson's, Aug. 22, 1682, all in *MHS Coll.*, Series 4, vol. viii.

81. In this period 54 new members joined the Church. In the preceding five years there were 88, and in the five years before that, 72. Copy of original records, owned by the Church.

82. *MHS Coll.*, Series 5, v, 155.

Leverett and John Cotton, who were on the ground and were those "as have done ye work, y^t appertains to ye President." [83] In the next year Dudley's council appointed Mather "Rector" of Harvard, making Leverett and Brattle tutors.[84] In their hands was to be the actual management, while the "Rector" remained nominally the chief authority and continued his "usual visitations."

Under Increase Mather's guidance the college developed greatly.[85] The advance of the times and the increase of population played a part, no doubt, but the new Rector carried Harvard through troubled days and left it more securely established than he found it. For the present the problem was one of its very existence. Harvard drew its being from a charter of the old colonial government, and that was no more. If, under the new régime, titles to individual holdings, conferred under the old government, were invalid, surely Harvard might fear lest the sole legal basis for its establishment be declared but a scrap of paper. Dudley, fortunately, was Puritan enough and New Englander enough to know that any radical attack on the college by the royal authorities would have been a sure road to popular disfavor. His making Mather Rector points to his desire to keep the old order at Harvard; and that there was no change under Andros shows that he, too, had political tact.

At the same time, Mather was awake to the danger, and took precautions against it. The Treasurer of the College was his friend and sympathizer, John Richards. He wrote in one of his account books: "1686, October 22. I tooke care againe of the Colledge stocke p psuasion of m^r Dudley, m^r Stoughton & m^r Incr. Mather, & rec^d of m^r Sam^1 Nowell, the late Treasurer, the severall Papers underneath written, & am ordered to new make all the Obligations, mortgages, &c., & take them in myne owne name, as by one Instrument of this date signed between us Interchangably appears." [86] Here was preparation for undue official interest in the college's titles to its holdings. Again, in the next year, another interesting transaction is recorded. Richards kept an account headed: "Stocke belonging to Harvard Colledge att Cambridge." "Stock is credited with moneys received by him, and charged

83. *Harv. Rec.*, pp. 76, 77, 78, 79, 257.
84. J. L. Sibley, *Biographical Sketches*, ii, 179.
85. J. Quincy, *History*, especially i, 38.
86. *Colonial Society Publications*, i, 183ff.

with his disbursements. On the first day of August, 1687, the credit entries footed up £130 11*s*. On that day he paid out 'for recording mortgage to m^r Dudley,' £1 8*s*. and 'to another for bonds, &c,' 13*s*., making £2 1*s*. This amount when added to previous disbursements apparently left in his hands £19 11*s*., which he paid over to Increase Mather. The entry in explanation of that payment is carefully erased, but the debit items are posted up, making . . . an exact balance. . . . An explanatory entry is made on each page to this effect: 'Thus farr an Accompt was demanded by Sr Edm^d Andros & delivered to him.'" The royal governor clearly insisted on his right to inspect the college books, and quite as plainly the payment of "Colledge Stocke" to Increase Mather shows that he was ready to shoulder, as an individual, the task of defending Harvard's property.[87] While he thus prepared for any invasion of the college's material holdings, he petitioned publicly, with Leverett and Brattle, "that the said Colledge may be confirmed in the hands it has bin in, & that they may have the same power which formerly they had," namely "to make laws for the government of their own Society, & to dispose of all moneys given, or that should be given, " and, if necessary, "to chuse another President, Fellow, or Treasurer." [88]

Apparently there was no effort to upset this scheme of things, and it does credit to the new government that there was none. Unmolested, Harvard continued its work. The Rector, devoting most of his time to his Boston church, rode out to Cambridge once or twice a week, going on horseback by way of the Charlestown ferry.[89] He was serving in a position he had not sought. He had refused it more than once, and after he took office, he threatened, in 1686 and 1687, to resign.[90] Yet he remained faithful to his trust, perhaps because there was no one else, perhaps because he felt that in troublous times experience counted heavily. He published a catalogue of graduates, a work of obvious historical importance.[91] At the request of Governor Dudley, he examined his son for entrance to the college.[92] And we are told that, at the Commencement in 1685, after his son Nathaniel had given a Hebrew oration, the Rector "after giving the Degrees"

87. *Colonial Society Publications*, i, 206.
88. *MHS Coll.*, Series 4, viii, 113, 114.
89. J. L. Sibley, *Biographical Sketches*, i, 597.
90. *MHS Proc.*, xxxiii, 257; *MHS Coll.*, Series 4, viii, 315.
91. *Colonial Society Publications*, xvii, 232.
92. *MHS Coll.*, Series 4, viii, 484.

spoke "in Praise of Academical Studies and Degrees" and the "Hebrew tongue." [93]

Whatever problems of scholarship were involved in such an inaugural, a different problem, and more subtle dangers, presented themselves at the Commencement of 1687. To this came His Excellency Sir Edmund Andros, with his chaplain, Mr. Ratcliffe, who "sat in the Pulpit by the Governour's direction." As the "Eleven Bachelors and Seven Masters proceeded," there was need for all Mather's urbanity.[94] Andros's presence marked the interest in the college of a royal government presumably unsympathetic with its standards. A Church of England clergyman in the pulpit was a further omen of evil to Puritan supporters of Harvard. At the same time, Mather and his colleagues held office by Andros's tolerance, and to oppose him publicly, or to treat him otherwise than courteously, must have been to expose the college to grave risk. So, though the Rector took good care to pray "forenoon and afternoon," apparently leaving the English chaplain no time to be heard, he must also have treated the Governor to some of the tact and courtesy which made possible in the next few years his personal appeal to men of all classes and tempers in England.

Diplomacy was needed for a man in Mather's position, even in the conduct of his daily life, in the Boston of 1683 to 1688. To become a mere defender of the charter, an opponent of the new government, or to remain content with preaching against what seemed to him the imported vices of the day, could have won him the support of but one party, the loyal Puritan church members. On the other hand, to accept the new order passively would have been to sacrifice for the approval of Andros not only the respect of the "faithful" in New England, but also the good-will of the man in the street, who found ground for complaint in such material burdens as the new taxes. To withdraw entirely from public affairs, to become a sequestered student and writer in a time of popular excitement, would have been to give up the basis of his prestige, personal influence among the people. Actually, his course avoided, on the one hand, open rupture with the new authorities, or too outspoken opposition to them, while, at the same time, he left no doubt as to the strength of his belief in the "rights" of New England. Accordingly, he appeared to the church member or the disgruntled layman as the leader of

SIR EDMUND ANDROS

ability and prudence, ready to serve when opportunity arose, and to the Governor and Council he seemed an opponent whose moderation made rational dealings possible, and one whose undoubted power in the town lent weight to his opinion.

More than one event of these years makes this clear. In 1686, when the news of Dudley's commission became known, "Mr. Phillips had very close Discourse with the President, to persuade him not to accept: 't was in Mr. Willard's Study Monday after noon just at night. Mr. Stoughton and Mather" were there, too.[95] Later in the year, when the old question of using the British flag with the cross of St. George was raised once more, and again stirred the Puritans' fear of Popery, Samuel Sewall staunchly refused to serve under the new colors. He "went and discoursed Mr. Mather," who judged it sin to have the cross "put in," but decided that Captain Eliot was "not in fault," inasmuch as he but acted under orders. Sewall's scruples were not so easily overcome.[96] Man of affairs that he was, he lacked Mather's insight into the fact that, as matters stood, resistance on minor points could serve no good end. When Andros arrived, in his "Scarlet Coat Laced," a dinner was given in his honor, and at the table, gay with the English uniforms, "Mr. Mather," in his sober garb, "crav'd a Blessing."

A courteous guest at his table, Mather was none the less quite ready to oppose Andros on a question of import. The Governor asked for one of the Boston churches in which to hold the English service, but "Mr. Mather and Willard thorowly discoursed his Excellency . . . in great plainness, showing they could not consent." [97] Andros yielded at the time, though he chose soon afterward to force his way into one of the meeting-houses, the use of which he had been refused. Once installed, his chaplain shared the building with the congregation which owned it, and, when their service followed his, the uninvited guests more than once kept the proprietors of the house waiting outside its doors.[98]

95. *MHS Coll.*, Series 5, v, 139.
96. *Ibid.*, 147, 148.
97. *Ibid.*, 162.
98. Cf. *MHS Coll.*, Series 5, v, 172, 177. J. T. Adams, *The Founding*, p. 421, speaks of the "inordinate length" of the Puritan sermons, and quotes a passage apparently intended to show that the length of the Puritan service interfered with the English church's service. Sewall's evidence is quite to the contrary. Prejudiced as he may have been, to draw the conclusion that the Puritans delayed the worship of Andros and his friends in the face of the story as told in his diary, is unsafe unless more evidence can be found to support such a view.

That no more resistance was shown is, perhaps, creditable to Boston. Certainly Mather's contenting himself with mere passing notes in his diary as to the affairs of the day,[99] the while he took good care to preserve friendly relations with Dudley, to dine with Andros, and to avoid open hostility, points either to a broadminded spirit of tolerance, or, at the least, to a prudent desire to bide his time.

If to one English clergyman he seemed the force which led the people to opposition,[100] one remembers that the writer appears not only to have been a dissentient from New England's church, but a violator of the orders of the colonial court.[101] And when all is said and done, one may not forget that when the King's declaration of liberty for all faiths reached Boston, Mather welcomed it.[102] Had he been a foe of toleration, he could hardly have pursued the way he chose. Others, narrower in spirit, saw in the royal order but the opening of New England to Popery or Quakerism.[103] It is not enough to explain Mather's attitude by saying that he did not see that the king's proclamation meant freedom, not only for Congregationalists, but for all. With as many sects as were represented in Boston, no dweller there can have been blind to what toleration implied. That Mather welcomed it is one more confirmation of his son's statement that he progressed more and more throughout his life toward the ideal of religious liberty.

He was not content merely to give thanks himself. In June, 1687, he suggested to the ministers in Boston that an expression of their gratitude be sent to James. He was commissioned to carry out the plan, and had the satisfaction of hearing from London "that it came very seasonably." [104] There seemed to be a chance here to build up strength for New England in public opinion abroad, and Mather continued the work. In October he suggested that "our churches, (and not the ministers only,) might thank the king for his Declaration, which was readily complied with by ten churches." [105] By this time he had been warned by the narrower party that the king's declaration was a

99. Cf. *MHS Proc.*, xxxiii, 399ff., June 6, 1686, and March 16 and April 17, 1687.
100. *Ibid.*, lii, 123.
101. *MHS Coll.*, Series 5, v, 98 and n.
102. *Parentator*, p. 102; *Autobiography*.
103. *MHS Coll.*, Series 4, viii, 507, 508; T. Hutchinson, *History*, i, 357, 358 and n.
104. *Autobiography*.
105. *Ibid.; Parentator*, p. 102; *MHS Coll.*, Series 4, viii, 697, 698.

danger, not a benefit, to Congregationalism. Moreover, Andros had forbidden public demonstrations of rejoicing on the part of the churches.[106] But, awake to what was involved, Mather knew that hope for the future lay not in clinging vainly to the dream of restoring the old exclusive Congregational control, but in facing, and accepting frankly, the newer ideal of tolerance, and, most important for the moment, in reëstablishing in England the belief that Massachusetts was not a land of narrowness and persecution, but the home of nonconformists of tolerant mind. No single episode in his life displays more clearly the broadening of his views, and none reveals more clearly his political foresight.

Beyond attack, perhaps, as the intolerant Puritan bigot, and too cautious in his public dealings in the town to lay himself open to serious charges, he paid the penalty of prominence by becoming the object of lampoons from those who differed from him.[107] Most serious was the enmity of Randolph. On July 16, 1684, Mather wrote in his diary: "I being in some distress of spirit bec. I hear, yt. some ltrs wh I sent to Holland, are fallen into ye hands of ym at Whitehall."[108] He had good reason for alarm. He had written to friends abroad frank criticism of the royal attacks on the charter, and such letters in the hands of royal authorities might well bring him an unwelcome share of their interest.[109] But a knowledge of the facts turned his fear to anger.[110]

One George Rosse, "being lately in Amsterdam," there found its way to him a letter from Boston which he "had time to copy," and sent promptly to Edward Randolph.[111] It contained matter perilously near sedition. It was dated December 3, 1683, and signed I. M.[112] To Randolph it was a treasure trove. At once he used it to build up hostility to Mather. To Samuel Shrimpton he wrote: "Mr. Mather, the Bellowes of Sedition & Treason has at last attained his end in setting his fools a horse-back." He told Sir Leoline Jenkins of the letter, and when that gentleman referred to Mather as "that star-gazer: that halfe distracted man," Randolph gleefully reported the conversation to Simon

106. *Parentator*, p. 103.
107. *Autobiography*, Aug. 29, 1684.
108. MS. *Diary*, 1680–84.
109. Cf. his letters in *MHS Coll.*, Series 4, vol. viii.
110. For the documents in the matter of the forged letter, see Palfrey, iii, 556–558 n.; *MHS Coll.*, Series 4, viii, 100–110; and C. W. Tuttle, *Capt. Francis Champernowne*, pp. 295–310.
111. *Ibid.*, pp. 295, 296.
112. For the letter, see *MHS Coll.*, Series 4, viii, 104ff.

Bradstreet.[113] Sir Roger L'Estrange [114] got wind of the affair, and in his "Observator" entertained his readers with an onslaught on New England bigotry as personified in Increase Mather.[115]

The latter, once the letter was in his hands, recognized it as none of his. Whatever he had written, he promptly knew the particular screed now in question to be a forgery. In his diary and autobiography, he declares the charge against him to be false. Later, he made the same statement in a printed work.[116] If such evidence be thrown out, there remains the fact that such men as Nathaniel Mather in Dublin and Simon Bradstreet in Boston found it impossible to believe the letter to be genuine. The latter wrote Randolph: "my charyty is such, that though I am afraid that hee [Mather] might write something inconvenient to his ffriends, yet I cañot think him soe foolish and absurd to write all that is contayned in that letter."[117] His contemporaries were not convinced of his guilt, and no one since has produced a shred of proof that the letter was his. Moreover, there are valid arguments against his authorship. Writing to Dudley, he displayed points of fact which marked the letter as not from his pen.[118] To quote: "The forger ... represents me as a person well assured of Shaftbury's happiness. . . . They that are acquainted with me knowe that I never had an high opinion of that Gentleman. This manifests the letter to be a peece of forgery. . . . He pretends as if I sent to Amsterdam for the New Covenant of Scotland, Caril upon Job, and Mr. Owen's last works. Now herein he has so grossly played the fool, soe as to discover the letter to be a meer peece of forgery. As for the new Covenant of Scotland, I never heard of such a thing, untill I saw it in this wicked letter, nor do I to this day vnderstand what is the meaning of it. Carill have been in my study this fiveteen years"—and we know he read Carill in 1675–76— [119] "& if I had him not, it is likely that I should send to Amsterdam, for Mr. Carill & Doct. Owen's works, which are here sould in Boston. I might obtaine them sooner and cheaper from London, then from Holland. . . . He farther represents me as that I knew by the signes in the Heavens, that

113. *MHS Coll.*, Series 4, viii, 525, 528, 529.
114. See *DNB*.
115. *Observator*, Nos. 173, 174, 176, 177; *Colonial Society Publications*, xxiv, 313.
116. I. Mather, *The Greatest Sinners Exhorted*, Preface.
117. *MHS Coll.*, Series 4, viii, 59, 533.
118. *Ibid.*, 108–110.
119. T. G. Wright, *Literary Culture*, pp. 130, 131.

the heathens should destroye [120] the whore of Babilon. . . . my judgement is declared in print express contradictory." Against this there is no evidence except a copy of a letter signed I. M., and Randolph's belief that these initials represented the signature of his Puritan enemy. One need not go further to seek to disprove a charge for which no basis can be found.

Unfortunately, Mather, sorely tried by the attacks made upon him in London and even in Barbadoes, did not content himself with writing to Dudley, or with the new solace he found in the Psalms.[121] In defending himself, he angrily accused Randolph. In his letter to Dudley he declared the forger was "Randolph himselfe," that Randolph was "a great knave." Once he seems to grant the possibility that the doubtful honor of the forgery may belong to Bernard rather than to Edward Randolph.[122] But in attacking either, prudence failed him. He was facing opponents likely to let no advantage slip.

In December, 1687, therefore, Randolph secured a warrant for Mather's arrest.[123] Very probably he was led to this action by the knowledge that in October the churches had urged "that some one should go to London with their thanks to the King for his declaration of religious freedom," and that several had suggested Mather for the task. He asked his church for permission, and "they unanimously consented." "My purpose for England was no sooner noised abroad," he writes, "than Randolph . . . caused an officer to arrest me, (on Saturday, December 24)." [124] Whether news of his projected mission to England lay back of Randolph's bringing suit, one cannot decide finally. Mather himself was sure of it,[125] and obviously any recital of the state of New England delivered in London by a man of his sympathies was likely to be wholly unflattering to Randolph. Whatever the motives behind it, the case came to trial on January 31. Mather had taken such legal advice as was to be had, and had written to Dudley, who was to judge him, a full statement of his position, insisting that he had believed, not Edward, but Bernard Randolph to be the author of the fraud. If one reads his letter, however, one cannot escape the feeling that, whatever he believed

120. Mather refers here to his *Kometographia*, pp. 129, 130.
121. *Autobiography*.
122. *MHS Coll.*, Series 4, viii, 100ff.
123. *Ibid.*, 702; C. W. Tuttle, *Capt. Francis Champernowne*, p. 304.
124. *Parentator*, pp. 103, 106; *Autobiography*.
125. *Ibid.*

in his more rational moments, Mather, in his wrathful excitement, had by no means spared Edward.[126]

At the trial "the overruling providence of God so ordered that there were but two Common Prayer-men of the jury, (where as it was thought all the jury would have been picked of such only to do me an ill turn;) & the whole jury cleared me, & Randolph was ordered to pay costs of court, instead of obtaining 500 lbs of me. which he hoped for." [127]

Freed from the charge of defamation, he bent himself to prepare for England. Prayer and fasting, and premonitions of good service to be done for God, filled his days. He went boldly to Andros and told him of the voyage he planned. He "did also give notice of it to the whole country in a lecture Sermon on Ex. 33:15." [128]

Randolph was not yet downed. In Mather's words: "Ed. Randolph, being assisted by Ben. Bullivant, the apothecary, who was then a justice of peace, (men whose names will stink in N. E. to the world's end,) & others of that fraternity, doubting that I might make complaints to the king of their irregular proceedings, especially of their contempt manifest of the king's Declaration for Indulgence, to Dissenters in matters relating to conscience ... caused an officer to go to my house with a design to arrest me in an action of scandal, on a pretended defamation of Randolph ... but it so happened that I had taken some ... physic that morning, which caused me to refuse to speak to the officer, although I knew nothing of his design." [129]

Plainly, Randolph's attempt to arrest Mather a second time had a motive deeper than a desire for damages. The case had been tried and settled, and Randolph's cause had been lost. How he arranged for the second attempt at arrest we can only guess, but it is hard to doubt that he had an end in view. He had much to fear from Mather, should he ever reach England, and, more particularly, the king. It is not easy to question Mather's conclusion that here was a deliberate effort to delay or prevent his departure from Boston. Indeed, the episode was so explained at the time, and the only answer offered was that Randolph did

---

126. *Autobiography; Parentator*, p. 106; Tuttle, *Capt. Francis Champernowne*, pp. 304 n., 305, 307, 308; *MHS Coll.*, Series 4, viii, 112ff.

127. *Autobiography.*

128. *Ibid.; Parentator*, p. 106; *MHS Coll.*, Series 5, v, 206.

129. *Autobiography; Parentator*, p. 107; MS. *Diary*, March 27, 1688; *MHS Coll.*, Series 5, v, 208. One remembers, of course, Hawthorne's sketch of "Dr. Bullivant."

not know of Mather's project and so could not have acted from a desire to detain him.[130] That Edward Randolph was ignorant of what Andros had been told, of what had been publicly declared at a lecture, and discussed by the church members of the town, is credible only if we believe that a trained diplomat and a practised observer of the smallest bubbles in the political broth, was as blind and as isolated from current talk as the dullest child in Boston streets. There remains only the obvious probability that he strove to check Mather's sailing. It is interesting to remember the theory that one of the liberties bestowed on New England by the Andros régime was freedom for all to go and come as they chose.[131] Mather's experience suggests that, in this respect, the privileges granted by the royal governor had more being on paper than in fact, and more charm for the twentieth century than for the seventeenth.

Randolph's agent left Mather's door without serving his warrant, but "within an hour there was a report in the town" that the arrest had been made.[132] The news spread quickly, and came soon to Mather himself. For several days he kept behind closed doors.[133] On March thirtieth, many of his church came, he writes, "desiring I wd not appear in Publick on ye Ld's day, bec. wicked men were lying in wayt to apprehend me." His mind was made up, and his heart was set on his voyage to England. It was a time to take no risks.

That evening, about ten o'clock, he commended his family to God, and bade them farewell. Putting on a wig and a long white cloak, he went out into the darkness.[134] There waited one Thurston, "one of Randolph's creatures," guarding the house and hoping for a chance to arrest its owner. But the sight of the tall figure, clothed in white, was too much for him,[135] and, unaware of his presence, "the Metropolitan Clergy-man" [136] of New England passed him in safety, and disappeared down the shadowy length of Middle Street.

An hour later, Increase Mather was under Captain Phillips's

---

130. *Andros Tracts*, i, 17, 52; *MHS Coll.*, Series 5, v, 209.
131. J. T. Adams, *The Founding*, p. 423.
132. *Autobiography*; *Parentator*, p. 107.
133. MS. *Diary*, March 30, 1688; *Autobiography*.
134. *Ibid.*
135. *Ibid.*; *Parentator*, p. 108.
136. J. Dunton, *Letters Written From New-England*, p. 74.

hospitable roof in Charlestown.[137] There he stayed throughout the next day. Meanwhile "Randolph's emissaries were searching for" him "in many places." On April first several of the young men of the Second Church came to their teacher and urged him to find some safer hiding-place. With them, at midnight, he once more made use of darkness to cover his flight and made his way to a hut on Rumney Marsh.[138] One more day he lay concealed there, and then, on April third, his faithful sons, Cotton and Samuel, the latter but a boy of thirteen, joined him. With friends they accompanied him to Pulling Point, where a ketch lay moored. On the shore he gave his blessing to Cotton, and, taking Samuel with him, put out to sea at dawn. Before night they reached the Gurnet, off Plymouth.[139]

For two longs days the ketch rode at anchor, or sailed idly up and down outside of the Pilgrims' harbor. Aboard, Increase Mather and young Samuel, sick, and in cramped quarters, grew weary with waiting. At last, on April seventh, a little sail bore down on them. It was a shallop, from Boston, manned by their friends. They brought news that the ship on which the Mathers were to have sailed had left port. Promptly "the ketch wherein I was," Increase writes, "sailed towards the ship." Her spars traced against the late afternoon sky must have been a welcome sight, and when, about six o'clock in the evening the ketch tossed alongside her high bulwarks, Mather and his son clambered aboard eagerly enough.[140] Once on deck, waving farewells to their friends in the ketch, and warmly welcomed by the master of the good ship *President*,[141] they could breathe more freely. Randolph and his machinations were left far behind, where the shore of Massachusetts was fast fading into blank horizon. Ahead in the twilight lay the dangers of the sea, and the burdens of a difficult diplomatic quest. Mather's face was turned toward an England greatly changed from that he had left a quarter of a century before, and his own mission was far weightier than any

137. *Autobiography; Parentator*, p. 107. Phillips was Cotton Mather's father-in-law.

138. *Autobiography; Parentator*, p. 108. Rumney Marsh is now part of Chelsea. Sewall says (*MHS Coll.*, Series 5, v, 210) that Mather went on April 1 to Aaron Way's by Hogg-Island (the Hog Island of to-day). Cf. also, *MHS Proc.*, xxvii, 138.

139. *Autobiography; Parentator*, p. 108; *MHS Coll.*, Series 5, v, 210; MS. *Diary*, 1688, April 3, 4.

140. *Ibid.*, April 4, 5, 6, 7; *Autobiography*.

141. One Arthur Tanner. *Ibid.*; MS. *Diary*, April 7, 1688; and *MHS Coll.*, Series v, 209, 210.

task he then had known. Then he had been a faithful preacher, bent on teaching the Word wherever he might find a peaceful living. Now he was an emissary, not to sedate Puritan congregations, but to a crowded and worldly royal court. Then he had only his own concerns in mind. Now there lay on his shoulders the weight of the colony's hopes.

By the time candles began to gleam from Boston windows that night, the news ran through the streets that Increase Mather was at sea.[142] Randolph, hearing it, turned into Bullivant's shop, perhaps, to pound his fist on the counter and speak a few angry words. But by more than one broad hearth that evening, good church members gave thanks. For Puritan or layman, merchant or divine, there was cheer in the knowledge that the case of taxpayer against Andros, and of the property holders against the king's officers, had been confided to an emissary of strong hands and a stout heart.

142. Cf. *MHS Coll.*, Series V, 209.

CHAPTER XIII

THE COURT OF JAMES THE SECOND

AFTER a voyage which Mather declared was "comfortable," in spite of torments from seasickness and toothache, and dangers from "islands of ice" and "sad Fogg," the travellers on the *President* on May sixteenth left the ship to board a Weymouth boat which they sighted in the English Channel. In a few hours Mather and his son landed in England. Weymouth, Increase wrote, "was ye last town wch I saw in E[ngland]. & pvidence has so ord[ere]d yt it is ye first town wch (after 27 years absence) I am agn brought unto." [1]

No troubles of the voyage were greater than those which faced a would-be diplomatic servant of the colonies in England in May, 1688. Shoals of fog still hang here and there over the tangled political history of that year, and for Mather, no lawyer, and a representative simply of a few congregations, the task of doing real service for a Massachusetts by no means sure of its exact status, in a court torn by many factions, might well have seemed too heavy to undertake. Certain elements of the situation he had clearly in mind. He knew what "rights" he sought for the colony. He knew that James II, turning a wistful eye toward a vision of Catholic England, was opposed by the English church and nation, so far as they upheld constitutional government against arbitrary rule. He realized that the nonconformists, so long despised by statesman and prelate alike, were now courted by both.[2] Their numbers, thrown on the king's side, would have done much to steady his throne. The English church, which saw in the king's first Declaration of Indulgence a lawless act, robbing it of its place as the authorized religious body, and found in the second royal proclamation of tolerance for all, equal defiance of constitutional rule, regarded an alliance of all English Protestants as the readiest weapon against tyranny and Rome. The Bishops' refusal to allow the king's most recent dictum to

1. *Autobiography*; MS. *Diary*, April 17 to May 16, 1688.
2. *Autobiography*; *Parentator*, p. 104.

be read in the churches had brought matters to a head. The issue was sure to be influenced by the numbers enlisted on either side, and thus every Puritan became a man to be wooed assiduously by James's favorites and orthodox churchmen. This much Mather saw, and he thanked God he had come when the king "and his ministers thought it their interest to be kind to Nonconformists." [3]

It was, none the less, far from plain sailing. The dissenters were divided as to how to receive the shower of fair words. Richard Baxter could not be bribed by sudden favor. Mather's old friend, John Howe, newly returned from exile, and courted by King James, listened rather to the Hampdens, and chose the popular side. His vote carried with it those of most of the divines who had discussed the problems with him. On the other hand, Stephen Lobb, whose father and Nathaniel Mather had married sisters, "a weak, violent and ambitious man," [4] had become a power at court through his willingness to serve as the king's agent with refractory Puritans. Henry Care and Thomas Rosewell took the same course, and Vincent Alsop, a prominent divine, linked hands with them. Where men who had watched the turn of events in England day by day, and had even played their part in them, could not agree as to the path to take, what guide had a New Englander who had not seen London for nearly thirty years?

To-day, of course, we see those Puritans who regarded alliance with the English church against the king as the best way to repel not only the agents of Rome but also royal attacks on popular rights, as men who chose with wisdom and foresight. The Declaration of Indulgence amounted to an overruling by royal decree of many laws legally established. The issue was not merely one of Protestant against Catholic, Puritan against prelate, but of constitutional prerogative against royal usurpation. Baxter and Howe chose the patriots' way. Lobb and Alsop built on the shifting sand of royal promises made, in defiance of law, by a fast weakening monarch. At the same time, as we have seen, the same Declaration of Indulgence, so grave a danger for England, was for the New England colonists visible in a different light. There was little peril from Catholicism in Massachusetts, and the constitutional rights of dwellers in England mattered little to

3. *Autobiography.*
4. T. B. Macaulay, *History*, chap. 7; *MHS Coll.*, Series 4, viii, 648 n., 651 n.

Boston citizens, provided they could have liberty for Congregationalism, and scope to continue their virtual autonomy.

How Mather felt in his heart of hearts on the choice thus presented between alliance with the English church, benighted as it seemed to him, and placid acceptance of privileges offered by a king who tolerated Puritans only that he might be free to aid their foes in Rome, is a question he took good care to leave unanswered. He came for a single object, the restoration of the Massachusetts charter. His only credentials were addresses of thanks to His Majesty for his first declaration of freedom for all creeds. Whatever his private views, as a diplomat he had but one resource. He must trade so far as might be upon the fact that New Englanders were Englishmen, and nonconformists; and so long as James II found dissenters useful to his ends, he must be reminded of his subjects in the colonies. If Mather were to espouse the cause of those hostile to the king, he must sacrifice any weight his words might have at court. So, although he distrusted all Catholics, however courteous, and dared not accept Father Petre's services, feeling that to do so would be "next [to] going to the devil for help," he adapted to his uses men of all views and ranks, received a welcome even from that "Goggle-Ey'd Monster," bloody Judge Jeffreys, and kept his own views carefully concealed.[5] Thus early he showed the diplomacy that made possible such success as he had in England.

Arriving in London, with his son, late on May twenty-fifth, he was "kindly entertained" by Major Robert Thompson, at Newington Green.[6] Samuel Nowell of Boston, ex-treasurer of Harvard, who had come to England in December, 1687, was, of course, one of the first to greet him.[7] On the twenty-eighth he "visited ye congregational ministers of London who mett" at Mr. Ford's. The next afternoon he visited Stephen Lobb. The latter, true to his mission at court, told the king of Mather's arrival, and, no doubt, suggested that nonconformity abroad as well as at home was worth catering to. King James lost no time and arranged that Mather should wait upon him the next day.[8] Mather arrived in London on Friday, and on Wednesday he

5. *Autobiography; Parentator*, pp. 114, 115; *Andros Tracts*, iii, 141 n.

6. MS. *Diary*, May 25, 1688. For Thompson, see T. Hutchinson, *Collection*, ii, 85, 181, 207, and J. Savage, *Genealogical Dictionary*, iv, 287ff.

7. MS. *Diary*, May 28, 1688; J. L. Sibley, *Biographical Sketches*, i, 335ff.

8. *Autobiography*; MS. *Diary*, May 28, 29, 30. For "Mr. Ford" see *DNB*, "Stephen Ford," and *Nonconformist's Memorial*, iii, 121.

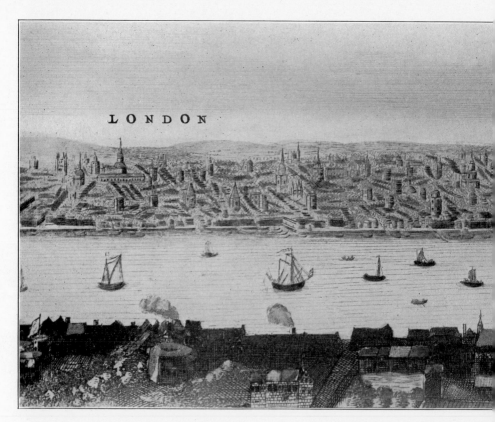

LONDON FROM SOUTHWARK

GN OF WILLIAM AND MARY

was in the presence of the king. He was not one to loiter in his quest. He waited for James in the Long Gallery at Whitehall,[9] so different from the Boston Townhouse, and a stage for actors who would have seemed quite out of place in the house of a Winthrop or a Leverett. Mather's garb may have marked him at Whitehall, but the loyalfollowers of the king had grown used to welcoming the sober Puritan dress, which they had despised of yore, and in speech and learning their guest was likely to prove at least their equal. From the beginning of his agency he met ladies of the court, and men of all classes, and fared as well with them as with his Boston friends. Here, as there, the chronicle of his visits, his dinings out, and his constant contact with the world, is voluminous.[10]

The story of Massachusetts' struggle for a charter covers the years from 1688 to 1692. In it alone there is material for a volume. To tell it with reference to all the interests, personalities, and consequences involved, demands more space than a biography of one of its actors can afford. The documents, published and unpublished, are legion, and many still lack places in any systematic bibliography or catalogue. For us, the central figure is Mather, the staunch New Englander, reared in a nursery that might well have produced a mere religious zealot. For our purposes, the central thread in the history of these eventful years must be his relation to them. The story as he told it, and as his son repeated it after him, is our first interest. His letters, and those written to him, the notes in his diary, and the comments of such eager allies as Samuel Sewall, must be the chief sources of our knowledge. If we see what his problem was, how he met it, how far his contemporaries believed he succeeded or failed, we have what we need to understand the English agency as a stage in his career. Having that, we may leave to the historian of the period the detailed examination of many papers and the task of relating Mather's agency to general English or American history. He must decide its relation to later growth in political theory. If any fact contributes to our judgment of Mather as a man seeking a goal beset by earthly obstacles, we may not neglect it. If any factor in the general situation helped to determine his thought or action, or makes it possible to judge

9. Cf. E. Sheppard, *The Old Royal Palace*. It is not clear just what Mather meant by the "Long Gallery."

10. Cf. MS. *Diaries*.

him more fairly, it is essential. Beyond that, within the limits of biography one cannot go.

As he waited in the Long Gallery, then, this Boston minister, formerly defiant of kings, foe of Catholics, and scorner of things of this life, first takes his place in the strange scene fortune had decreed for him. Had he been the Puritan so often painted for us, pious, fanatical, and an intolerant dogmatist, had he not been able to overlook minor scruples in the pursuit of noble ends, had he not been able to recognize beneath the gay coats of the court the same human nature he had studied in his parish, or had he failed to conform to their standards enough to be acceptable to them, he might, perhaps, have been a more ideally perfect figure, but he would have lacked the human quality that made him a force in the world. Moreover, he would have been useless as a diplomat, and New Hampshire, Plymouth, Connecticut, Harvard, and his own colony, all looking to him to win establishment for their futures, would have found him a broken reed. For the nonce, scholarship, divinity, and pious exhortation must be put aside. Only as a man able to use the slightest advantage given him by the character of the times or of those about him, always vigilant, and never forgetful of his aim, could he hope for progress.

At eleven o'clock the king entered. Mather offered to kneel, but James, only too willing to flatter, forbade it.[11] The first card in the hand of New England was the Address of Thanks. Mather presented it, and, at the king's request, read it aloud. He explained that it represented some twenty congregations in New England, and then offered a second document, this time from Plymouth.[12] James was all graciousness. He expressed joy that his Declaration met favor in the colonies, and promised largely that they should have "a *Magna Charta* for liberty of conscience."[13]

Two days later Mather was once more at Whitehall. This time he was admitted to the king's closet.[14] Once again he poured out New England's thanks for the "gracious Declaration of Indulgence." Once again the king expressed pleasure, and made broad statements as to his liberal aims. There was not much

11. *Autobiography*, which I follow in describing Mather's interviews with the king. Cf. also, *Parentator*, pp. 109, 110.
12. Cf. *Andros Tracts*, iii, 133 n.
13. *Autobiography; Parentator*, p. 110.
14. *Ibid.*, pp. 110ff.; *Autobiography*.

headway to be made thus, but James's question, as to how New England received Andros's rule, gave an opening for the real beginning of Mather's campaign. He had come not merely to give thanks. Massachusetts, as he saw it, demanded a change of government, and the first step must be the recall of Andros. To the king's query he replied that the royal governor would be agreeable to his subjects "if he would but duly attend to" the royal Declaration. Instead, said Mather, "there have been some of your subjects fined & imprisoned, because they, out of tenderness of conscience, declined swearing by the Book. I brought an address of thanks to your Majesty from more than twenty congregations. I believe all the congregations in New England would have concurred in that Address had not their Ministers been discouraged by Sir Edmond. . . . The ministers in Boston proposed to their congregations that they might keep a day of thanksgiving to bless God for his goodness in making your Majesty their king. Sir Edmond sent for them, & bid them keep the day at their peril." [15]

Probably the colonists' zeal to thank God for James II was not great, although they did wish to give praise for the Declaration of Indulgence. Mather's statement was admirably worded for the royal ears, if, perhaps, a somewhat too loyal coloring of Massachusetts' views.

The king declared himself surprised, and bade Mather put in writing his specific requests. Upon this he "kneeled to his Majesty, & he held out his hand to" him. His visitor kissed it, "& took" his leave "for that time." [16]

On June fourth Mather was hard at work drawing up New England's complaints.[17] On the seventh he dined with Mr. Lobb.[18] On the ninth, he visited "my Lord Fleetwood," that "weak man, but very popular with all the praying part of the army," son-in-law of Oliver Cromwell, and staunch fighter for his cause. He was an old man now, and, shorn of his honors, lived at Stoke Newington, a near neighbor of Mather's, and a former parishioner of his good friend, John Owen. Even in his last days, Fleetwood must have been an admirable figure to a New Englander, a friend of the Commonwealth, and no lover of the

15. *Autobiography.*   16. *Ibid.*
17. MS. *Diary*, June 4, 1688: "prprd complaints."
18. *Ibid.*, June 7, 1688. On June 23, Mather "lodged at Mr. Lob's" (*Ibid.*, June 23).

Stuarts.[19] The next day Mather "dined by Charing Cross with Sr. Nich. Butler," a member of the Privy Council and of the hated Ecclesiastical Commission, and "shewed him the memorial of N. E.'s present state.[20] Hee s[ai]d Sr. Ed. Andros deserved to have his ears cutt. That hee doubted not, but ye next time ye council sat there wld be an order for o[u]r relief. That hee wld shew ye memorial to ye Ld psident[21] & yt ye Ld psident & Himselfe wld introduce me with it to ye K." These were welcome words.

During the next week Mather talked with many, among them Mr. Griffith, a Puritan minister, in London, "very conversible, and much the gentleman";[22] Mr. Thomas Sergeant, in whom one would like to recognize a former unruly pupil at Harvard;[23] Mr. Alsop, influential at court, and noted for his "vividness of wit" and "nimbleness of raillery";[24] Mr. Baxter, "that excellent instrument of divine grace";[25] Lord Culpeper, erstwhile governor of Virginia,[26] and William Penn.[27] Mather may have distrusted him, as a Quaker, but he writes, "to give Mr. Penn his due,"[28] that he said "that Nicholson[29] ... should be removed; that

19. MS. *Diary*, June 9. The quotation in the text is from Lord Clarendon, *History*, iii, 1049, 1050.

20. MS. *Diary*, June 16, 1688. Cf. also, May 31. For Butler, cf. Luttrell, i, 400, 415, 416, 420, 421, 481, and iv, 655. He was a Catholic.

21. That is, the Lord President of the Privy Council, Robert Spencer, second Earl of Sunderland (1640–1702), who was a dominant power under King James, and, later, under William. He was brought up a Protestant, but joined the Roman church. He was called:

> A Proteus, ever acting in disguise;
> A finished statesman, intricately wise;
> A second Machiavel, who soar'd above
> The little tyes of gratitude and love. (See *DNB*.)

Macaulay in his *History* pictures him vividly.

22. MS. *Diary*, 1688, June 18; *Nonconformist's Memorial*, i, 107.

23. MS. *Diary*, 1688; J. L. Sibley, *Biographical Sketches*, ii, 443ff.

24. MS. *Diary*, 1688, June 19; *Nonconformist's Memorial*, iii, 48ff. See also, *DNB*, whence the quotations in the text are taken.

25. MS. *Diary*, 1688, June 20, "at Mr. Baxter's." Richard Baxter, one of the greatest English Puritans, needs no comment here. See *DNB*, and bibliography there given, and *Nonconformist's Memorial*, iii, 393ff. The quotation is from Dr. Bates's funeral sermon for Baxter, quoted in *Ibid.*, p. 401.

26. MS. *Diary*, 1688, June 20. "At Whitehall discourse with my Ld Culpeper." This was probably Thomas, Lord Culpeper. Cf. Luttrell, i, 163, 204, 215, and references to Culpeper in Channing, vol. ii, and J. A. Doyle, *The English in America. Virginia, Maryland and the Carolinas*, pp. 343ff.

27. Channing, ii, 102ff.; bibliography in *Ibid.*, p. 127; and Macaulay, *History*, chap. 7.

28. *Autobiography*.

29. Francis Nicholson, military representative of Andros. His commission as lieutenant governor of New England is cited in *Cal. State Papers, Am. and W. I.*, xii, #1709.

something should be sent to Andros that would nettle his nose, & that if he did not comply therewith he should be turned out of his government."[30] On Thursday the twenty-first he went to Whitehall and "wayted on my Ld psident"[31] of the Privy Council. Sunderland said "hee doubted Sr E. A. was not kind to dissenters, bad me tell him wt it was I desired for N. E. & it sld be done."[32] Once more, Mather found promises were cheap. In the afternoon he talked with "Nevil Payn," who wrote plays occasionally, plotted often, and was distrusted as one who "dealt with both hands."[33] Payne recommended that Mather see Father Petre.[34] This he did not do, the Puritan in him warning him not to trust so notorious a disciple of Rome. "Since," he writes, "I have seen that it was a gracious providence that did prevent me."[35] A last adviser was his brother Nathaniel, with whom he often discussed affairs.[36]

On Monday, July second, he saw the king again, in his closet at Whitehall, and presented a "Petition & Memorial in behalf of New England."[37] The king promised to take care of the matters mentioned in the paper. Mr. Lobb and "Counsellor Owen" were present,[38] and the former, eager that James should never forget his sect, remarked: "If his majesty would be kind to New England, it would have a good influence on Dissenters in England." Sir Hugh Owen, not to be outdone, and with a lawyer's liking for written articles, said: "If your Majesty would cause something to be published in behalf of the Dissenters in New England, that the world might see it, probably it would be of great advantage." Mather seized the opportunity to introduce a second of the great objects of his mission, asking a charter for the College. He declared: "If the church of England men had built a College for themselves, no one would object against it, but we think it hard that the College built by Non-conformists, should be put into the hands of Conformists."

30. *Autobiography;* MS. *Diary,* 1688, June 18.
31. *Ibid.,* June 21.   32. *Ibid.*
33. *Ibid.; DNB,* "Henry Neville Payne."
34. *Autobiography.* Edward Petre was the confessor of James II, and became a member of the Privy Council in 1687.
35. *Ibid.*
36. Cf., for example, MS. *Diary,* 1688, June 29, July 11.
37. *Autobiography; Parentator,* p. 113.
38. *Autobiography.* This was probably Sir Hugh Owen, who was admitted to the Inner Temple in 1672, and was M. P. for Pembrokeshire 1689-95. See G. E. C., *Complete Baronetage,* ii, 131.

To which James: "That's unreasonable, and it shall not be." [39] For the next three months Mather busied himself with more interviews with Alsop, Lord Bellasis, First Lord of the Treasury,[40] Lord Culpeper, Baxter, Matthew Mead,[41] the Attorney-General, Sir Thomas Powis,[42] Robert Boyle, Mr. Powell,[43] and William Ashurst. With a Yankee's delight in a bargain, he records that he "used to indent with some of" the nonconformist ministers at London, "that if they would spare time to go unto such or such a great person of their acquaintance, & improve their interest in him for New England, then I would gladly assist them in preaching." [44] Thus he preached for Thomas Cole,[45] for John Quick [46] at Bartholomew Close, and for many others, and established himself in the politicians' minds as a man whose connections with English Puritans made him a factor to be reckoned with.

On August twenty-first there is a peculiarly significant entry in his diary: "Discourse with Sir W. Phips about N. E." [47] Sir William Phipps [48] was born in Maine in 1650, of poor parents. He became apprentice to a ship's carpenter, and moved to Boston. There he married the widow of John Hull, "a young gentlewoman of good repute." [49] Fascinated by dreams of treasure trove, he managed to turn his savings to use, and, in 1683, took command of the English ship *Algier Rose*. After adventures befitting an age of romantic seafaring, he discovered a sunken wreck, whence he retrieved a considerable fortune. He came to

39. *Autobiography.*
40. John, Lord Bellasis. Cf. *DNB*, "John Belasyse (1614–1689)." He was a Catholic.
41. A Puritan divine of some prominence. *Nonconformist's Memorial*, ii, 461ff., and *DNB*.
42. Luttrell, i, 424. He became Speaker of the House of Commons during the interregnum.
43. Exact identification of this "Mr. Powell" is not possible, but I believe him to be Henry Powle, 1630–1692 (see *DNB*). He was not active in politics in 1688, but was a lawyer, and a member of the Royal Society. He was known as a historical and legal scholar, as well as an antiquarian.
44. *Autobiography.*
45. Thomas Cole, Puritan divine, tutor of Locke, schoolmaster in Oxfordshire, preacher at a church on Silver St., London, and lecturer at Pinners Hall. *Nonconformist's Memorial*, i, 249ff.; MS. *Diary*, 1688, July 29; *DNB*.
46. *Nonconformist's Memorial*, ii, 9ff.; MS. *Diary*, 1688, August 16.
47. *Ibid.*, August 21.
48. For him, see C. Mather, *Magnalia*, book II, Appendix, and *DNB*, "Sir William Phipps."
49. Mather, *Magnalia*, book II, Appendix, section 3.

London in 1687 with prosperity and a reputation, and was knighted by the king. He maintained an interest in Boston, and built a house there. He eagerly opposed Andros, and came to England in 1688, to use what influence he had in Mather's behalf. Adventurer as he was, and most happy when in some active and perilous quest, faced with a mutinous crew, or a stormy sea, he had, none the less, a persistent strain of piety.

He had, if Cotton Mather's quotation of him be correct, first become "sensible of his Sins" in 1674, when he heard Increase Mather "preach concerning, 'The day of trouble near.'" Thereupon, he adds, it "pleased Almighty God to smite me with a deep sense of my miserable condition, who had lived until then in the world, and had done nothing for God." [50] Thenceforth he combined with a talent for making money, political ambition, and boldness, if nothing more, in military enterprise, a taste for Puritan doctrine. His religious yearnings and, particularly, his reverence for the Mathers, stood him in good stead in his quest for power.

It is easier to picture Mather dealing successfully with Phipps, or with King James himself, than it is to think of him as a persuasive visitor to various ladies of the court. Diplomacy before and after him found court beauties useful. So he knew that the word of a lady-in-waiting sometimes has influence with a queen, and that a wife may prevail on a statesman when others fail. One must abandon, once and for all, any illusion that Mather, because he was a Puritan, was, therefore, no more than an underbred and obtrusively pious reformer. Instead, we find him "known to some ladies of honor" [51] who were of power in court circles. The Countess of Sutherland was later, as we shall see, a friend whose interest was used in his behalf. The Countess of Anglesey was another of his fair allies. "She was a member of Dr. Owen's church," [52] and the widow of Arthur Annesley, first Earl of Anglesey.[53] Lady Clinton, again a disciple of a Puritan, being "one of Mr. Alsop's church," [54] was another member of the court circle not immune to the persuasiveness of a New Englander's tongue, and Madam Lockhart, one of Queen Mary's

50. Mather, *Magnalia*, book II, Appendix, section 9.
51. *Autobiography*.
52. *Ibid.*
53. W. Orme, *Memoirs . . . of John Owen*, p. 374.
54. *Autobiography*.

ladies,[55] also did him services. These were all women versed in the ways of the world and, more especially, of the English court. There is no more vivid tableau in all his life's story than that evoked by the thought of Increase Mather received by the Countess of Anglesey, or by the Countess of Sutherland. He, soberly clad, and somewhat impressed by the glow of many candles and the brilliant costumes dear to Pepys's heart, was, none the less, able to capture the attention even of the patched, powdered, and worldly-minded, by his manner and speech. Surely he did not talk only of politics or theology. Surely some latent strain of courtliness, some aptitude for deft compliment, or, at least, for entertaining talk of the world, came to his aid. Without them he could hardly have won so easily the good offices of these "ladies of honor."

Most of them, of course, were influential in the years after 1688, but before he had been a year in England, we find him visiting Madam Lloyd,[56] a good friend of Bostonians. Moreover, he discovered early that a man deaf to his exhortations might have a wife more ready to hear. So on June eleventh, Stephen Mason wrote him:[57]

Just as you went from the booksellers, I with Mad^e Bl—— were there [to] wait on you, & suppose you took coach, or must haue overtaken you i[n] Cheapside; but missing you, & fearing a letter by the penny post might faile, I came hither to let you know that this day M^r. P. was at her lodgings, & that he assures her that you need not doubt all things [shall be] done to your content, and that he will labour in it, but not above board, [&] so as M^r. Blaithwaite shall know nothing of it, but saith it wilbe about 10 daies first, because of the present rejoycing, which hinders all buissinesse; & tels her that N. E. people have been represented as such who haue wronged his Majesty in his customes, & an odd humoured people, which occasioned what hath been transacted in N. E., but that he will undeceiue his Majesty. He aduised her to goe to my Lord Bellasise, as a person much in favour, which she resolues to doe on Thursday next.

Praying the Lord to succeed your endeauours, I remaine S^r., Yo^r sincerely affe^t ff^d & seru^t.

55. *Autobiography; Andros Tracts*, iii, 158 n.
56. *MHS Coll.*, Series 5, v, 248, 271; Series 6, i, 78, 98, ii, 204; MS. *Diary*, 1688, Sept. 5.
57. *MHS Coll.*, Series 4, viii, 699. For Mason, cf. *Ibid.*, Series 5, v, 254, 284, 286, vii, 63; and Series 6, i, 116, 118, 150, 151, 201; J. Savage, *Genealogical Dictionary*, iii, 170. MS. *Diary*, 1688, gives Mason's address as "at the three carved lions in Cañon Street."

Penn,[58] Mason, and Mather seem to have won over Mrs. Mary Blathwayt,[59] whose husband, William, was in high place, and by no means a whole-hearted supporter of the colonial cause.[60] One wishes that she had left a record as to how Mather and his sympathizers gained her active interest. Clearly his personality and skill turned varied human means to the uses of his diplomacy.

By September twenty-sixth, when he next visited the king's closet,[61] James II's usefulness to New England was waning, and his promises seemed less precious than in the days when William of Orange's shadow loomed less largely on the political horizon. On the other hand, it is said, he had but five days before publicly declared that he intended to establish liberty of conscience by legal means,[62] and in Mather's presence he was no less generous with assurances of the benefits he planned for the colonies. It is interesting to find Mather urging haste.

"I humbly pray," he said, "that the matter may be expedited, and I know that if your majesty shall be kind to New England it will have a good influence on your affairs here." James, remembering certain news that the Dutch were preparing against him, which had come but three days before,[63] can hardly have failed to see in his black-coated visitor one who was no mere novice in the day's politics.

James hastened, so far as England was concerned, to make a last attempt to rebuild his crumbling political foundations. On September twenty-ninth he proclaimed a general pardon; the

58. I identify the "Mr P." of the letter, as Penn, in view of Mather's frequent references to him in his diaries as "Mr P."

59. The identification of "Mad^e Bl——" as Mrs. Blathwayt seems clear from the context. She was Mary Wynter, daughter of John Wynter of Dyrham, Gloucestershire, and married Blathwayt December 23, 1686.

60. *DNB.* He became clerk of the Privy Council on October 22, 1686, and was a witness at the trial of the bishops. See reference to him, under the initials W. B., in Increase Mather's letter to Governor Hinckley, September 12, 1689, when he writes: "You have no enemy like your friend W. B., to whom you sent fifty guineas." *MHS Coll.*, Series 4, v, 211.

Blathwayt wrote Sir Robert Southwell, saying: "Increase Mather ... etc., are come hither from Massachusetts with addresses and have audiences of the great ones now. And there are joint endeavors to supplant Sir Edmund (Andros) and discredit the Cavaleros but I hope Sir Ed. Andros has taken such root in his Majestie's good opinion as to withstand some shocks." E. F. Ward, *Christopher Monck*, p. 301. (Quoted there from Welbeck MSS.)

61. *Autobiography; Parentator*, p. 114.

62. See memorandum of Thomas Prince, Sept. 21, 1688, in *MHS Coll.*, Series 4, viii, 713.

63. *Ibid.;* Macaulay, *History*, chap. 9.

next day he relieved the Bishop of London from his sentence of suspension; on October first London's charter was restored; on the fourth the Commission for Ecclesiastical Causes was dissolved; and on the twelfth, good augury for Harvard, Magdalen College was granted its former rights.

On October sixteenth Mather met James for the last time. Lord Wharton,[64] who had espoused the New Englander's cause, conducted him to the royal presence. Philip Wharton, fourth baron, was a good Puritan, and a benefactor to dissenters, whose name lives in more than one nonconformist's grateful letters or diary. Events had proved James to be in a mood to concede much, and Mather and Wharton may well have had high hopes, hearing his glib assurance "that property, liberty, & the college should all be confirmed to" New England.[65] Cotton Mather, who had before him, not only the autobiography and diaries still accessible to us, but also information drawn from talking over the whole affair with his father, when his memories of it were still fresh, tells us that Increase hoped the "Distress . . . of the Impending *Revolution*" would compel James to action; and, apparently, after the royal interview in October, Mather believed the king's promise was likely to be fulfilled. False rumors that the Prince of Orange's expedition was diverted lightened the pressure upon James, and destroyed New England's hopes. Whereupon Cotton Mather described his father as saying of the king: "I will see thy Face no more." [66]

It was clear at last that fair words were all James could give. With this October the first stage of Mather's agency ends. He had improved each week by efforts to add to his party every influential person, noble or lady, Presbyterian, Congregationalist, or Quaker, to whom he could gain access. In his personal interviews with the king, he had been unflagging in his determination not to allow it to be forgotten that nonconformists, in colonies as well as in mother country, were to be appeased. By October he was known in more than one great London house, and his name was familiar to the Attorney-General and to the lords of the Privy Council. He had made it impossible for any deft political architect to build, quite oblivious of New England and her agent.

64. Philip, fourth Baron Wharton. See *DNB*.
65. *Autobiography*. Cf. *Cal. State Papers, Am. and W. I.*, xii, ⚹1879, which seems to show that James meant to fulfil this promise.
66. *Parentator*, pp. 115, 116.

WHITEHALL PALACE FROM THE RIVER

Meanwhile he had been kept informed of affairs at home. From Samuel Sewall had come letters asking aid on the point in which the shoe pinched him most under Andros's laws.[67] John Cotton wrote, too, asking Mather's good offices with English promoters of missions among the American Indians.[68] Such letters brought the news of Boston streets, and Phipps, who sailed for England, probably in July,[69] brought first-hand impressions of colonial affairs.

Andros had journeyed in April, shortly after Mather's sailing, to the Penobscot, where a Frenchman, one Castine, ruled a little kingdom of his own in defiance of any English governor. He promptly vanished when Andros arrived, and the latter was content to take some of his unwilling host's belongings, sending word that he might regain his property by offering allegiance to Great Britain. Thence Andros turned to Pemaquid, where, with Randolph, he persuaded the Maine Indians to agree to keep the peace.[70]

Returning to Boston, he found awaiting him a new royal commission, dated in April, making him governor of all British America, save for Pennsylvania, Delaware, Maryland, and Virginia. His capital was to be at Boston, where he was to be assisted by a Council of forty-two members, of whom five constituted a quorum. The governor was empowered to remove councillors, provided he could show due cause to the king. He had authority to impose and collect taxes, and to make laws, subject to the English Privy Council's veto. Liberty of conscience was to be maintained, but strict censorship of the press was insisted upon.[71]

In July and August, Andros visited his new territories in the south, and in September went to Albany to try to reach some peaceful understanding with the Indians of the Five Nations. Sporadic outbreaks of the natives were causing trouble, and just prior to Mather's last interview with the king, the provisional government in Boston sent troops to Maine to protect the English there.[72]

While Andros thus extended his domain, untroubled, apparently, save for red-skinned neighbors, Mather was trying hard to undermine his standing in London. To see just what his weapons were, one must consider not only his speeches to the king, but

67. *MHS Coll.*, Series 4, viii, 517, 519.
68. *Ibid.*, pp. 226 n., 255, 257.
69. *Ibid.*, p. 712.
70. Palfrey, iii, 558ff.
71. *Ibid.*, pp. 561ff.
72. *Ibid.*

the various detailed statements he proffered to the English authorities.

At their first meeting Mather gave James the thanks of the Massachusetts churches for the Declaration of Indulgence, and with it a similar document from congregations in Plymouth.[73] The latter raised the issue of charter restoration, urging that the Pilgrim colony be allowed to keep what it held to be its charter rights.

When Mather saw the king on July second, he presented a "*Memorial* of the Grievances which filled his Country with the *Cry of the Oppressed.*"[74] In this he asserted that James's subjects in New England "dissenting from the Church of England are by much the greatest & wealthiest Part"; that Massachusetts was the first of the colonies to proclaim the king, and that they submitted quietly to the royal governor. They have, he declares, been maligned by the episcopal party, and the "Service of the Church of England has bin forced into their Meeteing Houses."[75]

All this was true, unless, perhaps, it was wrong to include all the accusations made against the colony by Randolph and others, under the head of attacks by "the episcopal party." But it was true that Church of England men had said and written hard things of New England Puritans, and to ascribe religious motives was as easy as it was natural.

The next item in the complaint was that Andros had not allowed the churches "to sett apart Days of Prayer and Thanksgiving: no, not even for the Blessing of your Gracious Declaration for Liberty of Conscience, Nor were the People there Encouraged to make humble Addresses of Thanks, but the Contrary."[76] It appears that although Andros had ordered thanksgiving from the whole colony for the king's liberality,[77] — a fact Mather does not mention, — he had forbidden special Congregational days of rejoicing over the Declaration of Indulgence.[78] One need not

73. *MHS Coll.*, Series 4, viii, 697, 698; *Andros Tracts*, iii, 133ff.; *Cal. State Papers, Am. and W. I.*, xii, ＃1793.

74. *Autobiography; Parentator*, pp. 112, 113; *MHS Coll.*, Series 4, viii, 113, 115, 699–702; *Andros Tracts*, iii, 136 n., 137 n., 138 n., 139 n.

75. *MHS Coll.*, Series 4, viii, 699, 700.

76. *Ibid.*, p. 700.   77. Palfrey, iii, 548 and n.

78. This was asserted by Mather, again and again, and by Cotton Mather in *Parentator*, p. 103. In the margin of the document we have been discussing, opposite the reference to this matter, is written "Three ministers in Boston, & one now in London doe attest to this." (*MHS Coll.*, Series 4, viii, 700.) It seems unlikely that a charge of this sort would have been brought without authority, inasmuch as Andros's side of the case was sure to be promptly heard.

blame him. He believed, soundly enough, that in His Majesty's Government, not in the Congregational church, lay the authority to call public days of thanksgiving.[79] Moreover, he was a military governor and versed in the ways of crowds. It could not but be dangerous for him to allow the party most bitterly averse to him to celebrate publicly a royal decree which weakened the position of the church he wished to uphold. On the other hand, his tact, not always to be relied upon, failed him here, for his action gave the Puritans a strong weapon with a king who promised "liberty of conscience" largely to win such men as they.

Mather then asserts that "there have bin threatnings to punish any Man that should give to the value of Two pence to maintaine a Nonconformist Minister."[80] This sounds perilously like mere rumor, but a marginal note declares "Sam[ll] Seawell, Theoph[s] Frary, & severall others in New-England can attest to this."[81] What the basis for the charge was, we do not know, but probably Sewall and Frary understood some English official's hasty speech to mean more than it did, and capitalized it as a ground for complaint. The accusation that New Englanders were fined and imprisoned for refusing to swear on the Bible, a practice forbidden by Puritan consciences, seems sustained,[82] although it is probable that imprisonment was not the penalty for failure to swear in the prescribed form, but for contempt of court, when the recalcitrants withheld their fines. The next three charges concern property, averring that dissenters' lands have been given to Episcopalians, that land was seized unless payments were made to hold it, that the people have been told by officials "that they are no better then Slaves, that they have no Title to Property or English Privilidges."[83] All this came from Andros's attack on land titles, and from John Wise's report of what Dudley said to him.[84] The statement of the case is not too strong for the facts as the Puritan saw them. As to the complaint that Massachusetts men had

79. W. D. Love, *The Fast and Thanksgiving Days*, pp. 228, 229.

80. *MHS Coll.*, Series 4, viii, 700.

81. *Ibid.*, p. 366, where is given a letter from Joshua Moodey to Mather, saying: "A copy of the Articles came over with some marginall notes of the names of sundry witnesses, some of which have been & are concerned to think whether it was so prudent & kind to expose them till the pinch came." See also, *Ibid.*, p. 700.

82. For the two sides of this, see *Andros Tracts*, i, 11ff., especially section 7, and i, 21ff., especially pp. 46, 47.

83. *MHS Coll.*, Series 4, viii, 700.

84. Cf., for example, Palfrey, iii, 526, 527, 529ff., and J. T. Adams, *The Founding*, pp. 417ff.

been jailed without reason, and fined for unknown offences, sufficient basis was found in the lack of printed laws under Andros, particularly noticeable in a commonwealth where printed statutes had come to be looked upon as a bulwark of popular rights.[85] Finally, in the copy of the "Memorial" preserved to-day, the last paragraph is in Mather's hand and refers to the college, repeating the Puritans' great fear lest Harvard might come to be governed by Anglican authorities.[86]

With the complaints Mather presented suggestions for their redress, in which Samuel Nowell and Elisha Hutchinson joined him.[87] They asked that land titles be confirmed to the colonists, on the terms in force before the loss of the old charter. They asked for "liberty of conscience in matters of Religion," recognition of the old way of taking oaths, and reservation of Congregational churches for the use of their owners. They hoped no taxes might be imposed without the consent of an assembly, and that town governments might exercise the same powers as in charter days. As for the College, they begged that it be left, as before, to the rule of its President and Fellows. These requests aimed at the obvious remedies for the colonists' chief grievances, and do not savor of a desire for an unreasonable degree of independence. Certainly they contain no hint of a longing for an intolerant religious government in New England. This is the more important, since Mather has been accused of having had primarily in view the preservation of the old religious restriction of the suffrage, and the salvation of Congregational power.[88] If this was his main desire, it is, to say the least, remarkable that he did not ask for it, and even more strange that he did petition for "liberty of conscience" and, later, even for the granting of the franchise to all "freeholders" without religious limitation. It is hard to see why he signed, with Nowell and Hutchinson, a petition seeking to have granted to Harvard a charter "confirming the Governm^t of that Society in such hands as layed the Foundation thereof, they taking Care that Persons of all Parswasions relating to Religion, that may desire to be admitted among

85. Palfrey, iii, 523, 524.
86. *MHS Coll.*, Series 4, viii, 700.   87. *Ibid.*, p. 701.
88. J. T. Adams (*The Founding*, p. 435) says: "In England, Mather was exerting every means to fasten the shackles permanently on the colony by insisting upon the old Congregational test for the suffrage." On pp. 445, 446, he repeats this view of Mather. As we shall see, he not only did not ask for the old limitation of the suffrage but signed a petition asking that it be granted to "freeholders."

them, shall be instructed in Academicall learning." [89] There was no diplomatic reason for feigning liberal views. James was catering to Puritans, and knew the English church was for the most part hostile. Mather believed his requests would be granted. To suppose, then, that he deliberately failed to ask for what he wanted, and asked, instead, for the contrary, is to make him not only an impossibly stupid bungler, but a bungler devoid even of instinct. One cannot realize too early in studying his agency that he fought for the popular cause, not the cause of his own sect. If land titles were assured, and an assembly provided, and if "liberty of conscience" was granted, he would have righted the greatest wrongs. With the popular support such success would assure him, his personal ends would be well served. A narrower programme might please his church, but must deny to him the general favor by which alone he could remain a force in public affairs or in the church itself. Only when this situation is clearly seen, can one understand the later course of Mather's mission in England.

Mather also petitioned the Committee for Trade and Foreign Plantations. They referred his requests to the Attorney-General.[90] But William Blathwayt, the Clerk of the Council, made a copy from which all mention of an assembly was omitted. "Being spoke to about it, he said the Earl of *Sunderland* blotted out that with his own hand," and "a Soliciter in this Cause" told the agents that the king had commissioned Andros to raise money without an assembly, and "would never consent to an Alteration." [91] Whether Blathwayt merely hid behind Sunderland, one cannot tell; but it is interesting to remember that his wife encouraged Mather by working in his interests, while her lord and master drew up documents denying popular government to New England.

We are fortunate in knowing just what Mather's petition to the Committee asked for, and just what the English authorities refused to grant. Among the State Papers, the document is preserved, signed by Mather, Nowell, and Hutchinson.[92] It asks that titles to land owned prior to May 24, 1686, be confirmed, that the register of titles to lands in New England be validated,

89. *MHS Proc.*, xii, 112.
90. *Cal. State Papers, Am. and W. I.*, xii, #1859, 1860.
91. *Andros Tracts*, ii, 10.
92. *Cal. State Papers, Am. and W. I.*, xii, #1860.

that the townships be allowed to decide questions as to commons and other business by vote of a majority of freeholders (not merely "freemen," members of a church, but all property owners), and that their commons be definitely granted to them. Courts of conscience [93] are asked for, one for each precinct, with jurisdiction up to the value of forty shillings. The petitioners sought to have probates of wills made in these courts, in cases where the estate did not exceed ten pounds. Larger estates were to go to the County Courts for probate. All marriages were to be registered and ratified in the Courts of Conscience, and there was to be a court of equity for all important cases. To these clauses no objection was made.

The colonists' other requests were less favorably received. Mather and his allies asked that, a revenue of five thousand pounds a year being first provided for the maintenance of the government, no other taxes should be levied except by the General Assembly. They wished to have this body the governor's council, elected by the freeholders of each precinct. No laws were to be made except by this assembly. There was to be liberty of conscience, no man was to be obliged to maintain a religion he did not profess, each sect was to be left to support itself, and the college was to be confirmed to those who founded it, while meeting-houses were to be left in the control of those who built them. All these proposals the Committee refused. [94]

This document clears up once and for all any questions as to whether Mather was illiberal, or narrow, in his zeal to serve his church at the popular expense. He asked votes for freeholders, no longer merely for the freemen who had formerly been required to be Congregationalists; he urged government by a popular assembly, sought liberty of conscience, and repudiated taxation of citizens for the support of churches other than their own. And, be it noted, not the bigoted Puritan of popular fancy, but the Earl of Sunderland and his fellow committee-men, defeated the prompt coming of a liberal popular government for New England.

The Committee's refusal of certain clauses, coupled with the rumors that the Dutch invasion was averted, [95] lulling James to fancied security on his throne, made it plain that the colonial demands would not be accepted in full. Accordingly, in October,

93. See *NED*, under "Court," definition IV, 11, c: "a small debt court."
94. *Cal. State Papers, Am. and W. I.*, xii, ⊛1860.
95. *Parentator*, p. 115.

Mather, Nowell, and Hutchinson resolved to get what they might, and once more petitioned the Committee.[96] If a popular assembly cannot be hoped for, they said, "the Council should consist of such persons as shall be considerable Proprietors of Lands within his Majesty's dominions"; and they asked "that the Countys being continued as at present, each County may have one, at least, of such of the Inhabitants of the same to be a member thereof." They begged that no laws be made without a majority vote of the Council, and that all laws, once passed, be printed. "So small a boon," writes Palfrey, "were men of Massachusetts content to ask from a King of England." [97] Most interesting of all, the boon concerned popular government, and, once more, there is no word of Mather's alleged preoccupation with church sovereignty.

James's temporary respite, based on the false report of the frustration of William's plan for invasion, was short. The events of the Revolution of 1688 need no discussion here. It is enough to recall that early in November Mather must have heard of the arrival of a manifesto from the Prince of Orange, and of James's wrath. William was already at sea, and on the fifth of November he landed at Torbay. On the ninth he was received in Exeter. There were disturbances in London, men of rank joined the invader, and, on the nineteenth, James took up quarters at Salisbury. Deserted by Churchill and his own daughter, Anne, he soon came back, almost alone, to London. On November thirtieth he began to prepare for a parliamentary election, but his game was lost. On December tenth he hurried his wife and son across the Channel. The next day he tried to follow, casting the Great Seal of England into the muddy waters of the Thames. He was captured two days later, and brought back, only to escape again on the eighteenth. On the twenty-third he sailed for France, leaving William safely in Whitehall, receiving the congratulations of his new subjects.

Meanwhile, in New England, Andros found the Indians amenable only to force. He led a small troop into Maine, and the failure of his campaign, coupled with the hardships suffered by his men, added one more grievance to the list New England

96. What seems likely to be a petition presented at this time is in *MHS Coll.*, Series 4, viii, 116. Palfrey (iii, 565) assigns it to October, 1688. The reference to the refusal of an Assembly makes this date probable.

97. Idem, iii, 566.

cherished against him. Popular animosity fed upon rumor, and more than one Massachusetts man saw the royal governor as the ally of the French and of King James, against the England which was striving to set up William of Orange as the constitutional leader of a popular government.[98] More than one Bostonian, seeking light in the darkness that had settled on New England, pinned his hopes on Increase Mather. In him his countrymen saw their one reliance against Andros and his visionary French allies. In him they saw the only means by which, whatever the event of the Revolution, whatever the temper of the English government, New England's cause might be sure of effective advocacy at Whitehall. They could record Andros's crimes, real and fancied, they could strive to unify popular feeling and turn it to effective use, but the real leadership could not be theirs. The ultimate success or failure of their hopes rested with a man who had fled in disguise from New England nine months before, and now, at the English court, bent every resource of a shrewd and active mind to the solution of his country's problem.

98. Cf. Palfrey, iii, 569; *MHS Coll.*, Series 4, viii, 707, 370, 372. In the last passage Moodey writes, "It will one day bee known whence this war rose." That Mather's attacks on Andros on this score were taken seriously enough to be answered shows that the matter was one which, in popular estimation, could not be laughed away.

CHAPTER XIV

THE NEGOTIATION WITH WILLIAM III

FOR Mather the change of government in 1688 meant more than that James II's promises were proved vain. His position changed at once on William III's advent. His nonconformity was no longer the support it had been. There was no longer any question of pitting one sect against another to serve the king's ends. On the other hand, there was much to be hoped for from William. He was looked upon as the savior of Englishmen's rights; and if English corporations were restored to their old prerogatives, there was hope that New England, too, might be confirmed once more in its charter privileges. But the argument from now on must be based, not on the Declaration of Indulgence, but on the colony's claims to the benefits conferred on English citizens at home. Massachusetts must justify the constitutionality of the institutions she hoped to save, and her future government must accord with whatever policy the new king saw fit to declare.

Mather continued busily at work. On November thirteenth, he had a last interview with Melfort,[1] the unscrupulous, of the "active, undertaking temper," whose influence in England was so nearly at an end. He kept in touch with other political leaders, and continued to preach for his brethren in London parishes. On December twentieth he "discoursed with Dr. Burnet about" New England.[2] Burnet had been active in William's interests, and was in high favor among the churchmen about the prince.[3] Major Thompson introduced Mather to him; and Lord Wharton

1. MS. *Diary*, 1688, Nov. 13. Melfort was John Drummond, first Earl and titular Duke of Melfort, Jacobite, "one of the handsomest men of his time, an accomplished dancer," but of a character which "never inspired confidence either in his political or religious professions." See *DNB*.

2. MS. *Diary*, 1688, Dec. 20; *Autobiography; Parentator*, pp. 126, 127. *Andros Tracts*, ii, 272, quotes Burnet on "New-England's Case" in a sermon before the House of Commons.

3. *DNB*, article "Gilbert Burnet, 1643–1715," and references there.

afterward declared that the agent's "having engaged the bishop of Salisbury to appear for New England was the best job" he "had done these seven years." [4] Sir John Thompson, later a member of the Convention Parliament, was another much-visited friend,[5] and we find Mather walking with him out to Hackney, pouring in his ears the sad tale of New England.[6] On December twenty-seventh he met once more "good old" Lord Wharton,[7] who had become an unflagging ally. He not only introduced Mather "unto many of the nobility," but himself urged the claims of New England "upon all occasions with the king, & with the Lords of the Council, as if he had been constituted as an agent for the country." [8] As early as December twenty-eighth, only ten days after William's coming to London, Mather was in consultation with the prince's chaplain, "honest William Carstares," called by Jacobites "the cardinal," [9] and with him "drew up a memorial" about New England. Carstares advised that it be carried to Bentinck, chamberlain and confidential adviser to William. And, on the last day of 1688, Mather not only saw Wharton once more, but dined with Sir Henry Ashurst, who, of all his English friends, was to be the most consistent and useful servant of the colony.[10]

Meanwhile Mather had been writing. Pamphleteering was too good a political instrument to be neglected. His unpublished diary tells us that, on December fifth, he finished his "Narrative of the state of New England." [11] If we accept this entry as a reference to a book called "A Narrative of the Miseries of New-England," ascribed with good reason to Mather, and definitely claimed by him, we can be sure, for the first time, of the exact

4. *Autobiography*.

5. See *Ibid.*; MS. *Diary*, 1688. He was Sir John Thompson, later first Baron Haversham. See *DNB*. He married a daughter of the Countess of Anglesey, referred to above as one of Mather's friends.

6. MS. *Diary*, 1688, Dec. 22.

7. *Ibid.*, Dec. 27; *Parentator*, p. 118.

8. *Autobiography*.

9. MS. *Diary*, 1688, Dec. 28. The entry reads: "A. M. with Mr. How, & after yt with Mr. Carstares (who came with ye prince of orange) about N. E. affair who drew up a memorial & advised to carry it to Mouns. Bentinck ye prince's chamberlain." For Carstares, see *DNB*, article "William Carstares, 1649–1715."

10. MS. *Diary*, 1688, Dec. 31. Sir Henry Ashurst was a son of a wealthy London merchant, Henry Ashurst (1614?–1680), for whom see *DNB*. Sir Henry was long a friend to New England. See references to him in Palfrey and similar works.

11. MS. *Diary*, 1688, Dec. 5.

date of its composition.[12] It was not printed until after January 2, 1689, for it refers to events of that day.[13]

The "Narrative" tells the troubles of the colony "by Reason of an Arbitrary Government Erected there Under Sir Edmond Andros." Beginning with a tribute to the character of the New Englanders, Mather points out that it is not for "the Honour & Interest of the *English Nation*" to discourage them (p. 3). English interests have been endangered, primarily by the *Quo Warranto* issued against the original charter. He asserts that the judgment against the colony was unjust, because no time was given to answer the charges. This statement is supported by what we know of the facts.[14] Mather continues, saying that "Evil Counsellours" desired to set up a French government in New England, and Sir Edmund Andros, "a *Gernsy-man*" was chosen as "a fit Instrument to be made use of" (p. 5).

This assertion, however improbable, was based on what the colonists believed of Andros's purposes, and letters from home may have given Mather the basis for the charge.[15] He goes on to decry the royal governor's failure to print the laws, his prohibi-

12. The title is: "A Narrative of the Miseries of New-England, By Reason of an Arbitrary Government Erected *there* Under Sir *Edmond Andros*." It is reprinted in *Andros Tracts*, ii, 3ff., to which edition all references in this book are made.

The ascription of this, and other books, to Mather during this period, rests on the following evidence. In a printed address, delivered in 1693 before the Governor and legislature of Massachusetts, Mather said that he "Published the *Narrative of the Miseries of New England*," and that afterwards he wrote "a *First, Second* and *Third Vindication of the people there*"; also that he wrote and dispersed "Reasons for the Confirmation of that Charter." It seems quite clear from the above that these works were all that Mather wrote bearing directly on his pleading of New England's cause, since his address was to justify himself, and he would not have been likely to omit anything he had written.

As to his authorship of the "Narrative," an unpublished manuscript of Mather's, preserved by the American Antiquarian Society with the *Autobiography*, says: "I drew up a Narrative of the Miseries of New England and shewed it to several lords, ministers, gentlemen, divines, who advised me to cause it to be printed, that so I might disperse many of them amongst the lords & commons to be assembled, January 22; which was accordingly done." As for the other works which Mather claims, an identification of them is attempted in the pages which follow.

On the whole matter, and this pamphlet, see *Andros Tracts*, ii, 2.

13. It reprints *The Address of the Nonconformist Ministers &c.*, delivered to William on Jan. 2, 1688–89 (see p. 12 of the "Narrative").

14. Mr. Whitmore, in *Andros Tracts*, i, 66 n., does not agree with Mather's view; but the account in Palfrey, iii, 392–394, especially 394, n. 1, seems to support Mather's statement.

15. Joshua Moodey wrote Samuel Nowell, as to Andros's Indian war, hinting darkly: "It will one day bee known whence this war arose." *MHS Coll.*, Series 4, viii, 372.

tion of frequent town meetings, his taxation without the vote of an assembly, the denial of *habeas corpus*, excessive charges for probates, and the invalidation of land titles, emphasizing the inconsistency of such measures with the best English practice. He then refers to his own agency, and James's kind reception of him. He prints a petition he presented in behalf of the town of Cambridge, stating its grievances under Andros. "Thus has New-England been dealt with," he concludes; "this has been and still *is* the bleeding state of that Countrey: they cannot but hope that *England* will send them speedy relief. . . . Many had fears that there is a Design to deliver that Countrey into the hands of the *French* King, except his Highness the Prince of *Orange*, whom a Divine Hand has raised up to deliver the Oppressed, shall happily and speedily prevent it" (pp. 10, 11).

At the close of his own remarks, Mather adds, "*The humble Application of* Henry *Lord Bishop of* London," to the Prince of Orange, and "*The Address of the* Nonconformist Ministers," including after each the prince's gracious reply, asserting his devotion to Protestantism.

This tract turns to account those items in New England's brief most likely to arouse governmental and popular response in England. There is no attack on the English church, but rather an appeal to the feelings of the Londoner of the time. For him, harping on the rights of English citizens, and dark hints of French aggression, had an obvious effect.

On January second, Sir Henry Ashurst went with Mather to St. James's Palace, and there the New England divine had his first glimpse of the Dutch prince.[16] A week later Lord Wharton conducted him to William, at the palace, and introduced him, saying that the people of New England were conscientious and godly and asked not for money or troops but for "their ancient privileges."[17] The prince promised to take care of the matter, and to give instructions in regard to it, to Mr. Jephson, his secretary.[18] Wharton then took Mather to Jephson. "Cousin," he said (for Jephson "was my Lord's kinsman"), "observe this gentleman, & whenever he comes to you, *receive him as if I came myself.*"[19]

16. MS. *Diary*, 1688–89, Jan. 2.
17. *Parentator*, pp. 118, 119, and *Autobiography*, describe this interview. I follow the latter.
18. Cf. Luttrell, i, 492, ii, 242.
19. *Autobiography*.

Soon after, an order was prepared, confirming in office all the colonial governors until further orders. Jephson remembered Mather, and showed him the document. Now Mather must have had more than a shrewd suspicion that Massachusetts, once aware of James II's fall, would not be likely to continue docilely under Andros. Should there be rebellion against him, and should there arrive a royal decree continuing him in power, he would not only be in a position to put down the revolt by as harsh means as he chose, but the colonists would be rebels against the Crown. Mather promptly spoke out, and Jephson reported to the prince, who commanded that his order be sent to all the colonies except New England.[20]

Mather then petitioned that Massachusetts, Plymouth, Rhode Island and Connecticut, should all be restored to charter privileges. The Lords of the Committee, after William Ashurst and Mather had appeared before them, recommended to the prince that a new governor be sent with provisional powers, and no authority to raise money by mere vote of the Governor and Council. It was implied that popular consent was necessary for taxation. The king referred this proposal back to the Committee, bidding them draw up a new charter for New England, to "preserve the rights and properties of those Colonies," and providing, not for a new governor, but for two commissioners to administer the colony for the present. No action seems to have been taken on this plan.[21]

On January eleventh Mather interviewed John Hampden;[22] on the twenty-fifth he discussed colonial affairs with Sir John Maynard, "the best old book lawyer of his time";[23] on February eighteenth, with Ashurst, he appeared before the Committee;[24] on the twenty-fifth he visited the Earl of Bedford;[25] and on the

20. *Autobiography; Parentator,* p. 119; *Andros Tracts,* ii, 274, 275; J. T. Adams, *The Founding,* pp. 431, 432; Palfrey, iii, 591.

21. Idem, iii, 592 and n.; *Cal. State Papers, Am. and W. I.,* xiii, ⚹18, 25, 28, 37.

22. MS. *Diary,* 1688–89, Jan. 11. Hampden was John Hampden, the younger, 1653–1696, and spokesman of the extreme Whigs in the Convention Parliament. See *DNB.*

23. MS. *Diary,* 1688–89, Jan. 25. Sir John Maynard was born in 1602, and died in 1690. His career was long and picturesque, as lawyer, and Member of Parliament, and on March 5, 1689, he became a lord commissioner of the great seal. See *DNB.*

24. *MHS Coll.,* Series 4, viii, 117.

25. MS. *Diary,* 1688–89, Feb. 25 and 27. The Earl of Bedford was William Russell, first Duke and fifth Earl of Bedford who was made a member of the Privy Council, Feb. 14, 1689, and bore the sceptre at William's coronation. See *DNB.*

twenty-seventh interviewed Sir Edward Harley.[26] On March ninth he went to "ye Temple about N. E. affair."[27] Meanwhile, on January sixteenth,[28] Samuel Sewall had arrived in London, and Mather spent the evening of the seventeenth with him,[29] and met him often thereafter.[30] Sewall was not only a Puritan but a business man, and knew, if anyone did, how Andros had wounded pocketbooks as well as consciences.[31] Supported by such advisers, and in touch with political leaders, Mather, on March fourteenth, visited William, now King of England.[32] Once more Wharton introduced him.

Mather congratulated William on his accession to the throne, and implored his favor for New England. The new king was shrewder than James, perhaps, and certainly had less reason to be conciliatory. He declared that he believed New Englanders were good people, but added, "I doubt [fear] there have been irregularities in their government there."

It was no longer a campaign of fair words, but one where facts were foremost. But Mather was not backward, and replied that he dared promise for his countrymen such reforms as were necessary. To which Wharton added, "And I'll be their guarantee, & here is Mr. Mather, the Rector of the College there shall be the other. We two will stand bound for New England, that for the future they shall act regularly." Such a promise was, on Mather's part, daring. He was not even the officially accredited agent of Massachusetts. He had no authority to speak for its government. But he had a clear idea of the ends which his fellow citizens sought, and enough confidence in his own leadership to believe that he could bring them to alter their ways as the king might demand, in return for his favor. William accepted the pledge, and to Mather's joy promised to order Andros's removal, and to summon him to account.[33] In return, the colony was to proclaim the new king and queen.

Mather hoped to turn this temporary success into permanent victory. Advised by his friends, he decided to try to get a

26. MS. *Diary*, 1688–89, Feb. 27. Sir Edward Harley was a member of the Convention Parliament, sitting for the county of Hereford. For him see *DNB*, article "Sir Edward Harley, 1624–1700."

27. MS. *Diary*, 1688–89, March 9.   28. See *MHS Coll.*, Series 5, v, 247.

29. MS. *Diary*, 1688–89, Jan. 17.

30. See entries in *MHS Coll.*, Series 5, vol. 5.

31. Sewall's letters to Mather in *Ibid.*, Series 4, vol. 8.

32. This interview is described in *Autobiography*, and *Parentator*, p. 120.

33. *Cal. State Papers, Am. and W. I.*, xiii, #28, 37.

reversal of the judgment against the charter, by act of Parliament.[34] He saw such leaders as Sir Edward Harley, Sir John Thompson, William Sacheverell, Alderman Love, John Hampden, and Sir John Somers.[35] He succeeded in having included in the Charter Bill a mention of the colonies. The Committee on Grievances reported that the "prosecutions of *quo warranto* against the . . . plantations" were wrongs deserving redress.[36] Mather had strong allies in the Commons, "and a great Interest-was also made in the *House of Lords*." [37]

New England's was, of course, but one of the many perplexing problems of the new government. Mingled opposition and welcome beset William. Whigs and Tories were mindful of their quarrels, and the new king's course was by no means easy to steer. In the face of Mather's importunity he took, naturally, temporary measures to satisfy Massachusetts, but he realized that time would be needed to reach a final settlement. But the colonists, meanwhile, had justified Mather's suspicions, and had taken the law into their own hands.

One or two ill-judged acts of Andros had stirred up popular feeling against him even further, in the beginning of 1689. News of William's projected invasion came in February, and there is reason to believe plans for revolt were soon under way. If the Prince of Orange were successful, a popular rising might be safe. If James II were reëstablished, the plotters might forget their rebellious schemes. Perhaps by April eighteenth news giving sufficient assurance of William's prosperous position had arrived. In any event, on that morning, rumors of an armed rising ran through Boston streets. The crowd, awake at once, captured Captain George of the frigate *Rose*. Randolph, Justices Bullivant and Foxcroft, and others, were hurried to jail. In the Townhouse, whither they had gone with an armed escort, Simon Bradstreet, John Richards, and others of the former colonial government, met to deliberate. About noon they came out on the balcony which looked down King Street, and read to the crowd a "Declara-

34. *Autobiography; Parentator*, p. 121; *Andros Tracts*, ii, 275.

35. *Autobiography*. Sacheverell, born in 1638, died in 1691, was indirectly, at least, and quite unintentionally, the cause of the defeat of the Corporation Bill. See p. 228, *post*, and *DNB*. Sir John Somers became in 1697 Lord High Chancellor of England, and was at this time Solicitor General. He was a man of ability and strength, and, one remembers, one of the famous "Kit-kat Club." See *Ibid*.

36. Palfrey, iv, 16; *Andros Tracts*, ii, 276; *Autobiography; Parentator*; T. Hutchinson, *History*, i, 389, 390 and n.

37. *Parentator*, p. 122; *Andros Tracts*, ii, 276.

tion,"[38] summing up the charges against Andros, and announcing the arrest of "those few *Ill Men* which have been (next to our Sins) the grand Authors of our Miseries." Andros was summoned by fifteen prominent citizens, who bade him yield the government and the fortifications, "to be preserved and disposed according to orders and direction from the crown of England." If he would consent to this, he was promised security. Otherwise, the fort where he had retired would be stormed. The messengers sent with the summons intercepted a boat coming from the frigate to take Andros off. He now asked a delay in the attack on the fort, and before night, came out with his men, and gave himself up. He was taken under guard to Mr. Usher's house, and his followers went to jail. On the next day the Castle was surrendered, and the frigate stripped. Andros was now imprisoned in the fort. Dudley was away, but returned inopportunely, only to be held prisoner at his own house.

The governor of James II was overthrown, be it noted, in the name of the Crown of England. On a small scale New England had revolted in the cause of what seemed popular liberty, and had defied a Stuart king, just as the mother country had done in the preceding months.[39]

A provincial government was set up at once, headed by a "Council for the Safety of the People." Bradstreet [40] was elected President. After a convention of delegates from all parts of the colony, it was decided to continue the old charter government. And, finally, on May twenty-sixth, a ship came in with an order to the local government to proclaim William and Mary, King and Queen of England. That night saw a great rejoicing in Boston — processions, a great public dinner at the Townhouse, and jubilant crowds in the streets.[41] Andros was in prison, a Protestant ruled England, and the old and tried friends of the colony governed it once more.

There is little doubt that the feeling that Andros had been a foe, not only of the colonists, but of England, as opposed to James II, and, possibly, an ally of France, was generally accepted, not only in Massachusetts where many events were translated by the popular imagination into evidence for it, but also in Eng-

38. *Andros Tracts*, i, 11ff.
39. I follow the account of the revolt given in Palfrey, iii, 577–587.
40. Idem, iii, 587, 329, 330.
41. Idem, iii, 589, 590.

land, where Mather took care to keep the idea in mind.[42] Therefore, the revolt could be seen as a justifiable enterprise of Englishmen who sought to crush tyranny and to save for England a
domain likely to be conveyed treacherously to a foreign power.
There is no evidence to support the theory that Andros was an
ardent follower of King James, even at the expense of disloyalty
to England, but it is by no means hard to see how he came to be
so regarded.[43]

Mather, at William III's court, must have got the news of the
revolution in Boston some time in June. On the fourth of July he
went to Hampton Court, where the king had taken up residence,
and, introduced by Wharton, hastened to make sure that William
saw New England's action as the colonists would have him see
it.[44] Mather's words are worth quoting.

"I presume," he said, "your Majesty has been informed of the
great service which your subjects in New England have done for
your Majesty, & for the nation, & for the Protestant interest, in
securing that territory for king William."

No apologies are here for a revolt against a royal governor.
There is simply a confident trading on the general belief that
Andros served not the nation but the Stuarts, and, particularly,
a Stuart rejected by his subjects.

William assured Mather that "he did kindly accept of what"
New England had done. In reply the agent asked that a statement to this effect be sent to the people. The king promised to
order the Secretary of State to write such a letter. Mather then
returned to the subject of "ancient rights & privileges." "To
which the king returned answer: 'I do assure you I will do all
that is in my power.'" Matthew Mead, a Puritan who "took
little pleasure in embroiling himself . . . in needless or fruitless
controversies," had come with his friend from Boston, and he
took occasion to say that William could do nothing more likely
to be approved by his dissenting subjects in England "than to be
kind to New England."[45]

42. It seems to me there is evidence sufficient for my statement in the frequency
with which the matter is alluded to in the State Papers, by Andros's enemies who made
the charge, and his friends, who denied it, and the seriousness with which it is discussed
in pamphlets such as those included in the *Andros Tracts*. See also, C. M. Andrews,
Colonial Self-Government, p. 276.

43. Palfrey, iii, 568–577.

44. This interview is described in *Autobiography*, and in *Parentator*, p. 122.

45. *Nonconformist's Memorial*, ii, 463; *Autobiography*.

They left the royal presence with assurance that their requests would be granted. And, on August twelfth, William was as good as his word, in that he issued a letter to the New England government, approving of their course.[46]

With New England's grievance as to the charter recognized in the House of Commons, with a provision for restoration of the old patent included in the Corporation Bill, which then seemed likely to pass,[47] and with a royal letter approving the overthrow of Andros, Mather's case seemed won. On August twentieth, he took leave of his friends, and went to Gravesend and so to Deal. A week later, with his son Samuel, he boarded the ship that was to take him to Boston.[48]

Meanwhile, several more pamphlets had been doing their work in Mather's cause. Before Andros fell, the colonial agent seems to have published in London a pamphlet called "New-England Vindicated From the Unjust Aspersions cast on the former Government there, by some late Considerations Pretending to Shew That the Charters in those Colonies were Taken from them on Account of their Destroying the Manufactures and Navigation of England."[49] This was an answer to a pamphlet probably presented to Parliament in 1689, during the discussion of the Corporation Bill.[50] It had maintained that the Massachusetts charter was annulled because the colonists had coined money, had taxed shipping and imports from England, had passed laws in opposition to Parliament, and had insisted upon an oath of fidelity to their Commonwealth. Massachusetts was also accused of aggressions against the property of other colonies, and was charged with making laws against all religions but the Congregational, especially against the English church. The colonists were declared to have ill-treated English naval officers who wished to recruit and provision their vessels, and it was further charged that the Bostonians entertained and encouraged pirates. The writer insisted, also, that only a few men, deprived of office under Andros, desired the old charter. To restore it would be to

46. *Cal. State Papers, Am. and W. I.*, xiii, ♯ 332.
47. *Autobiography;* Macaulay, *History*, chap. 15.
48. *Autobiography.*
49. For the reasons for ascribing the work to Mather, see *Andros Tracts*, ii, 113 n., and n. 12, *ante*. This would be, then, the first of the three "Vindications" which Mather says that he wrote. It is reprinted in *Ibid.*, pp. 113ff., to which edition all references here are made.
50. *Ibid.*, iii, 3ff.

draw laborers and manufacturers from England to the colony, and, by setting up a virtually independent state, to encourage French attempts upon it. If the charter were restored, New England mines would be developed without English capital, and colonial trade would rival, not complement, that of England. Finally, the old charter would dispossess all who had accepted grants from the royal governor.

This work, of course, stood frankly on considerations of pounds and pence. English trade and English interests must be preserved. Nothing more reasonable could be written, from the point of view of an English merchant. It was by no means an attack which could be laughed away. There is small wonder that Mather strove to defend the colony against it.

He limits his reply to the charges specifically directed against New England. He denies that many ships have been used to export to France and Holland, and to import manufactured articles from there, declaring that the colony had not enough vessels or goods for such enterprises, and could buy to better advantage than on the European continent. Most of the colony's trade was with Jamaica, Barbadoes, and the Caribbean islands, and many ships built in New England were paid for by English merchants and by them sold, or used in colonial trade. As for illegal commerce, he points to the Massachusetts law requiring observance of the Navigation Act.[51] Such breaches of law as there have been have not been sanctioned by the government, but represent no more than "the private Transgressions of some few particular persons" (p. 114).

He repeats once more the charge that the charter was unjustly vacated. He denies that the colony has coined base money, and reminds his readers that the mint was set up in 1652, when there was no king in England, and that, at the Restoration, a change in practice was decided upon. He shows that other colonies and the East India Company have coined money, and, when called to account, have been granted pardons. "Why then should *New-England* be esteemed more criminal than other Plantations?" (p. 116.)

As for taxes on English shipping, and duties on English goods imported, he says there has been but one tax, and that one less than in other colonies. Andros continued and increased this impost, without popular consent. He prints the "Oath of

51. *Mass. Rec.*, iv (part 2), 87.

Fidelity" required in Massachusetts, as a sufficient answer to the accusation in regard to it. He denies territorial aggressions, except that the colony aided Charles II to take New York, and captured St. John's, Penobscot, and Port-Royal from the French. If the Commissioners of Charles II were slighted, it was because their instructions "empowred them to *Hear and determine all Causes* (not by Law, but) *according to their sound* Discretion, which could not be submitted to by the *Massachusets*, without giving up at once their Charter and Priviledges."[52]

As to intolerance in religion, Mather admits "that there have been some severe and unjustifiable Laws there, in matters of Opinion" (p. 118). Here is more evidence, if any be needed, as to his own broad point of view. He adds, however, that Presbyterians are encouraged as well as Congregationalists, and that there are no laws against Anglicans. No congregation of the Church of England has ever been denied liberty to worship in Massachusetts. Naval captains have never been badly used, unless they have broken laws, and some of the king's ships have been provisioned without charge. No pirates have been received, unless their true character was unknown; and there is a law against piracy in Massachusetts as well as in England.

He argues that the colonists do pay taxes to England in that they pay duty on English goods, imported or exported, and that, under the old régime, they cost England nothing for protection or support. He denies flatly that most of the people are content under Andros's government. As for plots of the French, they must increase so long as the people are made dissatisfied with English rule. To appease the colony by restoring the Charter, would be to ensure complete loyalty to England. He reminds us, too, that the charter itself demanded a large measure of dependence, and that the old government was in the king's name.

If to restore the charter would be to draw artisans and manufacturers from England, it "is an unsufferable Reflection upon the Government of *England* As if People could live more easie under an unlimited and Arbitrary Power," such as the Massachusetts administration in the old days was called by its enemies, "than under the regular government of *England*" (p. 120). And if England would profit by the development of mines and other industrial undertakings in New England, she has much to gain

52. Cf. T. Hutchinson, *History*, i, 535ff., especially 536.

(1)

A FURTHER

VINDICATION
OF
New-ENGLAND,

FROM

Falſe Suggeſtions in a late Scandalous *Pamphlet*, pretending
to ſhew, *The Inconvenience of Joyning the* Plantation-
Charters *with thoſe of* ENGLAND.

IT was the Wiſe mans Advice, That in ſome caſes a Fool ſhould be Anſwered, leſt haply he ſhould be Wiſe in his own conceit: Which conſideration may indoce us to ſay
ſomething by way of Anſwer to a late ſcandalous Diſcourſer, who with his no leſs Folly
than Forgery, thought meet to Calumniate the good Proteſtants in *New-England*.

We may take an Eſtimate of this Anſwerer's Integrity, in that in the very firſt Paragraph
of his Diſcourſe he doth aſſert a palpable Untruth, only with a Deſign thereby to do Miſ-
chief to a good People.

For he ſuggeſts, That the Parliament in King *Charles* the Firſt's time, being ſenſible of
the Inconveniences that would ariſe by the Power granted to the *Maſſachuſets* Colony, pre-
ſented it as one of the Grievances of the Kingdom, doubting that they would ſhake off the
Royal Juriſdiction.

And will not the man that can deviſe ſuch Stories as this, ſay any thing?

The Charter of the *Maſſachuſets* Colony was granted in the Year 1628. and from that
Year till 1640. there was no other Parliament.

As for the Renowned Parliament of 1640. all the World knows, that they never had it
in their Thoughts to Leſſen the Priviledges of *New-England*, but rather to Confirm them:
Nor doth Sir *Ferdinando Gorges*, in his Account of *New-England*, p. 43. ſpeak as this Diſcourſer pretends. For he makes no mention of the Parliament, but what He aſſerts, was done
by King and Council, *Anno* 1622. which was Six years before the Charter of the *Maſſachuſets* was in being.

Such is the Forehead of this Diſcourſer, as that he fears not to Affirm, That it was never
known, that any of the Governours in *New-England* who were choſen by Charters, did take
the Oath preſcribed in the Act for Navigation. Whenas, there is nothing more certain, or
more known amongſt thoſe that are Acquainted with what hath been done in *New-England*.

Yet more: The Diſcourſer charges the Vindicator of *New-England* with Falſity, in ſay-
ing, That the word *Common-wealth* was Repealed in their Law-Book, and the word *Juriſdiction* inſerted inſtead thereof.

In Anſwer to this, we ſhall only ſubjoyn the Printed Law of the *Maſſachuſets* Colony,
made in the Year 1681. and then leave it to the Judgment of all unintereſted perſons, whether
our Diſcourſer be not a perſon devoid of all Faith and Truth.

In the printed Law-Book of the *Maſſachuſet's* Colony, *pag.* 81. are theſe words to be
ſeen.

IT *is Ordered by this Court, and Authority thereof, That the Twelfth Section of the Capital
Laws, Title* Conſpiracy, Rebellion; *and the Fourteenth Section of the ſaid Laws, Title* Rebellious Son, *and alſo the Law referring to* Chriſtmaſs, *p.* 57, 58. *and the word* Commonwealth, *where it Imports* Juriſdiction, *is hereby Repealed, and the word* Juriſdiction *is hereby Inſerted.*

As for what is inſinuated about Sir *John Weyborn* a Commander of one of the Kings Ships,
&c. We are ſorry for his ſake that any thing is mentioned about it. The thing was done
many years ago, before Capt. *Weyborn* was Sir *John*.

He attempted Forcibly to carry ſome of the Inhabitants in *Boſton* aboard his Veſſel, which
he had no Commiſſion to do. And was ſo Indiſcreet, as to ſtrike one or more of them,
which cauſed a Scuffle between his Men and ſome of the Inhabitants: And the Captain among
others got ſome blowes, for the which he might thank himſelf.

There

FIRST PAGE OF INCREASE MATHER'S SECOND
"VINDICATION OF NEW ENGLAND"

There was no Law on his fide, but on the contrary he broke the Peace: And the Government in *Bofton* is to be commended in that They did not countenance him in his Extravagancies.

The Difcourfer further faith, That the *Maffachufets* turn'd the Kings Juftices out of their Seats at. *Bofton* in the Year 1668. after They had been three Years Empowered, *&c.*

But this is very falfe. There was no fuch thing then done in *Bofton*, only in the Province of *Mayn*, they of *Bofton* did at the earneft Solicitation of the Inhabitants do fomething of that nature: Which Province the *Maffachufets* have fince that bought of the Proprietor Mr. *Gorges*, which has iffued all Controverfies.

As for the Commiffion granted by King *Charles* the Second, to thofe three Gentlemen who were fent to. *New-England* in the Year 1665. it did Empower them not only to determine the Bounds of the Colonies, which was not objected againft, but to hear all other Caufes by way of Appeal, and then to determine them according to their good and found Difcretion.

The Famous *Cook* faith, That fuch a Claufe in a Commiffion makes it illegal, but in as much as this Difcourfer juftifieth it, that is a fufficient Indication that he is one of thofe ill Men who of late have been carrying on defigns for Arbitrary Power.

For him thus to difcover himfelf at this time of day, does not argue him to be a wife Man.

He pretends that the *Maffachufetts* Colony is but a tenth of the Colonies of *New-England*, and that the People there will never unite againft the *French*, which things are notoriously untrue.

For the *Maffachufetts* are more than half the Country, and the four Colonies did many years ago enter into a Confederation, that if an Enemy fhould fall on any one of them, the reft would look on themfelves as concerned, and therefore they were for a long time called the united Colonies.

As for the foolifh Inftance he produces to confirm his Affertion, That when *one of the Colonies fighting againft the Indians, wanted Provifion, there was a fcruple whether they fhould accept of fupplyes from another, becaufe they were an unfanctified People.*

It is not to be endured with patience, that a Ridiculous formal Fop fhould impofe fuch Banter as this on the Honourable Parliament of *England*. Not one Colony, but all the Colonies in *New-England* were ingaged in that War with the *Indians*. *Rehoboth* and *Providence*, Towns as diftant in their Sentiments about Religion, as near in Situation, held a ftrict and Effectual Correfpondence at that Time.

And if we may conjecture what fhall be hereafter, by what is already paft, the Reftoring of Charters will have a very good Iffue, as that War had, without any Expence to *England* of either Men or Money.

As for what he afferts concerning the *Copper-mines*, fuppofed to be in *New-England*, it is but *Crambe bis Cocta*, the fame that was in the Confiderations formerly anfwered, which it would be naufeous here to repeat : Only it gives us juft caufe to fufpect that the fame venomous Pen wrote both thefe Pamphlets.

It is Nonfence to affirm, That the Charters of *New-England* make them independent on the Crown of *England* : Whereas if they be infpected, it will be found that by vertue thereof thofe Plantations are dependant on *England* ; nor have they any fuch unlimited Powers granted to them as this vain pretender has falfely and malicioufly fuggefted.

Befides, Intereft obliges them to a dependance on *England* : without it they cannot carry their Fifh and Lumber to the *Englifh* Plantations, to make Returns for *England*, wherein a very great part of their Livelihood doth confift.

Both the Charters in *England* and *New-England*, were taken away by the fame fort of Men, and on the fame Grounds, *viz.* in order to the Eftablifhing of Arbitrary Government. *England* has not been a gainer, but the contrary, by what has been done to *New-England*.

Inasmuch as the Honourable Houfe of Commons have Voted that the taking away the Charters of *New-England* was Illegal, and a Grievance, and that they fhould be reftored to them again; and inafmuch as the People there have of late done a great Service for King *William* (whom God grant long to Live and to Reign,) and for the *Englifh* Nation, and for the Proteftant Intereft, by fecuring the Fortifications in and near *Bofton*, for the Service of the Prince of *Orange*, (not knowing that He was then King) and for the Parliament of *England* ; whereby they have merited Encouragement : We no way doubt but they fhall partake in the common Deliverance : And we know that our Wife Senators will not regard the malevolent Infinuations of thofe ill Men, whofe defigns and defires are, that good Proteftants and good Subjects may be depriv'd of their ancient Rights and Priviledges.

SECOND PAGE OF INCREASE MATHER'S SECOND
"VINDICATION OF NEW ENGLAND"

by granting the charter, for, with the return of the old rulers, local capital would be offered to support local enterprise.

Finally, if to give back the patent would invalidate Andros's land grants, it would do no more than return property to its rightful owners, who "subdued a Wilderness, and . . . have maintained and defended it, to the enlargment of the King's Dominions; hoping, as in Reason they might, that their Posterity should enjoy the benefit thereof" (p. 122). What New England asks, is but the rights claimed by English corporations. Shall New England alone be denied?

Mather closes with a reference to another pamphlet, listing laws repugnant to those of England.[53] He is content with pointing out that the statutes referred to have, for the most part, been repealed, one never existed, the word Commonwealth "so much complain'd of" was changed to Jurisdiction, and the comments offered by the English writer are "but the Ebullitions of a spiteful Spirit" (p. 123).

Mather's work struck home enough to call forth an answer which does little more than reassert the original charges, or give the lie direct on one or two matters of fact.[54] At our distance we cannot fairly decide the merits of each point in debate. It is even harder now than it was in 1689 to decide just how many men longed for the old charter, or how prominent capitalists felt about the proposed change. But we can be sure that, where verification is possible, Mather was more than a match for his opponents. Exact authority can still be found for many of his statements in rebuttal. Of course, not all the laws he cites in support of his contentions were strictly enforced; but, even so, he has better basis for his argument than his enemies could find for theirs. When it came to general dicta, conditioned by personal views and local interests, his doctrine is certainly quite as easy to swallow as that urged against him.

It was in answer to the last pamphlet mentioned above that he wrote the second of his "Vindications" of New England. Of this, but one copy is known to me, and it has never been reprinted or ascribed to Mather. Through the courtesy of its owner, William Gwinn Mather, it is reproduced here in full. As for its authorship, it is most probably by the author of "New-England Vindicated," since it is a defence of that book. Moreover, we have Mather's statement that he wrote three vindications of New

England, and no known document is so likely to represent the second as this printed sheet of two pages. Its style and form accord with what we know of Mather's literary habit.[55]

In it he proceeds at once to answer the author of the "Short Discourse." He begins by showing the falsity of his opponent's suggestion that Parliament opposed New England's charter rights in the time of Charles I. This answer, compared with the "Short Discourse," leaves him the advantage.[56] He supports what he has said of the changing of the word "Commonwealth" to "Jurisdiction." He gives another side, at least, to a story about Sir John Weyborn. He explodes the statement that Massachusetts is but a tenth of New England.[57] One need go no further in comparing the answer and the book it attacked. It is enough to say that Mather spake whereof he knew, with more heat than he showed elsewhere, but always with a prudent eye on the facts. He winds up, cleverly, with a reference to the recognition of New England's case by the House of Commons, and with a reminder that the Andros revolt was "for the Service of the Prince of *Orange*."

On July 30, 1689, there was licensed for the press "A Brief Relation of the State of New England."[58] Whoever wrote the original draft, there is reason to believe that its final form was due to Mather.[59] Certainly there is nothing in the style to disprove his authorship, and the arguments offered are those with which he was most conversant. There are, too, some passages agreeing almost word for word with the "New-England Vindicated."[60] Purporting to be "a Letter to a Person of Quality," the pamphlet summarizes the story of the settling of New England. The action against the charter is called "a mere Rape" of "Priviledges." Since then, the colony has hastened toward ruin. Andros, sent with a commission "absolutely de-

---

55. See facsimile reproductions, facing pp. 223, 224.

56. Cf. *Andros Tracts*, ii, 138, with paragraphs 5 and 6 of Mather's work.

57. Cf. the facsimiles, and *Andros Tracts*, ii, 140, 141, 138. See also, Channing, ii, 160.

58. "A Brief Relation of the State of New England, From the Beginning of that Plantation To this Present Year, 1689." Printed in *Andros Tracts*, ii, 149ff. What seems to be a first draft of this is printed in *MHS Coll.*, Series 3, i, 93–101.

59. *Andros Tracts*, ii, 150.

60. Cf. *Ibid.*, p. 115, lines 15–17, and p. 155, lines 13–15. Cf. also, p. 114, "That the Act of Navigation should be strictly observed"; and p. 156, where identically the same phrase appears: (114) "the Government . . . is not to be blamed for the private Transgressions of some few particular persons"; (156) "the Transgression of some few particular Persons ought not to be charged as the fault of the Government"; and other correspondences apparent on a reading of the two tracts.

structive to the fundamentals of the *English* government," was overthrown by the people, who did "Unanimously Declare for *the Prince of Orange, and the Parliament of England.*" Admitting that the colony may have sinned against English law in the past, and that they have been too severe in regard to "matters relating to Conscience," the writer urges in defence that amends have been made and that now "leading men, and the generality of the People are of a more moderate Temper." The main argument is that England has much to gain from the continuance of Massachusetts in its former rights and privileges. In support Mather reminds his readers that other British colonies are largely dependent on New England for many commodities, that New England buys more English goods, and exports to the mother country such necessaries as "Sugars," "Tobacco," and "Indico" (pp. 155ff.). The colony has manifest advantages for cheap shipbuilding, and the people are well trained to serve the king in arms, against such enemies as the French. New England is the key to America. Sir Edmund Andros, of French extraction, and so of French sympathies, might have played into hostile hands, had not a loyal citizenry forestalled him by rebelling in the cause of King William. New England should, therefore, be given her old privileges, in order that she may prosecute the war against France without cost to England. The next paragraph, not in the original draft,[61] refers to the college and its growth. In this connection there is quoted a letter of Abraham Kick,[62] of Holland, to Queen Mary. It speaks of New England's achievements, and prays for royal favor to the dwellers there. This is followed up by a reference to the good work done in spreading the Gospel among the Indians; and here is quoted Mather's letter to Leusden, originally printed as "De Successu Evangelii." [63] The pamphlet ends with a plea to all Protestants to support New England. Surely none but Papists can be its enemies.

Another pamphlet, quite different in tone, called "A Vindication of New-England," probably issued some time in 1689, has been ascribed to Mather, or, at least, to someone writing largely

---

61. Cf. *Andros Tracts*, ii, 150. This, of course, is an argument for Mather's authorship of the pamphlet in its final form, since he urged the college's claims whenever he could.

62. This is also added to the original draft, and again there is evidence for Mather's authorship, since Kick was his friend. See *MHS Coll.*, Series 4, viii, 596–599, and *Andros Tracts*, ii, 162 n.

63. Also added to the original draft, and also likely to represent Mather's work.

from his dictation.[64] The arguments for this view are that it deals with matters which occurred in New England, and goes into such detail that one is led to believe a well-informed colonist must have had a hand in it. Again, Mather says that he wrote three vindications of New England, and before the "second vindication," discussed above, was discovered, it seemed necessary to include this tract as his, in order to identify the three he wrote. On the other hand, there are grave objections to a belief in his authorship of "A Vindication of New-England."

First of all, the work contains an express statement that it came from "the Pen of one, who altho' he never spent 7 years of his Life in any part of America, yet has been so inquisitive after the Affairs of *New-England*, and had so much acquaintance with the worthy Agents of that Country," [65] that he is able to write intelligently in the colony's behalf. This statement has been held to be a technical truth, meaning no more than that Mather dictated his book to an amanuensis, or that its final form was due to another hand than his.[66] But the book was printed in Boston and not, apparently, in London, where Mather was, and where his obvious field for controversy lay. Again, the style is not that used by him in any other book up to this time. Admitting that this is an insecure basis, by itself, for denying the tract to him, it has, none the less, great force when coupled with the fact that the work was anonymous, that Mather nowhere specifically claims it, and that it came out with an explicit statement that it was not by a New England man. Read it with the "Narrative of the Miseries of New-England," which Mather surely wrote, or with his later "Reasons for Confirming the Charter," and one must decide either that he wrote here in a style he used nowhere else, or that the book was not his. There is here a violence of phrase, a delight in the sound of words, and in playing upon them, frequent quotations, and a striving for effect — all not only foreign to the style of Mather's known works, and contrary to his often reiterated doctrine of simplicity in writing, but also likely to impress far from favorably those upon whose good opinion he relied for success.[67] Phipps could have given the same facts, or Ashurst, or Cotton Mather, or

---

64. This is printed in *Andros Tracts*, ii, 19ff. For the question of its authorship, see *Ibid.*, p. 20, and what follows below.

65. *Ibid.*, p. 78.

66. *Ibid.*, p. 20.   67. *Ibid.*, pp. 21ff.

Hutchinson, or Sewall, or Major Thompson, and without the same risk of discrediting a cause of which Mather was the diplomatic champion.

It seems probable that, if the "second vindication" we have glanced at had been known previously, the tract now under discussion would never have been linked with Mather's name. Denying it to him, we can still identify his three "vindications," and, therefore, there remains no ground for believing that he wrote it, while there is the evidence of style, of content, and of the writer's own statement, to dispel the belief that it was his.[68]

Whoever wrote it, "A Vindication of New-England" gave forceful utterance to New England's case. Its distinction lies not in its facts, which were those that the colonists believed to be true, but in its abuse of the opposition. It is an excursion into the field of downright vilification of political enemies, but it is the work of a man who could compose lively and heated special pleading designed for the ears of the man in the street. Such tracts were not uncommon, or by the standards of the time discreditable to their authors, but no one of them, in this period, is known to have come from Mather.[69]

Aboard ship, in the lower Thames, he knew that his printed works and his powerful friends were active in his interests. With the passing of the Corporation Bill, Massachusetts would have her charter once more. He could go back to Boston as the man who had restored his country's government, and relieved the people from what they felt to be tyranny. His letters gave his views, and extracts from two of them, together with a paragraph

68. The arguments in favor of Mather's authorship of this tract prove too much, for quite as many arguments can be adduced to support a theory that he wrote all the other anonymous tracts in defence of New England which are reprinted in the *Andros Tracts*. If we say that the fact that the style is unlike his and that the work is said to be by a writer not a native of New England, is not evidence against his having written the *Vindication*, then there is no reason for not assigning to him any other pamphlet of this period, provided it deals with New England's affairs, from the point of view held by his sympathizers. For other pamphlets avowedly not written by natives of New England, though dealing with New England's cause, cf. *Andros Tracts*, i, 194, ii, 268, iii, 190. Surely not all these were by Increase Mather, since he would certainly have claimed them; and yet it is quite as easy to believe that he did write them as to accept the *Vindication* as his.

69. Similar in tone is the tract printed in *Andros Tracts*, ii, 231ff., and not ascribed to Mather by Whitmore or anyone else, except J. T. Adams, who, in his *Founding of New England*, p. 445, quotes from it, as from a writing of Mather's. He, however, made a slip in reading the *Andros Tracts*, since in his footnote (445 n.), he refers to *Andros Tracts*, ii, 230, a passage which ascribes to Increase Mather not the tract Mr. Adams quotes, but the one which precedes it in the volume.

from an English journal, were printed as a broadside in Boston. The heading was "The Present State of the New-English Affairs," and a significant note explains that "This is Published to prevent False Reports." [70]

The citizen of Massachusetts, reading this sheet behind his counter or at the tavern, found much of good comfort. From Mather's pen he learned that the Corporation Bill had been twice read, and referred to a Committee on Emendations. The clauses referring to New England had met with no great opposition. He read that the king had approved the rising against Andros, and had sent a letter to this effect. He was assured that the Earl of Monmouth had espoused the colonial cause, as had most of the Privy Council and parliamentary leaders. And, in the last paragraph, there was the news that by an order dated July 30, 1689, the king had commanded the return of Andros, Randolph, and the other captives of the Boston revolution, to answer the charges against them in England.

Before the good people of Boston had a chance to hear of him through this "first newspaper," [71] Mather's plans suddenly changed. Little Samuel, his son, who accompanied him to England, keeps well in the background till September 3, 1689, but he then steps forward in no uncertain way. On that day he was taken very ill, and on the morrow he was known to have smallpox. So Mather stayed with him, and the ship sailed without them. By October third, Samuel could travel, and his father took him back to London. [72]

Once there, he saw that the delay in sailing might be no act of blind fate, but rather a manifestation of God's mercy. The Tories were gaining strength, and with the decline of the Whigs, the chances of the Corporation Bill grew less. There was much to do, to keep up his political fences, and Mather went once more to work. On January second, the select committee appointed to discuss the bill brought in its report. Too zealous Whigs, led by William Sacheverell, moved the adoption of a clause exacting severe penalties from many great Tories. The controversy which resulted ended only in William's prorogation of Parliament. So, in a dispute not of their making and fostered by one of their

---

70. Reprinted in *Andros Tracts*, ii, 15ff., and, in facsimile, for the Club of Odd Volumes, Boston, 1902.

71. Cf. W. G. Shillaber, Introduction with facsimile reprint of 1902, cited in note 70, above.

72. *Autobiography; Parentator*, p. 154.

allies, perished, for the present, New Englanders' hopes for regaining their charter by Parliamentary act. Nor did opportunity come again, for the Tories took the saddle, and Mather's Whig allies were for the present of little influence.[73]

The delay worked further harm, for the opponents of Mather's object had time to present their case in more detail than before. Randolph wrote constantly, tuning his recital of grievances to suit the prejudices of each Englishman he addressed. He urged that no decision be given as to the charter, until he had come to England.[74] The Episcopalians of Boston sharply accused the Puritans of a variety of crimes.[75] John Usher, who had been treasurer for Andros, came to London in the summer of 1689, and he was by no means silent.[76]

Massachusetts, meanwhile, governed itself as it had under the charter, without official sanction save for the king's letter granting those in office authority to continue. Mather and Sir Henry Ashurst were officially recognized as agents of the colony; and at the end of 1689, two physicians, Mather's classmate, Elisha Cooke, a staunch defender of the old charter, and Thomas Oakes, were associated with them in their mission.[77] Obviously New England was far from settled. No one could rest content until some form of government had royal approval. The present administration, under a temporary warrant, could be but a hand-to-mouth affair. And, as England had been at war with France since a few months after William's accession, so New England faced Indian enemies, and, sometimes, their French allies. In April, Massachusetts sent a small force to attack Port Royal in Acadia. The leader was no other than Sir William Phipps, who had turned from Mather's side in London, to volun-

73. *Autobiography; Andros Tracts,* ii, 276.

74. See letters from Randolph listed in *Cal. State Papers, Am. and W. I.,* vol. xiii, and Palfrey, iv, 62, 63, 64–66.

75. *Andros Tracts,* ii, 28ff.

76. Palfrey, iv, 66. In Sewall's diary for July 29, 1689, we read: "Standing in the Shop about 7. *mane,* Mr. John Usher comes to the door, which surpriseth me. . . . I go and acquaint Mr. Mather, who has heard nothing of it. He hastens to tother end of the Town. The Lord save N. E. I spoke to Mr. Usher not to do harm, as knowing the great King we must finally appear before: because he spoke of going to the King." *MHS Coll.,* Series 5, v, 268.

77. Palfrey, iv, 26 and n. For Cooke, see J. L. Sibley, *Biographical Sketches,* i, 520–525; and for Oakes, *Ibid.,* ii, 130–132. For the instructions to the agents, see *Cal. State Papers, Am. and W. I.,* xiii, ✻739. They were to wait upon the king, obtain a full confirmation of the ancient charter, correct misrepresentations as to the late Revolution, and represent matters relative to defence.

teer his services in the colonial campaign against the French. On May twenty-third Port Royal fell before him, and before he returned, he destroyed also the French defences at the mouth of the St. John.[78]

The four New England agents were no longer where words alone could serve. In March, Andros, Randolph, and their friends were in London, and on April tenth the agents were summoned before the Lords of the Committee to testify against their deposed governors. They asked for a week in which to prepare their charges.[79] One would give much to know what passed between them, but on April seventeenth no one volunteered to sign the accusations against Andros.[80]

Mather has left no doubt that he favored signing.[81] He could hardly feel otherwise. After charging Sir Edmund with many crimes, pamphleteering against him, and preventing his reappointment, to fail to sign the papers against him, would be to put himself and his cause in an awkward place. But there were now four agents, and unless all accused Andros, it must appear that New England was divided in its sentiment toward him. This would mean that the agents who did sign would have to fight alone against such allies as the ex-governor could muster, and, moreover, that their position might be easily interpreted as due to personal spite rather than as an expression of the will of their government.

Now, Cooke and Oakes were fresh from Massachusetts. They had not committed themselves in London, by preferring charges against James II's governor. How Ashurst felt we can only guess, but it seems probable that he shared Mather's views. There was a possibility for disagreement among the agents, and it was promptly realized.

On April seventeenth they appeared with Andros before the Lords of the Committee for Trade and Plantations. Sir Edmund was armed with a charge against the colony for revolt against lawful authority. Sir John Somers, who seems to have been the colonists' chief adviser, said that the agents were prepared to defend New England. Thus called upon, they recited their grievances against Andros. The President of the Committee, Sir

78. Palfrey, iv, 49.
79. Idem, iv, 66, 67; *Cal. State Papers, Am. and W. I.*, xiii, ※ 846.
80. *Ibid.*; Palfrey, iv, 67 and n. 3.
81. *Autobiography.*

JOHN LORD SOMERS
Baron of Evesham
Lord High Chancellor
of England
Obit 1716.

SIR JOHN SOMERS
From a painting in the National Portrait Gallery

Thomas Osborne, Marquis of Carmarthen, asked who imprisoned the governor. To which Somers replied, "The Country, my Lord." Osborne declared: "The country and the people, that is nobody. Let us see A. B. C. D. the persons that will make it their owne case. . . . That Paper is not signed by anybody." Somers insisted that the agents were there not as individuals but as representatives of a country. At this point, one of them, and, as we have seen, it is most likely to have been Mather, whispered to Somers that some of them would sign. But he advised against it. An investigation of Andros's acts would have been impolitic, as calling too much attention to others of James II's emissaries who had followed similar instructions with equal faithfulness. To inquire into their deeds would have been to annoy more than one man still in high place, and might even have directed unfavorable notice to certain members of the Committee itself. Cooke and, presumably, Oakes, took Somers's counsel at its face value. For Mather to sign alone, or with Ashurst only, would have been useless to his cause, and dangerous to his own position in influential circles. So the Privy Council received a report from the Committee affirming that no one appeared to sign charges against Andros. He was dismissed with no further trial, and, a year later, became Governor of Virginia.[82]

Mather inevitably lost ground at once. He had elaborately constructed something approaching a real political organization, with a definite platform — the rescue of New England from tyranny by the restoration of the charter. For this programme it was necessary to have a tyrant to show, and to have Andros go scot free, was to wipe out, so far as the average observer was concerned, all the force of Mather's complaints of the "grievous" state of the colony since the *Quo Warranto*. By the affair of April 17, 1690, "those oppressors did not only come off with flying colors, but insulted over their adversaries."[83] Powle, now a member of the Privy Council, assured Mather that great pressure was being brought to restore Andros to office in Boston. The Earl of Monmouth declared that the agents had cut New England's throat, by imprisoning a governor whom they could not prove guilty. The Earl of Devonshire, John Hampden, and others of Mather's friends, were "extremely scandalized."[84] William himself was not likely to be pleased with the turn of affairs. He had listened patiently to complaints against Andros, and had approved his overthrow, only to have him virtually acquitted of any crime.

With little room to hope for Parliamentary rehabilitation of the old charter, the agents turned to considering whether their colony's case might not be brought from Chancery before the King's Bench, presided over by Sir John Holt. This plan failed.[85] There remained but one other course. If the courts and Parliament could not or would not help, there was left only the trial of what might be done by a direct appeal to the king. A petition was prepared and presented by the Earl of Monmouth. William referred the matter to Holt and Pollexfen, the Lord Chief Justices, to Somers, and to Treby, the Attorney-General. Mather seems to have had some favor in their eyes, for he was allowed to be present at their deliberations. They drew up a new charter, and sent it to the king. He referred it, on January 1, 1691, to the Committee for Trade and Plantations.[86]

William was hardly accessible to the agents in 1690. In June he was busy with Irish rebels. July first was the day of the Battle of the Boyne, and the king did not come back to England till September. Then internal affairs demanded his care. He was content, perforce, to leave New England's case unsettled. Perhaps the agents, too, for most of the year, were glad to bide their time. News must have reached them, telling how Phipps, now the colonists' military leader, prepared an expedition against Quebec. Should he be successful, New England might well bear to William news of lands won from the French, with a reasonable hope that

---

85. Palfrey, iv, 70, and references given there.

86. *Andros Tracts*, ii, 276, 277; *Cal. State Papers, Am. and W. I.*, xiii, ※1276. There we find that the agents wished the King to reëstablish the old Corporation with a grant of all former lands or privileges. The Corporation should consist of all such as were formerly, or shall be hereafter, made free, and Maine should be included. New Hampshire, too, should be under the Corporation. There should be a general Assembly of representatives, and the election of general officers should be by majority of all the freemen present, or sending votes. The Assembly should have power to erect courts of judicature. It should be expressly denied the right to make laws repugnant to those of England, but should have power to impose necessary taxes for the support of the government, and increased authority to raise militia, pursue enemies, and erect fortifications. Grants made to individuals in New England should be confirmed. Liberty of fishing should be limited with respect to the rights of landowners.

It will be noted that this document provides for a suffrage restricted to freemen, but does not imply that freemen are to be chosen on religious grounds, but rather the contrary, since conformity to English law is emphasized.

he might, in return, be pleased to grant their requests. But insufficient preparations, faulty timing of two campaigns, internal dissensions in the colonial ranks, and Frontenac's promptness and skill, saved Quebec and New France. On November nineteenth Phipps was at home in Boston, a defeated man. He had lost two hundred lives, and the colony had spent fifty thousand pounds. Most of this fund had been borrowed. Paper currency was issued, and its prompt depreciation brought home to every man the gravity of the colony's reverses.[87]

In such straits, the government sent Phipps to England once more, to seek aid with which to renew the attack on Quebec, and, perhaps, in order that he might add his pleas to the agents', in their efforts at court. He was a general fresh from a disastrous venture, but he was not without some support from the colonists. He had sacrificed some of his own property in the public interest, and of him Sewall wrote Mather: "You will hear various Reports of Sir William Phips. I have discoursed with all sorts, and find that neither Activity nor Courage were wanting in Him; and the form of the Attack was agreed on by the Council of War." [88]

His Quebec expedition had afforded to the agents none of the political capital they had hoped for; but if Phipps, in person, could give them any help, he was surely welcome. If 1690 had been a year of little progress for them, it had offered abundant opportunity to their foes. Andros had made a skilful defence. Randolph, in England, was no less active and adroit in his attacks than he had been in Boston, and he pursued constantly his charges as to New England's violation of the English trade laws. Sponsored by him, there appeared "New England's Faction Discovered," a pamphlet which assailed the colonial cause in general, and Mather in particular, devoting most of its space to a pamphlet, "News from New-England," believed to have been his. This work, long unknown, has recently been discovered, but it is hard to find proof that Mather wrote it. There is nothing in its style or content which prevents our ascribing it to him, but he nowhere claims it specifically, nor is Randolph's laying it at his door based on anything more than personal opinion. Very probably Mather arranged for its publication, perhaps he edited

---

87. Palfrey, iv, 50–58. For the doings of the agents at this period cf. *MHS Proc.*, xlv, 644ff.

88. Palfrey, iv, 58; *MHS Coll.*, Series 6, i, 115.

it, and certainly he must have welcomed it as one more contribution to his cause.[89]

Randolph, or his deputy, in replying to it, answers ably the attack on Andros, so far as this concerned disloyalty or acts not sanctioned by his commission; but, on several points upon which we have knowledge to-day, "New England's Faction Discovered" shows a blithe tendency toward politically effective exaggeration or downright falsehood.[90]

John Palmer printed a more temperate defence of Sir Edmund,[91] and others took care that the authorities should no longer lack antidotes for Mather's persuasive arguments. Clearly the agents had much to do, to repel such opponents. To the Lords of the Committee they answered Randolph's remarks as to New England's observance of trade laws.[92] Some one of them, or of their friends, wrote "The Humble Address of the Publicans of New-England," a work as scurrilous as the "Vindication of New-England," [93] and one which suggests that it came from the same pen. Neither these, however, nor "Further Quaeries upon the Present State of New English Affairs," present any evidence of having been Mather's work.[94]

The agents were busy, then, in 1690, answering or explaining away the charges of their enemies. Early in 1691 William went to Holland and in his absence nothing definite could be done. But Mather was not idle, and printed his "Reasons for the

89. A copy of this work, a single sheet printed on both sides, is now in the library of W. G. Mather of Cleveland, by whose courtesy I have been enabled to examine it. The title is, "News from New-England: in A letter Written to a Person of Quality, wherein is a true Account of the present State of that Countrey, with respect to the late Revolution, and the present War with the Indians there. As Also Of A Pretended Miracle of the *French Jesuits* in that part of the World." It is marked "Licens'd *Febr.* 27, 1689. *J. F.*" [i.e. Febr. 27, 1689–90]. The imprint is, "*London*, Printed for John Dunton, at the *Raven* in the *Poultrey*, 1690."

90. For example, the writer says: "The Church of *England*, altho commanded to be particularly countenanced and encouraged, was wholly destitute of a place to perform Divine Service . . . until Sir. *E. A.* by advice of the Council, borrowed the new Meeting-house." (*Andros Tracts*, ii, 211.) As we have seen, the Church of England did have a place to worship, given them by the Puritans, and the word "borrowed" in connection with Andros's use of the meeting-house is obviously amusing. Mather is spoken of as a "pretended Teacher of the Gospel," a phrase more effective than truthful. One may find further evidences of Randolph's manner, by comparing the tract with such historical records as we have.

91. *Ibid.*, i, 21ff.
92. *Ibid.*, ii, 127ff.
93. *Ibid.*, pp. 231–270.
94. *Ibid.*, i, 194ff.

Confirmation of the Charters." [95] In this pamphlet he argues that the settlers in America enlarged the British empire, in the belief that they and their posterity might enjoy charter rights. "Nor may we suppose that in the Dayes of K. *William* They shall be deprived of what was granted to them by K. *James*, and K. *Charles* I and continued to them by K. *Charles* II untill the last year of his Reign" (p. 225). He refers to William's statement that he hoped to secure to the English their rights and liberties. He reminds his readers of the royal letter of August 12, 1689, which ordered that the government of New England be settled to the satisfaction of the English subjects in the colony. From this he argues for the charter, maintaining what he no doubt believed, that the majority of the people desired the return of the old government. To refuse it would be to breed discontent, and, thereby, to create increased danger from the French. New Englanders' loyalty was shown in their revolt against Andros, which Mather dubs "that glorious Cause which the Prince declared for" (p. 227). The Connecticut, Rhode Island, and Plymouth charters were never taken away by legal process. They are, therefore, still valid, and since Massachusetts asks merely the same rights that they conferred, she should not be denied, particularly since her own patent was illegally revoked. On this point, he urges the House of Commons' recognition of the prosecution of the *Quo Warranto*, as a grievance. Moreover, since the charters have been annulled, the colony has had to have financial aid from England, as never before. And, finally, the charters made the colonies dependent, and limited their activities to those prescribed by English law.

This pamphlet referred to the cases of all the New England

95. "Reasons *for the Confirmation of the* Charters *belonging to the several Corporations in* New-England," reprinted in *Andros Tracts*, ii, 225ff. A similar tract, referring only to Massachusetts, differing slightly, also appeared. The variations between the two are given in the reprint cited above. For the ascription to Mather, see note 12, *ante*. Mather's works written in the interest of New England, seem, then, to have been: (1) A Narrative of the Miseries of New England; (2) New England Vindicated; (3) A Further Vindication (not previously known); (4) A Brief Relation; (5) Reasons for the Confirmation, etc. Mr. Whitmore, in *Andros Tracts*, agrees on numbers (1), (2), (4), (5). Number (3) he did not know, and in place of it inserted "A Vindication of New England," which, as has been shown, was not by Mather. Some bibliographies have ascribed to Mather a tract called "The Revolution in New England Justified," in *Andros Tracts*, i, 63ff., but there seems no good evidence for this. Cf. *Ibid.*, p. 69 n. As to "News from New-England," there seems no good reason to ascribe it to Mather; and that he himself did not mention it in describing his writings for New England (cf. note 12, *ante*) argues against his authorship.

colonies, but a slightly altered version was issued in the specific interest of Massachusetts. In place of the clauses asserting that the colonies first became a financial burden after the revocation of the charter, and that the latter ensured dependence on England, the Massachusetts argument asserts, first, that no patent is asked for except one providing for subordination to England, and that no laws are desired repugnant to those of the mother country. To this is added a declaration that the colony is particularly eager to observe the statutes in regard to navigation and trade. After a brief reference to the increased cost incurred in supporting the colony since it became charterless, there is a complacent mention of the fact that Massachusetts "has lately reduced the *French* in *Acady* unto Obedience to the Crown of England." Similar success in Canada would mean "Millions to the *English* Crown and Nation"; and if the charters be restored, Massachusetts is likely to be encouraged to prosecute her military ambitions (p. 229 n.).

This tract Mather put into the hands of each member of the Privy Council. "His *Maxim* was, That in all Affairs, *a Few did All;* and his *Method* was, To find out the most *Potent Leaders* in all Affairs, and make sure of them." [96] Among the men he thus enlisted was Doctor Tillotson, that "man of a clear head, and a sweet temper," "the best preacher of the age." [97] Anglican as he was, he was liberal in his views toward the colony, and to Mather "did ... sometimes express ... his resentments of the injury which had been done to the first planters of New England, and his great dislike of Archbishop Laud's spirit towards them." Even in 1695, and in the heart of Puritan New England, Mather found it in his heart to write gratefully of Tillotson, to an audience by no means inclined to praise English bishops.

Burnet and Lord Wharton continued as allies, but Mather turned his persuasive powers upon a greater personage than either. Queen Mary was not to be neglected in any political drama of the court. Madam Martha Lockhart, one of the women of the bed-chamber, on April 9, 1691, introduced Increase to the royal presence, and left him alone with the queen.[98] She had already heard the colonial cause expounded by Abraham Kick, and she found her visitor from the far-away stronghold of Con-

96. *Parentator*, p. 125; *Andros Tracts*, ii, 277.
97. G. Burnet, *History*, i, 189; *Autobiography*. For Tillotson, cf. *DNB*.
98. *Autobiography; Parentator*, pp. 127ff.

gregationalism no less urgent in his pleas. He was ready, as usual, with compliments and assurances of loyalty. She, remarking that the matter had been long before the Council, declared: "I would have that which is *Just* done for" New England, "and not only so, but that something of *Favour* should be shown to them."

In October, Lady Jean Wemyss, Countess of Sutherland, who appeared to Mather "a very pious and admirably prudent lady," had told him that Queen Mary had promised her good offices for the colony.[99] The countess was a forceful person, used to pleading her own cause in official circles, and, no doubt, ready to turn such influence as she had to support a friend. Her husband sat in William's Privy Council, her son fought bravely for his king, and she herself, there is some reason to believe, went further than either in an interest in nonconformity. Perhaps her Scotch blood and the tradition of John Knox made her amenable to the type of doctrine Mather preached. Certainly she lent him a measure of the zeal she used in fighting to maintain her family fortunes, and her interest with the queen was great. The ring given her by Queen Mary bears witness to the closeness of their relation, and her voice must have counted, not only in determining her husband's vote at Council meetings, but in swaying the feeling of her sovereign. Thus, when Mather took occasion to thank Mary for her kind words to the countess, Her Majesty replied: "I have had a great character of you, from my Lady Southerland."[100]

One's imagination delights in the picture which reveals Mather and forceful Lady Jean Wemyss working in the same cause, and exchanging good opinions of one another. There were no ladies quite like the countess in Boston. In the Mather house, or even beside Boston-born Lady Phipps, she would have seemed a strange guest. Her garb and manners, and the queen's ring sparkling upon her hand, would have provoked interest, to say the least, had she appeared with Mrs. Maria Mather and her daughters in Boston's social circles. But in England Mather could adapt himself to meet women of the world, and she, knowing how to win a hearing from English lords, gay courtiers, or

---

99. *Autobiography;* W. Fraser, *The Sutherland Book*, i, 303ff. Mather spells her name "Southerland," as she herself did (*Ibid.*, ii, 196, 197; i, 305). T. Hutchinson, in the *History* (London, 1768 ed.), writes Sunderland (ii, 13) but has Sutherland in the edition of Boston, 1767.

100. *Autobiography; Parentator*, p. 127; Fraser, *The Sutherland Book*, i, 281ff., 299, 306ff., 295 and n., 303.

deviously minded politicians, was no less at home with a pious Puritan.

Mather now begged the queen that the articles approved by the small committee, considering the form of the new charter, might be approved. This was natural, inasmuch as he had helped to frame them. Mary found his request reasonable enough, and agreed to use her influence with the king. Mather adroitly introduced a mention of the tracts denouncing New England, and was, no doubt, reassured by her answer: "I have not seen all the Pamphlets." He continued with a reference to Phipps's Canadian venture, declaring that the colonists were "willing again to expose themselves in your Majesties Service." But here she was as well informed as he, and asked, "Are they Able to do it? I hear they are but in a Bad Condition?" He was able to deprive this of its force, by insisting that the uncomfortable state of New England resulted largely from the loss of the charter. With this she agreed, and then remarked: "I doubt, there have been Differences *There*, as well as Here, about *Church Government.*"

Mather's reply is so significant as to deserve quotation. "In *New-England*," he said, "they are generally those that are Called Non-Conformists: But they carry it with all due Respect unto others: We Judge some of them to be better Men than ourselves. This Nation has cause to Bless God, for the King, and for Your Majesty, in regard of that *Act of Indulgence*, and the *Liberty of Conscience*, which through Your Majesties Favour we now enjoy." Such words do not become a Puritan as intolerant and narrow as some would have us believe Mather to have been. Nor can they have been uttered simply for their effect, without expressing the speaker's real feeling, for we find them printed proudly by his son, and recorded by himself in his autobiography. It is hard to see this speech otherwise than as a statement of what Mather believed, and was willing to have made known.

Such views won ready acceptance with Queen Mary. Mather left her with her zealous expression of her love for tolerance and peace ringing in his ears.

William came back to London before the end of April, and Mather managed to interview him twice before he once more left England.[101] On the first occasion the agent offered a petition from some London merchants, asking that charter privileges be restored. This was a measure cleverly adapted to answer some of

101. *Autobiography; Parentator*, pp. 130ff.

the arguments brought against the colonial cause on the ground of its threatening of English commerce.

The next interview with William, on April twenty-eighth, was arranged through the good offices of William Cavendish, Earl of Devonshire. Mather does not notice it, but there seems to have been a certain curtness in the king's answers on this occasion. The agent was loud in his protestations of New England's devotion to the king. He pleaded for a settlement which would give their "ancient privileges" to the colonists, and that it might be speedily provided. He pointed out that New England was Congregational and Presbyterian, "so that such a governor will not suit with the people . . . as may be very proper for the other English plantations." The most William would say was that he had the Committee's report, and would see what could be done.

Mather followed up this interview, by enlisting the services of Francis Charlton, "with the wooden leg," a man devoted to Shaftesbury, and "a hot, indiscreet talker." He had plotted against James II, and had been sentenced for disloyalty. Under William the charges were dismissed, and perhaps he was not the less welcome to the new sovereign because of his hostility to the old. He and Bishop Tillotson both interviewed the king between April twenty-eighth and thirtieth, and "did . . . solicit & pray his majesty to be kind to New England." That a prelate of the English church pleaded thus, answered better than anything else could the complaint that Massachusetts sought a form of government opposed to all sects but one.[102]

On April thirtieth the Committee asked the king whether he would have a royal governor in New England, or allow the people to choose their own leader, and make their own laws. William asked that the charter provide for a governor appointed by the king.[103] Here, of course, was one of the great points in the whole

102. *Autobiography*. Francis Charlton, Luttrell says (i, 274), was one of those conspiring against James. In 1685 (*Ibid.*, p. 355) he was summoned to appear before the king. April 27, 1689 (*Ibid.*, p. 527) he, "outlawed for treason or misdemeanours in the late king James's time, came to the court of kings bench, and haveing writs of error allowed . . . , they revers'd the same." (Burnet), *A Supplement to Burnet's History*, ed. H. C. Foxcroft, p. 116, tells of Charlton's implication in the Rye House Plot. Thence are taken the quotations in the text. *Ibid.*, p. 151, says "the discontent that was over England made some hot men in London, such as . . . Charleton, fancy that it might be a fit time now for the duke of Monmouth to raise a rebellion." In his *Autobiography*, Mather calls him "Mr. Charlton." That Francis Charlton is referred to, is shown by Hutchinson, *History*, ii, 13.

103. *Cal. State Papers, Am. and W. I.*, xiii, ⚹1431, 1432, 1440.

debate. Most of the colonists desired, no doubt, to have no officers save those they elected themselves; but William saw too well that anything like an imperial policy demanded a royal governor in Massachusetts. His opinion, though it must have been foreseen, was a disappointment to the agents; but the king softened the blow by promising to nominate a governor satisfactory to the colony. The only stipulation was that a military man be chosen, to suit the needs of a time of war.[104]

Mather seems to have believed that the royal governor was to be of limited authority; but immediately after William sailed for Holland, the Privy Council issued an order providing that the governor should have the veto power in regard to acts and appointments passed by the colonial assembly. Mather was outraged, and won from several members of the Council opinions that the order did not accord with what the king had designed. He sent a copy of his protest to Henry Sidney, Secretary of State, "then with the King in *Flanders*," asking "That if that Order, Signed by one of the Clerks of the Council, was not according to the King's Mind, His Majesty would graciously please to signifie his Dis-approbation thereof." But there is no reason to believe that William meant to grant privileges other than those the Council had voted, and he did not answer Mather.[105]

The latter, meanwhile, was gratified by the Attorney-General, who drew up a charter "according to what he took to be the King's Mind, as expressed when his Majesty was last in Council. In that Draught, the Free-men (and not all Free-holders) had Power to Chuse the Deputy-Governour, and the other General Officers; and the King's Governour had not a Negative Voice allowed him in any Case." This proposal was presented to the Council on June 8, 1691, and met with the reasonable objection, "That by such a Charter ... the King's Governour would be made a *Governor of Clouts*." Orders were given for a new charter, which was drawn up, and shown to Mather. He was told that, if it did not satisfy him, he should make his objections to the Attorney-General. And he found at once that the new draft left out certain essential privileges which Massachusetts claimed.[106]

It is on the basis of the facts just recited that it has been said

104. *Andros Tracts*, ii, 280; *Parentator*, p. 133.
105. *Acts of the Privy Council, Colonial Series*, ii, 127; *Andros Tracts*, ii, 280.
106. *Ibid.*, 280, 181; *Cal. State Papers, Am. and W. I.*, xiii, № 1570.

that Mather particularly opposed the suggestion "relating to the suffrage," and that he had been "exerting every means to fasten the shackles permanently on the colony by insisting upon the old Congregational test for the suffrage." But such statements leave out of account the fact that we have in the Privy Council Records, and among the State Papers, a definite statement of the agents' objections to the proposed charter, as they made them to the Attorney-General. They complained, first, that "Judges, Justices of the Peace and Sheriffs" should "be chosen by the Generall Assembly, as well as other officers of all sorts, and not by the Governor," as the Lords planned. Their second protest was that the Committee's report provided "that the assistants or Council of State be chosen by the General Assembly, with the approbation of the Governor." Mather would allow the king's representative no power to veto the acts of the Assembly, and would not give the king an indefinite time in which to disapprove laws. And, far from insisting on the suffrage restriction, the agents specifically agreed that the Assembly be chosen by free-holders of £40 a year, and by inhabitants with £100 in money.[107]

The only other guide we have in this affair is the record that the Attorney-General's proposals denied the governor the veto power, and limited the suffrage to freemen, not including all "freeholders." In other words, only those could vote whom the government chose to admit to full citizenship, and the mere ownership of property did not qualify a man to vote. It is quite clear that Mather approved of this arrangement, and opposed the charter agreed on by the Council, which left the governor the right to negative acts and appointments and extended the suffrage to all freeholders. Therefore, we are safe in saying that he believed the voters should elect officers who might legislate and appoint to certain positions without being subject to the veto of an appointee of the king, and that he wished to limit the franchise to such men as the government saw fit to regard as qualified citizens. But, if this was his feeling, the fact remains that he did not press his objections, except in regard to the veto. He said not a word to the Attorney-General as to restricting the right to vote to "freemen." We know that he protested against endowing a royal governor with authority to reject popular acts

---

107. J. T. Adams, *The Founding*, pp. 435, 445, 446, and references given there; *Acts of the Privy Council*, ii, 126, 127; *Cal. State Papers, Am. and W. I.*, xiii, #1669, 1606, 1631.

that he disapproved, but we have no evidence that he uttered one word in favor of limiting the franchise. Nor can we imagine that he did, for the colony had voted, after the Andros revolt, to reduce the requirements for citizenship, basing them on non-religious grounds.[108] They had thus voluntarily surrendered what we are asked to believe that their accredited agent fought for as one of their dearest rights! And Mather not only made no specific plea for the religious test for voters, but never mentioned it in any one of the many arguments he offered during his agency. Indeed, he had on at least one occasion specifically petitioned for a government based on the votes of all freeholders. He sought the old charter, but he knew how often the colony had been warned that England would not tolerate the old suffrage restriction. He knew that the colonists had given up their old stand on the matter. With abundant evidence at hand, it would still be difficult to believe that he insisted on the colony's right to govern in a way specifically disapproved of in England, and by a method now no longer desired by his own people. No doubt he believed, personally, that the colonial government might well ask to be allowed to determine the amount of capital necessary to confer a vote upon its owner, or to fix the time of residence required for citizenship. If he did so believe, then he favored, so far as his own views were concerned, the limitation of the suffrage to "freemen"; but to say this, is not to declare that he thirsted for a state where all but those of his own faith were disenfranchised. Only speculation can determine what thoughts he had, in his private capacity. All we know is that he never spoke in favor of limiting the right to vote by means of any religious criterion, except in so far as this may have been included in the rights conferred by the old colonial charter, and that, when a new patent was under discussion, he objected to none of its provisions in regard to the suffrage. The records do not make him appear as the zealous servant of the old theocratic limitation of citizenship.[109]

108. Palfrey, iv, 26.

109. It should be remembered that to change the requirement for the suffrage from "freemen" to "freeholders" might disenfranchise men admitted to citizenship, but not property holders. No religious bias was needed to cause objection to this plan on the part of a representative of the colonists. So on July 17 we find it agreed that the agents may name certain freemen, not more than one hundred in number, who, though not freeholders, may vote. (*Cal. State Papers, Am. and W. I.*, xiii, ※1650.) We have here a clue to any objection Mather may be believed to have made to the change from

He did speak out as to the royal governor's being granted the right of veto, and his objections were strenuous. He went to Sir Henry Ashurst, and together they sought out the Attorney-General. To him, as we have seen, they protested against the authority given the governor.

At this time, Mather made one more of those slips to which his hot temper sometimes led him. As his anger had run away with him when he denounced Randolph, so, in declaring that he would rather die than accept the new charter, he said much more than he meant. Or, as he puts it, "I expressed my Dissatisfaction, perhaps, with a greater *Pathos* than I should have done"—a remark that deserves to be quoted when one charges him with imprudence. Imprudent he certainly was; for to vow to refuse the charter, and then to accept it, weakened his position when it became necessary for him to uphold the new form of government as one deserving popular support. Moreover, his lapse from diplomatic speech brought prompt retaliation. He was told that his consent to the charter was neither expected nor desired, that he was not a plenipotentiary for a foreign state, and that, if the proposed document was refused, Massachusetts must "take what would follow," since "his Majesty was resolved to settle the Countrey." [110]

The objections of Mather and Ashurst were given by the Attorney-General to the Privy Council, and sent also to the king. Some of Mather's friends wrote to the courtiers abroad with William, "entreating them to use their Interest with his Majesty that nothing might be Imposed on *New-England*, which would be grievous to his good Subjects there." Mather was sure that, if the king were in England, more influence might be brought to bear, and he prevailed on someone who was close to the queen, probably the Countess of Sutherland, to write her, urging that William be asked to delay all action until he returned to London. This Queen Mary did. [111]

Confident in her success, Mather, who had "By continual Attendance on this arduous Affair" lost sleep and "neglected" his "Necessary Food" until his "Health was greatly impaired,"

"freemen" to "freeholders." His objection would seem to be the act of a man not willing to see former citizens disenfranchised, not that of a zealot, eager to restrict the suffrage to his own sect.

110. *Andros Tracts*, ii, 281.

111. *Acts of the Privy Council*, ii, 127; *Cal. State Papers, Am. and W. I.*, xiii, ＃1670, 1675; *Andros Tracts*, ii, 282.

felt safe in retiring to rest in the country. He chose to go to Totteridge, eleven miles out of London, where his friend Richard Baxter had once lived, and where Mr. Charlton had an estate.[112]

William did not listen to his queen or to such courtiers as spoke for Mather. Wisely, he decided that New England must be settled at once, and that delay could serve no good end. The news of his determination to act at once surprised Mather, who hurried back to London, where he was shown the royal letter which disposed of his objections to the charter.[113]

There was nothing more for the agents to do, except to make the new form of government as satisfactory as might be. With Ashurst, Mather petitioned that no property of the colony or its citizens might be taken away, nor any privileges "which they have a Right unto." They asked that Maine be granted to Massachusetts, together with Nova Scotia.[114] All this was agreed to, although New Hampshire, which they also asked for, was denied.[115] Plymouth had desired a separate charter, but in view of the obvious disadvantages of having two colonies in a district most easily administered as a unit, such wishes had little chance of fulfilment. On the other hand, suggestions were made that Plymouth be joined to New York. Governor Hinckley wrote Mather, saying that if no separate charter could be secured, Plymouth men would choose union with Massachusetts. This, too, Mather arranged. True, he was harshly criticized by Ichabod Wiswall, agent of Plymouth, who stood on a platform of a separate charter or none, and, like Cooke, Mather's colleague, would accept no compromise. It is hard to see how Mather could have done better for Hinckley's people. Plymouth was obviously not likely to remain independent for long, and her citizens preferred Massachusetts to New York. One need hardly go behind their thanks to Mather for his action in regard to them.[116]

Mather begged for and won a chance to see the charter, as finally agreed upon. He succeeded in having inserted a clause preventing difficulty in future from the Puritans' repugnance to take oaths on the Bible. More important, an article was added "confirming Grants made by the General Court, notwithstanding

112. *Andros Tracts*, ii, 282, 283; *MHS Proc.*, xxviii, 348; *Nonconformist's Memorial*, iii, 397; G. Burnet, *Supplement*, p. 116 n.
113. *Andros Tracts*, ii, 283, 320.
114. *Ibid.*, 283, 284; *Cal. State Papers, Am. and W. I.*, xiii, #1731, 1738.
115. *Ibid.*, #1731, 1738, 1745; *Andros Tracts*, ii, 283.
116. See Appendix.

any defect that might attend the Form of Conveyance, that so Mens Titles to their Lands might not be invalidated, only for that the Laws which gave them their Right, had not passed under the Publick Seal in the time of the former Government." The colonists were thus insured against further attacks on their property, such as those which did so much to discredit Andros's régime. Other changes were asked for, but the agents could not persuade the Council to grant them. Their case was settled.[117] They had done their best. There remained only the question as to how they should receive such benefits as England would consent to give.

117. *Andros Tracts*, ii, 284; *Cal. State Papers, Am. and W. I.*, xiii, ※ 1731, 1758, 1759.

CHAPTER XV

THE NEW CHARTER

SHOULD the representatives of Massachusetts accept the new charter? Mather sought advice. It was pointed out to him that to refuse might bring a worse settlement for New England. To accept was not to sacrifice the old privileges, since judgment had been entered years ago against the original charter. The colonists under the new form of government would be by no means precluded from asking for more liberty, should a favorable time for such requests appear. A lawyer gave it as his opinion that the new charter was more advantageous than the old. Moreover, the king's power to settle the matter as he saw fit was undisputed. The agents might accept or not, but the royal will was sure to be carried out.[1]

Most interesting of all, we have Mather's own statement that he was told, and realized, that the old charter itself would not make it possible for New England to be governed as of yore. To attempt to repeat the acts of the past would be to make certain a new *quo warranto*.[2] Mather's acceptance of this doctrine is one more shred of evidence, if any be needed, that he cannot have supposed that in soliciting for the "ancient rights" of the colony he was working toward the reëstablishment of the religious test for the franchise, nor can he have hoped to restore it by any means whatsoever. He was too well informed as to what England would and would not allow in her colonies.

We need not stop for all the arguments he retails as those by which good advisers urged him to accept the proposed settlement.[3] Obviously they were wise. Massachusetts could hope for little if her agents rejected a document prepared with, at least, partial deference to their wishes. To stand out for the old order

---

1. *Andros Tracts*, ii, 285–287.

2. *Ibid.*, p. 287. See also, a letter of Charles Lidget to Francis Foxcroft, November 5, 1690: "Cook & Oakes run hard for the old Charter Mather & Ashurst for a new, finding by the former no power for the very necessarys of government, and openly own that no man of Estate or brain will subject himselfe to yᵉ injurys and perrils of giving judgment of any sort by that authority." *New England Historical and Genealogical Register*, xxxiii, 407.

3. *Andros Tracts*, ii, 285–292.

or none might be an effective gesture for a man wedded to the old ideas of theocratic government, but it could never be a practical measure. So long as there was a king and government in England, the colonies' destiny was to be shaped by them. Diplomats might hope to win changes and concessions, but not violations of what English statesmen saw as the fundamentals of colonial policy.

But, though his course might seem wise in London, if he signed the charter, how would the colonists greet Mather when he brought home to them a royal governor, and the loss of some of their former privileges? Inevitably there would be criticism. Elisha Cooke's sympathizers, the narrowest school, would take their chances under any government the king might choose, rather than accept voluntarily anything short of the rights they believed to have been granted to their fathers. So also, ardent Congregationalists might well blame the man who had gone to England as the emissary of the churches, should he return with no guarantee for the continued dominance of their religious establishment. The ordinary man in the street, however, would be glad to be sure that his property was in his own hands, and that he might once more vote for some, at least, of the officers who governed him.

The easiest course, undoubtedly, and the only one which agrees with the character sometimes bestowed on Mather, would be to refuse to sign the charter. If it were put in force in spite of his refusal, he might shrug his shoulders and declare that he had done his best. He might then pose before the strictest church party as a man who stood inflexibly for the old order or none, and criticism could not reach him, unless it were directed against his too rigid adherence to things overthrown by the progress of the colony and its ideas. So Elisha Cooke chose to refuse the new charter,[4] evading thus all responsibility for its effect upon New England, but, at the same time, writing himself down as a man unable to see the trend of the times and the inevitable consequences of England's imperial desires. If he was a defender of American independence, he insisted on independence at a time when it could not succeed. By his attitude he deprived himself of any chance to help in moulding the future course of Anglo-colonial relations. As an opponent of the only terms the king

4. Palfrey, iv, 82. Hutchinson (*History*, i, 408) says that Oakes signed, though he opposed the charter.

would grant, he was removed from the sphere of those nego-
tiators who could compromise when compromise was necessary,
and thereby save for themselves a chance to be of influence with
English statesmen in stating the colony's case and gaining concessions on such points as were not already settled by the nature
of England's policy.[5]

Mather and Ashurst wisely accepted the proposed charter. In
Mather's action lies the real success of his agency. He had
courage to face criticism at home, knowing that he brought to his
people, not the old independence, but a plan which allowed them
a large measure of popular government, guaranteed their property rights, and gave them, in place of a chaos in which they were
open to any tyrannical imposition, an established code ensuring
them certain privileges under English rule. Moreover, he could
well be proud to have it known that two of the most essential
clauses in the charter were due to his foresight, and written
at his dictation. True, he gave up power for his church by accepting the abandonment of the old religious restriction upon voters,
and by agreeing to articles providing for tolerance for all sects.
But the colony had made plain its own willingness to give up the
religious test for full citizenship, and Mather's consent to this,
and to the inauguration of "liberty of conscience" for all, is a
tribute to his enlightenment. We have seen that he never urged
anything but tolerance, while he was in England, and never insisted on any measure designed to give political power to his
church. He saw that Congregationalism could survive only by
suiting its policy to the times. He knew that its leaders could
strengthen themselves best by appearing to the English authorities as men with whom it was possible to deal without being
repelled by an outworn strictness of devotion to every jot and
tittle of the old order.

Accordingly he chose to sign the charter. If he had had his
own way, and a community shaped by his own wishes, he might
have tried to impose universal control by one church, intolerant
of all others; but, actually, he was dealing with human beings
who had interests outside as well as within the meeting-house,
and he turned his course with them in mind. That he did not
guess wrongly, from a practical point of view, is shown in that
the nomination of the new officers to be appointed for New Eng-

5. That Mather had in view a possible resumption of the fight for the "ancient
privileges" is shown by *Andros Tracts*, ii, 285.

land by the king was left virtually in his hands.[6] If he had sacrificed part of the old system by which Congregationalism had tried to rule, he gave up only what had to go, and, by so doing, made possible a new close alliance, of a different sort, between church leaders and governmental officers. Obviously, if he could choose the new governor and his colleagues, he could make sure that they were not men hostile to his church. Cooke and Oakes could find no such ready means to serve their ends. Their opposition to the new charter made it unlikely that they would be called to decide who should carry out its provisions. Mather, on the other hand, had put himself on record as accepting a form of government far better than any Massachusetts had owned since the *Quo Warranto*. He won, thereby, the chance to safeguard what he believed to be the will of Massachusetts, by suggesting men to govern it who were likely to meet the desires of those he represented.

Cooke seems to have wished to base his failure to accept the charter on grounds of expediency, declaring that he believed action should be delayed until the king returned to England. In this he acted with less knowledge of the true situation than Mather or Ashurst, who knew how the failure to push the charges against Andros must have impressed William, and realized how much pressure was being brought to hasten a settlement for the colony. Moreover, Mather had seen the king's approval of the charter and his explicit refusal of the agents' objections.[7] The finality in this royal letter was more apparent, probably, to Mather, who knew the true state of affairs, than to Cooke and Oakes, new to the English court, and without any close personal supporters there.

And so, on September 17, the Privy Council ordered the Secretary to "prepare a warrant for his Majesty's royal signature, for passing said charter under the great seal of England." Two weeks earlier Mather had been asked to nominate the new rulers for the colony. He had presented a list, his suggestions were all adopted, and on the 7th of October, the new charter was in force, and Sir William Phipps was governor in New England.[8] William Stoughton was chosen lieutenant-governor. Isaac

6. Palfrey, iv, 85; Hutchinson, *History*, i, 413; *Cal. State Papers, Am. and W. I.*, xiii, ＃1772.

7. *Andros Tracts*, ii, 315–317 (especially 316), 320.

8. *Cal. State Papers, Am. and W. I.*, xiii, ＃1769, 1806.

Addington, secretary under the provisional government, was continued in that office. As councillors, Simon Bradstreet, John Richards, Nathaniel Saltonstall, Wait Winthrop, John Phillips, James Russell, Samuel Sewall, Samuel Appleton, Bartholomew Gedney, John Hawthorn (Hathorne), Elisha Hutchinson, Robert Pike, Jonathan Curwin (Corwin), John Jolliffe, Adam Winthrop, Richard Middlecock (Middlecott), John Foster, Peter Serjeant, Joseph Lynd, Samuel Heyman, and Stephen Mason appeared as Mather's choices from Massachusetts. For Plymouth, he nominated Thomas Hinckley, William Bradford, John Walley, Barnabas Lothrop; and for Maine, Job Alcott, Samuel Daniel, and Silvanus Davis.[9]

We have already seen something of the new governor. Sir William Phipps was, undoubtedly, an admirer and follower of Increase Mather, and a good Congregationalist. He was, therefore, well adapted to favor Mather politically, and likely to try to defend the Congregational church against any loss of influence. Undoubtedly Mather remembered this in nominating Phipps, but he had other claims to advancement. The French were menacing, and colonial expeditions against them were constantly discussed. William felt that a military man should govern New England.[10] Now, great man or small, wise or foolish, Phipps excelled all New Englanders in military experience. However incapable a general he may have been, there was no one else to whom a large force could be trusted, unless a relatively untried leader were chosen, or unless an English soldier, with no interest in the colony except in so far as it could furnish troops, became governor in Boston. The last alternative would have pleased few in New England, and to select for a leader in time of war some good citizen whose prowess had been proved only on the drillground, would be too great a risk. It would be foolish to suggest that Phipps did not recommend himself to Mather as an ally of his church and a personal friend, but it is quite as idle to dispose of his appointment as nothing more than an ardent divine's choice of a pliant disciple. Phipps had served Massachusetts in time of need. He had won a military success, and had led one army to defeat. He had served faithfully, however mistakenly, and had been generous when the colonists were in straits. Sewall was not the only New Englander who knew that Phipps still commanded a share of their allegiance. Mather was lucky in that

9. *Cal. State Papers, Am. and W. I.*, xiii, ✻ 1806, 1772.
10. Cf. note 104, chap. xiv, *ante*.

he could choose a follower of his own, who was also a man who had friends in the colony and had proved his willingness to serve it.[11]

As for Stoughton, he had been agent from the colony to England in defence of the old charter. He knew something of negotiations in England, and one remembers that he urged upon the colony obedience to the Navigation Act. He was a close friend of Dudley, and had been a member of Andros's council, and a judge under him. On the other hand, he had aided in the revolt against Sir Edmund. He was a Puritan, and, at times, was marked by a stern narrowness of thought by no means to his credit. But he had been, for many years, a leader in Massachusetts public life, and if a governor who favored the Anglican Church had given him high place, one need not lay Mather's nomination of him solely to religious bias. He was not only a good Congregationalist, but a strong politician.[12]

Addington had been an Assistant under the old charter, and, since the revolution in Boston, had been secretary of the colony.[13] The freemen of Massachusetts obviously considered him worthy. Mather merely continued in office a man already approved by the voters.

Of the twenty-eight Assistants that Mather appointed, twenty-one were Massachusetts men, and of these all but five had held office in the provisional government elected to succeed Andros. All four of the Plymouth representatives had been elected to office before Mather chose them. Obviously, then, his selections, if conditioned by personal motives, were strangely consonant with the popular taste. Moreover, if it be urged that popular elections, prior to the enforcement of the new charter, meant little, since none but church members voted, the fact remains that, after the restriction of the suffrage was removed by the new form of government Mather brought back to Boston, twenty-eight of the officials he had chosen were voted upon by the people, and fifteen were reëlected.[14] Therefore, if the statement that Mather "succeeded in having the more important offices filled with the most fanatical, or the most subservient, of the men in

11. J. A. Doyle, *The Puritan Colonies*, ii, 379; Channing, ii, 286.

12. Palfrey, *passim;* J. L. Sibley, *Biographical Sketches*, i, 194–208.

13. Palfrey, *passim*.

14. See the lists in Palfrey, iv, 599, 600. The five who had not been in the government before were Jolliffe, Lynd, Heyman, Middlecott, and Mason, the last being a London merchant. The election of councillors was by the people, through their representatives chosen to the General Assembly.

the colony's public life" [15] be true, it must be admitted that the voters of Massachusetts, even after the religious test for the franchise had been weakened, had chosen just such "fanatical" and "subservient" men. And, after the suffrage was extended to all freeholders, they proceeded to choose the majority of this weak and bigoted group! Mather's governor was not subject to popular election, and there is no telling how he might have fared at the polls, but more than half of the Assistants kept their places.

One cannot show, then, that Mather nominated officers for New England purely on personal grounds. Of course, all his candidates were Puritans, and nearly all of them had been chosen by the voters in the reëstablished colonial government which followed the fall of Andros. Where were more representative men to be found, unless one went to those who had been allies of Randolph or of Sir Edmund, both rejected by the colony, or unless one sought some individual wholly inexperienced in public life? It was no time to crowd the Town-house with political novices, for the problem of the moment was no less than that of guiding New England through the difficult days which attended the beginning of a new political system.

A few leaders, in favor with the voters, were not chosen to office by Mather. Danforth had to give up his place to Stoughton, and John Smith, Peter Tilton, William Browne, William Johnson, Thomas Oakes, and Elisha Cooke, all lost their seats as Assistants. All but one of them were of Cooke's party, believing in the old charter at all costs.[16] Cooke and Oakes had opposed Mather's course during the agency. He could hope for nothing but criticism from them and their friends. But, leaving his personal feelings out of account, how could the colony, which must go on, willy-nilly, under the new charter, hope for constructive leadership from men who had fought the whole plan by which her destiny must be worked out? It is startling to find Mather painted as the advocate of the old charter, of the theocratic régime, and of intolerance, and then accused of nominating officers from "the clerical party" [17] to serve his own interests,

---

15. J. T. Adams, *The Founding*, p. 451. But Hutchinson (*History*, i, 414) says that the men Mather chose "were persons of the best characters in the several parts of the colonies."

16. Palfrey, iv, 86; Hutchinson, *History*, i, 414; and lists in Palfrey, iv, 599, 600.

17. J. T. Adams, *The Founding*, p. 451.

when the men whom he chose had been previously elected by the voters, and the only ones whom he displaced were themselves the champions of the strict old ways, and champions in opposition to him!

It would be idle to say that Mather made no mistakes in his nominations. His "slate" could not have been ideal, unless he were gifted with some uncanny power of reading the public mind a year in advance. With such a marvellous faculty, a scholar and divine, sure of peace and solitude, with no idea of carrying his teaching among men or making it of use in the world, could afford to fill the government with appointees chosen solely for their merit. But a practical man, intensely absorbed in religious matters, and, even more, in the carrying of light to the hearts and minds of men, the teacher of a church in the greatest town in New England, largely dependent on personal prestige for the satisfactory carrying on of his task, could not so easily shut his eyes to worldly truths. Such a one must do as Mather did, and select candidates, with an eye not only to their experience and past political successes, but also to their friendliness to him and his work. But, even had he wished, he could not have chosen solely with reference to himself. Those he nominated must be capable of winning the voters' favor, or their defeat would bring discredit to their sponsor. To elect weak and unpopular men in the hope that they, right or wrong, would carry him to success, would have been to err in a way foreign to Mather. He knew that most of the officers he chose could continue only if they were reelected by the people, he knew that the charter would win friends only in so far as the first rulers under it were successful, and he knew that his own prestige could not survive in the face of general hostility to the men and the form of government he had accepted for the colony. Had he foreseen how gravely he was to suffer from Phipps's faults, he might have chosen a different governor; but in 1692 Sir William had not revealed to Mather or to the colonists the weakness which later lost him the support of his subjects.

With the signing of the charter Mather's mission in England ended. His vanity was tickled by interviews with the king, and he was diplomat enough to wish to leave a favorable impression in William's mind. So, on the 23d of October, soon after the king's return to London, the Earl of Nottingham ushered Mather into the royal presence, in order that the agent might welcome his sovereign to England.[18] Again, on November 4, accompanied by the Earls of Nottingham, Devonshire, and Portland, he saw William, and thanked him for the charter.[19] At the same time, he hinted that the colonists' good behavior under the new government might warrant further favors in future.

Finally, on January 3, 1692, Mather and Phipps went together to Whitehall. They bade the king farewell, and Mather improved this last opportunity by asking and obtaining a promise of royal graciousness toward Harvard.[20]

Mather had found many friends in England, and more than once had longed to remain there. He lingered for two months more, among the bookshops and parish churches he had come to love, and with the Puritans, Anglicans, lords and ladies, from whom he had won a welcome. On March 7 he left town with Phipps and went to Southampton. Thence, in Sir William's yacht, they sailed to the Isle of Wight, and, a week later, to Dartmouth and Plymouth. On March 29 they finally put to sea, and headed toward Boston.[21]

With them they brought, as we have seen, a new form of government and new officers for it. The exact nature of the charter has been explained more than once, and its full text is accessible to-day.[22] We need only remind ourselves of its main features. It applied to a district including Massachusetts, Plymouth, Maine, and Nova Scotia, with a coast line almost unbroken from Martha's Vineyard and Nantucket to the mouth of the St. Lawrence. Inland the territory stretched to the Pacific coast. The old right of the people to elect their own executive officers was gone. The royal governor might reject laws passed by the popular assembly, or the king might veto them within three years of their enactment. The governor commanded the militia, and was authorized to appoint its officers, as well as the judges for the colonial courts. Admiralty affairs, the post-office, and the custom house, were all controlled from England. All this gave scope for a king to "oppress" the colonists if he chose

18. *Autobiography; Parentator*, pp. 144ff.   19. *Ibid.*
20. *Autobiography; Parentator*, p. 154.
21. *Autobiography; Parentator*, p. 155.
22. For discussions of the new charter, see, for example, Palfrey, iv, 75–83; J. T. Adams, *The Founding*, pp. 446–451; J. A. Doyle, *The Puritan Colonies*, ii, 374ff.; E. B. Greene, *Provincial America*, pp. 21, 22. The charter is printed in *Acts and Resolves, Public and Private, of the Province of Massachusetts Bay*, i, 1–20, and in *Colonial Society Publications*, ii, 7ff.

to do so, but the surest defence was the maintenance of close diplomatic ties with his court. For this Mather had done much to pave the way.

If the new charter fell short of the old in the amount of independent government it allowed, it contained, none the less, some distinct advantages. The General Court, elected by the people and their representatives, had the sole power to tax. The governor could use no funds except with the consent of the delegates of the people. Moreover, there were now legalized some things not expressly permitted before. The right to tax non-freemen, to govern by representatives, to inflict capital punishment, to set up courts, and to probate wills, were all confirmed to the colony. And, most immediately welcome, all titles to lands granted under the old government were recognized. However he felt on the broader questions of politics, the Massachusetts citizen was sure to feel relief in knowing that his farm, or his house in the North End of Boston, was guaranteed to him and his heirs. Probably his title had never really been in danger, but he certainly believed that it had, and the relief that came from reassurance on this point he clearly owed to Mather. How many of the other privileges now conferred were due to the same man, one may judge from the record of his work. Whether England would have been as liberal, had not her ministers been confronted by so able a defender of the colonies, is a question that cannot be answered; but we have seen that Mather spoke, wrote, and planned consistently to gain the very things seen to-day as the best elements of the new political scheme.

The agency is the climax of one side of his career. Here his talent for organization, for politics, and for clear argument in matters of statecraft, was used to the full. Here his personal qualities were most drastically tested by the need of winning sympathy and concessions from a court where many conflicting interests, and many personal ambitions, played a part. The years from 1688 to 1692 display the full vigor of some of the dominant qualities that marked, to a lesser degree, Mather's achievement at home.

For the most part, historians have seen in his agency the work of a man of ability and strength.[23] On the other hand, some

23. Cf. J. A. Doyle, *The Puritan Colonies*, ii, 330–332; Palfrey, vols. iii and iv, *passim;* and R. H. Murray, *Dublin University and the New World*, pp. 39, 40. C. M. Andrews (*The Fathers of New England*, pp. 196, 197) says: "Mather's success was note-

writers profess to see in it a partial failure for him. For us, then, some assessment of his accomplishment in England is needed, as a clue to his character and position as a man among men in a world of secular concerns.

His agency, of course, resulted in the new charter, and his acceptance of it committed him to it, so that it is possible to judge him, in part, by its merits or faults. It deprived New England of a measure of independence, and it withdrew from the Congregational Church some of its former aids to power. Therefore, if we believe that the colonists wished, and had a right to claim, virtual independence in 1692, Mather's mission was, indeed, a partial failure. Or, if we think that the undisputed supremacy of his church was vital to colonial interests, he served his country ill. But, however patriotic we may be as regards American independence or American Congregationalism, we must still admit that of the old privileges Mather yielded, most had never been sanctioned by English law. His failure to win them was but failure to secure "rights" unrecognized except by popular feeling, and without basis even in the old charter. They could not exist under any colonial policy then acknowledged by England, and to ask Mather to secure them would have been to ask him, single-handed, to accomplish, in four years, what it took a century and the labors of many men to achieve.

Admitting, then, that he failed to accomplish what some might have liked to see, one is still forced to remember that it is hard to imagine any American diplomat succeeding where he had failed. He was, of course, ignorant of law, but there was no New Englander at the time who was not, and his course was marked, as we have seen, by frequent conferences with English lawyers, and with Ashurst, who must have known something of the legal side. There is no evidence that he ever rejected the advice given him by such counsellors; and it is interesting to discover that, divine as he was, his advisers during his agency were not primarily his fellow clergymen, and his guide was not the letter of the Bible but such political wisdom as he had time to acquire in London. And we have concrete results from his work, in a government called better than that of the old charter.[24]

worthy"; and he cites some of the benefits he obtained for New England. Most interesting, perhaps, is Mr. Quincy's praise of Mather, doubly valuable as coming from a historian who, elsewhere, sees little in him to commend. See Quincy, *History*, i, 78, 122, 123.

24. J. T. Adams, *The Founding*, p. 446.

Certainly the new plan established a definite basis for colonial administration, and authorized some privileges that Massachusetts had hitherto claimed without authority. It confirmed the people's possession of some of their dearest prerogatives. The unpopular rule of Andros was replaced by a more liberal government, and a more or less chaotic provisional régime gave way to a body of law under which the state could proceed in full confidence as to her legal status. General tolerance in religion was expressly commanded, and by modern standards this was a great advance. To this, one remembers, Mather committed himself, by accepting it without protest, and, more than once, his specific requests in England were for changes in line with liberal development. He did fail to secure New Hampshire for Massachusetts, but he was defeated by a "not very reputable intrigue."[25] On the other hand, he did add Plymouth to his own state. If in this he failed to satisfy the dearest wishes of Plymouth men, he saved them from an alternative they dreaded, and gained the utmost England would grant. In Connecticut, the case was simpler, and thence, as from Plymouth and Massachusetts, Mather won the official thanks of the representatives.[26] He got from Treby and Somers, with whom he had so many other dealings, a legal opinion asserting that the old Connecticut charter was still in force. No more was necessary to make him seem to the people of that colony a ready aid in time of need.[27]

So Mather served three colonies, gave to one of them all she asked, to another more than she would otherwise have had, and bestowed upon his own state a new government far better than any she had known for years. He accepted without protest an extension of the suffrage and the legal establishment of religious tolerance. In return, he gave up only part of the virtual independence which the colony had claimed rather by custom than by right.

From our point of view, of course, quite as important as what he won, are the means by which he won it. On the side of char-

25. J. T. Adams, *The Founding*, p. 449; J. A. Doyle, *The Puritan Colonies*, ii, 379–381; J. Belknap, *History*, i, 239 (chap. 9); *MHS Coll.*, Series 4, viii, 37, letter of Moodey to Mather, Jan. 8, 1689, first paragraph of postscript.

26. Cf. Palfrey, iv, 89, 90.

27. B. Trumbull, *A Complete History of Connecticut*, i, 386, 387, and H. C. Lodge, *Short History of the English Colonies*, p. 380; also letter of Secretary Allyn of Connecticut to Mather, June 2, 1692, in *New England Historical and Genealogical Register*, xxiii, 341; and, on Connecticut's vote of thanks, *Ibid.*, 464.

acter and ability, no period of his life tells us so much. Going to England, a Puritan, a minister, and a colonist, unknown except to readers of current theology or New England history, he used the weapons he found so well that he nearly won from James II, no lover of popular liberty, the charter he sought for Massachusetts. He was defeated by no defect in his argument, but by a chance rumor that seemed to James to strengthen his hold on the throne. From this reverse, Mather continued his work with what must be seen as a talent for political warfare. Puritan preachers were enlisted in his service, and he impressed his views on the lords, judges, and politicians whose support was necessary for his success. Read the names of those whom he won over, and remember that the list represents only a part of those with whom he made his personality count. With such support he once more neared his goal, only to have restoration of the charter prevented by a conflict on a question of local English politics. But, finally, he won the inclusion in the new charter of the more essential terms he had sought. He left England with many friends in all classes, and there can have been few interested in the conduct of colonial affairs to whom the name of Mather did not have meaning, and few to whom his tall, soberly garbed figure was unfamiliar.

We look upon Benjamin Franklin's work as a diplomat as an achievement in statecraft. So it was; but it is interesting to speculate as to how much he was helped by Mather's mission, generations earlier. As one reads history, it is hard to escape the belief that Increase Mather was a pioneer in American diplomacy. His predecessors as colonial agents had neither the opportunity nor the daring to serve as he did. Whether he succeeded or failed, whether he was able or clumsy, he did more than any emissary from Massachusetts to England had done before. He made it clear to one group of English statesmen, at least, that the colonists had well-defined aims and men to speak for them. After his time, one finds more and more diplomatic intercourse between colonies and mother country; and it is quite clear that he himself believed that the friends he had made, and particularly the impression he had been able to give the king and queen, were guarantees of further progress in winning for the colonies a fair hearing and more favors from England. From this point of view his agency has deep meaning for subsequent history, and testifies plainly to the soundness of his political judgment.

The sort of ability that made his agency successful, whether revealed by Puritan or Papist, "ancient" or "modern," shows always a strong man. So also, his courage in accepting the charter is of the sort that has its place in the estimation of all ages and spheres of human life. He did not choose the easy course, which was to resign in the face of odds, but chose to link his fortunes with the success or failure of a new charter, because he believed it was likely to serve his country well. To face certain opposition, and to confide his own prestige to the chances of an administration which seemed the best that could be hoped for, was the act of a man who had political bravery of a sort which history always gives us cause to admire. And when such an act inaugurates a degree of liberality in government still to be regarded as in the line of progress, it offers still more to praise.

The new charter, it has been said, left a definite mark on the later development of New England.[28] From it, we are told, are derived some of her traditional institutions. To this we may agree; but it has been asserted that for the charter and its consequences the colony had only England and a Dutch king to thank.[29] We have seen too much of Mather and his fellow agents to assent to this. Certainly England was liberal, and her policy was far-sighted. Certainly William sincerely wished a government based on law and due recognition of popular rights. None the less, the State Papers of England to-day contain abundant proof that some of the most benevolent clauses in the new charter were suggested, not by English jurists, statesmen, or by William, but by Elisha Cooke, Thomas Oakes, Sir Henry Ashurst, and Increase Mather. That England went far in accepting their views is a tribute to her. But that they had to plead for their suggestions shows that neither England nor the agents alone won new political rights for Massachusetts. An able agency and a well-organized group of supporters, working with an enlightened and liberal government, established the new order. Less adroit diplomats, or more arbitrary English statesmen, would have changed the result. English liberality made the charter possible, and the agents' knowledge of the colony's demands, together with Mather's appreciation that the time had come to desert the ideal of a strictly intolerant theocracy, gave final form to many of the most essential clauses in the new patent. No New Englander who profited by the new régime at the time, and no

28. J. T. Adams, *The Founding*, p. 447.   29. *Ibid.*

one of his descendants, proud of his country's development, can forget William and his ministers, but still less can he lose sight of the fact that their good-will was turned to practical account by those men led by the first true colonial diplomat, Increase Mather.

In his London sojourn, at the height of his career, Mather found the personality which won friends and parishioners in Boston useful in securing in London champions of his cause. His pen, trained in theological writing, proved its skill in political pamphleteering. His mind, stored with Latin and Greek, bits of science, and scriptural lore, showed a faculty for quick insight into problems of government and trade. His yearning for practical service realized itself in work among men concerned with sordid human affairs. His tolerance, growing with the years and the changing feeling of his flock, showed full development in the decisions he made in London. His breadth of mind made it possible for him to treat with Anglicans and Presbyterians, and to mix on equal terms with such different types as were represented by Nevil Payne, William Penn, and the Countess of Sutherland. At fifty-three he showed the maturity of the worldly wisdom, the controversial skill, the liberality of mind, and, above all, the practical shrewdness, which we have seen developing throughout his life.

Characteristically, too, this highest growth of his stronger traits was accompanied by one more of those bursts of temper which are so often associated with vigorous natures like his. Just as he had flared up at Randolph, so he angrily said more than he meant to the counsellors of the king. Once more he paid the price in weakened influence. And, for our part, we may rejoice that his temper occasionally swept him off his feet. It is indispensable for us to remember that he was no model of perfection. Such a man could neither hold our interest nor win the footing he did in a court where human nature was to the fore. Most men at Whitehall were not paragons. So, if Mather lost his self-control on one occasion, sulked with Samuel Sewall,[30] or frankly combatted Cooke, Oakes, and Wiswall, it is but one more proof that his nature was not only vigorous but human. He had no place in a world where pious speech and abstract discussion ruled. He could find his way most easily where there were conflicting human interests, where passions, friendships and enmities of this world

30. Cf. *MHS Coll.*, Series 5, v, 266.

were rife, and where a sharp tongue was not without use. In such a *milieu* he could do God's work, as he saw it, by human means. There he could express himself fully, and thence he could win a measure of success for his country, and, for himself, the respect of all who recognize liberality, breadth and strength of mind, strong and compelling personality, and, in a good cause, self-forgetful courage.

CHAPTER XVI

THE BOSTONIAN IN LONDON

HAD Mather done no more in England than pursue his political negotiations, one could hardly call him idle. But England was too full of interest to allow him to become engrossed merely by his stated task. Books, friends, and a keen delight in observation, claimed him no less in 1689 or 1691 than in any other of his busy years. Wherever he went, — and he travelled as much as his duties in London allowed,— he made friends. Wherever there were new books, or old ones attractively offered, he was likely to be found among the purchasers. So also, when there were Puritan chapels with eager congregations, or ecclesiastical debates in which a trained nonconformist might be heard, he could not keep away.

He found old friends at Weymouth and at Dorchester,[1] where he broke his journey; but London was his goal. Thither he hastened, to be with Elisha Hutchinson and Samuel Nowell, to be invited to Congregational ministers' conclaves, and to be eagerly welcomed and lodged with Major Thompson at Newington Green. There were crowded streets, gay dress, and the new buildings of Christopher Wren to delight little Samuel, and bookshelves heaped high to lure his father into hours of the pursuit which is the student's and book collector's dearest joy. Whether he lived out at Newington, on bright days walking to and from the city with some good friend to whom he could talk and from whose advice he could profit, and, in bad weather, going by coach, hugging in his arms some calf-bound folio of sound divinity which he already saw proudly adorning the widest shelf of his study in the house on Middle Street, Boston; or whether he lived alone in his chambers in Copthall Court, Throgmorton Street,[2] in the heart of old London, amid the new building that was springing from the ruins of the Great Fire, he led a life of intoxicating wealth of opportunity. There were enough Puritan churches to fill many Sabbath mornings to his heart's content. In the Royal Exchange, at the Temple, on the

1. MS. *Diary*, 1688, May 16, 17.   2. *Autobiography; Parentator.*

elm-shaded Mall, or in the Parks, there was abundant diversion for many days.[3] A stone's throw from his London lodgings was the new Drapers' Hall; not far away was the Thames, where he may have joined Samuel Sewall in a morning swim; and his walk to Whitehall, or out to Hackney or Hoxton, was sure to be filled with glimpses, if no more, of persons and scenes which now fill some part in the historical pageant we conjure up as the London of the Revolution.[4]

Some of those he met were the human forces with whom he had to deal in winning his case for the colony, and still others he recognized as leaders not to be slighted by a student of contemporary learning. The men, in long coats embroidered and stiffened, wigs, and waistcoats which rivalled each other in their brocaded patterns, escorted ladies, some of whom had adopted Queen Mary's new fashion of wearing chintz or East India calico, while all displayed skirts which had begun "to heave and swell" in anticipation of the coming of the hoop. Such gay figures as Nell Gwyn may have appeared to Mather to be embodiments of earthly vanity, and he may have yearned for the vocabulary of a Nathaniel Ward to describe those "mymick Marmosets" in "Out-landish caskes," [5] but Samuel was still boy enough to delight in the color and brilliance they lent to the dusty, ill-paved streets.

But when Samuel had gone to bed, and such street lights as there were shone on the dirty pavements, Mather had plenty to do, even though he never joined the gay crowds flocking to Drury Lane to see Mrs. Barry, or Mrs. Bracegirdle, and Mr. Betterton, act in the latest play by Wycherley or Shadwell. If others sought out gaming houses or a cock-fight, or went to get a glimpse of the wits at "Will's," to smoke and talk politics at the "Grecian" or the "Rainbow," the height of Mather's dissipation is likely to have been an evening spent around the table at the New England Coffee House.[6] There would be Samuel Sewall, his head full of schemes for profitable importations to Boston, but none the less able to discuss with relish the most knotty of theological problems. There, too, would be Sir William Phipps, florid, fond of his tankard, letting an oath slip out now

---

3. MS. *Diary*, 1688, July 5; 1689, Feb. 9.
4. *Ibid.*, 1688, Nov. 25, July 25; *MHS Coll.*, Series 5, v, 264.
5. N. Ward, *The Simple Cobbler*, p. 28.
6. Cf., for example, *MHS Coll.*, Series 5, v, 285.

and then in his ardor to make apparent his zeal against the French.[7] With them would be Stephen Mason, confident in his prosperity as a city merchant, Elisha Hutchinson, Nowell, recalling old days at Harvard, Sir Henry Ashurst, and, in some subtle way the acknowledged leader of them all, Mather himself. It was to him that Phipps one evening tossed over an old brass snuff-box, bidding him keep it, telling, with a twinkle in his eye, how it had once been carried by no less a man than the brave Sir Walter Raleigh.[8]

When the tobacco smoke hung too thickly in the coffee-house, we might find Mather hurrying through the streets, mindful of the dangers of night-prowling bands of roisterers, seeking out the house of Robert Boyle or Richard Baxter.[9]

The former he saw often. "All modern thought, so far as it is scientific, is largely dependent upon the labors of three men — Isaac Newton, Robert Boyle and John Locke." [10] Boyle was sixty-two years old when Mather visited him in London. He was partly paralyzed, and handicapped by failing sight, but his mental powers were undimmed. To his house came such men as Burnet, Locke, Newton, and Halley, sure of finding there a modest, serious man, pale of face and slow of speech, who could talk to them of the Hebrew language, which he began to study in 1686, of theology, or of current literature, and could show them in his laboratory his latest experiments with magnets or gases. There lay his chief interest. Thence came the germs of most of his pamphlets and communications to the Royal Society, an institution in which he always maintained an active interest and to which he contributed much of the material it printed in its early years. A theory of his was useful to Pasteur, and we are told that "what Pasteur and his collaborators have done, is to explain and amplify the points experimentally established by Boyle." He designed and used an air-pump, independent of Guericke, and "established the science of pneumatics." Repeatedly he outlined theories later proved to be accurate, and incorporated, to-day, among the fundamental truths of science. To

7. Cf. N. Hawthorne, "Sir William Phips," in *Works*, vol. xii.

8. J. H. Tuttle, *The Libraries*, p. 311. The tobacco box is now owned by the American Antiquarian Society. The tale of its ownership seems to rest solely on family tradition.

9. Cf. MS. *Diaries*, 1688, May 29, June 20, July 16, Sept. 4, and elsewhere.

10. C. O. Thompson, "Robert Boyle," in *American Antiquarian Society Proceedings*, ii, 54ff.

ROBERT BOYLE

From a painting in the National Portrait Gallery

summarize in detail his varied activity would be impossible, but it is enough to remember that his cardinal principle was that scientific truth can be reached only by exact observation. He was a victorious opponent of scholasticism, and a pioneer in making experimental investigation the basis for scientific method. Surely, if any views were antipathetic to what we are told was the Puritan's attitude toward natural philosophy, his were. Yet it was with him that Increase Mather, sometimes labelled the superstitious theologian, spent many hours, and his books filled a large place on Mather's shelves. The New England divine, a humble admirer of Boyle's methods, tried, as we have seen, to record phenomena observed in the colonies. For his pains he is called, two hundred years later, a credulous bigot. Quite different must have been his reception by Boyle himself in 1688; for this leader among English scientists had an open mind and realized how much was then undreamed of in his, or anyone else's, philosophy. To-day, when the experiments of centuries have been made, and laws have been deduced from them, we can exclude many reported occurrences as unreal, or explain them away by some formula of the moment. But Boyle and Mather argued from no such accumulation of data, and, for them, the stuff of science was often just such "illustrious providences" as they both collected.[11]

Boyle's interest in Indians and in the Society for the Propagation of the Gospel among them[12] was sufficient reason for his receiving Mather; but his visitor was obviously not content to talk only of theology in the presence of an adventurer in science. This we should guess from Mather's previous dabbling in "natural philosophy," and we can be sure of it when we see how many of Boyle's scientific books he bought or received from their author's hands, or when we find him visiting Flamsteed, the Astronomer Royal, and with him "viewing the Stars" or going to a shop to see "about telescopes."[13] If Puritan theology was hostile to science, Boyle's laboratory and London telescope shops were not fit places for a New England divine. Mather frequented them, none the less, for his intellectual curiosity would not allow him to close his eyes to any movement of the day. In science, moreover, he had long had a peculiar interest, and more than

11. *American Antiquarian Society Proceedings*, ii, 57, 59, 75, 77, etc.
12. *Ibid.*, pp. 65ff.
13. MS. *Diary*, 1689, Feb. 7; *MHS Coll.*, Series 5, v, 252.

once he had in this connection exhibited a leaning toward modern and advanced thought.

If Richard Baxter [14] could not go far in discussing the dawnings of chemical research, he could talk from a memory well stored with tales of "illustrious providences." He was unique among Puritans in his breadth of activity, and his character, his patience, moderation, and truly Christian spirit, mark him above the rank and file of his brethren. In Mather he seems to have found a man he could trust and admire, and no divine in the colonies was so eminent as not to be gratified by the attention of the greatest English Puritan. From him Increase Mather had not only a kind reception, but letters which praised his books and his style, in such words as: "You have very much gratifyed me by your two books. Your very style & mode of writing is so suitable to my genius, y^t it pleases me even when I cañot consent to the matter. . . . I am so much taken with your history of prodigies, yt I purpose to put my scraps into yor hands (so much as is not lost) . . . if you will reprint your book while you stay here, & add these as a supplemt ffor I see you have good skill in selecting & contracting. I pray tell me whether you have any to sell (& where)." [15] In another letter Baxter wrote: "I loved your *father* . . . I love *you* better for your learning, labours, and peaceable moderation." [16] Baxter was one Puritan who knew what "peaceable moderation" was, and that he recognized it in Mather shows that we have not read the latter's character amiss.

The most tangible testimony of Baxter's feeling for Mather, and that most likely to have been grateful to the New Englander, was the dedication to "The Glorious Kingdom of Christ, *Described* and clearly *Vindicated*." Baxter published this discussion of the problem of the millennium in 1691, and dedicated it "To Mr. *Increase Mather*, the Learned and Pious Rector of the *New-England* Colledge (now in *London*)." He wrote on a theme that Mather had discussed in his "Mystery of Israel's Salvation," and disagreed on many points. But, he wrote, "I have read no man that hath handled it with so much Learning and Moderation as you have done. . . . I know no man fitter, if I err, to detect

14. Cf. *DNB*, and references there.

15. See an unpublished letter from Baxter to Mather, owned by Dr. Williams's library, in a volume of MS. letters of Baxter, pp. 217, 218. It is addressed to Mather "at Major Thompson's house at Newington."

16. Letter, August 3, 1691, in C. Mather, *Magnalia*, book III, part iii.

RICHARD BAXTER

From a painting in the National Portrait Gallery

my Errours. And as your Candour is rather for my publishing, than suppressing these Papers; so truly I am so far from disliking a true Confutation of this (or any Errour that I shall publish) that I therefore direct these lines to you, to intreat you, to write (whether I be alive or dead) your Reasons against any momentous or Dangerous Errour which you shall here find: That as we thus friendly consent to such a Collision, or rather Communication, as may kindle some further sparks of light, the Readers may be helpt by comparing all, the better to seek out the truth." The spirit of both men appears in these lines, and it is a spirit sometimes sadly to seek in later controversies of scholars. That Mather's "unworthy Fellow-Servant" dignified him by such consideration speaks volumes; and the little book, sure to be read widely, carried to all who took it up the news that out of New England and Harvard had come a theologian not to be neglected by any one who sought opinions of weight.

On other days Mather spent the morning with Goodwin Wharton, younger son of Lord Wharton, at Hatton Garden; or, sometimes, we might find him dining at the George Tavern in Cornhill.[17] He journeyed out to Windsor and Eton, and, when Sewall was in England, made a pilgrimage with him to the two great universities. At Oxford they saw "the Colledges and Halls, New-Colledge, Maudlin and Christ Ch. do most excell," and at New College "eat and drank Ale, wine, Lent Cakes full of Currants, good Butter and Cheese."[18] So also they visited Cambridge, with its memories of their own John Cotton. They broke their sight-seeing by good meals at the Red Lion in the "Petit Curie," and Sewall lovingly describes a dinner of "a Legg Mutton boiled and Colly-Flowers, Carrets, Roasted Fowls, and a dish of Pease."[19]

Faced with the problem of finding Mather as quickly as might be, we should probably do best to follow Stephen Mason's example and look for him at the booksellers'. If he were not at Whitehall or Hampton Court, at the Custom House, or at the sign of the Atlas in Cornhill, talking to his friend Robert Morden, writer on geography and maker of maps and globes, or if he were not bargaining for a new clock for the Middle Street house, he would be most likely to be found near St. Paul's Churchyard or

17. MS. *Diary*, 1688, July 4, 21.
18. *Ibid.*, Aug. 2-4; *MHS Coll.*, Series 5, v, 301.
19. *Ibid.*, pp. 259, 260.

in Little Britain.[20] There he must have become well known to such book-dealers as crack-brained John Dunton, or Richard Chiswell.[21] Probably he won the privilege of taking a volume or two home upon occasion, to be read and returned; and we can still trace many volumes that he bought in those happy days when he used to write in his diary, "At booksellers shops."

Among his purchases were more than fifty books still preserved, with inscriptions dating their acquisition during these years.[22] Of these more than half were theological, or manuals of Hebrew. There are a few current tracts, with titles such as "The State of Protestants of Ireland under King James's Government," "Articles Agreed upon by the Archbishops and Bishops," bound with other pamphlets, and "A Display of Tyranny."[23] The book-collector's perennial joy in a bargain is revealed in Mather's copy of Gisbert Voet's "Politicae Ecclesiasticae," where he has written "£2–15–0. In N. E. [New England] £3–14–0." Of especial interest are such works as Robert Cotton's "Answer to motives offered by military men to Prince Henry," the "BIAΘANATOΣ" of John Donne, King Edward the Sixth's "Own Arguments against the Pope's Supremacy," Richard Mather's "Heart Melting Exhortations," Hugo Grotius's "De Coenae Administratione," and a "Rituale Romanum," strangest book of all for a Puritan![24] Pointing to his interest in prodigies and witches, we find John Webster's "Displaying of Supposed Witchcraft," John Spencer's "Discourse concerning Prodigies," John Darrell's "Dialogical Discourses," and Elias Henckel's "Ordo et Methodus Cognoscendi Energumenos."[25] He would have classified these as science, and lumped them with the "Chemica Rationalis" of P. T., Erycius Puteanus's "De

20. MS. *Diary*, 1688, July 27, and memorandum as to a clock; I. Mather, *Cases of Conscience*, p. 283.

21. F. A. Mumby, *Romance of Book-Selling*, p. 189.

22. I include in this number books so inscribed listed by J. H. Tuttle, in *The Libraries of the Mathers*, and similar volumes owned by the American Antiquarian Society, but not listed in Tuttle, as well as one book noticed in the *New England Historical and Genealogical Register*, and one owned by W. G. Mather, Cleveland, Ohio.

23. The first of these is owned by the American Antiquarian Society, the last two by the Massachusetts Historical Society.

24. Of these books, all except the "Own Arguments" and the "Heart Melting Exhortation" are owned by the American Antiquarian Society. The other two are owned by the Massachusetts Historical Society and the Yale University library, respectively.

25. Of these the first is owned by the Harvard University library, the others by the American Antiquarian Society.

Cometa Anni 1618," and Boyle's "Experimentorum Novorum Physico-Mechanicorum," "Memoirs for the Natural History of Humane Blood," "Experiments and Considerations about the Porosity of Bodies," "Of the Reconcileableness of Specifick Medicines to Corpuscular Philosophy," "Short Memoirs for the Natural Experimental History of Mineral Waters," "Some Considerations touching Experimental Natural Philosophy," and "Essay of the Great Effects of even Languid and Unheeded Motion." [26] The last two have inscriptions which suggest that they were gifts of the author.[27] However he got them, such a group of authentic, up-to-date scientific writings shows, once more, Mather's intellectual progress in such matters.

Certainly given by the author was Baxter's "Church Concord," [28] and so also was Thomas Beverley's "Thousand Years Kingdom of Christ." [29] From Samuel Clark came his annotations to the New Testament.[30] Probably other books given to Mather are lost to-day, as must be many which he bought, and his library as it now exists contains many volumes which offer no hint as to when they were purchased. His London rooms in Copthall Court must have been crowded with the trophies of his literary quests. Probably he placed among them the two works which he noted particularly as ones to be sought in London.[31] Both, it is interesting to discover, were scientific. One was the "Germanic Ephemerides" for 1684,[32] and the other, the Philosophical Transactions of the Royal Society for 1685.

When he travelled, Mather carried certain books with him. Annotations on the Gospels, a general Biblical commentary, a work by Alstedius, the Bible, in English and in Hebrew, a psalter,

26. All owned by the American Antiquarian Society.

27. Both are inscribed, "For Mr. Mather at Mr. Whitings in Copthall Court in Throgmorton Street."

28. Owned by the American Antiquarian Society. It is inscribed, "ex dono Authoris."

29. Owned by the American Antiquarian Society. It is inscribed, "Mr. I. Mather ... Ex dono Authoris." Beverley was preacher at Cutlers' Hall, Cloak-Lane, London, and writer of prophecies. He believed and wrote that the millennial reign of Christ was to begin in 1697. See W. Wilson, *The History and Antiquities of Dissenting Churches*, ii, 63–65.

30. Inscribed, "I. Mather, given to me by the Revd Author Mr Samuel Clark at London 1689," *New England Historical and Genealogical Register*, xxxii, 420. Clark was the author of an annotated Bible which "is still a useful book." See *DNB*.

31. He noted these titles in a memorandum in the volume containing his diary for these years, as books to "Enquire after."

32. Cf. p. 175, note 78, *ante*.

a Latin grammar, and "Terentius." [33] Whether this was the Jesuit, Terentius, or, more probably, the dramatist, — profane, perhaps, but a fit comrade for Plautus, whose comedies Mather bought twenty years before,— we cannot tell; but either writer's presence among his luggage would mark the breadth of his tastes.[34]

Now and then he had to give up precious minutes among the bookstalls, to seek out John van der Spriett, a Dutch artist, then in London. He painted a portrait of Mather upon which we rely most for our mental image of him.[35] The strongly modelled face, far thinner than that of the 1683 engraving, the high cheekbones, the slender hands, the long fingers, and, most of all, the pose, in which Mather seems to be expounding from a text open before him, suggest that the work really reflects character. Certainly it is not the picture of a man to be likened to a tombstone.[36] There is too much life in the face and body, even as they appear on canvas, to make possible an impression other than that of a personality of force, even if of a pedagogic and dogmatic type.

We can be sure as to the time and place of painting the Van der Spriett portrait. In his diary for July 5, 1688, Increase writes, "At R. White's, who drew my effigies." Robert White engraved pictures of most of the great men of his time, and we know that he made an engraving from the Van der Spriett portrait, and dated it 1688. It seems, then, that by the first week in July, before he had been two months in England, Mather had had his portrait painted, and then engraved by one of the best-known workmen of the day. Before he left England a second print-maker had tried his hand at reproducing the likeness of the visitor from the colonies.[37]

With his portrait from the hands of a Dutch artist, and with engravings of it by the famous White and his pupil, Sturt, Mather's vanity, in one respect, should have been full fed. It must have been a further solace to see, here and there among the booksellers' stocks, books of his own offered for sale beside those

33. Memoranda in the volume containing his diary for these years list these books as "Libri mecum portandi."

34. The American Antiquarian Society owns to-day Mather's copy of Terence's comedies. I have found no record of his having owned the other "Terentius."

35. The painting is now owned by the Massachusetts Historical Society. Cf. K. B. Murdock, *The Portraits of Increase Mather*, and see frontispiece.

36. Cf. N. Hawthorne, *Works*, xii, 230.

37. K. B. Murdock, *The Portraits*.

of Baxter, Marvell, and Bunyan. To "The Wonders of Free Grace," printed probably in 1690,[38] was added his "Sermon Occasioned by the Execution of a Man," published earlier in Boston. But the most read of his signed works in these years, though by no means the most interesting to-day, was the widely reprinted "De Successo Evangelii," which appeared in 1688 in Latin, and, to judge by the number of its editions, seems to have been a singularly welcome tract.[39] This was due, probably, to no literary merit, but to its brevity and its subject. Since the first explorations in America, Catholics and Protestants alike had seized upon the opportunity to introduce their beliefs to the Indians. In London, the Society for the Propagation of the Gospel was active, and sent its agents throughout the colonies. French missionaries, bearing the standard of Rome, braved the St. Lawrence wilderness. Mather, himself sincerely interested in the Indian conversions in which John Eliot was leader, saw in them a subject sure to appeal to his brethren in all lands. His consciousness that his own reputation and that of his people would be well served abroad by some account of their success with their savage neighbors, led him to address to John Leusden, a Dutch scholar,[40] a Latin letter with the title "De Successo Evangelii Apud Indos in Nova-Anglia." This he published in London in 1688. There was a second edition in Latin in 1699, one in German in 1696, and, probably, one at Utrecht in 1693.[41] From a letter of Leusden to Mather we learn that the tract was also printed in French.[42] An English version appeared in "The Brief Relation," put out by Mather in connection with his agency,

38. The title as given by J. L. Sibley, *op. cit.*, i, 447, is: "Wonders of Free-Grace, Or, A Compleat History of all the Remarkable Penitents That have been Executed at Tyburn," etc. (London, 1691); and the title explains sufficiently the nature of the book. I am informed by Mr. T. J. Holmes that the date of the book is 1690, not 1691.

39. The title is: "De *Successu Evangelij* Apud Indos in Novâ-Angliâ Epistola. Ad Cl. Virum D. *Johannem Leusdenum*, Linguae Sanctae in Ultrajectinâ Academiâ Professorem, Scripta. A *Crescentio Mathero* Apud *Bostonienses* V.D.M. nec non Collegij *Harvardini* quod est *Cantabrigiae* Nov-Anglorum, Rectore. *Londini*, Typis *J. G.* 1688."

40. Leusden was "one of the most learned Hebraists of his day," professor at Utrecht from 1650 until his death in 1699. D. de S. Pool, *Hebrew Learning among the Puritans*, pp. 59ff.

41. "De Successu . . . Jam recusa, & successu Evangelii apud Indos Orientales aucta. Ultrajecti, Apud Wilhelmum Broedeleth Anno 1699."

"Ein Brieff von dem Gluecklichen Fortgang des Evangelii . . . Zum andernmahl gedruckt und mit dem gluecklichen Fortgang des Evangelii bey den Ost-Indianern vermehret. Utrecht gedurckt bey W. B. 1693 . . . Halle, Gedruckt bey Christoph Salfelden 1696."

42. *MHS Coll.*, Series 4, viii, 679.

and there are hints that there was an Indian translation.[43] Cotton Mather used an English version in his life of John Eliot, which reached four editions, and was included in his "Magnalia." Turner, in his "Compleat History of the most Remarkable Providences," also found a place for it.[44]

The letter is a brief matter-of-fact account of the triumphs of John Eliot, John Cotton, and Samuel Treat among the Indians. It is a news sheet rather than a literary work, but its subject gave it unique prominence. Leusden was delighted,[45] and besides having it translated, he expressed his gratitude by dedicating to Mather his edition of the Psalter in Latin and Hebrew, published at London in 1688.[46] He calls Mather "Maxime Reverendo & Clarissimo viro . . . Verbi Divini Ministro Vigilantissimo, atque Collegii Harvardini, quod est Cantabrigiae Nov-Anglorum Rectore & Doctori Celeberrimo ac Honorandissimo." Allowing for conventional excess of phrase, that a scholar of Leusden's rank thus addressed Mather in a book sold in the bookshops of St. Paul's Churchyard must have impressed more than one soberminded book-buyer, and gratified Mather's own pride in no small degree.

Meanwhile his "Testimony against Prophane and Superstitious Customs" was reprinted in Boston, and no doubt there was circulated with it in London his anonymous "Brief Discourse concerning the Unlawfulness of the Common Prayer Worship and of Laying the Hand on, and Kissing the Booke in Swearing,"[47] which, when it appeared in Boston, in 1686, aroused Randolph's ire, and seems to have involved Cotton Mather in difficulties with Andros and his following.[48] They ascribed the book, apparently, to Cotton rather than to Increase, but Prince assigns it to the elder Mather.[49] We have added confirmation of his authorship, for, in 1693, the book was answered in London, and

43. *Andros Tracts*, ii, 166, where it is said that the work was "translated into divers Languages in *New England*."

44. See p. 171, *ante*, for reference to this book.

45. *MHS Coll.*, Series 4, viii, 679.

46. *Ibid.* The title was: "*Liber* Psalmorum, *Editus* a Johanne Leusden," "Londini, . . . Sumptibus Samuelis Smith, ad insigne Principis in Caemiterio D. Pauli A. 1688." Mr. H. W. Van Loon kindly lent me his copy of the book, whence I have drawn the title, and the quotation below.

47. The title is: "*A Brief Discourse Concerning the unlawfulness of the Common Prayer Worship. And Of Laying the Hand on, and Kissing the Booke in Swearing.* By a Reverend and Learned Divine. Printed in the Year &c."

48. See p. 63, note 35, *ante*.

49. Cf. J. L. Sibley, *Biographical Sketches*, i, 449.

to this answer Increase Mather replied in 1713, speaking of the original tract as his own.[50] Moreover, a passage in the book itself makes Cotton's authorship impossible.[51]

The work, although written some years before Mather came to England, aroused most attention during his agency, and so is best discussed in this chapter. It purports to be a letter written to someone who asked Mather why it was "unlawful to be present at, or to partake in the Common prayer worship," and why one should not take oaths with one's hand upon the Bible, or kiss the book in swearing. The inquirer published the letter in order that others might be convinced by it. In it we find once more, not the able political debater, but the divine and scholar preaching from authorities and texts. Buttressed by a host of learned writers, making no effort toward literary form, but still keeping his usual direct and simple utterance, Mather denounces the Book of Common Prayer.

There is no better example of the stress placed by Puritans on what seem to us trivial details of worship than such books as this. But there are churches to-day which oppose the use of any liturgy; and if such views are now considered narrow, in Mather's day the question of the use of the Prayer Book was a serious one. Indeed, it was so grave as to separate from the Anglican Church some of its erstwhile followers. To us, time spent on such details seems wasted. To Mather and his brethren they were worthy of all the scholarly investigation he gave them.

Not content with his own book, Mather reinforced it, so far as it concerned the manner of taking oaths,— a matter of moment in connection with the agency and the new charter,—by bringing out, or, at least, prefacing a London edition, printed in 1689, of Samuel Willard's "A Brief Discourse Concerning that Ceremony of Laying the Hand on the Bible in Swearing." [52] In his preface Mather points to the authorities who have regarded "Kissing or Touching the Book in taking a solemn Oath" as an evil practice. Thence he turns to more practical arguments, men-

---

50. *Andros Tracts*, i, 180.

51. The author writes: "As for mee ... My Father was an Holy and a Learned man, and one that Suffered much for his *Non conformity;* should I once go to hear Common Prayer I ... Know not how I should bee able to look my Father in the Face in the other world." Obviously, Cotton could not have written this in 1686. Randolph's ascription to him throws an interesting sidelight on his denunciations of the Bostonians, since, in this case, he does not seem to have read the book on which he based a charge!

52. The work is reprinted in *Andros Tracts*, i, 179ff. The preface is signed M. I., as is Mather's preface to a book of his brother's. Cf. p. 97, *ante*.

tioning the method of oath-taking used in Scotland, in Europe, and in certain English Admiralty courts. He even quotes a vote of Parliament in 1649. He closes with the reason for the publication: "It is . . . hoped that this Disputation may excite others to enquire into, and further clear the controverted Question." [53]

A less controversial preface was that which Mather wrote for John Flavel's "Exposition of the Assembly's Catechism." [54] Flavel died in Dartmouth in 1691 and when Mather came there in March, 1692, on his way back to Boston, he took the opportunity to pay tribute to the memory of an old friend by adding an introduction to one of his books about to be published. In it, hastily written as it must have been, there speaks the sincere affection of an American Puritan for one of his English brethren.

One other book of Mather's dates from these years, his "Brief Account Concerning Several of the Agents of New-England, Their Negotiation at the Court of England." [55] Internal evidence makes it certain that Mather was the author of this anonymous tract.[56] It is a straightforward account of his negotiation, followed by a thorough exposition of the reasons for accepting the new charter and a complete defence of its good points. To this are added certain practical suggestions, advising the General Court to make good laws, and for "the Upholding of Religion" to pass acts to "Encourage an Able and Faithful Ministry." The college should be put "in such Hands, as will make it their Concern to Promote and Propogate Vertue and Learning" (pp. 295ff.). Mather also proposes that judges, sheriffs, and justices of the peace, be chosen from "Men fearing God" (p. 296). In these pages is made perfectly clear Mather's point of view toward the future. Congregationalism could thrive no longer by exclusive privilege. That

53. *Andros Tracts*, i, 182.

54. J. Flavel, *An Exposition of the Assembly's Catechism*. Mather also wrote, while in England, a preface for Flavel's *England's Duty, Under the present Gospel-Liberty*, dating it 1689. He also joined with his brother, John Howe, and others in signing a preface to Flavel's ΠΛΑΝΗΛΟΓΙΑ. *A . . . Discourse of . . . Mental Errors*, published in 1691.

55. "A Brief Account Concerning Several of the Agents of New-England, Their Negotiation at the Court of England: With Some Remarks on the New Charter Granted to the Colony of *Massachusets*. Shewing That all things duely Considered, Greater Priviledges than what are therein contained, could not at this Time rationally be expected by the People there." London, 1691. Reprinted in *Andros Tracts*, ii, 271ff., to which edition all references here are made.

56. The author writes in the second paragraph, p. 273: "When I began my Voyage from *Boston* for *London* (which was in *April*, 1688)." This fits no one of the agents but Mather.

Mather gave up without protest. Henceforth his church must succeed by a campaign of education, and by the appointment of such civil officers as would not shut their ears to the claims of the first settlers' religion. For the next ten years Mather worked along these lines.

He saw as early as 1691 that a real campaign was in store. He knew that he would have to face criticism, not only from too zealous advocates of American independence, opposed to any governor not of their own choice, but also from the ardent old-school Congregationalists, who believed that the right to vote should be linked with a religious test. To disarm such opponents he appended to his story of his work in England a letter from "the most Eminent *Nonconformist Divines* in *London.*" [57] Bates, Mead, Alsop, Howe, Annesley, Griffith, Quick, and others testified to his "inviolate Integrity, excellent Prudence, and unfainting Diligence," his "Talent to transact Affairs of State," and his insight into "the true Moment of things," which led him to prefer "the Publick Good to the vain Conceits of some, that more might have been obtained" (pp. 297, 298). Prejudiced testimony, perhaps, but confirmed by a private letter from an Englishman to his brother in New England. [58]

A decade after this tract appeared, an eager foe of Mather took occasion to remark that it was but an "*Embrio,*" stifled as soon as it was born. [59] But, as Mather's friends promptly pointed out, [60] a copy of the book was sent to the colony and read to the General Court, where it doubtless served its purpose, and we can be sure the printed work was never cancelled. On the other hand, the charge that Mather planned to have it appear after he left England, and that his friend, Mr. Baily, erred in bringing it to light too soon, thereby provoking its author to one more angry outburst, seems to be supported by the facts. But no harm was done, and Mather's ire quickly cooled.

In one paragraph the question of a charter for Harvard is discussed. To secure such a charter had been one of the main objects of Mather's pilgrimage. He could not, he says, achieve it, so long as the civil government of the colony was unsettled. When the new charter was granted, confirming, as it did, Harvard's owner-

57. Pp. 297ff. Cf. *Andros Tracts*, ii, 312.
58. *MHS Proc.*, xxxiv, 215.
59. S. G. Drake, *The Witchcraft Delusion*, iii, 150.
60. *Andros Tracts*, ii, 299, 317.

ship of its property, Mather was advised not to apply for a special patent incorporating the college, but to get the General Court to grant a charter and "make it an University, with as ample Priviledges as they should think necessary; and then transmit that *Act of the General Court* to *England*, for the Royal Approbation; which would undoubtedly be obtained." "I look upon this Particular alone," Mather adds, "to be well worth my going to *England*, and there serving half an Apprenticeship; for that no small Concernment of Religion, and the Happiness of future Generations, are comprehended in this Matter respecting the Colledge." [61] At our distance it certainly seems wiser to have planned to incorporate Harvard by vote of the colonial assembly, where local opinion could be represented, than to have secured by individual efforts, three thousand miles from Cambridge, a document which might be satisfactory to no one but the rector and the king and council.

Many years later, Cotton Mather, writing of his father's services to the college during his agency, quotes Increase as saying: "I procured in *Donations* to the Province and the College at least *Nine Hundred Pounds more than all the Expences of my Agency came to*"; and adds: "it was *His* Acquaintance with, and *His* Proposal to, That Good-Spirited Man, and Lover of all Good Men, Mr. THOMAS HOLLIS, that Introduced his Benefactions unto that *College;* to which his Incomparable Bounty has anon flow'd unto such a Degree, as to render him the *Greatest Benefactor* it ever had in the World." Mather, in his account of his work, refers to one legacy of five hundred pounds secured by him for Harvard.[62]

Thomas Hollis and his descendants were such good friends to the college that it is worth while to make some examination of the suggestion that Mather first interested them.[63] The facts accessible are these. In 1719 Hollis's first donation arrived. On Increase Mather's request, and because he "was instrumental in procuring these donations," the Corporation voted the interest of the gift to his grandson. Leverett, in his diary, says Mather "might be instrumental in procuring it." Benjamin Colman wrote Hollis as to Mather's claim and the use the money had been put to, and the donor replied, approving the application

61. *Andros Tracts*, ii, 295ff.
62. *Parentator*, pp. 151, 170; *Andros Tracts*, ii, 295.
63. For Hollis, cf., for example, Quincy, *passim*.

THOMAS HOLLIS

made of his bounty, and said, explaining the origin of his interest: "I have had many thoughts of showing some liberality to it [the college] ever since the death of my honored uncle, Robert Thorner, who made me one of his trustees." On these data Quincy rests his case, writing: "By thus carrying back the orgin of his good intentions to a time antecedent to any possible influence of Dr. Mather, he obviously intended to exclude any acknowledgment of it." To this he adds a remark that this "is sufficient to show the groundlessness of Dr. Mather's claim to instrumentality" in procuring Hollis's bounty.[64]

Fortunately we can go further. We know that Robert Thorner's will was not made at "a time antecedent to any possible influence of Dr. Mather" but was dated the 31st of May, 1690. Furthermore, the very wording of the will shows that Mather was in Thorner's mind. "I devise give and bequeath unto Harvard College in New England whereof Mr. Increase Matther is now President, the suñe of ffive hundred pounds to be paid unto the President of the said Colledge." [65] We know also that Thorner had known Nathaniel Mather for many years, and had been intimate with his father-in-law, William Benn, and that Increase saw Thorner in 1688 and, in 1689, had a letter from him which spoke of his purpose to help Harvard.[66] Also Hollis wrote Mather: "you seem ... to have forgotten me, thô in my letter to you I hinted, I was the man that gave you a minute out of my Unkle Thorner's will ... & you said you would cause it to be recorded in your Colledg Registers — approving of my said Unkles pious thought, thô as yet very distant — I was willing of my own substance to make a present to yᵉ same purpose." He approves using the interest of his gift as Mather suggested, and adds: "I have thôᵗˢ living — or by Will to order over to you a larger parsel [of] goods, the produce to be added for same uses to the summe you now have in hand." This letter, written in 1719, makes it clear that Hollis and Mather met in England, that Thorner's nephew then gave the Rector a minute from his uncle's will, and that, even after Mather left the President's chair at Harvard, Hollis wrote to him of his benevolent intentions and accepted his views as to how the gifts should be used.[67]

64. *Quincy*, i, 232, 235, 236; *Harv. Rec.*, pp. 446, 447.
65. *New England Historical and Genealogical Register*, xlv, 53, and cf. Quincy, i, 186.
66. *MHS Coll.*, Series 4, viii, 677 and n., 678; MS. *Diary*, Sept. 13, 1688.
67. For the letter, see *New England Historical and Genealogical Register*, ii, 265.

Therefore, by the same reasoning that Quincy employed, we can draw from the material now accessible the conclusion that Mather certainly played a part in interesting Thorner. We know that he knew Hollis, and kept up the friendship for years after 1691. Generosity of the sort that made Hollis an honored name in New England can rarely be traced to a single episode, or the influence of one man, but we can hardly escape the conclusion that Mather's relations to Thorner and to Hollis make it highly probable that he was, as his son declared, the agent whose efforts "Introduced" the generous Englishman's "Benefactions unto that *College*." Quincy's view, then, drawn as it was from an incomplete set of documents, seems to miss the truth. Instead, we may accept the "New England Weekly Journal's" statement, on April 19, 1731: "When the Rev. Dr. *Increase Mather* was Agent for the Province in *London, Anno* 1690, he was known in his Character of *President* or *Rector* of Harvard College to Mr. *Hollis*, who then told him that he purpos'd to remember said College in his Will, which was no doubt gratefully accepted & encouraged by Mr. *Mather*." [68]

If Leverett, not as thoroughly in touch with the records as it is possible for us to be, thought Mather "might be" the cause of Hollis's kindness, he was positive in his assertion that Mather directed the generosity of Nathaniel Hulton to Harvard.[69] We can verify this, inasmuch as Hulton wrote Mather, saying: "It is my resolution to give one hundred pounds, I say £100, which is as much as I can do . . . and this £100 I do wholly and absolutely leave to you to lay it out upon something that will bring in a yearly revenue forever." [70] Hulton died in 1693, and the last codicil of his will reads, "J give & Bequeath to Mr. Jncrease

---

68. Quoted in *New England Historical and Genealogical Register*, ii, 266. In 1731, Colman wrote: "To the Honour of my Country, I must add, that it was some Account Mr. *Hollis* received from us of the free and catholic Air we breath at our *Cambridge*, where *Protestants* of every Denomination may have their Children educated, and graduated in our *College*, if they behave with Sobriety and Virtue; that took his generous Heart and fix'd it on us, and enlarg'd it to us." B. Colman, *A Sermon* . . . Upon the News of the Death of . . . *Thomas Hollis*, Esq. But we have seen that Hollis himself said he was first interested when he learned of his uncle's bequest. If Harvard's liberality was what appealed, it must, then, have been its liberality prior to 1690, or, its liberality under Mather!

The *Religious History of New England* says (p. 154) that Mather's liberality toward Baptists led Hollis to be generous to Harvard — an attempt, apparently, to reconcile Colman's statement, given above, with the other facts we have cited.

On the whole matter, cf. also, *Harv. Rec.*, ii, 832, 833, and *Parentator*, p. 209.

69. Quincy, i, 235.

70. *New England Historical and Genealogical Register*, xlvi, 237.

Mather Minister of ye Gospel in New-England ye Suñe of one hundred pounds of Lawfull mony of England for ye use of ye Colledge there, of which He is President." [71] This gift, with Thorner's, made six hundred pounds — no mean contribution from Mather's labors for Harvard.

There were past benefactors to remember, too, and Mather, we have reason to believe, went to see Lady Holworthy, whose husband's generosity still keeps his name alive at Harvard.[72] In such errands, as in his interviews with two kings, the Rector of the New England college made sure that the name of his cherished "academy" should not be forgotten in England.

In corresponding with Anthony Wood, Mather turned his knowledge of Harvard and its graduates to the service of the cantankerous Oxford historian. Though "he never spake well of any man," Wood found Mather's information useful, and sent to him a presentation copy of the "Athenae Oxonienses." [73] More than that, he took pains to record in his diary that Mather, alone of all the nonconformists he had known, had been constantly civil — no mean admission for a man of Wood's acid temper toward dissenters.[74]

Such activities and sojournings, and, most of all, the conduct of his political skirmishings at court, took much money, and whatever his delight in his daily round, Mather could not close his eyes to sordid considerations of pounds and pence. In his tale of his agency he describes his need of funds, and how, failing prompt supplies from Boston, he had to borrow on his own security in order to meet the current expenses of his agency.[75] In a manuscript of his we read that he "was necessitated to give money to clerks, & to solicitors; sometimes 5 lb.; sometimes 10 lb.; sometimes 30 lb.; sometimes 40 lb.; at once. And that by the counsel and persuasion of friends of New England, I have borrowed 300 lb. & besides that, I have spent of my own money 150 lbs." He asked the colony to pay the £300, but "as for the 150 lbs.," was "willing to give it freely."[76] Sewall, we know, lent

71. *New England Historical and Genealogical Register*, xlv, 163, xli, 58, and *Harv. Rec.*, p. 386.

72. *MHS Coll.*, Series 4, viii, 502.

73. *DNB*, "Anthony Wood, 1632–1695"; J. L. Sibley, *Biographical Sketches*, i, 595, 597; *MHS Proc.*, xxviii, 28, 346ff.

74. *The Life and Times of A. Wood*, ed. A. Clark (Oxford, 1891–1900), iii, 396.

75. *Andros Tracts*, ii, 293.

76. Manuscript with his *Autobiography*, in the library of the American Antiquarian Society.

him one hundred and seventy pounds for use in New England's cause.[77] Stephen Mason lent one hundred and fifty pounds more, at a meeting at the New England Coffee House,[78] and wrote Bradstreet that the agents needed money, offering to supply Mather if payment could be guaranteed by the colony.[79] Richard Wharton estimated that two thousand pounds would be necessary in order to get "some effectual order . . . for releife of New England." [80] In view of this figure, Mather's answer to those who criticized his expenditures seems hardly necessary. "These little men," he writes, speaking of those who attacked him, "know not what it is to attend in the Courts of Kings for Four Years together. . . . I never demanded the least Farthing as a Recompence for the Time I spent in attending on their Affairs. . . . I suppose all Reasonable men will own That Reproaches cast on me for my *Expensiveness* in the Public Service are most Ungrateful and Unworthy." [81]

Such funds as Mather had for his own use, had, of course, to be shared with his family in Boston. There, in his deserted study, Maria Mather knelt, day after day, to pray for her absent husband.[82] But, whatever her zeal, she had little enough time for such devotions, with seven children, one of them failing in health, one very young, and one, Sarah, preparing for her marriage to Nehemiah Walter.[83] With political upheavals in Boston, soldiery often in the streets, and her husband abroad, a housewife had many pressing concerns. Cotton was able to help her somewhat, perhaps, but he was busy in the affairs of the colony, quarrelling with Moodey,[84] and producing books as fast as they could be printed.

Tragedy came to the Mather household in the death of Nathaniel, that boy so dear to father and brother as "Early Piety Exemplified." He died on October 17, 1688.[85] Increase Mather wrote in his diary on November 3 his fears "yt my Nathaniel is much indisposed as to his Health," and prayed for his recovery.

77. *MHS Coll.*, Series 5, v, 271, 286, 288.
78. *Ibid.*, 284, 285.
79. *Ibid.*, Series 4, v, 256.
80. *Ibid.*, Series 6, v, 17, 18.
81. *Andros Tracts*, ii, 322, 323.
82. I. Mather, *Sermon Concerning Obedience*, Preface.
83. Cf. J. L. Sibley, *Biographical Sketches*, iii, 300.
84. Cf. *MHS Coll.*, Series 5, v, 339.
85. "Early Piety Exemplified" was the title of Cotton Mather's life of his brother. It is reprinted in the *Magnalia*.

On December 3 he writes: "I had ye heavy tidings of ye death of my dear Nathaniel, for whom I must mourn many dayes. Alas yt so hopeful a branch of my Family is gone. A youth of 19 . . . very pious, his Learning such as I never knew his equall of his years. The church of God hath sustained a loss by his death. As for me I can not express how great my loss is in being deprived of such a praying son!" [86] To Anthony Wood he wrote of his son: "God saw meet to remove him to a better world. Hee was a young man of stupendous learning and great piety." [87] Great as was his grief, there was, in his faith, strength by which to bear it, and, in his devotion to his purpose, courage to keep him in England and hard at work.

In his writing during his years in London Mather wandered far from his usual theological paths, but he did not turn homeward without leaving his mark on a movement of importance for the history of nonconformity.[88] English Presbyterians and English Congregationalists, in 1691, made a sincere effort to wipe out minor points of difference by uniting on the essentials held by both sects. Into this movement, unfitting as it was for a hide-bound conservative, or for a champion of strict Congregationalism, Mather entered heartily. He saw that more breadth and, above all, more unity were needed, if the nonconformists were to survive and carry on their work in serving God according to His will.

The Presbyterians were distinguished from their Congregational brethren chiefly by their interest in church organization, and in their belief that each congregation should form part of a closely knit national church, with a definite scheme of government. Against this, Congregationalism asserted, as we have — seen, the virtual independence of the local congregation. Persecution, and a growing sense of the need of one strong body in place of two, in order to face better the united front of episcopal England and the hated army of Rome, brought Matthew Mead, friend of Mather and Congregational divine of rank, and John Howe, a Presbyterian, who, ever since 1659, had been an ally and guide of the Rector of Harvard, to take the lead in negotiating for the union of their sects. Howe held broad views, but, by his desire for a national organization, had been led gradually

86. MS. *Diary*, Nov. 3, Dec. 3, 1688.
87. *MHS Proc.*, xxviii, 347.
88. For what follows, see W. Walker, *Creeds and Platforms*, pp. 440ff.

from the Congregational to the Presbyterian fold. With him and Mead, Mather eagerly joined. Little difficulty was found in reaching an agreement. On April 6, 1691, there was brought forth formally a document designed to serve as a basis for the union of the two churches. Its ardent supporters hastened to carry its message throughout the country. Useful as the "Heads of Agreement" for the Union were, they suffered from a tendency, inherited by modern political platforms, to phrase broadly in order to cover divergent practice, rather than to define just what was the policy designed. The document was, moreover, largely Congregational in its view. For these reasons, and others, it did not survive in England, and failed to become the foundation for permanent unity among nonconformists. None the less, no one, who sees to-day constant efforts toward the breaking of denominational barriers defeated by the prejudices they attack, can criticize too harshly the deficiencies of this seventeenth-century attempt. Whatever its results, or its merits as a working arrangement, that it aimed toward church unity speaks highly for the liberality of its sponsors. It takes a churchman of broad vision to advocate to-day the merging of his form of worship with another's, and in 1691 denominational lines were no less carefully cherished than at the present.

Mather's connection with this progressive movement bore fruit in New England, at least. His son, receiving a copy of the English agreement, published it, and, as late as 1708, it bore a great part in shaping a new ecclesiastical constitution for Connecticut Congregationalism. There was little in it which differed from current colonial usage. That little chiefly concerned the ministers' authority to hold church councils without their congregations. In other words, the plan tended toward a less democratic order. It is, perhaps, not reading too much into the record to see here the first evidence of a belief that grew in Mather's mind in the coming years, when he conceived that the welfare of his church demanded firm leadership by trained men who could keep its traditions inviolate, and protect them from dangerous alteration which might proceed from a strictly democratic control. Possibly John Wise was right in believing that, in ecclesiastical as in civil government, the governed should guide. At the same time, if the original brand of Puritan piety was worth saving, and Mather believed it was, an oligarchic church government was the only safe means of securing it in an age when men were inclined to change their religious ideas as they changed their thought on other affairs. We may moralize, and declare that a church can live only by the support of its members, and that, therefore, their wishes should shape its course. True as this may be, Mather believed, as many wise men have done since his time, that leadership and education by strong men can influence the popular will and that, with such men to guard them, institutions can be kept in popular esteem.

With such new ideas, and with the accumulated experience of four years in the centre of the English-speaking world, Mather turned toward home. He left England reluctantly, for he had thought seriously of taking up his life-work there. He knew, too, that, however warm his fireside in Boston, however eager his welcome there, return to the colony meant the facing of odds new in his experience. His agency had committed him to the new charter. His fortunes were linked with its success, and with that of Sir William Phipps. We have seen that he had much to fear both from too zealous advocates of the old Congregational control of the state and from the dreamers who longed for complete colonial independence. His printed defence of his agency was no idle exercise in pamphleteering. It might well be necessary for him in the coming months. Cotton Mather, too, guessed the probable turn of affairs, and wrote political allegories which were by no means dull, and were certainly effective in their exaltation of his father's services and their exposition of the futility of the objections of his opponents.[89]

Mather came home as a man who had done much for New England. He had proved that he could see and accept the changes that progress demanded from church and state. He had met Anglicans and had learned to respect and admire more than one of them. He had embraced a code broad enough to include English Presbyterianism, and had advanced far beyond the stage of mere provincial divine. His pamphlets, in a style called even to-day not unworthy of Swift,[90] the master of the genre, had shown his ability to turn his pen to other subjects than popular science or theology. His tongue had proved persuasive among merchants and politicians, and his personality had served him well. But he had to pay for his winnings in the opposition of

89. *Andros Tracts*, ii, 325ff., and note on authorship, *Ibid.*, p. 324.
90. R. H. Murray, *Dublin University*, p. 51.

those whose idols he broke. Once in the full glare of the political stage, he must expect to take his share of abuse from the gallery.

All this he could talk over with Phipps on the long voyage. But the governor was, no doubt, more interested in what went on on deck. When the sea was rough, or the crew unruly, he could bear a hand, mindful of his prowess in the days when he commanded the *Algier Rose*. Puritanism, and introspection, were little remembered when he helped the crew to crowd on sail in a vain effort to overtake four French vessels sighted miles away. Mercifully, the chase was vain, for the enemy craft were men of war not merchantmen, and had they turned to fight, Mather might have found himself a captive in some French prison. His position, on the day when his ship and its convoy did come into contact with a French vessel, must have been like that of Dr. Burnet, aboard the Prince of Orange's fleet in the English Channel. While Phipps bustled about on deck, and joined heartily in the cheer that greeted the taking of the enemy as a prize, Mather, amid the excitement, may have remembered with a twinge of regret the good old days when he was a private citizen, little concerned with England's wars. Then the largest interests he had had at stake were the printing of his newest book, or the maintenance of his position against the criticism of his elders. He may well have thought of the days when he preached the duty of a minister to keep out of affairs of state. Surely he did not regret that he had ignored his own teaching in the interest of a cause which transcended in importance the duty of a pastor to his flock; but he may have had to contend, now and then, with a selfish yearning for the ease that had been his when he was no more than a student and a teacher of a devoted band of the faithful.[91]

But, on the 14th of May, 1692, he surely forgot all else in his joy at seeing on the horizon the first smoky outlines of the New England coast.[92] All day the shore came nearer, and he could point out to Samuel one after another of the landmarks grown familiar in the years he had lived among them. The sun was setting as they came up Boston harbor, and the beacon on the hill above the town was black against the crimson sky.

In the dusk, the frigate was at last safely moored beside the wharf. The street was thronged, and eight companies of militia were drawn up to receive the new governor. It was Saturday

91. *Autobiography.*   92. *Ibid.*

evening, and the Puritans' Sabbath had begun, so that no volleys could be fired to salute His Excellency; but here and there in the crowd, murmuring its curiosity and excitement, some bold spirits may have ventured a cheer of welcome.[93] With their military escort making a brave show, the new arrivals paraded up King Street toward the Town-house, the windows of which were now brightly lit by many candles. Within, Mather and Phipps were greeted by eager citizens of rank. The aged Bradstreet surely was there to welcome his successor in office. Stoughton, experienced in the political activities of the colony since its early days, cannot have been far away, and one likes to think that Danforth, although the coming of the new government deprived him of his high place, was none the less ready with his words of greeting.

In their presence, Phipps began to read his commission. Perhaps Mather, better versed in the technicalities of piety, frowned in warning, reminding him that on the Sabbath civil business should be forgotten. Perhaps the memory of the patient crowd in the street, or eagerness to see once more the wife who had stayed in Boston while he won, in England, new dignities for her, checked Phipps's speech. Certainly he broke off in the middle of his discourse, and once more took his place with the escort waiting for him before the Town-house door.[94]

The march continued across the Mill-Creek to the extreme north end of the town, and up the street whose name still commemorates the provincial charter, to Phipps's brick house near the Charlestown ferry.[95] Here, outside what was now the governor's mansion, Phipps parted for the time from the man who was now not only his spiritual mentor but his chief political ally. We may imagine how, standing in the lighted doorway, in his purple coat and with his sword by his side, he saluted gaily, as the eight companies took up their march once more.

This time they escorted little Samuel Mather and his father, who, that night, was second only to His Excellency Sir William Phipps. As the column turned into Middle Street, the sound of marching feet must have brought joy to Maria Mather's heart.

93. The basis of the description of Mather's arrival is Sewall's note in his diary for May 14, 1692 (*MHS Coll.*, Series 5, v, 360): "Sir William arrives in the Nonsuch Frigat: Candles are lighted before He gets into Townhouse. Eight Companies wait on Him to his house, and then on Mr. Mather to his. Made no volleys because 'twas Satterday night." For the rest, there is only fancy to guide.

94. *Cal. State Papers, Am. and W. I.*, xiii, #2283.

95. Cf. A. H. Thwing, *The Crooked and Narrow Streets*, pp. 63, 64.

Before her door the procession halted.[96] And, as she flung open the door, she saw hurrying to her the much-travelled boy of her heart and that tall familiar figure she loved and used to call "the best man in the whole world." [97]

For that evening, we may well believe, for those two, politics, church and all faded before the joy of home-coming. As the last curious spectator disappeared down the dark street, within doors Increase Mather sat once more at the head of the long pine table, with Abigail clinging to his hand, Cotton at his right, eagerly picking up every word, and Maria beaming her delight as she set out supper and filled the tankards. There, with the soft candlelight falling on the faces of his wife and children, and shining dimly through the door of his study on the dull calf of his precious books, he talked with a new zest of the glories of White-hall, and how he had been welcomed by the queen.

96. Mather's house was on Middle St. (now Hanover St.), near North Bennet St.
97. *Autobiography.*

CHAPTER XVII

"DOLEFULL WITCHCRAFT"

A MONTH after his arrival home, Mather wrote to the Earl of Nottingham, thanking him for his efforts toward securing the charter, and assuring him "that the Generallity of their Maj^{ties} Subjects (so far as I can understand) doe with all thankfulness receive the favours which by the new Charter are granted to them." The General Court ordered a day of thanksgiving for the safe installation of the new government, and the return of "Mr. Increase Mather." [1] Thus far the new régime seemed welcome and secure.

When Phipps and Mather landed, there were, however, grave troubles not far from Boston, and from them grew a series of events which cloud the record of New England history as it is read to-day. In jail were several score of colonists, awaiting final trial on the heinous charge of witchcraft. One of Phipps's first problems was how they should be treated; and his decision, however it may have appeared at the time, has tended in our day to bring discredit on his whole administration.

Nowhere more than in the tale of the "witchcraft delusion" in New England, is it necessary to confine one's self to the few facts surely established in contemporary records. Nowhere are conjectures, opinions, or generalizations of later times more misleading. This is particularly true when we consider the relation of Cotton and Increase Mather to the whole affair; for, with the human tendency to find individual scapegoats for all errors of the past, later history has delighted in laying the "persecution" of the Salem witches at the door of the two Mathers. Cotton has suffered most, for few critics have been so uninfluenced by the facts known in regard to Increase, as not to modify their statements as to his "cruelty" and "superstition," leaving Cotton to the fore as the villain of the piece. Too many writers, however, have found it easiest to link father and son together, to accept the legend that Cotton was a worker of dark deeds, and, accordingly,

1. *Acts and Resolves*, vii, 9.

to tar his father with the same brush.[2] Aside from the fact that the two men differed in temperament, that even their literary styles were unlike, and that their points of view on many questions were variously established, it would still be unjust to transfer Cotton's fancied faults to Increase merely because the two men stood in close blood relation.

For our purpose, fortunately, we may leave Cotton quite out of account, except in so far as Increase was obviously his partner in opinions or acts. Similarly, we may confide to physician, psychologist, or student of religious survivals, the explanation of just what was behind the strange behavior of certain Salem Village children, whose accusations brought many people to jail, and twenty to execution. And, best of all, we need not try to discuss or answer the many judgments passed on this chapter of New England history by writers viewing it from a later standpoint, with eyes opened by generations of scientific advance, except in so far as such judgments are based on facts which could have influenced the actors in the tragedy.

Very briefly, the story is that of a group of children in Salem Village, who, early in 1692, began to show signs of being tormented by agents of the devil. Their actions agreed with what was expected of victims of witchcraft, and their naming of their tormentors, and the popular excitement which ensued, led to the imprisonment of many citizens. These were charged with having entered into a contract with the devil, and with thus having secured power to molest others by the agency of infernal spirits. In May the disturbance was at its height. The jail was full. The ministers were alarmed by clear evidence that Satan was fighting for his erstwhile domain of New England, and had sent his emissaries there in force. From the pulpits came pleas for the detection and prosecution of the witches, and for popular reformation which alone could make the country inaccessible to diabolical attacks. The people, probably, were torn between rage against those they believed to have injured their neighbors' children, fear of this great revelation of the devil's might, and sympathy, growing as time went on, for those of good name who were drawn into the net.

For the twentieth-century mind it is almost impossible to appreciate as clearly as one must to understand what happened at Salem Village, how it was possible for the best-educated men

2. Cf., for example, A. D. White, *A History of the Warfare*, ii, 127.

of the day to accept without cavil the belief that witches existed and had power to do such things as were thought to have been done in this latest outbreak of Satanic power. It is even harder for us to realize how any man of reason could for one moment agree to sentence to death any human being on the charge of being a witch.

But the fact remains that, in England and America alike, the belief in witches and witchcraft was general.[3] Witchcraft was a crime punishable by death, not only in the colonies but in England. There were, of course, a few sceptics. Bekker, in Holland, greatest of all, later combatted the delusion.[4] Scot, in England, and Webster, had already argued against it with force. But, curiously enough, the basis of their pleas was hardly better founded in reason than that of the orthodox believers in witchcraft. The latter found in the Bible, in history, and in the phenomena of their own times evidence that witches were real, dangerous to men and to God's rule. This evidence they had to interpret without our present medical and psychological theories, and their opponents too often could not explain the facts observed and recorded. Denial of their reality was the only method the sceptics could rely upon, and they, too, were often forced to argue chiefly from written authority.[5]

Placed in the shoes of our predecessors in America, and faced with the conditions they found in 1692, what should we have done? The events agreed with what were commonly accepted as signs of witchcraft. Witchcraft was a crime. If we read the leading scholarly writers in America or Europe, we should find an overwhelming mass of testimony as to the reality of witches and their ability to do evil. If we consulted the greatest lawyers, or the best written legal authorities, we should find clear rules for the examination and trial of witches. If we went to the Royal Society, working as it was by methods of scientific experiment, we should find that Robert Boyle[6] had been, and his successors were, quite ready to accept certain phenomena as due to witchcraft. We should find students of current psychical research

3. Cf. G. L. Kittredge, "Notes on Witchcraft," in *American Antiquarian Society Proceedings*, xviii, 148 ff., and W. Notestein, *A History of Witchcraft*, p. 308.

4. Balthazar Bekker's "most telling attack upon the reality of witchcraft" was published in Dutch in 1691–1693, too late to have influenced the New England trials. The English translation appeared in 1695. Cf. Kittredge, "Notes," pp. 180ff.

5. *Ibid., passim*, and M. A. Murray, *The Witch-Cult in Western Europe*, p. 11.

6. Cf. Notestein, *A History*, pp. 305, 306. Boyle died in 1691.

sifting the evidence by the best tests known at the time, and concluding that the existence of witches could be proved by observation.[7] We should find among physicians no one to assert that disordered minds, hysteria, hypnotism, or any other "rational" explanation fitted the case; and in their libraries we should find books on witchcraft and the occult, just as there were volumes on fevers and remedies. The doctors would give "witchcraft" as their diagnosis. If, since it was a matter involving human life, and the controversy between God and Satan, we turned to the divines, we should find that they saw the affair as one in which unrighteousness and the powers of darkness had been given access by the unregenerate condition of mankind. Their answer would be that the laws of men must be obeyed in the interest of God, and the witches must be put to death. Here and there, among plain men of the world, not given either to historical or scientific reading, we might find a few scoffers, who would laugh at the idea that unearthly agents could cause human suffering, but they would be at a loss to give any authorities for their opinion. We might read Ady, or Scot, or Webster, but we should find only arguments no better founded, for the most part, than those of the English scholars, divines, judges, and philosophers, who drew their belief from human experience and from what their own eyes, or their friends', had seen.

If we were still sceptical, we should have to bear being suspected of disbelief in Christianity. We should be accused of rejecting the Bible. We should have to be content to align ourselves with a small minority of writers, and a minority made up of the least authoritative. And we should be constantly put to it to answer the facts adduced by Glanvill and More, who worked with scientific methods and, by the standards of the day, quite adequately proved the reality of witchcraft. To disbelieve would be to outlaw ourselves from the most authoritative school, to run counter to the accepted interpretation of the Bible, to link ourselves with a little-regarded group of radicals whose case rested on denial of what men of all ages believed they had seen and on an interpretation of Scripture rejected by the acknowledged masters in the use of such sources.[8] Moreover, we should

7. Cf., for example, H. S. Redgrove and I. M. L., *Joseph Glanvill and Psychical Research*, especially chaps. 5 and 6.

8. On all that precedes, a full and clear exposition with references to illustrative material is in Kittredge, "Notes"; and one should see also Notestein, *A History*, chaps.

have denied the existence of a crime for which in England, in the seventeenth century, more than a hundred persons had been executed, for which more than three thousand paid the penalty in Scotland, and one for which men were still haled before courts at home and abroad.[9]

But, as human thought developed, we should have come eventually to be vindicated. The reality of witches was at last denied once and for all, but, be it noted, not on the grounds urged by the seventeenth-century sceptics. Their claim to be regarded to-day as enlightened pioneers among an ignorant and reactionary majority rests neither on the blindness of the majority nor on their own anticipation of later discoveries of science. All honor to such men as saw, however vaguely, the delusion that the world labored under in its belief in witchcraft, but let us not forget that they, in their day and generation, were not the thinkers best grounded in learning or law, and that their opponents reasoned as most of us reason to-day about our peculiar current problems.

An analogy from later times is hard to draw. One remembers, of course, how long slavery was accepted as normal and right,

11 and 12. G. L. Burr (*New England's Place*, pp. 211, 212), in answering the question where one should seek doubters of the current view of witchcraft, says: "I should not look chiefly among the theologians, or even among the jurists," though "even among them doubters may be found." "I should not look first among teachers, university or other.... I would not look at all among the gossips or journalists.... I would look among the men of practical affairs, the men in touch with people and with facts; men of business, men of society, men of politics, men of travel, physicians, pastors. Yet, even among these, I should not listen first to those who talk — whether in books or outside them." It seems as if, to follow such advice, a seeker for truth in Boston in 1692 would have had to overthrow most of the usual standards for seeking information on questions of law and religion; nor on such a question in our day would one be likely to go first to business men, men of society, politicians, or travellers. Physicians and pastors we should seek, but if Phipps had done so, he would not have found sceptics on witchcraft. One remembers that Thomas Oakes, an eminent doctor in Boston, believed in witches, and that the New England ministers did so, so far as we can prove, to a man. I find no record of any New England minister of the time who disbelieved in witchcraft. Upham (*Salem Witchcraft*, ii, 304, 305) says that John Wise was enlightened, but he signed the preface to Increase Mather's *Cases of Conscience Concerning Evil Spirits*, and this work clearly upheld belief in witchcraft. J. Winsor, in *The Literature of Witchcraft*, p. 363, speaks of Joshua Moodey as more enlightened than the Mathers, because he helped to hide one of the accused. But in 1688 he wrote to Increase Mather describing "a very strange thing" which "we think ... must needs bee" witchcraft. He was no disbeliever. See *MHS Coll.*, Series 4, viii, 367. As to Oakes, see Sibley, *Biographical Sketches*, ii, 131; and on Boston physicians in general, C. Mather, *Magnalia*, book VI, chap. 7, "Ninth Example."

9. Kittredge, "Notes," pp. 203 and n., 204, 206ff.; Notestein, *A History*, pp. 418, 419.

and how completely it is now repudiated. Or, one may imagine that in 2000 A.D. murder may be proved always to be the result of disease, and so cease to be a crime. Murderers in that enlightened day may always be treated in hospitals, never tried or punished. Then those of us to-day who uphold our laws, who try to have murderers captured, and regard their conviction by juries as just, those lawyers who work in the interests of effective criminal procedure, those judges who do their duty as they see it, those ministers who preach against "crime waves," and those doctors who believe human passions may lead to the taking of human life, will all appear to our progressive descendants as barbarous followers of a "delusion," persecutors, exhorters to cruelty, and scientific dullards. Only the rare person in our generation who sees the death penalty as always wrong, or who believes imprisonment for life never justified, or who upholds the murderer's right to murder unrestrained by any law, will seem to posterity enlightened. They alone will be revered; and revered they will be, even though the reasons for their views are not those considered sound in the year 2000. The rest of us will be seen as backward victims of a cruel superstition.

Neither Phipps, then, hard-headed seaman that he was, nor Increase Mather, student of theology, amateur in science, and scholar of wide interests; not Thomas Oakes, physician, or any other recognized leader in the New England pulpit, college, politics, or business; not the lords of William's court, or his judges; not the scientists Boyle, More, or Glanvill; not that sceptical student of superstition, Thomas Browne; not the great divine, Richard Baxter, or any other save some radical challenger of received doctrine,[10] could see anything in the state of affairs at Salem Village in 1692, which called for anything more than a legal trial of the accused "witches" for a capital crime. In pursuance of what he cannot have seen otherwise than as a duty, Phipps promptly established a court to try the prisoners.[11] This body, headed by Lieutenant Governor Stoughton, set to work, and promptly found a certain Bridget Bishop guilty of witchcraft. She was hanged.

It is worth remembering, perhaps, that on the court sat not

10. *Acts of the Privy Council, Colonial*, ii, 242; *Cal. State Papers, Am. and W. I.*, xiv., 33; Notestein, *A History*, pp. 418ff.; Kittredge, "Notes," pp. 157, 158; Winsor, *The Literature of Witchcraft*, pp. 356, 357.

11. Palfrey, iv, 105.

only Stoughton, whom we like to call "bigoted," but Samuel Sewall, whose diary reveals to us a man hard to crowd within the limits of the conventional idea of Puritan pedantry, and one whose later attitude toward his share in the witch trials still wins praise; and not only men who can be called disciples of the Mathers, but other eminent citizens who were by no means solely dependent upon the favor of the two divines.[12]

After their first sentence, the court, though supported in their procedure by English precedents, showed a creditable interest in informing themselves as to the propriety of their course. Thus they sought the advice of the clergy. They were not content to leave it solely to their own church, but sought counsel from certain French and Dutch ministers, and even from a Church of England divine, serving as a chaplain in New York.[13] His answer was in no way more "advanced" than that of his French and Dutch colleagues,[14] nor was theirs a whit more "enlightened" than the reply of their Puritan brethren in Massachusetts.

Before considering the advice of the ministers, one must remind one's self of a legal question involved in the trials. The persons alleged to be the victims of witches often declared that they were attacked by spirits appearing to them in the likeness of this or that resident of the colony. Was this sufficient evidence to convict as a witch the person whose shape was taken by the fiend? Obviously, if it was, it was easy to bring to the gallows anyone against whom those "afflicted" by witchcraft chose to speak. On the other hand, if such "spectral evidence" were thrown out, or refused as the sole basis for conviction and considered of value only in a preliminary investigation, it was necessary, in order to prove a witch guilty, to show that he or she had revealed in some other fashion such supernatural powers as could be derived only from Satan. Such proof would be harder to find than an "afflicted" child ready to accuse a neighbor. Obviously, on the

12. The court was made up of William Stoughton, John Richards, Nathaniel Saltonstall, Wait Winthrop, Bartholomew Gedney, Samuel Sewall, John Hathorne, Jonathan Corwin, and Peter Sergeant, according to the records of Phipps's Council for May 27, 1692. See note by W. F. Poole, in his edition of T. Hutchinson, *The Witchcraft Delusion of 1692*, p. 32 n. Of these men only Corwin and Sergeant were not officeholders in the colony before Mather's selection of them under the new charter. Corwin was from Salem. Sergeant was of Boston, but not a member of Mather's church.

13. O. Manning and W. Bray (*The History and Antiquities of the County of Surrey*, ii, 714 n.) refer to this. See *MHS Proc.*, xxi, 348ff.

14. Manning and Bray, *The History*, ii, 714 n. For the answer of the foreign ministers, see *MHS Proc.*, xxi, 349ff.

weight given to "spectral evidence" depended the lives of many of the accused.[15]

Increase Mather joined the signers of the ministers' answer, and it is, therefore, our first clue as to his attitude toward the witchcraft excitement. The document is entirely clear. Like all good citizens in orderly commonwealths, its authors believed that the law should be enforced and the courts upheld. It praises the energy of the judges, but does not go into the question whether the evidence they had used thus far was sound or not. It urges the continuance of the fight against the devil's wiles. On the other hand, it denounces putting upon "spectral evidence" more weight than it will bear. It begs that "a very critical and exquisite caution" be used, and that there be followed "the directions given by such Judicious writers as Perkins and Barnard." [16] The ministers were not content with the common practice of English courts.[17] They objected to making mere "spectral evidence" the basis of convictions. They believed the devil could, at times, assume the shape of an innocent person, so that the appearance of a spectre in the likeness of a man was not in itself proof that the person represented was a witch. They did not, however, refuse to approve the admission of such evidence. It might serve to hold an accused person for further examination, and it might have consideration as corroborating other less dubious witnesses. Later criticism has sometimes wandered from the point, in debating whether or not the ministers opposed the "admission" of "spectral evidence." This they never considered. Their concern was with its use as evidence for conviction. To admit it to corroborate other testimony, or to hold a man for investigation, was entirely safe. More confusion has arisen from some historians' zeal to show the Puritans as bigoted as tradition declares them to have been, for their advice to the court has been twisted into a half-hearted warning against "spectral evidence" coupled with a vigorous and blood-thirsty

15. Cf. Kittredge, "Notes," pp. 197ff., 199 (note 165).

16. For William Perkins, see Notestein, *A History*, pp. 227ff. On his cautious views as to evidence, see especially, *Ibid.*, pp. 228, 229. On Richard Bernard (Barnard) and his *Guide to Grand-Jurymen . . . in cases of Witchcraft*, see *Ibid.*, pp. 234ff., especially p. 236: "The main aim of his discourse was, indeed, to warn judges and jurors to be very careful by their questions and methods of inquiring to separate the innocent from the guilty. . . . In his whole attitude, he was very nearly the mouthpiece of an age which, while clinging to a belief, was becoming increasingly cautious of carrying that belief too far into judicial trial and punishment."

17. Kittredge, "Notes," pp. 197, 198.

exhortation to continue sentencing the accused.[18] Read in the light of what is recorded again and again as to the ministerial point of view on "spectral evidence," the document of June 15, 1692, can be seen only as sound advice, including an appreciation of the conscientiousness of the judges, still undoubted by anyone, and a plea that they would continue with "exquisite caution" to put down an outbreak of crime. Such counsel was not only in the direction of safeguarding the innocent, but, for its day, liberal and advanced.

If the witchcraft delusion were, as later generations have sometimes been assured, fostered by the ministers to serve their own ends, and to glut their barbarous ambition to exalt their sect at whatever expense in human life, the answer of the clergy in 1692 would be hard to explain. But, remembering that the belief in witchcraft was too general to need fostering by anyone, that there is no proof that the New England divines tried to spread its influence or magnify its results, and that no end of theirs could have been served had they done so, their declaration still has meaning for us. It is an exact record, showing that the Puritan in Boston took a more humane position than the courts of King William III, in regard to methods of trying for witchcraft. However liberal England may have been, and however fanatically blind was the colony, on this one issue the Massachusetts minister dealt more mercifully than the judges in the courts across the sea.

In Winthrop's day, the advice of the ministers, right or wrong,

18. Upham says (*Salem Witchcraft*, ii, 268): "The reverend gentlemen, while urging, in general terms, the importance of caution and circumspection in the methods of examination, decidedly and earnestly recommended that the proceedings should be vigorously carried on." Again, in his *Salem Witchcraft and Cotton Mather*, pp. 21ff., he returns to the matter, but quite neglects the fact that the ministers did certainly urge caution, did wish prosecutions *according to the laws of God and England*, and that paragraph 2 of the answer refers, not to the execution, but to the "discovery" and investigation of witches.

J. T. Adams (*The Founding*, p. 455) says the ministers urged "speedy and vigorous prosecution," while "carefully hedging as to certain particulars." Sections 4, 5, and 6 of their reply, printed in Appendix B, do not seem to me to be "hedging," being perfectly explicit as to their views.

Neither Mr. Adams nor Mr. Upham remarks that the ministers urged the carrying on of the prosecutions only "according to the Direction given in the Laws of God, and the wholesome Statutes of the English Nation, for the Detection of Witchcrafts." In other words, they did just what most good citizens, divines or not, would do to-day — urged the prosecution of criminals, but prosecution according to the most humane legal practice of the time.

The much-misread answer of the ministers is given in full in Appendix B, pp. 405, 406.

would probably have been heeded. But William Stoughton held the view that the devil could never personate the innocent.[19] He was acting under a commission from Governor Phipps, not Minister Mather,— whose tool, we remember, he was called,[20]— and his court, throughout the summer, tried witches in opposition to the counsels of the brethren. Before September 2, nineteen persons were hanged, and one, in accordance with the old English criminal law, was pressed to death for refusing to plead.[21] It is hard to wipe away from our minds the impression of barbarity left by the bare relation of these executions. Yet Samuel Sewall, repentant as he became in later years, kept his diary in 1692 with no record of any revulsion of feeling caused by the bloody work in which he shared. Nor do we find any other good citizen of Massachusetts stirred to accuse the judges of wilful cruelty or cold-blooded persecution. John Evelyn, no Puritan and no fool, saw nothing to be distressed about in the affair, except in so far as he, Sewall, and everyone else were aghast at the extent of this most recent "crime wave." [22] Evil-doing was rampant, and the government was bringing the guilty to account. More could not be asked by any citizen with a respect for law.

There were, however, a few men who did honor to the community by objecting to what was done at Salem, not because the crime was a fancied one, but because they, like the ministers, distrusted the legal methods employed. They agreed with Increase Mather in thinking that "spectral evidence" was not enough to convict a witch. So thought Nathaniel Saltonstall,[23] again one of the "weak fanatics" Mather chose to office; and he refused to sit longer on the court because he disliked its methods. So also Samuel Willard had the courage to write and publish a little tract questioning the use of "spectral evidence." [24] And Thomas Brattle set forth in trenchant terms his opposition to some of the evidence accepted by the judges.[25] It has been said that in so doing he implied scepticism as to the reality of the

19. T. Hutchinson, *History*, ii, 23, 24; *MHS Coll.*, Series 1, v, 74.
20. Cf. p. 252, note 17, *ante*.
21. Hutchinson, ii, 59; Upham, *Salem Witchcraft*, ii, 338, 339.
22. Evelyn, *Diary*, Feb. 4, 1692–93; and cf. Kittredge, "Notes," pp. 162, 163 and n.
23. Upham, *Salem Witchcraft*, ii, 251; *MHS Coll.*, Series 1, v, 75.
24. *Memorial History of Boston*, ii, 164. A reprint is in *Congregational Quarterly* (1869), xi, 400ff.
25. *MHS Coll.*, Series 1, v, 61ff.

WILLIAM STOUGHTON

crime of witchcraft.[26] This is not susceptible of proof, but it is certain that he did give, together with his statement of his own attitude, invaluable evidence as to what the most enlightened New Englanders believed.

The letter in which he expressed his opinions takes pains to mention several men who were dissatisfied with what the court had done. Saltonstall and Willard are thus named, Bradstreet, Danforth, and Increase Mather.[27] Here is contemporary evidence of the best that the elder Mather held to what he had signed in the ministers' reply of June 15, and that he disapproved the methods of the court. Yet neither he, Saltonstall, Willard, Brattle, nor any one of the objectors spoke out against the executions. Brattle's letter was to a friend, not for publication, and was not printed until 1798.[28] So, if Mather be blamed, as he sometimes has been, for his "delay" in protesting against the "persecution" of the witches,[29] we must number with him those men most praised for their humanity, who kept quite as silent as he. And for the same reasons, no doubt. They knew, as he did, that the judges did what they saw as their duty, and followed accepted legal standards. Willard, Mather, and other divines, in June, protested against their methods, and then, being but private citizens, interfered no more with a constituted court of justice. In any other matter, had they done more, they would have been denounced for trying to restore theocracy by bringing their influence to bear in a case concerned only with the enforcement of

26. J. A. Doyle, *The Puritan Colonies*, ii, 393ff.

27. *MHS Coll.*, Series 1, v, 75.

28. *Ibid.*, v, 61. Doyle (*The Puritan Colonies*, ii, 393) says: "The honour of being the first to speak out fearlessly and to brave a mob, cruel with the cruelty of panic," belongs to Brattle. But Brattle did not "speak out publicly," but simply wrote a private letter to a friend, whereas Increase Mather's *Cases of Conscience*, questioning some of the evidence used by the court, was finished and read at a meeting of ministers five days before Brattle wrote.

Neither Mather nor Brattle believed it wise publicly to attack the conduct of the judges. The latter writes: "When errors of that nature are thus detected and observed, I never thought it an interfering with dutifulness and subjection for one man to communicate his thoughts to another thereabout; and with modesty and due reverence to debate the premised failings; at least when errors are fundamental, and palpably pervert the great end of authority and government." *MHS Coll.*, Series 1, v, 61, 62.

29. Cf. G. H. Moore, "Bibliographical Notes on Witchcraft in Massachusetts," in *American Antiquarian Society Proceedings*, v, 265, 266, who says that Increase Mather made no effort to stop the trials, and approved twenty executions before he was heard from. This leaves out of account his signing the answer of the ministers in June, does not explain why Brattle regarded him in October as one who had opposed the court's doings, and neglects the fact that Mather never, during the summer, specifically "approved" a single execution.

the laws of the state. As it is, they cannot be accused of officious meddling in government, and attacks shift to make them into inhumane upholders of superstition. So they seem to-day; but in their time, and for a generation thereafter, they appeared simply as would-be servants and teachers of their congregations, urging the most liberal attitude in witch trials, but not carrying their activity beyond the scope allowed them by the popular view, which still persists, of the place of the minister in public affairs.

Brattle's letter, with its unshakable testimony as to Mather's position, was written October 8, 1692. He not only tells us that Mather disliked the way the court proceeded, but tells how a certain Bostonian went to see one of the "afflicted" in Salem for advice as to strange symptoms observed in his own child. Thus he got "spectral evidence" against an individual, and attempted to secure a warrant for his arrest. This was denied him, and Increase Mather "took occasion severely to reprove the said man; asking him whether there was not a God in Boston, that he should go to the devil in Salem for advice; warning him very seriously against such naughty practices." [30] Mather appears in this incident as a man interested neither in upholding "spectral evidence" nor in keeping the witchcraft excitement alive.

Further testimony as to Mather's feeling during the summer of 1692 is afforded by a letter of John Proctor and others, protesting against the sentence imposed by the court, for it was addressed to several ministers, and Mather's name heads the list. Mr. Upham infers, reasonably, that this points to its having been known that the Teacher of the Second Church was doubtful as to the means by which the court arrived at convictions. [31] We know, too, that in all the fever of excitement about the trials, Mather not only kept silence, refraining from writing or saying anything that might fan the blaze, but also never went to Salem, even as a spectator, except on one occasion. [32] Then George Burroughs, a fellow minister, was on trial, and his colleague came to hear the

30. *MHS Coll.*, Series 1, v, 71.
31. Upham, *Salem Witchcraft*, ii, 310–312, 308, 309.
32. I. Mather, *Cases of Conscience Concerning Evil Spirits*," p. 286: "I was not myself present at any of the Tryals, excepting one, *viz.* that of *George Burroughs*." If this refers only to the few trials written of by Cotton Mather, the fact remains that we have no record of Increase's presence in Salem Village during the summer of 1692, in Sewall's Diary, or elsewhere, so far as I have been able to discover. Mather did go to Salem on October 19, after the trials were over, to visit the confessors. See *MHS Coll.*, Series 2, iii, 221.

evidence. In this case there was produced what seemed to Mather, as to the judges, clear evidence that Burroughs had used supernatural powers, so that his conviction was based by no means solely upon "spectral evidence." [33] Mather, therefore, found nothing to criticize in the conduct of the trial, and Burroughs's declaration of his own innocence, appealing as it seems to us, who judge on evidence then unknown, was no more striking to those who heard it, than are similar protestations from more than one legally condemned criminal of the present.

On October 3, the Cambridge Association of ministers met, and to them was read "a manuscript of cases of conscience relating to witchcraft, composed by the President of the College, the epistle commendatory whereunto was then signed by the" ministers at the meeting.[34] The "epistle commendatory," written by Willard, makes it plain that Mather, in accordance with the wishes of the Association, drew up a full statement of the ministers' position in regard to witch trials. It was intended as no shifting of ground, but simply as a fuller exposition of what had already been said by the clergy in June.[35]

Printed promptly, Increase Mather's "Cases of Conscience" gives, as definitely as one can ask, his views and his brethren's.[36]

33. Hutchinson, *History*, ii, 56, 57; Upham, *Salem Witchcraft*, ii, 296–304. The latter gives the facts of the trial, but some of the interpretations and inferences seem unsound.

34. *MHS Proc.*, xvii, 268.

35. I. Mather, *Cases of Conscience*, pp. 289–291.

36. The full title is (from the London edition): "Cases of Conscience Concerning Evil Spirits Personating Men; Witchcrafts, Infallible Proofs of Guilt in such as are Accused with that Crime. All Considered according to the Scriptures, History, Experience, and the Judgment of many Learned Men.... Printed at *Boston*, and Reprinted at *London*, for John Dunton, at the *Raven* in the *Poultrey*. 1693." There was an edition in Boston in 1693. The London edition also appeared as the second part of a book, with the title, "A Further Account of the Tryals of the New-England Witches. With The Observations Of a Person who was upon the Place several Days when the suspected Witches were first taken into Examination. To which is added, Cases of Conscience Concerning Witchcrafts and Evil Spirits Personating Men. Written at the Request of the Ministers of *New-England*. By *Increase Mather*, President of *Harvard* Colledge. Licensed and Entred according to Order. *London*. ... 1693."

This contains, first, "A True Narrative of some Remarkable Passages relating to ... *Witchcraft* at *Salem* Village in *New-England*," "Collected by Deodat Lawson." This is followed by "A Further Account of the Tryals of The ... Witches, Sent in a Letter from Thence, to a Gentleman in London." Then comes, as a separate part of the volume, Increase Mather's "Cases of Conscience."

The whole book has been often credited to Increase Mather, under the title of "A Further Account," etc., but it seems to me that only the "Cases of Conscience" can be called his. The first section was avowedly by Deodat Lawson, and the second, the letter, offers no proof that Mather wrote it. It begins, moreover, "Here were in *Salem*,"

It was the first publicly printed discussion of the methods of the witch court, with the possible exception of Willard's pamphlet, dated in 1692, which appeared in Philadelphia. Mather finished his work, and it was read to his colleagues, five days before Brattle wrote his letter. In other words, no one anticipated his protest unless Willard's little dialogue antedated it. The position of the "Cases of Conscience" in the history of the expression of opinion on New England witchcraft entitles it, therefore, to a detailed examination.

It begins with the question, "Whether it is not Possible for the Devil to impose on the imagination of Persons Bewitched, and to cause them to Believe that an Innocent, yea that a Pious person does torment them, when the Devil himself doth it; or whether Satan may not appear in the Shape of an Innocent and Pious, as well of a Nocent and Wicked Person to Afflict such as suffer by Diabolical Molestations?" And we are told at once: "The Answer to the Question must be Affirmative" (p. 225). No more explicit denial of the validity of "spectral evidence" can be framed. Mather's views, shared by the Salem judges, would have altered the whole course of the trials.

His main point decisively made, Mather goes on to support it by authorities. But here, as in the "Illustrious Providences," authority alone could not serve. "Our own Experience hath confirmed the Truth of what we affirm," Mather writes (p. 253), and proceeds to argue from the experience of Bostonians of his own and earlier generations. "Spectral evidence" is thoroughly repudiated. The Scriptures, the writings of scholars, and the observations of New Englanders, all prove that the Devil can disguise his agents in the shapes of the innocent.

Mather continues, taking up a second question of importance in relation to the trials. "If one bewitched is struck down at the Look or cast of the Eye of another, and after that recovered again by a Touch from the same Person, Is not this an infallible Proof, that the Person suspected and complained of is in League with the Devil? " (p. 255). The answer is once more based on

---

suggesting that a resident of Salem, not of Boston, was the author. Probably Increase Mather's connection with the volume included under the title of "A Further Account," etc., was that of a compiler, and even this much instrumentality cannot be proved. It is quite possible that the passage by Lawson and the letter were put together by the publisher.

The *Cases of Conscience* was reprinted in an edition of C. Mather: *The Wonders of the Invisible World*, London, 1862. To this edition all references here are made.

the opinions of learned authors, among them, be it noted, John Webster himself (p. 255 n.). The experience of recent investigators in English trials is also adduced. The final answer is clear. Testing witches by the methods discussed "is an unwarrantable Practice" (p. 269).

Mather, having cut the ground from under the advocates of two common proofs of witches' guilt, turns now to the query, "Whether there are any Discoveries of this Crime, which Jurors and Judges may with a safe Conscience proceed upon to the Conviction and Condemnation of the Persons under Suspicion?" He premises, first, that "The Evidence in this Crime ought to be as clear as in any other Crimes of a Capital nature," and, second, that "there have been ways of trying Witches long used in many Nations . . . which the righteous God never approved of." He denounces some superstitious "witch tests" used in "a Neighbor Colony." He argues against "ducking," together with other such popular measures, as contrary to Scripture, redolent of Paganism and the Devil, and as proved fallible by experience. But, leaving aside such unsound tests, "there are Proofs for the Conviction of Witches which Jurors may with a safe Conscience proceed upon, so as to bring them in guilty." These proofs are, first, "A free and voluntary Confession of the Crime made by the person suspected and accused," and second, the sworn statement of "two credible Persons . . . that they have seen the . . . accused speaking such words, or doing things which none but such as have Familiarity with the Devil ever did or can do." Testimony of one witch against another is not reliable, and its acceptance has caused the shedding of innocent blood. Only the two proofs cited are sufficient to convict.[37]

The book ends with a quotation from Perkins, urging no convictions without adequate proof (p. 283). It is impossible to read the "Cases of Conscience" as anything but a thoroughly documented answer to certain questions raised by the witch trials, and an answer insisting upon a caution which, had it been used in the summer of 1692, would have prevented much bloodshed.

To his book Mather added a Postscript. It has been conjectured that this was appended after the ministers' approval was secured,[38] but there is no evidence that, even if this was done,

37. Pp. 269, 270, 275, 276, 279ff., 282.
38. Cf. I. Mather, *Early History of New England*, etc. (a reprint of an early work of Mather's, given a new title by the editor, S. G. Drake, Boston, 1864), pp. xxii, xxiii. Mr.

the brethren failed to approve it. No one of them protested when it appeared in a book commended by them. In it Mather explains that he has written, not "to plead for Witchcrafts, or to appear as an Advocate for Witches." He has, he declares, written a discourse to prove that witches exist, but has not published it, although in "due time" he may do so (p. 285). He has not "designed any Reflection on those worthy Persons who have been concerned in the late Proceedings at *Salem;* They are wise and good Men, and have acted with all Fidelity according to their Light. . . . Pitty and Prayers rather than Censures are their due" (pp. 285ff.). Less could hardly be said in fairness. More approval of the trials Mather never expressed.

He then mentions Cotton's account of some of the doings of the court, condemns once more some of the popular tests for witchcraft, and, finally, writes of his son's book. "I perused and approved of" it "before it was printed; and nothing but my Relation to him hindred me from recommending it to the World" (p. 288). Such approval was entirely reasonable. Cotton Mather had argued that there were witches, had praised the faithfulness of the judges, and had given an account of some of the trials drawn from the records of the court. To this he added an unqualified disapproval of convictions based on the sort of evidence his fellow divines and his father denounced.[39] However they differed in their conduct during the excitement, Increase and Cotton shared certain fundamental beliefs; and the father's endorsement of the son's writings marks no more than his welcoming of one more statement of the position of the more liberal critics of the witch court.

The "Cases of Conscience" stands alone in its careful exposure of the most dangerous fallacies in the legal process by which the witches died.[40] It is far more explicit than Willard's pamphlet

Drake says here: "Perhaps the Fourteen [signers of the preface] did not include the Postscript in their Commendation. Indeed it is quite probable they knew Nothing of it until after the Book was printed. . . . The Postscript . . . did not probably appear in the original Edition of the *Cases of Conscience.* I have a manuscript copy of it (chiefly in the Autograph of the Author) to which there is no Postscript." The absence of the postscript from the manuscript as it reached Mr. Drake proves nothing, of course, and I know of no edition from which the Postscript can be proved to have been lacking originally. Moreover, as noted in the text, no one of the signers of the preface seems to have protested against the Postscript when it appeared as part of the book they had commended.

39. *Memorial History of Boston*, ii, 160, 161, 162.
40. *Ibid.*, 162.

on the same subject. It expressed the views of the foremost ministers, and it remains, for us, a landmark. With it at hand, there can be no doubt as to Mather's stand; seen in its pages, he must always be the intelligent critic who found the Bible, scholars, and human observation all in opposition to the court's methods. That he had courage to speak his views was much; that he wrote, "It were better that ten suspected Witches should escape, than that one innocent Person should be Condemned. . . . It is better that a Guilty Person should be absolved, than that he should without sufficient ground of Conviction be condemned. I had rather judge a Witch to be an honest woman, than judge an honest woman as Witch" (p. 283), proves him to have been mindful of humanity and caution in the face of a popular frenzy. No zeal to stamp out crimes ever drove him from his belief that, whatever the fate of the guilty, the innocent must never be in peril.

By autumn, whether because of this book,[41] the unanimity of the ministers, or a real dawning of light in Massachusetts minds, the opposition to the court's ways made itself heard. Stoughton, undeterred by a letter Mather had received from England denouncing "spectral evidence," uninfluenced by Brattle, Willard, Mather, Danforth, or any of the protesting clergy, persisted in his views of evidence.[42] Sewall significantly remarks that so great was the difference of opinion between the court and the ministers that the proceedings were halted.[43] The General Court had now voted to establish a Supreme Court, so that the temporary witch tribunal was automatically dissolved.[44] Judges for the new court were elected on December 7. Lest one fancy that popular feeling was in advance of the ministers', it is worth while to note that of all the new judges, Stoughton received most votes.[45] Danforth, who shared Mather's cautious views, came next, then John Richards who had also been on the former court, Winthrop, and Samuel Sewall. In other words, of those elected, four were among those who had tried and sentenced the witches, and there was included Stoughton, the man most opposed to the ministerial view. Only one of the new appointees was among

41. Cf. *Parentator*, p. 166.
42. Hutchinson, *History*, ii, 23 n. and 61; *Cal. State Papers, Am. and W. I.*, xiv, 112 (p. 30).
43. *MHS Coll.*, Series 5, v, 367.
44. *Ibid.*, 367, 368; Palfrey, iv, 111.
45. *MHS Coll.*, Series 5, v, 370.

those Brattle named as having questioned the proceedings of the summer.

The court did not meet at Salem until January, 1693. In the meanwhile the ministers' views had a chance to do their work, and the bringing of charges against some persons in high place and of unquestioned reputation, coupled with the time the people now had in which to think over more soberly what had been done, led to a decided change in feeling.[46] Governor Phipps was enough of a politician to detect it, and put himself on the side of the opponents of the trials. In so doing he gave as one of his reasons the advice he had received from Increase Mather and the other divines.[47] Thus, when the court met in January, all but three out of fifty were acquitted, and those three won pardons from Phipps.[48]

In England witchcraft trials continued well into the eighteenth century, and in Scotland bloody chapters in the history of witchcraft were still to be written.[49] But New England never again brought a witch to trial, and the "delusion," so far as it imprisoned human beings, brought them to trial, or to the gallows, was dead on her shores. Its tragic outbreak in 1692, however gruesome as a page in human history, was by no means so dreadful as similar occurrences in equally limited districts in older civilizations not under Puritan or "clerical" dominion.[50]

We have seen the facts in regard to Increase Mather's connection with the affair. They give no basis for the somewhat reckless ascription of motives which led to many eighteenth- and nineteenth-century accusations of him as one who fostered the "delusion," or, at least, delayed inexcusably in opposing its excesses. The facts refute such charges. They show that Mather was three thousand miles away from the scene of the tragedy until May, 1692; that, after the first execution, he publicly urged caution in the use of evidence; that he did not attend the trials; that he cautioned a parishioner against spreading the excitement; that he made plain to Brattle his discontent with what was done; that he was chosen to write the full statement of the ministers' position; that the book which resulted was the first

46. Hutchinson, *History*, ii, 60.
47. Cf. *Cal. State Papers, Am. and W. I.*, xiv, ⚹ 112 (p. 30); and *MHS Proc.*, xxi, 340, 341.
48. Hutchinson, *History*, ii, 60; Doyle, *The Puritan Colonies*, ii, 395.
49. *Kittredge*, "Notes," pp. 202ff.
50. *Ibid.*, pp. 205ff.

detailed argument against the procedure of the trials; and that, after it was printed, no witch was executed in Massachusetts. We know that Phipps, claiming credit for stopping the bloodshed, named Mather as one of those who advised the course he chose. And we know that Increase wrote and published a sentence which does not deserve to be forgotten when his reputation is at stake: "It is better that a Guilty Person should be absolved, than that he should without sufficient ground of Conviction be condemned."

But instead of finding him held up as a leader of the enlightened thought of his time, we have John Wise, Brattle, Pike, Moodey, Hale, and Willard singled out for praise.[51] Now Brattle, however worthy of honor, knew that Mather was liberally minded, and said so. As for Wise, his only public expression in the affair was his endorsement of what Mather wrote.[52] Willard, too, joined in commending the "Cases of Conscience," and himself criticized the court. But, it is well to remember that neither he nor Moodey doubted the reality of witchcraft, for both had studied and written about cases of diabolical possession.[53] Pike, advanced as were his views, went no further than Mather.[54] Hale wrote nothing till five years after the event, and then was still interested in discovering witches who deserved punishment. Wherever such men as these have a place as clear-sighted thinkers in a time of

51. Upham, *Salem Witchcraft*, ii, 304, 305; Doyle, *The Puritan Colonies*, ii, 393; Winsor, *The Literature of Witchcraft*, p. 363; and J. Quincy, *History*, i, 147, 148. As for Hale, Upham (*Salem Witchcraft*, ii, 475) speaks of his "rational view." In 1697 he wrote an expression of this view in *A Modest Enquiry Into the Nature of Witchcraft*, Boston, 1702. (The preface is dated 1697.) This is reprinted in part in G. L. Burr, *Narratives*, pp. 395ff. Hale, as Mather had done five years before, questions the method used in the trials, citing Mather as one authority, and urges repentance for the errors committed. He regrets that it is necessary to fear "that there hath been a great deal of innocent blood shed," but also, "that there have been great sinful neglects in sparing others, who by their divinings about things future, or discovering things secret, as stollen Goods, &c or by their informing of persons and things absent at a great distance, have implored the assistance of a familiar spirit," etc. He is concerned, not with denying witchcraft, but deciding who are witches, and feels that the Salem prosecution chose the wrong ones, leaving others deserving conviction! Such "rational views" do not compare favorably with Mather's.

52. Wise signed the commendatory preface to the *Cases of Conscience*, and, so far as we know, published nothing of his own on the subject.

53. *MHS Coll.*, Series 4, viii, 555, 360, 361, 367ff.

54. See J. S. Pike, *The New Puritan*, chap. 23. John Pike wrote a letter on August 9, 1692, in which he asserts his belief that there are witches, and recommends the same tests for guilt which were held by Mather to be the only reliable ones. Creditable as his view was to him, it was exactly Mather's; in view of which one wonders why Upham, in *Salem Witchcraft*, devotes so much space (ii, 449ff.) to praise of Pike and so little to commendation of Mather.

"delusion," Mather must join them, not as the blind tyrant from whose influence they had emancipated themselves,[55] but as the leader they publicly owned.

There are, however, one or two accusations brought against Increase Mather, which purport to have foundation in the recorded facts of his time. Perhaps it is necessary to say no more in answer to attacks of later generations, than that they are attacks of later generations and not those of Brattle and the men who knew Mather and his deeds. But his position among his contemporaries is important for any biography, and a glance at some of the charges brought against him may not be without use.

First, then, we are told that his "Illustrious Providences," published, one remembers, eight years before 1692, is shown by evidence from the Mathers' own time to have been largely responsible for the "delusion" centring about Salem Village.[56] This statement has been made again and again since Francis Hutchinson first gave grounds for it in his invaluable essay on witchcraft. But he said no more than that the Mathers' books prepared men's minds to become prey to the "delusion" of 1692.[57] Of course, all such statements are dangerous. To say to-day that moving pictures excite youth to crime, or that this or that book establishes false beliefs, is common, but in every case such statements, perforce, remain unproved. There is no harm in thinking that Increase Mather, who wrote of events which he

55. Winsor (*The Literature of Witchcraft*, p. 363) says: "There lived at the time of the Mathers some who were not enslaved by their influence," and that this "shows that society could have been saved, but for such misguided leaders. Such was Joshua Moody, who spirited away to a place of safety the accused Philip English and his wife. . . . Such was the outspoken Robert Pike." But Moodey wrote Mather to tell him of a witchcraft case, and we know he furnished for Mather's *Illustrious Providences* (which Mr. Winsor considers to have been instrumental in causing the outbreak of 1692) at least one narrative. Cf. note 53, *ante*. Whether or not they emancipated themselves from Mather's influence, Pike and Moodey shared his views, and never wrote, as he did, to make their liberal attitude public.

56. Cf. Winsor, *The Literature of Witchcraft*, pp. 355, 356, where, after making the charge referred to, he adds: "It is no merely modern propensity, prompted by a disregard of the tendency of that time, to charge so much upon the baleful misuse of literature, for these books were recognized even in the Mathers' day as an active agency, leading to direful events." In support of this he quotes Baxter, who said that the *Illustrious Providences* would overcome incredulity as to the existence of witches, and Hutchinson, whose essay on witchcraft came out thirty-four years after Mather's book. The same charge appears again and again in the work of other historians, less scholarly and careful than Justin Winsor.

57. F. Hutchinson, *An Historical Essay*, 2d ed., p. 101.

and other sober citizens believed to have occurred, strengthened in his readers' minds opinions which made it possible for them to see in the Salem Village excitement evidence of a real outbreak of crime.[58] This is well enough, if we are content to accept also what logically follows, and to admit that his responsibility was shared by those ministers who concurred in the idea that narratives of witchcraft cases were an indispensable part of any history of the "remarkable" events of New England. Willard, John Whiting, John Russell, and Joshua Moodey all furnished him material, by writing of cases which had come to their attention.[59] If his book was pernicious, they share with him the reproach of having unwittingly contributed to a tragedy — a reproach applicable also to all men who spoke of witches of which they had seen or heard. With them must be classed, too, the Englishmen who wrote of witches to their American friends, the German and English scientists whom Mather quoted, and the writers of a host of other books written before and after his and accessible to readers in New England. He did no more than edit a historical collection, to which he added his own denunciation of certain superstitions, one of which cost at least one life as late as 1863.[60]

But he did argue that witches existed, and this has excluded all else in the minds of some historians. This doctrine, however, needed no advocate in 1684; no one could have written a history of New England without including the witchcraft cases unless he were deliberately to omit a chapter of what was generally recognized as historical fact, and no one thus writing could have urged disbelief in witchcraft unless he had been a sceptic far in advance of any the colonies knew. Mather wrote history. Witchcraft filled but a small part of his book,[61] and he preached

58. Cf., for a modern expression of this point of view, J. A. Doyle, *The Puritan Colonies*, ii, 389. Mr. Doyle says, however, that to the *Illustrious Providences* "anyone might contribute an account of anything which sounded like a miracle." This is hardly fair, for one remembers that we have no proof that Mather printed any story simply because it was contributed. Cf. p. 174, *ante*.

59. Cf. *MHS Coll.*, Series 4, viii, 86ff., 466ff., 360ff., 555ff., and I. Mather, *Essay for the Recording of Illustrious Providences*, pp. 96, 99, 113, 114.

60. *Memorial History of Boston*, ii, 172 and n. Mather, one remembers, in his *Illustrious Providences*, argued against the "water-test" for witches.

61. In the edition of the *Illustrious Providences*, of London, 1890, 23 pages are devoted to "things Preternatural which have Hapned in New England," 24 to an argument proving "that there are Daemons and Possessed Persons," and 33 to "Apparitions." The book contains 262 pages of text. In other words, less than one third of its space is devoted to witchcraft cases. G. L. Burr (*Narratives*, p. 6 n.) says: "It is true the book of Mather is not wholly on 'the world of spirits': other 'providences' fill half

against superstition. If the work was of evil influence, so were most histories of the day, so was much other literature prior to 1700, and so is many a book written to-day in the interest of some theory now accepted but doomed to fall with time.

Yet a careful modern historian writes that Increase Mather deliberately sought to encourage credulity and superstition, and sees no way by which he can be forgiven![62] The reply to this is contained in what has been said above. And, had any man fancied that "superstition," as applied to witchcraft, needed aid from his pen, he could hardly have chosen a worse method than the writing of a book of narratives, which, for the most part, concerned nothing supernatural. He could hardly have been so addle-pated as to forget his aim, and challenge some points of popular credulity, and certainly he would have wasted no time on scientific discussions of magnetism and heat. Had his purpose been to encourage credulity, he could have committed no greater folly than to brand many tales of witchcraft as false! To say that his dark intention is proved by contemporary evidence, is to distort the facts. Baxter said, in 1691, that the "Illustrious Providences" was a sufficient answer to the disbeliever in witchcraft. Of course it was, just as was any standard history, or the Bible. But Baxter never hints that Mather, or Glanvill, or Boyle, or anyone else, wrote in order to egg on the credulous and superstitious. Hutchinson, writing in 1718, is no contemporary, and he, too, was careful to impute no motives. He wrote in a later generation, when belief in witchcraft was waning. His view of

the volume. But it is more largely so than any earlier collection of its sort, and in this the author's interest clearly centres." Two thirds, not half, of the volume, deals with other subjects. If it treats witchcraft more largely than other collections, it may be because witchcraft had been more prevalent in New England. I can find no evidence that Mather's interest centred more on the witchcraft narratives than on any other of his chapters.

62. Justin Winsor, in *The Literature of Witchcraft*, pp. 355, 356, says: "The systematic efforts of the Mathers, father and son, to engage the superstitious and reckless — and in this nefarious business Increase at a later day used his position as President of Harvard College, the better to accomplish his ends — led to many ministers and others helping, by offering a premium on invention and exaggeration, to pour in upon the expectant credulous, what Mather was pleased to call 'memorable or illustrious providences.'" He then goes on to say that this view is supported by evidence of writers in Mather's lifetime. The facts are that neither of the authorities Winsor cites (one of whom wrote thirty-four years after 1684) suggested that Mather wrote with any design to encourage superstition. Furthermore, as to his desire to "engage the superstitious," Mather writes in *Cases of Conscience*, p. 264, "The Laws and Customs of the Kingdom of darkness, are not always and in all places the same. And it is good for men to concern themselves with them as little as may be." This is a statement quite out of place in the mouth of a man with the motives Winsor ascribes to Mather!

a book written thirty-four years before is not good evidence as to its character or its writer's.

Cotton Mather has suffered more at the hands of later critics than his father, but now and then an attempt has been made to bring down both with the same stone. Leaving aside the fact that the younger Mather was himself advanced in his thought, and more than once took precautions to check the spread of the excitement in 1692,[63] it is easy to show that there is no reason to criticize Increase Mather for his relation to the doings of his son. The attempt to attack him through Cotton rests on the postscript to the "Cases of Conscience," where, as we have seen, he approves the publication of the "Wonders of the Invisible World." This was, to repeat, no more than an endorsement of a book which, while asserting the reality of witchcraft, urged the best known methods of arriving at the truth as to the guilt of the accused.

Cotton Mather abstracted the directions given by Perkins and Gaule, which would have worked mercifully had they been used in Salem, and cautioned against errors of passion or haste in fighting the devil's assault upon New England. He summarizes an English witch trial under Judge Hale and five of the Salem trials, getting Stoughton and Sewall to vouch for the correctness of his record. The whole was a thorough exposition of the orthodox view as to witches, and of the most cautious views as to the methods by which they should be tried. It contained nothing that Willard, Wise, Baxter, Boyle, Glanvill, Browne, or Evelyn would have been likely to disapprove, unless in the account of the trials, written with no protest as to the evidence accepted, we find some details repugnant to the best standards of the time. This account Cotton Mather wrote, one remembers, by order of the judges, who wished to have whatever could be said in favor of their procedure made public. The English trial described introduced much "spectral evidence," but it was regarded as insufficient, and the verdict came only when witnesses testified that the accused had performed supernatural acts. Proceeding to discuss Salem, Mather writes of five trials in no one of which was "spectral evidence" excluded, but in no one of which was it unsupported by other evidence, ridiculous to-day but of damning weight in an age when witches were common and their ways well known.

63. Cf. W. F. Poole, in *Memorial History of Boston*, vol. ii.

Thus Increase Mather lent his support to nothing which was repugnant to the most liberal theories as to the adequate proofs of a witch's guilt. And, when credulity is in question, it is only fair to remember that Cotton Mather wrote, not of what he had seen, but of the testimony accepted by a court of law and spread on its records as true.

Finally, Increase Mather has been accused of responsibility for establishing the witch court and continuing its activities through the summer of 1692.[64] The argument is simple. Mather was influential in making Phipps governor, and Phipps was his disciple. Had he not approved, the court would never have been appointed. Had he wished it, Phipps must have stopped the trials. Had he spoken out, his position as a leader was such that the whole excitement would have died away.

Nothing is more dangerous, of course, than an attempt to define the influence of one man upon another in politics. There can be no shred of proof that Mather approved, or failed to oppose, the establishment of the court. If every act of Phipps is to be ascribed to his pastor, then to Mather belongs the credit for ending the trials, and pardoning the victims. Moreover, Stoughton was as much Mather's appointee as Phipps, and Stoughton, we know, was opposed by the party whose views Mather expressed in the "Cases of Conscience." Only conjecture can support criticism of the Teacher of the Second Church as the dictator of all Phipps's acts, and if conjecture lays at his door all the governor's bad deeds, it cannot fairly deny him credit for the good works of his disciple. If Phipps was Mather's slave, we may with equal reason say that Stoughton was one, but records prove that this was not the case. Nathaniel Saltonstall, too, was chosen to office by Mather, and if Phipps represented the divine's influence, why not also Saltonstall, whose attitude we praise?

We have facts to prove Mather's position as member and leader of the liberal party in the discussion of legal methods. The charges against him rest on guesswork, and on a hypothesis which makes him, at one and the same time, the mentor of Saltonstall, Stoughton, and Phipps, men who held different views and chose different courses, and gives to him the credit for ending the trials. His reputation has nothing to fear from such conjectures or from the facts.

There remain to be considered the comments made by Robert

64. Cf., for example, Winsor, *The Literature of Witchcraft*, p. 360.

Calef.[65] Calef is an American of whom we may be proud, because he was "modern" enough to question some commonly accepted beliefs as to witchcraft. True, he argued, like those he criticized, from no purely rationalistic ground, but from his own interpretation of Scripture, and too often he confronted well-attested statements by flat denials, not convincing from a strictly logical point of view. He was no writer, and by no means a scholar, but he did mock some things that we now hold to be "delusions." He was a man of the world, and of common sense. He had definite views, however poorly supported they were. He wrote, unfortunately, too late to deserve any credit for the ending of the witchcraft excitement, and when his book came out, Sewall's public repentance for the methods he had used at Salem had said all that Calef could say.[66] Public opinion was, when his work was printed, as enlightened as he. He did not deny that there were witches, nor did his neighbors; but they had come to see, even before he did, that some innocent blood had been shed in 1692.

Most of his "More Wonders of the Invisible World" was an attack on Cotton Mather. He also found space for a paragraph or two directed against Willard, the clergy and judiciary in general, and against Increase Mather. To him he refers comparatively rarely. He mentions his presence with his son at the bedside of a suspected sufferer from witchcraft in Boston, after the Salem outbreak had passed, but does not record how scrupulously careful we know Cotton Mather to have been in avoiding anything that could lead to fresh accusations or a new stirring of popular superstition.[67] He bases his remarks on a paper written by the younger Mather, but printed without the author's consent.[68] He indulges in innuendoes which led the Mathers to bring

65. There is some doubt as to the identity of Calef. See W. F. Poole, in *Memorial History of Boston*, ii, 165 ff.; S. G. Drake, *The Witchcraft Delusion*, ii, xiff.; and G. L. Burr, *Narratives*, pp. 291 ff. Calef wrote *More Wonders of the Invisible World*, London, 1700, printed in Drake, *op. cit.*, ii, 1 ff.

66. January 14, 1697, Sewall made public statement of his regret for the errors of the court, but did *not* deny the reality of witchcraft. *MHS Coll.*, Series 5, v, 445. Nor did the government, in calling a fast day to atone for the errors at Salem, deny that Satan had been active. See *Ibid.*, 446 n.

67. Cf. R. Calef, *More Wonders*, ii, 49, 51, 55. As to Cotton Mather's caution, cf. W. F. Poole, in *Memorial History of Boston*, ii, 156, 157.

68. Of this document Calef writes (*More Wonders*, p. 14): "I received [it] of a Gentleman, who had it of the Author, and communicated it to use, with his express consent." To whom the "his" refers is not easy to decide, and "consent ... to use" is hardly consent to publish.

an action against him.[69] On his writing an apparently contrite letter, the proceedings were dropped.[70] But, curiously enough, in all this, Calef finds few specific charges to bring against Increase Mather individually, without deserting his subject to go afield in a discussion of the agents' work in England.[71] There are hints that Mather served his own interest rather than his country's. He is strangely silent as to the "Cases of Conscience," but he refers more than once to the paragraphs of the ministers' reply of June 15, 1692, which spoke of the need for continuing the court's efforts according to the laws of God and England.

On the whole, there is nothing here that needs answer. The book appeared when Increase Mather was opposed by many on grounds other than his views on witches, and such effect as it had in weakening his influence it owed, probably, not to any superior wisdom as to events of 1692 and 1693, but to its timely recapitulation of the arguments most useful to Mather's enemies in the church and in politics. Such a work, as we shall see, offered welcome material to those who sought weapons against the Mathers; but even so, it was quite adequately answered by certain citizens who thought with the leaders of the Second Church. To their reply, Mather himself added a few paragraphs, disposing of the attacks upon his conduct in England.[72] The witchcraft issue was, so far as Increase was concerned, the least important item in Calef's arsenal.

Summing up, we find Increase Mather in 1692 as a believer in witchcraft, an opponent of the methods of the court, and an ally and leader of those whom we see as the most liberal of the time. He wrote the first full statement of their views, and throughout the whole excitement he kept himself from any act or speech that could possibly have increased the harm that was done. His creed he epitomized himself, when he wrote: "It were better that ten

---

69. Calef, *More Wonders*, p. 55.

70. W. F. Poole, in *Memorial History of Boston*, ii, 167.

71. A reading of Calef makes this clear. He does, however, say (*More Wonders*, iii, 157): "It is rather a Wonder that no more Blood was shed, for if that Advice of his [Phipps's] Pastors could still have prevailed with the Governour, Witchcraft had not been so shammed off as it was." Calef seems not to have known that Phipps gave Increase Mather credit for his influence in stopping the trials. There is more excuse for this failure on Calef's part, than on that of later historians. As for Calef's attack on Mather as agent, see *Andros Tracts*, ii, 315–323, where the charges, and Mather's quite adequate reply, are given.

72. The answer was: *Some Few Remarks*, etc., Boston, 1701, by O. Gill and others. Cf. also, *Andros Tracts*, ii, 315–323.

suspected Witches should escape, than that one innocent Person should be Condemned."

This much can be shown by the evidence hitherto accessible to all students. To it we may now add Mather's own statement of his position in the witchcraft affair. Like "spectral evidence," what Mather says of himself must be supported by other records in order to pass current to-day, not because the Mathers' testimony can be proved to be unsound, but because those historians to whom they have seemed sinister figures have found it necessary to attack their veracity. We have seen how Increase Mather appears in the testimony of his contemporaries, and in the accessible records. With this picture agrees his own description of his attitude.

"I found ye country in a sad condition," he writes in May, 1692, "by reason of witchcraft & possessed persons. The judges & many of ye people had espoused a notion yt ye devill could not personate iñocent persons as afflicting others. I doubt [i. e. fear] yt iñocent blood was shed by mistakes of that nature. I therefore published my Cases of Conscience *de* witchcrafte, &c. By wch, (it is sayed) many were enlightened, juries convinced, & the shedding of more iñocent blood prevented." [73] The truth of this document remains unshaken.

The space devoted to Increase Mather's relation to the witchcraft outbreak is not justified, perhaps, by its importance in his life. But later criticism has so often determined its final judgment on inferences wrested from the events of 1692, that no biography can afford to let the matter go uninvestigated. For the purposes of twentieth-century eulogy, it would be possible to regret that he was not a Hutchinson thirty years ahead of his time, or even a Calef; but biography can hope for no more than to attempt a fair estimate of his position. Its verdict must be that, in witchcraft, he was not a radical on the side of what we now see as the truth, but an orthodox educated man, sharing the most liberal of the then orthodox doctrines.

Much has been said of the influence exerted by his stand on witchcraft in bringing down his power from the heights it reached in 1687 or 1692. [74] Nothing is harder to determine than such

73. *Autobiography.*

74. Cf. J. A. Doyle, *The Puritan Colonies*, ii, 400, 401. J. T. Adams (*The Founding*, p. 455) says that "public opinion was arrayed solidly against" Cotton Mather when, in 1693, he "tried to start another alarm in Boston." Cotton, of course, did

influences. Mather, in 1692, was open to attack, as we have seen, from opponents of the charter and of the officers he had chosen for the colony, and from all those to whom the government's acts were unwelcome. Nearly ten years later, when his prestige received its first serious blow, other forces than political enmity played a part. It is hardly necessary to feel that the community rebelled against his opinions on witchcraft, and that therein lay the cause of his partial loss of popular favor. Hostility to him can be shown to have many roots, but there is no evidence that any of his foes based their feeling on dislike for his relation to the events in Salem Village.

There is only one bit of evidence bearing on the popular view of those concerned in the witchcraft trials, and this has been curiously neglected by historians. We have a record of the result of the election of 1693. Those voting were not, it is true, the rank and file of the people, but they were their representatives, and as dependent on their favor as legislators of to-day. The issue was determined, of course, by other forces than approval or disapproval of what had been done in the witch court. Men were voted for, then as now, because they were personally liked, or because their decision on this or that question had pleased the voters. At the same time, a few of those who were candidates in 1693 were so involved in the Salem trials that their fate at the polls may reasonably be interpreted as partial evidence, at least, of the popular feeling toward their deeds in combating the wiles of Satan.

Twenty-eight councillors were elected.[75] Of these, eighteen

not "try to start another alarm" (cf. W. F. Poole, in *Memorial History of Boston*, ii, 146ff.), and his account of the 1693 case was not printed until Calef brought it out. There is no evidence that "public opinion was arrayed solidly against" him, though, seven years later, one man criticized him, making charges most of which he denied. Of course, by 1700, when Increase Mather was attacked on various grounds, and when public opinion had had seven years to develop a more enlightened point of view on witchcraft, an attack, like that of Calef, was useful, and played a part in stirring up feeling against the Mathers. It does not prove that in 1693 any popular reaction against their witchcraft views had occurred, or even that any had occurred in 1700, except on the part of one man. Probably it is safe to say that Calef's book in 1700 aroused some feeling against the Mathers' witchcraft attitude, among those who read it without examination of its facts, or memory of what, precisely, the Mathers had done; and so, by 1700, the witchcraft episode may have played a part in weakening Increase and Cotton. But it seems to me to be quite unsafe to say that immediately after the trials popular opinion turned against them, because of their witchcraft views. Such statements, however, are found in many histories. None of these, nevertheless, so far as I know, points to the election results in 1693, which are referred to in the text.

75. Palfrey, iv, 142; *MHS Coll.*, Series 5, v, 378.

had been chosen to office by Mather in the previous year. Nearly two thirds of his appointments were thus confirmed by the representatives of the people. Of those rejected, one, the aged Bradstreet, was probably unwilling to serve.[76] Of the others, three were men who had held office before Mather appointed them, and the remaining six were men whom he had chosen from those not previously endorsed by the voters. Now, of this class of men he chose but eight, and only two were reelected. In other words, though most of the government he had chosen was confirmed in office, the fortunate candidates were for the most part those who had been office-holders prior to 1692, and of the candidates who may be said to have been selected by him on personal grounds, three quarters failed of popular support. If all his appointees were under his influence, he still controlled the government; but most of those whom he had chosen on his own responsibility were rejected.

Why was this? Not on religious grounds, for but one of the defeated was a member of his congregation. Can we then say that the shift in the membership of the Council represented the voters' views on witchcraft, and their repudiation of Mather and some of his less distinguished friends? No such answer is possible. Of those rejected, not one, so far as we know, played any prominent part in the witch trials, or expressed his views in regard to them. But of the nine judges who sentenced the witches, every one was elected to the Council in 1693. The most liberal of all, Nathaniel Saltonstall, received fewer votes than Sewall, Winthrop, or Richards, and only a few more than Stoughton himself. Danforth, whom Brattle called an opponent of the court's methods, ran behind Winthrop and Sewall. There is here no evidence that the populace and their legislators saw those involved in condemning the witches as deluded or inhumane. Every judge received the stamp of popular approval, and the two who seem most likely to have been liberals did not head the list. The most popular name was that of Samuel Sewall, who felt, in later years, that he had erred enough to make necessary a public recantation.[77]

It is possible to explain the result of this election only by regarding the issue as in no way concerned with witchcraft, but as old charter *versus* new. From this point of view we can see why those men whose claim to office lay only in Mather's favor should

76. Palfrey, iv, 142.   77. *MHS Coll.*, Series 5, v, 378.

fail, if popular opinion to any considerable extent opposed the charter he had brought from England. We can see also why Danforth and Cooke were elected. Both held the old charter view of independence, and clung to a belief in the colony's right to dispense with royal governors. Hutchinson was near enough to 1693 to be able to judge more accurately than we can, and he was far better equipped with records. He gives no hint that the shift in the make-up of the Council was due to any but the obvious political motive.[78] There was, as yet, no overwhelming opposition to the new charter, for some of those retained in office supported the new order; but there was a feeling that a more truly representative character should be given to a body which Mather had composed solely of those who he felt sure would support the government to which he was himself committed.

The election of 1693, then, reveals no trace of a popular reaction against belief in witchcraft or Mather's views upon it, but shows the strength of the old charter party led by Elisha Cooke. The political rift was real, and widened with the passing years. Cooke came home from England in 1692, and kept a "Day of Thanksgiving for his safe Arrival." Neither Mather was there. Perhaps they were not invited; perhaps they refused to go. In any case, Samuel Sewall scented "Animosities," and prayed that "the Good Lord unite us in his Fear." [79] He was not heard, and the two parties grew away from one another. In the beginnings of this division between the advocates of colonial independence and the adherents of the new charter lies the explanation of the election of 1693, and what we should call to-day its political "rebuke" to Increase Mather.

Voters in May, 1693, saw him as we must see him when we free our minds from the authority of the last two centuries, and study his position as his neighbors knew it. He came through the witchcraft ordeal unscathed. He believed in witchcraft, but he urged moderation and justice, not fanatical zeal. The saving of innocent life interested him more than the hunting down of every guilty witch. Such men as Brattle, clearest sighted of all those who lived through the alarming events at Salem Village, saw him as a wise guide, and his writing was the most complete expression of their views. Once more he proved himself in the front rank of his day, and able to speak clearly and decisively for what he believed to be the right.

78. T. Hutchinson, *History*, ii, 70. 79. *MHS Coll.*, Series 5, v, 369.

ELISHA COOKE

CHAPTER XVIII

DEFENDING HIS FAITH

UNTIL 1692 the story of Increase Mather's life is that of a constant development in leadership. In that year he was of unique rank in the colony. He had printed more books than any other writer in New England. He was the close friend and spiritual adviser of the governor. He was the sponsor of the new charter. Phipps and Stoughton owed their offices to him, and, until 1693, the Council members held their places because he had seen fit to choose them. He was in fact, if not in name, the leader of the local Congregational Church, and he was President of Harvard College.

A scant decade after his return from England his fortunes had sharply declined. Then any single book he had ever written was surpassed in interest and importance, even in its own day, by the work of another New Englander,[1] and his writings were no longer printed more often in Boston than those of any other man. In 1701, if he still preserved influence with the governor, he dealt with a man less under his spell than Sir William Phipps. He was no longer the most active leader of his own congregation, and in general church councils, though he was still revered, his position was threatened by the well-organized opposition of promising young divines. And he was no longer president of the college. Worst of all, his loss of office at Harvard was due, essentially, to the efforts of those with whom he disagreed, and those whose ideas seemed to him to hold peril for New England.

Some elements in his decline brought no pangs. In literary preëminence the torch was not wrested from him, but gladly surrendered to his son. So also Cotton carried on the Mathers' tradition of dominance in the church, if, at times, deficiencies in his own nature, and his lack of sympathy with the changing ideals of the day, caused him to fail where his father had been consistently successful But in the passing of his hold on Harvard and the waning of his political influence there was a real reverse

1. Cotton Mather's *Magnalia* was finished by 1700.

for Increase Mather, and thence he drew more than one hour of discouragement.

For biography, of course, these years from 1692 to 1701 reveal more than most other periods of his life. The ideals to which a man clings in the face of opposition, those for which he will give up a part of his claim on popular esteem, and the qualities he shows when he has to defend doctrines previously unchallenged, offer a precious index of character.

It is in connection with a new religious movement in Boston, his relation to Harvard, and his efforts to serve New England in London once more before he died, that the fundamentals of Mather's position appear; but before coming to them, one may well glance at the background of events in the state and the round of minor concerns which continued to play their part in what was still a very active career. The key to what happened in Cambridge, and the antidote for a misconception of its meaning, lie in the day's politics. The attacks on Mather, which centred about innovations in church practice, struck not only at him but at his brethren in the pulpit, and some of the more virulent outbursts, purporting to be caused solely by a lofty zeal for truth, are best explained when we remember Cotton Mather's relation to his father. The son's violence of phrase, and the acidity of his vocabulary, are of themselves sufficient to explain certain counterblasts which, perforce, wounded both father and son.[2]

Increase was no longer the sole representative of his family to make his voice heard, nor can he have been lonely by his own fireside. Of his children, Jerusha was but eight years old in 1692. Hannah married John Oliver in 1697. Samuel, whose degree from Harvard was awarded while he was still in London, went soon to England to take up his life-work there. Sarah had married Nehemiah Walter, a minister consistently allied with the Mathers, and the first of the five children born to them in the next ten years was named Increase. Elizabeth became Mrs. William Greenough in 1696, and Maria married Bartholomew Green in 1688. By 1701 they had three children. Cotton, in 1692, had two, and five more were born to him before 1700. The Mather line had ramified throughout the colony, and a family party at the grandfather's house must have crowded its rooms.[3]

2. Cf. Cotton Mather's diary, *MHS Coll.*, Series 7, vol. vii, and his published writings in this period.

3. Cf. H. E. Mather, *Lineage of Rev. Richard Mather.*

Mather's church was his second home, and in the years 1692 to 1701, inclusive, he won, with Cotton, one hundred and seventy-three members. This was a decrease of fourteen from the record of the preceding decade, in spite of the natural increase in population, and points, probably, to some slackening of interest in church membership, at least in those congregations where the strictly orthodox tests for admission were maintained.[4] None the less, with a thousand or more hearers for his sermons,[5] and a steady accession of new communicants, he could draw from the statistics no conclusive proof of anything more than a slight change in popular sentiment. Nor does the evidence from other sources show us more than this.

Aside from the Second Church itself, the "Cambridge Association" of ministers was the centre of Mather's strictly religious activities. This body was formed on October 13, 1690, while Mather was in England. Probably he was consulted, for his name appears among its charter members.[6] He constantly refers in his writings to the duty of ministers to discuss questions of policy, and there are hints as to the obligation of individual churches to abide by their pastors' decisions. In such organization was the obvious safeguard for a Congregationalism weakened by the loss of its erstwhile political control. Certainly Mather was active in the councils of the "Association," and more than one of his books originated in a desire to publish the views of his brethren as they were expressed at its meetings.

In such undertakings, of course, his influence was not merely local. Boston was the seat of the government, and a preacher there inevitably came into touch with men from all parts of the colony. The latest books printed there circulated throughout New England, and, as religious enthusiasts to-day most often seek inspiring sermons in large metropolitan churches, so, in 1692, the colonist who longed for the heights of pulpit oratory rejoiced at the chance to hear Willard or Mather in Boston. Increase, as a young man, refused to serve elsewhere than in a Boston church, and however envious smaller congregations were of their favored neighbors who sat under his ministry, no one of them ventured to suggest that he leave his large parish for a more remote town. But, in 1692, when Nathaniel Gookin died,

4. My figures are from a MS. volume owned by the Second Church. Cf. F. B. Dexter, *Estimates of Population.*
5. I. Mather, *The Blessed Hope*, p. 27; Quincy, i, 499.
6. *MHS Proc.*, xvii, 263; W. Walker, *Creeds and Platforms*, pp. 470–472.

the church at Cambridge, which had long commanded the services of leading divines, unanimously called Mather.[7] Probably they were emboldened to hope by the knowledge that the President of Harvard was by necessity often in Cambridge, and they may have foreseen how much pressure was soon to be brought to force Mather to live at the college. Nevertheless he refused the invitation, though he manifested his interest in Gookin by turning over to his widow a part of his own income.[8]

He followed in Gookin's footsteps, too, by devoting part of his time to the conversion of the Indians. He had written to arouse interest in what was being done to turn red-skinned and carefree heathens into the most conventional of Puritans; and, in 1693, he signed with others a petition to Phipps asking that a mission be sent to carry on the work.[9] To him Samuel Treat wrote as to the savages' condition, and some of his correspondence with the London Society for the Propagation of the Gospel is preserved.[10] Whatever our feeling may be as to Mather's attitude toward King Philip's son, twenty years before, there is no doubt that he was merciful in 1698, when he expressed himself in favor of sparing the lives of certain captive Indians.[11] And in order that they and their compatriots might taste some of the pleasures of Puritan readers, several of Mather's sermons were translated into their language.[12]

From his diary we get glimpses of Mather dining with Phipps, or with Sir Francis Wheeler, that "brave, though unfortunate" officer of His Majesty's Navy.[13] We find Increase worrying about his brother-in-law, John Cotton, who was convicted of various "scandals" and ejected from his church at Plymouth.[14] His relative in Boston, stern in the cause of righteousness, is said to have declared that the punishment was too light.[15] A more godly member of the Mather family, Increase's brother Nathaniel, died in England in July, 1697, and the tidings brought grief to Boston.[16]

7. *MHS Coll.*, Series i, vii, 32.   8. J. L. Sibley, *Biographical Sketches*, ii, 479.

9. *MHS Coll.*, Series 3, i, 133.

10. Sibley, *Biographical Sketches*, ii, 305; J. W. Ford, *Some Correspondence*, etc., pp. 8off.

11. *New England Historical and Genealogical Register*, xviii, 166.

12. J. L. Sibley, *Biographical Sketches*, i, 454, Item 66; *MHS Coll.*, Series 6, i, 233.

13. MS. *Diary*, 1693; J. Charnock, *Biographia Navalis*, ii, 76ff. The quotation is from *Ibid.*, ii, 87. Cf. also, *MHS Coll.*, Series 5, v, 379.

14. MS. *Diary*, 1697, Sept. 4, Oct. 30; Sibley, *Biographical Sketches*, i, 501ff.

15. *MHS Coll.*, Series 5, v, 461.

16. Sibley, *Biographical Sketches*, i, 159; MS. *Diary*, 1697, Dec. 10; *MHS Coll.*, Series 5, v, 465.

There was disturbing news also of dissensions in Massachusetts congregations, especially at Watertown, and Increase Mather stated with some vigor his protest against the ordination of Simon Bradstreet in Charlestown.[17] The reason for this attitude comes out more clearly when one turns to his general hatred of deviations from the old ways of New England Congregationalism. Bradstreet was but one of several who believed that part of the discipline of the early churches was not founded on a proper reading of the truth.[18] If in his case Mather was inclined to be strenuous in his objections, he was more pacific in his dealings in the case of Mr. Parris. The latter had been notoriously involved in the witchcraft excitement, and if there was any imposture on the part of the "afflicted" children, or any wrongdoing in connection with their accusations, Parris can hardly be absolved from blame. His church, aware of this, sought to have him removed from their pulpit, and his case was referred to a committee of which Mather was a member. They proposed a compromise, but to no avail, and finally advised Parris to seek service elsewhere. They admitted frankly, of course, that "sundry unwarrantable and uncomfortable steps" had been taken in the days when the devil harried Salem Village, but the question was whether Parris himself had been imprudent. This the committee seems to have regarded as unproved, but efforts to smooth matters over failed in the face of a congregation which, whatever the facts may have been, had certain definite convictions as to their pastor.[19]

Further gleanings from these years give records of Mather's many friends and many books, of visits he made and received, of the dinners he attended, and of his patient study of the volumes in his library.[20] He bought new books, too, and it is interesting to note that of the four volumes which we can identify as having been purchased between 1692 and 1701, three were the works of scientists. They were the "Acta Medica and Philosophica" of Thomas Bartholin, erstwhile professor of medicine at Copen-

17. Cf. *MHS Coll.*, *passim*, and MS. *Diaries* for these years. For Watertown, see especially the entry for March 24, 1697. Cf. also, Sibley, *Biographical Sketches*, ii, 425. A letter of Cotton and Increase Mather to the Charlestown Church is in *MHS Coll.*, Series 4, viii, 119, and states the grounds of their objection to Bradstreet — principally that he denied the Congregational doctrine as to "church covenants."

18. W. Walker, *Creeds and Platforms*, pp. 476, 478.

19. *New England Historical and Genealogical Register*, xi, 318ff.

20. See MS. *Diaries*.

hagen, a man whose writings seem to have been in high favor with Mather.[21] In 1693 he bought David von der Beck's "Experimenta et Meditationes circa Naturalium Rerum Principia," again the work of a physician and scientist.[22] This was flanked by the "Epistolicae Quaestiones, cum Doctorum Responsis," of Johannes Beverovicius, a third physician, better known by his proper Dutch name of Jan van Beverwyck.[23] The fourth book Mather is known to have bought in these years is theological,[24] but, if his choice from the booksellers' lists is a criterion, his taste for the moment was more for medical science than for writings in the field where most of his own work had been done.

Turning from the books he read to those he wrote, we find another considerable pile of publications. Most of them reveal little not already expressed in his writings. One finds, for example, a preface for "The Spirit of Man," by Charles Morton,[25] whom Edward Randolph regarded as a dangerous religious radical, and most Puritans saw as a force for good in the councils of their church.[26] There is also a preface for a new book by Willard.[27] From a discussion by the Cambridge Association came Mather's "Judgment of Several Eminent Divines," and his statement of his views on the vexed question whether a man might marry his deceased wife's sister.[28] His interest in religious education dictated his "Solemn Advice to Young Men," interesting to us chiefly because it exhorts Boston boys to resist temptations to piracy, a career no longer accessible to most wayward youths.[29] One need not pause over his "Case of Conscience Concerning

21. Mather's copy of the *Acta Medica* is owned by the American Antiquarian Society. For other books of Bartholin owned by him, see J. H. Tuttle, *Libraries*, p. 316.

22. *Ibid.*, p. 316.

23. *Ibid.*, p. 317.

24. *Origenes contra Celsum*, etc., Cambridge (Eng.), 1658; now owned by W. G. Mather, Cleveland, Ohio.

25. Boston, 1693. The preface is signed by Mather, James Allen, Samuel Willard, John Baily, and Cotton Mather. There is no evidence that Mather was the sole author.

26. J. Quincy, *History, passim*; R. N. Toppan, *Edward Randolph*, iv, 90, 102.

27. S. Willard, *The Doctrine of the Covenant of Redemption*, Boston, 1693.

28. "The Judgment Of Several Eminent Divines Of The Congregational VVay Concerning A Pastors Power. Occasionally to Exert Ministerial Acts in another Church, besides that which is His Own Particular Flock." Boston, 1693. "The Answer Of Several Ministers in and near Boston, To that Case of Conscience, *Whether it is Lawful for a Man to Marry his Wives own Sister?*" Boston, 1695. Cf. *MHS Proc.*, xvii, 269.

29. "Solemn Advice To Young Men, Not to Walk in the Wayes of their Heart, and in the Sight of their Eyes; but to Remember the Day of Judgment." Boston, 1695.

Eating of Blood," [30] "Discourse Concerning the Uncertainty of the Times of Men," [31] or his "David Serving his Generation," [32] although it is well to remember those pages in the last-named book in which he emphasizes true devotion, not fear, as the mainspring of a godly life. "That keeping of the Commandments which proceeds from a slavish fear, and not from love, is not pleasing." [33] Intense faith, a real "love" for righteousness, made Puritanism for its disciples an ideal not grim and repellent, but one which could be accepted with the full vigor of heart and soul. In "Faithful Advice," [34] a book signed by Mather and his colleagues, among them Benjamin Colman, [35] a man too often painted as an object of the Mathers' persistent hatred, there is an accidental reference to another cardinal point of Puritanism, its emphasis on learning: "When the Knowledge of the *Tongues* and *Arts* Revived, *Religion* had a Revival with it: And though some *Unlearned* men have been useful to the Interests of *Religion*, yet no man ever decried *Learning*, but what was, an Enemy to *Religion*, whether he knew it or no." [36] Mere silveriness of tongue could not, Mather's friends believed, make amends for a lack of knowledge, and the significance of his words has not staled with time. A preface for Cotton Mather's "Everlasting Gospel" [37] shows no new element in Increase's development, nor does another preface, signed jointly with his son, for a new edition of a book by John Quick. [38] "A Vindication of the Divine Authority

30. "A Case of Conscience Concerning Eating of Blood, Considered and Answered." Boston, 1697. For the ascription of this work to Increase Mather, see J. L. Sibley, *Biographical Sketches*, i, 453. Cf. *MHS Proc.*, xvii, 274.

31. "A Discourse Concerning the Uncertainty of the Times of Men, And The Necessity of being Prepared for Sudden Changes & Death. Delivered in a Sermon Preached at Cambridge in *New-England*. *Decemb.* 6. 1696. On Occasion of the *Sudden Death* of Two Scholars belonging to Harvard *Colledge*." Boston, 1697.

32. "David Serving His Generation. Or, A Sermon Shewing What is to be done in order to our so Serving our *Generation*, as that when we Dy, we shall Enter into a Blessed *Rest* (Wherein Some account is given concerning many Eminent Ministers of Christ at *London*, as well as in *N. E.* lately gone to their *Rest.*) Occasioned by the Death, of the Reverend Mr. John Baily, Who Deceased at *Boston* in *New-England*. *December 12th.* 1697." Boston, 1698.

33. Page 7.

34. In C. Mather, *A Warning to the Flocks*. See Sibley, *op. cit.*, iii, 74, and reprinted in his *Magnalia*, book VII, chap. 5. The title of the preface in which Mather had a hand is: "A Faithful Advice from several Ministers of the Gospel, in and near *Boston*, unto the Churches Of *New-England*; relating to the Dangers that may arise from *Impostors*, pretending to be *Ministers*." It was dated December 28, 1699.

35. Colman's name is signed in the original edition, but not in the *Magnalia* reprint.

36. Pages 8 and 9.   37. Boston, 1700.

38. J. Quick, *The Young Mans Claim unto the Lord's Supper*. Boston, 1700.

of Ruling Elders" [39] contains nothing to detain the modern reader, and "The Blessed Hope," [40] aside from the fame it has won because it contained the first copper-plate engraving done in America, a portrait of its author,[41] demands attention for but one sentence. "Thoughts of the Blessed Hope," Mather declared, should make men "Joyful in their Serving God. And if they be otherwise, it will be a Blemish to Religion. If alwayes dejected and discouraged, it will discourage others, and make them think that Religion is a Malancholy thing." [42] If the nineteenth-century custom of regarding all joy as sinful was a heritage from the Puritans, it was handed down by those who ignored Increase Mather's behests. On such points as this, there is much light to be drawn from his writings from 1692 to 1701, even though most of the minor works just considered hold little else to repay the twentieth-century reader.

He had not forgotten how to write skilfully, however, and one or two passages written during these years testify to this fact. His preface to his son's "Johannes in Eremo" [43] — a book containing biographies of Cotton, Wilson, Norton, and Davenport, all "fathers" of New England and all men whom Increase Mather had known and loved — shows an informal manner, but the style of one who writes neither hastily nor without feeling. Here and there faint reflections of Cotton Mather's literary gestures appear, but for the most part effect is gained by simplicity of diction and structure. One paragraph gives not only an idea of the style but also a specific reminder that Mather's views as to his conforming brethren had been modified by experience.

"There are some," he writes, "who will not be pleased, that any Notice is taken of the hard Measure which these excellent Men had from those *persecuting Prelates*, who were willing to

---

39. "A Vindication of the Divine Authority of Ruling Elders In The *Churches of Christ:* Asserted by the Ministers & Elders, met together in a Provincial Assembly, *Novemb. 2d.* 1649. And Printed in *London,* 1650. Beginning at *Page* 34. to 48. Transcribed out of the Same Book. Whereunto is added, An Answer to the Question, *Whether are not the Brethren, and not the Elders of the Church only, to Judge concerning the Qualifications, and Fitness, of those who are Admitted into their Communion?* By the Reverend Mr. *Increase Mather,* in his Book Entituled, *The Order of the Gospel:* Printed in the year, 1700. Beginning at *Page* 23. to 29. Reprinted for Publick Good."

40. "The Blessed Hope, And the Glorious Appearing of the Great God our *Saviour,* Jesus Christ. Opened & Applied, In Several Sermons." Boston, 1701.

41. W. Dunlap, *History of the Rise and Progress,* iii, 299; K. B. Murdock, *The Portraits.*

42. Page 42.

43. This is printed in C. Mather, *Magnalia,* book III, part i.

have the World rid of them. But it is impossible to write the History of *New-England*, and of the *Lives* of them who were the chief in it, and yet be wholly silent in that matter. That eminent Person, Dr. *Tillotson* (the late Arch-Bishop of *Canterbury*) did, not above four Years ago, sometimes express to me, his Resentments of the Injury which had been done to the first Planters of *New-England*, and his great dislike of Arch-Bishop *Laud's* Spirit towards them. And to my knowledge, there are *Bishops* at this Day, of the same Christian *Temper* and *Moderation* with that Great and Good Man, lately dead. Had the *Sees* in *England*, fourscore Years ago, been filled with such Arch-Bishops, and Bishops, as those which King *William* (whom God grant long to Live and to Reign) has preferred to Episcopal Dignity, there had never been a New-England." [44]

Such a preface defies classification except as the work of a man of letters. It is of the seventeenth century, to be sure, and its manner is not always consonant with what we expect in similar efforts to-day. It shows no incontrovertible signs of literary genius, but, seen in its own age, it reveals some skill, much emotion, and a taste for writing because one has something to say which deserves to be well said.

In his "Folly of Sinning," [45] a sermon preached at the execution of a woman who had murdered her child, Mather once more shows a true literary instinct. The speech to the criminal is frank to the point of brutality; but the painting of the horrors of hell shows imagination and an instinct for what was likely to shake a hardened heart. But all this leads up to the main plea, which is for repentance. Christ can save, and His mercy is the one eternal fact never to be forgotten. *"Go to Jesus Christ,"* Mather said. "If you cannot go to him *with* a penitent heart, go to him *for* one. *Him has God Exalted to be a Prince and a Saviour to give Repentance unto Israel and forgiveness of Sins.* Oh Pray and Cry to him: Pray him to pour his Blood on thy Soul: That will break the Rockiest heart, the most *Adamantine* heart in the world. Pray as *David* did. *Wash me throughly from mine iniquity, and cleanse me from my Sin. Purge me with Hysop and I shall be clean.* Thus does he pray that his Soul might be washed in the blood of

44. Last paragraph of the Preface.

45. "The Folly of Sinning, Opened & Applyed, In Two Sermons, Occasioned by the Condemnation of one that was Executed at *Boston* in *New-England*, on *November 17th.* 1698." Boston, 1699.

Christ. And have not you need to pray after the same manner? If that precious blood be sprinkled on you, then notwithstanding your sins have been as Scarlet and red like Crimson they shall be as white as Snow" (p. 48). Again, in his "Two Plain and Practical Discourses,"[46] printed in London in 1699 from a shorthand transcript of two of Mather's sermons, there are one or two passages which show a feeling for the most vivid word and a realization of the possibilities of repetition and balance.

"How clear is it from the Scriptures, that Men may not Worship or Pray unto Angels, Saints, Graven Images? That one would think, that they that have the Scriptures, and own them to be the Word of God, should be convinced, that this ought not to be; yet come to a Papist, all the Scriptures you can produce to him, will not convince him of his Error. Alas, God hath shut their Eyes, and given them up to a Blind Mind! And when it is thus with [men] Miracles cannot Convert them; if God should work Miracles for them, they would not be Converted thereby; should God send Men from the Dead to them, neither would that Convert them. Should God break open the Barrs of the Bottomless Pit, and let loose Devils and Damned Wights, to come flying and crying into our Assemblies, with the chains of Darkness rattling about them to warn Sinners of the Wrath to come, and to tell them, what a Dreadful Place Hell is, neither would that Convert them" (pp. 99, 100). Those "Damned Wights," "flying and crying" with their "rattling chains" must have been real images before Mather's audience.

There remain one or two books written in this period which deserve attention because they express Mather's attitude toward events of the day or because they sum up important elements in his thought. Of the latter sort is his "Angelographia," published in 1696.[47] This was a collection of sermons on angels. He disclaims any desire to discuss the scientific aspect of his subject, but that he felt it necessary thus to limit his subject proves that he was aware of the rational trend of the times. Nor was he un-

46. "Two Plain and Practical Discourses Concerning I. *Hardness of Heart.* Shewing, That some, who live under the Gospel, are by a Judicial Dispensation, given up to that Judgment, and the Signs thereof. II. The Sin and Danger of *Disobedience to the Gospel.*" London, 1699.

47. "Angelographia, Or a Discourse Concerning the Nature and Power of the Holy Angels, and the Great Benefit which the *True Fearers* of God Receive by their Ministry: Delivered in several Sermons: To which is added, A Sermon concerning the Sin and Misery of the Fallen Angels: Also a Disquisition concerning Angelical-Apparitions." Boston, 1696.

critical in his views, for he declares in the preface that some so-called "Angelical apparitions" are delusions, and that "natural magic" may deceive men. He is frankly sceptical as to heavenly apparitions. Some such cases are due to disease; for if men "have been lately sick, and the disease wherewith they have been attended, has had any influence on the brain, that & Satan together will make them phansy very wonderful matters" (pp. 17, 18). Exclude Satan, and you have here an expression of a modern "rational" view. Nor is Mather prone to accept all history simply because it is in print. Speaking of a case described in books, he says: "I must confess, I am not easy to believe that *Christinas* death or her Ascension into Heaven was *real*, but that they were both *Phantastical*" (p. 34). And, with undeniable pertinence, he adds: "Nor do I know any cogent reason, why the Visions of one diseased with an *Apoplexy* should be thought to be of greater weight then the Visions of one diseased with a Fever or Calenture" (p. 34). His subject is close to what we call "psychical research," and the rudiments of a critical spirit which he shows were, in his time and for a divine, more important than they now seem.

In this book he decried, in passing, the dangers of apostasy. It was no straw man which he belabored. There were about him movements toward religious innovation and toward carelessness as to some of the old tenets of Puritanism. Some of his opponents seem to have construed his every reference to apostasy as an assault upon them. Yet he obviously aimed at no one man or party, but at all who receded from the old piety and the original New England form of worship. Because Mather's criticisms on such backsliders explain much in the controversies which followed, they cannot be overlooked.

He dated his preface to Cotton Mather's "Life of Jonathan Mitchel," [48] May 7, 1697, and addressed it "To the Church at Cambridge" and "the Students of the Colledge there." In this he defined what he saw as "apostasy" and made clear his attitude toward it.

He goes at once to the old question of admission to the church. He had at first, one remembers, clung to the strictest view, but had later accepted Mitchell's opinion in favor of the Half-Way Covenant, which provided for a relaxation of the tests for church

48. C. Mather, "Ecclesiastes: The Life of the Reverend and Excellent Jonathan Mitchel," in his *Magnalia*, book IV, part ii, chap. 4.

membership. With this much accepted, some New England Congregationalists, soon after the Synod of 1662, proceeded to the belief that such as were entitled to baptism under the new system should, even without experience of definite conversion, be entitled to full communion. As early as 1677, in his "Call from Heaven," Mather combatted this view.[49] He believed, as did most of his brethren, that full rights of membership belonged only to those who were consciously regenerate and could offer satisfactory evidence of their state. The controversy was long and ardent, but Mather never retreated from his stand.

The advocates of reducing the tests for membership strove, right or wrong, to alter what was generally regarded as a fundamental of polity.[50] Their plan would have made it possible for more men to come to communion. Thus far it was a democratizing process; but if, as Mather believed, it would destroy the meaning of communion to have it become anything less than a sacrament reserved for those who had won the right to it by a real trial of their faith, its merit is doubtful. Near the middle of the eighteenth century Jonathan Edwards went further in his wish to limit church membership,[51] and, later still, the tendencies represented by his opponents crystallized in the formation of a new sect. As to who was "right" and who was "wrong" in 1697, no decision is possible, except on the basis of such personal opinions as each of us may hold. The views Mather opposed were "thoroughly at variance with the older New England theory and practise."[52] If the Puritan experiment in Massachusetts had failed, they must be accepted. If it had worked well and still held promise, if it had influenced and guided strong men and women, and was still chosen by many of their descendants, it by no means deserved to be abandoned or denatured by any innovations however sincerely advocated.

Mather had loved Mitchell, and he reminded his readers of his tutor's views on baptism, taking the occasion to express his own convictions as well. "It cannot be denied," he says, "but that there has been an error in some churches, who have made this or that *mode* to be a '*divine institution*,' which Christ has not made to be so: and that there has been an unjustifiable severity in

49. Cf. W. Walker, *Creeds and Platforms*, pp. 279, 280.
50. Idem, *A History*, p. 182.
51. *Ibid.*
52. W. Walker, *Creeds and Platforms*, p. 477.

imposing *circumstantials* not instituted, whereby some truly gracious souls have been discouraged from offering themselves to joyn in fellowship with such churches. Thus it has been, when an oral declaration of *faith* and *repentance* has been enjoyned on all communicants, and that before the whole congregation; when as many an humble pious soul has not been gifted with such confidence." This is moderation, surely. "Nevertheless," he continues, "it concerns them [the churches] to beware of the other extream of laxness in admission to the Lord's holy table"; and he enlarges upon this point. Finally he turns to the Harvard students in his audience, with an appeal to them not to "deviate and degenerate from the Holy *Principles* and *Practises* of" their "Fathers."

His direct statement of his opinions met with little favor with some of his audience. But even had he known how strong a sentiment a few young men nourished against his views, it is not likely that he would have betrayed what he saw as an essential truth by keeping silence in order to preserve his own popularity. The president of a theological school to-day, who upholds his own beliefs, or his personal interpretation of the truth, although he knows that some of his faculty think him in error, or the college president who advocates compulsory Latin or Greek in opposition to some of his subordinates who would give up both, does just what Mather did, and deserves the same praise or blame we may bestow on him. If all such speakers managed to write such good prose as he did, judged by the standards of his time, if they were as sure of their authorities, and based their convictions on so wide an experience, whatever we might think of their theories, we should certainly be forced to a word of appreciation of their method.

Again, in "David Serving his Generation," printed in 1698, Mather returned to the question of innovations in church practice. "It was with respect unto Purity as to all Church Administrations," he said, that the first settlers "followed the Lord unto a Land which was not Sown. Wherefore notwithstanding too many of *this Generation*, who are lamentably Degenerated from the Principles and Spirit of their Fathers and Grandfathers, will rage at it, we cannot easily do a better service than to withstand Innovations which would prove fatal to the Churches, and to the Interest of Christ's Holy Kingdom among them. . . . We shall do well to remember, that there are Practices which in some other places of the World, would be a step towards Reformation; that in a people so Instructed and Enlightened as we have been, would deserve the Name of great Degeneracy & Apostasy" (p. 22). With this general statement, there are linked specific counsels. The ministry must be maintained at a high standard, the Indian missions must be supported, the government of Harvard must "be confirmed in faithful hands, that will transmit it unto such Successors" (p. 32). And, with a direct reference to certain difficulties which he had found in administering the college as he believed it should be administered, he adds that there should be "care that the *Tutors* there be such as shall make Conscience to Establish the Young Scholars in those Holy Principles of Truth" (p. 32). A harmless and general statement on the face of it, but one which could be easily construed by some hearers as a hint that the president was not altogether pleased with some of his subordinates at Harvard.

In 1700, Mather wrote a preface for Willard's "Peril of the Times Displayed." [53] Here he once more speaks of apostasy in New England, of the need for spiritual awakening, and to these familiar themes he adds a mention of the improvement which has come to the Church of England. For us the chief interest of the preface is not in its matter or style, but in the proof it offers that, in 1700, Mather and Willard were friends. In 1697 they fell out about the election of tutors at Harvard, and Mather sent his colleague a message saying, "He will never come to his House more till he give him satisfaction." [54] It has been suggested in some accounts that in 1700 or 1701 the two leading ministers of Boston were not on good terms. That they were, in 1700 at least, is proved by the fact that Mather wrote this preface for Willard. Moreover, that Mather wrote of apostasy here, and that Willard printed his remarks with his own work, is worth remembering when we find the former attacked as if he were the only minister in Boston who ever uttered or approved rebukes to those who fancied themselves the enlightened liberals of the day. Whatever their quarrel in 1697 may have been, in 1700 Mather and Willard were in close touch personally and in their beliefs as to doctrine. As his books outlined his attitude toward religious changes, so

53. S. Willard, "The Peril of the Times Displayed. Or The Danger of Mens taking up with a Form of Godliness, But Denying the Power of it. Being The Substance of several Sermons...." Boston, 1700.
54. *MHS Coll.*, Series 5, v, 464.

also his writings express much as to his political position. Two sermons, one delivered in 1693 and the other in 1699, testify to his attitude.

The first, printed with the title, "The Great Blessing of Primitive Counsellours,"[55] was preached by request of the government on the day of the election of 1693. On that day the officers whom Mather had chosen for the colony faced their first trial at the polls, in that the representatives voted as to who should sit in the Council for the coming year. The result was of obvious importance to Phipps, who was at the head of the government, and to Mather, who was responsible for its inauguration. If his choices were rejected, it could mean nothing but that the new charter which he had endorsed and the men he nominated were not acceptable to the colonists, and his personal prestige must suffer accordingly.

Under such circumstances we should expect few preachers to stick to abstract theology, and the practically minded Mather least of all. He began, to be sure, by outlining the general qualities which popular leaders should have. They should be pious, faithful, courageous, and wise. If such men were to be had, there would be good judges, and, as he said, "Religion and Reformation will be Encouraged" (p. 17). With this much general instruction, he becomes more specific. "This Informs and directs those in whose power it is to choose Counsellers what manner of persons they are to Elect," he remarks, "namely such as were at the Beginning" (p. 18), in the palmy days when New England was the invincible stronghold of Puritan faith. Still practical, he continues, "It is very meet that persons Nominated for Counsellers should be men of Estate, and of some Port in the World" (p. 19). This doctrine is often condemned to-day, and usually rejected in practice, but there are still heretics who regard it as wise.

Had Mather said no more, it would have been hard for us, or for any one of his hearers, to criticize him. But he proceeded, courageously at least, to touch one of the sorest spots in the people's political consciousness. "Let me also say to you . . . that it will not be prudence in you (at this time especially) to propose

55. "The Great Blessing of Primitive Counsellors. Discoursed in a Sermon, Preached in the Audience of the Governour, Council, and Representatives, of the Province of the *Massachusets-Bay*, in *New-England. May 31st.* 1693. Being the Day for the Election of *Counsellors*, in that Province . . . Bene agere & Male audire Regium est." Boston, 1693.

such Assistants to the Governour as you cannot but know, that He cannot Accept of, and so to necessitate him to make use of his Negative Voice, when He has no desire to do it. And you cannot but know that . . . no Governour will take those into his Council, who are *Malecontents*, and do what in them is to make others to be Disaffected to the Government. No Governour can take such men into his Bosome" (p. 19). And, turning to Phipps, he went on: "It is a very great Power which the Divine Providence has put into your Hands, that you should have a *Negative* on the *Elections* of this Day. A Power which I confess, neither you nor anyone else should have had, if any Interest that I was capable to make, could have prevented it. You know Sir, that I humbly argued against it to the Kings Majesty, and to many of His chief Ministers of State. But I now see that God has ordered it to be as it is in Mercy to this his People; what it may be for the future, when the Ingratitude of an unthankful Murmuring Generation of men, shall have provoked the Most High . . . the Lord knoweth: but at present there is more good than hurt in it, and will be so long as there shall be a Governour whose Heart is Engaged to seek not Himself but the Publick good. . . . No one that is Disaffected to the best and highest Interest, or, to the Government of Their Majesties in *England*, or that is an Enemy to the Government here, can be imposed on you" (pp. 19, 20).

Now, that a royal governor should have the right to veto the acts of the people's representatives seemed to Mather and to his fellow citizens a sore blow to their rights. His enemies, and those hostile to the new charter, could find no surer weapon against him than to point out that he had accepted for New England this loss of privileges. It was true that he had fought bitterly against it, but now, in May, 1693, he stood up before the leaders of the state and defended the hated clause.

Such a step was bold. Whether it was politically wise is open to question. In the first place, as Mather spoke, many a man in his audience must have felt that he was being threatened, in that he was assured that, if his vote did not fall on the side of Mather and Phipps, it would not count. And, secondly, those who regarded the matter as one of political justice or injustice cannot have been impressed by Mather's argument from present expediency, however kindly they felt toward the existing rulers. On the other hand, the governor's right to veto elections was legally established, and not to use it would have been to fly directly in the face of the letter and the spirit of his orders from the English authorities. The issue was one of independent colonial government *versus* partial independence subject always to royal control. Moderates, men who might have become Loyalists in 1776, believers in the colony as an English province, not an "American" nation, certainly upheld Mather. Elisha Cooke and those who believed with him that the old charter, as construed in Boston, represented the last word in political theory, must have squirmed rebelliously as Mather spoke. It would have been easy to conciliate them without offending the friends of the new régime, but to do so would have been for Mather to keep silence on a matter about which he felt deeply. Zealous as he may have been in his desire to protect his own popularity, he was not enough of a politician to sacrifice his principles for votes. He believed that men favorable to Phipps's government, with its sympathy for church and college, should be elected. Accordingly he spoke out, and explained without reserve just how far the popular will would be heeded. Probably he was unwise, and made enemies where a more evasive method might have won allies; but certainly he displayed his own independence without fear or favor.

The election, as we have seen, largely confirmed the existing government, but some of Mather's candidates were defeated, and a few of those avowedly in opposition to the result of his agency came into power. Their protests against the order of the day were sure to be heard. Among them was Elisha Cooke, the one man who centred about himself more and more each year Mather's political adversaries and those to whom strict independence seemed the ideal. Cooke was, to be sure, by no means the most popular candidate, and stood not far from the foot of the list in respect to the number of votes he received, but that he was chosen at all was a straw showing the direction of the political wind.[56]

He was so much of a "malcontent," and so frankly a foe of Phipps, in that he opposed the measures by which the new governor came into power, that his presence in the Council was a serious danger. Phipps promptly vetoed his election, and, as promptly, the people, no doubt mindful of Mather's remarks in his recent sermon, blamed not only the governor but his pastor.[57]

56. *MHS Coll.*, Series 5, v, 378.

57. Sewall wrote, on June 8, 1693: "Mr. Danforth labours to bring Mr. Mather and Cook together, but I think in vain. Is great wrath about Mr. Cook's being refused, and 'tis supposed Mr. Mather is the cause." *Ibid.*, p. 379. Cf. also, *Ibid.*, pp. 378, 379 n.

If Mather erred in defending the governor's right to veto, the latter blundered equally in making use of it. If his course was advised by the Teacher of his church, Mather must share the blame of having bungled the situation. It would have been safer to put up with Cooke's opposition in the Council than, by rejecting him, to crystallize at one stroke the enmity to the new régime by supplying its foes with a ready-made "martyr" to what seemed to them to be royal "tyranny." Cooke seems to have been a good politician and a believer in what he held to be colonial rights. He was not inclined to be diplomatic, and he knew how to fight. He was frank in his opposition to royal governors, and thus won the distinction of being turned out of office, not only by Phipps, but by another New Englander who later came to occupy the governor's chair.[58]

With the election past, its result known, and Cooke refused by Phipps, it was clear that any forebodings Mather may have had as to the political hostility drawn upon him by his action in accepting the charter were entirely justified. Knowing this, he wrote his preface to the printed version of his election sermon.

In it he recalls the happy days under the old charter, and admits the loss of some of its privileges, but he stoutly asserts that the new scheme of government still deserves support. He is chiefly concerned with his own vindication, and defends himself against talkers who chose to attack him. They proclaimed that he did nothing for the old charter, but he cogently reminds them of the chief events of his agency, and disposes of their accusations. "The *Whisperers* that have endeavoured to make people believe that the Ministers who Subscribed" the letter testifying to his efforts in England "did afterward repent of their so doing are *Forgers of Lies*," Mather declares. He alludes to warnings which he received in England from friends who assured him that the colonists would reward his work on their behalf with nothing but ingratitude. The events of 1693 gave him an inkling that the cynicism of his English acquaintances was well founded, and, as the years went by, he was made more and more aware of the wisdom of their prophecy.

By 1699, although opposition to Mather was nearly at its height, he was once more called upon to preach the election ser-

58. Palfrey, iv, 254.

mon.[59] The occasion was doubly significant in that a new governor, the Earl of Bellomont, an Englishman, and one whose feeling toward the colonists was as yet untested, had recently arrived in Boston. Mather combined in his discourse elements clearly adapted to impress His Excellency with a rugged refusal to sacrifice for any man on earth certain fundamental convictions as to truth. This last feature of his sermon he shows in his "This Honour of absolute Obedience is due to God alone. Inferiours are to obey their Superiours, but this Reserve always so far as shall consist with Obedience to the Will of God. If the Greatest man on Earth command a thing which God has forbidden he must not be obeyed. . . . Or, if men should inhibit what God Commands, we must honour God by obeying him rather than them" (p. 6). Here was the sort of talk Edward Randolph would have seized upon as seditious. One can imagine his delight in retailing it, with such embroidery as his prejudices dictated, to some chosen confidant among those of his friends most devoted to the doctrine of the divine right of kings. Mather's speech certainly showed no truckling before royal authority. But he had more to do than assert his independence, for matters that touched his faith were at stake. The new governor was a Church of England man, and some recognition of this was but prudent. So we read: "A man whose heart honours God, respecteth every Good, Holy man as such. He does not respect men meerly because they are of his party, or particular perswasion in matters not Essential to Salvation. Suppose him to be *Episcopalian, Congregational, Presbyterian, Antipedobaptist,* in his Opinion, if he is a Godly man he honours Godliness wherever he seeth it" (p. 15).

To the citizens Mather commented once more on the privileges they enjoyed under the new charter, but he had had, by 1699, enough experience of the popular temper to make him realize that references to the governor's veto power were not safe. So he said no more than, "It is a great priviledge which you enjoy this day, that there can be no Civil Rulers over the Province (excepting the Commander in Chief and his Deputy) but what the People by their *Representatives* shall approve of. No other Plantation enjoyes the like Priviledge. Nor should we, if the

59. "The Surest way to the Greatest Honour: Discoursed in a Sermon, Delivered In the Audience of His *Excellency* the Earl of *Bellomont,* Captain General and Governour in Chief, and of the Council, and Representatives of the General Assembly of the Province of the *Massachusetts-Bay,* Convened at *Boston* in *New-England, May 31st.* 1699. Being the day for the Election of *Counsellors* in that Province." Boston, 1699.

Senballats and *Tobijahs* amongst us could have had their desires" (p. 31). Who these "Senballats and Tobijahs" were, is obvious. That Mather referred thus to the implacable devotees of the old charter shows how little their opposition to his advocacy of the new order had shaken him.

He had not forgotten the old days when kings less good than William had held the throne and he had been a foe of English monarchs. "Let no man give a Vote for any one that has the slavish heart of a *Jacobite* in him" (p. 33). Other practical counsel he gave by exhortations to the clergy to emphasize Christ in their preaching, and by reminders that to deviate from the old religious "Platform" of New England would be to dishonor God. He urged the representatives to consider Harvard's situation, and, William being favorable and the time propitious, to take steps to secure a permanent establishment for the college. As for the voters, their best course, Mather declared, was to "Choose them that will Fear God & Honour the King" (p. 33).

One sentence in the preface to the printed sermon sums up one of Mather's sincerest beliefs. "Great men," he wrote, "are happier than others, chiefly in this Respect, That they have greater Opportunities to *Honour God*." His desire for high place in the church and in the respect of his fellow citizens cannot be ascribed to sordid ambition, if one accepts these words of his at their face value; and there is no reason to take them as anything but the expression of what he really thought.

His books, written between 1692 and 1701, give many clues as to his position in these years. Remembering some of the views he expressed, we can see better why his fortunes fared as they did in his relation to public affairs. But to understand fully what happened, we must turn from printed pages to the daily politics of seventeenth-century Massachusetts.

CHAPTER XIX

THE FIRST DEFEAT

HOW inextricably Mather's agency involved his fortunes with those of the new charter and its supporters, we have already seen, and we know that there was a party of some influence opposed to his views. Had Phipps been a stronger man, or had he been pursued by fewer foes abroad, he might have remained a popular governor, even though he was branded with what seemed to some of his compatriots the stigma of a royal appointment. But he was neither strong nor tactful. He lacked Dudley's adroitness and Stoughton's determination. His temper was that of a good seaman, and his bearing toward his subordinates was too often that of a captain toward his men. Moreover, whatever his character, the king's use of the veto power was in itself enough to weaken his governor's hold on the people. Wherever there were men loyal to William, with faith that Massachusetts could prosper best by continuing as a colony, there were also many who were repelled by the acts of the individual who, for the moment, represented the sovereign. When Phipps cudgelled a man in the streets for doing no more than his duty, or assaulted the captain of an English ship; when he wrote official letters with a vocabulary better suited to the forecastle, or quarrelled with the representatives about a question which they believed involved their rights, he offended many citizens, however they felt toward England and her authority. And those others who, with a complacent disregard of practical considerations, dreamed of a government subject to no royal governor, were not likely to receive with welcome any act performed under the new charter. Every colonial law, passed in Boston and vetoed in London, added fuel to the blaze of hostility, fanned by Elisha Cooke and his zealous "old charter" brethren. Thus, when Phipps pursued a wise and farsighted policy against the French, he found critics even for this.[1]

In 1694 Sir William was recalled to England, to answer charges, and, he knew, to try to escape from the net woven about him by

1. Cf. J. A. Doyle, *The Puritan Colonies*, ii, 405.

Joseph Dudley.[2] The latter was now a member of the Church of England, a political force, and an eager aspirant for the New England governorship. Inevitably he must have been against Phipps, and he became his most active foe in London. His intrigues were unnecessary, for Sir William died in February, 1695.

With the talents he had, he did his utmost for his country. He erred often, but he seems never to have allowed his personal interests to stand in the way of his country's. His defects were of vision, and when he did see clearly, he was brave and vigorous. He paid dearly for his hot temper and his lack of tact. But, in spite of his faults, New Englanders were "generally sad"[3] at the news of his death, and Increase Mather hastened to preach on "Merciful men taken away."[4]

The relation between Mather and Phipps made it inevitable that they should stand or fall together. Every charge against the governor was, less directly, one against his pastor. Mather lost a large share of his political influence at one stroke, when the man he had made ruler of New England was recalled to answer accusations of misconduct in office. Phipps died before he came to trial, so that he remained unvindicated, nor could Mather be quite removed from the shadow. In the governor's defeat alone there is enough to explain a greater reverse than that which came to Mather in 1701. That he kept as much influence as he did, in spite of Phipps's fall, argues for the strength of his position.

Much of this lay in the fact that Stoughton, the lieutenant-governor, who succeeded Phipps, was, as his predecessor had been, a friend, sympathizer, and appointee of Mather. Richard Coote, Earl of Bellomont, was made governor of New England in 1696; but he did not come to Boston until 1699, and in the meanwhile Stoughton ruled. Mather, therefore, had friends in high place. Nor did Bellomont, when he arrived, fail to listen sometimes to the leader of the colonial church.

In 1701 Stoughton served once more for a short time, but in that year both he and Bellomont died. The next governor was no other than Joseph Dudley. Cotton Mather aided him in

2. J. A. Doyle, *The Puritan Colonies*, ii, 407, 408; *MHS Coll.*, Series 5, v, 393; and *Cal. State Papers, Am. and W. I.*, xiv, ✻ 862.

3. *MHS Coll.*, Series 5, v, 404.

4. For a quotation from this sermon, see C. Mather, *Magnalia*, book II, Appendix, section 21.

securing his appointment.[5] How Increase felt toward his coming is not certain, but we know that until 1700 the elder Mather opposed his ambition. Dudley was a friend of Stoughton and a foe of Cooke. In his younger days he had been a Puritan. On the other hand, he was a bitter enemy of Phipps and therefore of the man who brought him to power. Probably, by 1701, Increase Mather had come to believe that Dudley had repented of his past errors. Indeed, there is a letter to Cotton Mather extant, in which Dudley explains and defends his course. It is very likely that the Mathers, with most New Englanders, preferred a native of the colony as their governor.[6] But, whatever the reasons for his appointment, Dudley's coming was a direct blow against the Cooke party and worked toward the continuing of the political division which existed as early as 1692.

Through all the public affairs of the time, Cotton Mather's voice is heard. He flayed his adversaries with gusto, meddled in public concerns, appeared wherever Boston ministers met, and kept his pen busy in the service of his opinions.[7] Curiously in contrast is the impression one gets of his father. Sewall's diary shows surprisingly little of the president during these years. Where the Mathers took sides in controversy, it was Cotton who spoke for their views. When Phipps sailed back to England, Increase did not go to see him off.[8] He seems to have been quite content to keep out of the active life of the town as much as might be. He was attacked by gout, he had much writing to do, and he had all the political campaigning he could manage in connection with Harvard. These were all good reasons for his keeping within doors. Cotton was quite capable of saying in public whatever needed to be said, and Increase, though he may have winced at his son's occasional lapses from diplomatic speech, seems to have been quite content that the younger man should bear the heat of the day.

To Harvard, however, Mather devoted not only much of his attention, but some of his old eager activity with voice and pen. He had returned from England with the advice that he should secure a charter for the college from an act of the local government. This he proceeded to do. The resulting document, passed

5. Cf. J. A. Doyle, *The Puritan Colonies*, ii, 440 n.
6. Cf. *MHS Coll.*, Series 6, v, 91, iii, 501f.
7. Cf. *Ibid.*, Series 7, vol. vii, and Series 5, vol. v, *passim*.
8. *Ibid.*, Series 5, v, 393.

under Phipps's eyes, and before Mather's political influence had been impaired, may fairly be taken as representing what the president saw as the ideal form of government for Harvard.[9]

Its essential feature was that it put all authority in the hands of a corporation of ten, which was to be self-perpetuating, and subject to no supervision by "visitors" or "overseers." Plainly, Mather felt that the only way to ensure Harvard's remaining a nursery, not only of learning but of piety, was to put it into the hands of men who felt as he did, and to allow them to choose their successors. Without outside supervision, they could then continue the traditions of the college under no necessity of conforming to any changes which might come in the views of its alumni or the community. Though undemocratic and narrow, such a scheme was a highly practical method of saving Harvard from changes in ideals or policy. With a wise Corporation, Harvard would be well governed, and to Mather and his friends good government, or what they believed to be good, was far more important than any catering to the educational whims of the moment. We may give thanks that Harvard was saved from his plan, but it is hard to criticize Mather's policy from the point of view of the interests he held dearest. Sound learning and Protestantism, particularly nonconformist Protestantism, were the essentials that he would have Harvard give to every pupil. The Congregational Church in the colony depended largely on its ability to draw well-trained ministers from the college. So long as his church, and the avoidance of what he saw as erroneous beliefs, were the greatest aims to be sought in education, Mather's policy was practically sound. He erred in choosing it, it seems to us, because experience has shown that his object was less desirable than he supposed. He seems more wrong to us than he did to his contemporaries, because we have developed aims of our own, and theories of our own, which we label "liberality," "democracy," or what not, and we, in our turn, adore these as the highest things in life.[10]

The Corporation chosen under the new charter which, under the law, remained in force unless it was vetoed by the king within three years, was headed by Increase Mather as president.[11] With him were elected James Allen, Samuel Willard, Nehemiah

Hobart, Nathaniel Gookin, Cotton Mather, John Leverett, William Brattle, Nehemiah Walter, and the treasurer, John Richards. Hobart refused to serve, and in his place Charles Morton was chosen. The board included, then, the minister of the First Church in Boston, the two leaders of the Second Church there, and the ministers of Cambridge and Charlestown. The two tutors, upon whom the administration had devolved during Mather's absence, were also chosen, and the former treasurer retained his office. All these men were Congregationalists, and all were good citizens. For the moment Harvard seemed likely to fare well at their hands.

The new charter gave the Corporation the right to confer higher degrees, and they promptly voted to Brattle and Leverett Bachelorships in Divinity. Upon Mather they conferred the title of Doctor of Divinity. All three men deserved honors, Leverett and Brattle for their faithful service, and Mather for his work as president and for his achievement in broader fields.

Such "self-gratification" on the part of the Corporation was not only innocent but recognized real distinction. None the less, no honor could come to Mather without arousing his political opponents. Thus we find in a letter to England, "Sir William and Council have given the College a charter, with power to receive gifts and confer degrees. They are proceeding to create Mather a doctor of divinity, which by some misunderstanding is to be obstructed. The deputies too are so displeased since Cooke's arrival that they will allow him [Mather] no salary unless he be resident and would have another man chosen." [12]

There is confirmation here of what might easily be surmised on other grounds. When Cooke, Mather's opponent during the agency, came home, "misunderstanding," discontent with the president, and a movement to replace him, all began. Cooke knew, as Randolph did, how influential a political agency the college might become. He could not easily stomach having the man whose stand on public questions he combatted from high and conscientious motives remain at the head of higher education in Massachusetts. So he sought for the weak spot in Mather's armor, and found it in his divided allegiance between his church and the college. Then, by advocating a law that the president of

when I disagree with Quincy, when there is more information to add, or when some particular document is referred to.

12. *Cal. State Papers, Am. and W. I.*, xiv, ⚹ 214 (March 23, 1693).

Harvard must live in Cambridge, Mather's foes took the readiest means of putting obstacles in the way of his keeping his office.

Probably it was better that the college should have a resident chief executive, but the letter we have quoted and the events of 1701 prove that not only high zeal for correct collegiate administration, but also certain definite political motives, lay back of the effort to require Mather's removal to the college or his retirement from the presidency. To ask him to leave Boston and one of the leading churches of New England, to wrestle with the daily conduct of what was still a small and struggling school, was to demand more than he or any other active divine was likely to grant. Should he refuse, Cooke's party could force his resignation. Should he accept, he would be less able to impose his will on the government in Boston, and his enemies would gain. Should he give up the control of Harvard, there would be a chance that it might be brought to train voters for Cooke.

So, for nearly ten years, the college was the centre of a battle. Against Mather were ranged his political enemies and, later, those who disagreed with him in ecclesiastical matters. Probably there joined with these some who resented what seemed to them to be the Mathers' too great dominance in the colony. Mather's task was to keep his position and prestige without sacrificing the principles he believed should govern church and state. The odds were too great for him, and, rather than compromise, he accepted the one great defeat of his life.

Before we look at this controversy, we may glance at one or two bits of evidence bearing on his administration of Harvard. That he was a good president, and that the college developed under him, is admitted even by those who dislike his attitude on some other matters.[13] We know from his diaries that he gave much time and thought to his duties and spent many days in going to and from Cambridge, then, of course, separated from Boston by a far greater journey than it is to-day. Seven or eight miles, on horseback, in all sorts of weather, was no slight undertaking; but such obstacles did not deter him. If he harangued the students on the dangers of Arminianism, he also took up subjects of broader interest. He advocated a "*liberal* mode of philosophizing, instead of floating about from school to school, as if you were literally Peripatetics." He denounced Aristotle, declaring, "Certainly an imp would be a fine interpreter of Aristotle!" But he was careful

13. Cf. J. Quincy, *History*, i, 116, 117.

to add: "You, who are accustomed to philosophize in a *liberal* spirit, are pledged to the formulas of no master: and you should moreover remember that one truly golden sentiment of Aristotle: 'Find a friend in Plato, a friend in Socrates' (and I say, a friend in Aristotle), but be sure, above all, to find a friend in truth." No advocate of intellectual freedom ever uttered a broader doctrine.[14]

Nor did he try ever to limit Harvard's curriculum to theology. He knew that New England must have not only ministers, but physicians, and that she could not afford to exclude all but divinity. In 1698 we find a student presenting a Commencement thesis on the question whether comets are meteors.[15] Under Mather's guidance the library bought scientific books and books of general scope.[16] Knowing his own broad interests, it is not hard for us to guess that the student who thirsted for a taste of astronomy, of chemistry, medicine, or experimentation in "natural philosophy," got what he sought.

Mather believed that the college had a duty toward historical research, especially when such studies might serve to support theological tenets. Such a duty could be performed in part by a further recording of the observed phenomena of nature. With exactly the same purpose which Mather had in writing his "Illustrious Providences," he, with the Corporation and at the request of the ministers' association,[17] put out in the name of the college "Proposals" asking for accounts of *unusual accidents*, in the heaven, or earth, or water: all wonderful *deliverances* of the distressed: *mercies* to the Godly; *judgments* on the wicked; and more glorious fulfilment of either the *promises* or the *threatnings* in the Scriptures of truth; with *apparitions, possessions, inchantments*, and all extraordinary things wherein the existence and agency of the *invisible world* is more sensibly demonstrated." The narratives are to be "written accounts . . . well attested with credible and sufficient witnesses." [18] Once more, experience was to support theological doctrines, and once more the method was essentially scientific.

Any mention of the "invisible world" made by a Mather has always excited certain historians to forget all else in their zeal to adorn more thoroughly the strange lay figure they have erected

14. C. Mather, *Magnalia*, book IV, part i, section 7.
15. *MHS Coll.*, Series 2, iv, 93n.
16. *Harv. Rec.*, p. 358.
17. *MHS Proc.*, xvii, 271.
18. C. Mather, *Magnalia*, book VI, Introduction.

to represent either Increase or his son. In their eyes both men strove to encourage belief in witches; the younger, at least, labored to spread popular excitement and persecution, and both would rather spy out a witch than inherit a fortune. Never is this fantasy more futile than when it is applied to the "Proposals" of the Harvard Corporation in 1694. Nowhere does the preservation of the myth require more resolute closing of one's eyes to the known facts and the existing records.

To cite but one example, it has been said that Increase Mather "used his position as President of Harvard College" in "the nefarious business" of trying "to engage the superstitious and reckless." [19] This is flatly contradicted, of course, by the "Proposals" themselves. They ask for narratives of apparitions and the like only as a part of a design which included everything else that was novel or unusual, or, as the Puritans put it, revealed God's wondrous works. Far from seeking to "engage" superstition, the Corporation asked for nothing except what could be supported by good witnesses. Indeed, a sufficient answer to the quotation given above is found in the fact that Mather was not the only signer of the "Proposals," and that among those who approved the plan was one whom our critic of the Mathers declares to have been enlightened in regard to witchcraft! [20] It is not enough to say that the document merely "purported" to represent the Corporation, for we have definite evidence that they signed it.[21] Only when we read the "Proposals" with the omission of all but one clause, forget all we know of Increase Mather's attitude during the witchcraft excitement, and believe that he secured for a document urging credulity and superstition the signature of a man who is said to have been his courageous opponent in such matters, can we see the document as anything but what it was. If we prefer to abide by the obvious facts, there is nothing more in the "Proposals" than an effort to secure materials for history and theology. Moreover, these materials were acceptable only when they were vouched for by good witnesses. The veriest child with a desire to encourage superstition

19. J. Winsor, *The Literature of Witchcraft*, p. 355.

20. The "Proposals" were signed by both Mathers, by Allen, Morton, Walter, Leverett, William Brattle, and Willard. William was the brother of Thomas Brattle, and his ally on other questions, and Willard is praised by Winsor for his "right-mindedness"! *Ibid.*, p. 363.

21. *MHS Proc.*, xvii, 271, entry for 1694, March 4. Quincy (*History*, i, 62), suggests that the "Proposals" only "purported" to be signed by the Corporation.

could turn out a plan which would serve his ends better than the sheet the Corporation issued. The "Proposals" were framed by men who knew what they wanted and asked for it, with explicit directions as to how it was to be presented. It has been reserved for later history to lose sight of the truth in the interests of prejudice.

As for details of his administration, Mather kept the old college rules in use.[22] The Bachelors of Arts were ordered to debate philosophical questions once each fortnight, and the Masters were to treat theological problems at such times as the President appointed.[23] In 1693 Richards resigned, and in his place no other than Thomas Brattle was elected treasurer.[24] So the two Mathers and their friends chose to dignify by high office a man who is called to-day the greatest of the sceptics as to witchcraft in 1692. The choice was natural, for Brattle was a citizen of standing; but it would be hard to explain if one accepted for a moment the idea that the Mathers differed from the new treasurer as to the power of Satan. We have Brattle's testimony that they agreed with him; and although he came later to oppose them on other grounds, so far as "the invisible world" was concerned, he was a Matherian.

Recorded with equal gravity is the vote forbidding "Plum-Cake" at Commencement; but one soon meets matters of more importance in the appearance of notes of a project to develop the college on the material side by new building.[25] This plan had already been discussed by the "Cambridge Association."[26] The first practical step seems to have been a vote to take down the old "Indian Colledge," which was, presumably, out of repair. There is also a vote appointing a committee to discuss with Stoughton his plan to build an "additional building to ye Colledg."[27] Thence came the first "Stoughton Hall," and the name of its successor, which still stands.

Within the Corporation Mather seems to have found little of the opposition which he had to contend with outside. While he was supported in the meetings of the Fellows, votes of those who sat in the Town-house were less favorable to him. As early as December 2, 1693, the General Court ruled that he should

---

22. *Harv. Rec.*, p. 339.
23. *Ibid.*, p. 340.
26. *MHS Proc.*, xvii, 270 (Oct. 2, 1693).
27. *Harv. Rec.*, pp. 357, 358.

24. *Ibid.*, pp. 341, 342.
25. *Ibid.*, p. 343.

reside at Harvard. To this he paid no attention. On June 5, 1695, the representatives passed a vote even more explicit in its terms. If Mather would go to Cambridge, he was to have a salary of one hundred and fifty pounds a year, but if he declined, another president was to be sought.

The Council, where Mather's appointees were still a majority, seems not to have concurred in either of the votes just mentioned. Mather was, none the less, awake to the feeling of the legislators, and he inclined to give up the presidency. On August 5 he told the Corporation that he wished to serve no longer and asked them to look for his successor; but they voted in entirely unambiguous terms to request him to stay, "not too deeply resenting the matters of discouragement laid before him." They gave material proof of their good will in the form of a donation of seventy pounds, and money with which he might buy a horse.

Then came the news that King William had refused his consent to the college charter of 1692.[28] The reason given was that no provision had been made for the sovereign and his governor to have visitatorial power.[29] The objection was reasonable, for no monarch was likely to approve the removal of the one great educational force in an important colony from all control by the royal government.

Meanwhile Mather had been impressed by a conviction that the Lord demanded his return to England, to serve Him there. This he regarded as "a special faith," and his diary is full of his spiritual debating of it.[30] We may easily scoff at this, saying that he was ambitious to become once more the honored agent of the colony. What was more natural than that, with such selfish desires, he should cheat himself into a belief that God called him to what he secretly craved? Such a view does not quite meet the facts. Mather's diaries were obviously not written for publication. He wrote them in very brief notes, setting down his doings without regard to their importance, and he gave much space to mentioning his sins. His autobiography he prepared for his children's eyes, and there, if one wills, he may have written for

28. Cf. *Cal. State Papers, Am. and W. I.*, xiv, ※ 1754, 1874.
29. *Ibid.*, ※ 874.
30. See *Autobiography; MS. Diary* (some extracts from which are in Quincy, *History*, i, 475ff.); *MHS Coll.*, Series 7, vol. vii (Quincy, *History*, i, 482ff., gives extracts); and *Parentator*, pp. 192ff.
It is well to remember, in using Quincy's extracts, that they are "selections" from the diary, and adapted to the author's theory as to Mather's motives.

posterity. If it were only there that he wrote of his conviction that God "called" him to return to England, we might ascribe his remarks to a desire to veil hypocritically his own ambition; but when we find his hastily scrawled diaries full of his perplexities as to the meaning of what seemed to him to be God's exhortations to service in London, we must admit that they represented something very real to him and that, if they but expressed his own secret desires, he deceived himself unconsciously and sincerely.[31]

England had always called him. He had left it reluctantly in 1662, and continued for years thereafter to dream of returning to the mother country. In 1688 his chance came, and he once more saw London. Four years there quickened the old love, and for the rest of his life he never forgot England's charms. Intellectually and socially there were opportunities better suited to the range of his nature than any offered by the colony. Even leaving aside such personal motives, he had thrown himself heartily into his diplomatic mission and was intensely eager that the new charter should succeed. When it was attacked and he was criticized, he would have been less than human had he not longed to try his hand once more in an effort to secure the changes the people desired. At the same time, his family were in Boston, he was growing old, and the North Atlantic was no less stormy than in his father's time. Sacrifice as well as self-gratification was involved in any plan to go to London, and, no doubt, he meant what he said when he called the defeat of his scheme for a new agency a "happy disappointment."[32]

Bits of his diary have been held up as hypocritical. Such interpretation is possible only if one is content to accept a part of what he wrote as expressing his feeling and the rest as mere striving for effect. To read his diary thus, one must select from his words in accordance with a preconceived idea of his character, and an idea which does not agree with the facts of his life. Nowhere else did his selfish ambition run counter to the best interests of his church and the state. Nowhere else do we find him eager for controversy for its own sake or desirous of forcing his own will upon the people except in so far as his own will was

31. On the whole question of the reading of the diaries, cf. Quincy's remarks as to Mather in these years, in vol. i of his *History*, and, for the other side, which seems better founded in justice, see Enoch Pond, *The Lives of Increase Mather and Sir William Phipps*, pp. 178ff., and C. Robbins, *History*, pp. 59–63.

32. *Autobiography.*

that of the religious and civil leaders. Even if his whole nature had altered in 1695, the fact still remains that the call he believed he heard demanding his return to England was not an unqualified delight to him. Instead, it was the source of many hours spent in introspective questioning as to where his duty lay.

However he felt, his political enemies were not likely to bid him "God speed" on a new voyage to England. Rumors ran through Boston streets that Cooke and Oakes had declared that, but for Mather, the old charter might have been saved, and that he had betrayed the country. Characteristically he challenged them directly as to their reported statement, which they promptly denied.[33] None the less, the very existence of such gossip showed the current of opinion.

With the rejection of the college charter of 1692, the need for an agency became more apparent. Though Stoughton, as acting governor, bade the officers of Harvard continue their adminis-tration as of yore, no one was content with such a makeshift. On September 5, 1696, Mather was "again discoursed of" as an agent to England. On December eleventh he "did acquaint" the representatives with his "purpose of undertaking a Voyage for E . . . (if ye Ld will) in order to ye obtaining of a govt settlement for ye Colledge." Later in the month, he records that the Cor-poration were eager to have him go, but his church was unwilling to release him.[34]

In November began a new attempt to pass a charter for Har-vard. Those who believed in New England's right to govern herself, with the minimum of attention to the king, were eager to incorporate the college on a basis that they decided upon, not by a patent secured from William III by one or two diplomatic emissaries. This had been Mather's own feeling when, in Eng-land, he chose to leave Harvard's problems to be solved by an act of the colonists' representatives rather than to try to secure a charter by his personal influence at court.

The new plan for the college contained few essential differences from that proposed in 1692. To it Allen, Willard, and both Mathers promptly objected. They protested against its requiring the chief officer of the college to live in Cambridge, declaring

---

33. MS. *Diary*, 1693, June 30, "discourse wth dr. Cooke & Oakes. yy both denied yt ever yy said yt yy could have got ye old charter agñ if it had not bin for me, or y^t I had betrayed ye countrey. I declared myselfe willing to forgive ye wrong yy had done to me." Quincy *History* (i, 475) gives his version of this diary entry.

34. MS. *Diary*, 1696, Sept. 5, Dec. 11, Dec. 28.

that this would render Harvard "incapable of action." This was, of course, a perfectly explicit notice that the president would resign rather than leave Boston. One or two minor clauses were also objected to, and the ministers finally declared that "the visitation" by the Governor and Council "is such as to make it extremely probable, that the act will not only miss of the Royal approbation, but also give offense by its variation from the direction of the Lords of the Council; which we intimate not from our dislike of the thing, but from our concern to have no part in any thing that may renew or prolong the unsettlement of the College." And "for such causes" they prayed "to be excused" from being named as officers of Harvard in the new draft for its government. In this last protest Willard, Mather, and the rest were entirely right. The royal authorities had made quite definite their insistence that the supervisory power should be vested in the king and his governor. The legislators were obstinately determined to include the Council, and highly indignant at criticism of their course; but obstinacy and anger could not drive English statesmen to change what they regarded as a necessary principle.

The 1696 charter came to nothing, and a new one was framed in 1697. Quincy says that it was drawn up by Mather. However this may be, the Council, in acting upon it, tried to remove Leverett from office in the Corporation. Sewall writes: "This day Mr. Leverett was by the Council denied to be of the Corporation for the College." Now, if Mather drew up the bill, he must have included Leverett's name. If this was the case, it speaks well for his liberality in appointing to office a man who was now known to be an ally of those who were arrayed against him in church matters. Of course, the Council may have been under the president's influence, but, as the record stands, all we can be sure of is that it was their act, not his, which aimed directly at Leverett's deposition.

The representatives restored Leverett's name. Once the new charter was passed, the Corporation pushed their plan to have Mather sent to England to secure the king's consent to what had been done. Their first petition was voted down by the representatives, and a second met the same fate. Quincy considers it "worthy of notice" that neither of "the petitions . . . signed by Mather, and stated to be 'by unanimous consent' appears to have been acted upon by the Corporation. There is no record of any meeting on either of the days mentioned in them." [35] This is true, but hardly "worthy of notice," since the college records as we have them are not complete, and, in the case of the first petition, there is an entry in Mather's diary, for June 7, the date given on the document, saying, "ye Corporation unanimously dsired me to undertake a voyage for E. on ye colledges account." [36]

Mather's enemies were hard at work. Robert Calef, whatever his motives were, was belaboring Cotton Mather for his association with the witchcraft trials and declaiming against Increase's deeds during his agency. The one thing that is absolutely certain as to Mather's whole connection with Harvard is that he never sought office there, simply as an office or a public distinction. He refused the presidency more than once, had tried to resign, was prepared to withdraw rather than move to Cambridge, and now, exposed to criticism from many sides, he called a special Corporation meeting in order that he might "(wth ye Lords Leave) . . . Resign" his "Relation to ye Colledge." [37] If we take his remarks as to his desire to go to England at their face value, it is no less than just to remember also the clear proofs he gives as to his lack of vanity and ambition in connection with his place at Harvard. So he wrote: "the Ld pvide & supply ye Colledge wth a better yn I am pdoning my many defects & yt I have done no more good for ye poore Colledge." [38]

The Corporation meeting was duly held, but the Fellows once more prevailed on Mather to remain in office, declaring that, now that a new governor was coming, there was a chance for a more hopeful turn of affairs. Mather stayed reluctantly, and difficulties promptly arose, reflecting, probably, a division already apparent in church councils. It was at this time that the president quarrelled with Willard; but, as we have seen, their friendship was not broken. Once more Mather tried to resign, but there was no quorum at the next Corporation meeting. After it he apparently decided to continue in office and seems to have been confident that he was to be sent to London. This hope encouraged him to remain.

In March he wrote to Blathwayt saying: "I suppose I had been

35. Quincy, *History*, i, 91.
36. MS. *Diary*, 1697, June 7. Moreover, *Cal. State Papers, Am. and W. I.*, xvi, ∦ 570, shows that the legislature had no doubts as to the authenticity of the other petition.
37. MS. *Diary*, 1697, Aug. 7, and Quincy, *History*, i, 478.
38. *Ibid.*

with you before this; but that it is necessary, that the Governour should arrive before my Going ... that so I may have his Countenance and Concurrence in what I am to sollicit for ... I leave only to entreat, that you would please to Improve your Interest at Court, that the Law for Incorporating Harvard-Colledge, which was sent over this Winter, may not come under Consideration until such Time, as I can be with you, which I hope may be in July or August next." [39] This can be read either as a sly bit of secret diplomacy, showing that Mather did not sincerely favor the 1697 charter as passed in the colony, or as a prudent measure to prevent its being refused before its friends could be heard.[40] Since it contained unaltered the clause which had caused the rejection of two earlier charters, it certainly needed defence if it was to pass. If Mather drew it up, as we are told he did, there can have been no motive for his trying secretly to defeat it. Probably his letter represented no more than an attempt to prevent the final rejection of the bill before he could get to London.

The Corporation continued to favor his agency. The new governor, Bellomont, arrived in New York in April, and the Fellows promptly sent to him an address asking that his influence be used to encourage Mather's being sent. To this the governor replied that the college charter as it stood would not pass, and that the sending of an agent would be helpful. The Assembly proceeded to consider the matter, but Mather's enemies were still vociferous. One of them declared that he deserved a year's imprisonment. Whereupon he wrote in his diary, "Is ys my Reward for taking so much pains to serve & save N. E.?" [41]

39. *Col. Soc. Pub.*, xix, 149. Cf. also, *Acts and Resolves*, i, 308.

40. For the adverse view, cf. *Acts and Resolves*, vii, 608, 609. The fact that Ashurst's letter (*Ibid.*, 609) was written *after* Mather wrote Blathwayt shows that Mather could not have known the charter was likely to succeed, at the time he wrote. And it is worth remembering that his request for delaying action on the bill was not heeded, and that the bill failed! In other words, his fears as to its passage were entirely justified, and Ashurst's opinion is beside the point. As to Mather's "disingenuousness" (*Ibid.*, 609), I fail to see where it lies. He told Bellomont just what he told Blathwayt, that is, that he waited for the former's arrival before going to England. Moreover, one remembers, he remained in office because he knew a new governor was coming. It seems clear that Mather planned to go to England; that, probably, he wished to delay action on the bill until he arrived, in order that he might help to save it; and, finally, that there is no evidence that he opposed its passage. Also, as stated in the text, Mather is said to have drawn up the very bill which, we are asked to believe, he hoped to defeat!

41. MS. *Diary*, 1698, June 28. The entry is reprinted, with changes, in Quincy, *History*, i, 479, 480.

The legislators refused Mather's plan, and again voted that he should live at the college. If he would consent, he was to have a salary of two hundred pounds a year. He refused, pointing out the unsettled legal status of Harvard, the claims of his church, and, with other objections, insisting that he could not give up preaching, which he "preferred before the gold and silver of the West Indies."

His formal answer he delivered in a letter to Stoughton. He rehearses his aversion to moving to Cambridge, speaks of his longing for England, and of the criticism heaped upon him by those who believed his policy was dictated by this desire. Therefore he told Stoughton that he would resign. There is no reason to doubt that he meant what he said, although his enemies declared his promise to give up office "was but a flourish." If so, it was a flourish which might have been disastrous. Insistence on the law, or Stoughton's advocacy of some other good divine, was all that was needed to defeat Mather, and this, of course, he knew. He would stay at Harvard as long as he could without giving up what seemed to him to be greater chances for usefulness.

Menwhile the 1697 charter had been refused in England, again because the king and governor were not made "visitors" of the college.[42] The colonial government's policy had been given a thorough trial and had been defeated. Mather's plan for an agency had not been tried at all, but was voted down by his enemies. Harvard still had no legal basis for its administration.

In this apparent impasse, Stoughton did not accept Mather's resignation, and the president now decided to make an effort to meet the wishes of the voters. He was the more ready to make some sacrifice in order to remain in office, probably, because the tendency toward changes in the church gained strength every day, so that orthodoxy in the college seemed more necessary than ever. But when Mather asked his church to allow him to move to Cambridge, they promptly refused their consent. None the less, on the twenty-third of the same month, he told the Corporation

42. The Council of Trade and Plantations reported to the Lord Justices, November 24, 1698: "An Act to incorporate Harvard College was formerly repealed because no power was reserved to the King to appoint visitors, and it was intimated that the Act would be passed if a clause were added giving a power of visitation to the King and to the Governor of the Province. Now the present Act to incorporate the College vests the power of visitation in the Governor and Council, and we therefore recommend that it be repealed." *Cal. State Papers, Am. and W. I.*, xvi, ♯ 1008. Cf. also, *Ibid.*, xvii, ♯ 73.

and the Council that, if his wife agreed and unless news from England prevented, he would come to live at Harvard.

At this juncture Bellomont arrived, with the advice that an address should be sent to the king, asking for a royal charter for the college. The representatives proceeded to draw up new suggestions for incorporating Harvard. These differed from the previous schemes in only two important features. One was that, at last, the visitatorial power was reserved to the king and governor. This was tempered for colonial consumption by a provision that five members of the Council should at all times be, *ex officio*, Fellows of Harvard.[43] The other innovation was the introduction of a clause restricting the right to hold office at the college to those men who were Presbyterians or Congregationalists, and, moreover, followers of the traditional orthodox policy.

This last requirement was an obvious attempt to preserve the sectarianism of Harvard. Nothing more illiberal can be imagined to-day, but it is worth while to remember that the college was founded as a Congregational school, and no idea of its being dominated by any other sect was by any means generally in favor among its alumni. To-day, with our theories of "national," "democratic" universities, sectarian restrictions savor of narrowness. Yet we should hardly blame the trustees of a theological seminary, or a school founded by one church, for refusing to elect officers representing opinions at variance with those for the teaching of which these institutions were founded. There is room to criticize the Mathers, Allen, Torrey, Willard, John Danforth, Peter Thacher, and Benjamin Wadsworth for their failure to grasp a vision of the college's future greater than any its founders had seen, but, however limited their foresight, they were faithful to what they conceived as the traditional ideals of Harvard. To-day we construe her traditions differently, but even so we cannot deny that Mather and the other ministers took a stand which was historically sound.

They introduced the proposal that the college officers should always be orthodox, but it is only fair to remember that the people's representatives stood solidly with them. The governor

43. Cf. here a letter of John Danforth, in *MHS Coll.*, Series 5, i, 448, who writes: "As for the Colledge, if ye present Act for its incorporation should be repeald in England, the Honble Gentlemen of ye Councill are likely to be made members of ye Corporation in ye next Act y^t may incorporate it." The rest of the letter refers to the writer's approval of Mather's being sent as agent, to Ashurst's and Bellomont's endorsement of the same plan, and to the "Generall Court's" refusal to consent.

refused to accept any bill containing a religious restriction, not because he had achieved a modern idea of non-sectarian education, but because the suggested clause excluded from office members of his own church.[44] But, in the face of his expressed opinion, the Council refused to omit the provision which ensured Harvard's continuing as the abiding place of the strict New England type of nonconformity.[45]

Now we have seen that the Council was, at other times, by no means eager to support Mather, and repeatedly opposed what they knew he desired. When it came to a question of religious conservatism, however, they joined forces with him. This is worth remembering, since it makes plain that the issue between Mather and his political antagonists was not one of liberality against reaction. Cooke and his followers were "old charter" men, adherents of the old order, under which Congregationalism had been far more powerful than under the system of government supported by Mather. His foes did not combat him because he was conservative as to church polity, but because he had accepted and favored the trial of a régime in which royal authority was more effectively exercised than before. Forgetful of this, some writers have tried to show that Mather's desire that the king and governor, not the governor and Council, should be visitors, was due to his yearning to protect Harvard's orthodoxy. Bellomont saw more clearly. One of his letters explains that the inclusion of the Council as a supervisory body was intended, not to favor religious liberty at the college, but to protect Congregationalism against a possibly hostile governor and king.[46] In opposing the Council's desire to exert some control over Harvard, Mather had no religious motives, but simply a very practical realization of the futility of trying to enact what the king was

44. Bellomont wrote: "I refused my assent to the Bill for Incorporation of the College, therefore, as it had already been twice rejected, and because of a clause excluding absolutely all members of the Church of England from the government of the College and consequently" (although this does not seem to have followed necessarily) "from being members thereof." Cal. State Papers, Am. and W. I., xvii, ※ 746.

45. Acts and Resolves, i, 308. Cf. also, Cal. State Papers, Am. and W. I., xvii, ※ 657.

46. Bellomont wrote: "The General Assembly do not desire there should be any clause in the Charter exclusive of Members of the Church of England, but they desire the power of visitation may be lodged in the Governor and Council, and not in the Governor singly, because, as this country is very remote from England, a Governor that were a violent man and an enemy to their religion might probably vex and disturb the whole by an attempt upon their College, in order to innovate in matters of discipline or religion, and that before they could make their complaint to the King, and be relieved against such a Governor." Cal. State Papers, Am. and W. I., xviii, ※ 641.

sure to veto. Moreover, the civil authorities proved that they agreed with him, when it came to preserving sectarian education. If a college should guide its policy by the will of the community and its alumni, what the ministers tried to do was right. When we are moved to objurgate Mather and his friends for their failure to abandon the traditions established by the founders and supported by the graduates of Harvard, and their failure to adopt an ideal of nonsectarianism not commonly accepted for generations after 1699, it is wholesome to remember that with them must be admonished the voters of Massachusetts and their representatives. In such company Mather, Willard, and the rest need not fear our censure for their reluctance to adopt standards which gained prominence a century or more after they were in their graves.

Bellomont's veto shipwrecked the 1699 charter plan. The Council, on June 11, 1700, voted to ask the king for a "royal charter of privileges"; but the representatives insisted that the patent should be framed in Boston. It was agreed that they should nominate the college officers, subject to the approval of the Council. The latter was to have visitatorial power, and Bellomont's letters show that this provision was regarded as a guarantee of orthodoxy and that he had altered his views to accept the colonists' position.[47]

The Council and the representatives left out of office the two Brattles and John Leverett, who were now openly advocating innovations in church discipline and fighting Mather with vigorous and continued attacks. He believed such unruly young men had no place in the college Corporation. That the legislators fell in with his view, in spite of their disagreement on other points, shows that they and their constituents had little use for what seemed the noisy radicalism of the time.[48]

At the same time that they joined him in selecting the most orthodox of leaders for Harvard, the Council and representatives gave a death-blow to his hopes of being sent to England. Instead of turning to him, they gave the task of seeking royal favor for Harvard to Bellomont. With his death ended the long struggle to secure a charter for the college.

The colonists had tried hard to gain their dearly longed-for

47. *Cal. State Papers, Am. and W. I.*, xviii, ⚓ 641.

48. Bellomont believed Mather's influence was responsible for keeping Brattle and Pemberton out of office. See *New England Historical and Genealogical Register*, xix, 236.

ends,[49] but consistently set their faces against a plan advocated by their agent in London, Sir Henry Ashurst,[50] by the Corporation, by the clergy, and by Bellomont himself. They would lose their case rather than send Mather to England. There is obvious here the hand of those who hated the new government and the diplomat who accepted it. They could not share his belief that there should be close relations between Boston and London and deference to English law. Mather's own hopes came to naught, and with them perished the colonists' dream of a legal establishment for Harvard.

In July, 1700, a new resolve was passed, requiring the President of Harvard to live at Cambridge and granting him two hundred and twenty pounds a year. Mather was elected president, and a committee waited upon him to urge him to accept office upon the prescribed terms. By this time the Second Church could see obvious dangers to Congregationalism which might threaten if Mather left Harvard. They voted to allow him to move to Cambridge. In July, 1700, he took up his residence across the river, several hours' journey from his beloved congregation and the busy life of Boston, endeared to him by the years he had shared in it.

He stood his exile until October 17, and then he wrote to Stoughton that he could stay no longer at the college, bidding him find another president. This resignation went to the legislators in February, 1701, and they voted that Samuel Willard should be made vice-president and that, if Mather refused to return to Cambridge, Willard and the Corporation should take over the control of Harvard. The president's house was repaired, and Mather made one last effort to endure life there. On June 30, 1701, he wrote to Stoughton:

I promised the last General Court to take care of the College until the Commencement. Accordingly I have been residing in Cambridge these three months. I am determined (if the Lord will) to return to Boston the next week, and no more return to reside in Cambridge; for it is not reasonable to desire me to be (as, out of respect to the public interest, I have been six months within this twelve) any longer absent

49. "The settlement of Harvard College seems to involve the ardent desires and affections of these people beyond all other things in this world; for as they have an extraordinary zeal and fondness for their religion, so anything that disturbs 'em in that, touches 'em in their tenderest part." *Cal. State Papers, Am. and W. I.*, xviii, ⚹ 641.

50. Cf. *MHS Coll.*, Series 6, v, 91.

from my family. And it is much more unreasonable to desire one, so circumstanced as I am, to remove my family to Cambridge, when the College is in such an unsettled state. I do therefore earnestly desire, that the General Court would, as soon as may be, think of another President for the College. It would be fatal to the interest of religion, if a person disaffected to the order of the Gospel, professed and practised in these churches, should preside over this society. I know the General Assembly, out of their regard to the interest of Christ, will take care to prevent it. It is, and has been, my prayer to God, that one much more learned than I am, and more fit to inspect and govern the College, may be sent hither, and one whom all the churches in New England shall have cause to bless the Lord for.

So I remain yours to honor and serve,

INCREASE MATHER.

From the College in Cambridge,
June 30th, 1701.

The General Court received this letter in August, and summoned Mather to appear before them. He came, and told them he would not live at the college, but, if they wished, he would retain the presidency on the old basis of non-residence.[51] They must have been thoroughly irritated by his persistent refusal to obey the laws they had made, and voted now to ask Willard to move to Cambridge and take control of Harvard.

He, like Mather, could not bring himself to leave Boston. The representatives, before his final decision was announced, passed once more a resolve urging Mather to continue in office and live at the college; but the Council knew how little they could hope for from such a plea and pursued their efforts with Willard. He at last agreed to undertake to govern Harvard, but only as a non-resident.

The Council now voted that Willard should be made vice-president, "to take the oversight of the College . . . and to reside there one or two days and nights in a week." The representatives concurred in this. Technically the law was complied with. By giving Willard the title of vice-president, this plan made it pos-

51. Quincy (*History*, i, 113) seems to neglect the fact that Mather said he would "continue his care of the College *as formerly*," that is, on a non-resident basis. Certainly Quincy's reflections on Mather's "caprice" in that he "would neither reside nor resign" are unjust. Mather steadfastly refused to "reside," and as steadfastly continued to "resign" when he had the chance. If the legislators were as annoyed as Quincy believed, all they had to do was accept any one of the resignations Mather offered.

sible for him to live in Boston. By giving him the actual authority in the college, it virtually ousted Mather. The long campaign against the Teacher of the Second Church was finished. He could not remain as President of Harvard unless he sacrificed his pride or gave up the most valuable part of his work. No idea of liberality in religion dictated his removal, for Willard shared with his predecessor a belief that orthodoxy must be safeguarded. No belief that Mather had been a witch-persecutor caused his fall, for all that could be said against him could be said against Willard.[52] The secret of Increase Mather's defeat lay in the political enmity aroused by his agency, in the general feeling, fostered by Cotton Mather's volubility, that the Mathers sought to control all men, in the ex-president's contempt for the desires of the legislature, and in certain personal attacks made upon him. Willard was his logical successor, as the next most prominent divine in Boston, and he was also the brother-in-law of Joseph Dudley, who was soon to become governor of the colony.

The assaults made upon Mather's personal motives and character undoubtedly played a part in defeating him. These connect themselves, for the most part, with the attempt made by the two Brattles, Leverett, and Ebenezer Pemberton to force certain alterations in church discipline upon their more orthodox brethren. One remembers Mather's pleas against apostasy, uttered in his writings for these years. The basis for his remarks appears in the story of the Brattle Street Church.[53]

The debate centred about the manner of admission to full communion in churches. The old practice required a relation of religious experience. The Brattle party wished to abolish this. They also felt that all baptized persons in the church who helped to pay the minister's salary should have a vote in choosing him to office. This was a deviation from the usual custom, by which ministers were selected only by those who had been admitted to

52. Quincy's comparison of Mather and Willard (*History*, i, 147, 148) is quite unjust. He implies that Willard kept out of the intolerant controversies to which Mather is said to have been addicted. Nothing is necessary here except the memory of Willard's *Ne Sutor Ultra Crepidam*, an attack on the Baptists, which Mather's views, expressed in his preface, do not rival in intolerance or zeal for controversy. Enough has been said to show how thoroughly erroneous is Quincy's comparison of Willard and Mather as to their witchcraft views.

53. For the controversy discussed in the text which follows, I have relied upon the accounts given in W. Walker, *Creeds and Platforms*, pp. 472–477, and *A History*, pp. 199–201; S. K. Lothrop, *A History of the Church in Brattle Street*; and *The Manifesto Church — Records of the Church in Brattle Square*.

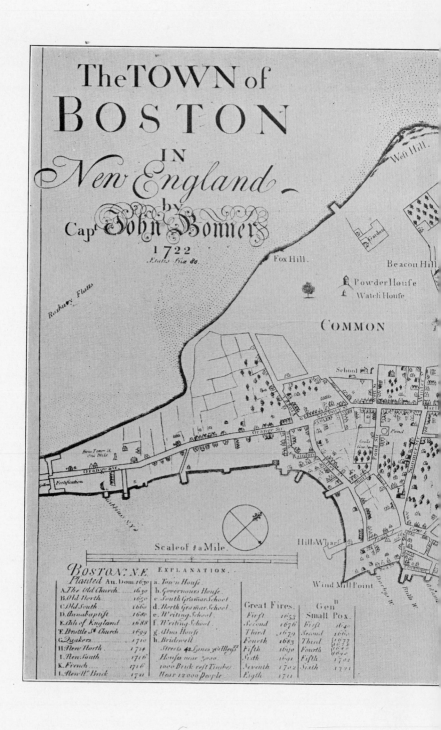

full communion. Again, certain divines advocated the use of the Lord's Prayer and the reading of passages from the Bible without exposition or comment. Such practices savored too much of the liturgical to comment themselves to the stricter brethren. Finally, the "radicals" advocated admitting to baptism any child presented and sponsored by a professing Christian.

Mather's church put itself on record in a vigorous protest to their brethren in Charlestown, who had chosen a minister by vote of all those who contributed to his support. On the other hand, Mather was content to preach when William Brattle, a champion of the proposed changes, was ordained in Cambridge.[54] Criticism and concessions alike failed to deter the innovators, and the Brattles and their followers proceeded to found a fourth Congregational Church in Boston. To its pulpit they called Benjamin Colman, a Harvard graduate of the class of 1692, who was then in England.[55] He secured ordination at the hands of the London Presbytery and came to Boston in November, 1699.

On the seventeenth of that month there was published "A Manifesto or Declaration, Set Forth by the Undertakers of the New Church."[56] This declared that, in order to prevent "all Misapprehensions and Jealousies," the new church expressed its "Aims and Designs." These were comprised in sixteen articles. They upheld the new doctrines we have glanced at, but approved and subscribed the Westminster "Confession of Faith," asserting the new church's intention to worship as God and the Scriptures demanded, in accordance with the methods followed by some Presbyterians and Congregationalists.

Cotton Mather saw in the "Manifesto" "articles that utterly subvert our churches." His father and James Allen, representing the Second and First Churches, refused to join in a fast with the Fourth or Brattle Street Church, set up by the innovators. Higginson and Noyes of Salem also wrote to the new congregation a letter of reproof. But Willard of the Third Church, Stoughton, Sewall, and Cotton Mather himself,[57] drew up a basis

54. *MHS Coll.*, Series 5, v, 438.

55. For him, see E. Turell, *Life and Character of Benjamin Colman*, and the works cited in note 53, *passim*.

56. *The Manifesto Church*, p. 5; S. K. Lothrop, *History*, pp. 20ff.

57. W. Walker, *Creeds and Platforms*, p. 477; Lothrop, *A History*, pp. 28ff.; Quincy (*History*, i, 135, 136) takes the view that Cotton Mather played no part in the reconciliation. This conclusion, however, seems to have been caused by neglect of the records, as is shown by B. Wendell, *Cotton Mather*, p. 143n., and A. P. Marvin, *The Life and Times of Cotton Mather*, pp. 211ff.

of agreement and on January 31, 1700, all the Boston Congregational organizations joined Colman's flock in worship. Both Mathers preached.

To unite in one religious service with the "radicals" was not to endorse their principles. Increase Mather took good care that he was understood to do no more than conform to the need of maintaining harmony among Boston churches, for he published a thorough exposition of the arguments which he believed could be urged against the tenets held by Colman's friends. This was his "Order of the Gospel," "one of the most interesting, but at the same time controversial, tracts of Congregational history." [58]

He has been blamed for writing it. It has been called a masked battery against the Brattles, and has been held up as a proof of his lust for controversy.[59] It is hardly just to stop with such views. Mather, believing sincerely in the correctness of the Congregational methods which Colman wished to alter, had a choice between keeping silence without striking a blow in defence of his doctrines, and writing his views. If he chose the latter course, he might criticize Colman, Brattle, Pemberton, and the rest, and confine his censure to them and their theories, or he might sum up in one book the arguments against all the current suggestions for altering Congregationalism, without limiting himself to those espoused by the Brattle Street Church. This was what he did. He mentioned no names, he attacked no man's motives, but he pointed out in detail what he felt to be the most cogent reasons against the critics of the old methods. He could hardly have done less. As for his raising a masked battery against the Brattles, such phrases have no meaning. He raised a frankly hostile battery against the Brattles, Stoddard,[60] and other new-school Congregationalists, but he confined his discussion to their ideas. If, to-day, a man writes a book arguing against Christian Science, if an Episcopalian bishop argues for the divinity of Christ, if a Unitarian challenges certain evangelical doctrines, or if a nonconformist criticizes the English liturgy, he does no more than write of his convictions on matters he believes to be important. But, forsooth, if he attacks opinions, not men, and does not

58. W. Walker, *Creeds and Platforms*, pp. 477, 478. "The Order of the Gospel, Professed and Practised by the Churches of Christ in *New-England*, Justified, by the Scripture, and by the Writings of many Learned men, both Ancient and Modern Divines In Answer to several Questions, relating to Church Discipline." Boston, 1700.

59. Quincy, *History*, i, 138ff.

60. Cf. Walker, *Creeds and Platforms*, p. 281.

mention any of those who fail to share his views, he raises a masked battery. He is an intemperate controversialist, as surely as Mather was. The only way to escape the reproaches bestowed upon the author of the "Order of the Gospel" is never to put pen to paper in defence of any opinion with which any human being disagrees. Such a programme would result in harmony and also in complete intellectual stagnation.

Mather attacked no individual and was moderate in his criticism of doctrines. Such was, as we have seen, his usual method in religious debates. As early as 1662 he proved that he could write on problems about which he felt deeply, without overstepping the bounds of courtesy toward his opponents. When he turned to defend the Half-Way Covenant, he was careful in his references to those who disliked it. It was only in his political tracts, where Andros and Randolph were his targets, that he indulged in heated personalities.

His "Order of the Gospel" he dedicates to the churches of New England. He summarizes certain doctrines, corresponding in part to those of the "Manifesto," and declares that, if they are accepted, "we then give away *the whole Congregational cause at once, and a great part of the Presbyterian Discipline* also." [61] It is presumptuous for an individual church to inaugurate one of these new principles except with the consent of a synod, and "to design all or most of these *Innovations* at once, is certainly a *bold Attempt.*" "Shall we then by Silence betray the Truth?" he asks. He declares that the cause he defends is Christ's cause, and says: "I am . . . very sensible that *young Divines*, who have not Studied these *Controversies*, are apt to think, that what has been *Ordinarily professed and practised in the Churches* of *New England*, is *Novelty and Singularity*. It may in that respect be a Service to the Churches that something be written, which may be for the Information and Illumination of such, in *Questions* of this nature, by means whereof they may be the more fit to Serve the *Churches of God* wherever the Divine Providence shall see fit to dispose of them." Some of the third generation in New England lack the "Principles, Spirit, and Grace of their Fathers and Grandfathers." The college needs prayers, and faithful tutors who will "not Hanker after new and loose wayes." This one phrase savors of a direct personal reflection, inasmuch as Pemberton, Leverett, and Brattle had all been tutors at Harvard. Even so,

61. Epistle Dedicatory. Cf. Walker, *Creeds and Platforms*, p. 475.

it is hard to see how Mather could have spoken of the need for orthodox teaching at the college without attacking in some measure his erstwhile subordinates. The climax of his preface comes in as true a sentence as he ever wrote. "*The Congregational Church Discipline*, is not suited for a Worldly Interest, or for a *Formal Generation* of Professors. It will stand . . . as *Godliness in the Power of it* does prevail." [62]

Nothing in this preface smacks unduly of personal malice against anyone, and only one or two phrases can be twisted into criticism of any individual or group. The same tone is kept in the body of the book, which considers seventeen questions relating to certain changes in church practice.

To summarize the most important of his answers, which he drew from the Bible, as he interpreted it, and from learned writers, he declares that individual churches consist of "Saints and true Believers on Christ." Candidates for communion should ordinarily be examined, but "a rigid Severity in Examination is to be avoided . . . Yea, it were better, . . . to admit diverse Hypocrites than to keep out one Sincere Child of God from coming into the Church." Then, in one of the few bits of intemperate phrasing in the volume, he brands those who do not share his opinion as believers in "pernicious error." He admits that there is a difference between Congregational and Presbyterian procedure in deciding the fitness of applicants for communion, and inclines toward the Congregational theory, though he sees nothing in this question to cause any "breach of Amity or *Union*" between the two sects. He denies that it is necessary for persons admitted to a church to make a public relation of their conversion, but he asserts the right of any congregation to demand such an account of religious experience, orally or in writing, in any individual case. Here he agrees essentially with the "Manifesto," although he does insist upon the church's right to demand "public relations" when they seem necessary. He admits the lawfulness of reading Scripture without exposition or comment, but he maintains that a minister who continues to explain what he reads is deficient in no part of his duty.

On the subject of baptism, the largest issue in debate, he once more goes beyond moderate speech, stating that the view expressed in the "Manifesto" (although he does not mention where it appeared) "is Popish and Anti-christian." He does not believe

62. Epistle Dedicatory.

that ministers should be chosen by all of those who are to pay for their support. Most of his arguments here seem very weak, but the essential point he makes is that the divine's main duty is toward communicants, that he is responsible to them as the active members of the congregation, and that, therefore, to them belongs the right to elect their pastor. He advocates close relations between churches, so that new congregations may not be organized, or new ministers ordained, without "Common Consent." Not only the divines but the brethren of each church may vote in ecclesiastical councils. The "Essence of a Ministers Call consists in a mutual Election between him and his People," and no pastor should be ordained except as an officer of a particular church and, preferably, in the presence of his congregation. "To say that a *Wandring* Levite who has no Flock is a Pastor, is as good Sense as to say, that he that has no Children is a Father, and that the man who has no Wife is a Husband." Here was a barbed shaft, probably intended as such, cast toward Benjamin Colman, whose ordination had been highly irregular according to Mather's standards. Finally, referring to his own work in 1691, he says that Presbyterian and Congregational churches can and should "maintain Communion with one another." [63]

Such was the essence of Increase Mather's plea for the old Congregational standards as opposed to Stoddard, Colman, and the others who believed that to them had been vouchsafed an ability to interpret the Scriptures in a way unknown to earlier Puritans. He wrote the "Order of the Gospel" as an argument upon the questions under discussion, and the few passages we have quoted contain the only bits of abusiveness that he included in his book. He defended not only his own views, but those of most of his brethren; and it is worth remembering that he was not a voice crying in a wilderness: of the three original churches in Boston two, and part of the third, opposed the Brattles' doctrine. Noyes, Higginson, and the legislators of the state proved that they, too, had no illusions as to the coming of new prophets to Boston in the shape of Benjamin Colman and his friends.[64]

63. Pages 13, 19, 22, 23, 61, 72, 91, 102, 136.

64. C. Mather, in *Thirty Important Cases*, tells of a general meeting of ministers from various parts of Massachusetts, on May 27, 1697. The following vote was passed: "We Ministers of the Gospel, in the Churches of *New-England*, being made Sensible of the Tendencies, which there are among us, towards Deviations from the Good Order, wherein our Churches have according to the Word of the Lord Jesus Christ, been happily Established and Continued:

Do here Declare and Subscribe, our full Purpose, by the Help of our Great Lord, to

There was room, of course, for the Brattle Street Church to defend its position, and not all of Mather's arguments were unanswerable. The reply to him came in "Gospel Order Revived," published in 1700.[65] This deserves reading. There is a humorous tone in many of its pages, a satirical spirit, and an occasional passage of lampooning wit, which make it seem like a cool breeze in a desert of too arid Puritan theological writing. Had its graces and skill been turned to account solely in the interests of honest opinion on religious problems, it would be hard to resist. As it is, many paragraphs are more than adequate as an answer to Mather. Others fall short, and many fail to observe what he actually wrote. But on almost every page there are spatterings of personal animosity, hints of malice against Mather, and a tendency to discuss, not issues, but the motives of the President of Harvard, which still prejudice the effect of the reasoning. Mather is said to have "obtruded" his own doctrines upon the churches. There are hints as to his "secret aim." "We hope," the authors write, "he has no private Interest to bribe him in this Affair; and we hope for a like favourable and candid Construction of this Reply." Mather's book is a "faulty treatise." There is a jibe at his early disapproval of the Half-Way Synod's decision, and a hint that he joined Chauncy in writing the "Anti-Synodalia." This Cotton Mather denied, and for it no proof exists. "Its known there was *Anti-Synodalia* printed, and who had a hand in it, *and how modest his Dissent was*, and in what terms they contradicted what the Synod had established, tho' the like is criminal and insufferable in any other." [66]

The tone of this is typical of too much of the book, and its assertions are quite unfounded. It was hardly fair to reproach a

mentain [*sic*] in our several Places, the *Purity*, and *Fellowship*, and *Liberties* of our *Churches*, upon all those Principles, which we apprehend Essential to the Congregational Church-Discipline, hitherto Professed in these Churches. And, that we will in matters of Moment calling for it, mutually Advise, and Assist, and Hearken to, each other in the Lord."

This was signed by Increase Mather, William Hubbard, Charles Morton, James Allen, Samuel Torrey, Samuel Willard, Samuel Cheever, Moses Fiske, Joseph Estabrook, Jabez Fox, Jeremiah Shepard, Thomas Clark, Peter Thacher, and, Cotton Mather says, "many others."

The "Order of the Gospel" was in direct defence of the principles expressed in this vote.

65. "Gospel Order Revived, Being an Answer to a Book lately set forth by the Reverend Mr. *Increase Mather.* . . . *By sundry Ministers of the Gospel in* New-England. Printed in the Year 1700."

66. Preface.

man with defiance of a Synod after he had altered his views, and had publicly owned his conversion in two printed books. Moreover, even when Mather did oppose the Synod, his "Apologetical Preface" was nothing if not moderate in its expression. Assuming that his recital of erroneous doctrines in his preface to the "Order of the Gospel" was meant to summarize the "Manifesto," which it never professed to do, his critics attack him for garbling the Brattle Street Church's declaration. Other charges as to his misuse of quotations may be more just, but seem based only on the inevitable disagreement in interpretation which arises when any two men of different views attempt to apply a given writing to their own uses. Mather is accused of an effort to terrify his readers, he is blamed for his lack of brevity, and, with a sneer hardly suited to anything purporting to be a serious document in an important controversy, the authors remark, "he may mean well." [67] One of his arguments is called "a pitious stumble" and "so miserable an inconsequence" (p. 15). That politics was not quite forgotten appears in the comment that, as the new charter and laws were made by men, they may be undone by men; and there is a vague hint as to Mather's deficiencies in serving the colony in London. And, finally, we read: "Should the Author grow angry, it would but cause us to suspect (what a bundance of people have long obstinately believed) that the contest for his part is more for Lordship and *Dominion* than for *Truth*" (p. 36).

To suggest that Mather relied upon a sort of tyrannical influence exerted upon New England, there was included in the "Gospel Order Revived" a statement that the book could not be printed in Boston, because the printers there were so in awe of the reverend doctor as to dare to take nothing which reflected upon him. To this the Boston publisher to whom the Brattles had offered the manuscript promptly replied, denying the charge. With this answer Cotton Mather published a heated denunciation of the authors of the "Gospel Order Revived." They, in turn, replied once more, answering personal attack by personal attack, and reasserting their accusation that Mather's influence had made it impossible for their book to be printed in Boston.[68]

The affidavits offered on both sides are preserved. On some minor points they disagree, but one or two bits of fact seem un-

67. Preface, p. 2.
68. I. Thomas, *History of Printing*, i, 415ff.

shaken. These are, first, that Thomas Brattle and three other men connected with the new church were responsible for printing the "Gospel Order Revived," that they refused to divulge its authors' names, and that the printer dared not assume the responsibility of printing an anonymous attack on a prominent citizen without the sanction of someone in authority. He suggested that Stoughton's approval be sought; but to this the authors' representatives would not consent, though the lieutenant governor had been tolerant toward the Brattle Street Church. They refused to submit the book to him because, they said, this would be to inaugurate a new custom, and there was no reason why they should be discriminated against. This specious plea the printer exploded, by reminding them that Samuel Sewall had been quite content to have a book of his judged by Stoughton. For their main contention the Brattles could produce no proof. They were not able to show that Mather directly or indirectly prevented the publication of their book in Boston. Moreover, they revealed themselves as daring to attack only from the ambush of anonymity and afraid to submit their manuscript to criticism by an open-minded arbitrator. There was nothing glorious in their course, and their remarks as to Mather's influence on the press, however useful to their ends, were sadly deficient in truth.

Had Colman and his friends chosen to debate with attention to the problems involved and with the same lack of personality and bad temper shown by Mather, they might easily have won a hearing and, perhaps, support from fair-minded readers of to-day. But they chose a course which inevitably casts suspicion on their motives. Presumably their interest was in matters of church polity. They chose to defend their views by personal attacks on the man who had written his criticism of their opinions. They chose to ascribe evil motives to him, to make malicious innuendoes, and, not content with this, they sought refuge in anonymity, a protection commonly used in such cases only by cowards or those whose arguments are weak. Had Mather not signed his book, they might have been excused for answering it anonymously. He had not added his name to the political pamphlets he wrote in reply to anonymous critics of New England, but the Brattle party had not his excuse. Their views were seriously discussed by a minister who was not ashamed to sign what he wrote and they retaliated by seeking to smirch his character while they dodged responsibility for what they said. It is hard, in the face of this, to forget what grounds the two Brattles and Leverett had for personal bias. It is hard to shut out the thought that, as Mather had combatted their remaining in office at Harvard, they may have had spite as well as zeal for truth when they cast stones at him. Such suspicions may be unjust, but the fact remains that it was they who dragged the controversy down from the plane of serious theological discussion to the level of spiteful abuse by men who dared not own what they wrote.

Nor is it possible certainly to whitewash the Brattle party by saying that they fought, however ill chosen their weapons, for "liberality" as opposed to reactionary intolerance. When one considers the tenets of this or that creed, it is hard to draw a sharp line between progress and reaction. Is an Anglican illiberal because he believes in a liturgy? Is a Unitarian illiberal because he does not acknowledge the divinity of Christ? Was Mather illiberal because he believed that the Congregational Church in New England had adopted methods which accorded with truth? If those who propose change are always progressive, then the Brattles were progressives; but so was Jonathan Edwards when, years after Mather's time, he turned to a discipline stricter than that the conservatives urged in 1700, and so was Mather when he opposed John Wise, who was combatting changes in the conventional polity and wished to maintain the old standard. How we judge Mather, Wise, or Edwards depends on our own individual views as to what is right in regard to forms of worship. All three of these men defended the existing order against those who wished to change it, but their opponents urged only what had been before employed in ecclesiastical organizations and so were, if one wishes to think of them as such, reactionary. The Brattles, too, fought for practices which were not new, but had been tried in other churches before their time. Were they progressives or reactionaries? To Mather that was not the question. They seemed to him to be men who wished to introduce into the Congregational church a discipline not in accord with its best interests. That his fears were not unfounded is shown by the fact that their views, once adopted and logically developed, are said to have led to the formation of a new sect not Congregational at all.[69] Nor can we find any sure basis by which to judge of their liberalism. If an innovation in polity could be shown to work undeniably in the interest of better life and sincerer worship for

69. Cf. E. Pond, *Lives of Increase Mather and Sir William Phipps*, p. 124.

most men, we should call it "progress"; but there is nothing in the Brattle Street Church's programme which can unhesitatingly be thus classified. If it was on the side of "progress" because it made available for more people the chief sacrament of the church and thus was "democratic," then, by the same reasoning, Mather was more liberal than his opponents when he declared that church members, not ministers alone, had a right to vote in church councils and that the brethren as well as the elders should pass on the qualifications of candidates for membership. Neither the reading of the Scriptures without comment, nor using the words of the Lord's Prayer, were practices essential to human progress, and Mather maintained that, although neither was unlawful, neither was necessary for salvation.

It is safest to leave "liberality" and "reaction" aside when one discusses the religious movements of 1700. Neither term fits either party in the debate. Nor should we forget that the Brattle Street Church soon took its place in the orderly day-to-day Congregationalism of Boston, where its individual tenets were not generally influential, and that its minister, if he is to be hailed as a "liberal," must be so named only in 1700, for he promptly distinguished himself by his conservatism and joined a movement designed to prevent just such innovations as that which he had fostered.[70]

But, if we still like to think of the Brattles as "liberals," fighting a bigoted majority, we may regret the more that their enlightenment could find no weapon better than personal abuse, and that their method had to be so nearly that of the irate fishwife. If the "Order of the Gospel" was the voice of blind reaction, it is deplorable that it could be answered only by malicious hints, sneers, and political innuendoes, all discharged by hidden adversaries. For thirty-eight years Mather had been writing in Boston, and his expressed views had often run counter to those of other men, who had answered him. Except in political squabbles, where no higher standards than those of the man in the street were demanded or of use, he never attacked an opponent's motives or had his own called into question in such terms as the self-styled advocates of new religious purity and freedom chose in 1700. If we must see bigotry in the old Congregationalism, it is unfortunate that we have to remember that Richard Mather, John Davenport, Charles Chauncy, Richard Baxter,

70. W. Walker, *A History*, p. 201; *Creeds and Platforms*, p. 483.

and Increase Mather, all old-school Puritans, managed many quarrels over doctrine with no spiteful denunciation of the characters of their foes, while the Brattles, Pemberton, Leverett, and Colman preferred to deal in malicious hints and veiled slights, directed against the motives of their antagonists, and did not even banish certain half-truths which came dangerously near plain falsehood. It is more comfortable to believe that such methods were not those selected by "liberals," but that the whole debate was but one of those common in politics, civil and ecclesiastic, of all times. Such controverises seem fundamental when they are under discussion, but usually have little bearing on the ultimate progress of mankind. Mather saw the issue in 1700 as one which affected the purity of his church. Larger interests were not involved on either side and, whatever we think of the merits of the argument, we cannot fail to see that the Brattles were those whose cause suffered by the methods they condescended to use.

A greater man than Mather might have received their onslaughts in silence; but his temper was too short, and he felt that his cause was too good to be allowed to go by default. He threw off his clerical habit, and seized the first cudgel that came to hand. He had tried to discuss serious matters in a dignified fashion. His answer had been abuse. Now he gave rein to his tongue and said what he would have considered unfit for scholarly debate, had not his foes shown him that in this dispute no rules of courtesy were to be observed.

He wrote the preface to "A Collection of Some of the Many Offensive Matters Contained in . . . The Order of the Gospel Revived." [71] Therein he poured out his resentment in terms quite worthy of a friend of the Brattles. He remarks that "as yet no minister will own" the "Gospel Order Revived," but he quite directly charges Colman with its authorship. "One that is of the same Spirit with him, viz. *T. B.* has ventured to own himself to be the Publisher of that which is an heap of Rude, Unmannerly and Unmanly Reflections: who likewise in Print Scornfully styles HIS Praesident, *a Reverend Scribler*, and complains of his *Cantings* . . . A *Moral Heathen* would not have done as he has done." [72] So

71. "A Collection Of Some Of the Many Offensive Matters, Contained in a Pamphlet, Entituled, *The Order of the Gospel Revived.*" Boston, 1701. The book itself was by Cotton Mather (*MHS Coll.*, Series 7, vii, 378). He answered the anonymous attack by an anonymous reply, but Increase Mather signed the preface.

72. Preface. For the expressions used by Brattle in his public answer to the printer's statement, see I. Thomas, *History*, i, 418, 419.

much for Brattle, in whose case there was reason to suspect motives not solely religious. As for the supposed author: "I have thought it not worth the while for me to take notice of the impotent *Allatrations* of so little a thing as that *Youth* is." [73]

The whole controversy is summed up as follows (page 5):

"The Book of *The Order of the Gospel*, was written at the desire of many principal Persons, in our Churches, and as it is inoffensively written, advancing Principles, and Arguments, without a *Manifesto* once mentioned, So it maintained nothing but what is according to the Ancient *Platform*, and *Practise*, and most Venerable *Synods* of our *Churches*. But some Younger men (as we suppose, To prove, it seems, That there is no *Apostasy* from the Order of the Gospel, among them!) have published a Volumn of Invectives against that Book and the Author of it."

The body of the book was written by Cotton Mather, who followed the example set by "Gospel Order Revived," and did not sign it; but Increase Mather frankly endorsed the whole by writing the preface over his name. The method of answering the Brattles' work is to quote passages from it, with brief and acid comments as to the irreverence, impiety, apostasy, or what not, of its authors. It was a clever procedure, provided most of the readers of the reply were in sympathy with it; and that Cotton Mather wrote in the way he did showed that the majority of church members agreed with the original "inoffensive" opinions and not with the "invective" brought against them.

Colman was a strong man in many respects. He wrote well and had the courage to be a radical and then to become a conservative. In the interest of his reputation, an attempt has been made to protect him from the doubtful honor of having written "Gospel Order Revived." [74] But no charity can save Thomas Brattle, who took steps to publish the book, and refused to make its author known. His enlightenment as to witchcraft cannot relieve him from the reproach of having helped to change a religious controversy into a personal quarrel. He could have shown his "liberality" quite as well by the sort of argument used by Mather and his adversaries for nearly forty years, or by John Wise in his equally vigorous and incomparably more fair criticism of those who differed from him as to ecclesiastical government. It is unfortunate to be obliged to remember that Brattle

73. Preface.
74. Cf. A. P. Marvin, *Life and Times*, p. 219.

had a political axe to grind and that "Gospel Order Revived" dealt in the sort of denunciation which is perennially useful in politics.

It is even more prejudicial to our good opinion of him and his friends, that his name and that of his brother have come to be linked, traditionally at least, with Calef's "More Wonders of the Invisible World." [75] This was, as we have seen, a criticism of what had been done in the witchcraft trials, saying only what had been said before, not denying the reality of witches, proposing no way by which the clergy could have prevented the tragedy of Salem Village, but distorting the advice they did give and using the witch prosecution, Phipps's career, and the agency to England as convenient grounds upon which to assail the Mathers. If Brattle had anything to do with this book, it is peculiarly discreditable to him. To have written in 1692 a private letter praising Increase Mather's attitude as to the witch court, and then to countenance a book which hinted that he was not as enlightened as Brattle had admitted him to be, would be the acts of a man for whom truth mattered little when weighed against a desire for revenge upon political foes. Brattle had nothing to gain from Calef's "enlightenment." The latter's book, with all its merits, followed, not heralded a change in popular opinion. But politically it was well timed, for 1700 was the year when the attacks on Mather were most vigorous. It is noticeable, too, that Calef often deserts his ostensible purpose of discussing witchcraft, in order to introduce material useful for a political onslaught on Mather.[76]

This book, too, was promptly answered, this time by certain members of the Second Church.[77] They printed Mather's own defence of his agency, which more than meets the vague charges brought against him.

Thus we see that, in 1701, when he lost the presidency of Harvard and indignantly recorded in his diary his sense of the injustice done him, Increase Mather fell before odds too great for him. Frank and honest political opposition from Cooke, playing upon the people's dread of "royal tyranny," had turned them against the agent who had compromised with England. Thus had de-

75. Cf. S. G. Drake, *The Witchcraft Delusion*, ii, p. xxix.

76. Tradition asserts that Mather had Calef's book burned at Harvard. This statement is made repeatedly, as fact, but I have not been able to find any basis for it in the College papers, Sewall's diary, or any other contemporary record.

77. Cf. p. 312, note 72, *ante*.

veloped, in the form of insistence upon a resident leader for Harvard, a movement which made Mather's position at the college untenable. Couple with this the fact that he had long been a leader, that his son tried to continue his power with no sparing of his vocabulary in the attempt to impose his views upon others, and remember that some citizens came very naturally, in accordance with the inevitable tendencies of human nature, to long for the day when someone other than the two Mathers might control the church.[78] Join with such men others who had new theories about church discipline, and one sees how many groups, and how many differing opinions, Mather must have conciliated if he were to remain unchallenged. There were no large questions of general importance involved in the contest against him. The election of a new head for the college represented no change in policy, and was merely change, not progress.

Much has been said of Increase Mather's ambition.[79] Ambitious he surely was, if it be ambitious to hold strong beliefs and an invincible desire to see them influential among men. But as to ambition for high office or personal power, one cannot be so sure. He was intensely desirous to go once more to England as colonial agent. No doubt he remembered the honor he had received in London and longed for more; but it is no less than just to remember that he seems to have meant what he said when he declared that he was eager to go abroad in order to serve the colony. In this hope he was defeated, and New England never gained what he had planned to seek, until a royal governor, less scrupulous than his predecessors, cut the Gordian knot by incorporating the college by a method they had not considered legal.[80] As for ambition at Harvard, it is perfectly clear that Mather valued his office there less than many other things. He defied repeatedly the wishes of those in whose power his appointment lay, and as often he refused to compromise in order to keep his place. Nor was ambition the root of his refusal to leave Boston. His position there was in no danger. His daily attendance at his church was not necessary for his leadership. When, years later, he tried to resign, his congregation would not allow him to do so. He had no interests at stake, so far as greed for office

78. For hints of the existence of such a class, see *MHS Coll.*, Series 7, vii, 317, 318, 323, 338, 377, 380, etc.

79. Cf., for example, J. A. Doyle, *The Puritan Colonies*, ii, 331.

80. *Ibid.*, 467.

was concerned, except at Harvard, and there he revealed the utmost indifference toward strengthening his defences. If he was ambitious, it was because he longed to serve Harvard in England and to continue what he saw as the policy of keeping friendly relations between colony and mother country; because he was eager to have his sermons turn many to righteousness; because he doted on the activity he found in Boston; and because he was devoted to Congregationalism and the carrying out of God's will by doing practical work in the largest community which offered him a hearing. Thus far he was ambitious, thus far he was proud, and thus far he was selfish. Such ambition, pride, and self-seeking are less ignoble than the same vices less directly connected with a practical ideal that the greatest power is synonymous with the greatest opportunity to be useful.

So in 1701 Mather turned back to his church and his study, keenly alive to the sharpness of popular ingratitude, sorely distressed by the heretical tendencies of the time, and mourning for the better days he remembered as he looked back over his sixty years of life. He had little with which to reproach himself. He had been both wise and bold in the decisions he made for the colony during his agency; he had been unflinching in his determination to yield nothing essential to his faith; and he had never been willing to compromise when it seemed to him that truth was at stake. Politically he had made enemies: he had frankly combatted those ministers who departed from his standards, and he had refused to truckle to any party in order to save his personal prestige. He had been attacked by those who sought change, by those who considered themselves prophets of religious advance, by those who hated the new charter, and, alas, by those who had personal grudges to repay. They had secured a partial victory. Willard was a man who held no ideas differing essentially from Mather's. No great cause was served by his becoming the president of the college. All that was accomplished was that a man who had done more than any other New Englander of his time in the interests of his people, his college, and his church, was deposed from an office which he would not struggle to keep.[81]

81. In his *Autobiography* he wrote: "The college was, through the malice of Drs. Cooper & Byfield, put in to the hands of Mr. Willard ... which showed great partiality in the Court. Thus have I been requited by them for all the service I have endeavored to do for them, & for the College. But why should I think much of it, when Moses, yea, the Lord himself was ill-rewarded by those whom he had laid under infinite obligations of gratitude.... Doubtless there is not any government in the world that has been

Surrender was not yet. Increase Mather never dreamed of turning from the plough. In the twenty-two years which remained to him, he wrote more than in all his previous life. President of Harvard or private citizen, beloved agent or rejected public servant, admired man of affairs or mere parish minister, his energy was devoted unflaggingly to the carrying on of his life's object. No worldly concern mattered if he could bring one human being to share with him his mystical devotion to God and Christ, his intense and passionate vision of them as the most real elements of life, and his absorption in their service as the one enthralling opportunity for self-development. The Town-house might be full of his enemies, his seat at Harvard might be filled by another, and scurrilous pamphlets might attack him, but in his ardent devotion, deep faith, and continual zeal for service, was a realm beyond the reach of human foes.

Whatever his personal defeat, the political system he believed in continued. Cooke was ousted from office. The radicals in the Congregational fold soon adapted themselves to the existing order. All that he had worked for persisted. There remained still the great task of turning men and women toward godliness. Upon him and his brethren devolved the labor of keeping alive the old faith, and he never lived to see it disappear. That it was as widespread as it was, was largely due to him; that it should continue a force among men, was the object to which he dedicated his remaining years.

laid under greater obligations by a greater man than this government has been by me. Nevertheless I have received more discouragement in the work of the Lord, by those in government, than by all the men in the world besides. Let not my children put too much confidence in men. It may be such as you have laid under the greatest obligations of gratitude, will prove most unkind to them. I have often had experience of it."

CHAPTER XX

OLD AGE AND THE NEW CENTURY

INCREASE MATHER'S childhood fell in the days of Milton, and now, in his age, he was to be a pilgrim in the world of Addison, Swift, and Pope. Samuel Johnson was fourteen years old in 1723, and, in Boston, Benjamin Franklin had left boyhood behind before the old minister of the Second Church, whom he remembered throughout his life,[1] gave up his work. Queen Anne came to the throne in England in 1702, and George I in 1714. Mather died in 1723. He lived through nearly one quarter of the new century which followed that in which he had been the leader of Massachusetts.

His last twenty-three years contain no less incident, no less activity, and more literary production than any others of his life. Their significance is, however, much less. He touched no new literary note after 1701, and in only one respect did he step in advance of his generation and become what we should call an "eighteenth-century thinker." In his old age there were developed further traits already apparent in him; then were written more books of theology, scholarly by the standard of his time; but there are no hints of anything distinctly new in his character or thought. The period from 1701 to 1723 may, therefore, be left comparatively unnoticed, provided one remembers that it contained Mather's vigorous expression of his faith and his carrying out of what he saw as his task among men.

He was not the man to slip back into reveries upon the dear dead days. There were institutions which still claimed his labors, and, alas, quarrels which his hot temper prolonged. He had aspirations toward his old influence in politics. He found new interests to which he could devote a zeal unweakened by age. And, finally, there was an opportunity to brave popular opposition once more, this time in order to further a scientific movement of such importance in the world's history that its beginning remains one of the brightest pages in the story of eighteenth-century thought.

1. Letter of B. Franklin to Samuel Mather, May 12, 1784.

Mather drew sadness from his defeat at Harvard. He made a last effort to share in guiding the political destinies of Massachusetts. In this he may have been actuated in part by a desire to regain his command of the college, either directly or through his son; and the story of the attempt forms the least attractive side of his activity from 1701 to 1710. It was the final struggle of an old man to recapture what had been wrested from him by the inevitable changes of human interests and ambitions. It was a contest in which he was foredoomed to defeat, and thence came more bitterness, a greater sense of man's ingratitude, and a greater longing for the day when he might be released from this world, to enter one not ruled by human passions. Yet the great aims of his life, the preservation of active faith among men and the safeguarding of Congregationalism, were not lost. He never saw the complete disruption of the religious system which was the centre of his activity. He did not live to see New England desert the political foundation he had helped to establish. He led his generation, survived it, and died before its ideals were superseded.

After 1701, however, it is Cotton Mather, not Increase, who is to the fore. The son fought the father's battles. The latter, perforce, withdrew more and more to his study. This appears even as early as the time of the quarrel with Sewall, which followed Increase Mather's departure from Harvard. Cotton, hearing rumors which led him to feel that Sewall's speech in the Council had been hostile to the erstwhile president, took pains to announce that the sturdy old merchant had treated Increase Mather worse than a negro. Sewall, grieved and, perhaps, a trifle conscience-stricken, resorted to a gift of "a Hanch of very good Venison" as a peace offering. Neither this, nor earnest conversation at "Mr. Wilkins'," sufficed to end this dispute, and even Increase himself declared that some misfortune would surely overtake Judge Sewall or his family.[2] But the breach was healed when the Mathers had a chance to read exactly what had been said in the Council; and soon thereafter we find Sewall, in time of stress, calling for his old friend Dr. Mather as of yore. Their relations survived the shocks of 1701, fomented as they were by Cotton Mather's too great haste in believing the worst.

It was toward Joseph Dudley, once Puritan and pillar of the state under the old charter, now Anglican and servant of England

2. *MHS Coll.*, Series 5, vi, 43-45.

rather than of Massachusetts, and always the adroit politician, that the Mathers found most opportunity to display their partisanship. Dudley came to Boston, as governor, in 1702. He was greeted by Sewall and other good citizens, many of whom were his political enemies, who took care to pay the proper tributes to his good qualities.[3] With them joined Increase Mather, preaching a sermon in which he exalted Dudley's virtues and exhorted him to serve his country well.[4]

Two views of such a discourse are possible. It may be that its author, still eager to do what he might to safeguard Harvard and the state, or desirous of power for its own sake, truckled to Dudley without sincerely approving of him. Or it may be that Mather, as his son declared, believed that a New Englander was better than an Englishman for a governor in Massachusetts. He may have been willing to forgive Dudley's past shortcomings, believing sincerely that there had been true repentance. We know that he welcomed the new executive and may have favored his appointment. This does not give us a sure basis on which to judge motives.

Dudley had not changed his coat, and some of the tendencies which led to his imprisonment by his fellow citizens in 1689 were still dominant in him. The Mathers discovered this at once, and labored to repair the harm that one of them, at least, had done in advocating Sir Joseph's promotion to the governorship. It has been said that Cotton Mather secretly opposed Dudley, while publicly he flattered him.[5] The same charge is not easily proved in the case of Increase. He had little to do with the governor after he took office, and the only evidence that there was a "selfish inconsistency" in the old divine's acts is that, on many points, he shared his son's views. All we can be sure of is that, after he had accepted Dudley, Increase Mather awoke to the faults still uncured in the new governor and opposed him by such means as he could, refraining meanwhile from any public announcement of his attitude. Perhaps this was base and hypocritical. Perhaps it was but prudence and the duty of a good citizen not to hasten too quickly to denounce a legally appointed representative of the crown. Perhaps Mather's course was dictated by a selfish hope

---

3. *MHS Coll.*, Series 5, vi, 57, 58.

4. In his *The Excellency of a Publick Spirit*, Boston, 1702. Cf. Quincy, *History*, i, 152.

5. Cf. *MHS Coll.*, Series 5, vi, 30.*

that, if Dudley were not antagonized, the old government of the college might be restored; or, quite as probably, he may have chosen his position because he did not wish to stir up further the existing dissensions between the Brattles, Leverett, and Pemberton, favored by Dudley, and himself.

The governor, soon after his arrival in Boston, went to see Cotton Mather. There he got a piece of good political advice, which has been often unjustly interpreted. Mather told Dudley not to let it be supposed that his acts were dictated by Byfield, Leverett, and their followers, or by the two ministers of the Second Church. That he advised a course controlled neither by himself nor his father, nor by their foes, speaks well for his wisdom and disinterestedness. The governor, however, informed Leverett and Byfield that he had been warned against them. Naturally they grew hot against Cotton Mather, and he against that "wretch," Joseph Dudley.[6]

In the next year Increase Mather expressed his opinion of the new executive, not publicly in Boston, but in a letter to the Earl of Nottingham.[7] He wrote:

The Generality of People throughout the Province have not the Love for the present Govern^r Mr Dudley that were to be desired. The old prejudices occasioned by his former mismanagements are revived. And his Conduct since his being Govern^r has in divers Instances been very dissatisfactory to those that have been his best friends.

Prudent men with us cannot but think that it would conduce much for the Interest of her Majesties affairs in the Province, as well as be for the happiness of her Subjects here, might they have a Govern^r that should have the Love of the People, the Consideration whereof I humbly leave with Yo^r Lordships wisdom.

Now we are asked to believe that Mather hoped to use Dudley in the service of his personal desires, and that his hostility to the governor was dictated by his failure of his hopes for renewed influence at Harvard. These hopes, if he had them, were not defeated for several years after the letter just quoted was written. There we find him urging a successor for the man whom, we are told, he was eager to conciliate in order to make him the tool of private ambition.

Meanwhile at Harvard the two Brattles had regained office. In 1707 Willard died, and there can be no doubt that the question

6. *MHS Coll.*, Series 1, iii, 137.　　　7. *Col. Soc. Pub.*, xix, 155.

of who was to succeed him interested the Mathers deeply. It is probably not unsafe to guess that Cotton had hopes for himself, and his father for him. But, actually, John Leverett, old foe of the Mathers, was elected president. He had eight votes, Increase Mather had three, and Cotton Mather but one. That the elder Mather, sixty-eight years old, could still win more than one fifth of the votes cast, testified that his power had not entirely gone.[8]

Before this election at Harvard, there had appeared in England a pamphlet directed against Dudley. It contained all the things that Cooke, Sewall, and the rest of the governor's foes would have liked to say, and raked up every charge against Sir Joseph. Almost certainly Cotton Mather had a hand in it, as in a second pamphlet which followed Dudley's answer to the first.[9] All we need remember is that Cotton Mather, and not Increase, seems to have been associated in this excursion into pamphleteering. Dudley, in referring to the attack, spoke only of Cotton Mather, and it does not seem possible to prove that Increase had any connection with the affair.[10] Perhaps he sympathized with what Cotton did; perhaps he questioned his course, as he did on a more personal matter.[11] All we can be sure of is that Increase Mather, whatever his motives, after consistent opposition to Dudley, may have advocated his becoming governor, certainly welcomed him, and, immediately after he began to serve, saw that he had not reformed, and schemed to oust him. It seems probable, too, that outwardly Mather was deferential to the governor, though he had little to do with him. The office Dudley held deserved respect, and he was the emissary of the queen. For a minister to attack him publicly would be neither polite nor safe.

But in 1707, after Leverett had been elected president of Harvard, after Dudley had retreated from his former assertion that the old college charter was dead and had put it into force once more, thus preventing any "reform" in its constitution such as might be desired by Mather and his brethren,[12] both Cotton and Increase were restrained no longer by official courtesy or prudence. Both wrote sharp letters to Dudley, accusing him of a variety of crimes, many of which he had not committed, but all of which were popularly laid at his door. Increase Mather's

8. Quincy, *History*, i, 156.
9. For the pamphlets, see *MHS Coll.*, Series 5, vi, 29*-131.*
10. *Ibid*, 200.
11. *Ibid.*, 81.*
12. Quincy, *History*, i, 159, 201.

letter has been called "vituperative." It is hardly that. It is a frank and harsh recital of Dudley's faults as the writer saw them, but it is guardedly phrased and its tone was not improper for the admonition of a pastor to one of his flock. Not rancor or vituperation but stern rebuke is its dominating note. Cotton's shows a more intemperate vocabulary, and infinitely more heat. The difference of the two Mathers in nature and in age appears nowhere more clearly than in these letters.[13]

To write them was a foolish move. Dudley made the obvious retort, asking why, if he was such a sinner, he had not been told of it before, and hinting that the defeat of the Mathers' hopes at Harvard lay back of their outburst. Probably it did, and if so, we must charge Increase Mather with one more hasty piece of imprudence arising from his quick temper and the sharp disappointment he felt at the coming of further perils to New England orthodoxy.

From now on there could be no reconciliation between Dudley and the Mathers. He wrote that he was pursued by them, and they seem to have written and schemed in an effort to replace him by Sir Charles Hobby or any other candidate less likely to favor the innovators in religion and education.[14] In 1709 Sir Henry Ashurst wrote Increase Mather, telling him that there was reason to hope for a new governor. It is interesting to find that he also said: "I hope you will use yr endeavors by an Act of yr Assembly to settle yt University upon so sure a foundation yt it shall not be in the power of any succeeding Govr to defeate ye religious designs of founders & benefactors, but that it may be a nursery of religion and godlinesse. The finishing of this noble work will well become you, as the last act of yr life; and if the Lord spare me my life, I shall make it my businesse to gett it confirm'd here."[15]

This sums up the Mathers' views as to the college, as well as showing that they were shared abroad. It also makes it unnecessary for anyone to assume personal ambition as the mainspring of Increase Mather's course toward Dudley, his foes at Harvard, and the innovators in the church. It is quite as easy, and quite as just, to believe that his stand was determined by what he, his brethren, and such men as Ashurst, saw as the need of preserving valuable traditions and protecting the interests of the alumni of, and donors to, Congregational Harvard.

13. *MHS Coll.*, Series 1, iii, 126ff.   14. *Ibid.*, Series 6, v, 163, 173, 199.
15. *Ibid.*, 199.

Whether his motives were good or bad, Mather's political power had gone, and his letters did not affect the course of affairs. Perhaps he became impatient at the little success Sir Henry Ashurst had in England, for he seems to have turned on him in a sharp letter of criticism.[16] This did not permanently affect their friendship, however, and they continued to correspond as to the state of public affairs.

As his political interests resulted in quarrels, so the old animosities did not die away. Colman was criticized by some of his flock for being too docile in his relations with the Mathers,[17] and Pemberton found plenty to do in making known that he for one did not forget the bickerings of 1700.[18] One remembers Sewall's immortal description of how "Mr. Pemberton with extraordinary Vehemency said, (capering with his feet) If the Mathers order'd it, I would shoot him thorow. I told him he was in a passion. He said he was not in a Passion. I said, it was so much the worse." [19]

On the other hand we find Mather, nearly twenty years after he left Harvard, speaking well of William Brattle.[20] Year by year he grew less active in current controversies, and thus he came to be more tolerant in his attitude toward those of his neighbors who once had differed from him.

In general church affairs he continued active. His books expressed his views on important questions of the day and he joined in the "Proposals" of 1705, thus linking himself with a movement which sought to change the old style Congregationalism. It came to nothing, partly because of the trend of the times, and especially because, in John Wise, the innovators met a conservative who excelled them all in the brilliance with which he defended the old order. Curiously enough he, who fought for the former method of church government, seems to-day the progressive, though, in his time, his views were toward rigid conservatism. The Mathers, Colman, and the others who joined in advocating the proposals, sought to strengthen the government of the church, and so to protect religion against the new ideas of the times. That they failed was a testimony to the strength of the pristine Congregational theory.[21]

16. *MHS Coll.*, Series 6, v, 216. 17. *Ibid.*, Series 3, v, 189.
18. *Ibid.*, Series 5, vi, 213.
19. *Ibid.*, p. 291.
20. J. L. Sibley, *Biographical Sketches*, iii, 201, 202.
21. W. Walker, *History*, pp. 202ff., and *Creeds and Platforms*, pp. 483ff.; H. M. Dexter, *Congregationalism*, pp. 491ff.

Mather opposed publicly the doctrine taught by George Keith,[22] an episcopal missionary who came over with Dudley,[23] once more showing a curious stupidity if his aim was to flatter the governor in the service of his own ends. His opposition was on doctrinal points, and that he was not aiming towards the old scheme of having no churches but Congregational, is conclusively brought out by his presence and preaching at the ordination of a Baptist minister in Boston.[24] He was interested in the Jew, Judah Monis, and wrote a preface to one of his books.[25] On the other hand, he expressed himself with heat when part of his own church separated to form a new congregation, not hostile in principles, but desirous of more space in which to worship.[26]

There is no doubt, too, that Mather was sincerely interested in the progress of Yale College. Certainly he had nothing to do with the inauguration of the plan which established it, but his advice was sought.[27] He suggested some means by which economy could be secured, advocated that ministers should be overseers, inveighed against public Commencements, hinted at the dangers to be feared from the civil government, and stated his belief that in the new college "ye welfare of yor Colony & Posterity is greatly concerned." To him, as to many others, Yale seemed likely to replace Harvard as the fountainhead of Congregationalism.[28] That it did not long remain as orthodox as its founders wished, was a sore blow.

There is some possibility that Cotton Mather tried to divert the bounty of Hollis from Harvard to Yale.[29] If so, it shows no

22. In his "Some Remarks On a late Sermon, Preached at *Boston* in *New-England*, By *George Keith*, M. A." Boston, 1702. Cf. *Religious History of New England*, p. 218.

23. *MHS Coll.*, Series 5, vi, 58.

24. I. Backus, *A Church History*, ii, 50.

25. *MHS Proc.*, lii, 292.

26. C. Robbins, *History*, pp. 65, 66; *MHS Coll.*, Series 3, v, 215. In *Autobiography* Mather wrote: "The year 1713 has been troublesome on occasion of a new meeting house, which some desired might be built in the north end of Boston. I declared that if they would set their meeting house in a place convenient for the prosperity of their end of the town, I would not only consent, but contribute to them towards it, & would do all for them that a father could do for his children. . . . At the same time I told them that if they set it in a place spoken of, too near the other meeting house, I would have nothing to do with them. Some of them that came to me in the name of all the rest, promised me they would not do it if grievous to me. Nevertheless, they do it. I am persuaded that a blasting from God will be upon them, first or last."

27. Cf. E. Oviatt, *The Beginnings of Yale*, chap. 4. Mather's letter, printed in F. B. Dexter, *Documentary History of Yale University*, pp. 6, 7, makes it clear that his advice was asked *after* the plan was under way.

28. Cf. Oviatt, *op. cit.*, chap. 5.   29. Quincy, *History*, i, 227ff.

more than that his interest was in no college as such, but in the spread of what he saw as good education. Whatever his attempts upon Hollis may have been, and however they seem to us, judging from our modern point of view of loyalty to one university in and for itself, we should remember that Increase Mather does not seem to have been involved in his son's active proselyting for Yale. The father is, however, accused of having fomented dissension at Harvard to discredit its administration.[30] Perhaps he did wish to bring disgrace upon his successors; perhaps he acted because he felt the issue was one of right and wrong; and perhaps he did no more than exert the prerogative of alumni in all generations, and asserted his right to tell the leaders of Harvard how it should be administered.

With Stoddard he debated in print the old question of baptism.[31] He joined his son and son-in-law in furthering singing at church,[32] he continued to work for the Indians,[33] and he aided in keeping up, year by year, a steady influx of new members to the Second Church.[34] It was to him that Michael Wigglesworth wrote, urging that some redress be made for the injuries done to innocent persons in the witchcraft prosecution.[35] That he was chosen as the man who should take up the matter with the brethren and with Dudley shows that he was, at once, not quite without influence and not suspected of favoring all that the Salem Court had done. Samuel Sewall, who found Cotton Mather often a trying neighbor, was consistent in his devotion to Increase. In 1719 we find him sending the old divine a ring, "as a Token of Thankfullness and Respect." [36] From his brother's widow, in London, Mather received a legacy of twenty-five pounds,[37] and from "Mrs. Mary Edwards" he had a similar bequest of five pounds.[38] In 1718 he made his own will. It is not only a legal document but a statement of faith, and deserves reading aside

30. Cf. Sibley, *Biographical Sketches*, iii, 187.

31. *Ibid.*, ii, 118, 119; *The New Englander*, iv, 350ff.; Walker, *Creeds and Platforms*, p. 282, and *A History*, pp. 180–182.

32. *The Second Church in Boston. Commemorative Services*, pp. vii–viii.

33. Cf. J. W. Ford, *Some Correspondence*, pp. 83ff., 95ff., and *MHS Coll.*, Series 6, v, 347, 355.

34. The number of new members added during these years was 338. This figure I have taken from a manuscript now in the possession of the Second Church.

35. *MHS Coll.*, Series 4, viii, 645.

36. *Ibid.*, Series 6, ii, 103.

37. *New England Historical and Genealogical Register*, xlv, 296.

38. His receipt for this is in the Haverford College Library.

from the information it contains. Cotton was the chief heir, and young Mather Byles, to become a famous wit and a delightful figure in the annals of Revolutionary Boston, was, as Mather's grandson, to have a fourth part of the estate, provided he entered the ministry. And at the end we read: "I do hereby signify to my executor that it is my mind & will y^t my Negro servant called [Speedgood?] shall not be sold . . . but I do . . . give him his liberty." [39]

Thoughts of death held no terror for him. Year by year he came more and more to feel that his work for God upon earth was done, and that the grave was the gateway for his entry to eternal peace. That he was weary is not to be wondered at. He was eighty years old in 1720. His "ephialtes" tormented him, and more serious physical ailments gave him hours of pain.[40] Nor had his last years been marked by success. If, in his church, the wounds of 1700 were healing, and no new changes seemed to threaten seriously, if his writing went well and each year added to the number of his publications, he had failed politically, and, we may think, he had been unwise in the steps he took. He had not conquered his temper, and, whether he wrote to reprove in good set terms a neighbor who seems to have delighted in malicious gossip,[41] or indulged in what Sewall called "plain home-dealing" [42] with Dudley, he proved that the quick anger, known to Randolph and the Committee on Trade and Plantations, had not weakened with years. And in a single event of 1714 there was sorrow enough to explain many melancholy hours.

In 1714 his wife died. For more than fifty years she had shared his work, and if we can be sure of anything, we can be sure that the union had been one of unbroken faith and love. Now, if ever, a reliance upon some power greater than those of earth was needed to carry him through his bereavement. Nor was he at a loss as to where to look for it. Speaking of his wife he said, "the Lord has now taken away that Blessing, I yet say, Blessed be the Name of the Lord. And as *David* said of his Dead child, so say I concerning my Dear Dead Consort, I shall go to her; (I trust in Christ that it will not be long first) but she shall not return to me. *Let the Will of the LORD be Done.*" [43]

39. New England Historical and Genealogical Register, v, 447.

40. *Autobiography.*   41. *American Antiquarian Society Proceedings*, xiv, 313, 314.

42. *MHS Coll.*, Series 5, vi, 212.

43. I. Mather, "A Sermon Concerning Obedience & Resignation to the Will of God in Every Thing. Occasion'd by the Death of that Pious Gentlewoman, Mrs. *Mariah*

INCREASE MATHER IN OLD AGE

In 1715 Increase Mather married Ann Cotton, widow of his nephew John Cotton of Hampton.[44] She was the daughter of an old friend,[45] and a member of his church.[46] She can never have filled the place Maria Mather's death had left, but her devotion may have brought some consolation to the old man.

Not all of his last years were given up to defeat, disappointment, sickness, and bereavement, nor did they ever conquer his spirit. It would be easy for such troubles as he underwent to make most men mere bitter contemners of the world. And, as one reads his autobiography, one finds there the heart of a man who had his hours of sadness, his moments of wrath, and tasted often the gall of disappointed hopes. He longed for England, probably, though he knew he was too old to go; he longed for the spirit his father found in the colony, but he must have realized how irrevocably it had gone. Yet he did not repine. He found that he had many causes for thanksgiving, and duly wrote them down. He found solace for woes in long hours at his desk; he found peace in devotion to study, to prayer, and to writing. And constantly he cherished the vision of a life to come and of the realization of those dreams which had made life livable for him — his dreams of God and Christ.

So in his age we see the climax of more than one side of his activity and his character. Then was his greatest literary productiveness, then his tolerance found its strongest concrete expression, and then his vices — temper, zeal for political intrigue, and longing to check the free development of men's religious institutions by narrowing and organizing the group which controlled them — all found a chance to reveal themselves. So also the faith that sustained him from boyhood flowered fully in making him meek in the face of adverse fate. And, finally, in one stroke he was able, when he was eighty years old, to show that his broad interests had served him well and to take his place with scientific liberals of the eighteenth century.

Cotton Mather, one remembers, did valiant work in introducing inoculation for smallpox into the colonies.[47] For his pains

Mather, Late Consort of *Increase Mather*, D.D. Who Entred into her Everlasting Rest, on the Lords Day, *April*. 4. 1714." Boston, 1714. See also *Autobiography*.

44. Cf. J. L. Sibley, *Biographical Sketches*, iii, 5. She was fifty-two years old in 1715.
45. Captain Thomas Lake.   46. C. Robbins, *History*, p. 239.
47. See G. L. Kittredge, Introduction to the Cleveland, 1921, reprint of I. Mather, *Several Reasons, etc.*, and *MHS Proc.*, xlv, 446, 447, 470, 471; *MHS Coll.*, Series 1, ix, 275.

he got criticism. The populace was not ready for the advance which the Puritan clergy favored, and the people's dislike for intellectual tyranny from the elders expressed itself in a bomb hurled into the window of the younger Mather's house. The advocates of inoculation are the more to be praised because they were ahead of current thought in Boston, and because experience of later generations seems to have confirmed their wisdom. That Cotton Mather, Colman, and other men, in their youth or middle age, took up the movement, is much to their credit, but they should normally have been more in touch with the latest science than a man whose career spanned sixty years of the seventeenth century, and whose age might have exempted him from the responsibility of keeping up with current medicine. But we have seen Mather's interest in science and his practical view of his mission. If science could save life, it mattered not how new its doctrine or how unpopular. Mather never feared the mob, and hastened to do his share in the war of pamphlets which marked the coming of a new and beneficent medical reform to Massachusetts.

In this is the final answer to the charge that he was of the seventeenth century alone, that he was a myopic theologian, the foe of science and blind to progress, and the proof that his mind was so broad and so active, even after he had lived for some years in a troublous world, that he could plunge eagerly into a new warfare for the service of mankind. When he was seventy years old, he wrote, excusing himself from undertaking new public office: "That which was a Recreation to me formerly, is now a Burden.... I may now rationally expect Liberty and Rest. Nothing suiteth with my Age so much as Retirement and Rest." [48] Yet, ten years later, his spirit was brave enough to carry him once more into the arena, there to do battle for the saving of human life.

It is pleasant, too, to remember that as the vague scientific questing of his younger days developed into a definite service to his countrymen in his age, they did their part for him by offering to fulfil for their old leader one of his dearest dreams. In 1715 the churches sought to send Mather on an embassy to England.[49] Nothing could have gratified him more. Nothing speaks more eloquently as to the sway he still held in the hearts of good church-goers in Boston. But there is pathos, too, in the thought that

48. *MHS Coll.*, Series 6, i, 394.   49. *Autobiography; Parentator*, p. 194.

opportunity came too late. He was too old, too determined to end his life quietly, and too resigned under disappointment and defeat, to be stirred even by the chance to see once more his beloved England. He was content to stay in Boston, there to dream of London while he lived out the little span of life which remained to him.

"To preach constantly at fourscore, and to so large an audience, and without notes, is a rare example, and scarcely to be found in history," declared one of his friends in England.[50] His was a "bright, wise, strong old age." [51] His efforts to resign from his pulpit were vain, and his congregation begged him to continue.[52] But after 1720 he began to realize the weight of his years. "Be sure, you don't pray, that you may Live beyond Fourscore!" was his counsel to his son.[53] In 1722 bad news came from New Haven, where there were events which seemed to herald Yale College's falling away from the old faith. The shock and his weakness were too much for Increase Mather. He never left his house again.[54] But even in his last months he talked of Congregational and Presbyterian unity, and expressed his belief that Boston would survive as a godly town. He saw no "settled good times" on earth until the second coming of Christ, and reasserted once more his belief in the religion of early New England. Most of all he warned against a "Lifeless Religion" and an "Irreligious Life." [55]

At the end of 1722 "he was extremely tortured and enfeebled with an obstinate *Hicket*." [56] Sometimes he was delirious, and sometimes mental tortures came with the fear that he might not be saved. He called to have the seventy-first psalm read to him again and again; and bade his son pray for him that he might "do good while he lived, and Honour Christ in his death." To Hollis he sent the message that he was going to the land of the living, for "this Poor World is the Land of the Dying." [57] His

50. J. Belknap, *History*, iii, 344.
51. *Parentator*, p. 196.
52. C. Robbins, *History*, p. 64.
53. *Parentator*, p. 200.
54. *Ibid.*, (p. 201) says that Mather's illness was largely due to an account of recent happenings at New Haven. In *MHS Coll.*, Series 2, iv, 297, there is a letter to the Mathers, dated September 25, speaking of the growth of episcopacy at Yale. The connection is obvious.
55. *Parentator*, pp. 201–203.
56. *Ibid.*, p. 207.
57. *Ibid.*, p. 209.

pain grew more severe, and when Sewall came to see him on July 30, he found him "agonizing and Crying out, Pity me! Pity me!" Sewall writes "I told him God pity'd him, to which he assented and seem'd pacify'd." [58]

On Friday August 23, a "Sacramental Lecture" was held in Boston. In the eighteenth-century town, the centre of New England, still far from the city we know to-day, but with changes on every hand, which would have impressed Richard Mather, faithful Congregationalists gathered to hear Mr. Thacher preach. No one of them can have lived to forget the thrill of startled emotion that ran through the audience when from the pulpit they were told that the oldest and greatest of the New England divines had died that noon.[59]

He died in Cotton Mather's arms. In his agony, his son gave him strength by reading the Scriptures, throughout his life his inexhaustible source of comfort in all the struggles of this world. As he grew weaker with each spasm of pain, Cotton said, "This Day thou shalt be in Paradise. Do you Believe it, Syr, and Rejoice in the Views and Hopes of it?" And, knowing his work was done, and mercifully relieved from the sense of his own unworthiness that had tormented him before, the old man found it in his heart to say with his dying breath, "I do! I do! I do!" [60]

58. *MHS Coll.*, Series 5, vii, 325, 326.
59. *Ibid.*, 326.
60. *Parentator*, p. 210.

CHAPTER XXI

INCREASE MATHER

MATHER'S was a "Greater *Funeral*, than had ever been seen for any *Divine*, in *these* . . . parts of the World. The Honourable, *William Dummer*, Esq; who was then lieutenant Governour and Commander in Chief; and his Honourable, Ancient, Cordial Friend, *Samuel Sewall*, Esq; the Chief Judge, of the Province; with the Præsident of the College," John Leverett, "Mr. Peter Thacher of Milton, Mr. Wadsworth," and "Mr. Colman" were "they that held the Pall; Before which, One Hundred and Three-score *Scholars* of the College, whereof he had once been the *Præsident*, walked in Order." There "were a vast number of Followers and Spectators," among them "about Fifty *Ministers* . . . All with an *Uncommon sadness* in their Countenance." [1]

So, on August twenty-ninth, 1723, Mather was buried beside his first wife "in the North burying place" on Snow Hill. The funeral procession passed the North Meeting House, the child of his own church, "and so up by Capt. Hutchinson's and along by his own House," with its deserted desk in the lonely, book-lined study, "and up Hull-Street," [2] to the burying-ground, whence those who followed his coffin could look over the green fields of a country town and the blue water of the river toward the villages of Charlestown and Cambridge. "The vast number att his funeral" [3] saw in the pall-bearers their governor and other prominent men of their Boston, and we should not forget that among them was Leverett, Mather's old foe, Colman, who had tasted the bitter rebukes the erstwhile president could give, and who himself had been by no means respectful to the Mathers, as well as faithful old Samuel Sewall, and the younger leaders in piety, Thacher and Wadsworth. Old quarrels had passed. Old differences were reconciled. In 1723 neither Leverett nor Colman could fail to do honor to a man who had served as well as man could serve. They had breadth to forgive private disputes, in order to do honor to Mather's high qualities; and Cotton Mather

1. *Parentator*, pp. 211, 212; *MHS Coll.*, Series 5, vii, 326.
2. *Ibid.*
3. *New England Historical and Genealogical Register*, xv, 199.

knew that the old man who used to delight in his last years in the thought that Bostonians were to him "a Loving People" [4] would rejoice that his forgiveness of his enemies should be marked by their being asked to join the friends about his grave.

Throughout New England ministers preached funeral sermons for the lost leader. Foxcroft, Cotton Mather, and Colman did the same office in Boston, and for more than two months the neighboring ministers took turns each week in preaching condolence to the Second Church.[5]

Surely, if he had lived, Willard would have joined the mourners. Surely Cooke would have done so, had he not died in 1715. He was a clean fighter, and a sincere lover of his country. He hated Mather's political views, but he never descended to the point where he attacked his rival's motives or character, and he would have been the first to wish to share in reverencing the best in the man whom he had fought.

In England Boyle, Baxter, Howe, and Nathaniel Mather were dead, but there were still men, nobles and commoners, to whom the latest news from Boston brought some personal sense of loss. They read in *The British Journal* that there had "died the Reverend Dr. *Increase Mather*, in the 85th Year of his Age, after a Life of many Years Service in *England* and *Ireland*, as well as in *New England*, and of many Sufferings, by a painful Sickness, in which he languished a long Time, before he expired. He was born at *Dorchester*, *June* 21, 1639, and signalized himself in many Publick Appearances; but especially in the Agency for his Country in the British Court, and as President of *Harvard-College*. He was Minister of the old *North-Church* at Boston 62 Years." [6]

We need little other reminder of his position in the eyes of his contemporaries. They knew him as the man who had written most, and had been most widely read, in New England, for fifty years of its history. They saw his work as "practical" and "seasonable," and they bought it year by year as each new volume came out. They knew that he was read abroad, that books of his were printed in England, in Scotland, in Holland, and translated into Dutch, German, French, and Indian. They would have been at a loss to find any American of his generation more worthy to be called a literary leader.

4. *Parentator*, p. 221.
5. *Ibid.*, pp. 212, 218ff.; B. Colman, *The Prophet's Death*. Boston, 1723.
6. *The British Journal*, Oct. 19, 1723.

INCREASE MATHER'S HOUSE AS IT WAS IN THE NINETEENTH CENTURY

A man who neither shared all his beliefs, nor was content to follow wherever he led, one who had joined in reviling him and had been sharply censured in his turn, spoke of Mather in terms which are doubly precious to us, because they give us the estimate of a man who knew him, and, at the same time, of one who was by no means prejudiced in his favor. Benjamin Colman said, of his learning:

He loved his study to a kind of excess; and in a manner lived in it from his youth to a great old age; where he gave himself to reading and doctrine; for he especially studied his Bible, and was mighty in the Scriptures; with which he began and ended; while, for sixty years together, he made himself master of all the learning of past ages, or that was passing in his own times, that was needful to furnish out an accomplished Divine.

A most excellent preacher he was, using great plainness of speech, with much light and heat, force and power. . . . He was very happy in his method, which was always distinct and perspicuous. . . . At the same time, there was a vein of learning and argument running through these laboured and plain discourses, which was a sufficient entertainment for the strongest and most curious (but serious) mind. . . . It was a soul-searching ministry. . . . His face as well as words were enough to teach and constrain devotion.[7]

His public services were recognized, and his contemporaries knew that no other American had performed any such diplomatic service as his. He had been the unquestioned leader of his people for more than half a century, always in the church, often in politics, and invariably in those human affairs where the example of a strong and active life can be made to count. "But what is more than barely to preach Christ Jesus the Lord, your excellent pastor lived here in the flesh by the faith in Him, in a holy conformity to His blessed life and law."[8] Once more Colman spoke justly, forgetful of personal prejudice, and recorded for us the estimate of those with whom Increase Mather lived.

Nor need we go further for a general summing up of his place among his fellow men, than another paragraph of Colman's:

He was the patriarch and prophet among us, if any could be so called: a holy man, and a man of God, holding fast the faithful word, and holding forth the word of life. . . . The prophets of old were sober,

---

7. W. B. Sprague, *Annals*, i, 158 (quoted from Colman).   8. *Ibid.*

grave, wise, virtuous, thoughtful, solid and judicious men, as well as devout and gracious. . . . In these respects truly the signs of a prophet of God were upon him. He had also the courage, zeal and boldness of a prophet in what he judged and esteemed to be the cause of God, his truth, his worship and his holiness.

Such words we shall hear applied to Mather, so long as we stay in the seventeenth century, delighting in the fresh green of Snow Hill, breathing the clear air of a country seaport, and rejoicing in the space and neatness of the community spread before us. But, when we give up this, and the stifling intellectual atmosphere we are taught to believe existed in the Boston of 1700, for our own Boston with its smoke, noise, crowds, foreign languages, and liberty, measured by modern tests, what shall we say then of our old friend Increase Mather, who is now no more than a dingy canvas portrait on the wall of a museum? Glad as we may be to exchange a town of native English and American for a city of many partially digested nationalities, shall we part without a pang from the old man who once knew New England and its people in such a way as to find the key to leadership in its counsels and their hearts? Shall we give up a country of traditions and venerated institutions, bad sanitation, high ideals, and strong leaders, for one which rejoices in the new, the untried, the progress it has made in the art of living, its freedom to think anything or nothing, and its readiness to follow any prophet who can make his voice heard, with unmixed joy and a sure conviction that we have found a better world?

However we may feel, when we come to our "historical estimate" of Mather, we find much more to say of him than we can safely postulate as to most of our prominent contemporaries. Right or wrong, living in good times or bad, in intellectual freedom or slavery, he stands in literature as a man who achieved unquestioned and long-continued leadership in his own country and his own time. No American author before John Wise and Benjamin Franklin rivalled him in the writing of English. He followed a definite creed, whether he preached or wrote, a creed of simplicity in diction and structure; and working thus, he presented few pages or few sermons which have not the stamp of sound style. Brilliance is usually to seek. Rhetorical ornament, perfect finish, or the precise reflection of emotion in words, we do not often find. But test him by comparison with his countrymen and he achieves superior rank, and place him among seventeenth-century English preachers and writers, and he may still stand unashamed. He did not write as Dryden did, and his style kept archaic turns, and a looseness of construction that some Englishmen left behind. But his best pages and his best discourses from the pulpit are not surpassed by any but the seventeenth-century English writers whom we call "great" in literary history.

As a scholar, too, the range of his reading, and his constant use of it, give him a proud place in his time.[9] Yet he was no slave to authority. He valued experience and observation as highly as learned dogma, and more than once his voice was heard on the side of tolerance for ideas and creeds which were new or different from his own. This breadth of view he carried into politics, and in that field he showed a skill unequalled in his generation among his countrymen. The result of his diplomacy was a governmental system which gave New England privileges enjoyed by no other English colony in America. It remained in operation for generations after his death. As a public force, as a leader of men, inside the church and out of it, there is no American of his era to whom he can be compared. He was, as has often been said, throughout his active life the one outstanding and dominant figure in the history of New England.

All this speaks for character, and there can be no doubt as to the strength of his. Where he seems deficient to us is in imagination, in the ability to conceive of better human institutions than those he knew, in the capacity to dream great dreams, to speculate romantically and lead men to realize his visions. We judge correctly in charging him with a lack of these qualities, if in so doing we say that he lacked the fanciful, the restless questing of the free imagination, where human affairs and human civilization were under discussion. He was not the man to evolve a new ideal political theory, to dream of Utopias on earth, or to turn the spectacle of human life into poetry or drama expressing the beauty of this world and revealing glimpses of inspired vision for its betterment. But we may admit this only when we qualify it in the same breath by saying that Mather did not lack the traits necessary for the sort of achievement to which he never aspired. That he had them is proved by his attitude toward his religion. There is imagination everywhere in his visualization of

9. In his books written up to and including 1701, Mather referred to 928 books or authors.

Heaven, of Hell, of angels, of devils, and in his ecstatic feeling of communion with God and Christ through prayer. No dreamer of dreams, no poet wrapt in mystic visions, ever did more than Mather did every time he knelt to wrestle with his sins, in passionate pleas for forgiveness and protestations of his love for the eternal fountainheads of his faith. Mysticism was the core of his religious attitude, but its outward expression was constantly practical. Therefore, judging him as we do by the fruits of his labor, we judge him falsely. Then, too, we have lost touch with the spirit which gave life to his devotion, and forget accordingly how real it was, and how thoroughly it called into play qualities of mind which, in another age, might have found an outlet in emotional and artistic expression. Colman knew, nor should we forget, how much true exaltation of the human spirit he described when he wrote of Mather: "But the first and last subject and object of all his sermons and prayers, among you, was Jesus Christ and Him crucified. This only he desired to know among you. With this he began, and with this he ended his ministry. . . . He saw much of His glory, and spake often of it with great pleasure and delight. . . . Christ was in him the hope of glory." [10]

Before we leave our "historical weighing" of Mather we should not fail to remind ourselves that, whatever he was, he was not a man who "opposed every liberal movement among the New England clergy." [11] What "liberal movements" there were in his day is hard to decide, but perhaps the Half-Way Covenant was one. This Mather supported heartily. For him to help in ordaining a Baptist was unquestioned liberalism. To join some others of the clergy in advocating inoculation in spite of the assaults of the people was liberalism. To advocate union between Congregationalists and Presbyterians was the sort of thing to which even to-day we should not deny the name of liberalism. If Mather had opposed all these things, he might be accused of narrowness. As it is, wherever any seventeenth-century Puritan can be exonerated from such a charge, he can.

So also we are told that "he was dictatorial and domineering, bearing himself arrogantly towards all underlings, unyielding in opposition to whoever crossed his will." [12] Dictatorial he may have been in his sermons, the poorest basis upon which to bring

10. W. B. Sprague, *Annals*, i, 158.
11. W. P. Trent and B. W. Wells, *Colonial Prose and Poetry*, ii, 216.
12. *Cambridge History of American Literature*, i, 49.

such a charge. Aside from what he spoke or printed in his capacity as minister, where he could hardly have been other than an asserter of the law, it is hard to find arrogance in his dealings with inferiors, nor does his tribute to Brattle suggest implacable enmity toward those who disagreed with him, or arrogance to his subordinates. Willard "crossed his will" in 1697, and in 1700 Mather did him a literary service. John Wise challenged a cause the Mathers favored, and helped to defeat it, and Increase paid him by aiding to win acceptance for one of his son's books.[13]

Of course he was not "a calculating dictator," except when he dictated measures in which he had the support of what he considered to be the best public opinion; nor did he ever rule the press "with an iron hand." [14] But the strangest charge of all is that he was "wholly lacking in intellectual curiosity." [15] To say this of a man who was a divine and yet bought and read the latest science, applied a scientific method to prove what he believed to be the facts of theology, followed up an interest in astronomy, formed a scientific society, and espoused the unpopular and radical venture of inoculation, is to leave many salient features of his career unaccounted for.

Such comments as we have quoted have no place in any estimate, "historical" or "universal." Yet, when we turn to the latter criterion, and try to judge him as a man not of one age but of all, we find manifest deficiencies in him.

As a writer, compared with the great spokesmen of human thought throughout its history, he never achieved greatness. If his literary theory was sound, and his models good, if his devotion to the Scriptures brought to his own writing an echoing of the rhythms and phrasing of the original, he never rose to heights of universal beauty in style and never recaptured in his own work the genius of the translators of the English Bible. As a scholar, widely learned as he appeared in his own day, we must see him as a voluminous reader too uncritical in the use of what he read. As a scientific student, he opened no new road. His utmost was an ability to be always in touch with the newest in thought, to discover the merit in what others originated, and to possess the courage to uphold them, however new and little

13. Mather wrote the preface for Jeremiah Wise's *Prayer in Affliction.* Boston, 1717.

14. The quotations are from *Cambridge History of American Literature*, i, 50.

15. *Ibid.*, p. 49.

favored their views. As a preacher, his influence was broad, but in his sermons as we read them there are but few scattered sentences which could justly be placed with the great spiritual exhortations of human history.

Admitting this, he is still preëminent in two respects. First, he had an unequalled share in guiding an important era of the history of a great nation, and his diplomacy, representing an innovation on all that his people had known before, achieved a result of long-enduring influence. So, too, his work at Harvard and in his church was important for human development in America, and, indirectly, as America has grown great, in other nations. As a modern writer, again no prejudiced idolater at his shrine, declares, "That Dr. Mather was well qualified for the office of President, and had conducted himself in it faithfully and laboriously, is attested by the history of the college, the language of the legislature, and the acknowledgment of his cotemporaries."[16] "His conduct in this great crisis of this country," when the new charter was obtained, "entitles him to unqualified approbation. It is scarcely possible for a public agent to be placed in circumstances more trying or critical; nor could anyone have exhibited more sagacity and devotedness to the true interests of his constituents. By his wisdom and firmness in acceding to the new charter, and thus assuming a responsibility of the weightiest kind, in opposition to his colleagues in the agency, he saved his country, apparently, from a rebellion or a revolution, or from having a constitution imposed by the will of the transatlantic Sovereign, possibly at the point of the bayonet."[17]

The explanation of this, as of all else in his life, lies in the second of his two claims to universal fame. This was the undying value of the sort of character he owned. Wherever we find a man able to lead a large community for half a century, inspiring them religiously, guiding them politically, and constantly impressing them with the example of a broad and useful career, we find a great man. Such was Mather. Essentially his life was the expression in practical form of the intense force of an ardent faith in God and man. His faith was so great, and his ability to turn its inspiration into service was so unfailing, that his time on earth

16. Quincy, as quoted by C. Robbins, *History*, p. 45. Cf. Robbins's remarks, there given.

17. Quincy, *History*, i, 123, 124.

was one of constant conquest over the hearts and minds of men. Such greatness is never dimmed by time.

If to-day we thread our way through busy streets, amid sights and sounds unknown to the seventeenth century, to that little oasis of quiet which we call Copps Hill Burying Ground, we may stand there beside the Mather tomb and marvel at the changes wrought by time since that August afternoon when Samuel Sewall turned sadly away from the grave of one of his oldest friends.[18] There have been changes in manners, customs, and creeds, as well as in nearly every material detail of existence. But, if our imagination be active and our feeling for the seventeenth century not too unsympathetic, we may wonder how Increase Mather would face our world.

I think we should find him a man whose power would not be vanquished by the scenes and conditions of an America of which he never dreamed. I think we should find him hostile to some of our modern institutions. His talk of "godliness," "faithfulness," and "service" might seem to some of us to be mere cant, and he in his turn would marvel at such modern shibboleths as "one hundred per cent Americanism," "efficiency," "the voice of the people," and "up-to-date religion." He might even exhort us to cease such insincere pratings, and, perhaps, we should be at a loss to prove that we work as hard for what we talk of in our "canting" as he did for his "godliness" and "service." He might disturb our complacency by an outburst of anger against some cherished theory of our time or against some of our popularly elected rulers.

But wherever there were fine human institutions, great hospitals, new discoveries of science opening vistas of hope for the saving and betterment of life, wise governments, good scholars, or strong churches, he would be the first to admire. When the talk was of history, of books, or of theology, wherever church union was broadly discussed, or the Bible still read, he would not only listen, but take part. Our only fear for him in a modern club or the faculty room of a university would be lest he might be too serious, too prone to sober thought, and too little blessed by a sense of humor. But I cannot feel that our fears would be justified, could we put him to the test.

18. On the Mather tomb, cf., for example, E. MacDonald, *Old Copp's Hill*, pp. 34 ff.

If we had to judge of Burne-Jones and his friends only by the permanent records they left in art, we should jump to the conclusion that they were serious-minded, preoccupied with the painting of fair but melancholy subjects, and possessed of no appreciation of the lighter side of life. We are near enough to them to know how they talked among themselves, we can laugh over their letters, and we are in no danger of picturing them as mortals as solemn as their art. So, perhaps, if we could know what Mather talked of, at Phipps's table, or when he dined with Sir Francis Wheeler, if we knew what was said when he left his study to join his friends in the beamed front room of some Boston dwelling where the fire was warm and the ale was good, we might not hasten to decide that what we know of his business letters, of his diaries, written to record his serious doings and emotions, and of his books, designed to teach or to explain, not to amuse, spells all there is to know of his impression upon the men who could hear his voice. Certainly a man who took the trouble to order the "Cabinet of Mirth," who came near a pun on so sober a subject as the views of a Puritan governor, and chose Plautus and Terence as travelling companions, does not seem the most likely candidate for the mantle of gloom in which we shroud our image of the conventional Puritan.

We cannot, alas, call Increase Mather back from "the tomb of the fathers." Nor would he wish to join us, unless we could show him new worlds to conquer and a new path to tread in the service of his ideals. All that remains for us is the chance to write his epitaph. We may choose to take Edmund Calamy's estimate, and to follow this eighteenth-century Englishman in declaring that "Dr. *Mather*, ... was vehemently set against all Sin and Impurity, and bent upon spreading Practical Godliness, and promoting Brotherly Love, in the whole Course of his Ministry; and securing the Peace and Liberties of his native Country, by his Conduct, to the utmost Extent of his Influence. And God was with him, and singularly own'd and bless'd him." [19] Or we may prefer to use the simpler summing up given by a modern scholar, no Puritan but a lover of good books and nobility of character, who called Mather "the greatest of the native Puritans." [20] Still, I think, we shall find all such phrases inadequate. Then, perhaps,

---

19. [Samuel Mather (of Witney)]; *Memoirs of the Life of the Late Reverend Increase Mather*, London, 1725, preface by E. Calamy.

20. B. Wendell, *Cotton Mather*, p. 287.

we may remember that Mather's best epitaph can never be put into words. The memory he would have us keep of him and the secret of his claim upon men of all time appear only in the deeds of his fourscore years of life. To realize what he made of his career, and how he turned to account the human means with which he had to work, is perforce to find a friend of whom we can say, "Whoso doeth these things shall never fall." More he would not ask of us.

APPENDICES

APPENDIX A

MATHER'S AGENCY AND THE PLYMOUTH COLONY

I GIVE brief references here to some sources in regard to the presentation of Plymouth's plea for restoration of her charter. On February 4, 1689, Governor Hinckley wrote Mather, thanking him for his services, and telling him that Wiswall was coming to England in Plymouth's interests (*MHS Coll.*, Series 4, v, 227). On August 13, Sir Henry Ashurst wrote Hinckley, saying, "I send you this by worthy Mr. Mather, who has been an indefatigable servant of your country." (*Ibid.*, p. 206.)

On April 26, 1690, Cotton Mather wrote Hinckley, saying that from Increase Mather's letters he learned the Governor of New York had Plymouth included in his commission, but that Increase "procured the dropping of it," and was told separate charters could not be hoped for. Accordingly he had Plymouth included with Massachusetts. To this Wiswall objected, and the Solicitor-General struck out the clause. Therefore, Cotton Mather believed there was again danger that Plymouth would be annexed to New York, because of Wiswall's action. (*Ibid.*, p. 248.)

On June 24, the General Court of Plymouth, "having information from England that the colony of Plimouth had been joyned to . . . New Yorke, but the same was prevented by . . . Mr Mather," and "also informed that Plymouth is likely to be annexed to Boston, although Mr. Wiswall has hindered it for the present," voted to ask the towns to raise money to secure an independent charter. (*Records of the Colony of New Plymouth in New England*, edited by N. B. Shurtleff, Boston, 1856, vi, 259.)

On October 17, Wiswall wrote Hinckley asking for more money, and more activity on the part of the colonies. (*MHS Coll.*, Series 4, v, 276.)

In 1691, Plymouth voted to make Ashurst, Mather and Wiswall, their Agents. (*Ibid.*, Series 2, iii, 190.)

On March 3, the colony voted thanks to these three men. (*Records of the Colony of New Plymouth, etc.*, vi, 260.)

In July, Wiswall wrote, urging action and saying no one in England has spoken a word for Plymouth. (*MHS Coll.*, Series 4, v, 285.)

On October 16, Hinckley informed Mather the colony would prefer annexation to Boston rather than to New York, but most wanted a separate charter. (*MHS Coll.*, Series 4, v, 287 ff.)

On October 17, he wrote Wiswall to the same effect, reminding him of Mather's experience and acquaintance at court. (*Ibid.*, pp. 292–294.)

On November 5, Wiswall wrote attacking Mather in vague terms. (*Ibid.*, p. 299.)

From such evidence F. Baylies, in his *Historical Memoir of New Plymouth* (Boston, 1866), part iv, pp. 134–138, concludes that Mather was active in saving Plymouth from New York, and uniting it to Massachusetts, but "faint and inefficient" in striving for a separate charter. But Mr. Drake, in the same work (part v, pp. 99–104), points out that no enemy of Mather, except Wiswall, charged him with lack of faith to Plymouth. Moreover, Ashurst was Mather's fellow-agent, and equally responsible, and no word is breathed against him. Drake wisely concludes the difficulty in getting a new charter was due to New England's geography. John Davis, in the appendix to his edition of N. Morton's *New England's Memorial* (Boston, 1826), thinks that Wiswall's remarks had no basis, pointing out that it was impossible for Plymouth to get a separate charter, however zealous her agents.

APPENDIX B

THE RETURN OF SEVERAL MINISTERS CONSULTED BY HIS EXCELLENCY, AND THE HONOURABLE COUNCIL, UPON THE PRESENT WITCHCRAFTS IN SALEM VILLAGE [1]

Boston, June 15, 1692.

I. The afflicted State of our poor Neighbours, that are now suffering by Molestations from the Invisible World, we apprehend so deplorable, that we think their Condition calls for the utmost help of all Persons in their several Capacities. II. We cannot but with all Thankfulness acknowledge, the Success which the merciful God has given unto the sedulous and assiduous Endeavors of our honourable Rulers, to detect the abominable Witchcrafts which have been committed in the Country; humbly praying that the discovery of these mysterious and mischievous Wickednesses, may be perfected. III. We judge that in the prosecution of these, and all such Witchcrafts, there is need of a very critical and exquisite Caution, lest by too much Credulity for things received only upon the Devil's Authority, there be a Door opened for a long Train of miserable Consequences, and Satan get an advantage over us, for we should not be ignorant of his Devices. IV. As in Complaints upon Witchcrafts, there may be Matters of Enquiry, which do not amount unto Matters of Presumption, and there may be Matters of Presumption which yet may not be reckoned Matters of *Conviction*; so 'tis necessary that all Proceedings thereabout be managed with an exceeding tenderness towards those that may be complained of; especially if they have been Persons formerly of an unblemished Reputation. V. When the first Enquiry is made into the Circumstances of such as may lie under any just Suspicion of Witchcrafts, we could wish that there may be admitted as little as is possible, of such Noise, Company, and Openness, as may too hastily expose them that are examined: and that there may nothing be used as a Test, for the Trial of the suspected, the Lawful-

1. The text given here is that of the London, 1693, edition of Mather's *Cases of Conscience*. This document has sometimes not only been misread but misprinted. Cf. W. F. Poole, in his edition of T. Hutchinson's *The Witchcraft Delusion* (Boston, 1870), p. 33 n.

ness whereof may be doubted among the People of God; but that the Directions given by such Judicious Writers as *Perkins* and *Bernard*, be consulted in such a Case. VI. Presumptions whereupon Persons may be committed, and much more Convictions, whereupon Persons may be condemned as guilty of Witchcrafts, ought certainly to be more considerable, than barely the accused Persons being represented by a Spectre unto the Afflicted; inasmuch as 'tis an undoubted and a notorious thing, that a Dæmon may, by God's Permission, appear even to ill purposes, in the Shape of an innocent, yea, and a vertuous Man; Nor can we esteem Alterations made in the Sufferers, by a Look or Touch of the Accused to be an infallible Evidence of Guilt; but frequently liable to be abused by the Devil's Legerdemains. VII. We know not, whether some remarkable Affronts given to the Devils, by our disbelieving of those Testimonies, whose whole force and strength is from them alone, may not put a Period, unto the Progress of the dreadful Calamity begun upon us, in the Accusation of so many Persons, whereof we hope, some are yet clear from the great Transgression laid unto their Charge. VIII. Nevertheless, We cannot but humbly recommend unto the Government, the speedy and vigorous Prosecution of such as have rendred themselves obnoxious, according to the Direction given in the Laws of God, and the wholesome Statutes of the *English* Nation, for the Detection of Witchcrafts.

APPENDIX C

LIST OF BOOKS REFERRED TO

NOTE. — I have not given complete titles in all cases but have tried to give sufficient data for identification. The titles marked with an asterisk (*) are those of books or collections containing articles by several authors. I have not listed these articles under the names of the individual authors except in cases where the article seemed of special importance or was very often referred to.

Acts and Resolves. *Acts and Resolves, public and private, of the province of Massachusetts Bay.* Boston, 1869-.

Acts of the Privy Council of England, Colonial Series. London, 1908-.

Adams, B., *The Emancipation of Massachusetts.* Boston, 1887.

Adams, J. T., *The Founding of New England.* Boston, 1921.

American Antiquarian Society, Proceedings of.* Worcester, various dates.

—— Transactions of.* Worcester, various dates.

American Historical Association, Papers of.* N. Y., 1886-.

American Society of Church History, Papers of.* N. Y., 1888-.

Andrews, C. M., *Colonial Self-Government.* N. Y. (1904).

—— *The Fathers of New England.* New Haven, 1919.

Andros Tracts, The. See Whitmore, W. H.

Autobiography. The manuscript autobiography of Increase Mather, owned by the American Antiquarian Society.

Backus, I., *A Church History of New-England.* Providence, 1784.

Bardsley, C. W., *A Dictionary of English and Welsh Surnames.* London,1901.

Barrows, S. J., and Trask, W. B. *Records of the First Church at Dorchester in New England 1636-1734.* Boston, 1891.

Bates, K. L., *American Literature.* N. Y., 1898.

Baxter, R., *The Glorious Kingdom of Christ.* London, 1691.

—— Letter to Increase Mather (manuscript) owned by Dr. Williams's Library, London.

Baylies, F., *Historical Memoir of New Plymouth.* Boston, 1866.

Bay Psalm Book, The. Facsimile reprint, with introd. by W. Eames. N. Y., 1903.

Beamont, W., *Winwick: Its History and Antiquities,* 2d ed. Warrington, n. d.

Belknap, J., *The History of New-Hampshire.* Phila., 1784.

Benton, J. H., *The Story of the Old Boston Town House 1658-1711.* Boston, 1908.

Boston Records Commission, Fourth Report 1880 (Dorchester Town Records). Boston, 1880.

Bowman, J. C., *The Hated Puritan,* in the Weekly Review (N. Y.), v, 10.

Boyle, R., The Works of. London, 1772.

Brinley Catalogue. Catalogue of the American Library of the late Mr. George Brinley of Hartford, Conn. Hartford, 1878-97.

British Journal, The, for October 19, 1723.

Brook, B., *The Lives of the Puritans.* London, 1813.

Browne, T., *Pseudodoxia Epidemica,* 2d ed. London, 1650.

Burnet, G., *History of His Own Time.* London, 1724.

(———), *A Supplement to Burnet's History of My Own Time,* ed. by H. C. Foxcroft. Oxford, 1902.

Burr, G. L., *Narratives of the Witchcraft Cases 1648-1706.* N. Y., 1914.

——— *New England's Place in the History of Witchcraft,* in American Antiquarian Society Proceedings, xxi, 185ff.

C., G. E., *Complete Baronetage.* Exeter, 1900.

Calamy, E., *Continuation of the Account of the Ejected Ministers.* London, 1727.

——— *Life of John Howe,* prefixed to The Works of John Howe. London, 1724.

——— *Memoirs of the life of the late Reverend Increase Mather. See* Mather, Samuel (of Witney).

Calef, R., *More Wonders of the Invisible World,* in S. G. Drake, *The Witchcraft Delusion in New England.* Roxbury, 1866.

Cal. State Papers, Am. and W. I.¹ *Calendar of State Papers, Colonial Series, America and West Indies,* ed. by Sainsbury and Fortescue. London, various dates.

*Cambridge History of American Literature.** N. Y., 1917-21.

*Cambridge History of English Literature.** Cambridge (Eng.), 1907-16.

Chambers, R., *The Book of Days.* Edinburgh, 1863.

Channing, E., *The History of the United States.* N. Y., 1917-.

Chaplin, J., *The Life of Henry Dunster.* Boston, 1872.

Charnock, J., *Biographia Navalis.* London, 1794-98.

Clarendon, E., *The History of the Rebellion and Civil Wars in England.* Oxford, 1807.

Clarke, S., *The Lives of Sundry Eminent Persons.* London, 1683.

Colman, B., *The Prophet's Death, Lamented and Improved.* Boston, 1723.

——— *A Sermon . . . Upon the News of the Death of the much Honoured* Thomas Hollis; *Esq.* Boston, 1731.

Colonial Society of Massachusetts, Publications of.* Boston, 1895-.

Colonial Society Publications. *See* item just preceding.

*Congregational Quarterly.** Boston, N. Y., 1859-78.

Criegern, H., *Johann Amos Comenius Als Theolog.* Leipzig, 1881.

Davis, A. M. F., *The Early College Buildings at Cambridge,* in American Antiquarian Society Proceedings, April, 1890, and separately. Worcester, 1890.

Davis, V. D., *Some Account of the Ancient Chapel of Toxteth Park, Liverpool . . . and of its Ministers, especially of Richard Mather, the first Minister.* Liverpool, 1884.

Dean, J. W., *Sketch of the Life of Rev. Michael Wigglesworth,* in New England Historical and Genealogical Register, April, 1863, and separately. Albany, 1863.

1. References to this work are to volume and number of entry, not to volume and page; *e. g.,* xiii, ✳ 1701 is vol. 13, entry 1701.

De Burigny, J. L., *The Life of the Truly Eminent and Learned Hugo Grotius.* London, 1754.

Densham, W., and Ogle, J., *The Story of the Congregational Churches of Dorset.* Bournemouth, 1899.

Dexter, F. B., *Documentary History of Yale University.** New Haven, 1916.

—— *Estimates of Population in the American Colonies*, in American Antiquarian Society Proceedings. October, 1887.

—— *Memoranda Respecting Edward Whalley and William Goffe*, in Papers of the New Haven Colony Historical Society, reprinted in F. B. Dexter, *A Selection from the Miscellaneous Historical Papers of Fifty Years*, 6ff.

—— *Selection from the Miscellaneous Historical Papers of Fifty Years.* New Haven, 1918.

—— *Sketch of the Life and Writings of John Davenport*, in F. B. Dexter, *Selection*, etc.

Dexter, H. M., *The Congregationalism of the Last Three Hundred Years*, etc. N. Y., 1880.

—— *Two Hundred Years Ago in New England*, in *Congregational Quarterly*, iv, 268.

Dictionary of National Biography, The. London, 1908–09.

Dixon, W. M., *Trinity College, Dublin.* London, 1902.

DNB. See *Dictionary of National Biography, The.*

Dorchester Town Records. *See* Boston Records Commission.

Doyle, J. A., *The English in America. Virginia, Maryland and the Carolinas.* London, 1882.

—— *The Puritan Colonies* (vols. ii and iii of his *The English in America*). London, 1887.

Drake, S. A., *Old Landmarks and Historical Personages of Boston.* Boston, 1901.

Drake, S. G., *The Early History of New England.* Boston, 1864.

—— *The History of King Philip's War.* Boston, 1862.

—— *The Pedigree of the Family of Mather*, in Mather, C., *Magnalia*, reprint of Hartford, 1853.

—— *The Witchcraft Delusion in New England.* Roxbury, 1866.

Duncan, J., *The History of Guernsey.* London, 1841.

Duniway, C. A., *The Development of Freedom of the Press in Massachusetts.* N. Y., 1906.

Dunlap, W., *A History of the Rise and Progress of the Arts of Design in the United States*, ed. by F. W. Bayley and C. E. Goodspeed. Boston, 1918.

Dunton, J., *Letters Written from New England*, ed. by W. H. Whitmore. Boston, 1867.

Eames, W.: See *Bay Psalm Book, The.*

Earle, A. M., *Customs and Fashions in Old New England.* N. Y., 1894.

Edwards, J., *A Faithful Narrative*, etc. Boston, 1737.

Ellis, G. W., and Morris, J. E., *King Philip's War.* N. Y., 1906.

Evelyn, J., *Diary* of. Various editions.

Force, P., *Tracts and Other Papers . . . of the Colonies in North America.** Washington, 1836–46.

Ford, J. W., *Some Correspondence between the Governors and Treasurers of the New England Company . . . and the Commissioners of the United Colonies in America.** London, 1897.

Ford, W. C., *The Boston Book Market, 1679–1700.* Boston, 1917.

Fosbrooke, T. D., *An Original History of the City of Gloucester.* London, 1819.

Fraser, W., *The Sutherland Book.* Edinburgh, 1892.

Gill, O., *et al., Some Few Remarks upon a Scandalous Book . . . written by one Robert Calef,* etc. Boston, 1701.

Gospel Order Revived . . . By sundry Ministers of the Gospel in New-England. (N. Y.), 1700.

Green, S. A., *Ten Fac-simile Reproductions . . . various subjects.* Boston, 1903.

Greene, E. B., *Provincial America 1690–1740.* N. Y. (1905).

Gribble, J. B., *Memorials of Barnstaple.* Barnstaple, 1830.

Hale, J., *A Modest Enquiry into the Nature of Witchcraft.* Boston, 1702.

Hammond, L., *Journal of. See* Mather, I., *Diary.*

Hanus, F. A., *Educational Aims and Educational Values.* N. Y., 1899.

Harrison, H., *Surnames of the United Kingdom.* London, 1912–18.

Harvard College Records. *See* Harv. Rec.

Harvard University. *Quinquennial Catalogue of Officers and Graduates.* Cambridge, 1920.

Harv. Rec. Harvard College Records, Parts 1 and 2. Corporation Records, 1636–1750, to be published as Colonial Society of Massachusetts Publications, vols. xv and xvi.

Hawthorne, N., The Works of. Cambridge, 1883.

Hazard, E., *Historical Collections consisting of State Papers.** Phila., 1792–94.

Hewlett, J. P., Edition of The Works of John Howe. London, 1848.

Hill, H. A., *History of the Old South Church.* Boston, 1890.

Historic Society of Lancashire and Cheshire, Transactions of. Liverpool, 1849–.

History of Dorchester. See next item.

History of the Town of Dorchester in Massachusetts, by a Committee of the Dorchester Antiquarian and Historical Society. Boston, 1859.

Howe, J., The Works of. London, 1724.

————, ed. by J. P. Hewlett. London, 1848.

Hutchins, J., *The History and Antiquities of the County of Dorset,* 3d. ed. Westminster, 1861–70.

Hutchinson, F., *An Historical Essay concerning Witchcraft,* 2d. ed. London, 1720.

Hutchinson, T., *A Collection of Original Papers,* reprinted as *Hutchinson Papers.** Albany, 1865.

———— *The History of the Colony of Massachusetts Bay,* vols. i and ii. London, 1765–68.

(————), *The Witchcraft Delusion of 1692,* ed. by W. F. Poole. Boston, 1870.

Jameson, J. F., *The History of Historical Writing in America.* Boston, 1891.

Johnson, E., *A History of New England.* London, 1654. Reprinted as *Johnson's Wonder-Working Providence,* ed. by J. F. Jameson. N. Y., 1910.

Josselyn, J., *An Account of Two Voyages to New England*, reprinted by W. Veazie. Boston, 1865.

Keith, G., *The Presbyterian and Independent Visible Churches*. London, 1691.

Kimball, E., *The Public Life of Joseph Dudley*. N. Y., 1911.

Kittredge, G. L., *Cotton Mather's Election into the Royal Society*, in Colonial Society of Massachusetts Publications, vol. xiv, and separately. Cambridge, 1912.

—— *Cotton Mather's Scientific Communications to the Royal Society*, in American Antiquarian Society Proceedings, xxvi, 18ff.

—— Introduction to Mather, I., *Several Reasons*, etc., reprinted. Cleveland, 1921.

—— *Notes on Witchcraft*, in American Antiquarian Society Proceedings, xviii, 148ff.

Lechford, T., *Plain Dealing: or, Newes from New-England*. London, 1642; reprinted, Boston, 1867.

Lectures on Massachusetts History. *Lectures delivered in a Course before the Lowell Institute in Boston, by Members of the Massachusetts Historical Society, on Subjects relating to the Early History of Massachusetts*. Boston, 1869.

LeRoy, P., *Notebook* of, ed. by G. E. Lee, in Publications of Guernsey Historical and Antiquarian Society. Guernsey, 1893.

Leusden, J., *Liber Psalmorum*. London, 1688.

Lodge, H. C., *A Short History of the English Colonies in America*. N.Y. (1881).

Long Island Historical Society Memoirs,* vol. i, Brooklyn, 1867.

Lothrop, S. K., *A History of the Church in Brattle Street, Boston*. Boston, 1851.

Love, W. D., *The Fast and Thanksgiving Days of New England*. Boston, 1895.

Lowndes, W. T., *The Bibliographer's Manual of English Literature*, ed. by H. G. Bohn. London, 1890.

Luttrell, N., *A Brief Historical Relation of State Affairs from September, 1678, to April, 1714*. Oxford, 1857.

Lyon, I. W., *The Colonial Furniture of New England*. Boston, 1891.

Macaulay, T. B., *History of England*. Various editions.

McCalmont, R. E., *Memoirs of the Binghams*. London, 1915.

MacCulloch, E., *Guernsey Folk Lore*, ed. by E. F. Carey. London, 1903.

MacDonald, E., *Old Copp's Hill and Burial Ground with Historical Sketches*, 19th ed. Boston, 1900.

Mahaffy, J. P., *An Epoch in Irish History: Trinity College, Dublin*, 2d ed. London, 1906.

Maitland, W. H., *History of Magherafelt*. Cookstown (Ireland), 1916.

Manifesto Church, The. Records of the Church in Brattle Square, Boston . . . 1699–1872. Boston, 1902.

Manning, O., and Bray, W., *The History and Antiquities of . . . County of Surrey*. London, 1802.

Marvin, A. P., *The Life and Times of Cotton Mather*. Boston (1892).

Massachusetts Historical Society. *See* MHS.

Mass. Rec. *Records of the Governor and Company of the Massachusetts Bay in New England*, ed. by N. B. Shurtleff. Boston, 1853–54.

Mather, C., *A Collection of Some of the Many Offensive Matters*, etc. Boston, 1701.

———— *A Faithful Man Described*. Boston, 1705.

———— *Magnalia Christi Americana: or, the Ecclesiastical History of New-England*. London, 1702.

———— *Parentator. Memoirs of Remarkables in the Life and Death of the Ever-Memorable Dr. Increase Mather*. Boston, 1724.

———— *Thirty Important Cases*. Boston, 1699.

———— *The Wonders of the Invisible World*, reprinted. London, 1862.

Mather, H. E., *Lineage of Rev. Richard Mather*. Hartford, 1890.

Mather, I., *Diary*, March, 1675–December, 1676, with the *Journal* of Capt. Hammond, ed. by S. A. Green. Cambridge, 1900.

———— *The Life and Death of . . . Mr. Richard Mather*, reprinted in Collections of Dorchester Antiquarian and Historical Society, No. 3. Boston, 1850.

———— MS. Diaries, various dates, in the possession of the American Antiquarian Society.

———— *A Sermon Concerning Obedience & Resignation to the Will of God*. Boston, 1714.

Mather, R., *Journal* of, Collections of Dorchester Antiquarian and Historical Society, No. 3. Boston, 1850.

[Mather, Samuel (of Witney)], *Memoirs of the Life of the Late Reverend Increase Mather, D.D.* London, 1725.

(This book has a preface by Edmund Calamy, and he is often given as the author of the whole work.)

Memorial History of Boston, The,* ed. by J. Winsor. Boston, 1880–81.

MHS Coll.* Massachusetts Historical Society Collections. Various dates.

MHS Proc.* Massachusetts Historical Society Proceedings. Various dates.

Morton, N., *New England's Memorial*, ed. by John Davis. Boston, 1826.

Mullinger, J. B., *Cambridge Characteristics in the Seventeenth Century*. London, 1867.

Mumby, F. A., *The Romance of Book Selling*. Boston, 1911.

Murdock, K. B., *The Portraits of Increase Mather*. Cleveland, 1924.

Murray, M. A., *The Witch-Cult in Western Europe*. Oxford, 1921.

Murray, R. H., *Dublin University and the New World*. London, 1921.

NED. *See* New English Dictionary.

New Englander, The.* New Haven, 1843–.

New England Historical and Genealogical Register.* Boston, 1847–.

New England's First Fruits. London, 1643; reprinted by J. Sabin. N. Y., 1865.

New English Dictionary. *A New English Dictionary on Historical Principles*. Oxford, 1888–.

New Hampshire Historical Society Collections.* Concord, 1824–.

Nonconformist's Memorial, The. . . . ed. by S. Palmer, 2d ed. London, 1802.

Notestein, W., *A History of Witchcraft in England from 1588 to 1718*. Washington, 1911.

Nutting, W., *Furniture of the Pilgrim Century*. Boston, 1921.

Observator, The. London, 1681–.

Oldmixon, J., *The British Empire in America*. London, 1708.

Orme, W., *Memoirs of the Life, Writings and Religious Connexions of John Owen, D.D.* London, 1820.

Oviatt, E., *The Beginnings of Yale.* New Haven, 1916.

Palfrey, J. G., *History of New England.* Boston, 1858–90.

Palmer, S. See *Nonconformist's Memorial.*

Parentator. See Mather, C., *Parentator.*

Peabody, W. B. O., *Life of Cotton Mather*, in J. Sparks, *The Library of American Biography*, vi, 163ff.

Pepys, S., *Diary.* Various editions.

*Philosophical Transactions, The, of the Royal Society.** London, various dates.

Picton, J. A., *Selections from the Municipal Archives and Records* [of Liverpool]. Liverpool, 1883.

Pike, J. S., *The New Puritan.* N. Y., 1879.

Polwhele, R., *History of Devonshire.* Exeter, 1797.

Pond, E., *The Lives of Increase Mather and Sir William Phipps.* Boston, 1870.

Pool, D. de S., *Hebrew Learning among the Puritans of New England prior to 1700*, in Publications of the American Jewish Historical Society, No. 20, 1911.

Poole, W. F. *See* Hutchinson, T.

—— *Cotton Mather and Salem Witchcraft.* Boston, 1869.

(——) *Cotton Mather & Witchcraft.* Two notices of Mr. Upham His Reply. Boston, 1870.

Porter, E. G., *Rambles in Old Boston.* Boston, 1887.

Potter, A. C., *Catalogue of John Harvard's Library.* Cambridge, 1919.

Prideaux, M., *An Easy and Compendious Introduction for Reading All Sorts of Histories*, 4th ed. Oxford, 1664.

Quincy, J., *The History of Harvard University.* Cambridge, 1840.

Records of the Colony of New Plymouth in New England, ed. by N. B. Shurtleff. Boston, 1856.

Records of the Governor, etc. *See* Mass. Rec.

Redgrove, H. S., and I. M. L., *Joseph Glanvill and Psychical Research in the Seventeenth Century.* London, 1921.

*Religious History of New England, The.** Cambridge, 1917.

Robbins, C., *History of the Second Church . . . in Boston.* Boston, 1852.

—— *The Regicides sheltered in New England*, in *Lectures on Massachusetts History, q. v.*

Roden, R. F., *The Cambridge Press.* N. Y., 1905.

Savage, E. A., *Old English Libraries.* London, 1911.

Savage, J., *A Genealogical Dictionary of the First Settlers of New England.* Boston, 1860–62.

*Second Church in Boston, The. Commemorative Service Held on the Completion of Two Hundred and Fifty Years since its Foundation.** Boston, 1900.

Second Church: Manuscript volume owned by, containing a copy of part of the original records.

Seymour, St. J. D., *The Puritans in Ireland 1647–1661.* Oxford, 1921.

Shelley, H. C., *John Harvard and His Times.* Boston, 1913.

Sheppard, E., *The Old Royal Palace of Whitehall.* London, 1902.

Sherman, S. P., *The Genius of America.* N. Y., 1923.

Shillaber, W. G., *Facsimile Reprint of The Present State of the New-English Affairs.* Boston, 1902.

Shurtleff, N. B. *See* Mass. Rec. and Records of the Colony, etc.

—— *Topographical and Historical Description of Boston*, 3d ed. Boston, 1890.

Sibley, J. L., *Biographical Sketches of Graduates of Harvard University.* Cambridge, 1873–85.

Sparks, J., *The Library of American Biography.** Boston, 1834–38.

Spingarn, J. E., *Critical Essays of the Seventeenth Century.** Oxford, 1908–09.

Sprague, W. B., *Annals of the American Pulpit.* N. Y., 1857–69.

Stedman, E. C., and Hutchinson, E. M., *A Library of American Literature.** N. Y., 1888–90.

Straus, O. S., *Roger Williams.* N. Y., 1894.

Stubbs, J. W., *The History of the University of Dublin.* Dublin, 1889.

Taylor, H. O., *The Mediaeval Mind.* N. Y., 1919.

—— *Thought and Expression in the Sixteenth Century.* N. Y., 1920.

Thomas, I., *The History of Printing in America*, 2d ed. Albany, 1874.

Thomson, J. A. (ed.), *The Outline of Science.** London (1921–).

Thoresby, R., *Diary* of. London, 1830.

Thwing, A. H., Card Index of land-owners in Boston, in the Library of the Massachusetts Historical Society.

—— *The Crooked and Narrow Streets of the Town of Boston.* Boston, 1920.

Toppan, R. N., *Edward Randolph.** Boston, 1898–1909.

Traill, H. D., and Mann, J. S., *Social England.** Illustrated edition. London 1902–04.

Trent, W. P., *A History of American Literature.* N. Y., 1903.

—— and Wells, B. W., *Colonial Prose and Poetry.** N. Y. (1903).

Tupper, F. B., *The Chronicles of Castle Cornet, Guernsey.* Guernsey, 1851.

—— *History of Guernsey.* Guernsey, 1876.

Turell, E., *The Life and Character of . . . Benjamin Colman.* Boston, 1749.

Turner, W., *A Compleat History of the Most Remarkable Providences.* London, 1697.

Tuttle, C. W., *Capt. Francis Champernowne. The Dutch Conquest of Acadie and other Historical Papers*, ed. by A. H. Hoyt. Boston, 1889.

Tuttle, J. H., *The Libraries of the Mathers*, in American Antiquarian Society Proceedings, xx, 269ff.

Tyler, M. C., *A History of American Literature, 1607–1765.* Students' edition. N. Y. (1878).

Upham, C. W., *Salem Witchcraft and Cotton Mather*, in *Historical Magazine* for September, 1869, and separately. Morrisania, 1869.

—— *Salem Witchcraft, with an Account of Salem Village and a History of Opinions on Witchcraft and Kindred Subjects.* Boston, 1867.

Urwick, W., *The Early History of Trinity College, Dublin.* Dublin, 1892.

Veazie, W. *See* Josselyn, J.

W., J., *The Life . . . of . . . Dr. . . . Winter.* London, 1671.

Waddington, C., *Ramus, Sa Vie, Ses Ecrits, et ses Opinions.* Paris, 1855.

Walker, G. L., *Thomas Hooker.* N. Y. (1891).

Walker, W., *Creeds and Platforms of Congregationalism.** N. Y., 1893.

—— *A History of the Congregational Churches in the United States.* N. Y., 1894.

—— *The Services of the Mathers in New England Religious Development*, in Papers of the American Society of Church History, v, 6ff.

—— *Ten New England Leaders*. Boston, 1901.

Ward, A. W., *A History of English Dramatic Literature*. London, 1875.

Ward, E. F., *Christopher Monck, Duke of Albermarle*. London, 1915.

Ward, N., *The Simple Cobbler of Agawam*, reprinted, Boston, 1843.

Ware, H., *Two Discourses containing the History of the Old North and New Brick Churches*. Boston, 1821.

Waters, T. F., *Ipswich in the Massachusetts Bay Colony*. Ipswich, 1905.

Wendell, B., *Cotton Mather, the Puritan Priest*. N. Y. (1891).

—— *Stelligeri and other Essays*. N. Y., 1893.

Westcote, T., *A View of Devonshire in 1630*. Exeter, 1845.

White, A. D., *A History of the Doctrine of Comets*, in Papers of the American Historical Association, vol. 2, no. 2.

—— *A History of the Warfare of Science with Theology in Christendom*. N. Y., 1919.

Whiting, J., *Truth and Innocency Defended*. London, 1702.

Whitmore, W. H. (ed.), *The Andros Tracts*.* Boston, 1868–74.

Wilson, W., *The History and Antiquities of Dissenting Churches and Meeting Houses in London*, etc. London, 1808–14.

Winsor, J., *The Literature of Witchcraft in New England*, in American Antiquarian Society Proceedings, x, 351ff.

Winthrop, J., *The History of New England from 1630 to 1649*, ed. by James Savage. Boston, 1853.

Winthrop, R. C., *Life and Letters of John Winthrop*. Boston, 1864–67.

Wood, Anthony, *The Life and Times of*, ed. by A. Clark. Oxford, 1891–1900.

Wood, W., *New Englands Prospect*, reprinted, Boston, 1897.

Worth, R. N., *A History of Devonshire*. London, 1886.

Wright, C. H. C., *History of French Literature*. N. Y., 1912.

Wright, T. G., *Literary Culture in Early New England*. New Haven, 1920.

APPENDIX D

CHECK LIST OF MATHER'S WRITINGS

NOTE. — This list is in two parts. The first contains those books published before 1702, and the second lists the later works. In neither list are full titles given, but simply a brief designation sufficient to make possible the identification of the book. This bibliography is based on data furnished me by Mr. T. J. Holmes and Dr. G. P. Winship, who are now editing a complete Mather bibliography, to be published by Mr. W. G. Mather, of Cleveland. In a few cases I have omitted titles usually ascribed to Mather, when the evidence seemed against his authorship; but I have done this only when Mr. Holmes and Dr. Winship have agreed with my conclusions.

Most of the books comprised in Part I of my list are mentioned in the text, and after each title I give a page reference to the passage in which it is discussed. The books listed in Part II are not discussed in the text.

PART I

BIBLIOGRAPHY TO 1702

Angelographia. Boston, 1696 . . . . 326, 327
Answer of several ministers . . . deceased wife's sister. Boston, 1695, 1711 322
Answer to the question whether are not brethren. — (In "A Vindication of the Divine Authority." See below.)
Arrow against . . . dancing. Boston 1684, 1686 163
Blessed Hope. Boston, 1701 324
Brief account concerning . . . agents of New England. London, 1691 274, 275
Brief discourse concerning Common Prayer worship. (Boston, 1686),
    London, 1689 . . . . 272, 273
Brief history of the war with the Indians. Boston, 1676, London, 1676,
    Boston, 1862 (with title "History of King Philip's War") . . . . 110ff.
Brief relation of the state of New England. London, 1689 . . . . 224, 225
——— The Same. In Force's *Tracts*.
——— The Same. In *Andros Tracts*.
——— The Same (earlier draft). *MHS Coll.*, Series 3, i, 93ff.
Brieff von dem glucklichen fortgang. Halle, 1696. . . . . 271n.
Call from Heaven. Boston, 1679, 1685 . . . . 135, 136
Case of Conscience concerning eating of blood. Boston, 1697. 323
Cases of conscience concerning evil spirits. Boston, 1693, London, 1693,
    London, 1862 . . . . 299ff., 309

David serving his generation. Boston, 1698. . . . . 323, 329, 330
Day of trouble is near. Cambridge, 1674 . . . . 101, 102
De successu evangelij. London, 1688, Utrecht, 1699 . . . . . 271, 272
Diatriba de signo. Amsterdam, 1682 140
Discourse concerning the danger of apostasy. Printed with Call from
   Heaven. Boston, 1679, 1685 . . . . 133ff.
Discourse concerning baptisme. Cambridge, 1675. 138
Discourse concerning the uncertainty of the times of men. Boston, 1697. 323
Disputation concerning church members and their children. London,
   1659 . . . . 80, n. 65
Disquisition concerning angelical apparitions. Boston, 1696. (Also in
   Angelographia.) . . . . 326, n. 47
Divine right of infant-baptisme. Boston, 1680. . . . . 138, 139
Doctrine of divine providence. Boston, 1684 . . . . 166, 167
Early history of New England. Albany, 1864.
   (This is a reprint of Relation of the Troubles, for which see below.)
Earnest exhortation to the inhabitants of New England. Boston, 1676 139
Essay for the Recording of Illustrious Providences. Boston, 1684,
   London, 1684, 1687, London, 1856 (with title "Remarkable Provi-
   dences"), London, 1890 (same as preceding) . . . . . . 167ff., 306ff.
Faithful advice from several ministers . . . imposters. Boston (1699) . 323
First principles of New England . . . baptisme. Cambridge, 1675 . . 98, 99
Folly of sinning. Boston, 1699 . . . . 325, 326
Further account of the tryals of . . . witches. London, 1693, 1862 299, n. 36
   (Probably not by Increase Mather.)
Further vindication of New-England. London, n. d. (1689?) . . . 223, 224
Great blessings of primitive counsellors. Boston, 1693, and in *Andros
   Tracts* 331, 332
Greatest sinners exhorted. Boston, 1686 164
Heaven's Alarm. Boston, 1681, 1682; also in *Kometographia*, and Lon-
   don, 1812 . . . . 143, 144
Historical discourse concerning prayer. Boston, 1677 . . . . . 139, 140
——— The Same. In Relation of the Troubles, see below.
History of King Philip's War. See Brief History, above.
Illustrious Providences. See Essay for the recording.
Judgment of several eminent divines. Boston, 1693 322
Kometographia.[1] Boston, 1683, London, 1811 . . . . 145ff.
Latter sign. (Boston, 1682) in 2d ed. of Heaven's Alarm 144
Letter concerning the success of the Gospel among the Indians. (Transla-
   tion of De Successu, *q. v.*)
Letter from some aged nonconforming ministers. Boston, 1712 (4th ed.).
   Contains preface by I. M. and seems to have been published by him
Life and death of Richard Mather. Cambridge, 1670 97
——— The Same. Boston, 1850, 1874.
Masukkenukeeg (an Indian translation of some of Mather's sermons).
   Boston, 1698 . . . . 320, n. 12
Mystery of Christ. (Boston) 1686 . . . . 164, 165

---

1. The title of this book is in Greek letters. I give the usual transliteration.

Mystery of Israel's salvation. (London) 1669 . . . . 94ff.

Narrative of the miseries of New England. (London, 1688), 1689, Boston, 1775, in *Andros Tracts* and Old South Leaflets, Annual Series, vol. ii, no. 3 . . . . 212ff.

Necessity of reformation. Boston, 1679 151

—— The Same. In Cotton Mather: Results of Three Synods. Boston, 1725.

New England vindicated. (London, 1688) and *Andros Tracts* . . . . 220ff.

News from New England. 233, 234
    (Probably not by Mather.)

Order of the Gospel. Boston, London, 1700 . . . . 360ff.

Practical truths tending to promote the power of godliness. Boston, 1682 137

Pray for the rising generation. Boston, 1678, 1679. (Also with Call from Heaven.) 133

Present state of New English affairs. Boston, 1689, 1902, and in New Hampshire Historical Soc. Coll., i, 252, and in *Andros Tracts*. . . . 228

Reasons for the confirmation of the charter . . . Massachusetts. N. p., n. d., 1689, and in *Andros Tracts*. 235, 236

Reasons for the confirmation of the charters . . . New England. N. p., n. d., 1689 . . . . 234, 235

Relation of the troubles. Boston, 1677 . . . . 128ff.

—— The Same (reprinted as Early History of New England). Albany, 1864 . . . . 128ff.

Remarkable Providences. See Essay for the recording of . . .

Renewal of covenant. Boston, 1677 132

Returning unto God. Boston, 1680 136

Sermon occasioned by the execution of . . . Boston, 1686, 1687 . . 165, 166

—— The Same. (In the Wonders of Free Grace.) London, 1691 165, 166

Sermon preached at the lecture in Boston. Second edition of The Wicked Man's Portion. Boston, 1685. See below.

Sermon wherein is shewed . . . Church . . . subject of . . . persecution. Boston, 1682 . . . . 136, 137

Solemn advice to young men. Boston, 1695, 1709? 322

Some important truths about conversion. London, 1674, Boston, 1721 . . . . 100, 101

Surest way to the greatest honour. Boston, 1699 . . . . 335, 336

Testimony against . . . prophane and superstitious customs. London, 1687, Boston, 1688 . . . . 163, 164

Times of men are in the hands of God. Boston, 1675 131

Two plain and practical discourses. London, Boston, 1699 326

Vindication of New England. N. p., n. d., 1688 . . . . 225ff.
    (Probably not by Increase Mather. See text.)

Vindication of the divine authority of ruling elders. Boston, 1700 . . . 324

—— The Same. In J. White: New England's Lamentations . . Boston, 1734.

Wicked man's portion. Boston, 1675, 1685 . . . . 131, 132

Wo to drunkards. Cambridge, 1673, Boston, 1712 . . . . 103, 104

PREFACES, ETC., IN WORKS BY OTHER AUTHORS

PART II

BIBLIOGRAPHY 1702–1723

NOTE. — I give here brief titles of such works as are noted by the editors of the forthcoming Mather bibliography in their preliminary check-list. This list does not pretend to be complete, nor can it be made so until the bibliography upon which Mr. Holmes and Mr. Winship are engaged is finished.

An account of the reasons, etc. (Contains letters by Increase and Cotton Mather, though it seems to be edited by A. Sears and others.) 1720.
Advice to the children of godly ancestors. Boston, 1721.
Awakening soul-saving truths. Boston, 1720.
Awakening truths tending to conversion. Boston, 1710.

Believers gain by death. Boston, 1713.

Burnings bewailed. Boston, 1711, 1712.

Call to the tempted . . . suicides. Boston, 1723.

Charge at the ordination of T. Prince. Boston, 1718.

Discourse concerning earthquakes. Boston, 1706.

Discourse concerning . . . prayer. Boston, 1710.

Discourse concerning the death . . . of John . . . and . . . Abigail Foster. Boston, 1711.

Discourse concerning the existence . . . of God. [Boston, 1716.]

Discourse concerning the grace of courage. Boston, 1710.

Discourse concerning the maintenance of . . . Boston, 1706, London, 1709.

Discourse on sacramental occasions (probably not a genuine title). Boston, 1711.

Discourse proving that the Christian religion . . . Boston, 1702.

Disquisition concerning ecclesiasticall councils. Boston, 1716.

. . . (Reprinted in Congregational Quarterly, Vol. 12). Boston, 1702.

—— The Same. Printed separately. Boston, 1870.

Disquisition concerning the . . . souls of men. Boston, 1707, London, 1707.

Dissertation concerning . . . conversion of the Jewish Nation. London, 1709, Boston, 1709.

Dissertation wherein the strange doctrine . . . Boston, 1708, Edinburgh, 1710, 1713.

Doctrine of singular obedience. Boston, 1707.

Duty of Parents. Boston, 1703, Boston, 1719.

Dying legacy of a minister. Boston, 1722.

Earnest exhortation to children of New England. Boston, 1711.

Elijah's Mantle. Boston, 1722, Boston, 1774.

Excellency of a publick spirit. Boston, 1702.

Five sermons on several subjects. Boston, 1719.

Four Sermons. Boston, 1708.

Further Testimony against . . . New North Church. Boston, 1720.

Ichabod. Boston, 1702, Boston, 1729.

Letter about the present state of Christianity . . . Indians. Boston, 1705.

Letter from some aged non-conforming ministers . . . 4th ed. Boston, 1712.

Meditations on death. Boston, 1707.

Meditations on the glory of the heavenly world. Boston, 1711.

Meditations on the glory of the Lord Jesus Christ. Boston, 1705.

Meditations on the sanctification of the Lord's day. Boston, 1712.

Now or never. Boston, 1713.

Original rights of mankind. Boston, 1722.

(Probably not by Mather.) Cf. Brinley Catalogue, #1012.

Plain discourse shewing who . . . enter . . . heaven. Boston, 1713, Boston, 1721.

Plea for the ministers. Boston, 1706.

Practical truths plainly delivered. Boston, 1718.

Practical truths tending to promote holiness. Boston, 1704.

Seasonable meditations . . . winter & summer. Boston, 1712.

Seasonable testimony to good order in churches. Boston, 1720.

Sermon concerning obedience & resignation. Boston, 1714.

Sermon shewing that ... wonderful revolutions in the world are near at hand. Edinburgh, 1710, Edinburgh, 1713.

Sermon wherein is shewed ... ministers ... need prayers. Boston, 1718.

Sermon wherein those eight characters ... Boston, 1718, Boston, 1719, Dublin, 1721.

Several reasons proving ... inoculating ... small pox. Boston, 1721, Boston, 1726, Cleveland, 1921; in *MHS Coll.*, Series 1, vol. 9, and in *Am. Journal of Public Health*, Feb. 1921.

Several sermons wherein is shewed. Boston, 1715.

Some further account ... of the small-pox inoculated. Boston, 1721.

Some important truths about conversion (new edition). Boston, 1721.

Some remarks on a late sermon ... by George Keith. Boston, 1702.

Some remarks on a pretended answer. London, Boston [1712].

Soul Saving gospel truths. Boston, 1703, 1712, Philadelphia, 1743.

Two discourses shewing. Boston, 1716.

Voice of God in stormy winds. Boston, 1704.

Wo to drunkards, 2d ed. Boston, 1712.

PREFACES, ETC., IN WORKS BY OTHER AUTHORS

Belcher, J.: God giveth the increase. Boston, 1722.

Boyd, W.: Gods way the best way. Boston, 1719.

Brown, J.: Divine Help. Boston, 1726.

Capen, J.: Funeral Sermon occasioned by the death of Joseph Green. Boston, 1717.

Danforth, J.: Blackness of sins against light. Boston, 1710.

Doolittle, T.: Treatise concerning Lord's supper, 20th ed. Boston, 1708.

Dummer, J.: Discourse on the Holiness of the Sabbath Day. Boston, 1704, 1763.

Flynt, H.: Doctrine of the Last Judgement. Boston, 1714.

Hillhouse, J.: Sermon ... state of saints. Boston, 1721.

Keith, J.: Bridgewater's Monitor. Boston, 1717, 1768, 1788.

Loring, I.: Duty and interest of young persons to remember their creator. Boston, 1718.

Mather, C.: Accomplished singer. Boston, 1721.

——— Brethren dwelling together in unity. Boston, 1718.

——— Coelestinus. Boston, 1723.

——— Course of Sermons on Early Piety. Boston, 1721.

——— Faithful Man. Boston, 1705.

——— Good evening ... best of dayes. Boston, 1708.

——— Hades look'd into. Boston, 1717.

——— Love triumphant. Boston, 1722.

——— Marah spoken to. Boston, 1718, 1721.

——— Ratio disciplinae. Boston, 1726.

——— Right way to shake off viper, 2d ed. Boston, 1720.

——— Serious address to those who ... frequent the Tavern. Boston, 1726.

——— Three letters from New England. London, 1721.

——— Utilia. Boston, 1716.

——— Winthropi Justa. London, 1709.

Mitchell, J.: Discourse of the Glory, 2d ed. Boston, 1721.

Monis, J.: Truth. Boston, 1722.

Moodey, S.: Vain Youth. Boston, 1707.

Praise out of the Mouth of Babes. Boston, 1709, 1741.

Prince, T.: God brings to the desired haven. Boston, 1717.

Reynolds, T.: Practical religion. Boston, 1713.

Sewall, J.: Precious treasure. Boston, 1717.

Symmes, T.: Monitor for delaying sinners. Boston, 1719.

Stoddard, S.: Guide to Christ. Boston, 1714, 1735, 1742, Edinburgh, 1763, Newburyport, 1801, and Northampton, 1816.

Wadsworth, B.: Death is certain. Boston, 1710.

Walter, N.: Discourse concerning the wonderfulness of Christ. Boston, 1713.

Webb, J.: Young man's duty. Boston, 1718.

White, J.: Secret prayer inculcated. Boston, 1719.

Wise, J.: Prayer in affliction. Boston, 1717.

INDEX

INDEX

Note. — Throughout the Index the initial *M.* stands for Increase Mather.

42, 45 ff.; Dunster first president of, 43; the first buildings, 44; the Indian college, 44, 45; charter of 1842, 45; curriculum of, 45, 46; library of, 46, 47; rigorous laws and rules of, 47, 48; Chauncy, second president of, 53; many early graduates of, return to England, 58; discussion in, 88; its early control of the press, 106; M. chosen a Fellow of, 107; presidency of, offered to M., and declined 107, 108; M.'s services to, 108; history of, from 1675 to 1685, 108; M. acting president of, 177, and rector, 178; status of, under Andros, 178, 179; extracts from treasurer's records, 178, 179; Commencement of 1687, 180; M. seeks charter for, 197; his request to James II concerning 206; William III's promise concerning, 254; question of charter for, renewed, 275, 276; Hollis's and other gifts to, 276 ff.; passing of M.'s hold on, 317; he secures charter for (1692), 339, 340; essential features of the charter, 340; members of Corporation of, thereunder, with M. as president, 340, 341; the centre of a battle between M. and his enemies, 342; M.'s administration of, 342 ff.; the "Proposals of 1694," 343, 344 and n., 345; project for new buildings, 345; M.'s several offers to resign as president, 346, 350, 352; William III withholds his consent to charter, and why, 348, 349; charter of 1697, 349 ff.; M. refuses to reside at, 352; 1697 charter rejected by William III, and why, 352 and n.; attempts to preserve sectarianism of, 353, 354; 1699 charter vetoed by Bellomont, 353, 354, 355; the long struggle to obtain a charter ended by Bellomont's death, 355, 356; M. elected president and finally takes up residence at Cambridge (1700), 356; end of his official connection with, 356 ff., 371, 372, 373; M. succeeded by Willard in control of affairs of, 357, 358; the true reason for M.'s removal, 358; M. hopes to regain his position at, 376, 378; Leverett president of, 379.

Hathorne, John, member of court to try witches, 293 n.; 250.
Haynes, John, 25.
"Health-drinking," condemned by M., 163, 164.
Hell-Fire Club, 139.
Herbert, George, 59.
Herrick, Robert, 40, 59.
Hevel, Johannes, 147.
Heyman, Samuel, 250, 251 n.
Higginson, John, 359, 363.
Hinckley, Thomas, Governor of Plymouth, 244, 250.
Hoar, Leonard, President of Harvard, 88; resigns, 107.
Hobart, Nehemiah, 341.
Hobbes, Thomas, 40, 59.
Hobby, Sir Charles, 380.
Holland, Henry, 77 and n.
Hollis, Thomas, and his gift to Harvard College, 276 ff.; C. Mather tries to divert his bounty to Yale, 382, 383; 387.
Holt, Katharine, marries R. Mather, 15. And see Mather, Katharine (Holt).
Holt, Sir John, 232.
Holworthy, Sir Matthew, 279.
Hook, Robert, 147.
Hook, William, 95.
Hooker, Thomas, 17 and n., 29, 30.
Hooper, John, Bishop of Gloucester, 65.
Horrocke, William, 12, 13.
Howe, John, his career and character, 63; M. goes to Great Torrington as his substitute, 63, 64; mentioned, 69, 144, 191, 281, 282, 390.
Hubbard, William, his history of King Philip's War, 110 n.
Hulton, Nathaniel, 278, 279.
Humble Address of the Publicans of New England, 234.
Hutchinson, Anne, 33.
Hutchinson, Captain, 112.
Hutchinson, Elisha, 206, 207, 209, 250, 262, 264.
Hutchinson, Francis, 306 n., 308.
Hutchinson, Thomas, *History of the Colony of Massachusetts Bay*, 57, 227, 252 n., 316.
Hyde, Edward, Earl of Clarendon, 86.

the use of the Bible, 132; his election sermon for 1677, 133, 134; on religious toleration, and persecution of heretics, 133, 134, 141–143; his attitude on divers religious matters, as illustrated by his sermons, 135 ff.; on baptism, 138, 139; on answers to prayer, 140; publishes a book on Holland, 140; his prefaces to other men's works, 140; his discourses on comets, 143, 144, 145–147; the Boston Philosophical Society, 148 and n.; Sewall's diary quoted on, 149; disinclined to take second place, 149; his critics, 149, 150; successful in gaining new members for the Second Church, 150; his personal appearance, 150, 151; and the Synod of 1679, 151; and the *quo warranto* against the charter, 152 ff.; his answer to the king's "Declaration," 153, 154, and its effect, 154; his manifold activities in the years following, 155, 156, 161; and Dudley, 157; books acquired in these years, 162, 163, 268, 269; books published by from 1683 to 1688, 163 ff.; denounces mixed "dancing," 163; attacks "Stage-Plays," 163, and "Health-drinking," 163, 164; on repentance and turning to Christ, 164, 165; on the execution of James Morgan, 165, 166; on manifestations of the divine Providence 166, 167.

Illustrious Providences, its readableness and importance, 167; its significance as one of the first scientific writings in America, 167 ff.; not concerned with witchcraft alone, 168; the main theme of the book, 168, 169, 170; the book considered in the light of Mather's scientific studies, 169, 170, 176; compared with similar books, of Clark and others, 170, 171; brief summary of the book, 171–173; compared with *Transactions* of the Royal Society, 173 and n., 174; contains Mather's own reflections on scientific matters, 175; the literary style of the book, 177.

The Flight to England. — Relations with his church, 177; becomes acting President of Harvard, 177; and "Rector," 178; development of the college under him, 178; takes precautions against attack on the college by royal authorities, 178; 179; his service to the college, 179; at the Commencement of 1687, 180; diplomatic necessities of his position, 180, 181; and Andros's request for a church in which to hold English services, 181; his attitude toward James II's declaration of liberty for all faiths, 182, 183; Randolph's enmity and the forged letter, 183–185; accuses Randolph of the forgery, 185; commissioned to carry to England the churches' thanks for the declaration, 185; Randolph causes his arrest and trial for libel, 185, 186; on his acquittal, prepares to go to England, 186; Randolph's attempt to cause his arrest a second time forces him to leave Boston in disguise, 187–189.

Diplomacy in England, 1688–1692. — Lands at Weymouth, 190; the sole purpose of his journey, 192; steers a middle course between factions, 192; in London, 192; his interviews with James II, 194, 195, 197, 201, 202; his charges against Andros, 195; visits Fleetwood, 195; other visits and interviews, 196, 197, 198; asks for a charter for Harvard, 197; preaches for Cole and others, 198; first meeting with Phipps, 198; and the ladies of honor, 199, 200; and Mrs. Blathwayt, 201; end of the first stage of his agency, 202; seeks to undermine Andros's standing in London, 203; items of his complaint, 204–206; his suggestions, 206; for their redress, his alleged wish to preserve Congregationalism in all its vigor, 206 and n., 207, 208; his petitions to the Committee on Trade, 207, 208, 209; his countrymen's reliance on him, 210; his position changed on accession of William III, 211; his relations with Bishop Burnet, Lord Wharton, and others, 211, 212; attacks Andros in his *Narrative of the Miseries of New England*, 212, 213 and n., 214; interviews with William III, 214, 216, 219, 238, 239; his petition for restoration of charter privileges, 215; seeks reversal of judgment against the charter, 217; takes ship to return to Boston, 220; his reply to *New England Vindicated*, 221–223, and its effect, 223; his other "Vindications," 223 ff.; was he the author of *A Vindication of New England?* 226, 227 and n.; his son's illness compels him to remain in England, 228; again in London, 228 ff.; and the Corporation Bill, 228, 229; why he failed to sign the formal charges against Andros, 230, 231; effect of whitewashing of Andros on his position, 231, 232; the petition to William III, 232; further war of pamphlets, 232, 233 ff.; and Tillotson, 236; obtains the support of Queen Mary, 236, 237, 238, 243; and the Countess of Sutherland, 236; and F. Charlton, 239; and the negotiations for a new charter, 239 ff.; his attitude on the religious test for the franchise, 241, 242, 246, 248; on the governor's right of veto, 243; his mistaken vehemence in opposition to the new charter, 243; his objections overruled by the king, 244; succeeds in obtaining certain modifications, 244, 245; seeks advice as to acceptance of charter, 246; arguments in favor of accepting, 246, 247; question as to the effect in America of his action, 247; in his decision to accept lies the real success of his agency, 248; his list of officials under the charter accepted, 249, 250; his relations with Phipps, 250, 251, Stoughton, 251, and Addington, 251; his nominations for Assistants not made purely on personal grounds, 251, 252; why some of the former officials were excluded, 252; Cooke and Oakes opposed to his course, 252; his nominations considered, 253; his mission in England ends with signing of charter, 253; last interviews with William III, 253, 254; sails for Boston, 254; his agency in England considered, 255 ff.; commits himself to general tolerance in religion, 257; his service to three colonies, 257; a pioneer in American diplomacy, 258, 260; his courage in accepting the charter, 259; his personality the source of his success, 260, 261; his skilful pen and his well-stored, 260; his uncertain temper, 260.

The Bostonian in London. — How he passed his time, 262 ff.; relations with Robert Boyle, 265, 266, and Richard Baxter, 266; Baxter dedicates his *Glorious Kingdom of Christ* to him, 266, 267; at Oxford and Cambridge, 267; among the bookshops, 267–269; his travelling library, 269, 270; Van der Spriett's and other portraits, 270; his *De Successo Evangelii*, 271, 272; his interest in the Indians, 271; divers other books and prefaces, 272 ff.; his account of his negotiations in England, 274; his point of view for the future — a campaign of education, 274 ff.; eminent divines testify to his character and ability 275; C. Mather quoted in his service to Harvard during his agency, 276; was it he who first interested Hollis in Harvard? 276 ff.; his large expenditures and consequent lack of funds, 279, 280; his grief for the death of his son Nathaniel, 280, 281; favors the movement to unite English Presbyterians and Congregationalists, 281; believes in need of an oligarchic church government, 282, 283; his opinions and standing on his return to America, 283; the voyage, 284; his welcome in Boston, 285.

The Witchcraft Delusion. — Responsibility for the persecution of "witches" in Salem, generally attributed to Mather and his son Cotton, 287; signs ministers' answer to the court's request for advice, 294; disapproves the court's methods, 297, 298; and the conviction of Burroughs, 298, 299; the *Cases of Conscience* gives his views on the trials, and on the subject of witchcraft, 299 and n., 300 ff.; his connection with the affair, 304, 305, 312, 313; his *Illustrious*

This Index was made for the author by George B. Ives of the Harvard University Press.